THE *unofficial* GUIDE®
TO Walt Disney World® with Kids

2012

THE *unofficial* GUIDE®

TO Walt Disney World® with Kids

2012

BOB SEHLINGER *and* LILIANE J. OPSOMER *with* LEN TESTA

(Walt Disney World® is officially known as Walt Disney World® Resort.)

WILEY

Produced by Menasha Ridge Press

Cover design by Paul Dinovo

Interior design by Vertigo Design

For information on our other products and services or to obtain technical support, please contact our Customer Care Department within the United States at 800-762-2974, outside the United States at 317-572-3993, or by fax at 317-572-4002.

John Wiley & Sons, Inc., also publishes its books in a variety of electronic formats. Some content that appears in print may not be available in electronic formats.

ISBN 978-1-118-01231-4

Manufactured in the United States of America

5 4 3 2 1

CONTENTS

List of Maps ix
Acknowledgments x

Introduction 1
How Come "Unofficial"? 1
    Declaration of Independence 1
    Your Unofficial Walt Disney World Toolbox 1
    The Music of Life 2
    Your Personal Trainers 3
About This Guide 5
    The Sum of All Fears 6
    Letters and Comments from Readers 7
    Reader Surveys 7
A Quick Tour of a Big World 12
    The Major Theme Parks 12
    The Water Theme Parks 14
    Other Walt Disney World Venues 14
    DisneySpeak Pocket Translator 18

PART ONE Basic Considerations 19
Is Walt Disney World for You? 19
    Different Folks, Different Strokes 19
    The Nature of the Beast 20
    Know Thyself and Nothing to Excess 20
The Age Thing 21
About Inviting Your Children's Friends 26
A Few Words for Single Parents 28
"He Who Hesitates Is Launched!" Tips and Warnings for Grandparents 29
Order and Discipline on the Road 31
    Six More Tips 34

PART TWO Getting Your Act Together 37
Gathering Information 37
    PassPorter's Guide 39
    Walt Disney World on the Web 39

Going High-tech with Liliane 41
Important Walt Disney World Phone Numbers 43

Allocating Time 43
When to Go to Walt Disney World 44
Holidays and Special Events at Walt Disney World 48
High-low, High-low, It's Off to Disney We Go 56

Planning Your Walt Disney World Vacation Budget 57
Walt Disney World Admission Options 57
Help Is on the Way! 59
Magic Your Way 60
Base-Ticket Add-On Options 60
A Cloud Is Just a Cloud 62
Big Brother Is Watching 63
How to Get the Most from Magic Your Way 64
Gotcha! 64
Where to Purchase Magic Your Way Tickets 64
How Much Does It Cost Per Day? 65

Babysitting 66
Special Programs for Children 68
Birthdays and Special Occasions 70

PART THREE **Where to Stay 72**
Some Basic Considerations 73
Cost 73
Location and Transportation Options 75
Commuting to and from the Theme Parks 76
Dining 78
The Size of Your Group 79
Staying in or out of the World: Weighing the Pros and Cons 79

Walt Disney World Lodging 81
Benefits of Staying in Walt Disney World 81

Walt Disney World Hotels: Strengths and Weaknesses for Families 87
Magic Kingdom Resorts 88
Epcot Resorts 93
Bonnet Creek/Downtown Disney Area Resorts 95
Animal Kingdom Resorts 100
HOTEL INFORMATION CHART 102–104
Independent Hotels of the Downtown Disney Resort Area 106
How to Get Discounts on Lodging at Walt Disney World 107

Lodging Outside Walt Disney World 110
Good Neighbor Hotels 110
Selecting and Booking a Hotel Outside Walt Disney World 111
The Best Hotels for Families Outside Walt Disney World 113
Getting a Good Deal on a Room Outside Walt Disney World 122
Condominiums and Vacation Homes 124

How to Childproof a Hotel Room 127

PART FOUR **Dining 129**
Eating Outside Walt Disney World 129
Buffets and Meal Deals Outside Walt Disney World 130
WHERE TO EAT OUTSIDE WALT DISNEY WORLD 132–133

Dining in Walt Disney World 134

 Disney Dining 101 135
 Advance Reservations: What's in a Name? 136
 Getting an Advance Reservation at Popular Restaurants 136
 Getting Your Act Together 141
 Dress 143
 Smoking 143
 Food Allergies and Special Requests 143
 A Few Caveats 144
 Walt Disney World Restaurant Categories 144
 WALT DISNEY WORLD BUFFETS AND FAMILY-STYLE RESTAURANTS 145
 Hard Choices 146
 THE TOP 10 SNACKS AT WALT DISNEY WORLD 148–149
 Fast Food in the Theme Parks 149
 Disney Dining Suggestions 153
 Readers' Comments About Walt Disney World Dining 155
 Counter-service Restaurant Mini-profiles 156
 Disney's Full-service Restaurants: A Quick Romp Around the World 165
 Magic Your Way Dining Plan 168
 Number Crunching 176
 Throw Me a Line! 177
 Purchasing Room-only Plus Passes Versus a Package 177
 Character Dining 178
 Walt Disney World Restaurants: Rated and Ranked 178
 WALT DISNEY WORLD RESTAURANTS BY CUISINE 179–181

PART FIVE **Disney Boot Camp: Basic Training for World-bound Families 182**

The Brutal Truth about Family Vacations 182
Mental and Emotional Preparation 183
 Division of Labor 183
 Togetherness 183
 Lighten Up 184
 Something for Everyone 184
 Whose Idea Was This, Anyway? 184
 Disney, Kids, and Scary Stuff 185
 SMALL-CHILD FRIGHT-POTENTIAL CHART 186–190
 A Magical Time for Mom and Dad 194
 Preparing Your Children to Meet the Characters 194
 Role-Playing 196
Physical Preparation 196
 The Agony of the Feet 197
 Sleep, Rest, and Relaxation 199
Developing a Good Plan 201
 The Great Walt Disney World Expedition 202
Logistic Preparation 203
 Clothing 203
 Accessories 206
 Miscellaneous Items 209
 Supplies for Infants and Toddlers 215

Tips for Pregnant Mothers 215
Remembering Your Trip 218
How to Have Fun Before and After Your Visit—
or the Things Bob Would Never Do 218
Trial Run 219

PART SIX **Get in the Boat, Men! 221**
Ready, Set, Tour! Some Touring Considerations 221
How Much Time Is Required to See Each Park? 221
Which Park to See First? 221
Operating Hours 222
Official Opening Versus Real Opening 222
The Rules 223
Your Daily Itinerary 226
Touring Plans 227
How to Find the Touring Plan That's Best for You 229
Fastpass 234
A Word about Disney Thrill Rides 238
A Word about Height Requirements 239
Waiting-line Strategies for Adults with Young Children 241

ATTRACTIONS AND RIDE RESTRICTIONS 244–245
Character Analysis 247
Character Watching 247
Character Dining: What to Expect 249

CHARACTER-MEAL HIT PARADE 251
Other Character Events 256
Strollers 257
When Kids Get Lost 259
Liliane's Tips for Keeping Track of Your Brood 262

PART SEVEN **The Magic Kingdom 264**
Main Street, U.S.A. 265
Adventureland 268
Frontierland 271
Liberty Square 274
Fantasyland 275
Tomorrowland 283
Live Entertainment and Parades in the Magic Kingdom 288
Magic Kingdom Touring Plans 292
Magic Kingdom Trivia Quiz 295

PART EIGHT **Epcot 297**
Kidcot Fun Stops 300
Future World 300
World Showcase 309
Live Entertainment at Epcot 317
Epcot Touring Plans 320
Epcot Trivia Quiz 322

PART NINE **Animal Kingdom 323**
The Oasis 326
Discovery Island 326
Camp Minnie-Mickey 327
Africa 328
Asia 331
DinoLand U.S.A. 333
Live Entertainment at Animal Kingdom 336
Animal Kingdom Touring Plans 338
Disney's Animal Kingdom Trivia Quiz 339

PART TEN **Disney's Hollywood Studios 340**
Live Entertainment at Disney's Hollywood Studios 355
Disney's Hollywood Studios Touring Plans 358
Disney's Hollywood Studios Trivia Quiz 360

PART ELEVEN **Universal Orlando and SeaWorld 361**
Universal Orlando 361
Universal Studios Florida 365
Disney's Hollywood Studios Versus Universal Studios Florida 366
Universal Studios Florida Attractions 373
Live Entertainment at Universal Studios 383
Universal Studios Florida Touring Plan 384
Universal's Islands of Adventure 384
Islands of Adventure Attractions 388
Islands of Adventure Touring Plan 402
SeaWorld 404

PART TWELVE **The Rest of the World 408**
The Water Theme Parks 408
Wet 'N Wild 413
Aquatica by SeaWorld 416
Downtown Disney 417
The Best of the Rest 424

Index 427
Clip-out Touring Plans 445
Unofficial Guide Reader Survey 469

LIST *of* MAPS

South Orlando and Walt Disney World
    Area 8–9
Walt Disney World 10–11
Hotel Concentrations around
    Walt Disney World 112
Magic Kingdom 266–267
Epcot 298–299
Where To View *IllumiNations* 319

Disney's Animal Kingdom 324–325
Disney's Hollywood Studios 342–343
Universal Orlando 368–369
Universal Studios Florida 370–371
Universal's Islands of
    Adventure 386–387
Downtown Disney 418–419

ACKNOWLEDGMENTS

THANKS TO OUR TEAM OF YOUNG PUNDITS, Idan Menin, Ian Geiger, Hannah Testa, Katie Sutton, and Shelton Siegel for their unique wisdom and fun-loving attitude (gotta have attitude, right?). Lou Mongello created the theme-park trivia quizzes, and Disney historian Jim Hill provided insightful and funny glimpses of the World behind the scenes. Cartoons in the guide were created by artist Tami Knight, possibly the nuttiest person in Canada. Much appreciation to Eve Zibart for her characteristically droll comments concerning Walt Disney World attractions, hotels, and dining. For research and contributions concerning family dynamics and child behavior, thanks to psychologists Karen Turnbow, Susan Corbin, Gayle Janzen, and Joan Burns. Kudos also to *Unofficial Guide* Research Director Len Testa and his team for the data collection and programming behind the touring plans in this guide.

Many thanks also to Amber Kaye Henderson, Holly Cross, Ritchey Halphen, Molly Merkle, and Darcie Vance for production and editorial work on this book. Annie Long earned our appreciation for her fine work in providing the typography. Cartography was provided by Scott McGrew and Steve Jones, and the index was prepared by Ann Cassar.

INTRODUCTION

HOW COME "UNOFFICIAL"?

DECLARATION OF INDEPENDENCE

THE AUTHORS AND RESEARCHERS OF THIS GUIDE specifically and categorically declare that they are and always have been totally independent of the Walt Disney Company, Inc.; of Disneyland, Inc.; of Walt Disney World, Inc.; and of any and all other members of the Disney corporate family not listed.

The authors believe in the wondrous variety, joy, and excitement of the Walt Disney World attractions. At the same time, we recognize that Walt Disney World is a business, with the same profit motivations as businesses the world over. In this guide we represent and serve you, the consumer. If a restaurant serves bad food, or a gift item is overpriced, or a certain ride isn't worth the wait, we can say so, and in the process we hope to make your visit more fun, efficient, and economical.

YOUR UNOFFICIAL WALT DISNEY WORLD TOOLBOX

YOU NEED DIFFERENT TOOLS TO WORK ON YOUR CAR than you do to fix your DVD player or trim the azaleas. It's much the same when it comes to a Walt Disney World vacation. If we think of information as tools, a couple with two toddlers in diapers will need different tools than a party of seniors going to the Epcot Flower and Garden Festival. Likewise, adults touring without children, families with kids of varying ages, and honeymooners all require their own special tools.

To meet the varying needs of our readers, we have created a very comprehensive guide, *The Unofficial Guide to Walt Disney World*. At about 850 pages, we call this guide the Big Book. The Big Book contains the detailed information anyone traveling to Walt Disney World needs to have a super vacation. It's our cornerstone guide.

As thorough as we try to make *The Unofficial Guide to Walt Disney World*, there isn't sufficient space for all the tips and valuable information that may be important and useful to certain readers. Thus, we've developed four additional Disney World guides, each designed to work in conjunction with the Big Book. All provide information tailored to specific Disney World visitors. Although some tips from the Big Book (such as arriving early at the theme parks) are echoed in these guides, most of the information is unique. You could think of the Big Book as a vacuum cleaner and the other guides as specialized attachments that certain users might need for a particular job (back to tools, you see). So here's what's in the toolbox:

This guide, *The Unofficial Guide to Walt Disney World with Kids* by Bob Sehlinger and Liliane J. Opsomer with Len Testa, presents detailed planning and touring tips for a family vacation, along with more than 20 special touring plans for families that are not published anywhere else. *The Unofficial Guide to Walt Disney World with Kids* is a complete guide and contains a wealth of family-specific information, tips, and advice not available in the Big Book or anywhere else. It's the only *Unofficial Guide* that is created with the guidance of a panel of kids, all of varying ages and backgrounds.

The Unofficial Guide: The Color Companion to Walt Disney World is a full-color visual feast that proves that a picture is worth 1,000 words. You can read everything you need to know about Disney's Wilderness Lodge Resort in the Big Book (even learn the best rooms to request), but in the *Color Companion* you can see the guest rooms, the pool, and the magnificent lobby. For the first time photographs illustrate how long the lines are at different times of day, how drenched riders get riding Splash Mountain, and how the parks are decked out for various holidays. The *Color Companion* whets your appetite for Disney fun, pictures all the attractions, serves as a keepsake, and as always, helps make your vacation more enjoyable. Most of all, the *Color Companion* is for fun. For the first time we are able to use photography to express our zany *Unofficial Guide* sense of humor. You might think of it as Monty Python meets Walt Disney in TechniColor.

Mini Mickey: The Pocket-Sized Unofficial Guide to Walt Disney World, by Bob Sehlinger and Len Testa, is a portable *CliffsNotes*-style version of *The Unofficial Guide to Walt Disney World.* It distills information from the Big Book to help short-stay or last-minute visitors decide quickly how to plan their limited hours at Disney World.

Beyond Disney: The Unofficial Guide to Universal Orlando, SeaWorld, & the Best of Central Florida, by Bob Sehlinger and Grant Rafter, is a guide to non-Disney attractions, restaurants, outdoor recreation, and nightlife in Orlando and central Florida.

THE MUSIC OF LIFE

ALTHOUGH IT IS COMMON in our culture to see life as a journey from cradle to grave, Alan Watts, a noted late–20th-century philosopher, saw it somewhat differently. He viewed life not as a journey but as a dance. In a journey, he said, you are trying to get somewhere, and are consequently always looking ahead, anticipating the way stations, and thinking about the end. Though the journey metaphor is popular, particularly in the West, it is generally characterized by a driven, goal-oriented mentality: a way of living and being that often inhibits those who subscribe to the journey metaphor from savoring each moment of life.

When you dance, by contrast, you hear the music and move in harmony with the rhythm. Like life, a dance has a beginning and an end. But unlike a journey, your objective is not to get to the end but to enjoy the dance while the music plays. You are totally in the moment and care nothing about where on the floor you stop when the dance is done.

As you begin to contemplate your Walt Disney World vacation, you may not have much patience for a philosophical discussion about journeys and dancing. But you see, it is relevant. If you are like most travel guide readers, you are apt to plan and organize, to anticipate and control, and you like things to go smoothly. And truth be told, this leads us to suspect that you are a person who looks ahead and is outcome-oriented. You may even feel a bit of pressure concerning your vacation. Vacations, after all, are special events and expensive ones as well. So you work hard to make the most of your vacation.

We also believe that work, planning, and organization are important, and at Walt Disney World they are essential. But if they become your focus, you won't be able to hear the music and enjoy the dance. Though a lot of dancing these days resembles highly individualized seizures, there was a time when each dance involved specific steps, which you committed to memory. At first you were tentative and awkward, but eventually the steps became second nature and you didn't think about them anymore.

Metaphorically, this is what we want for you and your children or grandchildren as you embark on your Walt Disney World vacation. We want you to learn the steps ahead of time, so that when you're on your vacation and the music plays, you will be able to hear it, and you and your children will dance with grace and ease.

YOUR PERSONAL TRAINERS

WE'RE YOUR WALT DISNEY WORLD PERSONAL TRAINERS. We will help you plan and enjoy your Walt Disney World vacation. Together we will make sure that it really is a vacation, as opposed to, say, an ordeal or an expensive way to experience heatstroke. Our objective, simply put, is to ensure that you and your children have fun.

Because this book is specifically for adults traveling with children, we'll concentrate on your special needs and challenges. We'll share our most useful tips as well as the travel secrets of more than 39,000 families interviewed over the years we've covered Walt Disney World.

So who are *we?* For starters, there's a bunch of us. Your primary trainers are Liliane and Bob. Helping out big time are Idan and

IDAN   **IAN**   **HANNAH**   **SHELTON**

Ian—also known as the I-Boys—as well as Hannah and Shelton. Idan is 20 years old and comes from the Queens borough of New York. He plays rock guitar (loudly), has kind of a sweetly grunge style (second-hand clothes are the coolest, right?), and wears shoes large enough for eagles to nest in. Ian is a 16-year-old from Tampa, Florida. His surfer mop-headed hair nearly covers his hazy blue peepers. He gets a kick out of playing soccer and hanging with his pet gecko, Iggie (not part of the I-Boys), and is addicted to saying "Sweet!" and "Awesome!"— punctuated with an occasional "Dude!" Hannah, age 12, lives near Winston-Salem, North Carolina, really knows Disney, and will read you the riot act if you mess up. The rest of us work for her. Our most recent team member is Shelton, who is a high school junior in Arlington, Virginia. He sings, plays keyboard, and loves to chow down on ethnic food. Maybe he'll team up with Idan to form an *Unofficial* rock band. The I-Boys, Shelton, and Hannah, needless to say, have a lot of opinions when it comes to Disney. So many, in fact, that they think Liliane and Bob are largely superfluous.

Liliane comes from Belgium and works in New York City. She's funny, very polite in the best European tradition, and puts more energy into being a mom than you'd think possible without performance-enhancing drugs. Optimistic and happy, she loves the sweet and sentimental side of Disney World. You might find her whooping it up at the *Hoop-Dee-Doo Musical Revue,* but you'll never see her on a roller coaster with Bob.

Speaking of whom, Bob is not exactly a curmudgeon, but he likes to unearth Disney's closely guarded secrets and show readers how to beat the system. His idea of a warm fuzzy might be the Rock 'n' Roller Coaster, but he'll help you save lots of money, find the best hotels and restaurants, and return home less than terminally exhausted. The caricatures on the next page pretty much sum up the essence of Bob and Liliane.

If you're thinking that the cartoons paint a somewhat conflicted picture of your personal trainers, you're right. Bob and Liliane—it must be admitted—have been known to disagree on a thing or two. Together, however, they make a good team. You can count on them to give you both sides of every story. As an analogy, Liliane will help you bask in the universal brotherhood theme of *It's a Small World.* Bob will show up later and help you get the infernal song out of your head. You get the idea.

BOB

LILIANE

Len is the research dude! Way! His really complicated scientific research will help you save a bundle of time (would you believe 4 hours in a single day) by staying out of those pesky lines.

Oops, almost forgot: There's another team member you need to meet. Called a Wuffo, she's our very own character. She'll warn you when rides are too scary, too dark, or too wet. You'll bump into her throughout the book doing, well, what characters do.

Why did we create our own character when Disney has dozens just sitting around? Simple—Disney characters toe the company line. We needed a tough (but lovable) independent character who would give you the straight skinny on what Disney rides do to your stomach and central nervous system.

▌ **ABOUT** *this* **GUIDE**

WALT DISNEY WORLD HAS BEEN OUR BEAT for more than two decades, and we know it inside out. During those years we have observed many thousands of parents and grandparents trying—some successfully, others less so—to have a good time at Walt Disney World. Some of these, owing to unfortunate dynamics within the family, were handicapped right from the start. Others were simply overwhelmed by the size and complexity of Walt Disney World; whereas still others fell victim to a lack of foresight, planning, and organization.

Walt Disney World is a better destination for some families than for others. Likewise, some families are more compatible on vacation than others. The likelihood of experiencing a truly wonderful Walt Disney World vacation transcends the theme parks and attractions offered. In fact, the theme parks and attractions are the only constants in the equation. The variables that will define the experience and determine its success are intrinsic to your family: things like attitude, sense of humor, cohesiveness, stamina, flexibility, and conflict resolution.

The simple truth is that Walt Disney World can test you as a family. It will overwhelm you with choices and force you to make decisions about how to spend your time and money. It will challenge you physically as you cover miles on foot and wait in lines touring the theme parks. You will have to respond to surprises (both good and bad) and deal with hyperstimulation.

This guide will forewarn and forearm you. It will help you decide whether a Walt Disney World vacation is a good idea for you and your family at this particular time. It will help you sort out and address the attitudes and family dynamics that can affect your experience. Most important, it will provide the confidence that comes with good planning and realistic expectations.

THE SUM OF ALL FEARS

EVERY WRITER WHO EXPRESSES an opinion is accustomed to readers who strongly agree or disagree: it comes with the territory.

Be prepared to read experienced Disney World visitors' opinions of the parks in this book and to apply them to your own travel circumstances.

Extremely troubling, however, is the possibility that our efforts to be objective have frightened some readers away from Walt Disney World or made others apprehensive. For the record, if you enjoy theme parks, Disney World is as good as it gets, absolute nirvana. It's upbeat, safe, fun, eye-popping, happy, and exciting. If you arrive without knowing a thing about the place and make every possible mistake, chances are about 90% that you'll have a wonderful vacation anyway. In the end, guidebooks don't make or break great destinations. Rather, they are simply tools to help you enhance your experience and get the most for your money.

As wonderful as Walt Disney World is, however, it's a complex destination. Even so, it isn't nearly as challenging or difficult as New York, San Francisco, Paris, Acapulco, or any other large city or destination. And, happily, there are numerous ways to save money, minimize hassle, and make the most of your time. That's what this guide is about: giving you a heads-up regarding potential problems or opportunities. Unfortunately, some *Unofficial Guide* readers add up the warnings and critical advice and conclude that Walt Disney World is too intimidating, too expensive, or too much work. They lose track of the wonder of Disney World and focus instead on what might go wrong.

Our philosophy is that knowledge is power (and time and money too). You're free to follow our advice—or not—at your discretion. But you can't exercise that discretion if we fail to present the issues.

With or without a guidebook, you'll have a great time at Walt Disney World. If you let us, we'll help you smooth the potential bumps. We're certain that we can help you turn a great vacation into an absolutely superb one. Either way, once there, you'll get the feel of the place and quickly reach a comfort level that will allay your apprehensions and allow you to have a great experience.

LETTERS AND COMMENTS FROM READERS

MANY OF THOSE WHO USE *The Unofficial Guide to Walt Disney World with Kids* write us to make comments or share their own strategies for visiting Walt Disney World. We appreciate all such input, both positive and critical, and encourage our readers to continue writing. Readers' comments and observations are frequently incorporated into revised editions of the *Unofficial Guide* and have contributed immeasurably to its improvement.

Privacy Policy

If you write us, you can rest assured that we won't release your name and address to any mailing-list companies, direct-mail advertisers, or other third party. Unless you instruct us otherwise, we will assume that you do not object to being quoted in a future edition.

How to Write or E-mail the Authors

Bob, Liliane, and Len
The Unofficial Guide to Walt Disney World with Kids
P.O. Box 43673
Birmingham, AL 35243
UnofficialGuides@MenashaRidge.com

When you write, be sure to put a return address on your letter as well as the envelope; sometimes envelopes and letters get separated. It's also a good idea to include your phone number.

Remember, our work often requires that we be out of the office for long periods of time, and *Unofficial Guide* mail and e-mail are not forwarded to us when we're traveling. So forgive us if our response is a little slow; we will respond as soon as possible when we return.

READER SURVEYS

A READER SURVEY IS LOCATED at the end of this guide. You'll notice throughout the book that we quote readers and publish the results of our several surveys. We'd love to hear from you and register your opinions. To this end you can either complete and mail the forms at the back of the book or take the Walt Disney World survey online at **touringplans.com/walt-disney-world/survey.** We're betting that you'll really like the advice and opinions of readers included in *The Unofficial Guide to Walt Disney World with Kids*. Be a contributor: Let us know what you think.

continued on page 12

South Orlando & Walt Disney World Area

Walt Disney World

continued from page 7

A **QUICK TOUR** *of a* **BIG WORLD**

WALT DISNEY WORLD ENCOMPASSES 43 SQUARE MILES, an area twice as large as Manhattan and roughly the same size as Boston. Situated strategically in this vast expanse are the Magic Kingdom, Epcot, Disney's Hollywood Studios, and the Animal Kingdom theme parks; two water parks; two nighttime entertainment areas; a sports complex; several golf courses, hotels, and campgrounds; almost 100 restaurants; four large, interconnected lakes; a shopping complex; three convention venues; a nature preserve; and a complete transportation system consisting of four-lane highways, elevated monorails, and a system of canals.

THE MAJOR THEME PARKS

The Magic Kingdom

When people think of Walt Disney World, most think of the Magic Kingdom. It comprises Cinderella Castle and the collection of adventures, rides, and shows symbolizing the Disney cartoon characters. Although the park is only one element of Disney World, it remains its heart. The Magic Kingdom is divided into six areas or lands arranged around a central hub. First encountered is Main Street, U.S.A., which connects the Magic Kingdom entrance with the central hub. Clockwise around the hub are Adventureland, Frontierland, Liberty Square, Fantasyland, and Tomorrowland. Mickey's Toontown Fair, the first new land in the Magic Kingdom since the park opened, was situated along Walt Disney Railroad on 3 acres between Fantasyland and Tomorrowland. (Mickey's Toontown Fair was also the Magic Kingdom's first land to go out of business. It closed forever on February 11, 2011, to make way for an expanded Fantasyland.) The Contemporary, Polynesian, and Grand Floridian Beach resorts are close to the Magic Kingdom and are directly connected to it by monorail and boat. Two additional hotels, Shades of Green (operated by the Department of Defense) and Wilderness Lodge Resort, are nearby but aren't served by the monorail.

Epcot

Epcot opened in October 1982. Divided into two major areas, Future World and World Showcase, the park is twice as big as the Magic Kingdom and comparable in scope. Future World consists of futuristic pavilions relating to different themes concerning humankind's creativity and technological advancement. World Showcase, arranged around a 41-acre lagoon, presents the architectural, social, and cultural heritages of almost a dozen nations, with each country represented by replicas of famous landmarks and local settings familiar to world travelers. Epcot is more education-oriented than the Magic Kingdom and has been repeatedly characterized as a sort of permanent World's Fair.

The five Epcot resort hotels—Disney's Beach Club & Villas, Disney's Yacht Club Resort, Disney's BoardWalk Inn & Villas, the Walt Disney World Swan, and the Walt Disney World Dolphin—are within a 5- to 15-minute walk of Epcot's "back door," the International Gateway entrance. The hotels are also linked to the park by boat. Disney's Caribbean Beach Resort is near Epcot but not linked to it. Epcot is connected to the Magic Kingdom and its resort hotels by monorail.

Disney's Hollywood Studios

This 100-acre theme park opened in 1989 and is divided into two areas. The first is a theme park focusing on the past, present, and future of the motion picture and television industries. This section contains movie-theme rides and shows and covers about half of the Studios complex. Highlights include a re-creation of Hollywood and Sunset boulevards from Hollywood's Golden Age; movie stunt demonstrations; a children's play area; and four high-tech rides: The Twilight Zone Tower of Terror, Star Tours, the Rock 'n' Roller Coaster, and Toy Story Mania.

The second area is a motion picture and television production facility encompassing three soundstages, a back lot of streets and sets, and creative support services. Public access to this area is limited to studio tours, which take visitors behind the scenes for crash courses on Disney animation and moviemaking, including (on occasion) the opportunity to witness the actual shooting of a feature film, television show, or commercial.

Disney's Hollywood Studios is linked to other Walt Disney World areas by highway and canal but not by monorail. Guests can park in the Studios' pay parking lot or commute by bus. Patrons staying in Epcot resort hotels can reach the Studios by boat.

Disney's Animal Kingdom

More than five times the size of the Magic Kingdom, the Animal Kingdom combines zoological exhibits with rides, shows, and live entertainment. The park is arranged somewhat like the Magic Kingdom, in a hub-and-spoke configuration. A lush tropical rain forest called The Oasis serves as Main Street, funneling visitors to Discovery Island at the center of the park. Dominated by the park's central icon, the 14-story-tall, hand-carved Tree of Life, Discovery Island is the park's center, with services, shopping, and dining. From Discovery Island, guests can access the theme areas: Africa, Asia, DinoLand U.S.A., and Camp Minnie-Mickey. Africa, the largest of the theme areas at 100 acres, features free-roaming herds in a re-creation of the Serengeti Plain. Guests tour in open-air safari vehicles. Rafiki's Planet Watch, unlike the other themed areas, is accessed from Africa.

Animal Kingdom has its own pay parking lot and is connected to other Walt Disney World destinations by the Disney bus system. Although no hotels are at Disney's Animal Kingdom, the Animal

Kingdom Lodge & Villas, All-Star, Art of Animation, and Coronado Springs resorts are nearby.

THE WATER THEME PARKS

THERE ARE TWO MAJOR SWIMMING THEME PARKS in Walt Disney World: Typhoon Lagoon and Blizzard Beach. Typhoon Lagoon is distinguished by a wave pool capable of making 6-foot waves. Blizzard Beach features more slides than Typhoon Lagoon. Both parks are beautifully landscaped, with great attention to aesthetics and atmosphere. The parks have their own adjacent parking lots and can be reached by Disney bus.

OTHER WALT DISNEY WORLD VENUES

Downtown Disney (Downtown Disney Marketplace, Pleasure Island, and Downtown Disney West Side)

Downtown Disney is a large shopping, dining, and entertainment complex encompassing the Downtown Disney Marketplace on the east, Pleasure Island in the middle, and Downtown Disney West Side on the west. The Marketplace is home to the largest Disney character merchandise store in the world, upscale resort wear and specialty shops, and several restaurants, including the tacky but popular Rainforest Cafe. Pleasure Island was converted in 2008 from an admission-required collection of nightclubs to a shopping-and-dining venue.

Downtown Disney West Side combines nightlife, shopping, dining, and entertainment. Dan Aykroyd's House of Blues serves Cajun-Creole dishes in its restaurant and electric blues in its music hall. Bongos, a Cuban nightclub and cafe created by Gloria and Emilio Estefan, offers Caribbean flavors and rhythms. Wolfgang Puck Café, sandwiched among pricey boutiques, is the West Side's prestige eatery. In the entertainment department, you'll find a 24-screen cinema; a permanent showplace for the extraordinary, 70-person cast of Cirque du Soleil; and DisneyQuest, a high-tech, interactive virtual reality and electronic games venue. Downtown Disney can be accessed via Disney buses from most Walt Disney World locations.

Disney's BoardWalk

Located near Epcot, Disney's BoardWalk is an idealized replication of an East Coast turn-of-the-20th-century waterfront resort. Open all day, the BoardWalk features upscale restaurants, shops and galleries, a brewpub, an ESPN sports bar, a nightclub with dueling pianos (New Orleans Pat O'Brien's–style), and a dance club. Though the BoardWalk does not have an admission fee per se, individual clubs levy a cover charge at night. Besides the public facilities, the Board-Walk fronts a 378-room deluxe hotel and a 532-unit time-share development. The BoardWalk is within walking distance of the Epcot resorts and the International Gateway of the Epcot theme park. Boat transportation is available to and from Epcot and Disney's Hollywood Studios, with buses serving other Disney World locations.

ESPN Wide World of Sports

Covering 200 acres, ESPN Wide World of Sports is a state-of-the-art competition and training facility consisting of a 7,500-seat ballpark, a field house, and venues for baseball, softball, tennis, track and field, beach volleyball, and more than 50 other sports. In addition to being the spring-training home of the Atlanta Braves, the complex hosts a mind-boggling calendar of professional and amateur competitions. Although Walt Disney World guests are welcome at the complex as paid spectators, none of the facilities are available for use by guests unless they are participants in a scheduled competition.

The Mouse at Sea

The Disney Cruise Line fleet consists of the **Disney Magic,** the **Disney Wonder,** and the **Disney Dream,** which joined the fleet in 2011. The **Disney Fantasy** will enter service in spring 2012. Though the foundation of its business is built on 3-, 4-, and 7-day Bahamian and Caribbean cruises out of Port Canaveral (about a 90-minute drive from Walt Disney World), the Disney Cruise Line also offers Alaska, Canada, New England, Pacific Coast, and Mexican Riviera cruises. All cruises originating in Port Canaveral make at least one port call at Disney's private island, Castaway Cay, and all can be combined in a land-sea package with a stay at Walt Disney World.

If you go for the cruise and Disney World package, visit the parks first; then sail away for more fun, as well as some much-deserved rest. *La dolce vita,* here I come. — Liliane

The Disney cruises are perfect for families and for kids of all ages. Although the cruises are family-oriented, extensive children's programs and elaborate child-care facilities allow grown-ups plenty of opportunities to relax and do adult stuff. The ships are modern ocean liners with classic steamship lines. Cabins are among the most spacious in the cruise industry, and the staff is very attentive and accommodating. From the waitstaff at breakfast, lunch, and dinner to the cabin stewards, yours truly has not experienced any better.

Cabin design reveals Disney's finely tuned sense of the needs of families and children and offers a cruise-industry first: a split bathroom with a bathtub and shower combo and sink in one room, and toilet, sink, and vanity in another. This configuration, found in all but standard inside cabins, allows any family member to use the bathroom without monopolizing it. All bathrooms have a tub and shower, except disabled rooms (shower only). Decor includes unusual features such as bureaus designed to look like steamer trunks. Cabins also have a

The room service gets a thumbs-up! Drinking pink lemonade and eating hot dogs, pizza, and cookies while watching a movie with friends is awesome. — Idan

telephone, TV, hair dryer, and a cooling box. In some cabins, pull-down Murphy beds or drop-down bunk beds allow for additional daytime floor space. Storage is generous, with deep drawers and large closets.

A big party with appearances by Mickey and Minnie marks departures, when the ship's horn toots "When You Wish upon a Star." Halfway through your voyage Disney throws a deck party, where Mickey saves all passengers from Captain Hook and his evil plans.

Dining is a true pleasure. Each night, passengers move to a different family restaurant—each with its own unique theme and menu—and take their table companions and waitstaff with them. In addition to the family restaurants, the ships have a range of cafes offering pizza, burgers, sandwiches, and ice-cream bars. Room service is available 24/7.

All the suits and ties in the world did not get me into Palo. I am still feeling the need for revenge, as I was denied access as a 17-year-old looking like Johnny Depp with a 20-year-old beauty on my arm.

For a night out without kids, Palo, which offers tables with a view, is a must. Reservations are also a must, and a surcharge of $20 is added for this service to your onboard bill. The food is excellent, and the ambience sophisticated. Disney enforces a strict policy for diners at Palo to be 18 years of age or older.

In addition to Palo, the *Dream* and the *Fantasy* crank it up a notch with Remy. Scott Hunnel of Victoria & Albert's and chef Arnaud Lallement from L'Assiette Champenoise—a Michelin two-star restaurant outside Reims, France—created the French-inspired menu. It is all delivered in an Art Nouveau–style dining room. This upscale dining experience on the high seas costs $75; an additional $99 is needed for wine pairing. If you think this is a little over the top, we completely agree. It remains to be seen if the wine list presented at the table by a sommelier is worth the hefty surcharge. Whatever happened to the no-frills, great food philosophy we learned from Remy in *Ratatouille*?

The Disney ships offer 15,000-plus square feet of playrooms and other kids' facilities. Programs include interactive activities, play areas supervised by trained counselors, and a children's drop-off service in the evening. Passengers can register their children for the nursery, and group babysitting is available for select hours every day. Cost is $6 per child per hour. The Oceaneer Club program with its Never Land theme is perfect for kids ages 3–7, though children up to age 10 can participate. (Programs on the *Wonder* allow children up to age 12.) Oceaneer Lab offers high-tech play. Kids wear ID bracelets, and parents receive pagers. There's a special club for teens.

Big with kids of all ages are the pools and the nightly entertainment on board, which show Disney at its best. The Walt Disney Theatre stages several musical productions each cruise, and the Buena Vista Theatre with its full-screen cinema shows first-run and digital 3-D movies as well as classic Disney films. Movies are also played poolside on a state-of-the-art 24- by 14-foot LED screen affixed to the forward funnel in the Goofy's Pool area.

The *Dream* features the first-ever on-board water coaster. At 765 feet long and the height of four decks, AquaDuck is a major attraction for kids and grown-ups alike. Following an initial drop, guests glide through a translucent tube in a loop that extends 12 feet over the side of the vessel, allowing them to look down on the ocean 150 feet below. The ride lasts about 90 seconds and comes with climbs and drops, twists and turns. If you can keep your eyes open while riding, the AquaDuck will provide you with a spectacular view of the ship.

Vista Spa & Salon (known as Senses on the *Dream* and the *Fantasy*) is an area reserved exclusively for adults and a great place to relax. The treatments are pricey, and there's a surcharge of $15 per day for the use of the saunas and steam rooms, as well as two aromatic showers. (The fitness center's showers and lockers are free of charge.)

Shore excursions depend on the itinerary, but all Cape Canaveral, New York, and Bahamian sailings make at least one call at **Castaway Cay,** Disney's 1,000-acre private island. The natural environment and miles of white-sand beaches have been nicely preserved. The best way to enjoy the island is to disembark first thing in the morning and secure a prime spot at the beach complete with hammock and shade. **Castaway family beach** is served by a tram running every 5 minutes. We walked the 0.25 mile to the beach but realize that it could be tiresome to walk in the blistering summer heat. **Cookie's BBQ** and **Cookie's Too** serve an array of food that is included in the price of your cruise. Programs for kids on Castaway Cay give parents a chance to enjoy **Serenity Bay,** the adults-only beach.

The Disney Cruise Line fared better than most during the recession, but throughout the industry, demand has declined and capacity, with the introduction of a number of new ships, has gone up. Disney Cruise Line offers a distinctive product and has a loyal client base. However, when other cruise lines heavily discount their cruises, the deals are often so good that Disney Cruise Line is forced to struggle to hang onto its market share. When you can buy a 7-night Alaska cruise on another line for less than a 4-day Disney cruise to Nassau and Castaway Cay, it strains the loyalty of even the most ardent Mouseketeer. Disney, therefore, has been discounting and offering Kids Sail Free specials for children who share a cabin with their parents.

The bottom line is that cruises are unequivocally the best deal in travel right now and for the foreseeable future. Deals abound. Check websites such as **cruisecritic.com, cruisemates.com, vacationstogo.com, lastminutetravel.com,** and **disneycruiseline.com** for the latest discounts. Search engine **kayak.com** is a great resource for uncovering cruise bargains. If you prefer to buy directly from Disney, here's how to get in touch:

Disney Cruise Line
800-951-6499 or 800-951-3532
disneycruise.com

Disney Cruise Line offers a free planning DVD that tells you all you need to know about Disney cruises and then some. To obtain a copy, call 888-DCL-2500, or order online at **disneycruise.com.**

DISNEYSPEAK POCKET TRANSLATOR

ALTHOUGH IT MAY COME AS A SURPRISE to many, Walt Disney World has its own somewhat peculiar language. Below are some terms that you are likely to bump into.

DISNEYSPEAK	ENGLISH DEFINITION
Adventure	Ride
Attraction	Ride or theater show
Attraction Host	Ride operator
Audience	Crowd
Backstage	Behind the scenes, out of view of customers
Bull Pen	Queuing area
Cast Member	Employee
Character	Disney character impersonated by an employee
Costume	Work attire or uniform
Dark Ride	Indoor ride
Day Guest	Any customer not staying at a Disney resort
Face Character	A character who does not wear a head-covering costume (Snow White, Cinderella, Jasmine, and the like)
General Public	Same as day guest
Greeter	Employee positioned at an attraction entrance
Guest	Customer
Hidden Mickeys	Frontal silhouette of Mickey's head worked subtly into the design of buildings, railings, vehicles, golf greens, attractions, and just about anything else
In Rehearsal	Operating, though not officially open
Lead	Foreman or manager, the person in charge of an attraction
On Stage	In full view of customers
Preshow	Entertainment at an attraction prior to the feature presentation
Resort Guest	A customer staying at a Disney resort
Role	An employee's job
Security Host	Security guard
Soft Opening	Opening a park or attraction before its stated opening date
Transitional Experience	An element of the queuing area and/or preshow that provides a story line or information essential to understanding the attraction

BASIC CONSIDERATIONS

IS WALT DISNEY WORLD *for* YOU?

ALMOST ALL VISITORS ENJOY WALT DISNEY WORLD on some level and find things to see and do that they like. In fact, for many, the theme park attractions are just the tip of the iceberg. The more salient question, then (because this is a family vacation), is whether the members of your family basically like the same things. If you do, fine. If not, how will you handle the differing agendas?

A mother from Toronto wrote a couple of years ago describing her husband's aversion to Disney's (in his terms) "phony, plastic, and idealized version of life." Touring the theme parks, he was a real cynic and managed to diminish the experience for the rest of the family. As it happened, however, dad's pejorative point of view didn't extend to the Disney golf courses. So mom packed him up and sent him golfing while the family enjoyed the theme parks.

If you have someone in your family who doesn't like theme parks or, for whatever reason, doesn't care for Disney's brand of entertainment, it helps to get the attitude out in the open. Our recommendation is to deal with the person up front. Glossing over or ignoring the contrary opinion and hoping that "Tom will like it once he gets there" is naive and unrealistic. Either leave Tom at home, or help him discover and plan activities that he will enjoy, resigning yourself in the process to the fact that the family won't be together at all times.

DIFFERENT FOLKS, DIFFERENT STROKES

IT'S NO SECRET THAT WE AT THE *Unofficial Guides* believe thorough planning is an essential key to a successful Walt Disney World vacation. It's also no secret that our emphasis on planning rubs some folks the wrong way. One author's sister and her husband, for example, are spontaneous people and do not appreciate the concept of detailed planning or, more particularly, following one of our touring plans when they visit the theme parks. To them the most important thing is to relax, take things as they come, and enjoy the moment. Sometimes they arrive at Epcot at 10:30 in the morning (impossibly late for us *Unofficial Guide* types), walk around enjoying the landscaping and architecture, and then sit with a cup of espresso, watching other guests race around the park like maniacs. They would be the first to admit that they don't see many attractions, but experiencing attractions is not what lights their sparklers.

Not coincidentally, most of our readers are big on planning. When they go to the theme park, they want to experience the attractions, and the shorter the lines, the better. They are willing to sacrifice some spontaneity for touring efficiency.

We want you to have the best possible time, whatever that means to you, so plan (or not) according to your preference. The point here is that most families (unlike my sister and her husband) are not entirely in agreement on this planning versus spontaneity issue. If you are a serious planner and your oldest daughter and husband are free spirits, you've got the makings of a problem. In practice, the way this and similar scenarios shake out is that the planner (usually the more assertive or type-A person) just takes over. Sometimes daughter and husband go along and everything works out, but just as often they feel resentful. There are as many ways of developing a win-win compromise as there are well-intentioned people on different sides of this situation. How you settle it is up to you. We're simply suggesting that you examine the problem and work out the solution *before* you go on vacation.

THE NATURE OF THE BEAST

Bob

Sehlinger's Law postulates that the number of adults required to take care of an active toddler is equal to the number of adults present, plus one.

THOUGH MANY PARENTS DON'T REALIZE IT, there is no law that says you must take your kids to Walt Disney World. Likewise, there's no law that says you will enjoy Walt Disney World. And although we will help you make the most of any visit, we can't change the basic nature of the beast . . . er, mouse. A Walt Disney World vacation is an active and physically demanding undertaking. Regimentation, getting up early, lots of walking, waiting in lines, fighting crowds, and (often) enduring heat and humidity are as intrinsic to a Walt Disney World vacation as stripes are to a zebra. Especially if you're traveling with children, you'll need a sense of humor, more than a modicum of patience, and the ability to roll with the punches.

KNOW THYSELF AND NOTHING TO EXCESS

THIS GOOD ADVICE WAS MADE AVAILABLE to ancient Greeks courtesy of the oracle of Apollo at Delphi, who gave us permission to pass it along to you. First, concerning the "know thyself" part, we want you to do some serious thinking concerning what you want in a vacation. We also want you to entertain the notion that having fun and deriving pleasure from your vacation may be very different indeed from doing and seeing as much as possible.

Because Walt Disney World is expensive, many families confuse "seeing everything" in order to "get our money's worth" with having a great time. Sometimes the two are compatible, but more often they are not. So, if sleeping in, relaxing with the paper over coffee, sunbathing by the pool, or taking a nap ranks high on your vacation hit parade, you need to accord them due emphasis on your Disney visit (are you listening?), even if it means you see less of the theme parks.

You can enjoy a perfectly wonderful time in the World if you are realistic, organized, and prepared.
Liliane

Which brings us to the "nothing to excess" part. At Walt Disney World, especially if you are touring with children, less is definitely more. Trust us, you cannot go full tilt dawn to dark in the theme parks day after day. First you'll get tired, then you'll get cranky, and then you'll adopt a production mentality ("we've got three more rides and then we can go back to the hotel"). Finally, you'll hit the wall because you just can't maintain the pace.

Plan on seeing Walt Disney World in bite-size chunks with plenty of sleeping, swimming, napping, and relaxing in between. Ask yourself over and over in both the planning stage and while you are at Walt Disney World: What will contribute the greatest contentedness, satisfaction, and harmony? Trust your instincts. If stopping for ice cream or returning to the hotel for a dip feels like more fun than seeing another attraction, do it—even if it means wasting the remaining hours of an expensive admissions pass.

Get a grip on your needs and preferences before you leave home, and
Bob
develop an itinerary that incorporates all the things that make you happiest.

The **AGE THING**

THERE IS A LOT OF SERIOUS COGITATION among parents and grandparents in regard to how old a child should be before embarking on a trip to Walt Disney World. The answer, not always obvious, stems from the personalities and maturity of the children, as well as the personalities and parenting style of the adults.

Walt Disney World for Infants and Toddlers

We believe that traveling with infants and toddlers is a great idea. Developmentally, travel is a stimulating learning experience for even the youngest of children. Infants, of course, will not know Mickey Mouse from a draft horse but will respond to sun and shade, music, bright colors, and the extra attention they receive from you. From first steps to full mobility, toddlers respond to the excitement and spectacle of Walt Disney World, though of course in a much different way than you do. Your toddler will prefer splashing in fountains and clambering over curbs and benches to experiencing most attractions, but no matter: He or she will still have a great time.

Somewhere between 4 and 6 years of age, your child will experience the first vacation that he or she will remember as an adult. Though more likely to remember the comfortable coziness of the hotel room than the theme parks, the child will be able to experience and comprehend many attractions and will be a much fuller participant in your vacation. Even so, his or her favorite activity is likely to be swimming in the hotel pool.

As concerns infants and toddlers, there are good reasons and bad reasons for vacationing at Walt Disney World. A good reason for taking your little one to Walt Disney World is that you want to go and there's no one available to care for your child during your absence. Philosophically, we are very much against putting your life (including your vacation) on hold until your children are older.

Traveling with infants and toddlers sharpens parenting skills and makes the entire family more mobile and flexible, resulting in a richer, fuller life for all.

Liliane

Especially if you have children of varying ages (or plan to, for that matter), it's better to take the show on the road than to wait until the youngest reaches the perceived ideal age. If your family includes a toddler or infant, you will find everything from private facilities for breast-feeding to changing tables in both men's and women's restrooms to facilitate baby's care. Your whole family will be able to tour together with fewer hassles than on a picnic outing at home.

An illogical reason, however, for taking an infant or toddler to Walt Disney World is that you think Walt Disney World is the perfect vacation destination for babies. It's not, so think again if you are contemplating Walt Disney World primarily for your child's enjoyment. For starters, attractions are geared more toward older children and adults. Even designer play areas like Tom Sawyer Island in the Magic Kingdom are developed with older children in mind.

By way of example, one author has a friend who bought a camcorder when his first child was born. He delighted in documenting his son's reaction to various new experiences on video. One memorable night when the baby was about 18 months old, he recorded the baby eating a variety of foods (from whipped cream to dill pickles) that he had never tried before. While some of the taste sensations elicited wild expressions and animated responses from the baby, the exercise was clearly intended for the amusement of Dad, not junior.

That said, let us stress that for the well prepared, taking a toddler to Walt Disney World can be a totally glorious experience. There's truly nothing like watching your child respond to the color, the sound, the festivity, and, most of all, the characters. You'll return home with scrapbooks of photos that you will treasure forever. Your little one won't remember much, but never mind. Your memories will be unforgettable.

Along similar lines, remember when you were little and you got that nifty electric train for Christmas, the one Dad wouldn't let you play with? Did you ever wonder who that train was really for? Ask yourself the same question about your vacation to Walt Disney World. Whose dream are you trying to make come true: yours or your child's?

If you elect to take your infant or toddler to Walt Disney World, rest assured that their needs have been anticipated. The major theme parks have centralized facilities for infant and toddler care. Everything necessary for changing diapers, preparing formula, and warming bottles and food is available. Dads in charge of little ones are welcome at the centers and can use most services offered. In addition, men's rooms in the major theme parks have changing tables.

Baby supplies—including disposable diapers, formula, and baby food—are for sale, and there are rockers and special chairs for nursing mothers.

Liliane

Infants and toddlers are allowed to experience any attraction that doesn't have minimum height or age restrictions. A Minneapolis mom suggests using a baby sling:

> We used a baby sling on our trip and thought it was great when standing in the lines—much better than a stroller, which you have to park before getting in line (and navigate through crowds). My baby was still nursing when we went to Walt Disney World. The only really great place I found to nurse in the Magic Kingdom was a hidden bench in the shade in Adventureland in between the snack stand (next to Tiki Room) and the small shops. It is impractical to go to the baby station every time, so a nursing mom better be comfortable about nursing in very public situations.

Two points in our reader's comment warrant elaboration. First, the rental strollers at all of the major theme parks are designed for toddlers and children up to 3 and 4 years old but are definitely not for infants. If you bring pillows and padding, the rental strollers can be made to work. You can bring your own stroller, but unless it's collapsible, you will not be able to take it on Disney trams, buses, or boats.

Even if you opt for a stroller (your own or a rental), we nevertheless recommend that you also bring a baby sling or baby/child backpack. Simply put, there will be many times in the theme parks when you will have to park the stroller and carry your child. As an aside, if you haven't checked out baby slings and packs lately, you'll be amazed by some of the technological advances made in these products.

The second point that needs addressing is our reader's perception that there are not many good places in the theme parks for breastfeeding unless you are accustomed to nursing in public. Many nursing moms recommend breast-feeding during a dark Disney theater presentation. This only works, however, if the presentation is long enough for the baby to finish nursing. *The Hall of Presidents* at the Magic Kingdom and *The American Adventure* at Epcot will afford you about 23 and 29 minutes, respectively.

Many Disney shows run back to back with only 1 or 2 minutes in between to change the audience. If you want to breast-feed and require more time than the length of the show, tell the cast member on entering that you want to breast-feed and ask if you can remain in the theater and watch a second showing while your baby finishes. Also keep in mind that many shows may have special effects or loud sound tracks that may make children even as old as 7 uncomfortable.

In addition to providing an alternative to carrying your child, a stroller serves as a handy cart for diaper bags, water bottles, and other items you deem necessary.

Liliane

If you can adjust to nursing in more public places with your breast and the baby's head covered with a shawl or some such, nursing will not be a problem at all. Even on the most crowded days, you can always find a back corner of a restaurant or a comparatively secluded park bench or garden spot to nurse. Finally, the Baby Care Centers, with their private nursing rooms, are centrally located in all of the parks except the Studios.

Walt Disney World for 4-, 5-, and 6-Year-Olds

Children ages 4–6 vary immensely in their capacity to comprehend and enjoy Walt Disney World. With this age group, the go/no-go decision is a judgment call. If your child is sturdy, easygoing, fairly adventuresome, and demonstrates a high degree of independence, the trip will probably work. On the other hand, if your child tires easily, is temperamental, or is a bit timid or reticent in embracing new experiences, you're much better off waiting a few years. Whereas the travel and sensory-overload problems of infants and toddlers can be addressed and (usually) remedied on the go, discontented 4- to 6-year-olds have the ability to stop a family dead in its tracks, as this mother of three from Cape May, New Jersey, attests:

> My 5-year-old was scared pretty bad on [the] Snow White [ride] our first day at Disney World. From then on, for the rest of the trip, we had to coax and reassure her before each and every ride before she would go. It was like pulling teeth.

If you have a tiring, clinging, and/or difficult 4- to 6-year-old who, for whatever circumstances, will be part of your group, you can sidestep or diminish potential problems with a bit of pretrip preparation. Even if your preschooler is plucky and game, the same prep measures (described later in this section) will enhance his or her experience and make life easier for the rest of the family.

Parents who understand that a visit with 3- to 6-year-old children is going to be more about the cumulative experience than it is about seeing it all will have a blast, as well as wonderful memories of their children's amazement.

The Ideal Age

Although our readers report both successful trips as well as disasters with children of all ages, the consensus ideal children's ages for family compatibility and togetherness at Walt Disney World are 8–12 years. This age group is old enough, tall enough, and sufficiently stalwart to experience, understand, and appreciate practically all Disney attractions. Moreover, they are developed to the extent that they can get around the parks on their own steam without being carried or collapsing. Best of all, they are still young enough to enjoy being with mom and dad. From our experience, ages 10–12 are better than 8 and 9, though what you gain in maturity is at the cost of that irrepressible, wide-eyed wonder so prevalent in the 8- and 9-year-olds.

Walt Disney World for Teens

Teens love Walt Disney World, and for parents of teens the World is a nearly perfect, albeit expensive, vacation choice. Although your teens might not be as wide-eyed and impressionable as their younger sibs, they are at an age where they can sample, understand, and enjoy practically everything Walt Disney World has to offer.

For parents, Walt Disney World is a vacation destination where you can permit your teens an extraordinary amount of freedom. The entertainment is wholesome, the venues are safe, and the entire complex of hotels, theme parks, restaurants, and shopping centers is accessible via the Walt Disney World transportation system. The transportation system allows you, for example, to enjoy a romantic dinner and an early bedtime while your teens take in the late-night fireworks at the theme parks. After the fireworks, a Disney bus, boat, or monorail will deposit them safely back at the hotel.

Because most adolescents relish freedom, you may have difficulty keeping your teens with the rest of the family. Thus, if one of your objectives is to spend time with your teenage children during your Disney World vacation, you will need to establish some clear-cut guidelines regarding togetherness and separateness before you leave home. Make your teens part of the discussion and try to meet them halfway in crafting a decision everyone can live with. For your teens, touring on their own at Walt Disney World is tantamount to being independent in a large city. It's intoxicating, to say the least, and can be an excellent learning experience, if not a rite of passage. In any event, we're not suggesting that you just turn them loose. Rather, we are just attempting to sensitize you to the fact that for your teens, there are some transcendent issues involved.

Most teens crave the company of other teens. If you have a solitary teen in your family, do not be surprised if he or she wants to invite a friend on your vacation. If you are invested in sharing intimate, quality time with your solitary teen, the presence of a friend will make this difficult, if not impossible. However, if you turn down the request to bring a friend, be prepared to go the extra mile to be a companion to your teen at Walt Disney World. Expressed differently, if you're a teen, it's not much fun to ride Space Mountain by yourself.

One specific issue that absolutely should be addressed before you leave home is what assistance (if any) you expect from your teen in regard to helping with younger children in the family. Once again, try to carve out a win-win compromise. Consider the case of the mother from Indiana who had a teenage daughter from an earlier marriage and two children under age 10 from a second marriage. After a couple of vacations where she thrust the unwilling teen into the position of being a surrogate parent to her stepsisters, the teen declined henceforth to participate in family vacations.

Many parents have written the *Unofficial Guide* asking if there are unsafe places at Walt Disney World or places where teens simply should not be allowed to go. Although the answer depends more on your family values and the relative maturity of your teens than on Walt Disney World, the basic answer is no. Though it's true that teens (or adults, for that matter) who are looking for trouble can find it anywhere, there is absolutely nothing at Walt Disney World that could be construed as a precipitant or a catalyst.

As a final aside, if you allow your teens some independence and they are getting around on the Walt Disney World transportation system, expect some schedule slippage. There are no posted transportation schedules other than when service begins in the morning and when service terminates at night. Thus, to catch a bus, for example, you just go to a bus station and wait for the next bus to your Disney World destination. If you happen to just miss the bus, you might have to wait 15–45 minutes (more often 15–20 minutes) for the next one. If punctuality is essential, advise your independent teens to arrive at a transportation station an hour before they are expected somewhere in order to allow sufficient time for the commute.

About **INVITING** *Your* **CHILDREN'S FRIENDS**

IF YOUR CHILDREN WANT TO INVITE FRIENDS on your Walt Disney World vacation, give your decision careful thought. There's more involved here than might be apparent. First, consider the logistics of numbers. Is there room in the car? Will you have to leave something at home that you had planned on taking to make room in the trunk for the friend's luggage? Will additional hotel rooms or a larger condo be required? Will the increased number of people in your group make it hard to get a table at a restaurant?

If you determine that you can logistically accommodate one or more friends, the next step is to consider how the inclusion of the friend will affect your group's dynamics. Generally speaking, the presence of a friend will make it harder to really connect with your own children. So if one of your vacation goals is an intimate bonding experience with your children, the addition of friends will probably frustrate your attempts to realize that objective.

If family relationship building is not necessarily a primary objective of your vacation, it's quite possible that the inclusion of a friend will make life easier for you. This is especially true in the case of only children, who may otherwise depend exclusively on you to keep them happy and occupied. Having a friend along can take the pressure off and give you some much-needed breathing room.

If you decide to allow a friend to accompany you, limit the selection to children you know really well and whose parents you also know. Your Walt Disney World vacation is not the time to include "my friend Eddie from school" whom you've never met. Your children's friends who have spent time in your home will have a sense of your parenting style, and you will have a sense of their personality, behavior, and compatibility with your family. Assess the prospective child's potential to fit in well on a long trip. Is he or she polite, personable, fun to be with, and reasonably mature? Does he or she relate well to you and to the other members of your family?

Because a Walt Disney World vacation is not, for most of us, a spur-of-the-moment thing, you should have adequate time to evaluate potential candidate friends. A trip to the mall including a meal in a sit-down restaurant will tell you volumes about the friend. Likewise, inviting the friend to share dinner with the family and then spend the night will provide a lot of relevant information. Ideally this type of evaluation should take place early on in the normal course of family events, before you discuss the possibility of a friend joining you on your vacation. This will allow you to size things up without your child (or the friend) realizing that an evaluation is taking place.

By seizing the initiative, you can guide the outcome. Ann, a Springfield, Ohio, mom, for example, anticipated that her 12-year-old son would ask to take a friend on their vacation. As she pondered the various friends her son might propose, she came up with four names. One, an otherwise sweet child, had a medical condition that Ann felt unqualified to monitor or treat. A second friend was overly aggressive with younger children and was often socially inappropriate for his age. Two other friends, Chuck and Marty, with whom she had had a generally positive experience, were good candidates for the trip. After orchestrating some opportunities to spend time with each of the boys, she made her decision and asked her son, "Would you like to take Marty with us to Disney World?" Her son was delighted, and Ann had diplomatically preempted having to turn down friends her son might have proposed.

We recommend that you do the inviting, instead of your child, and that you extend the invitation to the parent (to avoid disappointment, you might want to sound out the friend's parent before broaching the issue with your child). Observing this recommendation will allow you to query the friend's parents concerning food preferences, any medical conditions, how discipline is administered in the friend's family, how the friend's parents feel about the way you administer discipline, and the parents' expectation regarding religious observations while their child is in your care.

Before you extend the invitation, give some serious thought to who pays for what. Make a specific proposal for financing the trip a part of your invitation, for example: "There's room for Marty in the hotel room, and transportation's no problem because we're driving. So we'll just need you to pick up Marty's meals, theme park admissions, and spending money."

A **FEW WORDS** *for* **SINGLE PARENTS**

BECAUSE SINGLE PARENTS GENERALLY are also working parents, planning a special getaway with your children can be the best way to spend some quality time together. But remember, the vacation is not just for your child—it's for you too. You might invite a grandparent or a favorite aunt or uncle along; the other adult provides nice company for you, and your child will benefit from the time with family members. You might likewise consider inviting an adult friend.

Though bringing along an adult friend or family member is the best option, the reality is that many single parents don't have friends, grandparents, or favorite aunts or uncles who can make the trip. And while spending time with your child is wonderful, it is very difficult to match the energy level of your child if you are the sole focus of his or her world.

One alternative: Try to meet other single parents at Walt Disney World. It may seem odd, but most of them are in the same boat as you; besides, all you have to do is ask. Another option, albeit expensive, is to take along a trustworthy babysitter (18 or up) to travel with you.

The easiest way to meet other single parents at the World is to hang out at the hotel pool. Make your way there on the day you arrive, after traveling by car or plane and without enough time to blow a full admission ticket at a theme park. In any event, a couple of hours spent poolside is a relaxing way to start your vacation.

If you visit Walt Disney World with another single parent, get adjoining rooms; take turns watching all the kids; and, on at least one night, get a sitter and enjoy an evening out.

Throughout this book we mention the importance of good planning and touring. For a single parent, this is an absolute must. In addition, make sure that you set aside some downtime back at the hotel every day.

Finally, don't try to spend every moment with your children on vacation. Instead, plan some activities for your children with other children. Disney educational programs for children, for example, are worth considering. Then take advantage of your free time to do what you want to do: Read a book, have a massage, take a long walk, or enjoy a catnap.

While pricey, one of the best ways for single parents to relax is to add a three- or four-night cruise to their Disney stay. Onboard activities will keep your child occupied and give you time to relax.

"HE WHO HESITATES IS LAUNCHED!" *Tips and Warnings for Grandparents*

SENIORS OFTEN GET INTO PREDICAMENTS caused by touring with grandchildren. Run ragged and pressured to endure a blistering pace, many seniors just concentrate on surviving Walt Disney World rather than enjoying it. The theme parks have as much to offer older visitors as they do children, and seniors must either set the pace or dispatch the young folks to tour on their own.

An older reader from Alabaster, Alabama, writes:

The main thing I want to say is that being a senior is not for wusses. At Disney World particularly, it requires courage and pluck. Things that used to be easy take a lot of effort, and sometimes your brain has to wait for your body to catch up. Half the time, your grandchildren treat you like a crumbling ruin and then turn around and trick you into getting on a roller coaster in the dark. What you need to tell seniors is that they have to be alert and not trust anyone. Not their children or even the Disney people, and especially not their grandchildren. When your grandchildren want you to go on a ride, don't follow along blindly like a lamb to the slaughter. Make sure you know what the ride is all about. Stand your ground and do not waffle. He who hesitates is launched!

If you don't get to see much of your grandchildren, you might think that Walt Disney World is the perfect place for a little bonding and togetherness. Wrong! Walt Disney World can potentially send children into system overload and can precipitate behaviors that pose a challenge even to adoring parents, never mind grandparents. You don't take your grandchildren straight to Disney World for the same reason you don't buy your 16-year-old son a Ferrari: Handling it safely and well requires some experience.

Begin by spending time with your grandchildren in an environment that you can control. Have them over one at a time for dinner and to spend the night. Check out how they respond to your oversight and discipline. Most of all, zero in on whether you are compatible, enjoy each other's company, and have fun together. Determine that you can set limits and that they will accept those limits. When you reach this stage, you can contemplate some outings to the zoo, the movies, the mall, or the state fair. Gauge how demanding your grandchildren are when you are out of the house. Eat a meal or two in a full-service restaurant to get a sense of their social skills and their ability to behave appropriately. Don't expect perfection, and be prepared to modify your behavior a little too. As a senior friend of mine told her husband (none too decorously), "You can't see Walt Disney World sitting on a stick."

If you have a good relationship with your grandchildren and have had a positive one-on-one experience taking care of them, you might consider a trip to Walt Disney World. If you do, we have two recommendations. First, visit Walt Disney World without them to get an idea of what you're getting into. A scouting trip will also provide you with an opportunity to enjoy some of the attractions that won't be on the itinerary when you return with the grandkids. Second, if you are considering a trip of a week's duration, you might think about buying a Disney package that combines 4 days at Walt Disney World with a 3-day cruise. In addition to being a memorable experience for your grandchildren, the cruise provides plenty of structure for children of almost every age, thus allowing you to be with them but also to have some time off. Call the Disney Cruise Line at ☎ 800-951-3532 or visit **disneycruise.com**.

Tips for Grandparents

1. It's best to take one grandchild at a time, two at the most. Cousins can be better than siblings because they don't fight as much. To preclude sibling jealousy, try connecting the trip to a child's milestone, such as finishing the sixth grade.
2. Let your grandchildren help plan the vacation, and keep the first one short. Be flexible and don't overplan.
3. Discuss mealtimes and bedtime. Fortunately, many grandparents are on an early dinner schedule, which works nicely with younger children. Also, if you want to plan a special evening out, be sure to make the reservation ahead of time.
4. Gear plans to your grandchildren's age levels, because if they're not happy, you won't be happy.
5. Create an itinerary that offers some supervised activities for children in case you need a rest.
6. If you're traveling by car, this is the one time we highly recommend headphones. Kids' musical tastes are vastly different from most grandparents'. It's simply more enjoyable when everyone can listen to his or her own preferred style of music, at least for some portion of the trip.
7. Take along a night-light.

8. Carry a notarized statement from parents for permission for medical care in case of an emergency. Also be sure you have insurance information and copies of any prescriptions for medicines the kids may be on. Ditto for eyeglass prescriptions.

9. Tell your grandchildren about any medical problems you may have so they can be prepared if there's an emergency.

10. Many attractions and hotels offer discounts for seniors, so be sure you check ahead of time for bargains.

11. Plan your evening meal early to avoid long waits. And make advance reservations if you're dining in a popular spot, even if it's early. Take some crayons and paper to keep younger kids occupied.

ORDER *and* DISCIPLINE *on the* ROAD

OK, OK, WIPE THAT SMIRK OFF YOUR FACE. Order and discipline on the road may seem like an oxymoron to you, but you won't be hooting when your 5-year-old launches a screaming stem-winder in the middle of Fantasyland. Your willingness to give this subject serious consideration before you leave home may well be the most important element of your pretrip preparation.

Discipline and maintaining order are more difficult when traveling because everyone is, as a Boston mom put it, "in and out" (in strange surroundings and out of the normal routine). For children, it's hard to contain excitement and anticipation that pop to the surface in the form of fidgety hyperactivity, nervous energy, and sometimes, acting out. Confinement in a car, plane, or hotel room only exacerbates the situation, and kids are often louder than normal, more aggressive with siblings, and much more inclined to push the envelope of parental patience and control. Once in the theme parks, it doesn't get much better. There's more elbow room, but there's also overstimulation, crowds, heat, and miles of walking. All this coupled with marginal or inadequate rest can lead to meltdown in the most harmonious of families.

The following discussion was developed by leading child psychologist Dr. Karen Turnbow, who has contributed to the *Unofficial Guides* for years and who has spent many days at Walt Disney World conducting research and observing families.

Sound parenting and standards of discipline practiced at home, applied consistently, will suffice to handle most situations on vacation. Still, it's instructive to study the hand you are dealt when traveling. For starters, aside from being jazzed and ablaze with adrenaline, your kids may believe that rules followed at home are somehow suspended when traveling. Parents reinforce this misguided intuition by being inordinately lenient in the interest of maintaining peace in the family. While some of your home protocols (cleaning your plate, going to bed at a set time, and such) might be relaxed to good effect on vacation, differing from your normal approach to discipline can precipitate major misunderstanding and possibly disaster.

Children, not unexpectedly, are likely to believe that a vacation (especially a vacation to Walt Disney World) is expressly for them. This reinforces their focus on their own needs and largely erases any consideration of yours. Such a mind-set dramatically increases their sense of hurt and disappointment when you correct them or deny them something they want. An incident that would hardly elicit a pouty lip at home could well escalate to tears or defiance when traveling.

The stakes are high for everyone on a vacation; for you because of the cost in time and dollars, but also because your vacation represents a rare opportunity for rejuvenation and renewal. The stakes are high for your children too. Children tend to romanticize travel, building anticipation to an almost unbearable level. Discussing the trip in advance can ground expectations to a certain extent, but a child's imagination will, in the end, trump reality every time. The good news is that you can take advantage of your children's emotional state to establish pre-agreed rules and conditions for their conduct while on vacation. Because your children want what's being offered sooooo badly, they will be unusually accepting and conscientious regarding whatever rules are agreed upon.

Liliane

Discuss your vacation needs with your children and explore their wants and expectations as well before you depart on your trip.

According to Dr. Turnbow, successful response to (or avoidance of) behavioral problems on the road begins with a clear-cut disciplinary policy at home. Both at home and on vacation, the approach should be the same and should be based on the following key concepts:

1. LET EXPECTATIONS BE KNOWN. Discuss what you expect from your children but don't try to cover every imaginable situation. Cover expectations in regard to compliance with parental directives, treatment of siblings, resolution of disputes, schedule (including wake-up and bedtimes), courtesy and manners, staying together, and who pays for what.

2. EXPLAIN THE CONSEQUENCES OF NONCOMPLIANCE. Detail very clearly and firmly the consequences of unmet expectations. This should be very straightforward and unambiguous. If you do X (or don't do X), this is what will happen.

3. WARN YOUR KIDS. You're dealing with excited, expectant children, not machines, so it's important to issue a warning before meting out discipline. It's critical to understand that we're talking about one unequivocal warning rather than multiple warnings or nagging. These undermine your credibility and make your expectations appear relative or less than serious. Multiple warnings or nagging also effectively pass control of the situation from you to your child (who may continue to act out as an attention-getting strategy).

4. FOLLOW THROUGH. If you say that you're going to do something, do it. Period. Children must understand that you are absolutely serious and committed.

5. BE CONSISTENT. Inconsistency makes discipline a random event in the eyes of your children. Random discipline encourages random behavior, which translates to a nearly total loss of parental control. Long-term, both at home and on the road, your response to a given situation or transgression must be perfectly predictable. Structure and repetition, essential for a child to learn, cannot be achieved in the absence of consistency.

Although the above are the five biggies, there are several corollary concepts and techniques that are worthy of consideration.

First, understand that whining, tantrums, defiance, sibling friction, and even holding the group up are ways in which children communicate with parents. Frequently the object or precipitant of a situation has little or no relation to the unacceptable behavior. A fit may on the surface appear to be about the ice cream you refused to buy little Robby, but there's almost always something deeper, a subtext that is closer to the truth (this is the reason why ill behavior often persists after you give in to a child's demands). As often as not the real cause is a need for attention. This need is so powerful in some children that they will subject themselves to certain punishment and parental displeasure to garner the attention they crave.

To get at the root cause of the behavior in question requires both active listening and empowering your child with a "feeling vocabulary." Active listening is a concept that's been around a long time. It involves being alert not only to what a child says, but also to the context in which it is said, to the language used and possible subtext, to the child's emotional state and body language, and even to what's not said. Sounds complicated, but it's basically being attentive to the larger picture, and more to the point, being aware that there is a larger picture.

Helping your child to develop a feeling vocabulary consists of teaching your child to use words to describe what's going on. The idea is to teach the child to articulate what's really troubling him, to be able to identify and express emotions and mood states in language. Of course learning to express feelings is a lifelong experience, but it's much less dependent on innate sensitivity than being provided the tools for expression and being encouraged to use them.

It all begins with convincing your child that you're willing to listen attentively and take what he's saying seriously. Listening to your child, you help him transcend the topical by reframing the conversation to address the underlying emotional state(s). That his brother hit him may have precipitated the mood, but the act is topical and of secondary importance. What you want is for your child to be able to communicate how that makes him feel and to get in touch with those emotions. When you reduce an incident (hitting) to the emotions triggered (anger, hurt, rejection, and so on), you have the foundation for helping him to develop constructive coping strategies. Not only are being in touch with one's feelings and developing constructive coping strategies essential to emotional well-being, but they also beneficially affect behavior. A child who can tell his mother why he is distressed is a child who has discovered a coping strategy far more effective (not to mention easier for all concerned) than a tantrum.

Children are almost never too young to begin learning a feeling vocabulary. And helping your child to be in touch with, and try to communicate, his emotions will stimulate you to focus on your feelings and mood states in a similar way.

SIX MORE TIPS

UNTIL YOU GET THE ACTIVE LISTENING and feeling vocabulary going, be careful not to become part of the problem. There's a whole laundry list of adult responses to bad behavior that only make things worse. Hitting, swatting, yelling, name calling, insulting, belittling, using sarcasm, pleading, nagging, and inducing guilt (as in: "We've spent thousands of dollars to bring you to Disney World and now you're spoiling the trip for everyone") figure prominently on the list.

Responding to a child appropriately in a disciplinary situation requires thought and preparation. Following are key things to keep in mind and techniques to try when your world blows up while waiting in line for Dumbo.

1. BE THE ADULT. It's well understood that children can punch their parents' buttons faster and more lethally than just about anyone or anything else. They've got your number, know precisely how to elicit a response, and are not reluctant to go for the jugular. Fortunately (or unfortunately) you're the adult, and to deal with a situation effectively, you must act like one. If your kids get you ranting and caterwauling, you effectively abdicate your adult status. Worse, you suggest by way of example that being out of control is an acceptable expression of hurt or anger. No matter what happens, repeat the mantra, "I am the adult in this relationship."

2. FREEZE THE ACTION. Being the adult and maintaining control almost always translates to freezing the action, to borrow a sports term. Instead of a knee-jerk response (at a maturity level closer to your child's than yours), freeze the action by disengaging. Wherever you are or whatever the family is doing, stop in place and concentrate on one thing and one thing only: getting all involved to calm down. Practically speaking, this usually means initiating a time-out. It's essential that you take this action immediately. Grabbing your child by the arm or collar and dragging him toward the car or hotel room only escalates the turmoil by prolonging the confrontation and by adding a coercive physical dimension to an already volatile emotional event. If, for the sake of people around you (as when a toddler throws a tantrum in church), it's essential to retreat to a more private place, choose the first place available. Firmly sit the child down and refrain from talking to him until you've both cooled off. This might take a little time, but the investment is worthwhile. Truncating the process is like trying to get on your feet too soon after surgery.

3. ISOLATE THE CHILD. You'll be able to deal with the situation more effectively and expeditiously if the child is isolated with one parent. Dispatch the uninvolved members of your party for a Coke break or have them go on with the activity or itinerary without you (if possible) and arrange to rendezvous later at an agreed time and place. In addition to letting the others get on with their day, isolating the offending child with one parent relieves him of the pressure of being the group's focus of attention and object of anger. Equally important, isolation frees you from the scrutiny and expectations of the others in regard to how to handle the situation.

4. REVIEW THE SITUATION WITH THE CHILD. If, as discussed above, you've made your expectations clear, stated the consequences of failing those expectations, and have administered a warning, review the situation with the child and follow through with the discipline warranted. If, as often occurs, things are not so black and white, encourage the child to communicate his feelings. Try to uncover what occasioned the acting out. Lecturing and accusatory language don't work well here, nor do threats. Dr. Turnbow suggests that a better approach (after the child is calm) is to ask, "What can we do to make this a better day for you?"

5. FREQUENT TANTRUMS OR ACTING OUT. The preceding four points relate to dealing with an incident as opposed to a chronic condition. If a child frequently acts out or throws tantrums, you'll need to employ a somewhat different strategy.

Tantrums are cyclical events evolved from learned behavior. A child learns that he can get your undivided attention by acting out. When you respond, whether by scolding, admonishing, threatening, or negotiating, your response further draws you into the cycle and prolongs the behavior. When you accede to the child's demands, you reinforce the effectiveness of the tantrum and raise the cost of capitulation next time around. When a child thus succeeds in monopolizing your attention, he effectively becomes the person in charge.

To break this cycle, you must disengage from the child. The object is to demonstrate that the cause and effect relationship (that is, tantrum elicits parental attention) is no longer operative. This can be accomplished by refusing to interact with the child as long as the untoward behavior continues. Tell the child that you're unwilling to discuss his problem until he calms down. You can ignore the behavior, remove yourself from the child's presence (or visa versa), or isolate the child with a time-out. The important thing is to disengage quickly and decisively with no discussion or negotiation.

Most children don't pick the family vacation as the time to start throwing tantrums. The behavior will be evident before you leave home, and home is the best place to deal with it. Be forewarned, however, that bad habits die hard, and a child accustomed to getting attention by throwing tantrums will not simply give up after a single instance of disengagement. More likely, the child will at first escalate the intensity and length of his tantrums. By your consistent refusal over several weeks (or even months) to respond to his behavior, however, he will finally adjust to the new paradigm.

Children are cunning as well as observant. Many understand that a tantrum in public is embarrassing to you and that you're more likely to cave in than you would at home. Once again, consistency is the key, along with a bit of anticipation. When traveling, it's not necessary to retreat to the privacy of a hotel room to isolate your child. You can carve out space for time-out almost anywhere: on a theme park bench, in a park, in your car, in a restroom, even on a sidewalk. You can often spot the warning signs of an impending tantrum and head it off by talking to the child before he reaches an explosive emotional pitch.

Tantrums are about getting attention. Giving your child attention when things are on an even keel often preempts acting out.

Liliane

6. SALVAGE OPERATIONS. Children are full of surprises, and sometimes the surprises are not good. If your sweet child manages to make a mistake of mammoth proportions, what do you do? This happened to an Ohio couple, resulting in the offending kid pretty much being grounded for life. Fortunately there were no injuries or lives lost, but the parents had to determine what to do for the remainder of the vacation. For starters, they split the group. One parent escorted the offending child back to the hotel where he was effectively confined to his guest room for the duration. That evening, the parents arranged for in-room sitters for the rest of the stay. Expensive? You bet, but better than watching your whole vacation go down the tubes.

A family at Walt Disney World's Magic Kingdom theme park had a similar experience, although the offense was of a more modest order of magnitude. Because it was their last day of vacation, they elected to place the child in time-out, in the theme park, for the rest of the day. One parent monitored the culprit while the other parent and the siblings enjoyed the attractions. At agreed times the parents would switch places. Once again, not ideal, but preferable to stopping the vacation.

GETTING *Your* ACT TOGETHER

Visiting Walt Disney World is a bit like childbirth—you never really believe what people tell you, but once you have been through it yourself, you know exactly what they were saying!

—Hilary Wolfe, a mother and *Unofficial Guide* reader from Swansea, United Kingdom

GATHERING INFORMATION

IN ADDITION TO THIS GUIDE, our first recommendation is to visit our website, **touringplans.com,** which has essential tools for planning your trip and saving you time and money.

One of the most popular parts of **touringplans.com** is our crowd calendar, which shows crowd projections for each Disney and Universal theme park for every day of the year. Look up the dates of your visit, and the calendar will not only show the projected wait times for each day but will also indicate which theme park will be the least crowded.

We've also written more than 140 Disney-theme-park touring plans in addition to those in this book, featuring variations for holidays, seniors, Extra Magic Hours, and those who like to sleep in. If our plans aren't quite what you're looking for, **touringplans.com** lets you create your own, either from scratch or by using one of ours as a template (we'll automatically include restaurant information, hidden Mickeys, attraction trivia, park hours, and weather forecasts), and share them with family and friends.

To help you select the best resort for your family, we've also provided thousands of photos and dozens of online videos covering every inch of every Disney resort, plus many off-site accommodations.

Our most popular new Web feature is Lines, a mobile application providing continuous real-time updates on wait times at the Walt Disney World and Disneyland parks. Using a combination of our in-park researchers and updates sent in by readers, this new feature allows you to see all current wait and Fastpass-distribution times at every attraction in every park, as well as our estimated wait times for these attractions for the rest of that day and the next. If you have a Web-enabled cell phone, you'll be able to see instantly where the shortest lines are at any time of day. Apps are available via iTunes App Store (search for "touring plans") and Android App Store. Owners of other phones can use the Web-based version at **m.touringplans.com.** Touring plans are also available in Lines, providing step-by-step directions to the most popular attractions with minimal waiting in line.

And as long as you have that smartphone handy while visiting the World, we and your fellow *Unofficial Guide* readers would love it if you could report on the wait times you see while you're there. Go to **m.touringplans.com,** log in to your user account, and click the button labeled "+Time" in the upper right corner to help everyone out.

A big money-saving feature of the website is our Ticket Calculator, which tells you the least-expensive combination of tickets to buy (and where) to see everything you want in the theme parks and water parks.

Much of our Web content—including the online trip planner, resort photos and videos, and the Ticket Calculator—is completely free for anyone to use. Access to part of the site, most notably the crowd calendar, additional touring plans, and in-park wait times, requires a small subscription fee (current-book owners get 50% off). This nominal charge helps keep us online and costs less than a sandwich at Flame Tree Barbecue in the Animal Kingdom. Plus, **touringplans.com** offers a 45-day money-back guarantee—something we don't think Flame Tree can match.

Next, we recommend that you obtain the following:

Request information as far in advance as possible and allow 6 weeks for delivery. Make a checklist of information you request, and follow up if you haven't received your materials within 6 weeks.

Bob

1. **THE WALT DISNEY TRAVEL COMPANY FLORIDA VACATIONS BROCHURE AND DVD** These cover Walt Disney World in its entirety, list rates for all Disney resort hotels and campgrounds, and describe Disney World package vacations. They're available from most travel agents by calling the Walt Disney Travel Company at ☎ 407-828-8101 or 407-934-7639 or by visiting **disneyworld.com.** Be prepared to hold. When you get a representative, ask for the DVD vacation planner.

2. **THE DISNEY CRUISE LINE BROCHURE AND DVD** This brochure provides details on vacation packages that combine a cruise on the Disney Cruise Line with a stay at Disney World. Disney Cruise Line also offers a free DVD that tells all you need to know about Disney cruises and then some. To get a copy, call ☎ 800-951-3532 or order at **disneycruise.com.**

3. **ORLANDO MAGICARD** If you're considering lodging outside Disney World or if you think you might patronize out-of-the-World attractions and restaurants, obtain an Orlando Magicard, a Vacation Planner, and the *Orlando Official Vacation Guide* (all free) from the Orlando Visitors Center. The Magicard entitles you to discounts for hotels, restaurants,

ground transportation, shopping malls, dinner theaters, and non-Disney theme parks and attractions. The Orlando Magicard can be downloaded for printing at **visitorlando.com/magicard.** To order the accommodations guide, call ☎ 800-643-9492. For more information and materials, call ☎ 407-363-5872 weekdays during business hours or 9 a.m.–3 p.m. on weekends, or go to **visitorlando.com.**

4. *FLORIDA ROOMSAVER* Another good source of discounts on lodging, restaurants, and attractions statewide is *Florida RoomSaver*. The guide is free, but you pay $3 for handling ($5 if shipped to Canada). Call ☎ 800-332-3948, Monday–Friday, 8:30 a.m.–5:30 p.m. Eastern Time, or visit **roomsaver.com** for more information. Similar guides to other states are available at the same number.

5. *CHOOSE KISSIMMEE GUIDE* This full-color visitors guide is one of the most complete resources available and is of particular interest to those who intend to lodge outside of Disney World, featuring ads for hotels, rental houses, time-shares, and condominiums, as well as a directory of attractions, restaurants, special events, and other useful info. For a copy, call the Kissimmee Convention and Visitors Bureau at ☎ 800-327-9159 or 407-944-2400, or view it online at **visitkissimmee.com.**

6. **GUIDEBOOK FOR GUESTS WITH DISABILITIES** Pick one up at Guest Relations at any of the parks. Additional information is also available online at **disneyworld.disney.go.com/plain-text.**

7. *QUEENS IN THE KINGDOM: THE ULTIMATE GAY AND LESBIAN GUIDE TO THE DISNEY THEME PARKS* ($17.95) by Jeffrey Epstein and Eddie Shapiro.

PASSPORTER'S GUIDE

A SUPER RESOURCE FOR ANYONE WITH SPECIAL NEEDS is *PassPorter's Open Mouse for Walt Disney World and the Disney Cruise Line* by Deb Wills and Debra Martin Koma. The book covers everything from ADHD to asthma and is available from PassPorter Travel Press at ☎ 877-929-3273 or **passporter.com.**

WALT DISNEY WORLD ON THE WEB

SEARCHING THE INTERNET for Disney information is like navigating an immense maze for a very small piece of cheese: There's a lot of information available, but you may have to wade through list after list until you find the Internet addresses you want and need.

Many individuals maintain elaborate Disney-related websites and chat groups that can provide both correct and incorrect information, depending on who's chatting.

Recommended Websites

Unofficial Guide coauthor Len Testa has combed the Web looking for the best Disney sites. See his picks below.

BEST OFFICIAL THEME-PARK SITE While it still has room for improvement, the official **Walt Disney World website** (**disneyworld.com**) is slightly more useful than the official sites for Universal Studios (**universalorlando.com**) and SeaWorld (**seaworld.com**). All three sites contain information on ticket options, park hours, height requirements for attractions, disabled-guest access, and the like. Disney's site also allows you to make dining reservations online, which is really useful when you don't have enough time to do so on the phone. As an added bonus, you can make online reservations starting at 6 a.m. Eastern Time, an hour before the phone lines open. On the minus side, however, the site uses so many high-tech gimmicks that it sometimes just doesn't work. If you get an error message while trying to make a hotel or dining reservation, just restart your browser and try again. Also be aware that when making hotel reservations, Disney's website will automatically select the more expensive options, such as a water-view room instead of a standard view, and park hopper and water park admission instead of a base ticket. You have to manually undo each of those options every time you change your search criteria too.

BEST GENERAL UNOFFICIAL WALT DISNEY WORLD WEBSITE Besides **touringplans.com,** Deb Wills's **allears.net** is the website we recommend to friends who are interested in making a trip to Disney World. It contains information on virtually every hotel, restaurant, and activity in the World. Want to know what a room at a Disney resort looks like before you book one? This site has photos—sometimes for each floor of a resort. The site is updated several times per week and includes information for guests with special needs, menus from Disney restaurants, ticketing information, maps, and such.

BEST MONEY-SAVING SITE Mary Waring's **mousesavers.com** is the kind of site for which the Web was invented. It keeps an updated list of discounts and reservation codes for use at Disney resorts. The codes are separated into categories such as "For the general public" and "For residents of certain states." Anyone who calls Disney's central reservation office (☎ 407-W-DISNEY) can use a current code and get the discounted rate. Savings can be considerable—up to 40% in many cases. The site also displays discounts for AAA members and Disney Annual Pass holders, making it easy to determine if those options make sense for your trip. Two often-overlooked site features are the discount codes for rental cars and non-Disney hotels in the area.

BEST WALT DISNEY WORLD PREVIEW SITE If you want to prepare your children for the attractions, or if you just want to see what a particular attraction is like, visit **YouTube** (**youtube.com**). Enter the name of the desired attraction in the search bar at the top of the page, and several videos should come up. Videos of indoor ("dark") rides are usually inferior to those of outdoor rides due to poor lighting, but even the videos of indoor rides generally provide a good sense of what the attraction is about.

SOCIAL NETWORK SITES Social network sites such as Facebook and Twitter are popular forums for Disney fans to gather online and share comments, tips, and photos. Following fellow Disney fans as they share their experiences while they're in the parks can make you feel as if you're there, even if you're stuck in a cubicle at work.

BEST DISNEY DISCUSSION BOARDS The best online discussions of all things Disney can be found at **disboards.com.** With tens of thousands of members and millions of posts, these discussion boards are the most active and popular on the Web. And for information about just anything Disney, visit **wdwinfo.com.** For boards that feel more familiar than your neighborhood bar, try **disneyecho.emuck.com.** Disney visitors from the United Kingdom can say "cheerio" to one another whilst online at **thedibb.co.uk** or at **wdisneyw.com/forums,** where tips on transatlantic-airfare discounts, visa requirements, American customs, and more can be found. For the latest news on Disney Vacation Club, try **tagrel.com.**

MOBILE MAGIC Apps are the latest buzz, and Disney certainly knows when to seize an opportunity. Disney, together with Verizon, developed the Mobile Magic App, which for $9.99 is all yours for 180 days. Simply text MAGIC to 2777 on your Verizon phone, and the app will let you keep track of where to meet your kids' favorite characters. The app also lets you check the wait times and Fastpass return times for the park you're in. Finding a restaurant is part of the deal, and Disney will gladly help you plan the rest of your trip. For more information, go to **disneyparks. com/mobilemagic.**

Also check out the $4.99 Undercover Tourist app for the iPhone. The popular app gives you ride wait times, opening hours, and parade times, as well as restaurant and events information. The Traffic Light System helps you find the least-crowded attractions and parks. Interactive maps include Locate Me and Find a Friend features. The GPS tool can even help you find your car. For more information, visit **undercovertourist.com/ united-states/florida/orlando/attractions/avoid-the-lines.html.**

GOING HIGH-TECH WITH LILIANE

Podcasts

If you just can't make it through the year without the Mouse, don't despair. Sounds, images, and news from the World are available in abundance online. Here are some of our favorites.

WDW TODAY *Unofficial Guide* Research Director Len Testa cohosts three podcasts a week (Monday, Wednesday, and Friday) on all things Disney. Subscriptions are available free through iTunes. These programs consistently rank among the top 10 iTunes travel podcasts, drawing almost 40,000 listeners per show. Visit **wdwtoday.com.**

PASSPORTER MOMS PODCAST Two moms, Jennifer and Sara, share tips and chat with friends and guests about Walt Disney World, Disneyland, Disney Cruise Line, and general travel. So get some coffee and listen to some of the best advice out there at **passporter.com/ podcast/home.php.**

WINDOW TO THE MAGIC Paul Barrie, your smooth-voiced host, brings you all the magic with his weekly podcast. The show includes a game called "Where in the Park?" and delivers sounds, pictures, prizes, and more. Check it out at **windowtothemagic.com/podcast.html.**

SOUNDS OF DISNEY Every other Sunday you can join Jeff Davis, also known as The Sorcerer, as he delights his audience with music, news, and Disney songs right from the parks. In addition to the podcast, Davis's website, **srsounds.com,** provides music, videos, pictures, and a message board.

Blogs

Our all-time favorite blogger is Jim Hill, who has been writing about Disney for years at **jimhillmedia.com.** Although Jim undoubtedly loves the Mouse, he tempers his enthusiasm with the right dose of criticism and is perfectly attuned to what's going on behind the scenes.

Another fun place for the latest rumors is **thedisneyblog.com.** We especially like how easy it is to navigate the different categories. From A to Z, it's the way to go! The site is really on top of things, so much so that the *Orlando Sentinel* monitors it regularly and is even known to report on the posts.

BEST SITE FOR BREAKING NEWS AND RUMORS We try to check **wdwmagic. com** every few days for the latest news and rumors about Disney World. The site is popular with Disney fans and park cast members, who often provide insider information on upcoming attractions and developments. It also features pages dedicated to major rides, parades, and shows in each park, including audio and video clips. User forums allow you to read and post messages.

BEST TRIVIA SITES Louis Mongello's excellent *The Walt Disney World Trivia Book* has an equally good online magazine, *Celebrations*, at **celebrationspress.com**—with Disney theme park news and more. Lou also hosts the WDW Radio Show podcast. Check it out on iTunes and at **wdwradio.com.**

At long last, fans of Steven Barrett's *Hidden Mickeys Guide* now have an online destination where they can get updates on the latest tri-circle sightings at **hiddenmickeysguide.com.**

BEST ONLINE TOUR In early 2008, Disney teamed up with Google to present a 3-day virtual walk-through of the Orlando theme parks and resorts via Google Earth. While you can't yet go inside the attractions, you do get an unparalleled simulation of the park experience. Visit **disneyworld.com/3dparks** and hope for the day they're able to pipe the smell of the Main Street Bakery to your PC.

BEST INTERNET RADIO STATION We thought our 200-hour collection of theme-park digital audio was complete until we found **mouseworld radio.com.** Several different radio stations are available (some free, others for a small fee), playing everything from attraction ride scores and hotel background music to old sound clips from Disney-resort TV ads. What makes Mouse World Radio special is that the tracks match what the Disney parks are playing at the time of day you're listening. So every morning at 8 a.m., you'll hear essentially the same music that's currently playing at the Magic Kingdom before it opens.

BEST OFFICIAL MOM'S SITE Who knew? Walt Disney World has a Mom's Panel composed of more than a dozen moms and a few red herrings—er, dads—all chosen from among 10,000-plus applicants. The panelists have a website, **disneyworldmoms.com,** where they offer tips, discuss how to plan a Disney World vacation, and answer questions about how those guys got into the henhouse. The moms are unpaid and are free to speak their minds. One mom actually went from fan to cast member when Disney recruited her to head the panel. And the Mom's Panel is now on Facebook. Become a fan at **facebook. com/disneyworldmoms.**

There are hundreds of other Disney sites, as well as sites that rate and contrast thrill rides in theme parks in the United States and all over the world. Information about Disney World is also available at public libraries, travel agencies, and AAA.

IMPORTANT WALT DISNEY WORLD TELEPHONE NUMBERS

WHEN YOU CALL THE MAIN INFORMATION NUMBER, you'll be offered a menu of options for recorded information on operating hours, recreation areas, shopping, entertainment, tickets, reservations, and driving directions. If you have a question not covered by recorded information, press 8 at any time to speak to a representative. See pages 44–45 for a list.

ALLOCATING TIME

YOU SHOULD ALLOCATE 6 DAYS for a whirlwind tour (7–10 days if you're old-fashioned and insist on some relaxation during your vacation). If you don't have 6-plus days, be prepared to make some hard choices.

A seemingly obvious point lost on many families is that Walt Disney World is not going anywhere. There's no danger that it will be packed up and shipped to Iceland anytime soon. This means that you can come back if you don't see everything this year. Disney has planned it this way, of course, but that doesn't matter. It's infinitely more sane to resign yourself to the reality that seeing everything during one visit is impossible. We recommend, therefore, that you approach Walt Disney World the same

If you must visit during the busy summer season, cut your visit short by 1 or 2 days so that you will have the weekend or a couple of vacation days remaining to recuperate when you get home.

Bob

Important WDW Telephone Numbers

General Information	☎ 407-824-4321 or 407-824-2222
General Information for the Hearing Impaired	☎ 407-939-8255
General Information for Guests with Disabilities	☎ 407-939-7807
Accommodations/Reservations	☎ 407- W-DISNEY or 407-824-8000
Blizzard Beach Information	☎ 407-560-3400
Centracare	☎ 407-200-2273
Formosa Gardens	☎ 407-397-7032
Kissimmee	☎ 407-390-1888
Lake Buena Vista	☎ 407-934-2273
Dr. Phillips	☎ 407-291-9960
Dining Advance Reservations	☎ 407-939-3463
Disabled Guests Special Requests	☎ 407-939-7807
DisneyQuest	☎ 407-828-4600
ESPN Wide World of Sports	☎ 407-939-4263
Golf Reservations and Information	☎ 407-WDW-GOLF or 407-939-4653
Guided Tour Information	☎ 407-WDW-TOUR or 407-939-8687

way you would an eight-course Italian dinner: leisurely, with plenty of time between courses. The best way not to have fun is to cram too much into too little time.

WHEN TO GO TO WALT DISNEY WORLD

LET'S CUT TO THE ESSENCE: Walt Disney World between June 12 and August 18 is rough. You can count on large summer crowds as well as Florida's trademark heat and humidity. Avoid these dates if you can. Ditto for Memorial Day weekend at the beginning of the summer and Labor Day weekend at the end. Other holiday periods (Thanksgiving, Christmas, Easter, Halloween, spring break, and so on) are extremely crowded, but the heat is not as bad.

The least busy time is from Labor Day in September through the beginning of October. Next slowest are the second full week of November through the weekend preceding Thanksgiving, the week after Thanksgiving until the week before Christmas, January 4 through the first week of February (except the Martin Luther King holiday weekend and the weekend of the Disney World Marathon), and the last week of April through early June. Late February, March, and early April are

Lost and Found:	
Yesterday or before (all Disney parks)	☎ 407-824-4245
Yesterday or before (Downtown Disney)	☎ 407-828-3150
Today at the Magic Kingdom	☎ 407-824-4521
Today at Epcot	☎ 407-560-7500
Today at Disney's Hollywood Studios	☎ 407-560-4668
Today at Animal Kingdom	☎ 407-938-2785
Outdoor Recreation Reservations and Information	☎ 407-WDW-PLAY or 407-939-7529
Resort Dining and Recreational Information	☎ 407-WDW-DINE or 407-939-3463
Security	☎ 407-560-7959 (*routine*) or 407-560-1990 (*urgent*)
Tennis Reservations/Lessons	☎ 407-621-1991
Ticket Inquiries	☎ 407-566-4985
Typhoon Lagoon Information	☎ 407-560-6296
Walt Disney Travel Company	☎ 407-939-6244
Weather Information	☎ 407-827-4545
Wrecker Service (*or call Security after hours; see above*)	☎ 407-824-0976

dicey. Crowds ebb and flow according to spring-break schedules and the timing of Presidents Day weekend. Though crowds have grown in September and October as a result of promotions aimed at locals and the international market, these months continue to be good for weekday touring at the Magic Kingdom, Disney's Hollywood Studios, and Disney's Animal Kingdom, as well as for weekend visits to Epcot.

So, parents, what to do? If your children are of preschool age, definitely go during a cooler, less-crowded time. If you have school-age children, look first for an anomaly in your school-year schedule: in other words, a time when your kids will be out of school when most other schools are in session. Anomalies are most often found at the beginning or end of the school year (for example, school starts late or lets out early), at Christmas, or at spring break. In the event that no such anomalies exist, and providing that your kids are good students, our recommendation is to ask permission to take your children out of school either just before or after the Thanksgiving holiday. Teachers can assign lessons that can be made

You can't pick a less crowded time to visit Walt Disney World than the period between Labor Day and October 1.

Bob

Annual Attendance Patterns at the Magic Kingdom

Visitors per day (thousands)

Christmas   New Year's

Easter

Thanksgiving   Presidents   Memorial
                      Day   Day
Labor   College
Day   Spring Break

100
80
60
40
20
0

Sept Oct Nov Dec Jan Feb Mar Apr May June July Aug

up at home over the Thanksgiving holiday, either before or after your Walt Disney World vacation.

If none of these options are workable for your family, consider visiting Walt Disney World the week immediately before school starts (excluding Labor Day weekend) or the week immediately after school lets out (excluding Memorial Day weekend). This strategy should remove you from the really big mob scenes by about a week or more.

The time that works best for kids is the last week before school ends. Because grades must be finalized earlier, there is often little going on at school during that week. Check far in advance with your child's teacher to determine if any special exams or projects will occur in that last week. If no major assignments are on the child's schedule, then go for it.

Incidentally, taking your kids out of school for more than a few days is problematic. We have received well-considered letters from parents and teachers who don't think taking kids out of school is such a hot idea. A Fairfax, Virginia, dad put it thus:

> My wife and I do not encourage families to take their children out of school in order to avoid the crowds at Walt Disney World during the summer months. My wife is an eighth-grade science teacher of chemistry and physics. She has parents pull their children, some honor-roll students, out of school for vacations, only to discover when they return that the students are unable to comprehend the material. Several students have been so thoroughly lost in their assignments that they ask if they can be excused from the tests. Parental suspicions [about] the quality of their children's education should be raised when children go to school for 6 hours a day yet

supposedly can complete this same instruction with "less than an hour of homework" each night.

Likewise, a high-school teacher from Louisville, Kentucky, didn't mince words on this subject:

Teachers absolutely hate it when a kid misses school for a week because: (a) parents expect a neat little educational packet to take with them as if every minute can be planned—not practicable; (b) when the kid returns, he is going to be behind, and it is difficult to make up classroom instruction [at the time] when the kid needs it.

If a parent bothers to ask my opinion, I tell them bluntly it's their choice. If the student's grades go down, then they have to accept that as part of their family decision. I have a student out this entire week, skiing in Colorado. There's no way she can make up some of the class activities (and that's exactly what I told her mom).

Though we strongly recommend going to Disney World at less busy times of year, you should know that there are trade-offs. The parks often open late and close early in the off-seasons. When they open as late as 10 a.m., everyone arrives about the same time, making it hard to beat the crowd. A late opening coupled with an early closing drastically reduces the hours available for touring. Even when crowds are small, it's difficult to see a big park like the Magic Kingdom or Epcot 10 a.m.–6 p.m. Early closing (before 8 p.m.) may also mean that evening parades or fireworks are eliminated. And, because these are slow times at Disney World, some rides and attractions may be closed for maintenance or renovation. Finally, temperatures there fluctuate wildly during the late fall, winter, and early spring; daytime lows in the 40s are not uncommon.

BE UNCONVENTIONAL The Orange County Convention Center in Orlando hosts some of the largest conventions and trade shows in the world. Rooms anywhere near Walt Disney World are hard to find when there's a big convention, and as this Toronto, Ontario, reader points out, are also expensive:

If saving money on accommodations is an important part of your trip, be sure to check rates on the Net before you settle on a date. Trade shows at the Orange County Convention Center can host over 100,000 attendees, with most of them staying one to a room. This drives rates on even average properties to two or three times [normal] rates. Since all large conventions are scheduled over 1 year out, these spikes in room rates should be visible up to 12 months prior.

Check the convention schedule for the next 7 months at **occc.net/ global/calendar.**

DON'T FORGET AUGUST Kids go back to school pretty early in Florida (and in a lot of other places too). This makes mid- to late August a good time to visit Walt Disney World for families who can't vacation during the off-season. A New Jersey mother of two school-age children spells it out:

> *The end of August is the PERFECT [reader's emphasis] time to go*
> *(just watch out for hurricanes; it's the season). There were virtually*
> *no wait times, 20 minutes at the most.*

JUNE AND THE EARLY BIRD It's not an easy turnaround, but heading for Walt Disney World in late May or early June as soon as school is out will net big rewards. Late May through about June 12 is still considered shoulder season, so the crowds will not have spiked to summer levels. Also the weather is usually cooler than in late August. An exception to the above is the Memorial Day weekend, though the week following the holiday is one of the best crowd-wise of the whole summer.

HOLIDAYS AND SPECIAL EVENTS AT WALT DISNEY WORLD

YOU CAN'T BEAT THE HOLIDAYS FOR live entertainment, special events, parades, fireworks, and elaborate decorations at the theme parks and resort hotels. Unfortunately, you also can't beat holiday periods for crowds. A mom from Ogden, Utah, puts it this way:

> *Our family spends part of Christmas week at Walt Disney World*
> *every year. We know the lines will be outrageous, but the special*
> *shows, parades, and decorations more than make up for it. For first-*
> *timers who want to see the rides, Christmas is not ideal, but for us*
> *it's the most colorful and exciting time to go.*

A downside to holiday touring is that events held in the evening for which an additional admission charge is required cut into the touring time of those who elect not to attend. This complaint from a Georgia mom is a good example:

> *Mickey's Not-So-Scary Halloween Party seems to have taken over.*
> *Three of the six nights we were at Disney, Magic Kingdom closed*
> *early for the party. And I just refused to spend what amounts to*
> *almost another day's admission for a Halloween parade and spooky*
> *lighting. So, we got gypped out of a full day at MK, which is my kids'*
> *favorite park by far, not once, but three times.*

Here's a look at the larger special events and major holidays at Walt Disney World.

WALT DISNEY WORLD MARATHON Usually held the second weekend after New Year's, the marathon pulls in about 20,000 runners and their families, enough people to affect crowd conditions and pedestrian traffic throughout Disney World. The event expanded to 4 days in 2009 with the addition of kids' races and a health-and-fitness expo. In the spirit of participatory journalism, *Unofficial Guide* author and podcaster Len Testa usually runs the marathon, half marathon, or both. Check the **wdwtoday.com** podcast archives for tips and descriptions for all of Disney's running events.

BLACK HISTORY MONTH It is celebrated throughout Walt Disney World in February. There is no extra charge for the activities (displays, artisans, storytellers, and entertainers), and the celebration's effect on crowd levels is negligible.

CHINESE NEW YEAR Each year the China Pavilion in Epcot has a Chinese New Year celebration. Usually there are Chinese acrobats and special activities for kids.

PRINCESS HALF MARATHON At the end of February, this half marathon weekend draws a crowd. Focused on the female gender, the schedule for the weekend holds a health expo, kid races, and a family 5K in addition to the half marathon. You can expect that park attendance will be up and vehicular and pedestrian traffic will be affected.

MARDI GRAS A little-known event on Mardi Gras is the mini-parade through Port Orleans Resort. Several departments of the resort build floats on golf carts, and the floats are then judged and paraded through the grounds. During the parade they throw New Orleans–style trinkets (such as beads, candy, and doubloons) to the guests who line up to watch. If you will be at Port Orleans on Mardi Gras, ask at the front desk when this event will take place.

ATLANTA BRAVES SPRING TRAINING The Braves hold spring training and play a number of exhibition games at Disney's Wide World of Sports from mid-February through March. You can get the exhibition schedule and purchase tickets by calling TicketMaster at ☎ 800-745-3000 or visiting **ticketmaster.com.** You can watch the training sessions at no charge when you buy general admission to ESPN Wide World of Sports ($13.50 for adults, $10 for ages 3–9).

EASTER School is out; therefore, all the parks will be crowded. By far the most interesting event of the day is the Easter Parade at the Magic Kingdom. Outstanding floats carry Mickey, Minnie, and the gang, all dressed in their Sunday best, in a special parade. Of course, the appearance of the Easter Bunny is guaranteed. If you're staying in Walt Disney World, ask at the front desk about special activities (such as egg hunts) at your hotel and other Disney resorts.

This is also prime season for all restaurants, and special Easter menus are available. For dinner reservations, call ☎ 407-WDW-DINE. For dining options and actual menus, visit **allearsnet.com/din/dining.htm.**

EPCOT INTERNATIONAL FLOWER & GARDEN FESTIVAL Even if you don't have a green thumb, the 30 million blooms will make your eyes pop. This outstanding event is all yours to enjoy, and best of all, it doesn't affect crowd levels at the parks. The festival is held annually March–May.

STAR WARS WEEKENDS On several weekends, usually from mid-May to mid-June, Disney's Hollywood Studios becomes a mecca for *Star Wars* aficionados. It's characters, trivia games, and merchandise galore during these weekends, and kids can even sign up for a *Jedi Training Academy* and test their light-saber skills. Celebrities from the film series are available for autographs and appear in the *Star Wars* Celebrity Parade.

GAY DAYS Since 1991, gay, lesbian, bisexual, and transgendered (GLBT) people from around the world have converged on and around the World in June for a long weekend of events centered around the theme parks. Today, Gay Days attracts more than 140,000 GLBT visitors and their families and friends. Universal and Wet 'n Wild also participate, so be prepared: It's going to be crowded. For more information, visit **gaydays.com.**

FOURTH OF JULY AT WALT DISNEY WORLD Keep in mind that this particular holiday at Walt Disney World basically means crowds, crowds, and more crowds. All parks are in a festive and patriotic mood, and the fireworks are incredible. A very special place to visit is *The Hall of Presidents* at the Magic Kingdom. We recommend leaving the parks prior to the evening fireworks and watching them—from afar—at the Polynesian Resort. Keep in mind that most parks will reach full capacity by 10 a.m., and no advance reservations will get you into a park once it is closed. So pick your park and be prepared to stay there all day. If partying is your thing, consider Downtown Disney, which throws a DJ dance party and a fireworks show of its own.

SOUNDS LIKE SUMMER All summer long, you can dance to classic rock-and-roll hits under the skies of the open-air America Gardens Theater at Epcot. This summer concert series features a lineup of cover bands performing timeless tunes. There are three shows nightly at 5:45 p.m., 7 p.m., and 8:15 p.m., included in park admission.

NIGHT OF JOY For this Christian-music festival usually held the second weekend of September at the Magic Kingdom, crowds are manageable, but there is an extra fee of about $52 a night and $93 for both nights. The lineup of artists has included MercyMe, Jars of Clay, Skillet, Casting Crowns, Kirk Franklin, Rebecca St. James, Jeremy Camp, Todd Agnew, David Crowder Band, Smokie Norful, ZOEgirl, Building 429, Matthew West, and Vicky Beeching. For more information, visit **disneyworld.com/nightofjoy.**

EPCOT INTERNATIONAL FOOD & WINE FESTIVAL Held in the World Showcase late September–mid-November, the celebration represents 30 nations and includes demonstrations, wine seminars, tastings, and opportunities to see some of the world's top chefs. Though many activities are included in Epcot admission, the best workshops and tastings are by reservation only and cost extra. Call ☎ 407-WDW-DINE (939-3463) well in advance for more information. For what it's worth, we think the culinary demonstrations (around $6–$12) and wine and beverage seminars ($8–$13) are some of the best values at Food & Wine. If you think that Epcot's theme is a little too educational, there's nothing like a little wine to take the edge off.

Because most of the food kiosks are set up around World Showcase, it can be difficult to walk through the crowds around some of the popular spots. Wait times at Epcot's attractions, however, are affected only slightly.

WINE AND DINE HALF MARATHON In early October 2010, Disney launched this inaugural event—possibly the only half marathon run at night. The weekend revolves around this unique concept and ends with a post-race party in the midst of Epcot's Food & Wine Festival. Health expos, family races, and kid races are also part of the scheduled events. The number of runners and their cheer squads—combined with the guests who descend upon Epcot for the Food & Wine Festival alone—blow up the crowd levels like an agitated puffer fish. Again, vehicular and pedestrian traffic are disturbed by the running courses throughout Disney property.

HALLOWEEN AND MICKEY'S NOT-SO-SCARY HALLOWEEN PARTY Held each year on two dozen or so nights before Halloween until the night after Halloween, the party runs 7 p.m.–midnight at the Magic Kingdom. The event includes trick-or-treating, Mickey's Boo to You Parade, several DJ parties throughout the park, storytelling with Merlin, and *HalloWishes,* a special spooky fireworks show. Several times that evening, Disney villains will put on a great show followed by a Villains' Mix and Mingle in front of Cinderella Castle. Aimed primarily at younger children, the party is happy and upbeat rather than spooky and scary.

The park will be crowded, so arrive early (we recommend getting there an hour before the beginning of the party, as Disney starts letting guests with party tickets inside the park around 6:30 p.m., sometimes much earlier). Proceed directly to the table where the wristbands identifying you as a party guest are obtained. Also, get the special map for the event with details and hours of all the happenings. Go straight to the rides that are on your must-do list, and after that just enjoy the party. If trick-or-treating is a priority, do that first thing after you arrive or toward the end of the night, when crowds thin out and there are no long lines in front of the trick-or-treating stations.

An absolute must-ride is **The Haunted Mansion,** which is especially spooky but only in the sweetest way. Look for the ghost in the garden of the mansion when queuing up. His hilarious tales and interaction with the guests will make you forget you are standing in line. Characters are out in force all over the park, and the Boo to You Parade is pretty amazing. Our two favorite parts of the parade are the Headless Horseman riding at full speed through the park and The Haunted Mansion's groundskeeper, with his dim lantern in one hand and his bloodhound, followed by a large group of ghosts and gravediggers. The many special activities and the costumed kids and adults help you forget the crowds. So don't be shy: Wear a costume—about 50% of all the adults will be wearing a getup of some kind.

Tickets purchased in advance range $54–$68 plus tax for age 10 and up and $47–$62 plus tax for ages 3–9. Tickets at the gate, if available, typically cost an additional $6.

In addition to activities in the theme parks, Disney's **Fort Wilderness Cabins and Campground** offers haunted carriage rides. The carriage rides include a performer who tells the story of Ichabod Crane and the Headless Horseman from Washington Irving's story "The Legend of Sleepy Hollow." The rides leave from Pioneer Hall and cost $60 per carriage. A carriage can accommodate four adults, or two adults with three small children. This excursion can be booked up to 180 days in advance by calling ☎ 407-WDW-PLAY.

Teens and young adults looking for a non-Disney Halloween happening should check out the party at **Universal CityWalk.** And if you'd rather have a monster with a chain saw running after you, consider attending the Universal theme parks' **Halloween Horror Nights.** (*Note:* No costumes are allowed at the parks on these special nights.) For more information, visit **halloweenhorrornights.com.**

THANKSGIVING AT THE PARKS There are no special Thanksgiving events or decorations in the parks, so if you're looking for the equivalent of the Macy's Thanksgiving Parade, you're out of luck, although many of the Christmas decorations are normally in place the day after Thanksgiving. But if you think the lack of festivities translates to smaller crowds, think again—the kids are out of school, and this is the busiest travel weekend of the year. Your best bet for the least-crowded park will be Epcot.

Remember to make your dining arrangements long before your visit, especially if you want a traditional Thanksgiving meal. While there is plenty of food at the World, note that not all restaurants offer turkey with all the trimmings. Some that do include **Liberty Tree Tavern** at the Magic Kingdom; **50's Prime Time Cafe** at Disney's Hollywood Studios; **Citrico's** at the Grand Floridian; **Artist Point** at the Wilderness Lodge; and **'Ohana** (which means "family" in Hawaiian) at the Polynesian Resort, which is perfect for families with small children. For information and reservations, call ☎ 407-wdw-dine.

CELEBRATING CHRISTMAS AT WALT DISNEY WORLD If you're visiting during Christmas week, don't expect to see all the attractions in a single day of touring at any park. All parks, especially the Magic Kingdom, will be filled to capacity, and Disney will stop admitting visitors as early as 10 a.m. (Not to mention that women will have to wait up to 20 minutes to use the restrooms in the Magic Kingdom during Christmas week.) As you might have guessed by now, your only way in is getting there early. Be at the gates with admission passes in hand at least 1 hour before scheduled opening time. Most of all, bring along a humongous dose of patience and humor. The daily tree-lighting ceremonies and the parades are wonderful. Again, most parks will reach full capacity by 10 a.m., and no advance reservations will get you into the park once it is closed. So *pick your park* and be prepared to stay there all day.

Also, be sure to make dinner reservations long before your visit, especially if you are spending Christmas Eve and Christmas Day at the parks. Christmas festivities at Walt Disney World usually run

November 24–December 30. From the Monday following Thanksgiving weekend until December 20 or so, you can enjoy the decorations and holiday events without the crowds. This between-holidays period is one of our favorite times of year at Walt Disney World.

The **Magic Kingdom** is home to a stunning display of holiday decorations, a **tree-lighting ceremony** on Main Street, and **Mickey's Very Merry Christmas Parade** on select days. Check the *Times Guide* for days and hours. The Magic Kingdom is also the scene of **Mickey's Very Merry Christmas Party,** held from mid-November to mid-December, 7 p.m.–midnight. Separate admission is required, and costs run $52–$63, plus tax; call ☎ 407-W-DISNEY for dates, prices, and reservations. Admission includes holiday-themed stage shows, cookies and hot chocolate, performances of Mickey's Very Merry Christmas Parade, a magical snowfall on Main Street, Christmas carolers, a visit with Santa Claus, and fireworks. We do not recommend the party for first-time visitors.

Epcot is a good option on Christmas Day, when the Magic Kingdom is totally mobbed, but this doesn't mean it's a desolate place forgotten by the crowds, just somewhat less crowded than the Magic Kingdom. Again, if your heart is set on touring a park on Christmas Day, you will have to get up early.

At Epcot don't miss the **Candlelight Processional,** featuring a celebrity narrator accom-panied by a huge live choir and a full orchestra. The show takes place daily at the America Gardens Theatre and is included with regular Epcot admission. Special lunch and dinner packages are available for an additional charge and include preferred seating for the processional (call ☎ 407-WDW-DINE for reservations). If you don't want to spring for one of the packages, we recommend lining up at least 60 minutes prior to the show of your choice. Guests with preferred seating are well advised not to come at the last minute, either—instead, arrive at the reserved-seating entrance 30 minutes before the beginning of the show. Seats within this section are available on a first-come, first-served basis and are opened to general admission 15 minutes before the beginning of the show. Check the *Times Guide* for performance hours and information on the day's narrator.

A word of advice for families with small children: Reassure the kids that Santa knows where the family is on Christmas Day. You don't want your little ones to suddenly worry that Santa won't find them on Christmas because they're not at home. Consider shipping a small tree and holiday decorations to your hotel. Kids can decorate the window of your hotel room with their drawings.

Liliane

The nightly fireworks, water, and laser show *IllumiNations: Reflections of Earth* is always worth watching and has an extra-special holiday finale.

Our favorite Epcot holiday event, however, is **Holidays from Around the World.** While strolling from land to land, visitors can enjoy storytellers in each country. In **Canada,** Santa Claus explains how Christmas is celebrated by our neighbor to the north. At the **United Kingdom**

Pavilion, Father Christmas tells of his country's holiday customs. **France** is the home of Père Noël, and in **Morocco,** Taariji explains the Feast of Ashoora. In **Japan,** the Daruma Seller talks about how Japanese celebrate the New Year. (*Daruma* dolls are symbols of the New Year and are said to bring good luck.)

At the **American Adventure Rotunda,** you can visit Santa's Bakeshop, a life-size gingerbread house made with real gingerbread, candies, and icing. Santa himself is also on hand to tell Christmas stories. Special programs are held for Kwanzaa and Hanukkah as well. (To learn more about Kwanzaa, an African American celebration of family, community, and culture, visit **officialkwanzaawebsite.org.** The History Channel offers a nice description of Hanukkah, the Jewish Festival of Lights, at **history.com/topics/hanukkah.**)

In **Italy,** meet La Befana, the good witch who brings gifts to children on Epiphany. (For more information on La Befana, check out **en.wikipedia.org/wiki/befana.**) **Germany** honors St. Nicholas on December 6, and he welcomes visitors throughout the afternoon. Visitors can also hear the story of the nutcracker's origin. (To find out more about the legend of St. Nicholas, visit **kidsdomain.com/holiday/xmas/aroundstnicholas.html.**)

Did I mention that it's going to be packed? This is not a good time for first-time visitors, but fun can be had by all at the parks even at peak times. (I actually stayed at Walt Disney World on Christmas Eve and Christmas Day and loved it.) If all else fails, go to sleep—tomorrow is another day at Disney, and you should be rolling out of bed early!

Visit **China** and listen to the funny stories of the Monkey King. In **Norway,** meet the Christmas elf Julenissen, who represents simplicity and peace. (To learn more about Norway's Santa Claus, visit **tinyurl.com/NorwaySanta.**) In **Mexico,** the Three Sage Kings (Los Tres Reyes Magos) make appearances throughout the afternoon telling the story of Epiphany.

At **Disney's Hollywood Studios,** the park is also dressed for the season, but the big attraction is the **Osborne Family Spectacle of Lights.** Millions—yes, millions—of lights decorate the buildings on the Streets of America, and snow machines provide the perfect atmosphere. There is no additional fee to see the display, but be prepared for huge crowds. A little background: Jennings Osborne of Little Rock, Arkansas, began putting up Christmas lights on his house about 10 years ago and expanded his display by buying the two houses next to his home. As his collection grew, so did the displeasure of his neighbors. Eventually the matter was brought to court, and in 1994 the Arkansas Supreme Court ruled that his houses, with their 3 million lights, were a public nuisance. The Walt Disney Company brought Osborne's Christmas lights to Disney's Hollywood Studios in 1995 and has a special agreement with him to keep the display.

At the **Animal Kingdom,** don't miss **Mickey's Jingle Jungle Parade.** The park has festive holiday decorations and a gigantic Christmas tree with carolers performing throughout the day. At Camp Minnie-Mickey, kids can meet Santa Goofy and other favorite Disney characters all dressed in their holiday finest. If you don't mind the lines, this is the perfect place for taking holiday photographs.

Downtown Disney features holiday decor and offers photo ops with Santa but is mainly about shopping. The atmosphere is festive, with special window dressings at shops and restaurants.

You thought we were done? No way—there's much more to see outside of the parks.

The holiday decorations at the Walt Disney resorts are attractions in their own right. Generally speaking, each resort incorporates its theme into its holiday finery. At **Port Orleans Resort,** for example, expect Mardi Gras colors in the trees, while the **Yacht Club** has trees adorned with miniature sailboats. At the **Polynesian Resort,** kids will love the ginger-bread workshop complete with Santa sleeping in a hammock and elves taking it easy under the sun. For the mother of all Christmas trees, make sure to visit the **Grand Floridian,** where a five-story tree dominates the lobby, flanked by a gingerbread dollhouse and a miniature railroad. At the **Beach Club,** poinsettias, artificial snow, and a gingerbread carousel are the big draw. For a more natural approach, visit the **Wilderness Lodge** and **Animal Kingdom Lodge.**

If you're staying at a Walt Disney resort over Christmas, check with the concierge to see what holiday event your particular resort might be offering. Happenings can range from carolers, brass bands, and country singers to Christmas-cookie decorating, visits with Santa, and readings of *The Night Before Christmas.* Many hotels also offer free cookies and punch in their lobbies.

During December, Disney offers 25-minute "sleigh" rides through the woods from the Fort Wilderness Campground. (The horse-drawn vehicle is wheeled but made to look like a red sleigh, complete with sleigh bells!) The rides are offered every 30 minutes 5:30–9:30 p.m., departing from Crockett's Tavern at Fort Wilderness. The cost is $60 per sleigh. (Each sleigh can accommodate up to four adults or two adults plus up to three children age 9 and under.) You can book up to 180 days in advance by calling ☎ (407) WDW-PLAY (939-7529).

If you are looking for a perfect Christmas card, Downtown Disney is the place to go. Santa appears in his chalet at Downtown Disney Marketplace, and you can take pictures with your own camera or use PhotoPass. For a less classical picture, Santa Goofy appears in the chalet December 25–January 3. Ask Guest Relations for the daily schedule.

RINGING IN THE NEW YEAR WITH MICKEY AND FRIENDS If you're in the mood for a night of partying and live entertainment, there's no better place than **Downtown Disney** or **Universal CityWalk.** Both offer a choice of parties and midnight fireworks.

Though all parks, with the exception of the Animal Kingdom, have spectacular fireworks at midnight, here are a few different options for the last night of the year:

- Cirque du Soleil offers a special New Year's production of *La Nouba*. For more information, visit **cirquedusoleil.com.**
- Forget the rides—the lines will be long. Relax at your hotel pool and go out for a great dinner that night. If you have little children, get a baby-sitter. The trick is to arrive a day before New Year's, settle in, go to a water park, and start the touring after January 2, when crowds thin out.
- At Epcot, welcome the New Year several times. Have a drink before 6 p.m. at the Biergarten in Germany. (When the clock strikes 6, it will be midnight in Germany.) Then go over to the Rose & Crown Pub in the United Kingdom and repeat the celebration at 7 p.m., as guests and staff alike will be welcoming the New Year in the United Kingdom. Best of all, you get to start all over again a few hours later when the clock finally strikes midnight at Epcot.

HIGH-LOW, HIGH-LOW, IT'S OFF TO DISNEY WE GO

THOUGH WE RECOMMEND OFF-SEASON TOURING, we realize that it's not possible for many families. We want to make it clear, there-fore, that you can have a wonderful experience regardless of when you go. Our advice, irrespective of season, is to arrive early at the parks and avoid the crowds by using one of our touring plans. If attendance is light, kick back and forget the touring plans.

Selecting the Day of the Week for Your Visit

We receive thousands of e-mails and letters from readers each year asking which park is the best bet on a particular day. Because there are now so many variables (about 38) to consider when recommending a specific best park for a given date, we've created a computer program that weighs all the vari-ables and provides the answer. The results are posted in a Crowd Condition Calendar posted on our website, **touringplans.com.** Once you've decided the dates of your visit to Walt Disney World, access the website and check out your dates on the Crowd Condition Calendar (no charge). The calendar will tell you the park to visit (and to avoid) for each day of your stay. If you don't have regular Internet access, the information is worth a trip to an Internet cafe or to your local library to obtain.

You'll need to have a Park Hopper option on your theme-park admission to take advantage of Extra Magic Hours at more than one park on the same day.

Bob

Extra Magic Hours

Extra Magic Hours is a perk for families staying at a Walt Disney World resort, including the Swan, Dolphin, and Shades of Green, and the Hilton in the Downtown Disney resort area. On selected days of the week, Disney resort guests will be able to enter a Disney theme park 1 hour earlier, or stay in a selected theme park up to 3 hours later, than the official park-operating hours. Theme park visitors not stay-ing at a Disney resort may stay in the park for Extra Magic Hour evenings but cannot experience any rides, attractions, or shows. In other words, they can shop and eat.

WHAT'S REQUIRED? A valid admission ticket is required to enter the park, and you must show your Disney resort ID when entering.

WHEN ARE EXTRA MAGIC HOURS OFFERED? The Extra Magic Hours schedule is subject to constant change, especially during holidays and other periods of peak attendance. Gone are the days when you could be certain which park was running Extra Magic Hours.

You can phone Walt Disney World Information at ☎ 407-824-4321 (press 0 for a live representative), or access **disneyworld.disney.go.com/calendars** to check the schedule for the dates of your visit. The same information, along with tips for avoiding crowds during your Disney World vacation, is available at our website, **touringplans.com.**

Extra Magic Hours draw more Disney resort guests to the host park, which results in longer lines than you would otherwise experience.

Bob

We seriously hope that Disney will adopt a permanent schedule, but if it does not, use the information available from Walt Disney World Information or the website listed above to discover any schedule changes that might affect you. To avoid the most crowded park, simply steer clear of the one(s) offering morning Extra Magic Hours, or access **touringplans.com** for guidance.

WHAT DO EXTRA MAGIC HOURS MEAN TO YOU? Crowds are likely to be larger when the theme parks host an Extra Magic Hours session. If you're not staying at a Disney resort, we suggest avoiding the park hosting Extra Magic Hours, if at all possible.

If you're staying at a Disney resort, there are a couple of strategies you can employ to cut down on your wait in lines. One strategy is to avoid the park hosting Extra Magic Hours entirely, if possible. If you can be at the park when it opens, a second strategy would be to visit the park offering a morning Extra Magic Hours session until lunchtime, then visit another, less-crowded park in the afternoon.

PLANNING *Your* WALT DISNEY WORLD VACATION BUDGET

HOW MUCH YOU SPEND DEPENDS on how long you stay at Walt Disney World. But even if you only stop by for an afternoon, be prepared to drop a bundle. Later we'll show you how to save money on lodging. This section will give you some sense of what you can expect to pay for admissions and food. And we'll help you decide which admission option will best meet your needs.

WALT DISNEY WORLD ADMISSION OPTIONS

IN AN EFFORT TO ACCOMMODATE various vacation needs, Disney offers a number of different admission options. These range from the

WDW Theme Park Ticket Options

	1-day	2-day	3-day	4-day	5-day
BASE TICKET AGES 3–9					
	$84.14 –	$165.08 ($82.54/day)	$227.91 ($75.97/day)	$238.56 ($59.64/day)	$247.08 ($49.42/day)
BASE TICKET AGE 10 AND UP					
	$90.53 –	$178.92 ($89.46/day)	$247.08 ($82.36/day)	$258.80 ($64.70/day)	$267.32 ($53.46/day)

Base Ticket admits guest to one theme park each day of use. Park choices are Magic Kingdom,

	1-day	2-day	3-day	4-day	5-day
FOR PARK HOPPER, ADD:					
	$37.28 –	$58.58 ($29.29/day)	$58.58 ($19.53/day)	$58.58 ($14.65/day)	$58.58 ($11.72/day)

Park Hopper option entitles guest to visit more than one theme park on each day of use.

	1-day	2-day	3-day	4-day	5-day
FOR WATER PARK FUN AND MORE, ADD:					
	$58.58 2 visits	$58.58 2 visits	$58.58 3 visits	$58.58 4 visits	$58.58 5 visits

Water Park Fun and More option entitles guest to a specified number of visits (between 2 and 10)
park, Disney's Typhoon Lagoon water park, DisneyQuest, Oak Trail Golf Course,

	1-day	2-day	3-day	4-day	5-day
FOR NO EXPIRATION, ADD:					
	N/A –	$26.63 ($13.32/day)	$37.28 ($12.43/day)	$79.88 ($19.97/day)	$122.48 ($24.50/day)

No Expiration means unused admissions on a ticket have no expiration date.
All tickets expire 14 days after first use unless No Expiration is purchased.

basic 1-day, one park ticket, good for a single entry into one Disney theme park, to the top-of-the-line Premium Annual Pass, good for 365 days of admission into every Disney theme or water park, plus DisneyQuest.

The sheer number of ticket options available makes it difficult and, yes, daunting for a family to sort out which option represents the least expensive way to see and do everything they want. An average family staying for a week at an off-World hotel and planning a couple of activities outside the theme parks generally has about a dozen different ticket options to consider. To complicate matters, comparing options requires detailed knowledge of the myriad perks included with specific admissions. Finding the optimum admission, or combination of admissions, however, could save the average family a nice little bundle. Many families, we suspect, become overwhelmed trying to sort out the different options and simply purchase a more expensive ticket with features they will probably never use. Adding to the frustration, Disney's reservation

(*Note:* All ticket prices include 6.5% sales tax)

	6-day	7-day	8-day	9-day	10-day
BASE TICKET AGES 3–9					
	$255.60 ($42.60/day)	$264.12 ($37.73/day)	$272.64 ($34.08/day)	$281.16 ($31.24/day)	$289.68 ($28.97/day)
BASE TICKET AGE 10 AND UP					
	$275.84 ($45.97/day)	$284.36 ($40.62/day)	$292.88 ($36.61/day)	$301.40 ($33.49/day)	$309.92 ($30.99/day)

Epcot, Disney's Hollywood Studios, or Disney's Animal Kingdom.

	6-day	7-day	8-day	9-day	10-day
FOR PARK HOPPER, ADD:					
	$58.58 ($9.76/day)	$58.58 ($8.37/day)	$58.58 ($7.32/day)	$58.58 ($6.51/day)	$58.58 ($5.86/day)

Park choices are any combination of Magic Kingdom, Epcot, Disney's Hollywood Studios, or Disney's Animal Kingdom on each day of use.

	6-day	7-day	8-day	9-day	10-day
FOR WATER PARK FUN AND MORE, ADD:					
	$58.58 **6 visits**	$58.58 **7 visits**	$58.58 **8 visits**	$58.58 **9 visits**	$58.58 **10 visits**

to a choice of entertainment and recreation venues. Choices are Disney's Blizzard Beach water or ESPN Wide World of Sports Complex.

	6-day	7-day	8-day	9-day	10-day
FOR NO EXPIRATION, ADD:					
	$138.45 ($23.08/day)	$170.40 ($24.34/day)	$207.68 ($25.96/day)	$234.30 ($26.03/day)	$239.63 ($23.96/day)

Note: Check **touringplans.com** for the latest ticket prices, which are subject to change.

agents are generally trained to avoid answering subjective questions such as which ticket option is "best."

HELP IS ON THE WAY!

TO SIMPLIFY THINGS, we tried to define guidelines to help you choose the best ticket options for your vacation. Eight hours into this project, we sounded like a theme-park version of *Forrest Gump*. Remember that scene where Bubba rattles off 7,000 different ways to prepare shrimp? Well, that was kind of like us, babbling about tickets. Even saying some of the ticket names ("Adult Internet-only 7-day Base Ticket with Park Hopper Option") made us sound like our local Starbucks barista, only not as perky.

After a day or so, we realized that coming up with a handful of general guidelines was an impossible task, so we built a tool to figure it out. You can use it to determine the best ticket options for you by visiting our website, **touringplans.com,** and trying out the Disney Ticket Calculator. The tool aggregates ticket prices from a number of online ticket vendors, including Disney itself. Just answer a few simple questions relating to the size of your party and the theme parks you intend to visit. The tool then identifies your four least expensive ticket options.

The program will also make recommendations for considerations other than price. For example, Annual Passes, although they might cost more, make sense in certain circumstances because Disney often offers substantial resort discounts and other deals to Annual Pass holders. Those resort discounts, especially during off-season times, can more than offset a small incremental charge for the Annual Pass.

MAGIC YOUR WAY

WALT DISNEY WORLD has an array of theme-park ticket options, grouped into a program called Magic Your Way. The simplest option, visiting one theme park for 1 day, is called a 1-Day Base Ticket. Other features, such as the ability to visit more than one park per day ("park hopping") or the inclusion of admission to Disney's minor venues (Typhoon Lagoon, Blizzard Beach, DisneyQuest, and the like), are available as individual add-ons to the Base Ticket.

The more days of admission you purchase, the lower the cost per day. For example, if you buy an adult 5-day Base Ticket for $267.32 (taxes included), each day will cost $53.46, compared with $90.53 for a 1-day pass. Base Tickets can be purchased from 1 to 10 days and admit you to exactly one theme park per day. Base Tickets also expire 14 days from the first day of use. If, say, you purchase a 4-day Base Ticket on June 1 and use it that day for admission to the Magic Kingdom, you'll be able to visit a single Disney theme park on any of your 3 remaining days June 2–June 15. After that, the ticket expires and any unused days will be lost. Through another add-on, however, you can avoid the 14-day expiration and make your ticket valid forever. More on that later.

BASE-TICKET ADD-ON OPTIONS

NAVIGATING THE MAGIC YOUR WAY PROGRAM is much like ordering dinner in an upscale restaurant where all menu selections are à la carte: lots of choices, mostly expensive, virtually all of which require some thought.

Three add-on options are offered with the Magic Your Way Base Ticket, each at an additional cost:

PARK HOPPER Adding this feature to your Base Ticket allows you to visit more than one theme park per day. The cost is $58.58 on top of the price of any Base Ticket, except the 1-day ticket, which is $37.28. It's an exorbitant price for 2 days, but it does become more affordable the longer your stay. As an add-on to a 7-day Base Ticket, the $58.58 flat fee (including tax) would work out to $8.37 per day for park-hopping privileges. If you want to visit the Magic Kingdom in the morning and dine at Epcot in the evening, this is the feature you should request.

NO EXPIRATION Adding this option to your ticket means that unused admissions to the major theme parks, the swimming parks, and other minor venues, never expire. If you add this option to a 10-day Base Ticket and used only 4 days this year, the remaining 6 days could be used for admission at any date in the future. The No Expiration option ranges from $26.63 with tax for a 2-day ticket to $239.63 for a 10-day Base Ticket. This option is not available on 1-day tickets.

WATER PARK FUN AND MORE (WPFAM) This option gives you a single admission to one of Disney's water parks (Blizzard Beach and Typhoon Lagoon), DisneyQuest, Oak Trail Golf Course, or the ESPN Wide World of Sports Complex. The cost is a flat $58.58 (including tax). Except for the 1-day WPFAM ticket, which gives you two admissions, the number of admissions equals the number of days on your base ticket. If you buy an 8-day Base Ticket, for example, and add the WPFAM option, you get eight WPFAM admissions. What you *can't* do is, say, buy a 10-day Base Ticket with only three admissions or a 3-day Base Ticket with four admissions. You can, however, skip WPFAM entirely and buy an individual admission to any of these minor parks. This option is almost always the best deal if you want to visit only one of the venues.

Research indicates that less than 1 in 10 admission passes with unused days are ever used. I can report, however, that I have successfully kept track of Liliane all the partially used tickets I've taken home over the years. The secret? I keep them in the same place all the time with my passport, insurance papers, and other travel documents. And one more thing: I always keep a copy of my credit card receipt documenting the purchase. I even make a photocopy because receipts fade as time goes by.

The add-ons are available for purchase in any combination (except for the No Expiration add-on on 1-day tickets). If you buy a Base Ticket and then decide later on that you want one or more of the options, you can upgrade the Base Ticket to add the feature(s) you desire.

Annual Passes

An Annual Pass provides unlimited use of the major theme parks for one year; a Premium Annual Pass also provides unlimited use of the minor parks. Annual Pass holders also get perks, including free parking and seasonal offers such as room-rate discounts at Disney resorts. The Annual Pass is not valid for special events, such as admission to Mickey's Very Merry Christmas Party. Tax included, Annual Passes run $552.74 for adults and $509.07 for children ages 3–9. A Premium Annual Pass, at $691.19 for adults and $636.87 for children ages 3–9, provides unlimited admission to Blizzard Beach, Typhoon Lagoon, DisneyQuest, Oak Trail Golf Course, and ESPN Wide World of Sports complex, in addition to the four major theme parks. In addition to Annual Passes, Florida residents are eligible for discounts on 1-day theme-park Base Tickets (about 10%), as well as on various add-on options.

The new Disney Premier Passport is good for admission to all parks at the Disneyland and Disney World resorts. The Disney Premier Passport grants unlimited admission for one year to Disneyland and Disney California Adventure in Anaheim, California, as well as Magic Kingdom, Epcot, Disney's Hollywood Studios, Disney's Animal Kingdom, Typhoon Lagoon and Blizzard Beach water parks, DisneyQuest indoor interactive theme park, ESPN Wide World of Sports complex, and Disney's Oak Trail golf course in Orlando. Some events may require an additional charge. The pass includes parking at all four theme parks at Disney World (Magic Kingdom, Epcot, Animal Kingdom, Hollywood Studios) and parking at any pay-on-entry parking lot at Disneyland Resort. Also included are subscriptions to *Mickey Monitor, Backstage Pass,* and *Disney's Family Fun* magazine (one per household).

Those who already hold an annual pass for both resorts will automatically be issued a Disney Premier Passport, with an expiration date based on the later of the two annual passes. Guests can upgrade their annual or seasonal pass for one resort to a Disney Premier Passport for an additional fee. The new pass is available at Disneyland Resort ticket booths, Disney World Guest Relations windows, and at Disney World's Downtown Disney.

This pass may be a good thing, but our estimation is that it is largely a PR move. We estimate that the number of people who would actually benefit from this right now is less than 1,000.

Florida-resident Passes

Disney offers several special admission options to Florida residents. The Florida Resident Annual Pass ($414.29 adults, $381.27 children ages 3–9) and the Florida Resident Premium Annual Pass ($542.09 adults, $499.99 children ages 3–9) both offer unlimited admission and park-hopping privileges to the four major theme parks. The Florida Resident Premium Annual Pass also provides unlimited admission to Blizzard Beach, Typhoon Lagoon, DisneyQuest, Oak Trail Golf Course, and ESPN Wide World of Sports complex, in addition to the four major theme parks. AAA offers some nice discounts on these passes. And the Florida Resident Seasonal Pass ($286.49 adults, $264.12 children ages 3–9) provides unlimited admission to the four major theme parks except on select blackout dates but does not include free parking.

One final note: It doesn't cost as much to renew an Annual Pass as it does to buy it in the first place. When you renew any Annual Pass, you get 8% to 9% savings from the cost of the original pass.

A CLOUD IS JUST A CLOUD

THIS SECTION WAS FORMERLY TITLED "Every Cloud Has a Polyester Lining." In it we explained the few ways that Magic Your Way could save you money. Well, forget that—almost all good deals have gone the way of the dinosaur. The only exception is for folks who do not intend to park-hop and will require 4 or more days' admission, all to be used during a single vacation. If this describes your situation, you can realize some significant economies of scale. As you can see from our admissions chart, the more days you buy, the more you save. So what's changed for everybody else?

Consider that most guests only need 4 or 5 days' admission; the most cost-effective strategy, then, would seem to be to buy a 10-day Base Ticket plus the No Expiration option so you could roll over any unused admission days to a subsequent trip. When Disney first rolled out Magic Your Way, the No Expiration option was pretty reasonable.

Well, they couldn't let *that* continue, could they?

As of this writing, Disney has increased the cost of the No Expiration option by 242% from the time Magic Their, oops, *Your* Way (a joke any way you look at it) was introduced. If you buy an adult 10-day Base Ticket for $309.92 plus No Expiration for $239.63, you'll pay $549.55 including tax, or $54.96 a day—$1.50 per day *more* compared with simply buying a 5-day Base Ticket each time you visit Walt Disney World. While it is true that admission prices might go up before you visit again, in which case No Expiration would be to your benefit, it's equally true that you might misplace the tickets you bought in the previous scenario, or that you might have some better use for the $239.63 you shelled out on top of your ticket purchase.

BIG BROTHER IS WATCHING

ALL MAGIC YOUR WAY TICKETS are personalized, with the ticket holder's name and biometric information stored on the ticket. This doesn't mean, however, that you have to provide a DNA

Stay clear of passes bought on the black market or offered on eBay.

Liliane

sample when you plunk down your cash. Recording the biometric information requires a quick and painless measurement of one finger from your right hand, taken the first time you use the ticket. It has been used without incident for a number of years on Disney's Annual Pass.

The advantages of the bio scan are not altogether clear, though it's doubtless intended to prevent the original purchaser of the pass from selling unused days to a third party. If you're purchasing admission for your entire family and are worried about the difficulty in keeping everyone's tickets, we're told that Disney's computer system will link every family member's data to every ticket, allowing anyone to enter with anyone else's ticket. We've confirmed this by having a platoon of *Unofficial Guide* researchers (including men, women, and children) swap passes with each other; all were admitted.

This new scanning process is so cumbersome, however, that it has taken guests more than 30 minutes to enter some parks during peak periods—and occasionally more than an hour. In response to this, Disney frequently turns off the scanning process entirely (usually at Animal Kingdom).

HOW TO GET THE MOST FROM MAGIC YOUR WAY

FIRST, HAVE A REALISTIC IDEA of what you want out of your vacation. As with anything, it doesn't make sense to pay for options you'll never use. A 7-day theme-park ticket with seven WPFAM admissions might seem like a wonderful idea when you're snowbound and planning your trip in February. But actually trying to visit all those parks in a week in July might end up feeling more like Navy SEAL training. If you're going to make only one visit to a water park, DisneyQuest, or Wide World of Sports, you're almost always better off purchasing that admission separately rather than in the WPFAM option. If you plan to visit two or more WPFAM venues, however, you're better off buying the add-on.

What do you do with the kid's pass you bought when your now 6-foot teenager was less than 10 years of age? Go to Guest Relations and ask them to change the pass into a regular admission pass for the amount of days left on it. If you are lucky, they will do so without asking you to pay the price difference, but if not, you are still better off paying the difference and using the pass instead of wasting whatever value is left on it.

Liliane

Next, think carefully about paying for the No Expiration option. An inside source reports that fewer than 1 in 10 admission tickets with rollover days are ever reused at a Disney theme park. The rest are misplaced, discarded, or forgotten. Unless you are absolutely certain that you'll be returning to Walt Disney World within the next 1 or 2 years and have identified a safe place to keep those unused tickets, we don't think that the additional cost is worth the risk. (We've lost a few passes ourselves.)

GOTCHA!

EVIDENTLY AS A MATTER OF PRINCIPLE, Disney increases admission prices each year about a month after the *Unofficial Guide* goes to press. There's very high probability, therefore, that prices will be higher by the time you read this. Generally increases have run about 3% or 4% a year, but as we discussed above, specific categories of tickets are frequently bumped much more. This has been especially true for children's admissions over the past couple of years. In any event, if you're putting a budget together, assume at least a 3% increase.

WHERE TO PURCHASE MAGIC YOUR WAY TICKETS

YOU CAN BUY YOUR ADMISSION PASSES on arrival at Walt Disney World or purchase them in advance. Admission passes are available at Walt Disney World resorts and theme parks. Passes are also available at some non-Disney hotels and Orlando-area shopping centers, as well as through independent ticket brokers. Because Disney admission prices are not discounted in the greater Walt Disney World–Orlando area, the only reason for you to purchase from an independent broker is convenience. Offers of free or heavily discounted tickets abound, but they generally require you to attend a time-share sales presentation.

Magic Your Way tickets are available at Disney Stores and at **disney world.com** for the same prices listed in the chart on pages 58–59.

If you're trying to keep your costs to an absolute minimum, consider using an online ticket wholesaler, such as **Undercover Tourist, Kissimmee Guest Services, Maple Leaf Tickets,** or the **Official Ticket Center,** especially for trips with 5 or more days in the theme parks. All tickets sold are brand-new, and the savings can range from $2 to more than $41, depending on the ticket and options chosen. We've spoken with representatives from each company, and they're very well versed in the pros and cons of the various tickets and options. If the new options don't make sense for your specific vacation plans, the reps will tell you so.

Undercover Tourist	**undercovertourist.com**
Kissimmee Guest Services	**kgstickets.com**
Maple Leaf Tickets	**mapleleaftickets.com**
The Official Ticket Center	**officialticketcenter.com**

All four companies offer discounts on tickets for almost all central-Florida attractions, including Disney, Universal, SeaWorld, and Cirque du Soleil. Discounts for the major theme parks are about 6%–8.5%. Tickets for other attractions are more deeply discounted. **Undercover Tourist** (U.S.: ☎ 800-846-1302, Monday–Friday, 9 a.m.–4 p.m. Eastern Time; U.K.: ☎ 0800 081-1702, Monday–Friday, 2 p.m.–9 p.m. GMT; worldwide: ☎ +1 386 239-8624; fax +1 386 252-3469; **undercovertourist. com**) offers free delivery and has a sweetheart relationship with **mouse savers.com.** If you subscribe to the MouseSavers e-newsletter, you can access Undercover Tourist through a special "secret" link that provides additional savings on top of the normal discount. **Kissimmee Guest Services** (950 Celebration Blvd., Ste. H, in Celebration; ☎ 321-939-2057, Monday–Friday, 8 a.m.–8 p.m., Saturday, 8 a.m.–5 p.m., Sunday, 8 a.m.–noon Eastern Time; U.K.: ☎ 0208 432-4024; **kgstickets.com**) offers a lowest-price guarantee and will ship the tickets to you for $10, or you may pick up the tickets. The **Official Ticket Center** (3148 Vineland Rd., Kissimmee; ☎ 877-406-4836 or 407-396-9029, daily, 8 a.m.–8:30 p.m. Eastern Time; **theofficialticketcenter.com**) offers shipping for a flat $8 fee or $10 for delivery to Orlando-area hotels; it's of course free if you pick up at their office. **Maple Leaf Tickets** (4647 W. Irlo Bronson Hwy. [US 192], Kissimmee; ☎ 407-396-0300 or 800-841-2837, daily, 8 a.m.–6 p.m. Eastern Time; **mapleleaftickets.com**) offers the same deal on pickup at their store and for $6.95 delivery to Orlando-area hotels; U.S. Priority Mail service is a flat $6.95 per order.

HOW MUCH DOES IT COST PER DAY?

A TYPICAL DAY WOULD COST $616.91, excluding lodging and transportation, for a family of four—Mom, Dad, 12-year-old Tim, and 8-year-old Sandy—driving their own car and staying outside the

HOW MUCH DOES A DAY COST?

Breakfast for four at Denny's with tax and tip	$40.00
Epcot parking fee (free for passholders and resort guests)	$14.00
1 day's admission on a 5-day Base Ticket with Park Hopper Option	
Dad: Adult 5-day with tax = $325.90 divided by five (days)	$65.18
Mom: Adult 5-day with tax = $325.90 divided by five (days)	$65.18
Tim: Adult 5-day with tax = $325.90 divided by five (days)	$65.18
Sandy: Child 5-day with tax = $305.66 divided by five (days)	$61.13
Morning break (soda or coffee)	$11.90
Fast-food lunch (sandwich or burger, fries, soda), no tip	$38.00
Afternoon break (soda and popcorn)	$22.00
Dinner at Italy (no alcoholic beverages) with tax and tip	$195.34
Souvenirs (Mickey T-shirts for Tim and Sandy) with tax*	$39.00
1-day total (without lodging or transportation)	**$616.91**

Cheer up—you won't have to buy souvenirs every day.

World. They plan to stay a week, so they buy 5-day Base Tickets with Park Hopper Option. See breakdown below.

The cost of a Disney vacation almost always increases at a rate higher than either the rate of U.S. inflation (as measured by the Consumer Price Index) or the rate of the average U.S. worker's wages (as measured by the Bureau of Labor Statistics). The largest price hikes lately have been at Disney's sit-down restaurants. Our typical dinner at Italy—two shared appetizers, median-priced entrées for the adults, a child's dinner, two shared sides, two shared desserts, and four sodas —has increased by 7% in the past year. That's more than twice the rate of inflation (currently around 2.7%) and more than three times higher than the average U.S. worker's wages increase (about 2.1%). For comparison, the 1-day total also increased by about 4.4% since our last edition's update.

A Birmingham, Alabama, mom of two begs to differ with our budget recommendation above for souvenirs:

> Sorry, but Uncle Bob is totally out of touch when he says "you won't have to buy souvenirs every day." [In my experience,] you'll head home with several sets of character ears; enough dress-up costumes to outfit the neighborhood; and countless pins, toys, and knickknacks.

BABYSITTING

CHILD-CARE CENTERS Child care isn't available inside the theme parks, but three Magic Kingdom resorts connected by monorail or boat (Polynesian, Grand Floridian, and Wilderness Lodge & Villas), four Epcot resorts (the Yacht & Beach Club Resorts, the Swan, and the

CHILD-CARE CLUBS

HOTEL	NAME OF PROGRAM	AGES	PHONE
Animal Kingdom Lodge	Simba's Cubhouse	4–12	☎ 407-938-4785
Dolphin	Camp Dolphin	4–12	☎ 407-934-4241
Grand Floridian Resort & Spa	Mouseketeer Club	4–12	☎ 407-824-2985
Polynesian Resort	Never Land Club	4–12	☎ 407-824-1639
Swan	Camp Dolphin	4–12	☎ 407-934-4241
Wilderness Lodge & Villas	Cub's Den	4–12	☎ 407-824-1083
Yacht & Beach Club Resorts	Sandcastle Club	4–12	☎ 407-934-3750

*Child-care clubs operate afternoons and evenings. Before 4 p.m., call the hotels rather than the numbers listed above. All programs require reservations.

Dolphin), and Animal Kingdom Lodge have child-care centers for potty-trained children older than age 3 (see chart above). Services vary, but children generally can be left 4:30 p.m.–midnight. Milk and cookies and blankets and pillows are provided at all centers, and dinner is provided at most. Play is supervised but not organized, and toys, videos, and games are plentiful. Guests at any Disney resort or campground may use the services.

The most elaborate of the child-care centers (variously called clubs or camps) is **Never Land Club** at the Polynesian Resort. The rate for ages 4–12 is $12 per hour, per child (2-hour minimum).

All the clubs accept reservations (some six months in advance!) with a credit-card guarantee. Call the club directly or reserve through Disney central reservations at ☎ 407-WDW-DINE. Most clubs require a 24-hour cancellation notice and levy a hefty penalty of 2 hours' time or $23 per call for no-shows. A limited number of walk-ins are usually accepted on a first-come, first-served basis.

If you're staying in a Disney resort that doesn't offer a child-care club and you *don't* have a car, you're better off using in-room babysitting. Trying to take your child to a club in another hotel by Disney bus requires a 50- to 90-minute trip each way. By the time you've deposited your little one, it will almost be time to pick him or her up again.

IN-ROOM BABYSITTING Three companies provide in-room sitting in Walt Disney World and surrounding areas, including the International Drive–Orange County Convention Center area, the Universal Orlando area, and the Lake Buena Vista area. They are **Kid's Nite Out** (run by the KinderCare chain), **All About Kids,** and **Fairy Godmothers** (no kidding). Kid's Nite Out also serves hotels in the greater Orlando area, including downtown. All three provide sitters older than age 18 who are insured, bonded, and trained in CPR. Some sitters have advanced medical and first-aid training and/or education credentials. All sitters are screened, reference checked, and police checked. In addition to caring for your children in your guest room, the sitters

Babysitting Services

ALL ABOUT KIDS	KID'S NITE OUT	FAIRY GODMOTHERS
☎ 407-812-9300 or 800-728-6506 **all-about-kids.com**	☎ 407-828-0920 or 800-696-8105 **kidsniteout.com**	☎ 407-277-3724
HOTELS SERVED All WDW hotels and many outside the WDW area	HOTELS SERVED All WDW and Orlando-area hotels	HOTELS SERVED All WDW hotels and those in the general WDW area
SITTERS Men and women	SITTERS Men and women	SITTERS Mothers and grand-mothers, female college students
MINIMUM CHARGES 4 hours	MINIMUM CHARGES 4 hours	MINIMUM CHARGES 4 hours
BASE HOURLY RATES 1 child, $14 2 children, $16 3 children, $18 4 children, $20	BASE HOURLY RATES 1 child, $16 2 children, $18.50 3 children, $21 4 children, $23.50	BASE HOURLY RATES 1 child, $16 2 children, $16 3 children, $16 4 children, $18
EXTRA CHARGES Transportation fee, $12; starting before 7 a.m. or after 9 p.m., +$2 per hour	EXTRA CHARGES Transportation fee, $10; starting before 6:30 a.m. or after 9 p.m., +$2 per hour; additional fee for holidays	EXTRA CHARGES Transportation fee, $14; starting after 10 p.m., +$2 per hour
CANCELLATION DEADLINE More than 24 hours before service to avoid cancellation charge	CANCELLATION DEADLINE 24 hours before service when reservation is made	CANCELLATION DEADLINE 3 hours before service
FORM OF PAYMENT Cash or traveler's checks for actual payment; gratuity in cash; credit card to hold reservation	FORM OF PAYMENT AE, D, MC, V; gratuity in cash	FORM OF PAYMENT Cash or traveler's checks for actual payment; gratuity in cash
THINGS SITTERS WON'T DO Transport children	THINGS SITTERS WON'T DO Transport children in private vehicle, take children swimming, give baths	THINGS SITTERS WON'T DO Transport children, give baths. Swimming is at sitter's discretion.

will, if you direct (and pay), take your children to the theme parks or other venues. Many sitters arrive loaded with books and games. All three services offer bilingual sitters.

SPECIAL PROGRAMS FOR CHILDREN

Liliane

What will Disney think of next? A Bibbidi Bobbidi Boutique for Captain Jack Sparrow's hairdo? If only they had a package that included dinner with Johnny Depp.

SEVERAL PROGRAMS FOR CHILDREN are available, but they are somewhat lacking in educational focus.

DISNEY'S PIRATE ADVENTURE Children don bandannas, hoist the Jolly Roger, and depart on a boat trip to search for buried treasure following a treasure map. At the final port of call, the kids find the treasure (doubloons, beads, and rubber bugs!) and wolf down a PB&J sandwich. The treasure is divided among the kids. For children ages 4–12, the adventure costs $40 per child and is offered daily 9:30–11:30 a.m. at select Walt Disney World resort hotels. Though the setting is different at each resort, the program is largely the same. Call ☎ 407-WDW-PLAY for information. Kids of both genders really love this outing, many reporting it as the highlight of their vacation. Parents cannot accompany children on the outing.

If you want to go whole hog, check out The Pirate League in Adventureland at the Magic Kingdom, where scoundrels and rogues of all ages can acquire special pirate costumes and accessories, as well as an official pirate name. Two different packages are available:

FIRST MATE PACKAGE: Includes bandanna; choice of facial effects (scars, tattoos, fake teeth, earring, and eye patch); sword and sheath; pirate-coin necklace; one 5-by-7-inch photo; and personalized pirate oath for $30, plus tax.

EMPRESS PACKAGE: Comes with bandanna; shimmering makeup (face gem, tattoos, nail polish, earring, and eye patch); sword and sheath; pirate-coin necklace; one 5-by-7-inch photo; and personalized pirate oath for $30, plus tax.

These packages are available for boys, girls, and adults. Call ☎ 407-WDW-CREW to make an appointment.

WONDERLAND TEA PARTY Although the name of this enchanting event is enough to make most boys break out in hives, it is nevertheless available at the Grand Floridian on Monday–Friday afternoons, 2–3 p.m. The program consists of making cupcakes, arranging flower bouquets, and having lunch and tea with characters from *Alice in Wonderland*. Reservations can be made by calling ☎ 407-WDW-DINE up to 180 days in advance.

MY DISNEY GIRL'S PERFECTLY PRINCESS TEA PARTY If your daughter loves princesses and dressing up, then My Disney Girl's Perfectly Princess Tea Party at the Grand Floridian will give you a boost toward the Parent of the Year Award. Your own little princess can sip tea, listen to stories, and join in sing-alongs led by hostess Rose Petal, all while decked out in her favorite regal attire. Princess Aurora or another princess will drop by to visit all the junior royalty. Plus your daughter goes home with a variety of souvenirs, including a special 18-inch My Disney Girl doll dressed in a matching Princess Aurora gown with accessories, her own ribbon tiara, silver link bracelet, fresh rose, scrapbook set, and a Best Friend certificate. To receive the royal treatment, you'd better be prepared to pay a royal bill. The 2011 price for one adult and one child (ages 3–11) was $250. A light lunch is included. Each additional adult costs $85, each additional child an extra $165. Princes who attend the tea party will receive a plush Duffy, the Disney bear, and a Mickey pirates cap. Call ☎ 407-939-6397 for reservations or more information.

> I guess I still have to be grateful that mom did not make me go to the Princess Tea Party. Believe it or not, it is also available for young Idan
>
> princes. She took me at age 17 to the Princess Storybook Dining at Akershus, you know. Anything for the research!

Important: Disney is tinkering with prices and availability of packages more than ever. Always check for availability and prices prior to promising your kids any activity.

MAGIC KINGDOM FAMILY MAGIC TOUR This is a 2-hour guided tour of the Magic Kingdom for the entire family. Even children in strollers are welcome. The tour combines information about the Magic Kingdom with the gathering of clues that ultimately lead the group to a character greeting at the tour's end. Definitely not for the self-conscious, the tour involves skipping, hopping, and walking sideways as you progress from land to land. There's usually a marginal plot such as saving Wendy from Captain Hook, in which case the character at the end of the tour is Wendy. You get the idea. The tour departs daily at 10 a.m. The cost is $34 per person plus a valid Magic Kingdom admission. The maximum group size is 18 persons. Reservations can be made up to one year in advance by calling ☎ 407-WDW-TOUR.

DISNEY'S THE MAGIC BEHIND OUR STEAM TRAINS You must be age 10 or older for this 3-hour tour, presented every day except Sunday. The tour kicks off at 7:30 a.m., when you join the crew of the Walt Disney World Railroad as they prepare their steam locomotives for the day. The cost is $49 per person plus a valid Magic Kingdom admission. Call ☎ 407-WDW-TOUR for additional information and reservations.

BIRTHDAYS AND SPECIAL OCCASIONS

ALL GUESTS WHO CELEBRATE A BIRTHDAY or are visiting Walt Disney World for the first time can pick up a button corresponding to the celebration at Guest Relations when entering any of the parks. Often upon check-in the hotel clerks will ask if any member of your party is celebrating a special event. It is especially fun for birthday kids, as cast members will congratulate your child throughout the day in the hotel, on the bus, in the park, and at restaurants throughout the World. A Lombard, Illinois, mom put the word out and was glad she did:

> My daughter was turning 5 while we were there, and I asked about special things that could be done. Our hotel asked me who her favorite character was and did the rest. We came back to our room on her birthday and there were helium balloons, a card, and a Cinderella 5x7 photo autographed in ink! When we entered the Magic Kingdom, we received an It's My Birthday Today pin (FREE!), and at the restaurant she got a huge cupcake with whipped cream, sprinkles, and a candle. IT PAYS TO ASK!!

Another great and reasonably priced treat is to have your hair cut at the Harmony Barber Shop on Main Street at the Magic Kingdom. Rest assured that you or your kid will walk away with a good haircut, and you may even be treated to a song by the Dapper Dans, Disney's famous barbershop quartet! The best time to go is during a parade. You get a good view and the staff sings along with the parade music. It is a great photo op. An Ohio mom celebrated her child's first haircut at the barber shop:

> The barber shop at the entrance of MK makes a big deal with baby's first haircut—pixie dust, photos, a certificate, and "free" mouse ears hat! ($14 total)

A fashion- and dollar-conscious Kalamazoo, Michigan, family writes:

> The tip that tickled me the most in your book, that we have used every year, is the Main Street Barber Shop hair-do for little girls. The cost is so low; I want to say I spent about $12 including tip. You don't need reservations, and in my opinion, they do a better job than Bibbidi Bobbidi Boutique. We never waited more than an hour for my daughter to have her hair done. They put it into a teased bun and use bright-colored paints and colorful confetti to match whatever princess dress she has on. I understand that Disney doesn't want it to compete with Bibbidi, so I don't know if I want you telling anyone this great secret or not! I am afraid they might take it away if it becomes too widely known. Maybe you should charge an extra $10 for this tip.

WHERE *to* STAY

WHEN TRAVELING WITH CHILDREN, your hotel is your home away from home, your safe harbor, and your sanctuary. Staying in a hotel, an activity usually reserved for adults, is in itself a great adventure for children. They take in every detail and delight in such things as having a pool at their disposal and obtaining ice from a noisy machine. Of course, it is critical that your children feel safe and secure, but it adds immeasurably to the success of the vacation if they really like the hotel.

In truth, because of their youth and limited experience, kids are far less particular about hotels than adults tend to be. A Spartan room and a small pool at a budget motel will make most kids happier than a beagle with a lamb chop. But kids' memories are like little steel traps, so once you establish a lodging standard, that's pretty much what they'll expect every time. A couple from Gary, Indiana, stayed at the pricey Yacht Club Resort at Walt Disney World because they heard that it offered a knockout swimming area (true). When they returned two years later and stayed at Disney's All-Star Resorts for about a third of the price, their 10-year-old carped all week. If you're on a budget, it's better to begin with more modest accommodations and move up to better digs on subsequent trips as finances permit.

In our opinion, if you are traveling with a child age 12 or younger, one of your top priorities should be to book a hotel within easy striking distance of the parks.

Bob

"You Can't Roller-skate in a Buffalo Herd"

THIS WAS A SONG TITLE FROM THE 1960s. If we wrote that song today, we'd call it "You Can't Have Fun at Disney World if You're Drop-dead Tired." Believe us, Walt Disney World is an easy place to be penny-wise and pound-foolish. Many families who cut lodging expenses by booking a budget hotel end up so far away from Walt Disney World that it is a major hassle to return to the hotel in the middle of the day for swimming and a nap. By trying to spend the whole day at the theme parks, however, they wear themselves out quickly, and the dream vacation suddenly disintegrates into short tempers and exhaustion. And don't confuse this advice with a sales pitch for Disney hotels. There are, you will find, dozens of hotels outside Walt Disney World that are as close or closer to certain Disney theme parks than some of the resorts inside the World. Our main point—in fact, our only point—is to make it easy on yourself to return to your hotel when the need arises.

SOME BASIC CONSIDERATIONS

COST

A NIGHT IN A HOTEL AT DISNEY WORLD or the surrounding area can run anywhere from $40 to $900. Clearly, if you are willing to sacrifice some luxury and don't mind a 10- to 25-minute commute, you can really cut your lodging costs by staying outside Walt Disney World. Hotels in Walt Disney World tend to be the most expensive, but they also offer some of the highest quality, as well as a number of perks not enjoyed by guests who stay outside of the World.

Bay Lake Tower, BoardWalk Villas, Wilderness Lodge Villas, Animal Kingdom Villas, Old Key West Resort, Saratoga Springs Resort, Treehouse Villas, and Beach Club Villas offer condo-type accommodations with one-, two-, and (at Saratoga Springs, BoardWalk Villas, Animal Kingdom Villas, Bay Lake Tower, and Old Key West) three-bedroom units with kitchens, living rooms, DVD players, and washers and dryers. Prices range from about $345 per night for a studio at Animal Kingdom Villas to $2,550 per night for a three-bedroom Grand Villa at Bay Lake Tower. Fully equipped cabins at Fort Wilderness Resort & Campground cost $275–$450 per night. A limited number of suites are available at the more expensive Disney resorts, but they don't have kitchens.

Before you choose a resort based on price alone, consider this: Our reader surveys indicate that you'll be more satisfied with your hotel choice if it's slightly more expensive than the hotels at which you typically stay. In general, readers report that they're most

WHAT IT COSTS TO STAY IN THE DOWNTOWN DISNEY RESORT AREA	
Best Western Lake Buena Vista Resort Hotel	$104–$250
Buena Vista Palace Hotel & Spa	$179–$1,009
DoubleTree Guest Suites	$82–$505
Hilton Walt Disney World	$95–$329
Holiday Inn at Walt Disney World	$94–$159
Royal Plaza	$109–$249
Wyndham Lake Buena Vista Resort	$77–$399

COSTS PER NIGHT OF DISNEY RESORT HOTEL ROOMS

All-Star Music Resort Family Suites	$194–$365
All-Star Resorts	$82–$179
Animal Kingdom Lodge	$250–$615
Animal Kingdom Villas (Jambo House and Kidani Village)	$280–$2,330
Art of Animation Resort (opens summer 2012)	$194–$365
Bay Lake Tower	$395–$2,550
Beach Club Resort	$335–$815
Beach Club Villas	$345–$1,250
BoardWalk Inn	$345–$885
BoardWalk Villas	$345–$2,330
Caribbean Beach Resort	$154–$309
Contemporary Resort	$300–$905
Coronado Springs Resort	$159–$284
Dolphin (Sheraton)	$169–$459
Fort Wilderness Resort & Campground (cabins)	$275–$450
Grand Floridian Resort & Spa	$440–$1,145
Old Key West Resort	$305–$1,780
Polynesian Resort	$385–$1,020
Pop Century Resort	$82–$179
Port Orleans Resort	$154–$269
Saratoga Springs Resort & Spa	$305–$1,780
Swan (Westin)	$189–$479
Treehouse Villas	$570–$965
Wilderness Lodge	$250–$840
Wilderness Lodge Villas	$340–$1,245
Yacht Club Resort	$335–$990

satisfied staying at a hotel one category up from their typical, non-Disney choices. The Disney moderate resorts do particularly well overall. Note that these results explicitly take into account the price differences among the resorts. That is, even after taking into account that moderate resorts are more expensive than value resorts, readers who typically stay at value resorts are still more satisfied at a moderate than a value when at Disney.

Also at Disney World are the seven hotels of the Downtown Disney Resort Area (DDRA), also known as the Disney Village Hotel Plaza. Accommodations range from fairly luxurious to Holiday Inn quality. Though not typically good candidates for bargains, these hotels surprised us with some great deals during the past few years. While the DDRA is technically part of Disney World, staying there is like visiting a colony rather than the motherland. Free parking at theme parks isn't offered—nor is early entry, with one exception, the Hilton—and hotels operate their own buses rather than use Disney transportation.

LOCATION AND TRANSPORTATION OPTIONS

ONCE YOU HAVE DETERMINED YOUR BUDGET, think about what you want to do at Walt Disney World. Will you go to all four theme parks or will you concentrate on one or two? If you intend to use your own car, the location of your Disney hotel isn't especially important unless you plan to spend most of your time at the Magic Kingdom. (Disney transportation is always more efficient than your car in this case because it bypasses the Transportation and Ticket Center and deposits you at the theme park entrance.)

> For the record, the resorts within walking distance of the International Gateway (the back door, so to speak, of Epcot) are expensive and are a long, long walk from Future World, the section of Epcot where families tend to spend most of their time.
>
> *Liliane*

Most convenient to the Magic Kingdom are the monorail hotels, which are the Grand Floridian, the Contemporary, Bay Lake Tower, and the Polynesian resorts. The Wilderness Lodge is linked by direct boat to the Magic Kingdom.

Most convenient to Epcot and Disney's Hollywood Studios are the BoardWalk Inn & Villas, Yacht & Beach Club Resorts, the Swan, and the Dolphin. Though all are within easy walking distance of Epcot's International Gateway, boat service is also available. Vessels also connect Epcot hotels to Disney's Hollywood Studios. Epcot hotels are best for guests planning to spend most of their time at Epcot and/or the Studios.

Centrally located are Caribbean Beach, Art of Animation, and Pop Century resorts. Along Bonnet Creek, Disney's Old Key West and Port Orleans resorts also offer a central location.

Though not centrally located, the All-Star, Animal Kingdom Lodge & Villas, and Coronado Springs resorts have very good bus service to all Walt Disney World destinations and are closest to the Animal Kingdom. Independent hotels on US 192 near the entrance to Walt Disney World are also just a few minutes

> If you plan to use Disney transportation and intend to visit all four major parks and one or both of the swimming theme parks, book a centrally located resort with good transportation connections. The Epcot resorts and the Polynesian, Caribbean Beach, Art of Animation, Pop Century, and Port Orleans resorts fill the bill. Disney's Old Key West Resort is centrally located but offers only limited bus service noon–6 p.m.
>
>
> *Bob*

from the Animal Kingdom. Wilderness Lodge and Fort Wilderness Campground have the most convoluted and inconvenient transportation service of the Disney hotels. The Old Key West Resort is also transportation challenged—that is, buses run less frequently than at other Disney resorts. The same is true of the Saratoga Springs Resort and Treehouse Villas.

COMMUTING TO AND FROM THE THEME PARKS

FOR VISITORS LODGING INSIDE WALT DISNEY WORLD With three important exceptions, the fastest way to commute from your hotel to the theme parks and back is in your own car. And although many Walt Disney World guests use the Disney Transportation System and appreciate not having to drive, based on timed comparisons, it is almost always less time-consuming to drive. The exceptions are these: (1) commuting to the Magic Kingdom from the hotels on the monorail (Grand Floridian, Polynesian, Bay Lake Tower, and Contemporary Resorts); (2) commuting to the Magic Kingdom from any Disney hotel by bus or boat; and (3) commuting to Epcot on the monorail from the Polynesian Resort via the Transportation and Ticket Center.

If you stay at the Polynesian Resort, you can catch a direct monorail to the Magic Kingdom, and by walking 100 yards or so to the Transportation and Ticket Center, you can catch a direct monorail to Epcot. Located at the nexus of the monorail system, the Polynesian is certainly the most convenient of all hotels. From either the Magic Kingdom or Epcot, you can return to your hotel quickly and easily whenever you desire. Sound good? It is, but it costs $365–$990 per night.

Second to the Polynesian in terms of convenience are the Grand Floridian and Contemporary resorts, also on the Magic Kingdom monorail, but they cost as much as or more than the Polynesian.

DRIVING TIME TO THE THEME PARKS

MINUTES TO: FROM	MAGIC KINGDOM PARKING LOT	EPCOT PARKING LOT	DISNEY'S HOLLYWOOD STUDIOS PARKING LOT	DISNEY'S ANIMAL KINGDOM PARKING LOT
Downtown Orlando	35	31	33	37
North International Drive and Universal Studios	24	21	22	26
Central International Drive–Sand Lake Road	26	23	24	27
South International Drive and SeaWorld	18	15	16	20
FL 535	12	9	10	13
US 192, north of I-4	10–15	7–12	5–10	5–10
US 192, south of I-4	10–18	7–15	5–13	5–12

Less expensive Disney hotels transport you to the Magic Kingdom by bus or boat. For reasons described below, this is more efficient than driving a car.

DRIVING TIME TO THE THEME PARKS FOR VISITORS LODGING OUTSIDE WALT DISNEY WORLD For vacationers staying outside Walt Disney World, we've calculated the approximate commuting time to the major theme parks' parking lots from several off-World lodging areas. Add a few minutes to our times to pay your parking fee and to park. Once parked at the Transportation and Ticket Center (Magic Kingdom parking lot), it takes an average of 20–30 more minutes to reach the Magic Kingdom. To reach Epcot from its parking lot, add 7–10 minutes. At Disney's Hollywood Studios and the Animal Kingdom, the lot-to-gate transit time is 5–10 minutes. If you haven't purchased your theme park admission in advance, tack on another 10–20 minutes.

Our hotel information chart on pages 102–104 shows the commuting time, with no consideration of getting to and from the parking lot to the turnstiles, to the Disney theme parks from each hotel listed. Those commuting times represent an average of several test runs. Your actual time may be shorter or longer depending on many variables.

The commuting times in the Hotel Information Chart show conclusively that distance from the theme parks is not necessarily the dominant factor in determining commuting times. Among those we list, the hotels on Major Boulevard opposite the Kirkman Road entrance to Universal Orlando, for example, are the most distant from the Disney parks. But because they're only one traffic signal from easy access to I-4, commuting time to the parks is significantly less than for many closer hotels.

SHUTTLE SERVICE FROM HOTELS OUTSIDE WALT DISNEY WORLD Many hotels in the Walt Disney World area provide shuttle service to the theme parks. They represent a fairly carefree alternative for getting to and from the parks, letting you off near the entrance (except for the Magic Kingdom), and saving you the cost of parking. The rub is that they might not get you there as early as you desire (a critical point if you take our touring advice) or be available at the time you wish to return to your lodging. Also, be forewarned that most shuttle services do not add vehicles at park opening or closing times. In the morning, your biggest problem is that you might not get a seat. At closing time, however, and sometimes following a hard rain, you can expect a lot of competition for standing space on the bus. If there's not room for everyone, you might have to wait 30 minutes to an hour for the next shuttle.

CONVENIENCE CONVENIENTLY DEFINED Conceptually, it's easy to grasp that a hotel that is closer is more convenient than one that is far away. But nothing is that simple at Walt Disney World, so we'd better tell you exactly what you're in for. If you stay at a Walt Disney World resort and use the Disney transportation system, you'll have a 5- to 10-minute walk to the bus stop, monorail station, or dock (whichever applies). Once there, buses, trains, or boats generally run about every 15–25 minutes, so you might have to wait a short time for your transportation to arrive. Once you're on board, most conveyances make additional stops en route to your destination, and many take a less-than-direct route. Upon arrival, however, they deposit you fairly close to the entrance of the theme park. Returning to your hotel is the same process in reverse and takes about the same amount of time.

Regardless of whether or not you stay in Walt Disney World, if you use your own car, here's how your commute shakes out. After a 1- to 5-minute walk from your room to your car, you drive to the theme park, stopping to pay a parking fee or showing your Disney ID for free parking (if you are a Disney resort guest). Disney cast members then direct you to a parking space. If you arrive early, your space may be close enough to the park entrance (Magic Kingdom excepted) to walk. If you park farther afield, a Disney tram will come along every 5 minutes to collect you and transport you to the entrance.

At the Magic Kingdom, the entrance to the park is separated from the parking lot by the Transportation and Ticket Center (TTC) and the Seven Seas Lagoon. After parking at the Magic Kingdom lot, you take a tram to the TTC and then board a ferry or monorail (your choice) for the trip across the lagoon to the park. All this is fairly time-consuming and is to be avoided if possible. The only way to avoid it, however, is to lodge in a Disney hotel and commute directly to the Magic Kingdom entrance via Disney bus, boat, or monorail. Happily, all of the other theme parks are situated adjacent to their parking lots.

Because families with children tend to spend more time on average at the Magic Kingdom than at the other parks, and because it's so important to return to your hotel for rest, the business of getting around the lagoon can be a major consideration when choosing a place to stay; the extra hassle of crossing the lagoon (to get back to your car) makes coming and going much more difficult. The half hour it takes to commute to your hotel via car from the Animal Kingdom, Disney's Hollywood Studios, or Epcot takes an hour or longer from the Magic Kingdom. If you stay in a Disney hotel and use the Disney transportation system, you may have to wait 5–25 minutes for your bus, boat, or monorail, but it will take you directly from the Magic Kingdom entrance to your hotel, bypassing the lagoon and the TTC.

DINING

DINING FIGURES INTO THE DISCUSSION of where to stay only if you don't plan to have a car at your disposal. If you have a car, you can go eat wherever you want. Alternatively, if you plan on using the Disney Transportation System (for Disney hotel guests) or the courtesy shuttle of your non-Disney hotel, you will either have to dine at the theme parks or at or near your hotel. If your hotel offers a lot of choices or if other restaurants are within walking distance, then there's no problem. If your hotel is somewhat isolated and offers limited selections, you'll feel like I did on a canoe trip once when we ate northern pike at every meal for a week because that's all we could catch.

At Walt Disney World, although it's relatively quick and efficient to commute from your Disney hotel or campground to the theme parks, it's a long, arduous process requiring transfers to travel from hotel to hotel. Disney hotels that are somewhat isolated and that offer limited dining choices include the Old Key West, Caribbean Beach, All-Star, Pop Century, Art of Animation, Animal Kingdom Lodge, Coronado Springs, and Wilderness Lodge resorts, as well as the Fort Wilderness Campground and most of the Saratoga Springs Resort.

If you want a condo-type accommodation so that you have more flexibility for meal preparation than eating out of a cooler, the best deals in Walt Disney World are the Wilderness Cabins (prefab log cabins) at Fort Wilderness Campground. Other Disney lodgings with kitchens are available at the BoardWalk Villas, Old Key West, Saratoga Springs, Wilderness Lodge Villas, Animal Kingdom Villas, Bay Lake Tower, and the Beach Club Villas, but all are much more expensive than the cabins at the campground. Outside Walt Disney World, an ever-increasing number of condos are available, and some are very good deals. See our discussion of lodging outside of Walt Disney World later in this chapter.

THE SIZE OF YOUR GROUP

LARGER FAMILIES AND GROUPS MAY BE interested in how many people can stay in a Disney resort room, but only Lilliputians would be comfortable in a room filled to capacity. Groups requiring two or more rooms should consider condo/suite/villa accommodations, either in or out of Walt Disney World. If there are more than six in your party, you will need either two hotel rooms, a suite (see Wilderness Lodge), or a condo.

> If you share a room with your children, you all need to hit the sack at Liliane the same time. Establish a single compromise bedtime, probably a little early for you and a bit later than the children's usual weekend bedtime. Observe any nightly rituals you practice at home, such as reading a book before lights out.

STAYING IN OR OUT OF THE WORLD: WEIGHING THE PROS AND CONS

1. COST If cost is your primary consideration, you'll lodge much less expensively outside Walt Disney World.

2. EASE OF ACCESS Even if you stay in Walt Disney World, you're dependent on some mode of transportation. It may be less stressful to use Disney transportation, but with the single exception of commuting to the Magic Kingdom, the fastest, most efficient, and most flexible way to get around usually is a car. If you're at Epcot, for example, and want to take the kids back to Disney's Grand Floridian Beach Resort for a nap, forget the monorail. You'll get back much faster in your own car.

A reader from Raynham, Massachusetts, who stayed at the Caribbean Beach Resort (and liked it very much) writes this:

HOTEL | MAXIMUM OCCUPANCY PER ROOM

All-Star Resorts | 4 people plus child in crib

Animal Kingdom Lodge:Jambo House | *Studio:* 4 people; *2-bedroom:* 8 people; both plus child in crib

Animal Kingdom Lodge:Kidani Village | *Studio:* 4 people; *2-bedroom:* 8 people; *3-bedroom:* 12 people; all plus child in crib

Art of Animation | *The Little Mermaid buildings:* 4 people; *The Lion King, Cars, and Finding Nemo buildings:* 6 people; all plus child in crib

Bay Lake Tower at the Contemporary Resort | *Studio:* 4 people; *2-bedroom:* 8 people; *3-bedroom:* 12 people; all plus child in crib

Beach Club Resort | 5 people plus child in crib

Beach Club Villas | *Studio:* 4 people; *2-bedroom:* 8 people; *Grand Villa:* 12 people; all plus child in crib

BoardWalk Inn | 4 people plus child in crib

BoardWalk Villas | *Studio:* 4 people; *2-bedroom:* 8 people; *Grand Villa:* 12 people; all plus child in crib

Caribbean Beach Resort | 4 people plus child in crib

Contemporary Resort | 5 people plus child in crib

Coronado Springs Resort | 4 people plus child in crib

Dolphin(Sheraton) | 4 people

Fort Wilderness Homes | 6 people plus child in crib

Grand Floridian Beach Resort | 4 or 5 people plus child in crib

Old Key West Resort | *Studio:* 4 people; *2-bedroom:* 8 people; *Grand Villa:* 12 people; all plus child in crib

Polynesian Resort | 5 people plus child in crib

Pop Century Resort | 4 people plus child in crib

Port Orleans French Quarter | 4 people plus child in crib

Port Orleans Riverside | 4 people plus child in crib or trundle bed

Saratoga Springs | *Studio:* 4 people; *2-bedroom:* 8 people; *Grand Villa:* 12 people; all plus child in crib

Swan(Westin) | 4 people

Treehouse Villas | 9 people

Wilderness Lodge | 4 people plus child in crib; junior suites with bunk beds accommodate 6 people

Wilderness Lodge Villas | *Studio:* 4 people; *2-bedroom:* 8 people

Yacht Club Resort | 5 people plus child in crib

Even though the resort is on the Disney bus line, I recommend rent-ing a car if it [fits] one's budget. The buses do not go directly to many destinations, and often you have to switch at the Transporta-tion and Ticket Center. Getting a [bus] seat in the morning is no problem. Getting a bus back to the hotel after a hard day can mean a long wait in line.

The Disney Transportation System is about as efficient as is humanly possible. No matter where you're going, you rarely wait more than 15–20 minutes for a bus, monorail, or boat. It is only for the use and benefit of Disney guests; nevertheless it is public transportation, and users must expect the inconveniences inherent in any transporta-tion system: conveyances that arrive and depart on their schedule, not yours; the occasional need to transfer; multiple stops; time lost loading and unloading large numbers of passengers; and, generally, the chal-lenge of understanding and using a complex transportation network.

3. YOUNG CHILDREN Although the hassle of commuting to most non-World hotels is only slightly (if at all) greater than that of commuting to Disney hotels, a definite peace of mind results from staying in the World. Regardless of where you stay, make sure you get your young children back to the hotel for a nap each day.

4. SPLITTING UP If your party will likely split up to tour (as frequently happens in families with children of widely varying ages), staying in the World offers more transportation options, thus more indepen-dence. Mom and Dad can take the car and return to the hotel for a relaxed dinner and early bedtime, while the teens can remain in the park for evening parades and fireworks.

5. SLOPPING THE PIGS If you have a large crew that chows down like pigs at the trough, you may do better staying outside the World, where food is far less expensive.

6. VISITING OTHER ORLANDO-AREA ATTRACTIONS If you plan to visit SeaWorld, Kennedy Space Center, the Universal theme parks, or other area attractions, it may be more convenient to stay outside the World. Don't, however, book a hotel halfway to Orlando because you think you might run over to Universal or SeaWorld for a day. Remember the number-one rule: "Stay close enough to Walt Disney World to return to your hotel for rest in the middle of the day."

WALT DISNEY WORLD LODGING

BENEFITS OF STAYING IN WALT DISNEY WORLD

IN ADDITION TO PROXIMITY—especially easy access to the Magic Kingdom—Walt Disney World resort hotel and campground guests are accorded other privileges and amenities unavailable to those staying outside the World. Though some of these perks are only advertising gimmicks, others are potentially quite valuable. Here are the benefits and what they mean:

1. EXTRA MAGIC HOURS AT THE THEME PARKS Disney World lodging guests (excluding guests at the independent hotels of Downtown Disney Resort Area, except for the Hilton) are invited to enter a designated park 1 hour earlier than the general public each day or to enjoy a designated theme park for 3 hours after it closes to the general public in the evening. Disney guests are also offered specials on admission, including discount tickets to the water parks. These benefits are subject to change without notice. Early entry can be quite valuable if you know how to use it. It can also land you in gridlock.

2. THEME All of the Disney hotels are themed, in pointed contrast to non-Disney hotels, which are, well, mostly just hotels. Each Disney hotel is designed to make you feel that you're in a special place or period of history. See the chart on the opposite page depicting the various hotels and their respective themes.

Themed rooms are a huge attraction for children, firing their imaginations and really making the hotel an adventure and a memorable place. Some resorts carry off their themes better than others, and some themes are more exciting. **The Wilderness Lodge & Villas,** for example, is extraordinary. The lobby opens eight stories to a timbered ceiling supported by giant columns of bundled logs. One look eases you into the Northwest wilderness theme. The isolated lodge is heaven for kids.

The **Animal Kingdom Lodge & Villas** replicate the grand safari lodges of Kenya and Tanzania and overlook their own private African game preserve. By far the most exotic of the Disney resorts, it's made to order for families with children.

Another kid's favorite is the exotic **Treehouse Villas at Saratoga Springs Resort.** Originally introduced in 1975, the tree house accommodations were closed and demolished in 2002. The new tree houses, designed in the adventurous image of their predecessors, are nestled in the woods adjacent to the Lake Buena Vista Golf Course.

The **Polynesian Resort,** also dramatic, conveys the feeling of the Pacific islands. It's great for families. Waterfront rooms in the Moorea building offer a perfect view of Cinderella Castle and the Magic Kingdom fireworks across Seven Seas Lagoon. Kids don't know Polynesia from amnesia, but they like those cool "lodge" buildings and all the torches at night.

Grandeur, nostalgia, and privilege are central to the **Grand Floridian, Yacht & Beach Club Resorts, Beach Club Villas, Saratoga Springs Resort,** and the **BoardWalk Inn & Villas.** Although modeled after Eastern Seaboard hotels of different eras, the resorts are amazingly similar. Kids appreciate the creative swimming facilities of these resorts but are relatively neutral toward the themes.

WALT DISNEY WORLD RESORT HOTEL THEMES

HOTEL	THEME
All-Star Resorts	Sports, movies, and music
Animal Kingdom Lodge & Villas	East African game preserve lodge
Art of Animation	Disney's animated films
Bay Lake Tower at the Contemporary	Ultra-modern high-rise
Beach Club Resort and Villas	New England beach club of the 1870s
BoardWalk Inn	East Coast boardwalk hotel of the early 1900s
BoardWalk Villas	East Coast beach cottage of the early 1900s
Caribbean Beach Resort	Caribbean islands
Contemporary Resort	The future as perceived by past and present generations
Coronado Springs Resort	Northern Mexico and the American Southwest
Dolphin (Sheraton)	Modern Florida resort
Grand Floridian Beach Resort	Turn-of-the-20th-century luxury hotel
Old Key West Resort	Key West
Polynesian Resort	Hawaii/South Sea islands
Pop Century	Icons from various decades of the 20th century
Port Orleans French Quarter	Turn-of-the-19th-century New Orleans and Mardi Gras
Port Orleans Riverside	Antebellum plantation and bayou theme
Saratoga Springs	1880s Victorian lakeside resort
Swan (Westin)	Modern Florida resort
Treehouse Villas	Rustic vacation homes with modern amenities
Wilderness Lodge	National park grand lodge of the early 1900s in the American Northwest
Yacht Club Resort	New England seashore hotel of the 1880s

The **Port Orleans Resort** lacks the real mystery and sultriness of the New Orleans French Quarter, but it's hard to replicate the Big Easy in a sanitized Disney version. The Riverside section of Port Orleans, however, hits the mark with its antebellum Mississippi River theme, as does **Old Key West Resort** with its Florida Keys theme. Children like each of these resorts, even though the themes are a bit removed from their frame of reference. The **Caribbean Beach Resort**'s theme is much more effective at night, thanks to creative lighting. By day, the resort looks like a Miami condo development. In 2009 the hotel created pirate-themed suites, which are a big hit with little buccaneers. The playground and swimming pool fit in nicely with the pirate theme, and the shop has a large collection of toys from the *Pirates of the Caribbean* movies. All three resorts are more spread out and the buildings built to a more human (two- or three-story) scale.

Coronado Springs Resort offers several styles of Mexican and Southwestern American architecture. Though the lake setting is lovely and the resort is attractive and inviting, the theme (with the exception of the main swimming area) isn't particularly stimulating. Coronado Springs feels more like a Scottsdale, Arizona, country club than a Disney resort.

Coronado Springs is my favorite Disney resort, and Pepper Market is the best food court in the Mouse empire.

Liliane

The **All-Star Resorts** encompass 30 three-story, T-shaped hotels with almost 6,000 guest rooms. There are 15 themed areas: five celebrate sports (surfing, basketball, tennis, football, and baseball), five recall Hollywood movie themes, and five have musical motifs. The resorts' design, with entrances shaped like musical notes, Coke cups, and footballs, is somewhat adolescent, sacrificing grace and beauty for energy and novelty. Guest rooms are small, with décor reminiscent of a teenage boy's bedroom. Despite the themes, the All-Star Resorts lack sports, movies, and music. For children, staying at the All-Star Resorts is like being a permanent resident at a miniature golf course. They can't get enough of the giant footballs, dalmatians, and guitars. On a more subjective level, kids intuit that the All-Star Resorts are pretty close to what you'd get all the time if Disney had 12-year-olds designing their hotels. They're cool, and the kids feel right at home.

The **Pop Century Resort** is almost a perfect clone of the All-Star Resorts—three-story, motel-style buildings around a central pool, food court, and registration area. Aside from location, the only differences between the All-Star and Pop Century resorts are the decorative touches. Where the All-Star Resorts are distinguished (if you can call it that) by larger-than-life icons from sports, music, and movies, Pop Century draws its icons from various decades of the 20th century. Look for such oddities as building-size Big Wheel tricycles, hula hoops, and the like.

Slated to open at the end of 2012 and located adjacent to the Pop Century Resort, the **Art of Animation Resort** draws its inspiration from four classic Disney animated films: *The Lion King, The Little Mermaid,* and Disney/Pixar's *Finding Nemo* and *Cars.* Be ready for some larger-than-life figures, similar to the Pop Century Resort, such as a 35-foot-tall King Triton.

Pretense aside, the **Contemporary, Bay Lake Tower, Swan,** and **Dolphin** are essentially themeless but architecturally interesting. The Contemporary is a 15-story, A-frame building with monorails running through the middle. Views from guest rooms in the Contemporary are among the best at Walt Disney World. Bay Lake Tower at the Contemporary Resort is a sleek, curvilinear high-rise offering bird's-eye views of Bay Lake. The Swan and Dolphin resorts are massive yet whimsical. Designed

Just in case your luggage is delayed or your room isn't ready, always pack a change of clothes and bathing suits for all family members in your carry-on luggage.

Liliane

by Michael Graves, they're excellent examples of "entertainment architecture." Children are blown away by the giant sea creature and swans atop the Dolphin and Swan and love the idea of the monorail running through the middle of the Contemporary.

3. GREAT SWIMMING AREAS Walt Disney World resorts offer some of the most imaginative swimming facilities that you are likely to encounter anywhere. Exotically themed, beautifully landscaped, and equipped with slides, fountains, and smaller pools for toddlers, Disney resort swimming complexes are a quantum leap removed from the typical, rectangular hotel swimming pool. Some resorts, such as the Grand Floridian and the Polynesian, even offer a sand beach on the Seven Seas Lagoon in addition to swimming pools. Others, such as the Caribbean Beach and Port Orleans resorts, have provided elaborate themed playgrounds near their swimming areas. Incidentally, lest there be any confusion, we are talking about Disney hotel swimming areas and not the Disney paid-admission water theme parks (Typhoon Lagoon and Blizzard Beach).

4. DISNEY'S MAGICAL EXPRESS SERVICE Checked baggage for those arriving in Orlando by commercial airliner are collected by Disney and sent via bus directly to your Walt Disney World resort, allowing you to bypass baggage claim. There's also a bus waiting to transport you to your hotel. If your flight arrives in Orlando close to or after 10 p.m., you must collect your own bags and bring them with you on the bus. Magical Express Transportation runs 24 hours a day.

If you are flying within the United States or Puerto Rico, when it's time to go home, you can check your baggage and receive your boarding pass at the front desk of your Disney resort. This service is available to all guests at Disney-owned resorts—but not the Swan, Dolphin, Shades of Green, or Downtown Disney resorts—even those who don't use the Magical Express service (folks who have rental cars, for example). Resort check-in counters are open 5 a.m.–1 p.m., and you must check in no later than 3 hours before your flight. At press time the following airlines participated in the program: American, Continental, Delta, JetBlue, US Airways, Air Tran, Alaska Airlines, United, and Southwest. All participating airlines have restrictions on the number

WALT DISNEY WORLD RESORT SWIMMING POOLS: *Rated and Ranked*	
HOTEL	POOL RATING
1. Yacht & Beach Club Resorts and Beach Club Villas (shared complex)	★★★★★
2. Animal Kingdom Villas (Kidani Village)	★★★★¹/₂
3. Port Orleans Resort	★★★★¹/₂
4. Saratoga Springs Resort & Spa–Treehouse Villas	★★★★¹/₂
5. Wilderness Lodge & Villas	★★★★¹/₂
6. Animal Kingdom Lodge & Villas (Jambo House)	★★★★
7. Bay Lake Tower at the Contemporary Resort	★★★★
8. Coronado Springs Resort	★★★★
9. Dolphin	★★★★
10. Polynesian Resort	★★★★
11. Swan	★★★★
12. BoardWalk Inn & Villas	★★★¹/₂
13. Contemporary Resort	★★★¹/₂
14. Grand Floridian Resort	★★★¹/₂
15. All-Star Resorts	★★★
16. Caribbean Beach Resort	★★★
17. Fort Wilderness Resort and Campground	★★★
18. Old Key West Resort	★★★
19. Pop Century Resort	★★★
20. Shades of Green	★★★
21. Art of Animation *(not yet open at press time)*	

of bags, checking procedures, and various other related items. Consult your carrier before leaving home for specifics.

If your flight departs from Orlando before 8 a.m., Magical Express will pick you up before the Magical Express desk at your resort is open. In this case, because the desk isn't manned until 5 a.m., you cannot use the resort check-in for your bags or get your boarding pass. You'll need to handle your own luggage and get your boarding pass at the airport.

Travel agents report very few complaints about Magical Express. Still, the service is not without its faults. Luggage is transported by truck to Walt Disney World instead of accompanying you on the bus. Readers complain of luggage delivered to their hotel rooms hours late, sometimes in the middle of the night. If you want, you can collect your own luggage at the baggage claim and bring it along with you on the

Magical Express bus. It isn't much extra trouble and you will be at peace knowing where your luggage is at all times. If you arrive at your hotel with luggage in hand and your room isn't ready, the hotel will store your luggage and provide a phone number you can call to check the status of your room. Be forewarned that some buses go directly to your resort while others make multiple stops at other resorts. Regarding the return trip to the airport, we've received reports both of readers barely getting to the airport in time for their flight and of others made to depart from their hotel very early. One reader, for example, was picked up at 4:35 a.m. for a 7:40 a.m. flight.

5. BABYSITTING AND CHILD-CARE OPTIONS A number of options for babysitting, child-care, and children's programs are offered to Disney hotel and campground guests. All the resort hotels connected by the monorail, as well as several other Disney hotels, offer "clubs," or themed child-care centers, where potty-trained children ages 4–12 can stay while their adults go out.

Though somewhat expensive, the clubs do a great job and are highly regarded by children and parents. On the negative side, they're open only in the evening, and not all Disney hotels have them. If you're staying at a Disney hotel that doesn't have a child-care club, you're better off using one of the private in-room babysitting services (see page 68). In-room babysitting is also available at hotels outside Disney World.

6. GUARANTEED THEME PARK ADMISSIONS On days of unusually heavy attendance, Disney resort guests are guaranteed admission to the theme parks. In practice, no guest is ever turned away until a theme park's parking lot is full. When this happens, that park most certainly will be packed to the point of absolute gridlock. Under such conditions, you would have to possess the common sense of an amoeba to exercise your guaranteed-admission privilege. The privilege, by the way, doesn't extend to Blizzard Beach and Typhoon Lagoon.

7. CHILDREN SHARING A ROOM WITH THEIR PARENTS There is no extra charge per night for children younger than age 18 sharing a room with their parents. Many hotels outside Walt Disney World also observe this practice.

8. FREE PARKING Disney resort guests with cars don't have to pay for parking in the theme-park lots or at the resorts, which saves about $14 per day.

WALT DISNEY WORLD HOTELS:
Strengths and Weaknesses for Families

FOR THE SAKE OF ORIENTATION, we've grouped the Disney resorts, as well as the Swan and Dolphin resorts, by location. Closest to the Magic Kingdom are the Grand Floridian, the Polynesian, the

Bay Lake Tower, and the Contemporary resorts, all on the monorail; the Wilderness Lodge & Villas and Fort Wilderness Campground, which are connected to the Magic Kingdom by boat; and the U.S. military resort, Shades of Green, served exclusively by bus.

Close to Epcot are the Yacht & Beach Club Resorts, the Beach Club Villas, the BoardWalk Inn & Villas, and the non-Disney-owned Swan and Dolphin resorts. These are the closest hotels to Disney's Hollywood Studios.

Closer to Downtown Disney and Bonnet Creek are the Old Key West, Saratoga Springs, Port Orleans, Caribbean Beach, Pop Century, and Art of Animation resorts. Also nearby are the seven independent hotels of the Downtown Disney Resort Area.

The All-Star and the Coronado Springs resorts are located near both Disney's Hollywood Studios and the Animal Kingdom. Closest to the Animal Kingdom is The Animal Kingdom Lodge & Villas.

MAGIC KINGDOM RESORTS
Grand Floridian Resort & Spa

GRAND FLORIDIAN RESORT & SPA

STRENGTHS	WEAKNESSES
On Magic Kingdom monorail	Somewhat formal
Ferry service to Magic Kingdom	Cavernous, impersonal lobby
Excellent guest rooms	Overly large physical layout
Children's programs, character meals	Children don't get theme
Excellent children's pool	Only one on-site restaurant suitable
Beach	for younger children
Recreational options	Imposing, rather formal public areas
Restaurant selection via monorail	Distant guest self-parking
Child-care facility on-site	

The Grand Floridian has a lot to offer: a white sand beach, a spa and fitness center, tennis courts, elaborate theatrical dining from high tea to personal butler service, and so on. But the tone strikes some people as rather hoity-toity; the music in the lobby can be disconcertingly loud, the rooms are not so expansive or good-looking as the public spaces, and the complex is frequently crowded with sightseers and plantation nostalgics waving fat cigars. Also, because the Wedding Chapel is located on the grounds of the Grand Floridian, there are frequently receptions, photo sessions, and tizzies—which, depending on your outlook, add charm or are inconveniences. Word on the street is that the Grand Floridian is the next resort to be added to Disney's Vacation Club lineup. We're not sure whether this will involve construction of new buildings or the renovation of existing structures.

Polynesian Resort

POLYNESIAN RESORT	
STRENGTHS	Recreational options
Relaxed and casual	Restaurant selection via monorail
Ferry service to Magic Kingdom	WDW's best child-care facility
Exotic theme that children love	on-site
On Magic Kingdom monorail	Easily accessible self-parking
Epcot monorail within walking distance	
Transportation and Ticket Center	**WEAKNESSES**
adjoins resort	Overly large and confusing layout
Rooms among the nicest at WDW	Walkways exposed to rain
Children's programs, character meals	Noise from nearby motor speedway
Beach and marina	Front-desk inefficiency
Excellent swimming complex	

The Polynesian is arrayed along the Seven Seas Lagoon facing the Magic Kingdom. It's a huge complex, but the hotel buildings, laid out like a South Sea island village around a ceremonial house, are of a decidedly human scale compared to the hulking Grand Floridian or Contemporary resorts. From the tiki torches at night to the bleached sand beach, kids love the Polynesian. The resort's location at WDW's transportation nexus makes it the most convenient resort for those without a car. Though the Polynesian is one of Disney's oldest resorts, periodic refurbishments keep it well maintained.

Contemporary Resort and Bay Lake Tower

CONTEMPORARY RESORT AND BAY LAKE TOWER	
STRENGTHS	Recreational options including super
On Magic Kingdom monorail	games arcade
10-minute walk to Magic Kingdom	Restaurant selection via monorail
Interesting architecture	Child-care facility on-site
Nicest rooms at WDW	Good restaurant on-site
Super views of the Magic Kingdom or	
Bay Lake	**WEAKNESSES**
Character meals	Sterility of theme and decor in
Excellent children's pool	public areas
Marina	Monorail aside, theme leaves
	children cold

The Contemporary Resort has a sleek, almost Asian look, although the pyramid structure itself is a period piece, of course. And it has lots to offer the active family: six lighted tennis courts, three swimming pools, a health club, volleyball courts, a beach, and a marina that rents sail-boats of various sizes—you must be at least 18 years old, which helps limit the traffic a little—and offers parasailing and waterskiing. For 2012 Disney has added health and wellness suites, which feature in-room exercise equipment, bamboo floors, non-allergenic mattresses, and organic fruit and vegetables at the concierge desk. Guest rooms were completely refurbished and are now the nicest to be found at Walt Disney World. There's no compelling theme, but then show me a child who isn't wowed by monorails tearing though the inside of a hotel. With a 2009 debut, the Bay Lake Tower is a high-rise Disney Vacation Club property situated on Bay Lake between the Contemporary Resort and the Magic Kingdom. Like other DVC developments, it offers one-, two-, and three-bedroom suites. Features include a fireworks-viewing deck, a rooftop lounge, a lakeside pool, and a sky bridge linking the tower to the Contemporary Resort's monorail station.

Wilderness Lodge & Villas

WILDERNESS LODGE & VILLAS	
STRENGTHS	Child-care facility on-site
Magnificently rendered theme that children can't get enough of	Convenient self-parking
Good on-site dining	**WEAKNESSES**
Great views from guest rooms	Boat service only to Magic Kingdom
Extensive recreational options	No direct bus to many destinations
Romantic setting and interesting architecture	No character meals
Elaborate swimming complex	Rooms sleep only four people (plus child in crib)
Health and fitness center	Must take boat or bus to access off-site dining options

This deluxe resort is inspired by national-park lodges of the early 20th century. Wilderness Lodge & Villas ranks with Animal Kingdom Lodge & Villas as one of the most impressively themed and meticulously detailed Disney resorts. It's also by far the hands-down favorite hotel of children. You won't have any trouble convincing the kids to abandon the theme parks for rest and a swim if you stay at the Wilderness Lodge.

Situated on the shore of Bay Lake, the lodge consists of an eight-story central building flanked by two seven-story guest wings and a wing of studio and one- and two-bedroom condominiums. The hotel features exposed timber columns, log cabin–style facades, and dormer windows. The grounds are landscaped with evergreen pines and pampas grass. The lobby boasts an 82-foot-tall stone fireplace and two 55-foot Pacific Northwest totem poles. Timber pillars, giant tepee chandeliers, and stone- and wood-inlaid floors accentuate the lobby's rustic luxury. Although the resort isn't on vast acreage, it does have a beach and a delightful pool modeled on a mountain stream complete with waterfall and geyser. Adjoining the Wilderness Lodge is the Wilderness Lodge Villas, a Disney Vacation Club property offering condo accommodations.

Shades of Green

SHADES OF GREEN	
STRENGTHS	Video arcade
Large guest rooms	Game rooms with pool
Informality	Ice-cream shop
Quiet setting	
Views of golf course from guest rooms	**WEAKNESSES**
	No interesting theme
Convenient self-parking	Limited on-site dining
Swimming complex	Limited bus service
Fitness center	

This deluxe resort is owned and operated by the U.S. Armed Forces and is available only to U.S. military personnel (including members of the National Guard and reserves, retired military, and employees of the U.S. Public Health Service and the Department of Defense; others may be eligible; call for additional information). Shades of Green consists of one three-story building nestled among three golf courses. Tastefully nondescript, Shades of Green is at the same time pure peace and quiet. There's no beach or lake, but there are several pools, including one shaped like Mickey's head. Surrounding golf courses are open to all Disney guests. If you qualify to stay here, don't even think about staying anywhere else.

Fort Wilderness Campground

If camping is one of your hobbies, you can rough it in beautiful territory at Fort Wilderness for as little as $46 per campsite. Either set up a tent and use the restrooms, showers, and Laundromat down the lane, or borrow your parents' RV. With the accessibility of two markets on-site, most visitors here choose to do their own cooking; do so and this becomes the absolute rock-bottom priced Disney World vacation.

784 campsites	$46–$125 per night	boat/bus service
408 wilderness homes and cabins **(sleep 4–6)**	$275–$450 per night	boat/bus service

Fort Wilderness is ideal for nature lovers. For the less active, electric carts are for rent. Also available are pools, a marina, a beach, and outdoor games such as basketball, volleyball, shuffleboard, fishing, canoeing, biking, and even tennis and horseback riding. If you really get into

---

FORT WILDERNESS CAMPGROUND

STRENGTHS

Informality

Children's play areas

Best selection of recreational options
    at WDW

Special day and evening programs

Campsite amenities

Number of showers and toilets

Limited automobile traffic

Hoop-Dee-Doo Musical Revue
    dinner show

Off-site dining options via boat at
    Magic Kingdom resorts

Convenient self-parking

Free Wi-Fi

WEAKNESSES

Isolated location

Complicated bus service

Confusing campground layout

Lack of privacy

Very limited on-site dining options

Extreme distance to store and restau-
    rant facilities from many campsites

Crowding at beaches and pools

Small baths in cabins

---

the mood, you can sit around the evening campfire and watch a movie with the other happy campers. The campgrounds are the only accommodations that allow you to have pets (not running loose, of course).

Here's what you cannot do: drive anywhere within the campground, not even from your campsite back to the trading post. You must take the bus, bike, or golf cart (both are for rent), or walk (it's not far). And bus or boat transportation to the theme parks can be laborious.

All loops have a comfort station with showers, toilets, phones, an ice machine, and a coin laundry.

Bob

Obviously, Fort Wilderness draws a lot of families (did we mention the petting farm and the hay rides?), and in hot weather, a lot of bugs and thunderstorms. If you want things a little more comfortable, ask for a full-service hookup and get water, electricity, an outdoor grill, sanitary disposal, and even a cable TV connection. If you want super privacy and even more amenities, rent one of the prefab log cabins, which get you a full kitchen, housekeeping services, air-conditioning, a daily newspaper, voice mail, and, yes, cable TV.

For tent and RV campers, there's a fairly stark trade-off between sites convenient to pools, restaurant, trading posts, and other amenities, and those that are most scenic, shady, and quiet. RVers who prefer to be near Guest Services, the marina, the beach, and the restaurant and tavern should go for loops 100, 200, 700, and 400 (in that order). Loops near the campground's secondary facility area with pool, trading post, bike and golf-cart rentals, and campfire program are 1400, 1300, 600, 1000, and 1500, in order of preference. If you're looking for a tranquil, scenic setting among mature trees, we recommend loops 1800, 1900, 1700, and 1600, in that order, and the backside sites on the 700 loop. The best loop of all, and the only one to offer both a lovely setting and proximity to key amenities, is loop 300. The best loops for tents and pop-up campers are loops 1500 and 2000, with 1500 being nearest a pool, convenience store, and the campfire program.

EPCOT RESORTS

Yacht & Beach Club Resorts and Beach Club Villas

YACHT & BEACH CLUB RESORTS AND BEACH CLUB VILLAS	
STRENGTHS	15-minute walk to DHS
Fun and nautical New England theme	Best swimming complex at WDW
Attractive guest rooms	Health and fitness center
Good on-site dining	Convenient self-parking
Children's programs, character meals	View from waterside guest rooms
Excellent selection of nearby off-site dining	Child-care facility on-site
Boat service to Disney's Hollywood Studios and Epcot	**WEAKNESSES**
10-minute walk to rear entrance of Epcot	No transportation to Epcot main entrance, except by taxi
10-minute walk to BoardWalk	No convenient counter-service food
	Poor room-to-hall soundproofing

Situated on Crescent Lake across from Disney's BoardWalk, the Yacht & Beach Club Resorts are connected and share a boardwalk, marina, and swimming complex. The Yacht Club Resort has a breezy Nantucket and Cape Cod atmosphere with its own lighthouse and boardwalks, lots of polished wood, and burnished brass (and boxes of chess or checkers pieces available for your room on request). Its sibling resort, the Beach Club, shares most of the facilities but is a little sportier and more casual in atmosphere. The Disney Vacation Club Villas at the Beach Club are available for rental, have their own small pool, and may offer more privacy. The resorts offer a shared mini–water park, Stormalong Bay, with a white-sand beach and marina, and an unusual number of sports facilities, such as croquet, tennis, and volleyball, plus fitness rooms, and so on. Many of the rooms have balconies with views looking out across the lagoon toward the BoardWalk.

BoardWalk Inn & Villas

On Crescent Lake, the BoardWalk Inn is another of the Walt Disney World deluxe resorts. The complex is a detailed replica of an early-20th-century Atlantic coast boardwalk. Facades of hotels, diners, and shops create an inviting and exciting waterfront skyline. In reality, behind the facades, the BoardWalk Inn & Villas are a single integrated structure. Restaurants and shops occupy the boardwalk level, while accommodations rise up to six stories above. Painted bright red and yellow along with weathered pastel greens and blues, the BoardWalk resorts are the only Disney hotels that use neon signs

BOARDWALK INN & VILLAS

STRENGTHS

Lively seaside and amusement pier theme

Newly refurbished guest rooms

10-minute walk to Epcot rear entrance

15-minute walk to DHS

Boat service to Disney's Hollywood Studios and Epcot

Modest but well-themed swimming complex

3-minute walk to BoardWalk midway and nightlife

Selection of off-site dining within walking distance

Health and fitness center

View from waterside guest rooms

Child-care facility on-site

WEAKNESSES

No restaurants in hotel

Limited children's activities and no character meals

No restaurants within easy walking distance suitable for younger children

No transportation to Epcot main entrance

Distant guest self-parking

as architectural detail. The complex shares one pool with an old-fashioned amusement-park theme and also has two quiet pools.

The BoardWalk Inn & Villas have a lot to offer in terms of entertainment, in that the ESPN Club, the carnival midway, street performers, and for adults, BoardWalk nightspots, are all literally at your feet. But think about what that will mean when you're ready to call it quits; the sound can come right up through the building, and odd lights are glaring at all hours.

Walt Disney World Swan and Dolphin Resorts

THE SWAN AND THE DOLPHIN

STRENGTHS

Exotic architecture

Extremely nice guest rooms

Good on-site and nearby dining

Excellent beach and swimming complex

Health and fitness center

Child-care facilities on-site

Children's programs, character meals

Varied recreational offerings

10-minute walk to BoardWalk nightlife

Boat service to Disney's Hollywood Studios and Epcot

Participates in Extra Magic Hours program

View from guest rooms

WEAKNESSES

Primarily adult convention and business clientele

No transportation to Epcot main entrance

Distant guest self-parking, requires daily fee

Do not qualify for Disney's Magical Express service

Confusing layout

The Walt Disney World Swan and Dolphin resorts were not designed by Disney Imagineers, though you might certainly think they were. They were the playgrounds of post-modern architect Michael Graves; in fact, they are not Disney-owned properties at all, though guests have most of the perks. The Swan and Dolphin are patronized by business types and adult travelers rather than families, and their theme runs more to the surrealistic rather than to the whimsical. That being said, a quick glance at the Swan and Dolphin's strengths will verify that they have as much or more to offer families than the Disney resorts.

BONNET CREEK/ DOWNTOWN DISNEY AREA RESORTS

Caribbean Beach Resort

CARIBBEAN BEACH RESORT

STRENGTHS	WEAKNESSES
Attractive Caribbean theme	Lackluster on-site dining
Children's play areas	No easily accessible off-site dining
Convenient self-parking	No character meals
Walking, jogging, biking	Extreme distance of many guest rooms from dining and services
Lakefront setting	Occasionally poor bus service
	Large, confusing layout
	Long lines to check in

The huge Caribbean Beach Resort occupies 200 acres surrounding a 45-acre lake called Barefoot Bay. This mid-priced resort, modeled after resorts in the Caribbean, consists of the registration area (Custom House) and six two-story "villages" named after Caribbean islands. Each village has its own pool, laundry room, and beach. The Caribbean motif is maintained with red-metal roofs, widow's walks, and wooden-railed porches. The atmosphere is cheerful, with buildings painted blue, lime green, and sherbet orange. Many of the rooms have been refurbished and re-themed to include characters from *Finding Nemo* and *Pirates of the Caribbean.* In addition to the five village pools, the resort's main swimming pool is themed as an old Spanish fort, complete with slides and water cannons.

Port Orleans French Quarter and Riverside Resorts

Port Orleans's Riverside and French Quarter resorts are good-looking, lower-cost hotel alternatives that combine steamboat-era Southern décor and fairly easy access to Downtown Disney, and they're pretty popular among families too.

The 1,008-room French Quarter section is a sanitized Disney version of the New Orleans French Quarter. Consisting of seven three-story buildings next to Bonnet Creek, the resort suggests what New

---

PORT ORLEANS FRENCH QUARTER AND RIVERSIDE RESORTS

STRENGTHS	WEAKNESSES
Extremely creative swimming areas	No character meals
Nice guest rooms, especially in the French Quarter	Insufficient on-site dining
	No easily accessible off-site dining
Pleasant setting along Bonnet Creek	Extreme distance of many guest rooms from dining and services
Food courts	
Convenient self-parking	Large, confusing layout
Children's play areas	Congested bus-loading areas
Varied recreational offerings	
Boat service to Downtown Disney	

Orleans would look like if its buildings were painted every year and garbage collectors never went on strike. There are prim pink-and-blue guest buildings with wrought-iron filigree, shuttered windows, and old-fashioned iron lampposts. In keeping with the Crescent City theme, the French Quarter is landscaped with magnolia trees and overgrown vines. The centrally located Mint contains the registration area and food court and is a reproduction of a turn-of-the-19th-century building where Mississippi Delta farmers sold their harvests. The registration desk features a vibrant Mardi Gras mural and old-fashioned bank-teller windows. The section's Doubloon Lagoon swimming complex surrounds a colorful fiberglass creation depicting Neptune riding a sea serpent. We think that the French Quarter has the most attractive and tasteful rooms of any of the Disney moderate resorts.

Port Orleans's Riverside Resort draws on the lifestyle and architecture of Mississippi River communities in antebellum Louisiana. Spread along Bonnet Creek, which encircles Ol' Man Island (the section's main swimming area), Riverside is subdivided into two more themed areas: the mansion area, which features plantation-style architecture, and the bayou area, with tin-roofed rustic (imitation) wooden buildings. Mansions are three stories tall, while bayou guesthouses are a story shorter. The river-life theme is augmented by groves of azalea and juniper. Riverside's food court houses a working cotton press powered by a 35-foot waterwheel. New at Riverside for 2012 is a set of 512 rooms themed after Disney's *The Princess and The Frog, Beauty and the Beast,* and *Aladdin* films.

Disney's Old Key West Resort

This was the first Disney Vacation Club property. Although the resort is a time-share property, units not being used by owners are rented on a nightly basis. Old Key West is a large aggregation of two- to three-story buildings modeled after Caribbean-style residences and guesthouses of the Florida Keys. Arranged subdivision-style around a golf

DISNEY'S OLD KEY WEST RESORT

STRENGTHS	WEAKNESSES
Extremely nice studios and villas	Old Key West theme meaningless to children
Full kitchens in villas	
Quiet, lushly landscaped setting	Large, confusing layout
Convenient self-parking	Substandard bus service
Small, more private swimming pools in each accommodations cluster	Limited on-site dining
	No easily accessible off-site dining
Recreation options	Extreme distance of many guest rooms from dining and services
Boat service to Downtown Disney	
	No character meals

course and along Bonnet Creek, the buildings are in small neighborhood-like clusters. They feature pastel facades, white trim, and shuttered windows. The registration area is in Conch Flats Community Hall, along with a full-service restaurant, modest fitness center, marina, and sundries shop. Each cluster of accommodations has a quiet pool; a larger pool is at the community hall. A waterslide in the shape of a giant sand castle is the primary kid pleaser at the main pool.

Saratoga Springs Resort & Spa

SARATOGA SPRINGS RESORT & SPA

STRENGTHS	WEAKNESSES
Extremely nice studio rooms and villas	Traffic congestion at resort's southeast exit
Lushly landscaped setting	
Best fitness center at Walt Disney World	Small living areas in villas
	Distance of some accommodations from dining and services
Convenient self-parking	
Close to Downtown Disney	Limited dining options
Best spa at Walt Disney World	No character meals
Golf on property	Most distant of all Disney resorts from the theme parks
Excellent themed swimming complex	
Hiking, jogging, and water recreation	Theme and atmosphere not very kid-friendly

The main pool is the resort's focal point. Called High Rock Spring, it tumbles over boulders into a clear, free-form heated pool. The area offers a waterslide that winds among the rocks, two whirlpool spas, and an interactive wet-play area for children. The Saratoga Springs complex will eventually be the largest Vacation Club resort, with well over 800 units. It's expanding toward the Downtown Disney shopping area (across the lake) via a path and a pedestrian bridge. There is boat as well as bus service at the facility, although the boats are prohibited from running if lightning threatens. The resort's décor plays on the history and retro-Victorian style of the upstate New York racing resort, with traditional horse-country prints and drawings, stable boy uniforms for the bellhops, and so on. The spa, probably Disney's best, has a fitness center attached. The Downtown Disney fireworks are visible from some areas. Favorites for children are the Treehouse Villas nestled in a pinewood bordering the golf course. With the entire living and sleeping area about 12 feet off the ground, you really feel like you're living in a tree house. Opened in 2009, the rustic Treehouse Villas are among Walt Disney World's most inventive accommodations. There are only 60 three-bedroom units, so if you want a reservation for one of those larger units, book well in advance.

Pop Century Resort

POP CENTURY RESORT

STRENGTHS	WEAKNESSES
Kid-friendly theme	Small guest rooms
Low (for Disney) rates	No full-service dining
Large swimming pools	Large, confusing layout
Food court	No character meals
Convenient self-parking	Limited recreation options
Fast check-in	

On Victory Way near the ESPN Wide World of Sports Complex is Disney's Pop Century resort. Originally designed to be completed in phases, the first section opened in 2004. The long-planned second phase of Pop Century was canceled in favor of a new value resort, Disney's Art of Animation. While not open at press time, a summary of Art of Animation's features follows.

The All-Star, Pop Century, and Caribbean Beach resorts are infamous for long lines at check-in time, which is usually 3 or 4 p.m. To avoid the lines, check in 11 a.m.–1 p.m. Your room might not be ready for occupancy, but odds are that they'll check you in and issue your room keys. If you have luggage, you can check it with bell services and have it delivered or pick it up later.

Pop Century is an economy resort. In terms of layout, architecture, and facilities, Pop Century is almost a clone of the All-Star Resorts (that is, four-story, motel-style buildings built around a central pool, food court, and registration area). Decorative touches make the difference. Where the All-Star Resorts display larger-than-life icons from sports, music, and movies, Pop Century draws its icons from decades of the 20th century. Look for such oddities as building-size Big Wheels, hula hoops, and the like, punctuated by silhouettes of people dancing the decade's fad dance.

The public areas at Pop Century are marginally more sophisticated than the ones at the

All-Star Resorts, with 20th-century period furniture and décor rolled up in a saccharine, those-were-the-days theme. A food court, bar, playground, pools, and so on emulate the All-Star Resorts model in size and location. A Pop Century departure from the All-Star precedent has merchandise retailers thrown in with the fast-food concessions in a combination dining and shopping area. This apparently is what happens when a giant corporation tries to combine selling pizza with hawking Goofy hats. (You just know the word *synergy* was used like cheap cologne in those design meetings.) As at the All-Star Resorts, there is no full-service restaurant. The resort is connected to the rest of Walt Disney World by bus, but because of the limited dining options, we recommend having a car.

If you're considering one of the Disney "value" resorts, this reader from Dublin, Georgia, thinks Pop Century beats the All-Star Resorts hands-down.

> *Pop Century is now my favorite. 1. It is far superior to the All-Stars but the same price. 2. There is a lake at a value resort and a view of fireworks. 3. The courtyards have Twister games, neat pools, and a Goofy "surprise fountain" for little children. 4. The memorabilia is interesting to us over 18 years old. 5. I love the gift shop, food court, and bar combo. 6. There are frozen Cokes in the refillable-mug section. 7. Bus transportation is better than anywhere else, including Grand Floridian! 8. You can rent surrey bikes. 9. The rooms have real soap instead of the All-Stars' yucky globby stuff. 10. The layout is more convenient to the food court. 11. I never hear construction noise, and the noise from neighbors is not worse than anywhere else. 12. Where else do the [cast members] do the shag to oldies? Also, the shrimp lo mein is the best bargain and among the best food anywhere.*

Art of Animation Resort

The Art of Animation Resort, scheduled to open late 2012, draws its inspiration from four classic Disney animated films: *The Lion King, The Little Mermaid,* and Disney/Pixar's *Finding Nemo* and *Cars.*

The new value resort, located across Hour Glass Lake from Pop Century, will have 864 rooms and 1,120 family suites. These suites have two separate bathrooms, a master bedroom, three separate sleeping areas within the living space, and a kitchenette. The resort will consist of three-story buildings and exterior-facing rooms and a series of

ART OF ANIMATION RESORT	
STRENGTHS	**WEAKNESSES**
Kid-friendly theme	Small guest rooms
Low (for Disney) rates	No full-service dining
Large swimming pools	Large, confusing layout
Food court	No character meals
Convenient self-parking	Limited recreation options

themed swimming pools, including a large feature pool at the Finding Nemo courtyard of the resort. A water play area is planned, as well as a 68,800-square-foot commercial building with shopping and dining space. Expect to see large, colorful icons of the film's characters throughout the grounds.

ANIMAL KINGDOM RESORTS
Animal Kingdom Lodge & Villas

ANIMAL KINGDOM LODGE & VILLAS	
STRENGTHS	On-site nature programs and storytelling
Exotic theme	
Uniquely appointed guest rooms	Health and fitness center
Most rooms have private balconies	Child-care center on-site
View of savanna and animals from guest rooms	Proximity to non-Disney restaurants on US 192
Themed swimming areas	**WEAKNESSES**
Excellent on-site dining, including a buffet	Remote location

The Animal Kingdom Lodge is a snazzy take on safari chic, with balcony views of wildlife that alone may be worth the tabs, but its distance from the other parks may be a drawback for those planning to explore all of Disney World. On the other hand, if you have a car, it's the closest resort to all of the affordable family restaurants lining US 192 (Irlo Bronson Parkway). By far the most exotic Disney resort, it's made for families.

Designed by Peter Dominick of Wilderness Lodge fame, Animal Kingdom Lodge fuses African tribal architecture with the rugged style of grand East African national-park lodges. Five-story, thatched-roof wings fan out from a vast central rotunda housing the lobby and featuring a huge mud fireplace. Public areas and many rooms offer panoramic views of a private 33-acre wildlife preserve punctuated with streams and elevated kopje (rock outcrops) and populated with 100 types of free-roaming animals and 130 birds. Most guest rooms boast hand-carved furnishings and richly colored upholstery. Almost all have full balconies.

Having stayed at Kidani Village shortly after its opening, we think it's a quiet, relaxed resort. The lobby and rooms have a smaller, more personal feel than Jambo House. The building exterior isn't anything special—essentially a set of green rectangles with oversize African-themed decorations attached. Kidani's distance from Jambo House makes it feel even more remote than Jambo. The bus stops are a fair distance from the main building too, and it's easy to head in the wrong direction when you're coming back from the parks at night.

Coronado Springs Resort

CORONADO SPRINGS RESORT	
STRENGTHS	**WEAKNESSES**
Nice guest rooms	Insufficient on-site dining
View from waterside guest rooms	*Extreme* distance of many guest rooms from dining and services
Food court	
Mayan-themed swimming area with waterslides	No character meals
	Low-flow showerheads make rinsing off take longer
Fitness center	
Nightclub on property	
Convenient self-parking	

To save a little money without giving up services, consider the Coronado Springs Resort, a rich, Old Mexico–style complex with courtyards, fountains, stucco and terra-cotta buildings, a few Mayan ruins here and there, several swimming pools, a mini water park, a white-sand beach, a fitness center, a walking path circling a 22-acre lake, and so on. Because it is also used as a convention hotel, expect a high percentage of guests to be business travelers. Coronado Springs has particularly good access to the Animal Kingdom and Blizzard Beach.

All-Star Resorts

ALL-STAR RESORTS	
STRENGTHS	**WEAKNESSES**
Super kid-friendly theme	Remote location
Low (for Disney) rates	Small guest rooms (except family suites)
Large swimming pools	
Food courts	No full-service dining
Convenient self-parking	Large, confusing layout
	Congested bus-loading areas
	No character meals
	Limited recreation options
	Close to McDonald's (kidding!)

Disney's version of a budget resort features three distinct themes executed in the same hyperbolic style. Spread over a vast expanse, the resorts comprise almost 35 three-story motel-style guest-room buildings. Although the three resorts are neighbors, each has its own lobby, food court, and registration area. All-Star Sports Resort features huge sports icons: bright football helmets, tennis rackets, and baseball

continued on page 105

Hotel Information Chart

All-Star Resorts ★★★

Walt Disney World
1701–1901 W. Buena Vista Dr.
Lake Buena Vista, FL 32830
☎ 407-934-7639
disneyworld.com

LOCATION	WDW
ROOM RATING	73
COST ($ = $50)	$$$–

commuting times to parks (in minutes)

MAGIC KINGDOM	6:15
EPCOT	5:45
ANIMAL KINGDOM	4:15
DHS	5:15

Animal Kingdom Lodge ★★★★

Walt Disney World
2901 Osceola Pkwy.
Lake Buena Vista, FL 32830
☎ 407-938-3000
disneyworld.com

LOCATION	WDW
ROOM RATING	89
COST ($ = $50)	$ x 6 +

commuting times to parks (in minutes)

MAGIC KINGDOM	8:15
EPCOT	6:15
ANIMAL KINGDOM	2:15
DHS	6:00

Animal Kingdom Villas (Kidani Village and Jambo House) ★★★★½

Walt Disney World
2901 Osceola Pkwy.
Lake Buena Vista, FL 32830
☎ 407-938-3000
disneyworld.com

LOCATION	WDW
ROOM RATING	93
COST ($ = $50)	$ x 8

commuting times to parks (in minutes)

MAGIC KINGDOM	8:15
EPCOT	6:15
ANIMAL KINGDOM	2:15
DHS	6:00

Beach Club Villas ★★★★½

Walt Disney World
1900 Epcot Resorts Blvd.
Lake Buena Vista, FL 32830
☎ 407-934-2175
disneyworld.com

LOCATION	WDW
ROOM RATING	90
COST ($ = $50)	$ x 8

commuting times to parks (in minutes)

MAGIC KINGDOM	7:15
EPCOT	5:15
ANIMAL KINGDOM	6:45
DHS	4:00

BoardWalk Inn ★★★★

Walt Disney World
2101 Epcot Resorts Blvd.
Lake Buena Vista, FL 32830
☎ 407-939-5100
disneyworld.com

LOCATION	WDW
ROOM RATING	89
COST ($ = $50)	$ x 8 +

commuting times to parks (in minutes)

MAGIC KINGDOM	7:15
EPCOT	5:30
ANIMAL KINGDOM	7:00
DHS	3:00

BoardWalk Villas ★★★★½

Walt Disney World
2101 Epcot Resorts Blvd.
Lake Buena Vista, FL 32830
☎ 407-939-5100
disneyworld.com

LOCATION	WDW
ROOM RATING	90
COST ($ = $50)	$ x 7 –

commuting times to parks (in minutes)

MAGIC KINGDOM	7:15
EPCOT	5:30
ANIMAL KINGDOM	7:00
DHS	3:00

Dolphin ★★★★½

Walt Disney World
1500 Epcot Resorts Blvd.
Lake Buena Vista, FL 32830
☎ 407-934-4000
swandolphin.com

LOCATION	WDW
ROOM RATING	90
COST ($ = $50)	$$$$–

commuting times to parks (in minutes)

MAGIC KINGDOM	6:45
EPCOT	5:00
ANIMAL KINGDOM	6:15
DHS	4:00

Fort Wilderness Resort (cabins) ★★★★

Walt Disney World
4510 N. Fort Wilderness Trl.
Lake Buena Vista, FL 32830
☎ 407-824-2900
disneyworld.com

LOCATION	WDW
ROOM RATING	86
COST ($ = $50)	$ x 7

commuting times to parks (in minutes)

MAGIC KINGDOM	13:15
EPCOT	8:30
ANIMAL KINGDOM	20:00
DHS	14:00

Grand Floridian Resort & Spa ★★★★½

Walt Disney World
4401 Floridian Way
Lake Buena Vista, FL 32830
☎ 407-824-3000
disneyworld.com

LOCATION	WDW
ROOM RATING	93
COST ($ = $50)	$ x 10

commuting times to parks (in minutes)

MAGIC KINGDOM	on monorail
EPCOT	4:45
ANIMAL KINGDOM	11:45
DHS	6:45

Art of Animation
(not yet open at press time)

Walt Disney World
1850 Animation Way
Lake Buena Vista, FL 32830
☎ 407-934-7639
disneyworld.com

LOCATION	WDW
ROOM RATING	N/A
COST ($ = $50)	$$–

commuting times to parks (*in minutes*)

MAGIC KINGDOM	8:30
EPCOT	6:30
ANIMAL KINGDOM	6:15
DHS	5:00

Bay Lake Tower at Contemporary Resort
★★★★½

Walt Disney World
4600 N. World Dr.
Lake Buena Vista, FL 32830
☎ 407-824-1000
disneyworld.com

LOCATION	WDW
ROOM RATING	95
COST ($ = $50)	$ x 9 +

commuting times to parks (*in minutes*)

MAGIC KINGDOM	on monorail
EPCOT	11:00
ANIMAL KINGDOM	17:15
DHS	14:15

Beach Club Resort
★★★★½

Walt Disney World
1800 Epcot Resorts Blvd.
Lake Buena Vista, FL 32830
☎ 407-934-8000
disneyworld.com

LOCATION	WDW
ROOM RATING	90
COST ($ = $50)	$ x 8

commuting times to parks (*in minutes*)

MAGIC KINGDOM	7:15
EPCOT	5:15
ANIMAL KINGDOM	6:45
DHS	4:00

Caribbean Beach Resort
★★★½

Walt Disney World
900 Cayman Way
Lake Buena Vista, FL 32830
☎ 407-934-3400
disneyworld.com

LOCATION	WDW
ROOM RATING	80
COST ($ = $50)	$$$$–

commuting times to parks (*in minutes*)

MAGIC KINGDOM	8:00
EPCOT	6:00
ANIMAL KINGDOM	7:15
DHS	4:15

Contemporary Resort
★★★★½

Walt Disney World
4600 N. World Dr.
Lake Buena Vista, FL 32830
☎ 407-934-7639
disneyworld.com

LOCATION	WDW
ROOM RATING	93
COST ($ = $50)	$ x 7

commuting times to parks (*in minutes*)

MAGIC KINGDOM	on monorail
EPCOT	11:00
ANIMAL KINGDOM	17:15
DHS	14:15

Coronado Springs Resort
★★★★

Walt Disney World
1000 W. Buena Vista Dr.
Orlando, FL 32830
☎ 407-939-1000
disneyworld.com

LOCATION	WDW
ROOM RATING	83
COST ($ = $50)	$ x 8

commuting times to parks (*in minutes*)

MAGIC KINGDOM	5:30
EPCOT	4:00
ANIMAL KINGDOM	4:45
DHS	4:45

Old Key West Resort
★★★★½

Walt Disney World
1510 N. Cove Rd.
Lake Buena Vista, FL 32830
☎ 407-827-7700
disneyworld.com

LOCATION	WDW
ROOM RATING	90
COST ($ = $50)	$ x 7 –

commuting times to parks (*in minutes*)

MAGIC KINGDOM	10:45
EPCOT	6:00
ANIMAL KINGDOM	14:30
DHS	10:30

Polynesian Resort
★★★★½

Walt Disney World
1600 Seven Seas Dr.
Lake Buena Vista, FL 32830
☎ 407-824-2000
disneyworld.com

LOCATION	WDW
ROOM RATING	92
COST ($ = $50)	$ x 9 +

commuting times to parks (*in minutes*)

MAGIC KINGDOM	on monorail
EPCOT	8:00
ANIMAL KINGDOM	16:15
DHS	12:30

Pop Century Resort ★★★

Walt Disney World
1050 Century Dr.
Lake Buena Vista, FL 32830
☎ 407-938-4000
disneyworld.com

LOCATION	WDW
ROOM RATING	71
COST ($ = $50)	$$$–

commuting times to parks (*in minutes*)

MAGIC KINGDOM	8:30
EPCOT	6:30
ANIMAL KINGDOM	6:15
DHS	5:00

Hotel Information Chart (continued)

Port Orleans Resort (French Quarter) ★★★★

Walt Disney World
2201 Orleans Dr.
Lake Buena Vista, FL 32830
☎ 407-934-5000
disneyworld.com

LOCATION	WDW
ROOM RATING	84
COST ($ = $50)	$$$$–

commuting times to parks (*in minutes*)

MAGIC KINGDOM	12:00
EPCOT	8:00
ANIMAL KINGDOM	16:15
DHS	12:30

Port Orleans Resort (Riverside) ★★★★

Walt Disney World
1251 Riverside Dr.
Lake Buena Vista, FL 32830
☎ 407-934-6000
disneyworld.com

LOCATION	WDW
ROOM RATING	83
COST ($ = $50)	$$$$–

commuting times to parks (*in minutes*)

MAGIC KINGDOM	12:00
EPCOT	8:00
ANIMAL KINGDOM	16:15
DHS	12:30

Saratoga Springs Resort & Spa ★★★★½

Walt Disney World
1960 Broadway
Lake Buena Vista, FL 32830
☎ 407-827-1100
disneyworld.com

LOCATION	WDW
ROOM RATING	90
COST ($ = $50)	$ x 7 –

commuting times to parks (*in minutes*)

MAGIC KINGDOM	14:45
EPCOT	8:45
ANIMAL KINGDOM	18:15
DHS	14:30

Shades of Green ★★★★½

Walt Disney World
1950 W. Magnolia Palm Dr.
Lake Buena Vista, FL 32830
☎ 407-824-3400
shadesofgreen.org

LOCATION	WDW
ROOM RATING	91
COST ($ = $50)	$$

commuting times to parks (*in minutes*)

MAGIC KINGDOM	3:30
EPCOT	4:45
ANIMAL KINGDOM	9:30
DHS	6:15

Swan ★★★★½

Walt Disney World
1200 Epcot Resorts Blvd.
Lake Buena Vista, FL 32830
☎ 407-934-3000
swandolphin.com

LOCATION	WDW
ROOM RATING	90
COST ($ = $50)	$$$$

commuting times to parks (*in minutes*)

MAGIC KINGDOM	6:30
EPCOT	4:45
ANIMAL KINGDOM	6:15
DHS	4:00

Treehouse Villas at Disney's Saratoga Springs Resort & Spa ★★★★½

Walt Disney World
1960 Broadway
Lake Buena Vista, FL 32830
☎ 407-827-1100
disneyworld.com

LOCATION	WDW
ROOM RATING	90
COST ($ = $50)	$ x 14 –

commuting times to parks (*in minutes*)

MAGIC KINGDOM	12:45
EPCOT	7:15
ANIMAL KINGDOM	16:45
DHS	12:30

Wilderness Lodge ★★★★

Walt Disney World
901 Timberline Dr.
Lake Buena Vista, FL 32830
☎ 407-824-3200
disneyworld.com

LOCATION	WDW
ROOM RATING	86
COST ($ = $50)	$ x 6 +

commuting times to parks (*in minutes*)

MAGIC KINGDOM	N/A*
EPCOT	10:00
ANIMAL KINGDOM	15:15
DHS	13:30

Wilderness Lodge Villas ★★★★½

Walt Disney World
901 Timberline Dr.
Lake Buena Vista, FL 32830
☎ 407-824-3200
disneyworld.com

LOCATION	WDW
ROOM RATING	90
COST ($ = $50)	$ x 8 –

commuting times to parks (*in minutes*)

MAGIC KINGDOM	N/A*
EPCOT	10:00
ANIMAL KINGDOM	15:15
DHS	13:30

Yacht Club Resort ★★★★

Walt Disney World
1700 Epcot Resorts Blvd.
Lake Buena Vista, FL 32830
☎ 407-934-7000
disneyworld.com

LOCATION	WDW
ROOM RATING	89
COST ($ = $50)	$ x 8

commuting times to parks (*in minutes*)

MAGIC KINGDOM	7:15
EPCOT	5:15
ANIMAL KINGDOM	6:45
DHS	4:00

*Primary transportation is by ferry boat rather than car.

continued from page 101

bats—all taller than the buildings they adorn. Similarly, All-Star Music Resort features 40-foot guitars, maracas, and saxophones, while All-Star Movies Resort showcases giant popcorn boxes and icons from Disney films. Lobbies of all are loud (in both decibels and brightness) and cartoonish, with checkerboard walls and photographs of famous athletes, musicians, and film stars. At 260 square feet, guest rooms at the All-Star Resorts are very small. They're so small that a family of four attempting to stay in one room might redefine family values by week's end. Definitely a family resort, young children exercising their lungs make the All-Stars the noisiest Disney resorts, though guest rooms are well soundproofed and quiet.

To the rejoicing of parents everywhere, Disney opened 192 family suites at its All-Star Music Resort. Located in the Jazz and Calypso buildings, these suites measure roughly 520 square feet, slightly larger than the cabins at Fort Wilderness. Each suite, formed from the combination of two formerly separate rooms, includes a kitchenette with mini-refrigerator, microwave, and coffeemaker. Sleeping accommodations include a queen bed in the bedroom, plus a pullout sleeper sofa and two chairs that convert to beds in the family room.

We get more reader mail about the All-Star Resorts than about all the other Disney hotels combined. The following comments are pretty representative. First from a Baltimore family that had a very positive experience:

We were pleasantly surprised. Yes, the rooms are small. But the overall magic there is amazing. The lobby played Disney movies . . . [and] there are great photo ops everywhere. . . . The food court—let's face it—is crap . . . except for the refrigerator cases where you can buy fresh-tasting (albeit expensive) fruit, water, healthy snacks, and great chicken-salad sandwiches. Further, despite forewarnings of loud children, we were in the Love Bug building and found it very quiet. The express-checkout service was also a godsend.

But a Massachusetts family of four had this to say:

I would never recommend the All-Star for a family. It was like dormitory living. Our room was about one mile from the bus stop, and the food court got old very quickly. Buses were great, but the room was tiny. . . . You needed to step into the bathroom, shut the door, then step around the toilet which blocked half the tub.

Finally, a dad from Rogers, Arkansas, had this to say:

Make sure that people understand how inconvenient the shuttle service becomes when you have to share one bus for all three All-Star resorts. This one issue ruined what was an otherwise very pleasant experience.

INDEPENDENT HOTELS OF THE DOWNTOWN DISNEY RESORT AREA

THE SEVEN HOTELS OF THE Downtown Disney Resort Area (DDRA) were created in the days when Disney had far fewer of its own resorts. The hotels—the Holiday Inn at Walt Disney World, DoubleTree Guest Suites, Wyndham Lake Buena Vista Resort, Hilton, Royal Plaza, Best Western Lake Buena Vista Resort, and Buena Vista Palace Hotel & Spa—are chain-style hotels with minimal or nonexistent themes, though the Buena Vista Palace especially is pretty upscale. All were hit hard by the tourism slump in recent years, and several of the larger properties shifted their focus to convention and business travelers. Now that Disney has trouble filling its own massive inventory of rooms, DDRA properties are struggling to refurbish or re-create themselves while clinging tenaciously to the Disney World connection.

The main advantage to staying in the DDRA is being in Disney World and proximal to Downtown Disney. Guests at the Hilton, Wyndham Lake Buena Vista Resort, Buena Vista Palace, and Holiday Inn are an easy 5- to 15-minute walk from Disney Marketplace. Guests at the Royal Plaza, Best Western, or DoubleTree are about 10 minutes farther by foot. Disney transportation can be accessed at Downtown Disney, though the Disney buses take a notoriously long time to leave due to the number of stops throughout the shopping and entertainment complex. Although all DDRA hotels offer shuttle buses to the theme parks, the service is provided by private contractors and is somewhat inferior to Disney Transportation in frequency of service, number of buses, and hours of operation. Get firm details in advance about shuttle service from any DDRA hotel you're considering. All these hotels are easily accessible by car and are only marginally farther from the Disney parks than several of the Disney resorts (and are quite close to Typhoon Lagoon).

All DDRA hotels try to appeal to families, even the business and meeting hotels. Some have pool complexes that rival those at any Disney resort, whereas others offer a food court or all-suite rooms. A few

AMENITIES AT DOWNTOWN DISNEY RESORT AREA HOTELS					
RESORT	PROGRAMS	DINING	KID-FRIENDLY	POOLS	RECREATION
Best Western LBV Resort	—	★★½	★★★	★★½	★★
Buena Vista Palace	★★★★	★★★★	★★★½	★★★½	★★★★
DoubleTree Guest Suites	—	★★	★★★	★★½	★★½
Hilton WDW	—	★★½	★★½	★★★	★★½
Holiday Inn at WDW	—	★★	★★	★★★	★★
Royal Plaza	★★½	★★	★★½	★★½	★★★
Wyndham LBV Resort	★★½	★★½	★★★	★★★	★★★

sponsor Disney character meals and organized children's activities; all have counters for buying Disney tickets, and most have Disney gift shops. In addition, we've seen some real room deals in the DDRA, especially in the off-season. To help you decide if the DDRA is right for you, take a peek at the combined website for the DDRA hotels at **downtown disneyhotels.com**. Finally, check the comparative chart above.

HOW TO GET DISCOUNTS ON LODGING AT WALT DISNEY WORLD

THERE ARE SO MANY GUEST ROOMS in and around Walt Disney World that competition is brisk, and everyone, including Disney, wheels and deals to keep them filled. This has led to a more flexible discount policy for Walt Disney World hotels. Here are tips for getting price breaks:

If all you need is a room, booking through Disney Central Reservation is better Bob than booking online or through the Walt Disney Travel Company because Central Reservation offers better terms for cancellation and payment dates.

1. SEASONAL SAVINGS You can save $15–$50 or more per night on a Walt Disney World hotel room by scheduling your visit during the slower times of the year.

2. ASK ABOUT SPECIALS When you talk to Disney reservationists, ask specifically about specials. For example, "What special rates or discounts are available at Disney hotels during the time of our visit?" Being specific and assertive paid off for an Illinois reader:

I called Disney's reservations number and asked for availability and rates. . . . [Because] of the Unofficial Guide warning about Disney reservationists answering only the questions posed, I specifically asked, "Are there any special rates or discounts for that room during the month of October?" She replied, "Yes, we have that room available at a special price. . . ." I saved $440.

3. KNOW THE SECRET CODE The folks at **mousesavers.com** keep an updated list of discounts and reservation codes for Disney resorts. You can sign up for the MouseSavers newsletter and hot deals for discount announcements, Disney news, and exclusive offers not available to the general public. The codes are separated into categories such as "For anyone," "For residents of certain states," and "For Annual Pass holders." For example, the site once listed a code published in an ad in some Spanish-language newspapers and magazines, offering a rate of $65 per night for Disney's All-Star Resorts April 22–August 8. Dozens of discounts are usually listed on the site, covering most Disney hotels. Anyone calling the Disney Reservation Center at ☎ 407-WDW-MAGIC can use a current code and get the discounted rate.

You should be aware that Disney is shying away from room-only codes that anyone can use. Instead, Disney is targeting people with pin codes in e-mails and direct mailings. Pin-code discounts are offered to specific individuals and are correlated with that person's name and address. Pin-code offers are nontransferable. When you try to make a reservation using the code, Disney will verify that the street or e-mail address to which the pin code was sent is yours.

To get your name in the Disney system, call the Disney Reservation Center at ☎ 407-824-8000 or 407-WDW-MAGIC and request that written info or the free trip-planning DVD/video be sent to you. If you've been to Walt Disney World previously, your name and address will of course already be on record, but you won't be as likely to receive a pin-code offer as you would by calling and requesting to be sent information. On the Web, go to the official site, **disneyworld.com,** and sign up to automatically be sent offers and news at your e-mail address.

Our blog, **blog.touringplans.com,** often provides advance notice on discount details and their dates of availability. Two other sites, **allears. net** and **wdwinfo.com,** have discount codes for up to 50% off rack rates at the Swan and Dolphin.

4. INTERNET SELLERS Expedia (**expedia.com**), Travelocity (**travelocity. com**), and One Travel (**onetravel.com**) discount Disney hotels. Most breaks are in the 7% to 25% range but can go as deep as 40%. Disney also places its hotel rooms on Priceline (**priceline.com**).

5. WALT DISNEY WORLD WEBSITE Particularly with the economic recovery moving slowly, Disney has become more aggressive about offering deals on its website. Go to **disneyworld.com** and look for "Special Offers" under "Tickets and Packages" at the bottom of the page. Also look for seasonal discounts, usually listed as "Summer-time Savings," "Fall Savings," or something similar. You must click on the specific special to get the discounts: If you fill out the information on "Price Your Vacation," you'll be charged the full rack rate with no mention of available discounts.

6. RENTING DISNEY VACATION CLUB POINTS The Disney Vacation Club (DVC) is Disney's time-share condominium program. DVC resorts at Walt Disney World include Old Key West, Saratoga Springs Resort & Spa, the Beach Club Villas, Villas at Wilderness Lodge, Animal Kingdom Villas, Bay Lake Tower at the Contemporary Resort, and the BoardWalk Villas. Each resort offers studios and one- and two-bedroom villas (Saratoga Springs, BoardWalk Villas, Animal Kingdom Villas, Bay Lake Tower, and Old Key West also have three-bedroom units). All accommodations are roomy and luxurious. The studios are equipped with wet bars and fridges, and the villas come with full kitchens. Most accommodations have patios or balconies.

DVC members receive a number of points annually that they use to pay for their Disney accommodations. Sometimes members elect to "rent" (sell) their points instead of using them in a given year. Though Disney is not involved in the transaction, it allows DVC members to make these points available to the general public. The going rental rate is usually in the range of $12–$13 per point. A studio for a week at the BoardWalk Villas would run you $2,330 plus tax for the regular season if you booked through the Disney Reservation Center. The same studio costs the DVC member 105 points for a week (in peak season). If you rented his points at $12 per point, the BoardWalk Villas studio would cost you $1,260—almost $1,200 less.

You have two options when renting points: Locate and deal directly with the selling DVC member or go through a company that specializes in DVC points rental. The popular Disney discussion board Disboards (**disboards.com**) has a specific forum for matching DVC sellers and renters. When you deal directly with the selling DVC member, you pay him or her directly, such as by certified check (few will accept credit cards). The DVC member makes a reservation in your name and pays Disney the requisite number of points. Arrangements vary, and some trust is required from both parties. Usually your reservation is documented by a confirmation sent from Disney to the owner, and then passed along to you. Though the deal you cut is strictly up to you and the owner, you should always insist on receiving the aforementioned confirmation before making more than a 1-night deposit.

Finding a seller yourself can sometimes yield good deals but takes time and effort with no guarantees you'll find a match. For a fixed rate of around $13 per point, the folks at **dvcrequest.com** will act on your behalf as a points broker, matching your request for a specific resort and dates to its available supply. It will also take requests months in advance and notify you as soon as something becomes available—a big benefit to those who can't surf the Web every day. Plus they accept major credit cards.

We suggest using the discussion boards if you're going during the off-season, if you could stay at any of several resorts, and if you have the time and skills to invest in finding a seller at a low rate. If you're trying to book a particular resort, especially during a busy time of year, there's something to be said for the low-hassle approach of a points broker.

7. TRAVEL AGENTS Travel agents are active players and particularly good sources of information on limited-time programs and discounts. We believe a good travel agent is the best friend a traveler can have. And though we at the *Unofficial Guide* know a thing or two about the travel industry, we always give our agent a chance to beat any deal we find. If she can't beat it, we let her book it anyway if she can get a commission. We nurture a relationship that gives her plenty of incentive to roll up her sleeves and work on our behalf.

As you might expect, there are travel agents and agencies that specialize, sometimes exclusively, in selling Walt Disney World. These agents have spent an incredible amount of time at Walt Disney World and have completed extensive Disney education programs. They are usually the most Disney-knowledgeable agents in the travel industry. Most of these specialists and their agencies display the "Earmarked" logo stating that they are an authorized Disney vacation planner.

These Disney specialists are so good we use them ourselves. The needs of our research team are many, and our schedules are complicated. When we work with an authorized Disney vacation planner, we know we're dealing with someone who knows Disney inside and out, including where to find the deals and how to use all the tricks of the trade that keep our research budget under control. Simply stated, they save us time and money, sometimes lots of both.

Each year we ask our readers to rate the travel agent who helped plan their Disney trip. The best of the best include Sue Pisaturo, whom we've used many times and who contributes to this guide (**sue@smallworld vacations.com**); Kathy McCullock (**kathymcc@nc.rr.com**); Marion Carlson (**marionwdwtravel@comcast.net**); Anne Cook (**annewdwtravel@ comcast.net**); and Lori Bandera (**banderawdwtravel@aol.com**).

Our reader-survey results indicate that for Walt Disney World, you'll be much more satisfied using a travel agent who specializes in Disney and much more likely to recommend those agents to a friend. While the names above are the ones most consistently recommended in our surveys, there are good Disney specialists throughout the country if you prefer to work with someone close to home.

LODGING *outside* WALT DISNEY WORLD

AT THIS POINT YOU'RE PROBABLY WONDERING HOW, as mentioned above, a hotel outside Walt Disney World could be as convenient as one inside Walt Disney World. Well, Mabel, Walt Disney World is a *muy largo* place, but like any city or state, it has borders. By way of analogy, let's say you want to stay in a hotel in Cincinnati, Ohio, but can't find one you can afford. Would you rather book a hotel in Toledo or Cleveland, which are both still in Ohio but pretty darn far away, or would you be willing to leave Ohio and stay just across the river from Cincinnati in Covington, Kentucky?

Just south of Walt Disney World on US 192 are a bunch of hotels and condos, some great bargains, that are closer to the Animal Kingdom and Disney's Hollywood Studios than are many hotels in Walt Disney World. Similarly, there are hotels along Disney's east border, FL 535, that are exceptionally convenient if you plan to use your own car.

Lodging costs outside Walt Disney World vary incredibly. If you shop around, you can find a clean motel with a pool within a few minutes of the World for as low as $40 a night. You also can find luxurious, expensive hotels. Because of hot competition, discounts abound.

GOOD NEIGHBOR HOTELS

A GOOD NEIGHBOR HOTEL is a hotel that has paid Disney a marketing fee in order to display that designation. Usually there is a ticket shop in the lobby that sells full-price Disney tickets. Other than that, the Good Neighbor designation means nothing for the consumer. It does not guarantee quality. Some Good Neighbor hotels really aren't very nice, while others are excellent. Some are close to Walt Disney World, while others are quite far away. Disney requires Good Neighbor hotels to provide free shuttle service to Walt Disney World but prohibits them from offering shuttle service to Universal or SeaWorld.

SELECTING AND BOOKING A HOTEL OUTSIDE WALT DISNEY WORLD

THERE ARE FOUR PRIMARY out-of-the-World areas to consider:

1. INTERNATIONAL DRIVE AREA This area, about 15–25 minutes northeast of Walt Disney World, parallels I-4 on its eastern side and offers a wide selection of both hotels and restaurants. Accommodations range from $60–$430 per night. The chief drawbacks of the International Drive area are its terribly congested roads, countless traffic signals, and inadequate access to westbound I-4. While the biggest bottleneck is the intersection with Sand Lake Road, the mile of International Drive between Kirkman Road and Sand Lake Road stays in near-continuous gridlock. It's common to lose 25–35 minutes trying to navigate this 1-mile stretch.

Hotels in the International Drive area are listed in the *Orlando Official Vacation Guide,* published by the Orlando/Orange County Convention and Visitors Bureau. For a copy, call ☎ 800-972-3304 or 407-363-5872.

2. LAKE BUENA VISTA AND THE I-4 CORRIDOR A number of hotels are situated along FL 535 and west of I-4 between Walt Disney World and I-4's intersection with the Florida Turnpike. These properties are easily reached from the interstate and are near a large number of restaurants, including those on International Drive. Most hotels in this area are listed in the *Orlando Official Vacation Guide.*

3. US 192 (IRLO BRONSON MEMORIAL HIGHWAY) This is the highway to Kissimmee, south of Walt Disney World. In addition to a number of large, full-service hotels, there are many small, privately owned motels that are often a good value. Several dozen properties on US 192 are closer to the Disney theme parks than are the more expensive hotels in the Downtown Disney Resort Area. The number and variety of restaurants on US 192 has increased markedly in the past several years, easing the area's primary shortcoming. Hotels on US 192 and in Kissimmee can be found in the *Kissimmee Visitor's Guide;* call ☎ 800-327-9159 or check **floridakiss.com.**

4. UNIVERSAL ORLANDO AREA In the triangular area bordered by I-4 on the southeast, Vineland Road on the north, and Turkey Lake Road on the west are Universal Orlando and the hotels most convenient to it. Running north-south through the middle of the triangle is Kirkman

Hotel Concentrations around Walt Disney World

1. International Drive Area
2. Lake Buena Vista Resort Area & the I-4 Corridor
3. US 192–Kissimmee Resort Area
4. Universal Orlando Area

Road, which connects to I-4. On the east side of Kirkman are a number of independent hotels and restaurants. Universal hotels, theme parks, and CityWalk are west of Kirkman. Traffic in this area is not nearly as congested as on nearby International Drive, and there are good interstate connections in both directions.

THE BEST HOTELS FOR FAMILIES OUTSIDE WALT DISNEY WORLD

WHAT MAKES A SUPER FAMILY HOTEL? Roomy accommodations, in-room fridge, great pool, complimentary breakfast, child-care options, and programs for kids are a few of the things the *Unofficial Guide* hotel team researched in selecting the top hotels for families from among hundreds of properties in the Disney World area. Some of our picks are expensive, others are more reasonable, and some are a bargain. Regardless of price, be assured that these hotels understand a family's needs.

Though all the following hotels offer some type of shuttle to the theme parks, some offer very limited service. Call the hotel before you book and ask what the shuttle schedule will be when you visit. Because families, like individuals, have different wants and needs, we haven't ranked the following properties here. They're listed geographically and then alphabetically.

INTERNATIONAL DRIVE & UNIVERSAL ORLANDO AREAS

DoubleTree Resort Orlando–International Drive
★★★★½

10100 International Dr., Orlando; ☎ 407-352-1100 or 800-327-0363; doubletreeorlandoidrive.com

Rate per night $89–$499. **Pools** ★★★½. **Fridge in room** In some rooms; otherwise available for $10 per day. **Shuttle to parks** Yes (Disney, Universal, SeaWorld, Aquatica, and Wet 'n Wild). **Maximum number of occupants per room** 4. **Special comments** A good option if you're visiting SeaWorld.

FORMERLY THE INTERNATIONAL PLAZA RESORT & SPA, this hotel with Balinese décor has undergone a comprehensive $35-million renovation. Situated on 28 lush, tropical acres, the DoubleTree is adjacent to SeaWorld and Aquatica water park. All 1,094 rooms and suites, classified as resort or tower, have been completely refurbished and are equally suitable for business travelers or families. We recommend the tower rooms for good views and the resort rooms for maximum convenience. The Bamboo Grille serves steak and seafood along with breakfast; you can also get a quick bite at the deli, pool bar, or Bangli lounge. Relax and cool off at one of the three pools (there are two more just for kids) or indulge in a spa treatment. A fitness center, mini-golf course, kids' game area, and children's day camp round out the amenities. The resort is about a 15-minute drive to Walt Disney World, a 12-minute drive to Universal, or a short walk to SeaWorld.

Hard Rock Hotel ★★★★½

5800 Universal Blvd., Orlando; ☎ 407-503-2000; hardrockhotelorlando.com

Rate per night $234–$724. **Pool** ★★★★. **Fridge in room** Minibar; fridge available for $15 per day. **Shuttle to parks** Yes (Universal, SeaWorld, Discovery Cove,

Aquatica, and Wet 'n Wild). **Maximum number of occupants per room** 5 for standard double queen rooms; 3 for standard king rooms. **Special comments** Microwaves available for $15 per day.

LOCATED ON UNIVERSAL PROPERTY, the 650-room Hard Rock Hotel is nirvana for any kid older than 8, especially those interested in music. Architecture is California Mission–style, and rock memorabilia is displayed throughout. If you plan to spend at least a few days at Universal parks, this is an excellent upscale option. Guests receive theme park privileges such as all-day access to the Universal Express line-breaking program, delivery of packages to their rooms, and priority seating at select Universal restaurants. The music-filled pool area has a white-sand beach, a waterslide, a 12,000-square-foot pool, an underwater audio system, and an ultrahip pool bar. You'll also find four restaurants and lounges, a fitness center, and a Hard Rock merchandise store. Guest rooms are ultrahip too, with cutting-edge contemporary décor, a CD sound system, TV with pay-per-view movies and video games, coffeemaker, iron and board, robes, hair dryer, and two phones. A supervised activity center, Camp Lil' Rock, serves kids ages 4–14. Pet-friendly rooms available.

Holiday Inn Castle Hotel ★★★½

8629 International Dr., Orlando; ☎ 407-345-1511 or 877-317-5753; thecastleorlando.com

Rate per night $100–$230. **Pool** ★★★. **Fridge in room** Available for $15. **Shuttle to parks** Yes (Disney and Universal; additional fee). **Maximum number of occupants per room** 4. **Special comments** Pets up to 75 pounds welcome for a $75 fee.

YOU CAN'T MISS THIS ONE; it's the only castle on I-Drive. Inside you'll find royal colors (purple dominates), opulent fixtures, European art, Renaissance music, and a mystic Castle Creature at the door. The 216 guest rooms also receive the royal treatment in décor, though some guests may find them gaudy. All, however, are fairly large and well equipped with TV with PlayStation, fridge, three phones, coffeemaker, iron and board, hair dryer, and safe. The Castle Café off the lobby serves full or Continental breakfast. For lunch or dinner, you might walk next door to Vito's Chop House (dinner only) or Café Tu Tu Tango (an *Unofficial* favorite). The heated circular pool is 5 feet deep and features a fountain in the center, a poolside bar, and a whirlpool. There's no separate kiddie pool. Other amenities include a fitness center, gift shop, lounge, valet laundry service and facilities, and guest services desk with park passes for sale and babysitting recommendations. Elevators require an electronic key card.

Loews Portofino Bay Hotel ★★★★½

5601 Universal Blvd., Orlando; ☎ 407-503-1000 or 888-430-4999; loewshotels.com/en/portofino-bay-hotel

Rate per night $269–$714. **Pools** ★★★★. **Fridge in room** Minibar; fridge available for $15 per day. **Shuttle to parks** Yes (Universal, SeaWorld, Discovery Cove, and Wet 'n Wild). **Maximum number of occupants per room** 4. **Special comments** Character dinner on Friday.

LOCATED IN UNIVERSAL ORLANDO, the 750-room Portofino Bay Hotel is themed like an Italian Riviera village. Guests receive theme park privileges such as all-day access to the Universal Express line-breaking program, delivery of packages to their room, and priority seating at select Universal restaurants. The rooms are ultraluxurious, with opulent baths and soothing neutral hues. Standard guest-room amenities include minibar, coffeemaker, iron and board, hair dryer, safe, and TV with pay-per-view movies. Microwaves are available ($15 per day). Campo Portofino offers supervised activities at night (movies, video games, crafts, and such) for children ages 4–14. The cost is $15 per hour plus $15 per meal, per child; hours vary. Trattoria del Porto restaurant offers a character dinner 6:30–9:30 p.m. on Friday, with characters such as Scooby-Doo and Woody Woodpecker in attendance. Portofino has four other Italian restaurants (each with a children's menu), an Italian bakery (also serves gelato), and two bars. Three elaborate pools, gardens, jogging trails, pet-friendly rooms, and a spa and fitness center round out major amenities. If you can pay for it and plan to spend time at Universal, you can't go wrong here.

Nickelodeon Suites Resort Orlando ★ ★ ★ ½

14500 Continental Gateway, Orlando; ☎ 407-387-5437 or 877-NICK-111; nickhotel.com

Rate per night $159–$529. **Pools** ★★★★. **Fridge in room** Yes. **Shuttle to parks** Yes. **Maximum number of occupants per room** 8 (for three-bedroom suites). **Special comments** Daily character breakfast; resort fee of $25/night.

SPONGEBOB SQUAREPANTS, EAT YOUR HEART OUT. This revamped resort is as kid-friendly as they come. Decked out in all themes Nickelodeon, the hotel is sure to please any fan of the Nick TV shows. Nickelodeon characters from the channel's many shows hang out in the resort's lobby and mall area, greeting kids while parents check in. Guests can choose from among 777 one-, two-, and three-bedroom suites executed in a number of different themes—all very brightly and creatively decorated. All suites include kitchenettes or full kitchens; also standard are a microwave, fridge, coffeemaker, TV, iron and board, hair dryer, and safe. KidSuites (two- and three-bedroom units) feature a semiprivate kids' bedroom with bunk or twin beds, pull-out sleeper bed, 32-inch TV, CD player, and activity table. The master bedroom offers ample storage space that the kids' bedroom lacks. Additional amenities include a high-tech video arcade, Studio Nick—a game-show studio that hosts several game shows a night, a buffet (kids 3 and younger eat free with a paying adult), a food court, the full-service Nicktoons Cafe (offers character breakfasts), a convenience store, a lounge, a gift shop, a fitness center, a washer and dryer in each courtyard, and a guest-activities desk (buy Disney tickets and get recommendations on babysitting). Not to be missed—don't worry, your kids won't let you—are the resort's two pools, Oasis and Lagoon. Oasis features a water park complete with water cannons, rope ladders, geysers, and dump buckets, as well as a hot tub for adults (with a view of the rest of the pool to keep an eye on little ones) and a smaller play area for younger kids. Kids will love the huge, zero-depth-entry Lagoon Pool, replete with 400-gallon dump bucket, plus nearby basketball court and nine-hole mini-golf course.

Rosen Shingle Creek ★ ★ ★ ★

9939 Universal Blvd., Orlando; ☎ 407-996-9939 or 866-996-9939; rosenshinglecreek.com

---

Rate per night $99–$285. **Pools** ★ ★ ★ ★. **Fridge in room** Yes. **Shuttle to parks** Yes (Universal, Wet 'n Wild, Discovery Cove, Aquatica, and SeaWorld only). **Maximum number of occupants per room** 4.

BEAUTIFUL ROOMS (east-facing ones have great views) and excellent restaurants distinguish this mostly meeting- and convention-oriented resort. Pools are large and lovely and include a lap pool, a family pool, and a kiddie wading pool. There's an 18-hole golf course on-site, as well as a superior spa and an adequate fitness center. On-site babysitting is offered. A state-of-the-art video arcade will gobble up your kids' pocket change, but the real kicker, especially for the 8-and-up crowd, is a natural area encompassing lily ponds, grassy wetlands, Shingle Creek, and an adjacent cypress swamp. Running through the area is a nature trail complete with signs to help you identify wildlife. Great blue herons, wood storks, egrets, mallard ducks, and ospreys are common, as are sliders (turtles), chameleons, and skinks (lizards). Oh yeah, there are alligators and snakes too—real ones, but that's part of the fun. If you stay at Shingle Creek and plan to visit the theme parks, you'll want a car. Shuttle service is limited, departing and picking up at rather inconvenient times and stopping at three other hotels before delivering you to your destination.

LAKE BUENA VISTA & I-4 CORRIDOR

Buena Vista Palace Hotel & Spa ★ ★ ★ ½

1900 Buena Vista Dr., Lake Buena Vista; ☎ 407-827-2727 or 866-397-6516; buenavistapalace.com

---

Rate per night $99–$380. **Pools** ★ ★ ★ ½. **Fridge in room** Yes. **Shuttle to parks** Yes (Disney only). **Maximum number of occupants per room** 4. **Special comments** Sunday character breakfast available at Watercress Café.

IN THE DOWNTOWN DISNEY RESORT AREA, the Buena Vista Palace is upscale and convenient. Surrounded by a man-made lake and plenty of palms, the spacious pool area contains three heated pools, the largest of which is partially covered; a whirlpool and sauna; a basketball court; and a sand volleyball court. Plus, a pool concierge will fetch your favorite magazine or fruity drink. The 897 guest rooms are posh and spacious; each comes with a desk, coffeemaker, hair dryer, satellite TV with pay-per-view movies, iron and board, and minifridge. There are also 117 suites. In-room babysitting is available through the All about Kids service. One lighted tennis court, a European-style spa, a fitness center, an arcade, a playground, and a beauty salon round out amenities. Two restaurants and a mini-market are on-site, as well as the Lobby Lounge and a full-menu sports bar. *Note:* These amenities and services come at a price—a $17-per-night resort fee will be added to your bill.

Hilton Walt Disney World ★ ★ ★ ★

**1751 Hotel Plaza Blvd., Lake Buena Vista; ☎ 407-827-4000 or
800-782-4414; hilton-wdwv.com**

Rate per night $99–$309. **Pools** ★★★½. **Fridge in room** Minibar; fridge available on
request. **Shuttle to parks** Yes (Disney theme and water parks only). **Maximum number of occupants per room** 4. **Special comments** Sunday character breakfast.

THE HILTON OCCUPIES 23 ACRES in the Downtown Disney Resort Area.
Since it's an official Walt Disney World hotel, guests can take advantage of
the Disney Extra Magic Hours program. The Hilton's 814 guest rooms and
suites are spacious, luxurious, and tasteful. Decorated in earth tones, all standard rooms have granite baths, iron and board, hair dryer, two phones, desk,
minibar, coffeemaker, and cable TV with pay-per-view movies and video
games. One big plus is the character breakfast, offered 8:30–11 a.m. on Sunday. (Reservations are recommended.) Food is served buffet-style, and five
characters attend (only two are present at a time). Other important family
amenities include babysitting services; an arcade and pool table; and two
beautifully landscaped heated swimming pools, as well as a kiddie pool. Six
restaurants, including Benihana, add to the hotel's convenience.

Holiday Inn SunSpree Resort Lake Buena Vista ★ ★ ★ ½

**13351 FL 535, Orlando; ☎ 407-239-4500 or 866-808-8833;
hisunspreelbv.com**

Rate per night $80–$175. **Pool** ★★★. **Fridge in room** Yes. **Shuttle to parks** Yes
(Disney, Universal, and SeaWorld). **Maximum number of occupants per room**
4–6. **Special comments** Resort fee of $9.53/night entitles guests to numerous
perks, including use of fitness center and daily fountain drinks for kids.

THE BIG LURE IS KIDSUITES, rooms with a separate children's area. Themes
include a tree house, jail, space capsule, and fort, among others. The kids' area
sleeps two to four children in two sets of bunk beds or one bunk bed and a
twin. The separate adult area has its own TV, safe, hair dryer, and kitchenette
with fridge, microwave, sink, and coffeemaker. Standard guest rooms offer
these adult amenities. Other kid-friendly amenities include the tiny Castle
Movie Theater, which shows movies all day every day; a playground; an
arcade; and a basketball court. Also offered are a large, free-form pool, complete with kiddie pool and two whirlpools, and a fitness center. Applebee's
serves breakfast and dinner. There's also a mini-mart. Another perk: Kids age
12 and younger eat free from a special menu when dining with one paying
adult (maximum four kids per adult). Finally, pets weighing 30 pounds or less
are welcome (for an additional $40 nonrefundable fee).

Hyatt Regency Grand Cypress ★ ★ ★ ★ ½

**1 Grand Cypress Blvd., Orlando; ☎ 407-239-1234;
grandcypress.hyatt.com**

Rate per night $215–$355. **Pools** ★★★★★. **Fridge in room** Yes. **Shuttle to parks**

Yes (Disney, Universal, and SeaWorld). **Maximum number of occupants per room** 4. **Special comments** Wow, what a pool! Resort fee of $23.

THERE ARE MYRIAD REASONS TO STAY at this 1,500-acre resort, but the pool ranks as number one. The 800,000-gallon tropical paradise has two waterslides, waterfalls, grottos, and a bridge. Your kids may never want to leave the pool to visit the theme parks. The Hyatt is also a golfer's paradise. With 45 holes of Jack Nicklaus–designed championship golf, a 9-hole pitch-and-putt course, and a golf academy, there's something for golfers of all abilities. Other recreational perks include a racquet facility with hard and clay courts; a private lake with beach; a fitness center; and miles of trails for biking, walking, and jogging. The 683 standard guest rooms are 360 square feet and have a Florida ambience and private balconies. Amenities include high-speed Internet, iron and board, safe, hair dryer, ceiling fan, and cable TV with pay-per-view movies. Suite accommodations offer even more amenities. Camp Hyatt provides supervised programs for kids ages 3–12; in-room babysitting is available. Five restaurants offer dining options; three lounges provide nighttime entertainment; and a coffee bar offers another ambience.

Marriott Village at Lake Buena Vista ★★★

8623 Vineland Ave., Orlando; ☎ 407-938-9001 or 800-761-STAY; marriottvillage.com

Rate per night $119–$219. **Pools ★★★**. **Fridge in room** Yes. **Shuttle to parks** Yes (Disney only; $7 fee). **Maximum number of occupants per room** 4 (5 at Spring-Hill). **Special comments** Free Continental breakfast at Fairfield and SpringHill.

THIS GATED HOTEL COMMUNITY INCLUDES a 388-room Fairfield Inn, a 400-suite SpringHill Suites, and a 312-room Courtyard. Whatever your budget, you'll find a room here to fit it. If you need a bit more space, book SpringHill Suites; if you're looking for value, try the Fairfield Inn; if you need limited business amenities, reserve at the Courtyard. Amenities at all three properties include fridge, cable TV, iron and board, and hair dryer. Additionally, all SpringHill suites have microwaves. Cribs and rollaway beds are available at no extra charge at all locations. Swimming pools at all three hotels are attractive and medium-size, featuring children's interactive splash zones and whirlpools; in addition, each property has its own fitness center. The incredibly convenient Village Marketplace food court includes Pizza Hut, Village Grill, and Village Coffee House, along with a 24-hour convenience store. Several full-service chain restaurants are within walking distance. Other services and amenities include a Disney planning station and ticket sales, an arcade, and a Hertz car-rental desk. Shoppers will find the Orlando Premium Outlets adjacent.

Sheraton Safari Hotel & Suites Lake Buena Vista ★★★★

12205 S. Apopka–Vineland Rd., Orlando; ☎ 407-239-0444 or 800-325-3535; sheratonsafari.com

Rate per night $89–$174. **Pool ★★★**. **Fridge in room** Suites only; available for $10 per night in other rooms. **Shuttle to parks** Yes (Disney free; other parks for a fee). **Maximum number of occupants per room** 4–6. **Special comments** Cool python waterslide. Dogs up to 80 pounds allowed.

THE SAFARI THEME IS NICELY EXECUTED throughout the property—from the lobby dotted with African artifacts and native décor to the 79-foot python waterslide dominating the pool. The 393 guest rooms, 90 safari suites, and six executive suites sport African-inspired art and tasteful animal-print soft goods in brown, beige, and jewel tones. Amenities include cable TV, coffeemaker, iron and board, hair dryer, and safe. Suites are a good option for families because they provide added space with a separate sitting room and a kitchenette with a fridge, microwave, and sink. The first thing your kids will probably want to do is take a turn on the python waterslide. It's pretty impressive, but as one *Unofficial Guide* researcher pointed out, it's somewhat of a letdown: The python doesn't actually spit you out of its mouth. Instead you're deposited below its chin.

Sheraton Vistana Resort Villas ★ ★ ★ ★ ½

8800 Vistana Centre Dr., Orlando; ☎ 407-239-3100 or 866-208-0003; starwoodhotels.com

Rate per night $139–$279. **Pools** ★★★½. **Fridge in room** Yes. **Shuttle to parks** Yes (Disney only; Universal and SeaWorld for a fee). **Maximum number of occupants per room** 4–8. **Special comments** Though time-shares, the villas are rented nightly as well.

THE SHERATON VISTANA IS DECEPTIVELY LARGE, stretching across both sides of Vistana Centre Drive. Because Sheraton's emphasis is on selling the time-shares, the rental angle is little known. But families should consider it; the Vistana is one of Orlando's best off-Disney properties. If you want a serene retreat from your days in the theme parks, this is an excellent base. The spacious villas come in one-bedroom, two-bedroom, and two-bedroom-with-lock-off (two rooms joined by a door) models. All are decorated in beachy pastels, but the emphasis is on the profusion of amenities. Each villa has a full kitchen (including fridge/freezer, microwave, oven/range, dishwasher, toaster, and coffeemaker, with an option to pre-stock with groceries), washer and dryer, TVs in the living room and each bedroom (one with DVD player), separate dining area, and private patio or balcony in most. Grounds offer seven swimming pools; four playgrounds; two restaurants; game rooms; fitness centers; a mini-golf course; sports equipment rental; and courts for basketball, volleyball, tennis, and shuffleboard. A mind-boggling array of activities for kids (and adults) ranges from crafts to games and sports tournaments. Of special note: Vistana is highly secure, with locked gates bordering all guest areas, so children can have the run of the place without parents worrying.

Wyndham Bonnet Creek Resort ★ ★ ★ ★

9560 Via Encinas, Lake Buena Vista; ☎ 888-743-2687 or 800-610-9558; wyndhambonnetcreek.com

Rate per night $179–$359. **Pool** ★★★★. **Fridge in room** Yes. **Shuttle to parks** Yes (Disney only). **Maximum number of occupants per room** 4 (plus child in crib) to 12 (depending on condo). **Special comments** A non-Disney suite hotel within Walt Disney World.

WYNDHAM BONNET CREEK RESORT is a condo hotel on the south side of Buena Vista Drive, about a quarter mile east of Disney's Caribbean Resort. The property has an interesting history: When Walt Disney began secretly buying up real estate in the 1960s under the names of numerous front companies, the land on which this resort stands was the last holdout and was never sold to Disney, though the company tried repeatedly to acquire it through the years. The site was ultimately bought by Marriott, which put up a Fairfield Inn time-share development in 2004. The Wyndham is part of a luxury-hotel complex on the same site that includes a 500-room Waldorf Astoria and a 1,000-room Hilton. The development is surrounded on three sides by Disney property and on one side by I-4.

The Bonnet Creek Resort offers upscale, family-friendly accommodations: one- and two-bedroom condos with fully equipped kitchens, washer-dryers, jetted tubs, and balconies. Activities and amenities on-site include five outdoor swimming pools, a "lazy river" float stream, a children's activities program, a game room, a playground, and miniature golf. There is free scheduled transportation to all the Disney parks. One-bedroom units are equipped with a king bed in the bedroom and a sleeper sofa in the living area; two-bedroom condos have two double beds in the second bedroom and an additional bath.

US 192 AREA

Comfort Suites Maingate ★★★½

7888 W. Irlo Bronson Memorial Hwy., Kissimmee; ☎ 407-390-9888 or 888-390-9888; comfortsuiteskissimmee.com

Rate per night $70–$170. **Pool** ★★★. **Fridge in room** Yes. **Shuttle to parks** Yes (Disney, Universal, and SeaWorld). **Maximum number of occupants per room** 4–6. **Special comments** Complimentary Continental breakfast daily.

THIS PROPERTY HAS 150 SPACIOUS one-room suites, each with double sofa bed, microwave, fridge, coffeemaker, TV, hair dryer, and safe. The suites aren't lavish, but they are clean and contemporary. Extra bathroom counter space is especially convenient for larger families. The heated pool is large and has plenty of lounge chairs. A kiddie pool, whirlpool, and poolside bar complete the courtyard. Maingate's big plus is its location next door to a shopping center with about everything a family could need. There, you'll find restaurants, a supermarket, a bank, a dry cleaner, a tourist information center with park passes for sale, and a Centra Care walk-in clinic.

Gaylord Palms Hotel & Convention Center ★★★★½

6000 W. Osceola Pkwy., Kissimmee; ☎ 407-586-2000; gaylordpalms.com

Rate per night $129–$279. **Pool** ★★★★. **Fridge in room** Yes. **Shuttle to parks** Yes (Disney). **Maximum number of occupants per room** 4. **Special comments**

Probably the closest you'll get off-World to Disney-level extravagance. Resort fee of $15/day.

THIS DECIDEDLY UPSCALE RESORT has a colossal convention facility and strongly caters to business clientele but still is a nice (if pricey) family resort. Hotel wings are defined by the three themed, glass-roofed atriums they overlook. Key West's design is reminiscent of island life in the Florida Keys; Everglades is an overgrown spectacle of shabby swamp chic, complete with piped-in cricket noise and a robotic alligator; and the immense, central St. Augustine harks back to Spanish Colonial Florida. Lagoons, streams, and waterfalls cut through and connect all three, and walkways and bridges abound. Rooms reflect the colors of their respective areas, though there's no particular connection in décor (St. Augustine atrium-view rooms are the most opulent, but they're not Spanish). A fourth wing, Emerald Bay Tower, overlooks the Emerald Plaza shopping and dining area of the St. Augustine atrium. These rooms are the nicest and the most expensive, and they're mostly used by convention-goers. Though rooms have fridges and alarm clocks with CD players (as well as other perks, such as high-speed Internet access), the rooms themselves really work better as retreats for adults rather than kids. However, children will enjoy wandering the themed areas or playing in the family pool (with water-squirting octopus). In-room babysitting is offered.

Orange Lake Resort ★★★★½

8505 W. Irlo Bronson Memorial Hwy., Kissimmee; ☎ 407-239-0000 or 800-877-6522; orangelake.com

Rate per night $126–$270. Pools ★★★★. Fridge in room Yes. Shuttle to parks Yes (fee varies with destination). Maximum number of occupants per room Varies. Special comments This is a time-share property, but if you rent directly through the resort, you can avoid time-share sales pitches.

YOU COULD SPEND YOUR ENTIRE VACATION never leaving this property, located about 6–10 minutes from the Disney theme parks. From its 10 pools and 2 mini water parks to its 36 holes of championship golf and 2 nine-hole executive courses, Orange Lake offers an extensive menu of amenities and recreational opportunities. If you tire of lazing by the pool, try waterskiing, wakeboarding, tubing, fishing, or other activities on the 80-acre lake. There's also a live alligator show, exercise programs, organized competitive sports and games, arts-and-crafts sessions, and miniature golf. Activities don't end when the sun goes down. Karaoke, live music, a Hawaiian luau, and movies at the resort cinema are some of the evening options.

The 2,412 units are tastefully decorated and comfortably furnished, ranging from suites and studios to three-bedroom villas, all containing fully equipped kitchens. If you'd rather not cook on vacation, try one of the seven restaurants scattered across the resort: two cafes, three grills, one pizzeria, and a fast-food eatery. If you need help with (or a break from) the kids, babysitters are available to come to your villa, accompany your family on excursions, or take your children to attractions for you.

Radisson Resort Orlando-Celebration ★ ★ ★ ★

2900 Parkway Blvd., Kissimmee; ☎ 407-396-7000 or 800-634-4774;
radissonorlandoresort.com

Rate per night $107–$168. **Pool** ★★★★½. **Fridge in room** Yes. **Shuttle to parks** Yes (Disney and Downtown Disney). **Maximum number of occupants per room** 5. **Special comments** $12.50/day resort fee; kids age 10 and younger eat free with a paying adult for breakfast at Mandolin's restaurant and dinner at the Sports Lounge. Free Internet access.

THE POOL ALONE IS WORTH A STAY HERE, but the Radisson Resort gets high marks in all areas. The free-form pool is huge, with a waterfall and waterslide surrounded by palms and flowering plants, plus a smaller heated pool, two whirlpools, and a kiddie pool. Other outdoor amenities include two lighted tennis courts, sand volleyball, a playground, and jogging areas. Rooms are elegant, featuring Italian furnishings and marble baths. They're of above-average size and include a minibar (in some rooms), coffeemaker, TV, iron and board, hair dryer, and safe. Dining options include Mandolin's for breakfast and dinner, and a 1950s-style diner serves burgers, sandwiches, shakes, and Pizza Hut pizza, among other fare. A sports lounge with an 11-by-6-foot TV offers nighttime entertainment. Guest services can help with tours, park passes, car rental, and babysitting. Children can be kept occupied by board games, coloring, a face-painting clown, and juggling classes for starters.

GETTING A GOOD DEAL ON A ROOM OUTSIDE WALT DISNEY WORLD

HOTEL DEVELOPMENT AT WALT DISNEY WORLD has sharpened the competition among lodgings throughout the Orlando/Kissimmee area. Hotels outside Walt Disney World, in particular, struggle to fill their guest rooms. Unable to compete with Disney resorts for convenience or perks, off-World hotels lure patrons with bargain rates. The extent of the bargain depends on the season, day of the week, and local events. Here are tips and strategies for getting a good deal on a room outside Walt Disney World.

1. ORLANDO MAGICARD Orlando MagiCard is a discount program sponsored by the Orlando/Orange County Convention and Visitors Bureau. Cardholders are eligible for discounts of 20–50% at about 50 participating hotels. The MagiCard is also good for discounts at area attractions, including several dinner theaters. Valid for up to six persons, the card isn't available for groups or conventions.

To obtain an Orlando MagiCard and a list of participating hotels and attractions, call ☎ 800-643-9492 or 407-363-5872. Visit **visit orlando.com/magicard;** the MagiCard and accompanying brochure can be printed from a personal computer.

Anyone older than 18 is eligible, and the card is free. If you miss getting a card before you leave home, you can get one at the Convention and Visitors Bureau at 8723 International Drive in Orlando.

When you call for a MagiCard, also request the *Orlando Official Accommodations Guide.*

2. FLORIDA ROOMSAVER *RoomSaver* is a book of discount coupons for bargain rates at hotels statewide and is available free in many restaurants and motels on main highways leading to Florida. Because most travelers make reservations before leaving home, picking up the coupon book en route doesn't help much. However, you can obtain the guide by calling ☎ 800-332-3948, Monday–Friday, 8:30 a.m.–5:30 p.m. or by visiting **roomsaver.com.** You will pay $3 ($5 U.S. for Canadian delivery) for handling.

3. HOTEL SHOPPING ON THE INTERNET Websites we've found most dependable for Walt Disney area hotel discounts are shown below.

The secret to shopping on the Internet is . . . shopping. When we're really looking for a deal, we check all the sites listed. Flexibility on dates and location are helpful, and we always give our travel agent the opportunity to beat any deal we find.

Always call the hotel in question, not the hotel chain's national 800 number.

Bob

We recommend choosing a hotel based on location, room quality, price, commuting time to the parks, plus any features important to you. Next, check each of the applicable sites below. You'll be able to ferret out the best Internet deal in about 30 minutes. Then call the hotel to see if you can save more by booking directly. Start by asking the hotel for specials. If their response doesn't beat the Internet deal, tell them what you've found and ask if they can do better.

Begin your hotel shopping on a search engine such as **kayak.com.** Kayak searches hotel and Internet-seller websites to find the cheapest

---

OUR FAVORITE ONLINE HOTEL RESOURCES

mousesavers.com   Best site for hotels in Disney World.

dreamsunlimitedtravel.com   Excellent for both Disney and non-Disney hotels.

2000orlando-florida.com   Comprehensive hotel site.

valuetrips.com   Specializes in budget accommodations.

travelocity.com   Multidestination travel superstore.

roomsaver.com   Provides discount coupons for hotels.

floridakiss.com   Primarily US 192–Kissimmee area hotels.

visitorlando.com   Good info; not user-friendly for booking.

orlandovacation.com   Great rates for condos and home rentals.

expedia.com   Largest of the multidestination travel sites.

hotels.com   Largest Internet hotel-booking service; many other sites link to this site and its subsidiary, **hoteldiscounts.com.**

rates for more than 200 Disney-area hotels and provides links to the sellers. Kayak offers search filters such as price, quality rating, and proximity to a specific location (Walt Disney World, Universal Studios, SeaWorld, the convention center, airport, and so on) to help you narrow your search.

4. IF YOU MAKE YOUR OWN RESERVATION Reservationists at the toll-free number are often unaware of local specials. Always phone the hotel directly and ask about specials before you inquire about corporate rates. Don't hesitate to bargain, but do it before you check in. If you're buying a hotel's weekend package, for example, and want to extend your stay, you can often obtain at least the corporate rate for the extra days.

CONDOMINIUMS AND VACATION HOMES

VACATION HOMES ARE FREESTANDING, while condominiums are essentially one- to three-bedroom accommodations in a larger building housing a number of similar units. Because condos tend to be part of large developments (frequently time-shares), amenities such as swimming pools, playgrounds, game arcades, and fitness centers often rival those found in the best hotels. Generally speaking, condo developments do not have restaurants, lounges, or spas. In a condo, if something goes wrong, someone will be on hand to fix the problem. Vacation homes rented from a property-management company likewise will have someone to come to the rescue, though responsiveness tends to vary vastly from company to company. If you rent directly from an owner, correcting problems is often more difficult, particularly when the owner doesn't live in the same area as the rental home.

In a vacation home, all the amenities are contained in the home (though in planned developments there may be community amenities available as well). Depending on the specific home, you might find a small swimming pool, hot tub, two-car garage, family room, game room, and even a home theater. Features found in both condos and vacation homes include full kitchens, laundry rooms, TVs, DVD players, and frequently stereos. Interestingly, though almost all freestanding vacation homes have private pools, very few have backyards. This means that, except for swimming, the kids are pretty much relegated to playing in the house or front yard.

Time-share condos are clones when it comes to furniture and décor, but single-owner condos and vacation homes are furnished and decorated in a style that reflects the taste of the owner. Vacation homes, usually one- to two-story houses located in a subdivision, very rarely afford interesting views (though some overlook lakes or natural areas), while condos, especially the high-rise variety, sometimes offer exceptional ones.

The Price Is Nice

The best deals in lodging in the Walt Disney World area are vacation homes and single-owner condos. Prices range from about $65 a night for two-bedroom condos and town homes to $200–$500 a night for three- to seven-bedroom vacation homes. Forgetting about taxes to keep the comparison simple, let's compare renting a vacation home to staying at one of Disney's Value Resorts. A family of two parents, two teens, and two grandparents would need three hotel rooms at Disney's Pop Century Resort. At the lowest rate obtainable, that would run you $82 per night per room, or $246 total per night. Rooms are 260 square feet each, so you'd have a total of 780 square feet. Each room has a private bath and a television.

Renting at the same time of year from **All Star Vacation Homes** (no relation to Disney's All-Star Resorts), you can rent a 2,053-square-foot, four-bedroom, three-bath vacation home with a private pool three miles from Walt Disney World for $219—a savings of $27 per night over the Disney Value Resort rate. With four bedrooms, each of the teens can have his or her own room. Further, for the dates we checked, All Star Vacation Homes was running a special in which they threw in a free rental car with a one-week home rental.

Location, Location, Location

The best vacation home is one that is within easy commuting distance of the theme parks. If you plan to spend some time at SeaWorld and the Universal parks, you'll want something just to the northeast of Walt Disney World (between the World and Orlando). If you plan to spend most of your time in the World, the best selection of vacation homes is along US 192 to the south of the park.

To get the most from a vacation home, you need to be close enough to commute in 20 minutes or less to your Walt Disney World destination. This will allow for naps, quiet time, swimming, and dollar-saving meals you prepare yourself. Though traffic and road conditions are as important as the distance from a vacation home to your Disney destination, we recommend a home no farther than 5 miles away in areas northeast of Walt Disney World and no farther than 4.5 miles away in areas south of the park.

The only practical way to shop for a rental home is on the Web. This makes it relatively easy to compare different properties and rental companies. On the downside, there are so many owners, rental companies, and individual homes to choose from that you could research yourself into a stupor. There are three main types of websites in the home-rental game: those for property-management companies, which showcase a given company's homes and are set up for direct bookings; individual owner sites; and third-party listings sites, which advertise properties through different owners and sometimes management companies as well. Sites in the last category will usually refer prospective renters to an owner's or management company's site for reservations.

The best websites provide the following:

- Numerous photos and in-depth descriptions of individual homes to make comparisons quick and easy

- Overview maps or text descriptions that reflect how distant specific homes or developments are from Walt Disney World
- The ability to book the specific individual rental home of your choice on the site
- A prominently displayed phone number for non-Internet bookings and questions

The best sites are also easy to navigate and let you see what you're interested in without logging in or giving personal information.

Recommended Websites

After checking out dozens upon dozens of sites, here are the ones we recommend. All of them meet the criteria listed above. If you're stunned that there are so few of them, well, so were we. (For the record, we elected not to list some sites that met our criteria but whose homes are too far away from Walt Disney World.)

All Star Vacation Homes (**allstarvacationhomes.com**) is easily the best of the management-company sites, with photographs and plenty of details about featured homes. The company's rental properties are within either 4 miles of Walt Disney World or 3 miles of Universal.

Orlando's Finest Vacation Homes (**orlandosfinest.com**) represents both homeowners and vacation-home-management companies. Offering a broad inventory, the Orlando's Finest website features photos and information on individual homes. Although the info is not as detailed as that offered by the All Star Vacation Homes site, friendly sales agents can fill in the blanks.

The website for the **Orlando–Orange County Convention and Visitors Bureau** (**visitorlando.com**) is the place to go if you want to rent a condominium at one of the many time-share developments (click on "Places to Stay" at the site's home page). You can call the developments directly, but going through this website allows you to bypass sales departments and their high-pressure invitations to sit through sales presentations. The site also lists hotels and vacation homes.

Vacation Rental by Owner (**vrbo.com**) is a nationwide vacation-homes listings service that puts prospective renters in direct contact with owners of rental homes. The site is straightforward and always lists a large number of rental properties in Celebration, Disney's planned community situated about 8–10 minutes from the theme parks. Two similar listings services with good websites are **Vacation Rentals 411** (**vacationrentals411.com**) and **Last Minute Villas** (**lastminutevillas.net**).

We frequently receive letters from readers extolling the virtues of renting a condo or vacation home. This endorsement by a family from St. Joe, Indiana, is typical:

We rented a home in Kissimmee this time, and we'll never stay in a hotel at WDW again. It was by far the nicest, most relaxing time we've ever had down there. Our rental home was within 10–15 *minutes of all the Disney parks and 25 minutes from SeaWorld. We had three bedrooms, two baths, and an in-ground pool in a screened enclosure out back. We paid $90 per night for the whole shootin' match. We used AAA Dream Homes Rental Company and . . . [they] provided us with detailed info before we went down so we would know what we needed to bring.*

From a New Jersey family of five:

I cannot stress enough how important it is if you have a large family (more than two kids) to rent a house for your stay! . . . We stayed at Windsor Hills Resort, which I booked through **globalresorthomes. com** *. . . It took us about 10 minutes to drive there in the a.m., and we had no traffic issues at all. We had a brand-new four-bedroom, four-bathroom house with our own pool. . . . All for $215 a night! This was in October, but rates never climb above $300, even in the high season. We loved getting away from the hubbub of Disney and relaxing back at the house in "our" pool.*

AAA Dream Homes (**floridadreamhomes.com**) has a good reputation for customer service and now has photos of and information about the homes in its inventory online.

HOW *to* CHILDPROOF *a* HOTEL ROOM

TODDLERS AND SMALL CHILDREN up to 3 years of age (and sometimes older) can wreak mayhem—if not outright disaster—in a hotel room. They're mobile, curious, and amazingly fast, and they have a penchant for turning the most seemingly innocuous furnishing or decoration into a lethal weapon. Chances are you're pretty experienced when it comes to spotting potential dangers, but just in case you need a refresher course, here's what to look for.

Always begin by checking the room for hazards that you cannot neutralize, like balconies, chipping paint, cracked walls, sharp surfaces, shag carpeting, and windows that can't be secured shut. If you encounter anything that you don't like or is too much of a hassle to fix, ask for another room.

If you use a crib supplied by the hotel, make sure that the mattress is firm and covers the entire bottom of the crib. If there is a mattress cover, it should fit tightly. Slats should be 2.5 inches (about the width of a soda can) or less apart. Test the drop sides to ensure that they work properly and that your child cannot release them accidentally. Examine the crib from all angles (including from underneath) to make sure it has been assembled correctly and that there are no sharp edges. Check for chipping paint and other potentially toxic substances that your child might ingest. Wipe down surfaces your child might touch or mouth to diminish the potential of infection transmitted from a previous occupant. Finally, position the crib away from drape cords, heaters, wall sockets, and air conditioners.

A Monteno, Illinois, mother of a 2-year-old offered this suggestion:

> *You can request bed rails [at the Disney resorts]. Our two-and-a-half-year-old is way too big for the pack and play. The bed rails worked perfectly for us.*

If your infant can turn over, we recommend changing him or her on a pad on the floor. Likewise, if you have a child seat of any sort, place it where it cannot be knocked over, and always strap your child in.

If your child can roll, crawl, or walk, you should bring about eight electrical outlet covers and some cord to tie cabinets shut and to bind drape cords and the like out of reach. Check for appliances, lamps, ashtrays, ice buckets, and anything else that your child might pull down on him- or herself. Have the hotel remove coffee tables with sharp edges, and both real and artificial plants that are within your child's reach. Round up items from table and countertops such as matchbooks, courtesy toiletries, and drinking glasses, and store them out of reach.

If the bathroom door can be accidentally locked, cover the locking mechanism with duct tape or a doorknob cover. Use the security chain or upper latch on the room's entrance door to ensure that your child doesn't open it without your knowledge.

Inspect the floor and remove pins, coins, and other foreign objects that your child might find. Don't forget to check under beds and furniture. One of the best tips we've heard came from a Fort Lauderdale, Florida, mother who crawls around the room on her hands and knees in order to see possible hazards from her child's perspective.

If you rent a suite or a condo, you'll have more territory to childproof and will have to deal with the possible presence of cleaning supplies, a stove, a refrigerator, cooking utensils, and low cabinet doors, among other things. Sometimes the best option is to seal off the kitchen with a folding safety gate.

PART FOUR

DINING

DINING OPTIONS ABOUND BOTH IN AND OUT of Walt Disney World, and if you're so inclined, there are a lot of ways to save big bucks while keeping your crew nourished and happy.

EATING *outside* WALT DISNEY WORLD

1. **A CAR HELPS** Access to restaurants outside of Walt Disney World can really cut the cost of your overall vacation, but you need to have wheels. If you eat only your evening meal outside the World, the savings will more than pay for a rental car.

2. **PLENTY OF CHOICES** Eating outside of Walt Disney World doesn't relegate you to dining in lackluster restaurants. The range of choices is quite broad and includes elegant dining options, as well as familiar chain restaurants and local family eateries.

3. **DISCOUNTS ARE EVERYWHERE** Visitor magazines and booklets containing discount coupons to dozens of out-of-the-World restaurants are available everywhere except in Walt Disney World. The coupons are good at a broad selection of eateries, ranging from burger joints to some of the best restaurants in the area. Though coupon booklets and freebie visitor mags are pretty much everywhere, the mother lode can be found at the Visit Orlando Official Visitor Center at 8723 International Dr., Ste. 101, at the corner of Austrian Row, open 8:30 a.m.–6:30 p.m.; ☎ 407-363-5872. Here you'll find copies of every magazine and booklet available. The center also sells slightly discounted tickets to the theme parks. Also see **visitorlando.com.**

4. **WHEN YOU DON'T HAVE A CAR** If you're staying in a hotel outside Disney World, Room Service Orlando (7041 Grand National Dr., Ste. 109; ☎ 407-352-1170; **roomserviceorlando.com**) will deliver a meal from your choice of several area restaurants, including T.G.I. Fridays, TooJay's

Gourmet Deli, Saffron, Kim Wu Chinese, and Cariera's Cucina Italiana. The delivery charge is $5 per restaurant if ordered online or $6 by phone, with a minimum $15 order. Gratuity is added to the bill. Cash, traveler's checks, MasterCard, Visa, American Express, and Discover are accepted. Hours are 4:30–11 p.m.

BUFFETS AND MEAL DEALS OUTSIDE WALT DISNEY WORLD

BUFFETS, RESTAURANT SPECIALS, and discount dining abound in the area surrounding Walt Disney World, especially on US 192 (known locally as the Irlo Bronson Memorial Highway) and along International Drive. The local visitor magazines, distributed free at non-Disney hotels among other places, are packed with advertisements and discount coupons for seafood feasts, Chinese buffets, Indian buffets, breakfast buffets, and a host of combination specials for everything from lobster to barbecue. For a family trying to economize, some of the come-ons are mighty appealing. But are these places any good? Is the food fresh, tasty, and appealing? Are the restaurants clean and inviting? Armed with little more than a roll of Tums, the *Unofficial* research team tried all the eateries that advertise heavily in the free tourist magazines. Here's what we discovered.

CHINESE SUPER BUFFETS Whoa! Talk about an oxymoron. If you've ever tried preparing Chinese food, especially a stir-fry, you know that split-second timing is required to avoid overcooking. So it should come as no big surprise that Chinese dishes languishing on a buffet lose their freshness, texture, and flavor in a hurry.

For the past few editions of this guide, we were able to find several Chinese buffets that were better than the rest and that we felt comfortable recommending. Unfortunately, however, our endorsements seem to be the kiss of death: We return the next year to discover that quality has slipped precipitously. We attempted to find a new buffet to replace the ones we deleted from the guide, and we can tell you that wasn't fun work. At the end of the day, **Mei Asian Bistro** (8255 International Dr.; ☎ 407-352-0881) is the only Chinese buffet we've elected to list. To call it a *super* buffet might be stretching things, but aside from a lackluster dessert selection, it's pretty good.

INDIAN BUFFETS Unlike Chinese food, Indian food actually improves as the flavors marry. In the Walt Disney World area, most Indian restaurants offer a buffet at lunch only—not too convenient if you plan on spending your day at the theme parks. If you're out shopping or taking a day off, here are some Indian buffets worth trying:

Aashirwad Indian Cuisine 5748 International Dr., at the corner of International Drive and Kirkman Road; ☎ 407-370-9830

Punjab Indian Restaurant 7451 International Dr.; ☎ 407-352-7887

BRAZILIAN BUFFETS A number of Brazilian buffets have sprung up along International Drive. The best of these is **Vittorio's** (5159 International

Dr., near the outlet malls at the northern end of International Drive; ☎ 407-352-1255; **vittoriosrestaurant.com**).

SEAFOOD AND LOBSTER BUFFETS These affairs don't exactly fall under the category of inexpensive dining. The main draw (no pun intended) is all the lobster you can eat. The problem is that lobsters, like Chinese food, don't wear well on a steam table. After a few minutes on the buffet line, they make better tennis balls than dinner. If, however, there's someone in the kitchen who knows how to steam a lobster, and if you grab your lobster immediately after a fresh batch has been brought out, it will probably be fine. There are three lobster buffets on US 192 and another two on International Drive. Although all five do a reasonable job, we prefer **Boston Lobster Feast** (6071 W. Irlo Bronson Memorial Hwy.; ☎ 407-396-2606; and 8731 International Dr., five blocks north of the Convention Center; ☎ 407-248-8606; **bostonlobsterfeast.com**). Both locations are distinguished by a vast variety of seafood in addition to the lobster. The International Drive location is cavernous and insanely noisy, which is why we prefer the Irlo Bronson location, where you can actually have a conversation over dinner. There's ample parking at the International Drive location, while parking places are in short supply at the Irlo Bronson restaurant. At about $35 for early birds (4–6 p.m.) and $40 after 6 p.m., dining is expensive at both locations.

SALAD BUFFETS The most popular of these in the Walt Disney World area is **Sweet Tomatoes** (6877 S. Kirkman Rd.; ☎ 407-363-1616; 12561 S. Apopka–Vineland Rd.; ☎ 407-938-9461; **sweettomatoes. com**). During lunch and dinner, you can expect a line out the door, but fortunately it moves fast. The buffet features prepared salads and an extensive array of ingredients to build your own. In addition to the rabbit food, Sweet Tomatoes offers a variety of soups, a modest pasta bar, a baked-potato bar, an assortment of fresh fruit, and ice cream sundaes. Dinner runs $9.99 for adults, $5 for children ages 6–12, and $3.49 for children ages 3–5. Lunch is $8.59 for adults and the same prices as dinner for children (not including tax).

BREAKFAST AND ENTRÉE BUFFETS Entrée buffets are offered by most chain steak houses in the area, such as **Ponderosa, Sizzler,** and **Golden Corral.** Among them, they have 18 locations in the Walt Disney World area. All serve breakfast, lunch, and dinner. At lunch and dinner, you get the buffet when you buy an entrée, usually a steak. Generally speaking, the buffets are less elaborate than a stand-alone buffet but considerably more varied than a salad bar. Breakfast service is a straightforward buffet (that is, you aren't obligated to buy an entrée). As for the food, it's chain-restaurant quality but decent all the same. Prices are a bargain, and you can get in and out at lightning speed— important at breakfast when you're trying to get to the theme parks

continued on page 134

Where to Eat outside Walt Disney World

AMERICAN

J. Alexander's   7335 Sand Lake Rd., Orlando; ☎ 407-345-1039; **jalexanders. com**; moderate. Chic, relaxed ambience; large portions of steak and seafood.

The Ravenous Pig*   1234 N. Orange Ave., Winter Park; ☎ 407-628-2333; **theravenouspig.com;** moderate–expensive. New American cuisine with an award-winning menu that changes frequently, with seasonal ingredients.

Seasons 52   7700 W. Sand Lake Rd., Orlando; ☎ 407-354-5212; **seasons52. com;** moderate–expensive. Delicious, creative New American food (and low in fat and calories). Solid wine list.

BARBECUE

Bubbalou's Bodacious Bar-B-Que   5818 Conroy Rd., Orlando (near Universal Orlando); ☎ 407-295-1212; **bubbalous.com;** inexpensive. Tender, smoky barbecue; tomato-based "killer" sauce.

CHINESE

Ming Court   9188 International Dr., Orlando; ☎ 407-351-9988; **ming-court. com;** moderate–expensive. Wok-fired dishes, sushi.

CUBAN/SPANISH

Columbia   649 Front St., Celebration; ☎ 407-566-1505; **columbiarestaurant. com;** moderate. Cuban/Spanish creations such as paella and the 1905 Salad.

FRENCH

Le Coq au Vin*   4800 S. Orange Ave., Orlando; ☎ 407-851-6980; **lecoqauvin restaurant.com;** moderate–expensive. Country French cuisine in a relaxed atmosphere. Reservations suggested.

INDIAN

Tabla Bar and Grill   5827 Caravan Ct., Orlando; ☎ 407-248-9400; **tablabar.com;** moderate. Near Universal Orlando entrance; family-owned; authentic, innovative.

ITALIAN

Bice Orlando Ristorante   Loews Portofino Bay Hotel, 5601 Universal Blvd., Orlando; ☎ 407-503-1415; **bicegroup.com;** expensive. Authentic Italian; great wines.

JAPANESE/SUSHI

Amura   7786 W. Sand Lake Rd., Orlando; ☎ 407-370-0007; **amura.com;** moderate. A favorite sushi bar for locals. The tempura is popular too.

Hanamizuki   8255 International Dr., Orlando; ☎ 407-363-7200; **hanamizuki. us;** moderate–expensive. Usually filled with Japanese visitors; pricey but authentic.

*20 minutes or more from Walt Disney World

Nagoya Sushi   7600 Dr. Phillips Blvd., Ste. 66, in the very rear of The Marketplace at Dr. Phillips; ☎ 407-248-8558; **nagoyasushi.com;** moderate. A small, intimate restaurant with great sushi and an extensive menu.

MEXICAN

Cantina Laredo   800 Via Dellagio Way, Orlando; ☎ 407-345-0186; **cantina laredo.com;** moderate–expensive. Authentic Mexican in upscale atmosphere.

Chevys Fresh Mex   12547 FL 535, Lake Buena Vista; ☎ 407-827-1052; **chevys. com;** inexpensive–moderate. Conveniently located across from the FL 535 entrance to WDW.

Don Pablo's   8717 International Dr., Orlando; ☎ 407-354-1345; **donpablos. com;** inexpensive. Good food but can be a bit noisy.

El Patron   12167 S. Apopka–Vineland Rd., Orlando; ☎ 407-238-5300; **elpatronrestaurantcantina.com;** inexpensive. Family-owned restaurant serving freshly prepared Mexican dishes. Full bar.

Moe's Southwest Grill   7541-D W. Sand Lake Rd., Orlando; ☎ 407-264-9903; **moesorlando.com;** inexpensive. Dependable southwestern fare.

SEAFOOD

Bonefish Grill   7830 W. Sand Lake Rd., Orlando; ☎ 407-355-7707; **bonefishgrill. com;** moderate. Casual setting along busy Restaurant Row on Sand Lake Road. Choose your fish; then choose a sauce to accompany. Also steaks and chicken.

STEAK/PRIME RIB

The Capital Grille   Pointe Orlando, 9101 International Dr., Orlando; ☎ 407-370-4392; **thecapitalgrille.com;** expensive. Dry-aged steaks, good wine list, and classic decor.

Del Frisco's*   729 Lee Rd., Orlando; ☎ 407-645-4443; **delfriscosorlando.com;** expensive. Family-owned; rated top steak house in Central Florida. Prime steaks, lobster, over 6,500 bottles of wine, world-class selection of single-malt scotch.

Texas de Brazil   5259 International Dr., Orlando; ☎ 407-355-0355; **texasde brazil.com;** expensive. All-you-care-to-eat in a Brazilian-style *churrascaria*. Ribs, filet mignon, chicken, lamb, and salad bar. Kids age 6 and under free, ages 7–12 half price.

Vito's Chop House   8633 International Dr., Orlando; ☎ 407-354-2467; **vitos chophouse.com;** moderate. Upscale meat house with a taste of Tuscany.

THAI

Red Bamboo   6803 S. Kirkman Rd. at International Drive, Orlando; ☎ 407-226-8997; **redbamboothai.com;** moderate. Acclaimed by Orlando dining critics for its authentic Thai dishes. Delicious vegetarian options; impressive wine list.

continued from page 131

early. Some locations offer lunch and dinner buffets at a set price without you having to buy an entrée.

Though you can argue about which chain serves the best steak, Golden Corral wins the buffet contest hands down, with at least twice as many offerings as its competitors. While buffets at Golden Corral and Ponderosa are pretty consistent from location to location, the buffets at the various Sizzlers vary a good deal. The pick of the Sizzlers is the one at 7602 W. Irlo Bronson Memorial Hwy. (☎ 407-397-0997). In addition to the steak houses, area **Shoney's** also offer breakfast, lunch, and dinner buffets. Local freebie visitor magazines are full of discount coupons for all of the previous restaurants.

MEAL DEALS Discount coupons are available for a wide range of restaurants, including some wonderful upscale-ethnic places such as **Ming Court** (Chinese; 9188 International Dr.; ☎ 407-351-9988; ming-court.com). Our favorite prime-rib joint is **Wild Jack's Steaks & BBQ** (7364 International Dr.; ☎ 407-352-4407). The decor is strictly cowboy modern, but the beef is some of the best in town, and the price is right.

A meat eater's delight is the Feast for Four at **Sonny's Real Pit Bar-B-Q**, a Florida chain that turns out good barbecue. For $40 per family of four, you get sliced pork and beef, plus chicken, ribs, your choice of three sides (beans, slaw, or fries), garlic bread or corn bread, and soft drinks or tea, all served family-style. The closest Sonny's location to the Walt Disney World and Universal tourist areas is at 7423 S. Orange Blossom Trl. in Orlando (☎ 407-859-7197); for a listing of other restaurants within a wider radius, visit **sonnysbbq.com.** No coupons are needed or available for Sonny's, but they are available for the other "meateries."

COUPONS Discounts and twofer coupons for many of the restaurants mentioned can be found in freebie visitor guides available at most hotels outside of Walt Disney World. The **Visit Orlando Official Visitor Center** (8723 International Dr., Ste. 101; ☎ 407-363-5872; open daily, 8:30 a.m.–6:30 p.m.) offers a treasure trove of coupons and free visitor magazines. Check out **couponsalacarte.com** and **orlandocoupons.com** for printable coupons.

DINING *in* WALT DISNEY WORLD

ONCE YOU COULD HAVE JOKED that a chapter about dining in Walt Disney World was an oxymoron. Whatever else it was (and it was many wonderful things), Disney World was no gourmet paradise. For the most part, in fact, the restaurants were as much entertainment as the rest of Disney World: The fast-food joints feature character decor, and the international pavilions sport native costumes.

Disney's food and beverage department has vastly expanded, and it has succeeded in launching a remarkable upgrade of the full-service restaurants around the World. Now there are nine or ten first-class restaurants and perhaps an equal number of B+ establishments. The wine lists have been seriously improved and expanded—there is even a full-fledged wine bar, Martha's Vineyard, at the Yacht & Beach Club.

Of course, if the average parents roaming the Walt Disney World parks were primarily concerned with pleasing their palates, the hottest dinner ticket at the park would not be the *Hoop-Dee-Doo Musical Revue*. In fact, if you want to know what Disney World visitors really like, look at the numbers: Every year, they consume 1.6 million turkey legs, nearly 10 million hamburgers, 7.7 million hot dogs, 46 million sodas, and 5 million bags of popcorn.

So, for many families, food is a secondary consideration, but if you do care more about dining out on your vacation or would like to experiment with different cuisines, *The Unofficial Guide to Walt Disney World*, referred to in the Introduction, includes more detailed reviews not only of the sit-down establishments in Disney World itself but also some of the better restaurants outside the World.

One thing parents should be aware of is that both full- and counter-service restaurants at Walt Disney World serve very substantial portions. You can easily put aside parts of dinners for lunches the next day (if you have a refrigerator in your room), split an entrée, or load up at lunch and go light on dinner.

DISNEY DINING 101

It's the Economy, Pluto

As the aftermath of the recession affects the number of travelers visiting the World, Disney scrambled furiously to make up for lost revenue. Unfortunately, this translates to higher and higher prices at Disney restaurants. Main-course prices at some restaurants have risen more than 35%; plus, Disney levies a dining surcharge during the summer and other busy times of year. Recently we dined at the Wave restaurant at the Contemporary Resort and ordered a wine that retails for about $11. It was $9 a glass (!)—about a five-times markup. Believe us, if you rent a car and simply eat each dinner off of Disney property, you'll save enough to more than pay for the rental cost.

These comments from a Tennessee reader spell it out:

The first time we ate at Liberty Tree Tavern a few years ago, the cost was about $23 per person for each adult. This year, the cost would have been about $33 per person with the increased prices and the holiday dining surcharge they add during the summer months. This is a nearly 40% price increase over a period of 3 years for basically the same experience! We decided that turkey and mashed potatoes weren't worth the $33 and ended up eating elsewhere.

And from a New Orleans mom:

Disney keeps pushing prices up and up. For us, the sky is NOT the limit. We won't be back.

ADVANCE RESERVATIONS: WHAT'S IN A NAME?

DISNEY TINKERS CEASELESSLY with its restaurant-reservations policy. In 2005 Disney decided to change the name from Priority Seating to the rather redundant Advance Reservations. Indeed, the name is all that changed: When you call, your name and essential information are taken as if you were making an honest-to-goodness reservation. The Disney representative then tells you that you have Advance Reservations for the restaurant on the date and time you requested. Though they're called Advance Reservations, most reservations at Disney World don't guarantee you a table at a specific time, as they would at your typical hometown restaurant. The Disney rep usually explains that you'll be seated ahead of walk-ins—that is, those who do not have Advance Reservations.

The no-show rate in January, a slow month, is about 33%, while in July it's less than 10%.

Bob

GETTING AN ADVANCE RESERVATION AT POPULAR RESTAURANTS

CINDERELLA'S ROYAL TABLE, in Cinderella Castle in the Magic Kingdom, hosts the immensely popular character breakfast starring Cinderella and other Disney princesses. The toughest character-meal ticket at Disney World is an 8 a.m. Advance Reservation for this venue when the Magic Kingdom opens at 9 a.m. Why? Cinderella's Royal Table is Disney's tiniest character-meal restaurant, accommodating only about 130 diners at a time. Demand so outdistances supply for this event that some Walt Disney World visitors find themselves going to unbelievable lengths to secure an Advance Reservation.

This frustrated reader from Golden, Colorado, complains:

I don't know what you have to do to get an Advance Reservation for Cinderella's Royal Table in the castle. I called Disney Dining every morning at 7 a.m., which was 5 a.m. where I live! It was like calling in to one of those radio shows where the first person to call wins a prize. Every time I finally got through, all the tables were gone. I am soooo frustrated and mad I could spit.

On the upside, Disney now offers online reservations, which open at 6 a.m. Eastern time, a full hour before their phone reservations open. If you have access to a computer in the morning, this is by far the easiest way to secure a table for any restaurant you'd like. Visit **disneyworld. com/reservations/dining** to make reservations. We suggest trying this site out a couple of days before you need to make reservations, so you become familiar with how it works.

To reserve via phone, you must call ☎ 407-WDW-DINE at 7 a.m. EST. If you're visiting during the off-season and you're not too fussy about

Advance Reservations: The Official Line

You can make reservations up to 180 days in advance for:

Afternoon tea and children's programs **at the Grand Floridian Resort & Spa**

All Disney table-service restaurants and character-dining venues

Cirque du Soleil's *La Nouba* **at Downtown Disney**

Fantasmic! dinner package **at Disney's Hollywood Studios**

Hoop-Dee-Doo Musical Revue **at Fort Wilderness Resort**

Mickey's Backyard BBQ **at Fort Wilderness Resort**

Spirit of Aloha Dinner Show **at the Polynesian Resort**

Guests staying at Walt Disney World resorts—these do not include the Swan, the Dolphin, Shades of Green, or the hotels of the Downtown Disney Resort Area—can make Advance Reservations up to 10 additional days ahead, effectively giving them a maximum window of 190 days.

Advance Reservations Go Online

To reserve online, go to **disneyworld.com/reservations/dining.** An e-form will come up where you can enter the name of the restaurant you want to book, your party size, and the date and time for which you'd like to make your reservations. If you're on the Disney Dining Plan and want to use dining credits, there's a prompt for that as well. After selecting a date, you must enter your preferred reservation time or, alternatively, a meal period. If, for example, you select "breakfast" instead of entering a specific time, you're essentially saying that anytime during the hours breakfast is served is fine. If you enter a particular time, say 9:30 a.m., and no tables are available, the online reservation system will display alternative locations at the same time, but it won't show you alternative days for the same location. For instance, if you want Cinderella's Royal Table for breakfast on July 1 and it isn't available, Disney might tell you that The Crystal Palace is; it won't tell you, however, if Cindy's is available on July 2 instead. The advantage of booking online is that you can submit your request 1 hour earlier than on the phone. The disadvantage is that you can't speak with a live person who can help you explore other options if your preferred reservation time is unavailable. *Note:* **Disney's online-reservations system opens at 6 a.m. Eastern time— 1 hour earlier than the phone-reservations system.**

which meal you get or what time you eat, our research has found that you can usually book a few weeks out from your desired date (see page 138). If you're visiting Disney World during summer or around a major holiday, or you want to dine at a specific popular time, read on.

The only way to get a table is to obtain an Advance Reservation directly through Disney. Your best chance of getting that reservation is to book online at 6 a.m. Eastern time, exactly 180 days before the day you want to eat. If you live in California and have to get up at 3 a.m. Pacific time to go online, Disney couldn't give a mouse's patoot. There's

Number of Days in Advance Needed to Book Theme-park Sit-down Restaurants

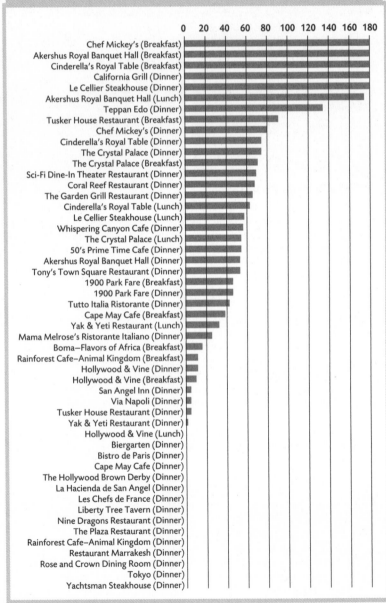

Advance Reservations: The Unofficial *Scoop*

USING DOZENS OF VOLUNTEERS with free long-distance plans and access to the online Advance Reservations system, we have built profiles of each theme-park restaurant, showing how many days in advance (on average) that restaurant filled up for various meals at the most popular times (for example, an 8 a.m. breakfast at Cinderella's Royal Table when the park opens at 9 a.m.). Our results are shown in the chart on the opposite page. All meals are dinner unless otherwise noted.

Not surprisingly, you'll need to book highly rated restaurants such as Canada's **Le Cellier Steakhouse** and the breakfast buffet at **Chef Mickey's** a full 180 days in advance if you want to get a prime seating time. One notable difference from last year is the increased popularity of Epcot's **Teppan Edo** restaurant at Japan. It now takes more than 4 months of planning to get a prime 6 p.m. dinner spot during busier times of the year, up from around 100 days last year.

Surprisingly, and slightly farther down the list, the Magic Kingdom's **Cinderella's Royal Table** lunch and dinner generally need to be booked within 2–3 months of your trip, except during the busiest times of the year (see opposite page). Breakfast here is still the hottest ticket in the parks, but price increases and additional capacity at lunch and dinner have made tables somewhat easier to get then.

It's possible to snag reservations at Italy's **Via Napoli** and Germany's **Biergarten** buffet within 3 weeks of your trip, which is surprising because both are well regarded by both our dining reviewer and our readers. If you're looking for a last-minute sit-down meal in the Magic Kingdom, the **Liberty Tree Tavern** is your best bet.

Bringing up the rear are World Showcase's **Nine Dragons Restaurant** (China) and most of the sit-down restaurants at Animal Kingdom. Nine Dragons' placement is well deserved due to its overpriced, underwhelming food. Regarding Animal Kingdom's eateries, we think that our findings don't have so much to do with these restaurants' quality as they do with the fact that people don't need to hang around until dinnertime to see the entire park.

no limit to the number of hoops they can make their patrons jump through if demand exceeds supply.

To be among the fortunate few who score an Advance Reservation during peak times, try the following. First, try on the correct morning. Use a calendar and count backward exactly 180 days from (but not including) the day you wish to dine. (Disney's computers don't understand months, so you can't, for example, try on January 1 to make an Advance Reservation for July 1 because that's more than 180 days.) If you want to eat on May 1, for example, begin your 180-day backward count on April 30. If you count correctly, you'll find that the correct morning to try is November 2. If you don't feel like counting days, call ☎ 407-WDW-DINE and the Disney folks will calculate it for you. Call them during the afternoon, when they're less busy, about 185 days before your trip. Let them know when you'd like your Advance Reservation, and they'll tell you which morning to make reservations.

To get a table, you must be online on Disney's dining reservations page at almost exactly 6 a.m. Eastern time. Once there, you'll see a place to enter a restaurant name (type "Cinderella's Royal Table"—without the quotes), a place to specify the time of your meal, and your party size; fill these in ahead of time. You'll also see a text box where you can specify the date of your visit. Click on the date text box, enter the date of your visit in MM/DD/YYYY format (for example, 07/01/2012 for July 1, 2012) and press the tab key on your keyboard. (You can also click on the blue calendar icon to flip through a month-by-month calendar, but this is slower.) If your date isn't yet available, a message will appear saying that you've chosen a date more than 180 days in advance of today. If this happens, refresh the page within your browser and start over. If you don't see an error message, however, click the button labeled "Search for a Table" to send your request to Disney's computers.

Disney kids' meals are now for ages 3–9; the cutoff used to be age 11.

Liliane

Disney doesn't calibrate its clock with the correct time as determined by the U.S. Naval Observatory or the National Institute of Standards and Technology, but we conducted synchronizing tests and determined that Disney reservation-system clocks are accurate to within a handful of seconds. Several Internet sites will give you the exact time. Our favorite is **atomictime.net,** which offers the exact time in displays that show hours, minutes, and seconds. Once the Atomic Time home page is up, click on "HTML multizone continuous" and look for the Eastern time zone. Using this site or your local Time of Day number from the phone directory, synchronize your computer to the second. About 3 minutes before 6 a.m., start trying to enter your dates to see if they're accepted.

Bear in mind that while you're typing, other guests are trying to make Advance Reservations too, so you want the transaction to go down as fast as possible. Flexibility on your part counts. It's much harder to get a seating for a large group, so give some thought to breaking your group into numbers that can be accommodated at tables for four. Also make sure that you have your credit card out where you can read it.

All Advance Reservations for Cinderella's Royal Table character meals require complete prepayment with a credit card at the time of the booking. The name on the booking can't be changed after the Advance Reservation is made. Advance Reservations may be canceled with the deposit refunded in full by calling ☎ 407-WDW-DINE at least 24 hours before the seating time.

While many readers have been successful using our strategies, some have not been:

I got up extra early 180 days before our trip to get Thanksgiving reservations at Le Cellier for my husband's birthday. Even though I logged on to Disney's website right at 6 a.m., by the time I got done typing and clicking, the only table that was available was at 8:40 p.m.—too late for our children and we would have missed IllumiNations.

On most days, a couple hundred users slam Disney's computer system within milliseconds of one another. With this volume, a 20th of a second or less can make the difference between getting a table and not getting one. As it happens, there are variables beyond your control. One is the number of computers through which your request passes before it reaches Disney's reservation system. The explanation is somewhat technical, but the same principle applies whether you're trying to get dining reservations online with Disney or concert seats through Ticketmaster.

If you don't have access to a computer at 6 a.m. on the morning you need to make reservations, Disney's phone agents begin taking calls at 7 a.m. Eastern. Call ☎ 407-WDW-DINE at 7 a.m. EST and follow the prompts to speak to a live person. You may still get placed on hold if call volume is higher than usual, and you'll be an hour behind the early birds with computers. Still, you'll be well ahead of those who couldn't make it up before sunrise.

If You Can't Get an Advance Reservation

If you insist on a meal at a specific restaurant but can't get an Advance Reservation, go to the restaurant on the day you wish to dine and try for a table as a walk-in. This is a long shot, though it's possible during the least busy times of year. There's also a fair shot at success on cold or rainy days when there's an above-average probability of no-shows. If you try to walk in, your chances are best during the last hour of serving.

Landing an Advance Reservation for Cinderella's Royal Table at dinner is somewhat easier, but the price is a whopping $57 for adults and $35 for children ages 3–9. As at breakfast and lunch, five photos of your group and a photo of the castle, along with a Cinderella-themed photo holder, are included in the price (like it or not). If you're unable to lock up a table for breakfast or lunch, a dinner reservation will at least get your children inside the castle.

A Snellville, Georgia, mom recalls:

We ate [dinner] at Cinderella Castle to fulfill my longtime dream. The menu was very limited and expensive. For three people, no appetizers or dessert, the bill was $100.

And no booze, either. Alcohol isn't served in the Magic Kingdom.

GETTING YOUR ACT TOGETHER

IF YOU WANT TO PATRONIZE any of the Walt Disney World Resort full-service restaurants, buffets, character meals, or dinner shows, you should make Advance Reservations; the chart on page 138 shows a listing of how far ahead of time you can make them. Note that you can now make Advance Reservations online (see page 137) as well as by calling ☎ 407-WDW-DINE.

Concerning the online method, it will save time when you want to book advanced dining reservations if you set up an account on the Disney dining website, **disneyworld.com/reservations/dining,** before the 180-day booking window. For the busiest full-service restaurants, buffets, and character meals, you should make Advance Reservations 90–180 days ahead of time—although there are exceptions to the rule (see page 138).

If you fail to make Advance Reservations before you leave home, or if you want to make your dining decisions spontaneously, your chances of getting a table at the restaurants of your choice aren't the best, especially during the hours when most folks prefer to eat dinner.

For Advance Reservations, make sure you bring your confirmation number to the restaurant.

If you visit Walt Disney World during a very busy time of year, it's to your advantage to make Advance Reservations before you leave home, as this Houston couple attests:

Make reservations if you plan on having table service. Even trying to walk in for full service at off-times was impossible.

Another reader warns of a sea change in Advance Reservations policy that practically eliminates same-day reservations and walk-ins:

While walking around the parks and resorts this weekend, I think literally every sit-down restaurant we passed had a sign out front saying something like, IN ORDER TO SERVE OUR GUESTS WITH DINING RESERVATIONS IN A TIMELY MANNER, WE ARE NOT ACCEPTING WALK-UP DINING REQUESTS AT THIS TIME. *I believe every World Showcase country had this sign, as did the Magic Kingdom, the Yacht & Beach Club, and Animal Kingdom Lodge's two sit-downs, all weekend, so I don't think this is a one-time thing. This may also explain why the World Showcase restaurants are going through refurbishments one by one—must be to add capacity.*

A dad from St. Paul, Minnesota, changed course, much to his and his family's satisfaction:

We had so much difficulty booking the Disney restaurants that we just threw up our hands and reread the part of the guide about places to eat outside of WDW. We ended up eating only one meal (a character breakfast) in a Disney restaurant. The rest of the time we followed your suggestions for non-Disney restaurants in the general area. I'm happy to report that we had some super meals and that the money we saved more than paid for our rental car.

Though securing Advance Reservations before you leave home is more important than ever, there's no need, except as stated previously, to call 90–180 days in advance. For most restaurants, calling 45 days in advance will get you the restaurants that you desire. If you're visiting during an extremely busy time of year, try to call as far in advance as possible.

If you poop out at the theme park and you don't feel like using your Advance Reservations that night, be aware that some restaurants have penalties for being a no-show and will charge you a cancellation fee. Note that you must pay in full at the time of booking for all meals at Cinderella's Royal Table, the *Hoop-Dee-Doo Musical Revue,* the *Spirit of Aloha* Dinner Show, and *Mickey's Backyard BBQ.* If you're a no-show, you lose the entire amount, so be sure to get the exact cancellation policy at the time that you book your meal. Incidentally, if you're asked for a credit card to secure a seating, be aware that it's a *real* reservation as opposed to an Advance Reservation. Also be aware that if you're a no-show for a particular reservation, it will not affect any other Advance Reservations you may have made.

If you've lined up many Advance Reservations, it's a good idea to phone ☎ 407-WDW-DINE a few days before you arrive to make sure everything's in order. If you stay at a Disney resort, Guest Relations can print out a summary of all your Advance Reservations.

If you have an Advance Reservation for a theme-park restaurant at a time prior to opening, simply proceed to the turnstiles and inform a cast member, who will admit you to the park. If you fail to make Advance Reservations, most full-service theme-park restaurants will take walk-ins 2:30–4:30 p.m.

DRESS

DRESS IS INFORMAL AT MOST THEME-PARK restaurants, but Disney has instituted a business casual dress code for some of its resort restaurants: khakis, dress slacks, jeans, or dress shorts with a collared shirt for men and Capris, skirts, dresses, jeans, or dress shorts for women. Restaurants with this dress code are **Jiko—The Cooking Place** at Animal Kingdom Lodge & Villas, the **Flying Fish Café** at Disney's BoardWalk, the **California Grill** at the Contemporary Resort, **Bistro de Paris** at Epcot's France Pavilion, **Citricos** and **Narcoossee's** at the Grand Floridian Resort & Spa, **Artist Point** at Wilderness Lodge, **Yachtsman Steakhouse** at the Yacht Club Resort, **Todd English's bluezoo** and **Shula's Steak House** at the Dolphin, and **Il Mulino** at the Swan. **Victoria & Albert's** at the Grand Floridian is the only Disney restaurant that requires men to wear a jacket to dinner.

SMOKING

WALT DISNEY WORLD RESTAURANTS adopted a nonsmoking policy several years ago, after Florida voters passed an amendment to the state's constitution that prohibits smoking in restaurant lounges. (Freestanding bars—less than 10% of revenues from food sales—are exempt.)

FOOD ALLERGIES AND SPECIAL REQUESTS

IF YOU HAVE FOOD ALLERGIES or observe some specific type of diet (such as eating kosher), make your needs known when you make your Advance Reservations. Does it work? Well, a Phillipsburg, New Jersey, mom reports her family's experience:

> *My 6-year-old has many food allergies, and we often have to bring food with us to restaurants when we go out to eat. I was able to make reservations at the Disney restaurants in advance and indicate these*

allergies to the reservation clerk. When we arrived at the restaurants, the staff was already aware of my child's allergies and assigned our table a chef who double-checked the list of allergies with us. Each member of the waitstaff was also informed of the allergies. The chefs were very nice and made my son feel very special.

A FEW CAVEATS

BEFORE YOU BEGIN EATING your way through the World, you need to know:

1. Theme-park restaurants rush their customers in order to make room for the next group of diners. Dining at high speed may appeal to families with young children, but to people wanting to relax, it's like eating in a pressure chamber.

   If you want to linger over your expensive meal, don't order your entire dinner at once. Study the menu, and then order appetizers. Tell the waiter that you need more time to decide among entrées. Order your main course only after appetizers have been served.

2. If you're dining in a theme park and cost is an issue, make lunch your main meal. Entrées are similar to those on the dinner menu but are usually less expensive.

3. Disney adds a surcharge of $4 per adult and $2 per child to certain popular restaurants during weeks of peak attendance, including Presidents Day, Easter, mid-June to mid-August, Thanksgiving, and Christmas. The following restaurants participate in the gouging: Akershus Royal Banquet Hall (Princess Storybook Meals), Biergarten, Boma (breakfast and dinner), Cape May Café (breakfast and dinner buffet), Chef Mickey's (breakfast and dinner), Cinderella's Royal Table, The Crystal Palace, The Garden Grill Restaurant, Hollywood & Vine (Play 'n Dine character buffets), the *Hoop-Dee-Doo Musical Revue,* Liberty Tree Tavern (dinner), *Mickey's Backyard BBQ,* 1900 Park Fare (breakfast and dinner), 'Ohana (breakfast and dinner), the *Spirit of Aloha* Dinner Show, Trail's End Restaurant at Fort Wilderness (only a $2 surcharge for adults and $1 for kids), and Tusker House Restaurant. Not to be left out, folks on the Disney Dining Plan pay their own special surcharge—$2 for adults and $1 for kids during peak times—at every restaurant on the plan.

WALT DISNEY WORLD RESTAURANT CATEGORIES

IN GENERAL, FOOD AND BEVERAGE offerings at Walt Disney World are defined by service, price, and convenience.

FULL-SERVICE RESTAURANTS These are found in Disney resorts (except the All-Star complex, Art of Animation, Pop Century, and Port Orleans French Quarter), all major theme parks, Downtown Disney Marketplace, and Disney's West Side. Advance Reservations (see page 137) are recommended for all full-service restaurants except those in the Downtown Disney Resort Area. The restaurants accept American Express, Carte Blanche, Diners Club, Japan Credit Bureau, MasterCard, and Visa.

BUFFETS AND FAMILY-STYLE RESTAURANTS There has been an explosion of buffets at Disney World during recent years. Many have Disney characters in attendance, and most have a separate children's menu featuring dishes such as hot dogs, burgers, chicken nuggets, pizza, macaroni and cheese, and spaghetti and meatballs. In addition to the buffets, several restaurants serve a family-style, all-you-can-eat, fixed-price meal.

Advance Reservations arrangements are required for character buffets and recommended for all other buffets and family-style restaurants. Most major credit cards are accepted.

Walt Disney World Buffets and Family-style Restaurants

ANIMAL KINGDOM LODGE
RESTAURANT Boma–Flavors of Africa
CUISINE American (B), African (D)
MEALS SERVED B, D
CHARACTERS No

BEACH CLUB RESORT
RESTAURANT Cape May Café
CUISINE American
MEALS SERVED B, D
CHARACTERS Yes (B)

CONTEMPORARY RESORT
RESTAURANT Chef Mickey's
CUISINE American
MEALS SERVED B, D
CHARACTERS Yes

CORONADO SPRINGS
RESTAURANT Maya Grill
CUISINE American
MEALS SERVED B*, D
CHARACTERS No

DISNEY'S ANIMAL KINGDOM
RESTAURANT Tusker House
CUISINE American (B), African (L, D)
MEALS SERVED B, L, D
CHARACTERS Yes (B)

DISNEY'S HOLLYWOOD STUDIOS
RESTAURANT Hollywood & Vine
CUISINE American
MEALS SERVED B, L, D
CHARACTERS Yes (B, L)

EPCOT
RESTAURANT Akershus Royal Banquet Hall
CUISINE American (B), Norwegian (L, D)
MEALS SERVED B, L, D
CHARACTERS Yes

EPCOT
RESTAURANT Biergarten
CUISINE German
MEALS SERVED L, D
CHARACTERS No

EPCOT
RESTAURANT The Garden Grill
CUISINE American
MEALS SERVED D
CHARACTERS Yes

FORT WILDERNESS
RESTAURANT Hoop-Dee-Doo Musical Revue
CUISINE American
MEALS SERVED D
CHARACTERS No

FORT WILDERNESS
RESTAURANT Mickey's Backyard BBQ
CUISINE American
MEALS SERVED D
CHARACTERS Yes

FORT WILDERNESS
RESTAURANT Trail's End Restaurant
CUISINE American
MEALS SERVED B***, L, D***
CHARACTERS No

GRAND FLORIDIAN
RESTAURANT 1900 Park Fare
CUISINE American
MEALS SERVED B, D
CHARACTERS Yes

THE MAGIC KINGDOM
RESTAURANT Cinderella's Royal Table
CUISINE American
MEALS SERVED B*, L, D
CHARACTERS Yes

THE MAGIC KINGDOM
RESTAURANT The Crystal Palace
CUISINE American
MEALS SERVED B, L, D
CHARACTERS Yes

THE MAGIC KINGDOM
RESTAURANT Liberty Tree Tavern
CUISINE American
MEALS SERVED L, D†
CHARACTERS No

POLYNESIAN RESORT
RESTAURANT 'Ohana
CUISINE Polynesian
MEALS SERVED B, D
CHARACTERS Yes (B)

POLYNESIAN RESORT
RESTAURANT Spirit of Aloha Dinner Show
CUISINE American
MEALS SERVED D
CHARACTERS No

SWAN
RESTAURANT Garden Grove
CUISINE American
MEALS SERVED B‡, L‡, D
CHARACTERS Yes (B**, D)

WILDERNESS LODGE
RESTAURANT Whispering Canyon Café
CUISINE American
MEALS SERVED B, L, D
CHARACTERS No

YACHT CLUB RESORT
RESTAURANT Captain's Grille
CUISINE American
MEALS SERVED B*, L, D
CHARACTERS No

* *Serves family-style meals only at breakfast.*
** *Character-breakfast buffet served only on weekends.*
*** *Serves buffet-style meals only at breakfast and dinner.*

† *Serves family-style meals only at dinner.*
‡ *Serves family-style meals only at breakfast and lunch.*

If you want to eat a lot but don't want to stand in yet another line, then try one of the all-you-can-eat family-style restaurants. These feature platters of food brought to your table in courses by a server. You can sample everything and eat as much as you like. You can even go back to a favorite appetizer after you finish the main course. The food tends to be a little better than what you'll find on a buffet line.

The table on page 145 lists buffets and family-style restaurants (where you can belly up for bulk loading) at Walt Disney World.

FOOD COURTS Featuring a collection of counter-service eateries under one roof, food courts can be found at the moderate (Coronado Springs, Caribbean Beach, and Port Orleans) and value (All-Star, Pop Century, and Art of Animation) Disney resorts. (The closest things to a food court at the theme parks are Sunset Ranch Market at DHS and Sunshine Seasons at Epcot; see below.) Advance Reservations are neither required nor available at these restaurants.

COUNTER SERVICE Counter-service fast food is available in all theme parks, Downtown Disney Marketplace, Disney's BoardWalk, and Disney's West Side. The food compares in quality with Captain D's, McDonald's, or Taco Bell but is more expensive, though often served in larger portions.

FAST CASUAL Somewhere between burgers and formal dining are the establishments in Disney's fast casual category, including three in the theme parks: **Tomorrowland Terrace** in the Magic Kingdom, **Sunshine Seasons** in Epcot, and **Studio Catering Co.** in Disney's Hollywood Studios. Fast-casual restaurants feature menu choices a cut above what you'd normally see at a typical counter-service location. At Sunshine Seasons, for example, chefs will prepare grilled salmon on an open cooking surface while you watch, or you can choose from rotisserie chicken or pork, tasty noodle bowls, or large sandwiches made with artisanal breads. These locations all feature Asian or Mediterranean cuisine, something previously lacking inside the parks. Entrées cost about $2 more on average than traditional counter service, but the variety and food quality more than make up for the difference.

VENDOR FOOD Vendors abound at the theme parks, Downtown Disney Marketplace, Disney's West Side, and Disney's BoardWalk. Offerings include popcorn, ice cream bars, churros (Mexican pastries), soft drinks, bottled water, and (in theme parks) fresh fruit. Prices include tax, and payment must be in cash.

HARD CHOICES

DINING DECISIONS WILL DEFINITELY affect your Walt Disney World experience. If you're short on time and you want to see the theme parks, avoid full service. Ditto if you're short on funds. If you want to try a Disney full-service restaurant, arrange Advance Reservations—again, they won't actually reserve you a table, but they can minimize your wait.

THE COST OF COUNTER-SERVICE FOOD

Bagel or muffin	$2.59
Brownie	$2.39–$3.29
Cake or pie	$4.00
Cereal with milk	$3.19
Cheeseburger with fries	$6.59–$9.29
Chicken-breast sandwich (grilled)	$7.00 ($8.59 basket)
Children's meals	$5.00
Chips	$1.50–$3.0
Cookies	$2.00
Fish basket (fried) with fries	$7.09–$9.69 (shrimp)
Fried-chicken strips with fries	$7.69
Fries	$2.66
Fruit (whole piece)	$1.00–$2.75
Fruit cup/fruit salad	$3.00–$3.39
Hot dogs	$4.25–$7.50 ($6.59 basket)
Ice cream bars	$2.50–$3.75
Nachos with cheese	$7.95
PB&J sandwich	$5.00
Pizza	$5.59–$8.69
Popcorn	$3.25–$4.75
Pretzel	$3.79–$4.29
Salad (entrée)	$7.79–$8.19
Salad (side)	$3.00
Smoked turkey leg	$7.59
Soup/chili	$2.79–$4.49
Sub/deli sandwich	$8.00 (cold), $9.39 (hot)
Taco salad	$7.69
Taco with yellow rice	$5.49 (veggie), $6.00 (beef)
Veggie burger (basket)	$7.09

DRINKS	SMALL	LARGE
Beer (not available in the Magic Kingdom)	$5.50	$6.25
Bottled water	N/A	$2.50
Cappuccino/espresso	$2.69/$3.69	$4.25/$5.25 (double)
Coffee	$2.09	$3.75
Floats/milk shakes/sundaes	$3.79	$4.59
Fruit juice	$1.69	$2.59
Hot tea and cocoa	$1.89	$2.09
Milk	$1.29	$2.19
Soft drinks, iced tea, and lemonade	$2.19	$2.49

Refillable souvenir mugs cost $14 (free refills) at Disney resorts and $10.75 at water parks; mugs sold at Animal Kingdom cost $7.00 (refills $1).

The Top 10 Snacks at Walt Disney World

FOLLOWING IS A TOP-10 LIST of particularly decadent or unusual snacks available at WDW. We've omitted the usual funnel cakes, popcorn, and ice cream available anywhere. Also absent are the truly bizarre snacks, such as the squid treats sold at the Mitsukoshi Department Store in the Japan Pavilion at Epcot's World Showcase. These are the goodies worth scouring the parks and resorts for, in ascending order:

10. Kaki Gori at the Japan Pavilion, Epcot World Showcase A little on the sweet side but lighter than ice cream, the shaved ice at this small stand comes in such unique flavors as honeydew melon, strawberry, and tangerine. And at $3.28, it's a bargain.

9. Turkey legs Available at every theme park, these must come from 85-pound turkeys because they're huge, not to mention extra-juicy and flavorful. Grab some napkins and go primal on one of these bad boys, and don't worry about the stares you might attract—they're all just jealous.

8. Tie-Dyed Cheesecake at Disney's Pop Century Resort This fun and colorful dessert is delicious. Part red-velvet cake and part cheesecake, the dessert is so popular that many discussion boards offer recipes such as this one: tinyurl.com/tie-dyedcheesecake.

7. Main Street Bakery at the Magic Kingdom Homemade goodies, including some sugar-free offerings. Try the blueberry loaf, hot French-toast loaf, and Mickey Bundt cakes (but probably not all at once). Also check out the assortment of Mickey Mouse crisped-rice treats, available plain, dipped in chocolate, or with sprinkles.

6. Cadbury chocolate bars at the U.K. Pavilion, Epcot World Showcase If you've never had an English Cadbury bar, you just don't know what you're missing.

Integrating Meals into the *Unofficial Guide* Touring Plans

Arrive before the park of your choice opens. Tour expeditiously, using your chosen plan (taking as few breaks as possible), until about 11 or 11:30 a.m. Once the park becomes crowded around midday, meals and other breaks won't affect the plan's efficiency. If you intend to stay in the park for evening parades, fireworks, or other events, eat dinner early enough to be finished in time for the festivities.

Character Dining

A number of restaurants, primarily those that serve all-you-can-eat buffets and family-style meals, offer character dining. At character meals, you pay a fixed price and dine in the presence of one to five Disney characters who circulate throughout the restaurant, hugging children (and sometimes adults), posing for photos, and signing autographs. Character

5. **Milk shakes from Beaches & Cream at the Beach Club Resort** Hand dipped, thick, and creamy. When was the last time you sported a milk shake mustache? For large crowds, or large appetites, try the Kitchen Sink: a huge sundae consisting of mountains of ice cream and toppings that is actually served in a kitchen sink.

4. **Selma's cookies at the BoardWalk** Oddly enough, these are available at the candy store, Seashore Sweets, rather than at the BoardWalk Bakery (go figure), but they're worth tracking down for their rich, buttery, homemade taste.

3. **Ghirardelli Soda Fountain and Chocolate Shop at Downtown Disney Marketplace** Everything is good, and the atmosphere has a sophisticated ice-cream-shop–plus–coffee-bar vibe. *Very* San Fran.

2. **Zebra Domes at Animal Kingdom Lodge** Offered as a dessert on the Boma buffet, they're also available at the Mara food court, on the lower level of the resort near the pool. They consist of a layer of sponge cake topped with chocolate mousse, and then covered in white- and dark-chocolate ganache stripes. Fun and yum rolled into one!

And the number-one snack at the Walt Disney World Resort is . . .

1. **Two words: Dole Whip!** Available in Adventureland at the Magic Kingdom, a Dole Whip is a soft-serve pineapple–ice cream dream. Adding to the ecstasy, Dole Whips are also paired with pineapple juice in Dole Floats. Heavenly!

There's another goody that even trumps the Dole Whip, but Bob says we can't tell you. Maybe if you behave, we can slip it in at the end of the chapter.

Liliane

breakfasts, lunches, and dinners are served at restaurants in and out of the theme parks.

FAST FOOD IN THE THEME PARKS

BECAUSE MOST MEALS DURING a Disney World vacation are consumed on the run while touring, we'll tackle counter-service and vendor foods first. Plentiful in all theme parks are hot dogs, hamburgers, chicken sandwiches, green salads, and pizza. They're augmented by special items that relate to the park's theme or the part of the park you're touring. In Epcot's Germany, for example, counter-service bratwurst and beer are sold. In Frontierland in the Magic Kingdom, vendors sell smoked turkey legs. Counter-service prices are fairly consistent from park to park. Expect to pay the same for your coffee or hot dog at Animal Kingdom as at Disney's Hollywood Studios.

Getting your act together in regard to counter-service restaurants in the parks is more a matter of courtesy than necessity. Rude guests rank fifth among reader complaints. A mother from Fort Wayne, Indiana, points out that indecision can be as maddening as outright discourtesy, especially when you're hungry:

Every fast-food restaurant has menu signs the size of billboards, but do you think anybody reads them? People waiting in line spend enough time in front of these signs to memorize them and still don't have a clue what they want when they finally get to the order taker. If by some miracle they've managed to choose between the hot dog and the hamburger, they then fiddle around another 10 minutes deciding what size Coke to order. Tell your readers PULEEEZ get their orders together ahead of time!

A North Carolina reader on counter-service food lines:

[Many] counter-service registers serve two queues each, one to the left and one to the right of each register. People are not used to this and will instinctively line up in one queue per register, typically on the right side, leaving the left vacant. We had register operators wave us up to the front several times to start a left queue instead of waiting behind others on the right.

Healthful Food at Walt Disney World

One of the most commendable developments in food service at Disney World has been the introduction of healthier foods and snacks. People who are diabetic, vegetarian, or on a diet, or those who require kosher meals, should have no trouble finding something to eat. The same goes for anyone seeking wholesome, nutritious food. Health-conscious choices are available at most fast-food counters and even vendors. All the major theme parks, for example, have fruit stands.

Cutting Your Dining Time at the Theme Parks

Even if you confine your meals to vendor and counter-service fast food, you lose a lot of time getting food in the theme parks. At Walt Disney World, everything begins with a line and ends with a cash register. When it comes to fast food, *fast* may apply to the time you spend eating it, not the time invested in obtaining it.

Here are suggestions for minimizing the time you spend hunting and gathering food:

1. **Eat breakfast before arriving.** Don't waste touring time eating breakfast at the parks. Besides, restaurants outside the World offer some outstanding breakfast specials. Some hotels furnish small refrigerators in their guest rooms or offer to rent them. If you can get by on cold cereal, rolls, fruit, and juice, having a fridge in your room will save a ton of time. If you can't get a fridge, bring a cooler.

2. **Buy snacks from vendors** in the parks as you tour, or stuff some snacks in a hip pack. This is very important if you're on a tight schedule and can't spend a lot of time waiting in line for food.

3. **All theme-park restaurants are busiest** 11:30 a.m.–2:15 p.m. for lunch and 6–8:15 p.m. for dinner. For shorter lines and faster service, don't eat during these hours, especially 12:30–1:30 p.m.

4. **Many counter-service restaurants sell cold sandwiches.** Buy a cold lunch (except for drinks) before 11:30 a.m. and carry it until you're ready to eat. Ditto for dinner. Bring small plastic bags in which to pack the food. Purchase drinks at the appropriate time from any convenient vendor.

5. **Most fast-food eateries have more than one service window.** Regardless of time of day, check the lines at all windows before queuing. Sometimes a window that's manned but out of the way will have a much shorter line or none at all. Note, however, that some windows may not offer all items.

6. **If you're short on time** and the park closes early, stay until closing and eat dinner outside Disney World before returning to your hotel. If the park stays open late, eat dinner about 4 or 4:30 p.m. at the restaurant of your choice. You should miss the last wave of lunchers and sneak in just ahead of the dinner crowd.

Tips for Saving Money on Food

Every time you buy a soda at the theme parks, it's going to set you back about $3, and everything else from hot dogs to salad is comparably high. You can say, "Oh well, we're on vacation," and pay the exorbitant prices, or you can plan ahead and save big bucks. For comparison purposes, let's say that a family of two adults and two young teens arrives at Walt Disney World on Sunday afternoon and departs for home the following Saturday after breakfast. During that period the family eats six breakfasts, five lunches, and six dinners. What those meals cost depends on where and what they eat. It is possible for them to rent a condo and prepare all of their own meals, but they didn't travel all the way to Walt Disney World to cook. So, let's be realistic and assume that they will eat their evening meals out (which is what most families do, because, among other reasons, they're too tired to think about cooking). It may be just burgers or pizza, but they eat dinner in a restaurant.

That leaves breakfast and lunch to contend with. Here, basically, are the options. Needless to say, there are dozens of other various combinations. They could eat all of their meals in full-service restaurants, for example, but the bottom line is that most people don't, so we'll just keep this relatively simple.

1. Eat breakfast in their room out of their cooler or fridge and prepare sandwiches and snacks to take to the theme parks in their hip packs. Carry water bottles or rely on drinking fountains for water. Cost: $121 for family of four for 6 days (does not include dinners or food purchased on travel days).

2. Eat breakfast in their room out of their cooler or fridge, carry snacks in their hip packs, and buy lunch at Disney counter-service restaurants. Cost: $298 for family of four for 6 days (does not include dinners or food purchased on travel days).

3. Eat breakfast at their hotel restaurant, buy snacks from vendors, and eat lunch at Disney counter-service restaurants. Cost: $604 for family of four for 6 days (does not include dinners or food purchased on travel days).

In case you're wondering, these are the foods on which we've based our grocery costs for those options where breakfast, lunch, and/or snacks are prepared from the cooler:

Liliane

If you are an Entertainment Club member, don't forget to take your card and coupons for Orlando. Publix currently offers $5 off any purchase over $50.

BREAKFAST Cold cereal (choice of two), breakfast pastries, bananas, orange juice, milk, and coffee.

LUNCH Cold cuts or peanut butter and jelly sandwiches, condiments (mayo, mustard, and such), boxed juice, and apples.

SNACKS Packaged cheese or peanut butter crackers, boxed juice, and trail mix (combination of M&Ms, nuts, raisins, and so on).

If you opt to buy groceries, you can stock up on food for your cooler at the Publix at either the intersection of International Drive and US 192 or at the intersection of Reames Road and FL 535. There's also a Winn-Dixie on Apopka-Vineland Road about a mile north of Crossroads Shopping Center.

Projected costs for snacks purchased at the theme parks are based on drinks (coffee or sodas) twice a day and popcorn once each day. Counter-service meal costs assume basic meals (hot dogs, burgers, fries, and a drink). Hotel breakfast expense assumes eggs, bacon, and toast or pancakes with bacon and juice, milk, or coffee to drink.

DISNEY DINING SUGGESTIONS

BELOW ARE SUGGESTIONS FOR DINING at each of the major theme parks. If you are interested in trying a theme-park full-service restaurant, be aware that the restaurants continue to serve after the park's official closing time. We showed up at the Hollywood Brown Derby just as Disney's Hollywood Studios closed at 8 p.m. We were seated almost immediately and enjoyed a leisurely dinner while the crowds cleared out. Don't worry if you are depending on Disney transportation: Buses, boats, and monorails run 1–3 hours after the parks close.

The Magic Kingdom

Food at the Magic Kingdom seems to improve a little each year. The **Crystal Palace** at the end of Main Street offers a good (albeit pricey) buffet chaperoned by Disney characters, while the **Liberty Tree Tavern** in Liberty Square features hearty family-style dining. **Cinderella's Royal Table,** a fixed-price full-service restaurant on the second floor of the castle, features characters at all meals.

Authors' Favorite Counter-service Restaurants

Cosmic Ray's Starlight Café (limited kosher items) Tomorrowland
Pecos Bill Tall Tale Inn & Café Frontierland

Fast food at the Magic Kingdom is, well, fast food. It's more expensive, of course, than what you would pay at McDonald's, but what do you expect? It's like dining at an airport—you're a captive. On the positive side, portions are large, usually large enough for children to share. Overall, the variety of fast food offerings provides a lot of choice, though the number of selections at any specific eatery remains quite limited.

Epcot

From the beginning, dining has been an integral component of Epcot's entertainment product. The importance of dining is reflected in the number of restaurants and in their ability to serve consistently interesting and well-prepared meals. This is in stark contrast to the Magic Kingdom, where food service was once seemingly an afterthought, with quality and selection a distant runner-up to logistical efficiency.

For the most part, Epcot's restaurants have always served decent food, though the World Showcase restaurants have occasionally been timid about delivering an honest representation of the host nation's cuisine. While these eateries have struggled with authenticity and have sometimes shied away from challenging the meat-and-potatoes palate of the average tourist, they are bolder now, encouraged by America's exponentially expanding appreciation of ethnic dining. True, the less adventuresome can still find sanitized and homogenized meals, but the same kitchens will serve up the real thing for anyone with a spark of curiosity and daring.

Authors' Favorite Counter-service Restaurants

Kringla Bakeri og Kafe Norway	Sunshine Seasons The Land
Sommerfest Germany	Yakitori House Japan

Many Epcot restaurants are overpriced, most conspicuously the **Coral Reef** (The Seas). Representing relatively good value through the combination of ambience and well-prepared food are **Biergarten** (Germany) and **Restaurant Marrakesh** (Morocco). Biergarten and Restaurant Marrakesh also have entertainment.

If you want to sample the ethnic foods of World Showcase without eating in restaurants requiring Advance Reservations, we recommend these counter-service specialties:

France Boulangerie Patisserie, for French pastries

Germany Sommerfest, for bratwurst and Beck's beer

Japan Yakitori House, for yakitori (meat or vegetables on skewers)

Morocco Tangierine Café, for hummus, tabbouleh, and lamb

Norway Kringla Bakeri og Kafe, for pastries, open-face sandwiches, and Ringnes beer (our favorite)

United Kingdom Rose & Crown Pub, for Guinness, Harp, and Bass beers and ales

Disney's Hollywood Studios

Dining at Disney's Hollywood Studios is more interesting than in the Magic Kingdom and less ethnic than at Epcot. The Studios has five restaurants where Advance Reservations are recommended: the **Hollywood Brown Derby, 50's Prime Time Café, Sci-Fi Dine-In Theater Restaurant, Mama Melrose's Ristorante Italiano,** and the **Hollywood & Vine** cafeteria. The upscale Brown Derby is by far the best restaurant at the Studios. For simple Italian food, including pizza, Mama Melrose's is fine. Just don't expect anything fancy. At the Sci-Fi Dine-In, you eat in little cars at a simulated drive-in movie of the 1950s. Though you won't find a more entertaining restaurant in Walt Disney World, the food is

Liliane

If visiting with small children, the lunch buffet at Hollywood & Vine in Disney's Hollywood Studios by far surpasses the offerings of The Crystal Palace buffet at the Magic Kingdom. We were surprised by the many healthy and tasteful dishes available at the Hollywood & Vine restaurant.

quite disappointing. Somewhat better is the 50's Prime Time Café, where you sit in Mom's kitchen of the 1950s and scarf down meat loaf while watching clips of vintage TV sitcoms. The 50's Prime Time Café is fun, and the food is a step up. The best way to experience either restaurant is to stop in for dessert or a drink 2:30–4:30 p.m. Hollywood & Vine features singing and dancing characters from *Disney Junior* during breakfast and lunch.

Authors' Favorite Counter-service Restaurants

ABC Commissary Commissary Lane   Fairfax Fare Sunset Boulevard

Backlot Express Echo Lane   Pizza Planet Streets of America

Animal Kingdom

Because touring the Animal Kingdom takes less than a day, crowds are heaviest 9:30 a.m.–3:30 p.m. Expect a mob at lunch and thinner crowds at dinner. We recommend you tour early after a good breakfast, and then eat a very late lunch or graze on vendor food. If you tour later in the day, eat lunch before you arrive, and then enjoy dinner in or out of the theme park.

The Animal Kingdom offers a lot of counter-service fast food but has converted **Tusker House** to a buffet-style restaurant and added **Yak & Yeti,** a table-service restaurant, in Asia. You will find plenty of traditional Disney theme-park food—hot dogs, hamburgers, deli sandwiches, and the like—in the Animal Kingdom, but even the fast food there is a cut above the average Disney fare. The third restaurant in the Animal Kingdom is the **Rainforest Cafe,** with entrances both inside and outside the theme park (you don't have to purchase theme-park admission, in other words, to eat at the restaurant). Unlike the Rainforest Cafe at the Downtown Disney Marketplace, the Animal Kingdom branch accepts Advance Reservations.

Although grilled meats are available, don't expect a broad choice of exotic dishes in the Animal Kingdom.

Authors' Favorite Counter-service Restaurants

Anandapur Local Foods Cafés Asia

Flame Tree Barbecue Discovery Island

The sit-down Yak & Yeti also serves above-average dishes from China, Thailand, Vietnam, and Japan.

READERS' COMMENTS ABOUT WALT DISNEY WORLD DINING

EATING IS A POPULAR TOPIC AMONG *Unofficial Guide* readers. In addition to participating in our annual restaurant survey, many readers like to share their thoughts with us. The following comments are representative of those we receive.

A reader from Glendale, Illinois, had a positive experience with Disney food, writing:

On the food: In general, we were pleasantly surprised. I expected it to be overpriced, generally bad, and certainly unhealthy. There were a lot of options—and almost all restaurants (including counter service) had generally good food and some healthy options. It is not the place to expect fine cuisine—and is certainly overpriced—but if you understand the parameters, you can eat quite well. One thing I appreciated

*was having a children's menu that did not consist only of hot dogs
and fries. My children ate well, and we were able to get them a good
variety of food—with plenty of fruits and vegetables.*

We've received consistent raves for Boma:

Boma (the African buffet at the Animal Kingdom Lodge) is terrific!

A Lombard, Illinois, mom underscores the need to make Advance
Reservations:

*Please stress that if you want a "normal" dining hour at a specific
restaurant, call them 90 or 60 days in advance—IT IS WORTH IT!
One reservation I wanted to change about 2 weeks before our arrival
date, and I had a choice of dinner times of either 7:45 or 9 p.m. (not
feasible with little ones).*

A Greenwood, Indiana, family had this to say:

*The food was certainly expensive, but contrary to many of the views
expressed in the* Unofficial Guide, *we all thought the quality was excellent. Everything we had, from chicken strips and hot dogs in the parks
to dinner at the Coral Reef, tasted great and seemed very fresh.*

A family from Youngsville, Louisiana, got a leg up on other guests:

The best thing we ate were the smoked turkey legs.

A mom from Aberdeen, South Dakota, writes:

*When we want great food, we'll be on a different vacation. Who
wants to waste fun time with the kids at a sit-down restaurant when
you know the food will be mediocre anyway?*

On the topic of saving money, a Seattle woman offered this:

*For those wanting to save a few bucks (or in some cases several
bucks), we definitely suggest eating outside WDW for as many meals
as possible. To keep down our costs, we ate a large breakfast before
leaving the hotel, had a fast-food lunch in the park, a snack later to
hold us over, and then ate a good dinner outside the park. Several
good restaurants in the area have excellent food at reasonable prices,
notably Café Tu Tu Tango and Ming [Court], both on International
Drive. We also obtained the* Entertainment Book *for Orlando, which
offers 50% off meals all over town.*

COUNTER-SERVICE RESTAURANT MINI-PROFILES

TO HELP YOU FIND PALATABLE FAST-SERVICE FOOD that suits
your taste, we have developed mini-profiles of Walt Disney World
theme-park counter-service restaurants. The restaurants are listed
alphabetically by theme park.

The restaurants profiled on the following pages are rated for quality and portion size (self-explanatory), as well as for value. The value
rating ranges A–F as follows:

A	=	Exceptional value, a real bargain
B	=	Good value
C	=	Fair value, you get exactly what you pay for
D	=	Somewhat overpriced
F	=	Significantly overpriced

MAGIC KINGDOM

Casey's Corner

QUALITY Good **VALUE B** **PORTION** Medium **LOCATION** Main Street, U.S.A.
READER-SURVEY RESPONSES 83% 👍 17% 👎 **DISNEY DINING PLAN** Yes

Selections Quarter-pound hot dogs, fries, corn dog nuggets, chili, Cracker Jacks, and brownies.

Comments A little pricey on the dogs and very crowded—keep walking.

Columbia Harbour House

QUALITY Fair **VALUE B** **PORTION** Medium **LOCATION** Liberty Square
READER-SURVEY RESPONSES 90% 👍 10% 👎 **DISNEY DINING PLAN** Yes

Selections Fried fish and shrimp; hummus and tuna-salad sandwiches; child's plate with mac and cheese, PB&J, chicken nuggets, or garden chicken salad with grapes; New England clam chowder; coleslaw; chips; fries; garden or BLT salad; chocolate cake, apple crisp, or strawberry yogurt.

Comments No trans fats in the fried items, and the soups and sandwiches are a cut above most fast-food fare. Upstairs seating is usually less hectic.

Cosmic Ray's Starlight Café

QUALITY Good **VALUE B** **PORTION** Large **LOCATION** Tomorrowland
READER-SURVEY RESPONSES 85% 👍 15% 👎 **DISNEY DINING PLAN** Yes

Selections Rotisserie chicken and ribs; turkey-bacon and vegetarian wraps; hot dogs; hamburgers, including veggie burgers; Greek salad; Caesar salad with chicken; chicken-noodle soup; chili-cheese fries; carrot cake, triple-chocolate cake, and no-sugar-added brownies for dessert. Kosher choices include a burger, chicken strips, and corned beef on rye.

Comments Big, noisy place. Inside tables usually available. Plenty of options, including kosher food. Generous toppings bar.

Friar's Nook

QUALITY Good **VALUE B** **PORTION** Medium–large **LOCATION** Fantasyland
READER-SURVEY RESPONSES Too New to Rate **DISNEY DINING PLAN** Yes†

†Premium and Platinum plans only

Selections Hot dogs, fries, and frozen drinks.

Comments Part of the Fantasyland expansion.

Golden Oak Outpost

QUALITY Good **VALUE** B+ **PORTION** Medium–large **LOCATION** Frontierland
READER-SURVEY RESPONSES 92% 👍 8% 👎 **DISNEY DINING PLAN** Yes

Selections Chicken nuggets, fried-chicken-breast sandwich, and vegetable or chicken flatbreads. Chocolate cake, carrot cake, and cookies.

Comments Entrées are served with apple slices or fries.

The Lunching Pad

QUALITY Good   VALUE B–   PORTION Medium   LOCATION Tomorrowland
READER-SURVEY RESPONSES 80% 👍   20% 👎   DISNEY DINING PLAN Yes

Selections Hot dogs, sweet cream-cheese pretzels, and frozen sodas.

Comments Smack in the middle of Tomorrowland, The Lunching Pad now serves "designer dogs": a Philly cheese-steak hot dog, a Coney Island dog, and a taco dog.

Pecos Bill Tall Tale Inn & Café

QUALITY Good   VALUE B   PORTION Medium–large   LOCATION Frontierland
READER-SURVEY RESPONSES 89% 👍   11% 👎   DISNEY DINING PLAN Yes

Selections One-third-pound Angus cheeseburger, barbecued-pork sandwich, veggie burgers, chicken wraps, chicken Caesar salad, taco salad, chili, child's plate with burger or salad with grilled chicken, fries and chili-cheese fries, strawberry yogurt, and carrot cake.

Comments Use the great fixin's station to garnish your burger. Combos come with fries or carrots.

The Pinocchio Village Haus

QUALITY Fair   VALUE C   PORTION Medium   LOCATION Fantasyland
READER-SURVEY RESPONSES 76% 👍   24% 👎   DISNEY DINING PLAN Yes

Selections Personal pizzas, chicken nuggets, Caesar salad with chicken, Mediterranean salad, meatball sub; kids' meals of pizza, mac and cheese, or PB&J; fries plain or with toppings.

Comments An easy stop for families in Fantasyland, but it's usually crowded and takes some patience. Consider Columbia Harbour House and Pecos Bill Tall Tale Inn & Café, both only a few minutes' walk away (and with better food).

Storybook Treats

QUALITY Good   VALUE B   PORTION Medium   LOCATION Fantasyland
READER-SURVEY RESPONSES 95% 👍   5% 👎   DISNEY DINING PLAN No

Selections Sundaes, including fudge brownie and strawberry shortcake; floats and shakes; cookies; drinks.

Comments An ice cream stop. Good options and decent value.

Tomorrowland Terrace Noodle Station

QUALITY Good   VALUE B   PORTION Medium–large   LOCATION Tomorrowland
READER-SURVEY RESPONSES 67% 👍   33% 👎   DISNEY DINING PLAN Yes

Selections They've added burgers, a fried-chicken sandwich, and a deli wrap sandwich to the Asian-inspired menu. There's also orange chicken with rice; beef and broccoli; tofu; Caesar salad with chicken; child's plate of chicken nuggets, beef and mac, mac and cheese, and PB&J sandwiches. Strawberry yogurt, chocolate cake, and carrot cake for dessert.

Comments Only open during busy park times.

Tortuga Tavern (open seasonally)

QUALITY Fair   VALUE B   PORTION Medium–large   LOCATION Adventureland
READER-SURVEY RESPONSES 85% 👍   15% 👎   DISNEY DINING PLAN Yes

Selections Beef taco salad, vegetarian or beef tacos, and quesadillas for kids.
Comments Large, shaded eating area.

EPCOT
Africa Coolpost

QUALITY Good	VALUE B–	PORTION Small	LOCATION Between Germany and China
READER-SURVEY RESPONSES 88%	12%	DISNEY DINING PLAN Yes	

Selections Hot dogs, ice cream (waffle cone), floats, sundaes, frozen slushes (frozen soda), coffee or tea, and draft Safari Amber beer ($6.25).
Comments Mainly prepackaged food for a quick drink or snack.

Boulangerie Patisserie

QUALITY Excellent	VALUE B	PORTION Small–medium	LOCATION France
READER-SURVEY RESPONSES 94%	6%	DISNEY DINING PLAN Yes	

Selections Coffee, croissants, pastries, chocolate mousse, sandwiches, baguettes, cheese plate, ham-and-cheese croissant, and quiche.
Comments There is always a crowd, savoring the French pastries, at this tucked-away spot. No indoor seating, but a few shaded outside tables.

La Cantina de San Angel

QUALITY Good	VALUE B	PORTION Medium–large	LOCATION Mexico
READER-SURVEY RESPONSES 77%	23%	DISNEY DINING PLAN Yes	

Selections Chicken and beef tacos, nachos, cheese empanada, guacamole and chips, churros, fruit Popsicles, and margaritas.
Comments The new Cantina is a popular spot for a quick meal, with 150 covered outdoor seats. Also new to the scene: a companion full-service restaurant, La Hacienda de San Angel.

Crêpes des Chefs de France

QUALITY Excellent	VALUE B+	PORTION Medium	LOCATION France
READER-RESPONSE SURVEYS 89%	11%	DISNEY DINING PLAN No	

Selections Crêpes with chocolate, strawberry, or sugar; vanilla and chocolate ice cream; specialty beer (Kronenbourg 1664); espresso.
Comments These crêpes rate high—even with French guests.

Electric Umbrella Restaurant

QUALITY Fair–good	VALUE B–	PORTION Medium	LOCATION Innoventions East
READER-RESPONSE SURVEYS 79%	21%	DISNEY DINING PLAN Yes	

Selections Bacon double cheeseburger; chicken nuggets with fries; Caesar and Greek salads; child's plate with cheeseburger, wrap, or chicken nuggets; fruit cups, cookies, cheesecake, no-sugar-added brownie.
Comments There's more-interesting fast food in the World Showcase.

Fife & Drum Tavern

QUALITY Fair	VALUE C	PORTION Large	LOCATION United States
READER-RESPONSE SURVEYS 74%	26%	DISNEY DINING PLAN Yes	

Selections Turkey legs, popcorn, pretzels, ice cream, smoothies, draft beer.
Comments Better for a cold drink or a quick snack than an actual meal. Seating is available in and around the Liberty Inn, behind the Fife & Drum.

Fountain View Ice Cream

QUALITY Fair	VALUE C+	PORTION Medium–large	LOCATION Future World West
READER-SURVEY RESPONSES 88%	12%	DISNEY DINING PLAN Yes	

Selections Ice cream cones, sundaes, floats, ice cream sandwiches, raspberry smoothies, frozen cappuccinos, soda, coffee, and tea.

Comments Good for a late-morning treat on a hot day. Long lines develop just after lunch and around dinner.

Kringla Bakeri og Kafe

QUALITY Good–excellent	VALUE B	PORTION Small–medium	LOCATION Norway
READER-SURVEY RESPONSES 94%	6%	DISNEY DINING PLAN Yes	

Selections Cakes and pastries; rice cream; sandwiches (club, ham and apple, salmon and egg, or roast beef); green salad; espresso, cappuccino, and imported beers (Carlsberg beer for $8).

Comments Delicious and different but pricey. Try the rice cream (not a typo, by the way). Shaded outdoor seating.

Liberty Inn

QUALITY Fair	VALUE C	PORTION Medium	LOCATION United States
READER-SURVEY RESPONSE 72%	28%	DISNEY DINING PLAN Yes	

Selections Bacon double cheeseburger; barbecued pork; hot dogs; veggie burgers; chicken nuggets; Caesar chicken salad; chili; iceberg wedge salad; child's plate of chicken nuggets, chicken wrap, or PB&J.

Comments The menu offers more than dogs and burgers; kosher items also available. Still, World Showcase has more-inspired selections.

Lotus Blossom Café

QUALITY Fair	VALUE C	PORTION Medium	LOCATION China
READER-SURVEY RESPONSE 62%	38%	DISNEY DINING PLAN Yes	

Selections Egg rolls, pot stickers, veggie stir-fry, sesame chicken salad, shrimp fried rice, orange chicken with steamed rice, and beef-noodle soup bowl. For kids, sweet-and-sour chicken.

Comments Middling, overpriced Chinese food.

Promenade Refreshments

QUALITY Fair	VALUE C	PORTION Large	LOCATION Between World Showcase Promenade
READER-SURVEY RESPONSES 88%	12%	DISNEY DINING PLAN Yes	

Selections Hot dogs, pretzels, popcorn, ice cream, and beer.

Comments Best for a quick snack, especially if you have a reservation at one of the World Showcase's full-service restaurants. Seating is limited to nonexistent—be prepared to walk and chew.

The Refreshment Port

QUALITY Good	VALUE B	PORTION Medium	LOCATION World Showcase
READER-SURVEY RESPONSES 96%	4%	DISNEY DINING PLAN Yes	

Selections Crispy fried shrimp or chicken with tostones (green plantains), beef or cheese empanada, frozen Bacardi mojito, iced lattes, and *dolce de leche* ice cream sundae.

Comments Latino-inspired quick service; great tastes for nibbling and sipping as you begin your walk around World Showcase.

Rose & Crown Pub

QUALITY Good	VALUE C+	PORTION Medium	LOCATION United Kingdom
READER-SURVEY RESPONSES 91%	9%	DISNEY DINING PLAN Yes	

Selections Fish-and-chips; Scotch egg (hard-boiled, wrapped in sausage, and deep-fried); corned-beef sandwich; English Bulldog (split sausage stuffed with mashed potatoes, bacon, and Irish Cheddar); Guinness, Harp, and Bass beers, as well as other spirits.

Comments The attractions here are the pub atmosphere and the draft beer. Outside the pub is Yorkshire County Fish Shop, which serves food to go. The full-service restaurant Rose & Crown Dining Room requires Advance Reservations.

Sommerfest

QUALITY Good	VALUE B-	PORTION Medium	LOCATION Germany
READER-SURVEY RESPONSES 90%	10%	DISNEY DINING PLAN Yes	

Selections Bratwurst and frankfurter sandwiches with kraut; soft pretzels; apple strudel; German wine and beer.

Comments Tucked in the entrance to the Biergarten restaurant, Sommerfest is hard to find from the street. Very limited seating. Not for picky eaters, but a good place to grab a cold brew and bratwurst.

Sunshine Seasons

QUALITY Excellent	VALUE A	PORTION Medium	LOCATION The Land Pavilion
READER-SURVEY RESPONSES 92%	8%	DISNEY DINING PLAN Yes	

Selections Comprises the following four areas: (1) wood-fired grills and rotisseries, with rotisserie half-chicken or slow-roasted pork chop and wood-grilled sustainable catch fish with sun-dried-tomato tapenade; (2) sandwich shop with made-to-order sandwiches such as oak-grilled veggie flatbread, Reuben panini, and turkey and cheese on focaccia; (3) Asian shop, with noodle bowls and various stir-fry combos; (4) soup-and-salad shop, with soups made daily and unusual creations such as seared tuna-noodle salad and roasted-beet-and-goat-cheese salad.

Comments Everything is prepared fresh. Perfect for picky eaters.

Tangierine Café

QUALITY Good	VALUE B	PORTION Medium	LOCATION Morocco
READER-SURVEY RESPONSES 92%	8%	DISNEY DINING PLAN Yes	

Selections Chicken and lamb *shawarma;* hummus; tabbouleh; lentil salad; couscous salad; chicken, lamb, and falafel wraps; olives; child's hamburger or chicken tenders with carrot sticks and apple slices and small beverage; Moroccan wine and beer; baklava.

Comments No belly dancers as at Restaurant Marrakesh, but the food here is authentic. The best seating is at the outdoor tables.

Yakitori House

QUALITY Excellent	VALUE B	PORTION Small–medium	LOCATION Japan
READER-SURVEY RESPONSES 85%	15%	DISNEY DINING PLAN Yes	

Selections Shogun combo meal with beef and chicken teriyaki, vegetables, and rice; beef curry; vegetable tempura with shrimp and udon noodles;

side salad; sushi; miso soup; green tea; sponge cake with ginger-flavored frosting; Kirin beer, sake, and plum wine.

Comments An easy place to explore new tastes. Limited seating.

Yorkshire County Fish Shop

QUALITY Good	VALUE B+	PORTION Medium	LOCATION United Kingdom
READER-SURVEY RESPONSE 93%	7%	DISNEY DINING PLAN Yes	

Selections Fish-and-chips, shortbread, and Bass Ale draft.

Comments There's usually a line for the crisp, hot fish-and-chips at this convenient fast-food window attached to the Rose & Crown Pub. Outdoor seating overlooks the lagoon.

ANIMAL KINGDOM

Anandapur Local Foods Cafés

QUALITY Fair	VALUE B	PORTION Large	LOCATION Asia
READER-SURVEY RESULTS 88%	12%	DISNEY DINING PLAN Yes	

Selections Crispy honey chicken with steamed rice, sweet-and-sour chicken, kung pao beef, Mandarin chicken salad, Asian chicken sandwich, egg rolls, and chicken fried rice. Kids' menu includes chicken bites or cheeseburger with applesauce and carrots.

Comments The crispy honey chicken is the best choice.

Flame Tree Barbecue

QUALITY Excellent	VALUE B–	PORTION Large	LOCATION Discovery Island
READER-SURVEY RESPONSES 93%	7%	DISNEY DINING PLAN Yes	

Selections Half slab St. Louis–style ribs; smoked half chicken; smoked-beef and -pork sandwiches; crisp green salad with barbecued chicken; fruit plate with honey yogurt; child's plate of baked chicken drumsticks or hot dog; fries, coleslaw, and onion rings; Key lime or chocolate mousse; Safari Amber beer, Bud Light, and wine.

Comments One of our favorites for lunch. Try the covered gazebo overlooking the water.

Kusafiri Coffee Shop

QUALITY Good	VALUE B	PORTION Medium	LOCATION Africa
READER-SURVEY RESPONSES 86%	14%	DISNEY DINING PLAN No	

Selections Fruit turnovers, Danish and other pastries, muffins, croissants, bagel with cream cheese, cookies, brownies, cake, fruit cup, yogurt, coffee, cocoa, and juice.

Comments A good early-morning sugar rush on the way to Kilimanjaro Safaris. Shares space with Tusker House; easy walk-up window.

Pizzafari

QUALITY Fair	VALUE B	PORTION Medium	LOCATION Discovery Island
READER-SURVEY RESULTS 84%	16%	DISNEY DINING PLAN Yes	

Selections Cheese, pepperoni, and veggie personal pizzas served with Caesar salad; grilled-chicken Caesar salad; antipasto salad; hot Italian-style sandwich; child's mac and cheese or cheese pizza; chocolate mousse or no-sugar-added strawberry parfait; beer and wine.

Comments A favorite with children. Hectic at peak mealtimes. The pizza is pretty unimpressive. Kosher menu is available.

Restaurantosaurus

QUALITY Good	VALUE B+	PORTION Medium–large	LOCATION DinoLand U.S.A.
READER-SURVEY RESPONSES 77%	23%	DISNEY DINING PLAN Yes	

Selections Cheeseburgers; shrimp po'boy; chicken nuggets; grilled-veggie sub; Dig Site Salad (romaine, beef chili, tortilla chips, corn relish, and Cheddar); chocolate mousse and cheesecake; child's cheeseburger or chicken nuggets; coffee, tea, and cocoa; apple and orange juice; beer.
Comments Fast food with a good toppings bar for the burgers.

Royal Anandapur Tea Company

QUALITY Good	VALUE B	PORTION Medium	LOCATION Asia
READER-SURVEY RESPONSES 98%	2%	DISNEY DINING PLAN No	

Selections Wide variety of hot and iced teas; lattes; coffee, espresso, and cappuccino; fruit and cheese Danishes; cookies.
Comments Halfway between Expedition Everest and Kali River Rapids, this is the kind of small, eclectic food stand unique to the Animal Kingdom that you wish could be found at other parks. Offers loose-leaf teas from Asia and Africa, many of which can be made either hot or iced.

Tamu Tamu

QUALITY Good	VALUE C	PORTION Large	LOCATION Africa
READER-SURVEY RESPONSES 81%	19%	DISNEY DINING PLAN No	

Selections Turkey and swiss on focaccia, tuna salad on pita, cheeseburgers on multigrain buns, and chocolate and vanilla shakes.
Comments Seating is behind building and could easily be overlooked.

DISNEY'S HOLLYWOOD STUDIOS

ABC Commissary

QUALITY Fair	VALUE B–	PORTION Medium–large	LOCATION Echo Lake
READER-SURVEY RESPONSES 67%	33%	DISNEY DINING PLAN Yes	

Selections Asian salad; chicken bleu sandwich; chicken curry; cheeseburgers with apple slices or fries; fried fish with apple slices or fries; child's chicken nuggets, cheeseburger, or ham-and-cheese wrap; chocolate mousse; no-sugar-added strawberry parfait; wine and beer.
Comments Indoors, centrally located, air-conditioned, and usually not too crowded. Hard to find. Offers kosher food.

Backlot Express

QUALITY Fair	VALUE C	PORTION Medium–large	LOCATION Echo Lake
READER-SURVEY RESPONSES 79%	21%	DISNEY DINING PLAN Yes	

Selections Burgers with fries or carrot sticks, Southwest salad with chicken, grilled turkey and cheese, chicken nuggets, hot dogs, grilled-vegetable sandwich, and desserts. For children, chicken nuggets or meaty macaroni. Soft drinks and beer.
Comments A big dining space that's often overlooked. Great burger-fixin's bar. Indoor and outdoor seating.

Fairfax Fare

QUALITY Fair	VALUE B	PORTION Medium–large	LOCATION Sunset Boulevard

READER-SURVEY RESPONSE 100% 👍 0% 👎 DISNEY DINING PLAN Yes

Selections Barbecue chicken and ribs, salads, hot dogs, and pulled pork sandwiches. For kids, peanut butter and jelly or mac and cheese.

Comments Breakfast options are limited but can be a good value when on the Disney Dining Plan, as most entrées cost $10–$14.

Min and Bill's Dockside Diner

QUALITY Fair	VALUE C	PORTION Small–medium	LOCATION Echo Lake

READER-SURVEY RESPONSE 81% 👍 19% 👎 DISNEY DINING PLAN No

Selections Italian sausage, chicken Caesar sandwich, frankfurter on a pretzel roll, shakes and soft drinks, beer, chips, and cookies.

Comments Walk-up window with limited outdoor seating.

Pizza Planet

QUALITY Good	VALUE B+	PORTION Medium	LOCATION Streets of America

READER-SURVEY RESPONSE 75% 👍 25% 👎 DISNEY DINING PLAN Yes

Selections Cheese, pepperoni, and vegetarian pizzas; meatball subs; salads; child's meatball sub or cheese pizza; cookies and crisped-rice treats.

Comments *The* place for pizza at the Studios.

Starring Rolls Cafe

QUALITY Good	VALUE B	PORTION Small–medium	LOCATION Sunset Boulevard

READER-SURVEY RESPONSES 87% 👍 13% 👎 DISNEY DINING PLAN Yes

Selections Giant deli sandwiches, salads, sushi, oversize pastries and desserts, and coffee.

Comments Open for breakfast on some mornings. Slowest service of any counter-service eatery.

Studio Catering Co.

QUALITY Good	VALUE B	PORTION Small–medium	LOCATION Sunset Boulevard

READER-SURVEY RESPONSES 87% 👍 13% 👎 DISNEY DINING PLAN Yes

Selections Grilled-veggie sandwich, grilled-turkey club, buffalo chicken sandwich, pressed Tuscan deli sandwich, chicken Caesar wrap, and Greek salad. PB&J and chicken nuggets for kids. The adjacent High Octane Refreshments serves cocktails, including a variety of margaritas.

Comments Good place for a break while your kids enjoy the Honey, I Shrunk the Kids playground. Shady outside seating.

Sunset Ranch Market

QUALITY Fair	VALUE B–	PORTION Medium–large	LOCATION Boulevard

READER-SURVEY RESPONSES 78% 👍 22% 👎 DISNEY DINING PLAN Yes

Selections Five restaurants in one location offering everything from smoked turkey legs, hot dogs, and beer at Toluca Legs; pizzas, hot Italian deli sandwiches, salads, and chocolate fudge cake at Catalina Eddie's; and veggie burgers, soups, and child's mac and cheese or chicken nuggets with grapes, carrot sticks, or applesauce at Rosie's.

Comments Seldom crowded; nearby picnic tables. Backlot Express is a better option than Rosie's for the same fare.

DISNEY'S FULL-SERVICE RESTAURANTS: A QUICK ROMP AROUND THE WORLD

DISNEY RESTAURANTS OFFER AN EXCELLENT (though expensive) opportunity to introduce young children to the variety and excitement of ethnic food. No matter how formal a restaurant appears, the staff is accustomed to wiggling, impatient, and often boisterous children. **Les Chefs de France** at Epcot, for example, may be the nation's only French restaurant where most patrons wear shorts and T-shirts and at least two dozen young diners are attired in basic black . . . mouse ears.

Almost all Disney restaurants offer children's menus, and all have booster seats and high chairs. They understand how tough it may be for kids to sit for an extended period of time, and waiters will supply little ones with crackers and rolls and serve your dinner much faster than in comparable restaurants elsewhere. Letters from readers suggest that being served too quickly is much more common than having a long wait.

> Bottom line: Young children are the rule, not the exception, at Disney restaurants.

Liliane

In **Epcot,** preschoolers most enjoy the **Biergarten** in Germany, **San Angel Inn** in Mexico, and **Coral Reef** in the Seas Pavilion in Future World. The Biergarten combines a rollicking and noisy atmosphere with good basic food, including roast chicken and German sausages; a German oompah band entertains. Children often have the opportunity to participate in Bavarian dancing. San Angel Inn is in the Mexican village marketplace. From the table, children can watch boats on Gran Fiesta Tour drift beneath a smoking volcano. With a choice of chips, tacos, and other familiar items, picky children usually have no difficulty finding something to eat. Be aware that the service is sometimes glacially slow. The Coral Reef, with tables beside windows looking into The Seas' aquarium, offers a colorful mealtime diversion for all ages. If your kids don't eat fish, Coral Reef also serves beef and chicken. The downside is that the food is extremely expensive. For a more affordable splurge, forget lunch or dinner and drop in during off-hours for one of the Coral Reef's decadent desserts. The San Angel Inn is likewise overpriced but not in the same league as Coral Reef. The Biergarten offers reasonable value, plus good food.

Cinderella's Royal Table in Cinderella Castle is the big draw in the **Magic Kingdom.** Interestingly, other Magic Kingdom full-service restaurants hold little appeal for children. For the best combination of food and entertainment, book a character meal at the **Liberty Tree Tavern** or **The Crystal Palace.**

At **Disney's Hollywood Studios,** all ages enjoy the atmosphere and entertainment at the **Sci-Fi Dine-In Theater Restaurant** and the **50's Prime Time Café.** Unfortunately, the Sci-Fi's food is close to dismal except for dessert, and the Prime Time's is uneven. Theme aside, children enjoy the character meals at **Hollywood & Vine,** and the pizza at **Mama Melrose's** never fails to please.

There are three full-service restaurants at the **Animal Kingdom**: the **Rainforest Cafe,** which is a great favorite of children; **Yak & Yeti,** a 300-seat table-service restaurant near Expedition Everest; and **Tusker House,** a buffet-style restaurant.

As you've undoubtedly noticed by now, Disney World is a trend-savvy place, and every market share has its niche. But Disney World is also about stars, fantasies, and meeting characters. So if you've become habituated to wood-fired pizza, the **California Grill** atop the Contemporary Resort will oblige. Great sushi can be had at **Teppan Edo** at Japan in Epcot and at **Kimonos** in the Swan. The best and biggest steaks are at **Shula's** in the Dolphin, **Le Cellier Steakhouse** of Canada, or the **Yachtsman Steakhouse** at the Yacht Club, albeit way overpriced. **Kouzzina** is a family-style eatery at Disney's BoardWalk that features celebrity chef Cat Cora's Mediterranean-style recipes. Epcot saw two additions as of fall 2010: In Italy **Via Napoli,** an authentic Neapolitan pizzeria, features wood-burning ovens and imports water from a source that most resembles the water in Naples, Italy, home of some of the world's best pizza dough. The 300-seat pizzeria is inspired by the Naples 45 pizzeria on East 45th Street in New York City and has both indoor and outdoor dining. In Mexico, popular **La Cantina de San Angel** expanded, adding a new full-service restaurant, **La Hacienda de San Angel** (dinner only), which together features 400 seats with alfresco seating for lunch and a perfect place for viewing *IllumiNations,* the nightly Epcot fireworks spectacular.

The **Planet Hollywood** at Downtown Disney (teens love it) famously belongs to and has memorabilia from the likes of Demi Moore, Bruce Willis, and Sylvester Stallone (and because this branch of the chain really looks like a planet, it becomes the "globe" entrance that matches Epcot's Spaceship Earth, which just goes to show you how big an attraction it is). The West Side has two other celebrity-connected restaurant-nightclubs: the **House of Blues,** a New Orleans–style nightspot partly owned by surviving Blues Brother Dan Aykroyd and James Belushi; and **Bongos,** a Cuban-flavored café created by Gloria Estefan and her husband, Emilio.

Not only film and sports stars but also Food Network and food-magazine stars have been enlisted in the Disney World parade. Paul Bocuse was one of the eponymous **Chefs de France** who designed the menu for that restaurant and the **Bistro de Paris** in Epcot (and now that the building actually has a kitchen rather than hauling in food from outside commissaries, it does them much more credit). Boston star chef Todd English created **bluezoo** for the Dolphin. California's Wolfgang Puck is so celebrity-kitchen conscious that the TV monitors at his café-plex in the West Side show not sports or movies but the cooks at work (a fad English has also adopted).

Celebrity status notwithstanding, neither Wolfgang Puck's Café nor the Estefans' Bongos have drawn much praise from diners, though bluezoo is very good (but also quite adult). The House of Blues, surprisingly enough, has done much better with its New Orleans–style jambalayas and gospel brunch.

If your kids haven't had their fill of robotic crocodiles, Abraham Lincolns, singing parrots, and the like, **T-REX** and Rainforest Cafe will serve up all they can handle. T-REX features animatronic dinosaurs and an occasional woolly mammoth, while Rainforest Cafe is stuffed with jungle critters. Both of course have gift shops. There are not one but two super-trendy Rainforest Cafe branches, one at the renovated Disney Village Marketplace and a super-theatrical version at the entrance to Animal Kingdom, where the decor and audio-animatronic elephants make it fit right into the scenery there. Not surprisingly in a place where the sky "rains" and the stars flicker overhead, more thought went into naming the dishes than perfecting the recipes.

If your kids prefer dinosaurs to pachyderms, try T-REX, which is located within spitting distance of the Rainforest Cafe and operated by the same folks. The food is better than Rainforest, and children go nuts about being surrounded by a life-size animatronic brontosaurus, triceratops, and such.

In fact, although Disney's official guides to Walt Disney World describe various restaurants as *delicious, delectable,* or *delightful*— George Gershwin, call your agent—the truth is that only perhaps a dozen of the nearly 100 full-service establishments are first-rate. And some of the most disappointing restaurants, in general, are the often attractive but commissary-bland ethnic kitchens.

Though a blessing in disguise to many children and picky eaters of all ages, most of the "ethnic" food at Walt Disney World is American-ized, or rather homogenized, especially at Epcot, where visitors from so many countries, as well as the United States, tend to have pre-conceived notions of egg rolls and enchiladas. **Teppan Edo** in the Japan Pavilion happens to be one of the better restaurants in the World, with pretty good teppanyaki (and good tempura next door)— but it specializes in a particularly Westernized form of Japanese cuisine, first produced in New York only about 30 years ago. The **Nine Dragons** restaurant in the China Pavilion has been seriously recon-ceived and now features not only quite satisfying dim sum but handmade noodles (taffy-pulled out in the dining room), a respect-able five-spiced fish, and really crisp vegetables. The **San Angel Inn** in the Mexico Pavilion is associated with the famous Debler family of Mexico City. And **Les Chefs de France/Bistro de Paris,** with executive chefs Paul Bocuse, Gaston LeNotre, and Roger Verge, is now a fairly serious destination—one with an old-world view.

The buffet at Norway's **Akershus** isn't bad, but it's stodgy, smoky, and cheese- and mayonnaise-heavy. (Frankly, if smoked meats are your thing, the smoked turkey legs from the carts, which are enough for at least two people and cost $7.59, are far better.)

Among the places the culinary staff actually recommends (off the record) are the classic-continental prix-fixe **Victoria & Albert's** at the Grand Floridian, where you pay $125 a head to have every waitress introduce herself as Vicky and all the waiters as Al; the **Flying Fish Café; Artist Point; Jiko; Sanaa; Citricos;** and the **California Grill,** which has one of only seven ultra-chic Tom Shandley soufflé ovens in the United States. All of the above are best reserved for a parents' night out.

Another thing: A lot of the food at Disney World, particularly the fast food, is not what you'd describe as healthy. (Funnel cakes? Happy Meals?) But this is an area that the parks have started to address. **Artist's Palette** at Saratoga Springs Resort and **Sunshine Seasons** in The Land Pavilion at Epcot have been reconceived as fast casual spots, where the food is prepared fresh, often when you order it, but can be carried out or taken to nearby tables. At Sunshine Seasons, there are four different fully staffed kitchens, one preparing entrée salads with seared tuna or roasted beets with goat cheese, as well as soups du jour; another stir-frying veggies and preparing Asian noodle soup; a third wood-grilling chicken and beef to be wrapped in grilled flatbread or salmon with pesto; and a fourth preparing deluxe focaccia sandwiches. Artist's Palette offers everything from French toast to individual wood-grilled pizzas to gourmet-prepared entrées for carryout. See the nice **Turf Club Bar & Grill** next door for roasted and grilled specialties.

And yes, OK, because you've been good, I'll tell you the one junk food to blow your calorie budget on: As you cross the bridge between Future World and the World Showcase in Epcot, there's a little wagon just to the right, toward Canada, that sells cones of glazed pecans called sticky beavers. Don't say we never spoiled you.

Beyond that, there are fruit stands and juice bars scattered around, veggie sandwiches and chili, wraps, rotisserie chicken, soft pretzels as well as the deceptively simple popcorn, baked potatoes (not, frankly, prepared with the apparent care of the turkey legs but about one-tenth the calories and salt), as well as the frozen fruit bars in the ice cream freezers and frozen yogurt or smoothies at the ice cream shops. Yes, it's hard, especially with all those fudge and cookie stands blasting chocolate at you, but stick to your guns. Look for the fruit markets in Liberty Square in the Magic Kingdom, on Sunset Boulevard in Disney's Hollywood Studios, and in the Harambe marketplace at Animal Kingdom.

MAGIC YOUR WAY DINING PLAN

THIS DINING PLAN PROVIDES for each member of your group, for each night of your stay, one counter-service meal, one full-service meal, and one snack at participating Disney dining locations and restaurants, including room service at some Disney resorts (type "Disney Dining Plan Locations 2011 [or 2012]" into your favorite Internet search engine to find sites with the entire list). For guests age 10 and up, the price is $46–$48 per night (varies seasonally); for guests ages 3–9, the price is $12–$13 per night, tax included. Children younger than age 3 eat free from an adult's plate.

The counter-service meal includes a main course (sandwich, dinner salad, pizza, or the like), dessert, and nonalcoholic drink, or a complete combo meal (a main course and a side dish—think burger and fries), dessert, and nonalcoholic drink, including tax. The full-service sit-down meals include a main course, dessert, a nonalcoholic drink, and tax. If you're dining at a buffet, the full-service meal includes the buffet, a nonalcoholic drink, and tax. The snack includes items normally sold from carts or small stands throughout the parks and resorts: ice cream, popcorn, soft drinks, fruit, chips, apple juice, and the like.

For instance, if you're staying for three nights, each member of your party will be credited with three counter-service meals, three full-service meals, and three snacks. All those meals will be put into an individual meal account for each person in your group. Meals in your account can be used on any combination of days, so you're not required to eat every meal every day. Thus, you can skip a full-service meal one day and have two on another day.

Disney's top-of-the-line restaurants (dubbed Disney Signature restaurants in the plan), along with all the dinner shows, count as two full-service meals. If you dine at one of these locations, two full-service meals will be deducted from your account for each person dining.

In addition to the preceding, the dining plan comes with several other important rules:

- Everyone staying in the same resort room must participate in the plan.

- Children ages 3–9 must order from the kids' menu, if one is available. This rule is occasionally not enforced at Disney's counter-service restaurants, enabling older children to order from the regular (adult) menu.

- In-room minibars are not included in the plan.

- Refillable mugs are only included in some of the dining plans, such as the Magic Your Way Quick Service Dining Plan.

- A full-service meal can be breakfast, lunch, or dinner. The greatest savings occur when you use your full-service meal allocations for dinner.

- The meal plan expires at midnight **on the day you check out** of the Disney resort. **Unused meals are nonrefundable.**

- The dining plan is occasionally unavailable when using certain room-only discounts.

QUICK SERVICE DINING PLAN This plan includes meals, snacks, and non-alcoholic drinks at most counter-service eateries in Walt Disney World. The cost is $35 per day for guests age 10 and up, $13 per day for kids ages 3–9. The plan includes two counter-service meals and two snacks per day, plus one refillable drink mug per person, per package (eligible for refills only at counter-service locations in your Disney resort), and 30 minutes of play at a Disney-resort arcade. The economics of the plan are difficult to justify unless you're drinking gallons of soda or coffee to offset Disney's inflated prices.

MAGIC YOUR WAY DELUXE DINING PLAN This one offers a choice of full-service or counter-service meals for three meals a day at any participating restaurant. In addition to the three meals a day, the plan also includes two snacks per day and a refillable drink mug. The

Deluxe Plan costs $79 for adults and $22 for children for each night of your stay. Cranking it up another notch, there are even more extravagant dining plans associated with Magic Your Way Premium and Platinum packages, both described a little later.

In addition to food, all the plans include deal sweeteners such as a free round of miniature golf, a certificate for a 5-by-10-inch print from Disney's PhotoPass, a sort of two-for-one certificate for use of Sea Raycers watercraft, a commemorative luggage tag, and such.

Disney ceaselessly tinkers with the dining plans' rules, meal definitions, and participating restaurants. For example, it's possible (though not documented) to exchange a sit-down-meal credit for a counter-service meal, although doing this even once can negate any savings you get from using a plan in the first place. Any Magic Your Way package that includes table-service dining can be upgraded—for a fee—to a Wine and Dine Plan, which includes one wine entitlement per night, per room.

In addition to ceaselessly tinkering with the plan and raising the prices, Disney also constantly cuts benefits. As of 2011, when redeeming your Quick Service credits for breakfast, you get one drink instead of two, so no more juice and hot beverage—you need to make a choice or pay additional.

THINGS TO CONSIDER WHEN EVALUATING THE PLUS DINING PLAN If you prefer to always eat at counter-service restaurants, you'll be better off with the Quick Service plan. Other poor candidates for the Plus plan include finicky eaters, light eaters, families who can't agree on restaurants, and those who can't get reservations at their first- or second-choice sit-down restaurants. It's usually not cost-effective during the holidays or summer either. In addition, if you have children age 10 and up, be sure that they can eat an adult-size dinner at a sit-down restaurant every night; if not, you'd probably come out ahead just paying for everyone's meals without the plan.

When the dining plan was first introduced, it included an appetizer and gratuity for each full-service meal, making it a pretty good deal; by our estimate, savings of up to 13% per person per day were possible in some of Disney's best restaurants. As a result, the dining plan was one of the most requested of Disney's package add-ons.

Alas, with the initial success of the plan, Disney saw an opportunity to make more money. In 2008, Disney eliminated the appetizer and gratuity from the plan, increasing the cost of a full-service meal by at least 15%–18% for the gratuity alone, and an additional 15%–20% per appetizer per person. (To be fair, many appetizers are large enough to share.) Some of the pricier entrées were modified or eliminated from menus.

If you decide to opt for the plan, keep in mind that skipping a single full-service meal during a visit of 5 or fewer days can mean the difference between saving and losing money. In our experience, having a scheduled sit-down meal for every day of a weeklong vacation can be mentally exhausting, especially for kids and teens. One option might be to schedule a meal at a Disney Signature restaurant, which requires two full-service credits. Because you have a full dinner credit for the day you check out, and because it's not likely that you'll still be around for dinner, you have an extra credit to use during your stay to dine in a signature restaurant without skipping a full-service meal one night.

Many of the most popular restaurants are fully booked as soon as their reservation window opens, so book your restaurants as soon as possible. Then decide whether the dining plan makes economic sense.

If you're making reservations at restaurants in Disney hotels other than your own, a car allows you to easily access all the participating restaurants. When you use the Disney transportation system, dining at the various Disney-resort restaurants can be a logistical nightmare. Those without a car may want to weigh the immediate services of a taxi (typically at $10–$12 each way across Disney property) versus a 45- to 60-minute trip on Disney transportation each way.

For an in-depth discussion of the various plans, including number-crunching (and even algebra!), visit **touringplans.com** (click "Dining" on the home page, then "Disney Dining Plan").

Readers who tried the Disney dining plan had varying experiences. A mother of two from Marshalltown, Iowa, volunteered this:

> *The dining plan is great in theory, but it had way too much food and used too much valuable park time for the table-service meals. We won't use it again.*

From a Minnesota family of three:

> *We purchased the basic Disney Dining Plan, and my wife and I were almost overwhelmed by the amount of food we received. I skipped a counter-service meal one day, which allowed my son to use [the meal credit] for breakfast from the resort food court the next day.*

A St. Louis family of three comments:

> *We purchased the dining plan and would never do it again. Far too expensive, far too much food, and then you have to tip on top of the expense. Additionally, table-service meals were hard to use for us, and reservations hard to obtain. Much easier to purchase what you want, where and when you want. (Intended to use a counter-service meal at McDonald's at Epcot for 12-year-old. Found out you had to get the large [nine-piece] nuggets, the large fries, a large drink, and a McFlurry in order to use the counter-service meal. Most adults I know wouldn't eat that much food, let alone a 12-year-old!) Food is a "gotcha" at Disney, but the dining plan proved to be a poor choice for us.*

A Toronto family says gratuities add up:

> *Families should be warned that tips in Disney table-service restaurants can add up quickly in a week. The tip for our party of five at Le Cellier alone was $45.*

A Belmont, Massachusetts, dad likes the Quick Service Dining Plan:

If you intend to eat Disney food, the counter-service meal plan is a good option. We didn't want the full plan because the restaurants seemed overpriced, and the necessity of reservations months in advance seemed crazy and a bar to flexibility. You get two counter-service meals (entrée/combo, dessert, drink) and two snacks (food item or drink) per person as part of the plan, and even though kids' meals are cheaper, there is no distinction when you order—kids can order (more-expensive) adult meals.

But a reader from The Woodlands, Texas, laments that the plan has altered the focus of her vacation:

For me, the Disney Dining Plan has taken a lot of the fun out of going to Disney World. No longer are we free to enjoy the parks and fit in meals as a secondary matter. Now, dining for each day must be planned months in advance, unless one is to eat just hot dogs, pizza, and other walk-up items. As heretical as it may sound, I'm actually less inclined to go to WDW now. I want to have fun. I don't want to be locked into a tight schedule, always worrying about where we need to be when it's time to eat. I don't want to eat when I'm not hungry just because I have a reservation somewhere. Eating has become the primary consideration at WDW, not the parks and entertainment.

Along similar lines, a Bethany, Connecticut, dad adds this:

We took the dining plan and were disappointed. It was a lot of work to coordinate. We made travel plans 6 weeks prior to departure and were unable to procure reservations in our favorite restaurants (or they were at inconvenient times—9:50 p.m. at Boma).

A Midland Park, New Jersey, family of four says ditto:

With so many people now using the dining plan, it seems that if you were to book a last-minute trip or miss one of your reservations, you might not be able to get a table-service meal at all—reservations were hard to come by, even though I called 2 months before our trip!

A mom from Orland Park, Illinois, comments on the difficulty of getting Advance Reservations:

I purchased the dining plan for this trip and must say I will never do that again. It's impossible to get table reservations anywhere good— the [restaurants] that are available are available for a reason. We found ourselves taking whatever was open and were unhappy with every sit-down meal we had, except for lunch at Liberty Tree Tavern. I do not enjoy planning my day exclusively around eating at a certain restaurant at a certain time, but that is what you must do 6 months in advance if you want to eat at a good sit-down restaurant in Disney. That is ridiculous.

As this reader from San Jose, California, explains, guests who are not on the dining plan need to know how the plan has affected obtaining Advance Reservations:

> *The Disney Dining Plan has almost eliminated any chance of spontaneity when visiting any of the sit-down restaurants. When planning 90 days out for the off-season, I was told by the Disney rep to make all my priority-seating reservations then because the restaurants are booked by people on the dining plan. In fact, I was told that most of the sit-down restaurants don't even take walk-ins anymore. Sure enough, even though I was well over 90 days away from my vacation, a lot of my restaurant choices were unavailable. I had to rearrange my entire schedule to fit the open slots at the restaurants I didn't want to miss.*

We should add to this discussion that during the recession and now in its aftermath, Disney lures guests to Walt Disney World by including the dining plan free with certain vacation packages. This vastly increases the number of people on the dining plan and makes getting Advance Reservations much more difficult.

Pesky Technicalities and Administrative Problems

Readers report experiencing a host of problems with both understanding and using the Disney Dining Plan. A dad from Tonawanda, New York, opines:

> *The dining plan is great, but unfortunately, not enough guests actually read the literature about it and become confused, leading to long, slow lines at some counter-service locations.*

A family of four from Mount Pleasant, South Carolina, observes:

> *The impact of the Disney Dining Plan was amazing. It created longer lines at the registers because they were programmed to ring up each thing individually, or so it seemed. For instance, for a Mickey Meal, the checkout guy had to push buttons for chicken nuggets, applesauce, milk, and fries—not just one button for the entire meal. It took the guy about 7 minutes to figure it and process us.*

A woman from Atco, New Jersey, warns:

> *The Disney Dining Plan does not always work for snacks, even though vendors have signs posted stating they accept the card. We were told many times, "Oh, the machine isn't working today."*

An Atlanta reader has this to say:

> *The downside to our stay was [using credits] at the fast-food counter at Coronado Springs. I thought I was prepared. . . . not! Servers didn't seem to know what was included as a snack or what comprised a meal with the dining plan. It was a very frustrating experience. We spent the majority of our [credits] at the parks or other resorts.*

Many families purchase the dining plan without understanding how limited the menu choices are for kids age 9 and under. First from a Westchester, Ohio, mom:

We had only one complaint in our 6 days there, and that was with the Disney Dining Plan. All three of our girls are under 9 and had to choose Kid's Picks wherever offered. We did not come across any offerings like hamburgers, hot dogs, or pizza the whole time we were there. My kids couldn't even get pizza at Pizzafari in Animal Kingdom! They were so sick of mac and cheese and chicken nuggets after day two that going out to eat wasn't that exciting for them. We were given a hard time by food-service workers when we asked about substituting something different, and we were turned down 50% of the time. On our last day, a sympathetic employee told us we could get any counter-service food we wanted and just not tell the cashier that it was for a child (apparently, for counter service, Disney doesn't keep track of whether it is for an adult or child). It did work for us on that last day, but I wish we would have known that sooner. Hope this info will help some families with young kids.

A Pittsburgh mother of three recounts a similar experience:

My two kids were actually sick of eating macaroni and cheese and chicken fingers. The amount of food they get is also very small—OK for my 4-year-old but not for my 9-year-old, who ended up eating off my plate; otherwise, I would have had to buy something extra to fill him up. Plus, we went to a pizza place in Animal Kingdom park, and there was NO pizza on the [dining plan's] kids' menu. No pizza at a pizza place?

From a Midwestern reader:

We could almost relate our dining experience to that of a person who receives food stamps—very restricted and always at the mercy of someone else for food selection. We spent close to $1,000 on food and were extremely frustrated with the entire experience. I would prefer to be able to eat whatever I want rather than be restricted to certain food items at certain places.

From a Wisconsin father of two:

On the last day of our visit, we were still learning about acceptable substitutions. For example, you can have two drinks for lunch, but you have to give up your dessert. In the 90° heat, I would have gladly given up my fattening dessert to have a bottle of cold water to bring along.

The dining plan left a family of five from Nashville, Tennessee, similarly dazed and confused:

What was annoying was the inconsistency. You can get a 16-ounce chocolate milk on the kids' plan but only 8 ounces of white milk at many places. At the Earl of Sandwich, you can get 16 ounces of either kind. A pint of milk would count as a snack (price $1.52), but they wouldn't count a quart of milk (price $1.79) because it wasn't a single serving. However, in Animal Kingdom, my husband bought a water-bottle holder (price $3.75) and used a snack credit. The kids choices' were limited as well, maybe one or two per restaurant.

Readers also report difficulties in keeping their accounts straight. A Saskatoon, Saskatchewan, father of three says you have to watch vendors like a hawk:

We had a problem with a vendor who charged us meal service for each of the ice cream bars we purchased. This became evident at our final sit-down meal, when we didn't have any meal vouchers left. Check the receipts after every purchase!

A Havre de Grace, Maryland, mom had a similar experience:

I did want to tell you that we used the dining plan and found it to be not at all user-friendly. There was a lot of confusion on how many meals were on which card, and each place charged differently. It was very frustrating to use. Anyone else using this plan should make sure they put the correct number of meals on the correct cards.

A mom from Shawnee, Kansas, found the dining plan too complex on the restaurants' end:

A comment on Disney Dining—a great savings for us, but it seems like it was tough on the servers at the restaurants. It always took FOREVER for everything to be settled. They just seemed to really dislike dealing with the plan.

Reader Tips for Getting the Most Out of the Plan

A mom from Radford, Virginia, shares this tip:

If you eat a late lunch (where, by the way, they feed you the same ungodly amount of food), you WILL NOT be hungry for dinner. Also, depending on where you go, different Disney employees give you different answers on what counts as a snack. One employee told us anything under $5, and another one said anything under $3. Hint: *Use the snacks as your breakfast once you get in the park—we did this the last 2 days and it worked out great!*

A mom from Overland Park, Kansas, who has children with dietary restrictions submitted this comment:

Our children are allergic to dairy products, and I found the staff were pretty willing to provide a nondairy dessert option so the kids didn't feel left out.

Magic Your Way Premium Package

With the Magic Your Way Premium Package you get lodging; Magic Your Way Premium tickets with Park Hopping and Plus Pack features; breakfast, lunch, and dinner, including character meals and dinner shows; unlimited golf, tennis, fishing excursions, and water sports; select theme-park tours; **Cirque du Soleil** show tickets; unlimited use of child-care facilities—everything you can think of except for alcoholic beverages. (*Note:* The length of the Magic Your Way Premium Package must equal the total number of nights you stay at a Disney resort, plus 1 day. Package length cannot be customized to fit your touring plans.) The premium package costs $165 for adults and $114 for kids ages 3–9, plus the cost of the standard Magic Your Way package.

Disney, needless to say, has built a nice profit into every component of the Magic Your Way Premium Package. If you don't use all features of the plan and did not purchase the No Expiration option on your tickets, Disney makes out even better.

PLATINUM PACKAGE REPRISE The favorite of high rollers who want to prepay for everything they might desire while at Walt Disney World, the Platinum Package gets you lodging; tickets; breakfast, lunch, and dinner in full-service restaurants; unlimited golf, tennis, boating, and recreation; unlimited dinner shows and character breakfasts; primo Cirque du Soleil seats; private in-room child care; unlimited use of child-care facilities; personalized itinerary planning; dinner at Victoria & Albert's restaurant; a spa treatment; a fireworks cruise; admission to select tours; reserved seating for *Fantasmic!*; and (here's the kicker) nightly turndown service! Everything you can think of, in other words, except alcoholic beverages. Per diem prices for the Platinum Package are $220 for adults and $155 for kids in addition to the cost of a standard Magic Your Way package—but anyone who buys this package doesn't really care what the prices are anyway.

NUMBER CRUNCHING

COMPARING A MAGIC YOUR WAY PACKAGE with purchasing the package components separately is a breeze.

1. Pick a Disney resort and decide how many nights you want to stay.

2. Next, work out a rough plan of what you want to do and see, so you can determine the admission passes you'll require.

3. When you're ready, call the Disney Reservations Center (DRC) at ☎ 407-934-7639 and price a Magic Your Way package with tax for your selected resort and dates. The package will include both admissions and lodging. It's also a good idea to get a quote from a Disney-savvy travel agent.

4. Now, to calculate the costs of buying your accommodations and admission passes separately, call the DRC a second time. This time, price a room-only rate for the same resort and dates. Be sure to ask about the availability of any special deals. While you're still on the line, obtain the prices, with tax, for the admissions you require. If you're not sure which of the various admission options will best serve you, consult our free Admissions Option analyzer at **touringplans.com.**

5. Add the room-only rates and the admission prices. Compare this sum to the DRC quote for the Magic Your Way package.

6. Check for deals and discounts for packages, room-only rates, and admission.

When you upgrade to a Magic Your Way Premium Package, you load the plan with so many features that it's extremely difficult to price them individually. For a rough comparison, price the plan of your choice using the previous steps. To complete the picture, work up a dining budget, excluding alcohol. Add your estimated dining costs to the room-only quote and admissions quote, and compare this to the price of the plan.

THROW ME A LINE!

IF YOU BUY A VACATION PACKAGE FROM DISNEY, don't expect reservationists to offer suggestions or to help you sort out your options. Generally, they respond only to your specific questions, ducking queries that require an opinion. A reader from North Riverside, Illinois, complains:

I have received various pieces of literature from WDW, and it is very confusing to figure out everything. My wife made two telephone calls, and the representatives from WDW were very courteous. However, they only answered the questions posed and were not eager to give advice on what might be most cost-effective. [The] WDW reps would not say if we would be better off doing one thing over the other. I feel a person could spend 8 hours on the phone with WDW reps and not have any more input than you get from reading the literature.

If you can't get the information that you need from Disney, contact a good travel agent. Chances are that the agent can help you weigh all of your options.

PURCHASING ROOM-ONLY PLUS PASSES VERSUS A PACKAGE

*Sue Pisaturo of Small World Vacations (**smallworldvacations.com**), a travel agency that specializes in Disney, also thinks there is more involved in a package-purchase decision than money. Her suggestions follow.*

Should you purchase a Walt Disney World package or buy all the components of the package separately? There's no single answer to this confusing question.

A Walt Disney World package can be compared to a store-bought prepackaged kids' meal, the kind with the little compartments filled with meat, cheese, crackers, drink, and dessert: You just grab the package and go. It's easy, and if it's on sale, why bother doing it yourself? If it's not on sale, it still may be worth the extra money for convenience.

Purchasing the components of your vacation separately is like buying each of the meal's ingredients, cutting them up into neat piles and packaging the lunch yourself. Is it worth the extra time and effort to do it this way? Will you save money if you do it this way?

You have two budgets to balance when you plan your Disney World vacation: time and money. Satisfying both is your ultimate goal. Research and planning are paramount to realizing your Disney vacation dreams. Create your theme-park touring plan prior to making a final decision with regard to the number of days and options on your theme-park passes. Create your dining itinerary (along with advance dining reservations, if possible) to determine if Disney's dining plan can save you some money.

CHARACTER DINING

ALL THE RAGE AT WALT DISNEY WORLD for more than a decade, character dining combines a meal with meeting the characters. The characters circulate throughout the meal, stopping at each table to sign autographs, pose for photos, and lavish attention on mostly adoring (but sometimes stupefied) children. For a detailed description of this Disney ritual, see pages 249–257.

WALT DISNEY WORLD RESTAURANTS: RATED AND RANKED

STAR RATING The star rating represents the entire dining experience: style, service, and ambience, in addition to taste, presentation, and quality of food. Five stars is the highest rating and indicates that the restaurant offers the best of everything. Four-star restaurants are above average, and three-star restaurants offer good, though not necessarily memorable, meals. Two-star restaurants serve mediocre fare, and one-star restaurants are below average. Our star ratings don't correspond to ratings awarded by AAA, Mobil, Zagat, or other restaurant reviewers.

COST RANGE The next rating tells how much a complete meal will cost. We include a main dish with vegetable or side dish and a choice of soup or salad. Appetizers, des-

Inexpensive	$12 or less per person
Moderate	$13–$23 per person
Expensive	More than $23 per person

serts, drinks, and tips aren't included. We've rated the cost as inexpensive, moderate, or expensive.

QUALITY RATING The food quality is rated on a scale of one to five stars, five being the best rating attainable. The quality rating is based on the taste, freshness of ingredients, preparation, presentation, and creativity of food served. There is no consideration of price. If you are a person who wants the best food available and cost is not an issue, you need look no further than the quality ratings.

VALUE RATING If, on the other hand, you are looking for both quality and value, then you should check the value rating, expressed as stars.

★★★★★	Exceptional value, a real bargain
★★★★	Good value
★★★	Fair value, you get exactly what you pay for
★★	Somewhat overpriced
★	Significantly overpriced

Walt Disney World Restaurants by Cuisine

RATING CUISINE	LOCATION	OVERALL RATING	COST	QUALITY RATING	VALUE RATING
AFRICAN					
Jiko— The Cooking Place	Animal Kingdom Lodge	★★★★½	Exp	★★★★½	★★★½
Boma— Flavors of Africa	Animal Kingdom Lodge	★★★★	Exp	★★★★	★★★★½
Tusker House Restaurant	Animal Kingdom	★½	Mod	★	★★
AMERICAN					
California Grill	Contemporary	★★★★½	Exp	★★★★½	★★★
The Hollywood Brown Derby	DHS	★★★★	Exp	★★★★	★★★
Artist Point	Wilderness Lodge	★★★½	Exp	★★★★	★★★
Cape May Café	Beach Club	★★★½	Mod	★★★½	★★★★
Whispering Canyon Café	Wilderness Lodge	★★★	Mod	★★★½	★★★★
Captain's Grille	Yacht Club	★★★	Mod	★★★½	★★★
The Crystal Palace	Magic Kingdom	★★★	Mod	★★★½	★★★
House of Blues	West Side	★★★	Mod	★★★½	★★★
50's Prime Time Café	DHS	★★★	Mod	★★★	★★★
Liberty Tree Tavern	Magic Kingdom	★★★	Mod	★★★	★★★
Cinderella's Royal Table	Magic Kingdom	★★★	Exp	★★★	★★
T-REX	Downtown Disney	★★★	Mod	★★	★★
The Wave . . . of American Flavors	Contemporary	★★★	Mod	★★	★★
ESPN Club	BoardWalk	★★½	Mod	★★★	★★★
ESPN Wide World of Sports Café	ESPN Wide World of Sports Complex	★★½	Mod	★★★	★★★
Hollywood & Vine	DHS	★★½	Mod	★★★	★★★
1900 Park Fare	Grand Floridian	★★½	Mod	★★★	★★★
Chef Mickey's	Contemporary	★★½	Exp	★★★	★★★
Boatwrights Dining Hall	Port Orleans	★★½	Mod	★★★	★★
Grand Floridian Café	Grand Floridian	★★½	Mod	★★★	★★
Beaches & Cream Soda Shop	Beach Club	★★½	Inexp	★★½	★★½
Sand Trap Bar & Grill	Osprey Ridge Golf Course	★★½	Mod	★★½	★★½
Planet Hollywood	West Side	★★½	Mod	★★	★★
Rainforest Cafe	Downtown Disney & Animal Kingdom	★★½	Mod	★★	★★

Walt Disney World Restaurants by Cuisine

RATING CUISINE	LOCATION	OVERALL RATING	COST	QUALITY RATING	VALUE RATING
AMERICAN (CONTINUED)					
Garden Grove	Swan	★★	Mod	★★★	★★
Olivia's Cafe	Old Key West	★★	Mod	★★½	★★
Sci-Fi Dine-In Theater Restaurant	DHS	★★	Mod	★★½	★★
The Garden Grill Restaurant	Epcot	★★	Exp	★★	★★★
Big River Grille & Brewing Works	BoardWalk	★★	Mod	★★	★★
The Fountain	Dolphin	★★	Mod	★★	★★
The Plaza Restaurant	Magic Kingdom	★★	Mod	★★	★★
Trail's End Restaurant	Fort Wilderness Resort	★★	Mod	★★	★★
Turf Club Bar & Grill	Saratoga Springs	★★	Mod	★★	★★
Wolfgang Puck Grand Café	West Side	★★	Exp	★½	★½
LakeView Restaurant	Wyndham LBV	★★	Mod	★	★★★
Tusker House Restaurant	Animal Kingdom	★½	Mod	★	★★
Maya Grill	Coronado Springs	★	Mod	★	★
BUFFET					
Boma— Flavors of Africa	Animal Kingdom Lodge	★★★★	Exp	★★★★	★★★★½
Cape May Café	Beach Club	★★★½	Mod	★★★½	★★★★
Biergarten	Epcot	★★★½	Exp	★★★	★★★★
The Crystal Palace	Magic Kingdom	★★★	Mod	★★★½	★★★
Akershus Royal Banquet Hall	Epcot	★★★	Exp	★★★	★★★★
Hollywood & Vine	DHS	★★½	Mod	★★★	★★★
1900 Park Fare	Grand Floridian	★★½	Mod	★★★	★★★
Chef Mickey's	Contemporary	★★½	Exp	★★★	★★★
Garden Grove	Swan	★★	Mod	★★★	★★
Trail's End Restaurant	Fort Wilderness Resort	★★	Mod	★★	★★
Tusker House Restaurant	Animal Kingdom	★½	Mod	★	★★
CHINESE					
Nine Dragons Restaurant	Epcot	★★★	Mod	★★★	★★

CUISINE	LOCATION	OVERALL RATING	COST	QUALITY RATING	VALUE RATING
CUBAN					
Bongos Cuban Café	West Side	★★	Mod	★★	★★
ENGLISH					
Rose & Crown Dining Room	Epcot	★★★	Mod	★★★½	★★
FRENCH					
Bistro de Paris	Epcot	★★★	Exp	★★★½	★★
Les Chefs de France	Epcot	★★★	Exp	★★★	★★★
GERMAN					
Biergarten	Epcot	★★★½	Exp	★★★	★★★★
GLOBAL					
Paradiso 37	Downtown Disney	★★½	Inexp	★★★	★★★
GOURMET					
Victoria & Albert's	Grand Floridian	★★★★★	Exp	★★★★★	★★★★
INDIAN/AFRICAN					
Sanaa	Animal Kingdom Villas–Kidani Village	★★★★	Exp	★★★★	★★★★
IRISH					
Raglan Road Irish Pub & Restaurant	Downtown Disney	★★★★	Mod	★★★½	★★★

DISNEY BOOT CAMP:
Basic Training for World-bound Families

The **BRUTAL TRUTH** *about* **FAMILY VACATIONS**

IT HAS BEEN SUGGESTED THAT THE PHRASE *family vacation* is a bit of an oxymoron. This is because you can never take a vacation from the responsibilities of parenting if your children are traveling with you. Though you leave your work and normal routine far behind, your children require as much attention, if not more, when traveling as they do at home.

Parenting on the road is an art. It requires imagination and organization. Think about it: You have to do all the usual stuff (feed, dress, bathe, supervise, teach, comfort, discipline, put to bed, and so on) in an atmosphere where your children are hyperstimulated, without the familiarity of place and the resources you take for granted at home. Although it's not impossible—and can even be fun—parenting on the road is not something you want to learn on the fly, particularly at Walt Disney World.

The point we want to drive home is that preparation, or the lack thereof, can make or break your Walt Disney World vacation. Believe us, you do *not* want to leave the success of your expensive Disney vacation to chance. But don't confuse chance with good luck. Chance is what happens when you fail to prepare. Good luck is when preparation meets opportunity.

Your preparation can be organized into several categories, all of which we will help you undertake. Broadly speaking, you need to prepare yourself and your children mentally, emotionally, physically, organizationally, and logistically. You also need a basic understanding of Walt Disney World and a well-considered plan for how to go about seeing it.

MENTAL *and* EMOTIONAL PREPARATION

THIS IS A SUBJECT THAT WE WILL TOUCH on here and return to many times in this book. Mental preparation begins with realistic expectations about your Disney vacation and consideration of what each adult and child in your party most wants and needs from their Walt Disney World experience. Getting in touch with this aspect of planning requires a lot of introspection and good, open family communication.

DIVISION OF LABOR

TALK ABOUT WHAT YOU AND YOUR PARTNER NEED and what you expect to happen on the vacation. This discussion alone can preempt some unpleasant surprises mid-trip. If you are a two-parent (or two-adult) family, do you have a clear understanding of how the parenting workload is to be distributed? We have seen some distinctly disruptive misunderstandings in two-parent households where one parent is (pardon the legalese) the primary caregiver. Often, the other parent expects the primary caregiver to function on vacation as she (or he) does at home. The primary caregiver, on the other hand, is ready for a break. She expects her partner to either shoulder the load equally or perhaps even assume the lion's share so she can have a *real* vacation. However you divide the responsibility, of course, is up to you. Just make sure you negotiate a clear understanding *before* you leave home.

TOGETHERNESS

ANOTHER DIMENSION TO CONSIDER is how much togetherness seems appropriate to you. For some parents, a vacation represents a rare opportunity to really connect with their children, to talk, exchange ideas, and get reacquainted. For others, a vacation affords the time to get a little distance, to enjoy a round of golf while the kids are participating in a program organized by the resort.

At Walt Disney World you can orchestrate your vacation to spend as much or as little time with your children as you desire, but more about that later. The point here is to think about your and your children's preferences and needs concerning your time together. A typical day at a Disney theme park provides the structure of experiencing attractions together, punctuated by periods of waiting in line, eating, and so on, which facilitate conversation and sharing. Most attractions can be enjoyed together by the whole family, regardless of age ranges. This allows for more consensus and less dissent when it comes to deciding what to see and do. For many parents and children, however, the rhythms of a Walt Disney World day seem to consist of passive entertainment experiences alternated with endless discussions of where to go and what to do next. As a mother from Winston-Salem, North Carolina, reported:

*Our family mostly talked about what to do next with very little shar-
ing or discussion about what we had seen. [The conversation] was
pretty task oriented.*

Two observations: First, fighting the crowds and keeping the family moving along can easily escalate into a pressure-driven outing.
Having an advance plan or itinerary eliminates moment-to-moment
guesswork and decision making, thus creating more time for savoring
and connecting. Second, external variables such as crowd size, noise,
and heat, among others, can be so distracting as to preclude any
meaningful togetherness. These negative impacts can be moderated,
as previously discussed, by your being selective concerning the time of
year, day of the week, and time of day you visit the theme parks. The
bottom line is that you can achieve the degree of connection and
togetherness you desire with a little advance planning and a realistic
awareness of the distractions you will encounter.

LIGHTEN UP

PREPARE YOURSELF MENTALLY to be a little less compulsive on vacation about correcting small behavioral deviations and pounding home
the lessons of life. Certainly, little Mildred will have to learn eventually
that it's very un-Disney-like to take off her top at the pool. But there's
plenty of time for that later. So what if Matt eats hamburgers for breakfast, lunch, and dinner every day? You can make him eat peas and broccoli when you get home and are in charge of meal preparation again.
Roll with the little stuff, and remember when your children act out that
they are wired to the max. At least some of that adrenaline is bound to
spill out in undesirable ways. Coming down hard will send an already
frayed little nervous system into orbit.

SOMETHING FOR EVERYONE

IF YOU TRAVEL WITH AN INFANT, TODDLER, or any child who
requires a lot of special attention, make sure that you have some
energy and time remaining for your other children.
In the course of your planning, invite each child
to name something special to do or see at Walt Disney World with mom or dad alone. Work these
special activities into your trip itinerary. Whatever
else, if you commit, write it down so that you don't
forget. Remember, a casually expressed willingness
to do this or that may be perceived as a promise by
your children.

Try to schedule some
time alone with each of
your children, if
not each day,
then at least a
couple of times
during the trip.

Liliane

WHOSE IDEA WAS THIS, ANYWAY?

THE DISCORD THAT MANY VACATIONING FAMILIES experience
arises from the kids being on a completely different wavelength from
mom and dad. Parents and grandparents are often worse than children
when it comes to conjuring up fantasy scenarios of what a Walt Disney

World vacation will be like. A Disney vacation can be many things, but believe us when we tell you that there's a lot more to it than just riding Dumbo and seeing Mickey.

In our experience, most parents and nearly all grandparents expect children to enter a state of rapture at Walt Disney World, bouncing from attraction to attraction in wide-eyed wonder, appreciative beyond words of their adult benefactors. What they get, more often than not, is not even in the same ballpark. Preschoolers will, without a doubt, be wide-eyed, often with delight but also with a general sense of being overwhelmed by noise, crowds, and Disney characters as big as tool sheds. We have substantiated through thousands of interviews and surveys that the best part of a Disney vacation for a preschooler is the hotel swimming pool. With some grade-schoolers and pre-driving-age teens you get near-manic hyperactivity coupled with periods of studied nonchalance. This last,

Short forays to the parks interspersed with naps, swimming, and quiet activities such as *Liliane* reading to your children will go a long way toward keeping things on an even keel.

which relates to the importance of being cool at all costs, translates into a maddening display of boredom and a "been there, done that" attitude. Older teens are frequently the exponential version of the younger teens and grade-schoolers, except without the manic behavior.

As a function of probability, you may escape many—but most likely not all—of the above behaviors. Even in the event that they are all visited on you, however, take heart, there are antidotes.

For preschoolers you can keep things light and happy by limiting the time you spend in the theme parks. The most critical point is that the overstimulation of the parks must be balanced by adequate rest and more mellow activities. For grade-schoolers and early teens, you can moderate the hyperactivity and false apathy by enlisting their help in planning the vacation, especially by allowing them to take a leading role in determining the itinerary for days at the theme parks. Being in charge of specific responsibilities that focus on the happiness of other family members also works well. One reader, for example, turned a 12-year-old liability into an asset by asking him to help guard against attractions that might frighten his 5-year-old sister.

The more information your children have before arriving at Walt Disney *Liliane* World, the less likely they will be to act out.

Knowledge enhances anticipation and at the same time affords a level of comfort and control that helps kids understand the big picture. The more they feel in control, the less they will act out of control.

DISNEY, KIDS, AND SCARY STUFF

DISNEY ATTRACTIONS, BOTH RIDES AND SHOWS, are adventures. They focus on themes common to adventures: good and evil, life and

continued on page 190

Small-child Fright-potential Chart

This is a quick reference to identify attractions to be wary of, and why. The chart represents a generalization, and all kids are different. It relates specifically to kids ages 3–7. On average, children at the younger end of the range are more likely to be frightened than children in their sixth or seventh year.

The Magic Kingdom

MAIN STREET, U.S.A.

Main Street Vehicles   Not frightening in any respect.

Walt Disney World Railroad   Not frightening in any respect.

ADVENTURELAND

The Enchanted Tiki Room   A thunderstorm, loud volume level, and simulated explosions frighten some preschoolers.

Jungle Cruise   Moderately intense, some macabre sights. A good test attraction for little ones.

The Magic Carpets of Aladdin   Much like Dumbo. A favorite of young children.

Pirates of the Caribbean   Slightly intimidating queuing area; intense boat ride with gruesome (though humorously presented) sights and a short, unexpected slide down a flume.

Swiss Family Treehouse   May not be suitable for kids who are afraid of heights.

FRONTIERLAND

Big Thunder Mountain Railroad   Visually intimidating from outside, with moderately intense visual effects. The roller coaster is wild enough to frighten many adults, particularly seniors. Switching-off option provided (see page 242).

Country Bear Jamboree   Not frightening in any respect.

Frontierland Shootin' Arcade   Not frightening in any respect.

Splash Mountain   Visually intimidating from outside, with moderately intense visual effects. The ride culminates in a 52-foot plunge down a steep chute. Switching-off option provided (see page 242).

Tom Sawyer Island   Some very young children are intimidated by dark walk-through tunnels that can be easily avoided.

LIBERTY SQUARE

The Hall of Presidents   Not frightening, but boring for young ones.

The Haunted Mansion   Name raises anxiety, as do sounds and sights of waiting area. In attraction with humorously presented macabre sights. The ride itself is gentle.

Liberty Belle Riverboat   Not frightening in any respect.

FANTASYLAND

Dumbo the Flying Elephant A tame midway ride; a great favorite of most young children.

The Great Goofini May frighten some preschoolers.

It's a Small World Not frightening in any respect.

Mad Tea Party Midway-type ride can induce motion sickness in all ages.

The Many Adventures of Winnie the Pooh Frightens a small percentage of preschoolers.

Mickey's PhilharMagic Some preschoolers may be a little scared at first, but taking off the 3-D glasses tones down the effect.

Peter Pan's Flight Not frightening in any respect.

Prince Charming Regal Carrousel Not frightening in any respect.

Princess Fairytale Hall Not frightening in any respect.

Seven Dwarfs Mine Train Not open at press time.

Snow White's Scary Adventures Moderately intense spook-house-genre attraction with some grim characters. Absolutely terrifies many preschoolers. Ride to close sometime in 2012.

Under the Sea: Journey of the Little Mermaid Moderately intense effects; Ursula may frighten children under 7 years of age..

TOMORROWLAND

Astro Orbiter Visually intimidating from the waiting area, but the ride is relatively tame.

Buzz Lightyear's Space Ranger Spin Dark ride with cartoonlike aliens may frighten some preschoolers.

Monsters, Inc. Laugh Floor May frighten a small percentage of preschoolers.

Space Mountain Very intense roller coaster in the dark; the Magic Kingdom's wildest ride and a scary roller coaster by any standard. Switching-off option provided (see page 242).

Stitch's Great Escape! Very intense. May frighten children age 9 and younger. Switching-off option provided (see page 242).

Tomorrowland Speedway Noise of waiting area slightly intimidates preschoolers; otherwise, not frightening.

Tomorrowland Transit Authority PeopleMover Not frightening in any respect.

Walt Disney's Carousel of Progress Not frightening in any respect.

Small-child Fright-potential Chart (continued)

Epcot

FUTURE WORLD

Captain EO/Honey, I Shrunk the Audience   Extremely intense visual effects and loudness frighten many young children.

The Circle of Life   Not frightening in any respect.

Innoventions East and West   Not frightening in any respect.

Journey into Imagination with Figment   Loud noises and unexpected flashing lights startle younger children.

Living with the Land   Not frightening in any respect.

Mission: SPACE   Extremely intense space-simulation ride that has been known to frighten guests of all ages. Preshow may also frighten some children. Switching-off option provided (see page 242).

The "Mom, I Can't Believe It's Disney!" Fountain   Not frightening in any respect.

The Seas Main Tank and Exhibits   Not frightening in any respect.

The Seas with Nemo & Friends   Very sweet but may frighten some toddlers.

Soarin'   May frighten children age 7 and younger. Really a very mellow ride.

Spaceship Earth   Dark, imposing presentation intimidates a few preschoolers.

Test Track   Intense thrill ride may frighten any age. Switching-off option provided (see page 242).

Turtle Talk with Crush   Not frightening in any respect.

Universe of Energy: *Ellen's Energy Adventure*   Dinosaur segment frightens some preschoolers; visually intense, with some intimidating effects.

WORLD SHOWCASE

The American Adventure   Not frightening in any respect.

Germany   Not frightening in any respect.

Gran Fiesta Tour Starring the Three Cabelleros   Not frightening in any respect.

IllumiNations   Not frightening in any respect.

Impressions de France   Not frightening in any respect.

Italy   Not frightening in any respect.

Japan   Not frightening in any respect.

Kim Possible World Showcase Adventure   Not frightening in any respect.

Maelstrom Visually intense in parts; features trolls. Ride ends with a plunge down a 20-foot flume. A few preschoolers are frightened.

Morocco Not frightening in any respect.

O Canada! Not frightening in any respect, but audience must stand.

Reflections of China Not frightening in any respect.

United Kingdom Not frightening in any respect.

Disney's Hollywood Studios

The American Idol Experience At times, the singing may frighten anyone.

Beauty and the Beast—Live on Stage!/Theater of the Stars Not frightening in any respect.

Disney Junior—Live on Stage! Not frightening in any respect.

The Great Movie Ride Intense in parts, with very realistic special effects and some visually intimidating sights. Frightens many preschoolers.

Fantasmic! Terrifies some preschoolers.

Honey, I Shrunk the Kids Movie Set Adventure Not scary (though oversize).

Indiana Jones Epic Stunt Spectacular! An intense show with powerful special effects, including explosions, but young children generally handle it well.

Jedi Training Academy It does involve battle with Darth Vader, but the good guys always win; children typically love it.

Jim Henson's Muppet-Vision 3-D Intense and loud, but not frightening.

Lights, Motors, Action! Extreme Stunt Show Super stunt spectacular; intense with loud noises and explosions, but not threatening in any way.

The Magic of Disney Animation Not frightening in any respect.

Rock 'n' Roller Coaster The wildest coaster at Walt Disney World. May frighten guests of any age. Switching-off option (see page 242).

Sounds Dangerous with Drew Carey Noises in the dark frighten children as old as 8.

Star Tours: The Adventure Continues Extremely intense visually for all ages; too intense for children under age 8. Switching-off option (see page 242).

Streets of America Not frightening in any respect.

Studio Backlot Tour Sedate and nonintimidating except for Catastrophe Canyon, where an earthquake and a flash flood are simulated. Prepare younger children for this part of the tour.

Toy Story Mania! Dark ride may frighten some preschoolers.

Small-child Fright-potential Chart (cont'd)

Disney's Hollywood Studios (*continued*)

The Twilight Zone Tower of Terror Visually intimidating to young children; contains intense and realistic special effects. The plummeting elevator at the ride's end frightens many adults as well. Switching-off option (see page 242).

Voyage of the Little Mermaid Not frightening in any respect.

Walt Disney: One Man's Dream Not frightening in any respect.

Disney's Animal Kingdom

The Boneyard Not frightening in any respect.

Conservation Station and Affection Section Not frightening in any respect.

DINOSAUR High-tech thrill ride rattles riders of all ages. Switching-off option (see page 242).

Expedition Everest Frightening to guests of all ages. Switching-off option (see page 242).

Festival of the Lion King A bit loud but otherwise not frightening in any respect.

Flights of Wonder Swooping birds alarm a few small children.

Kali River Rapids Potentially frightening and certainly wet for guests of all ages. Switching-off option (see page 242).

Kilimanjaro Safaris A "collapsing" bridge and the proximity of real animals make a few young children anxious.

Maharajah Jungle Trek Some children may balk at the bat exhibit.

Pangani Forest Exploration Trail Not frightening in any respect.

Primeval Whirl A beginner roller coaster. Most children age 7 and older will take it in stride. Switching-off option (see page 242).

Theater in the Wild/*Finding Nemo—The Musical* Not frightening in any respect, but loud.

The Tree of Life/*It's Tough to Be a Bug!* Very intense and loud with special effects that startle viewers of all ages and potentially terrify young children.

TriceraTop Spin A midway-type ride that will frighten only a small percentage of younger children.

Wildlife Express Train Not frightening in any respect.

continued from page 185

death, beauty and the grotesque, fellowship and enmity. As you sample the attractions at Walt Disney World, you transcend the spinning and bouncing of midway rides to thought-provoking and emotionally powerful entertainment. All of the endings are happy, but the adventures' impact, given Disney's gift for special effects, often intimidates and occasionally frightens young children.

There are rides with burning towns and ghouls popping out of their graves, all done with a sense of humor, provided you're old enough to understand the joke. And bones. There are bones everywhere: human bones, cattle bones, dinosaur bones, even whole skeletons. There's a stack of skulls at the headhunter's camp on the Jungle Cruise, a platoon of skeletons sailing ghost ships in Pirates of the Caribbean, and a haunting assemblage of skulls and skeletons in The Haunted Mansion. Skulls, skeletons, and bones punctuate Peter Pan's Flight and Big Thunder Mountain Railroad. In the Animal Kingdom, there's an entire children's playground made up exclusively of giant bones and skeletons.

My first roller coaster experience was with my mom. We rode The Barnstormer at Goofy's Wiseacre Farm [a coaster for the under-7 crowd]—and she screamed my ears off. Next she took a ride with you know who: Bob. He somehow managed to get her on Idan The Incredible Hulk Coaster at Universal's Islands of Adventure. I can't begin to imagine what she must have said to him. [*Editor's Note:* Bob is still deaf in one ear.]

Monsters and special effects at Disney's Hollywood Studios are more real and sinister than those in the other theme parks. If your child has difficulty coping with the ghouls of The Haunted Mansion, think twice about exposing him or her to machine-gun battles, earthquakes, and the creature from *Alien* at the Studios.

One reader tells of taking his preschool children on Star Tours:

We took a 4-year-old and a 5-year-old, and they had the *^%#! scared out of them at Star Tours. We did this first thing in the morning, and it took hours of Tom Sawyer Island and Small World to get back to normal.

Our kids were the youngest by far in Star Tours. I assume that other adults had more sense or were not such avid readers of your book. Preschoolers should start with Dumbo and work up to the Jungle Cruise in late morning, after being revved up and before getting hungry, thirsty, or tired. Pirates of the Caribbean is out for preschoolers. You get the idea.

Before lining up for any attraction, check out our description of it and see our Small-child Fright-potential Chart on pages 186–190.

Bob

At Walt Disney World, anticipate the almost inevitable emotional overload of your young children. Be sensitive, alert, and prepared for practically anything, even behavior that is out of character for your child at home. Most young children take Disney's macabre trappings in stride, and others are easily comforted by an arm around the shoulder or a squeeze of the hand. Parents who know that their children tend to become upset should take it slow and easy, sampling more benign adventures, gauging reactions, and discussing with the children how they felt about what they saw.

Some Tips

1. START SLOW AND WARM UP Although each major theme park offers several fairly nonintimidating attractions that you can sample to determine your child's relative sensitivity, the Magic Kingdom is probably the best testing ground. At the Magic Kingdom, try Buzz Lightyear's Space Ranger Spin in Tomorrowland, Peter Pan's Flight in Fantasyland, and the Jungle Cruise in Adventureland to measure your child's reaction to unfamiliar sights and sounds. If your child takes these in stride, try Pirates of the Caribbean. Try the Astro Orbiter in Tomorrowland, the Mad Tea Party in Fantasyland, or The Great Goofini also in Fantasyland to observe how your child tolerates certain ride speeds and motions.

You know I scream a lot on roller coasters, but did you know that I don't leave my feet on the floor during the *It's Tough to Be a Bug!* 3-D show at the Animal Kingdom? Well, now you know I do not like bugs, and they sting too; they do, they do.

Liliane

Do not assume that because an attraction is a theater presentation it will not frighten your child. Trust us on this one. An attraction does not have to be moving to trigger unmitigated, panic-induced hysteria. Rides such as the Big Thunder Mountain Railroad and Splash Mountain may look scary, but they do not have even one-fiftieth the potential for terrorizing children as do theater attractions such as *Stitch's Great Escape!*

2. BE ATTUNED TO PEER AND PARENT PRESSURE Sometimes young children will rise above their anxiety in an effort to please parents or siblings. This doesn't necessarily indicate a mastery of fear, much less enjoyment. If children leave a ride in apparently good shape, ask if they would like to go on it again (not necessarily now, but sometime). The response usually will indicate how much they actually enjoyed the experience. There's a big difference between having a good time and just mustering the courage to get through.

3. ENCOURAGE AND EMPATHIZE Evaluating a child's capacity to handle the visual and tactile effects of Walt Disney World requires patience, understanding, and experimentation. Each of us, after all, has our own demons. If a child balks at or is frightened by a ride, respond constructively. Let your children know that lots of people, adults and children, are scared by what they see and feel. Help them understand that it's OK if they get frightened and that their fear doesn't lessen your love or respect. Take pains not to compound the discomfort by making a child feel inadequate; try not to undermine self-esteem, impugn courage, or ridicule. Most of all, don't induce guilt by suggesting the child's trepidation might be ruining the family's fun. It is also sometimes necessary to restrain older siblings' taunting or teasing.

A visit to Walt Disney World is more than just an outing or an adventure for a young child. It's a testing experience, a sort of controlled rite of passage. If you help your little one work through the challenges, the time can be immeasurably rewarding and a bonding experience for you both.

The Fright Factor

Of course, each youngster is different, but there are eight attraction elements that alone or combined can push a child's buttons:

1. NAME OF THE ATTRACTION Young children will naturally be apprehensive about something called The Haunted Mansion or The Twilight Zone Tower of Terror.

2. VISUAL IMPACT OF THE ATTRACTION FROM OUTSIDE Big Thunder Mountain Railroad and Splash Mountain look scary enough to give even adults second thoughts, and they visually terrify many young children.

3. VISUAL IMPACT OF THE INDOOR QUEUING AREA Pirates of the Caribbean's caves and dungeons and The Haunted Mansion's "stretch rooms" can frighten kids even before they board the ride.

4. INTENSITY OF THE ATTRACTION Some attractions are overwhelming, inundating the senses with sights, sounds, movement, and even smell. *It's Tough to Be a Bug!* in the Animal Kingdom, for example, combines loud sounds, lights, smoke, animatronic insects, and 3-D cinematography to create a total sensory experience. For some preschoolers, this is two or three senses too many.

5. VISUAL IMPACT OF THE ATTRACTION ITSELF Sights in various attractions range from falling boulders to lurking buzzards, from grazing dinosaurs to attacking white blood cells. What one child calmly absorbs may scare the bejeebers out of another.

6. DARK Many Disney World attractions operate indoors in the dark. For some children, darkness alone triggers fear. A child who is frightened on one dark ride (The Haunted Mansion, for example) may be unwilling to try other indoor rides.

While there is no certain way to know what will scare your kids or what will garner a big smile, many rides are so intense that they can even eat adults. I make a huge Liliane detour around The Twilight Zone Tower of Terror or Space Mountain, but I can't get enough of Star Tours, Mission: SPACE, and the Kali River Rapids—and I have survived the Mad Tea Party and Expedition Everest. Parents know their children best. I do remember braving The Twilight Zone Tower of Terror once because I felt that I could not deprive my 10-year-old just because I was a chicken. I didn't let on that this was not my cup of tea. My prayers to exit the attraction were answered when he asked me shyly if we could ask a cast member to get out. The request was granted instantly by both me and the cast member.

7. THE RIDE ITSELF; THE TACTILE EXPERIENCE Some rides are wild enough to cause motion sickness, to wrench backs, and to discombobulate patrons of any age.

8. LOUD The sound levels in some attractions and live shows are so loud that younger children flip out even though the general content of the presentation is quite benign. For toddlers and preschoolers especially, it's good to have a pair of earplugs handy.

Disney Orientation Course

We receive many tips from parents telling how they prepared their young children for the Disney experience. A common strategy is to acquaint children with the characters and stories behind the attractions by reading Disney books and watching Disney DVDs at home. A more direct approach is to watch Walt Disney World travel DVDs that show the attractions. You can order the free Walt Disney World Vacation Planning DVD by calling Disney reservations at ☎ 407-824-8000, or log on to **disneyworld.com** and click on "FREE Vacation Planning DVD" at the top of the page to order. Ignore all prompts, and the phone system will assume that you're on a rotary phone and patch you through to a live person (though you may be on hold a couple minutes). This DVD isn't as comprehensive as travelogues you might rent, but it's adequate for giving your kids a sense of what they'll see. Also, as discussed in a previous chapter, you can find a video of every Disney attraction on **youtube.com.**

A MAGICAL TIME FOR MOM AND DAD

OK, LILIANE WRITING HERE. Because Bob's idea of a romantic evening is watching Monday Night Football on the sofa with his honey instead of sitting in his La-Z-Boy, I'm going to tackle this subject solo. Let's face it: We all know that moms and dads deserve some special time. But the reality on the ground is that the kids come first. And when the day is over, mom and dad are way too tired to think about having a special evening alone. It is difficult enough to catch a movie or go out for a romantic dinner in our hometowns, so how realistic is a romantic parents' night out while on vacation at Walt Disney World?

The answer is: No planning, no romance! With a little magic and some advance preparation, you can make it happen. Here we offer a few suggestions.

Staying at a hotel that offers great kids' programs is a big plus. Consider signing up small children for a half-day program with lunch or dinner while you enjoy your resort. Go to the pool and read a book, and then have a meal in calm and peace. Rent a bike, a boat, or just take off outside the World. This is also a great opportunity to enjoy the thrill rides you passed up when you were busy worshipping at the altar of Dumbo.

PREPARING YOUR CHILDREN TO
MEET THE CHARACTERS

ALMOST ALL DISNEY CHARACTERS ARE QUITE LARGE; several, like Br'er Bear, are huge! Young children don't expect this and can be intimidated if not terrified. Discuss the characters with your children before you go. If there is a high school or college with a costumed mascot nearby, arrange to let your kids check it out. If not, then Santa Claus or the Easter Bunny will do.

On the first encounter at Walt Disney World, don't thrust your child at the character. Allow the little one to deal with this big thing from whatever distance feels safe to him or her. If two adults are present, one should stay near the youngster while the other approaches the character and demonstrates that it's safe and friendly. Some kids warm to the characters immediately; some never do. Most take a little time and several encounters.

At Walt Disney World there are two kinds of characters: those whose costume includes a face-covering headpiece (animal characters and such humanlike characters as Captain Hook) and face characters, those who resemble the characters so no mask or headpiece is necessary. Face characters include Mary Poppins, Ariel, Belle, Jasmine, Aladdin, Cinderella, Snow White, Tarzan, Esmerelda, and Prince Charming.

Tell children in advance that headpiece characters don't talk.

Ian

Only face characters speak. Headpiece characters don't make noises of any kind. Because cast members couldn't possibly imitate the distinctive cinema voice of the character, Disney has determined that it's more effective to keep them silent. Lack of speech notwithstanding, headpiece characters are very warm and responsive and communicate very effectively with gestures. Disney is currently testing new technology that will allow headpiece characters to speak. It is assumed that the technology is a portable version of that used in *Turtle Talk With Crush* at Epcot, where an animated turtle converses in real time with audience members. A less advanced option is a menu-driven selection of recorded phrases such as, "Hi, I'm Mickey," or "What's your name?"

Some character costumes are cumbersome and give cast members very poor visibility. (Eye holes frequently are in the mouth of the costume or even on the neck or chest.) This means characters are somewhat clumsy and have limited sight. Children who approach the character from the back or side may not be noticed, even if the child touches the character. It's possible in this situation for the character to accidentally step on the child or knock him or her down. It's best for a child to approach a character from the front, but occasionally not even this works. Duck characters (such as Donald, Daisy, and Uncle Scrooge), for example, have to peer around their bills.

If a character appears to be ignoring your child, pick up your child and hold him or her in front of the character until the character responds.

Liliane

It's OK for your child to touch, pat, or hug the character. Understanding the unpredictability of children, the character will keep his feet very still, particularly refraining from moving backward or sideways. Most characters will sign autographs or pose for pictures.

Another great way to show young kids how the characters appear in the parks is to rent or buy a Disney SingAlong Songs DVD. Not unlike

If your child wants to collect character autographs, it's a good idea to carry a pen the width of a magic marker. Costumes make it exceedingly difficult for characters to wield a pen, so the bigger the writing instrument, the better.

similar Barney videos, they are children's sing-along programs showing the costumed Disney characters interacting with real kids. At a minimum the shows will give your kids a sense of how big the Disney characters are. The best two are *Flik's Musical Adventure* SingAlong Songs at Disney's Animal Kingdom and *Campout* SingAlong Songs at Walt Disney World. *It's a Small World* SingAlong Songs—Disneyland Fun is a third offering, but then there's THAT SONG. No sense turning your brain to mush before even leaving home.

ROLE-PLAYING

ESPECIALLY FOR YOUNGER CHILDREN, role-playing is a great way to inculcate vital lessons concerning safety, contingency situations, and potential danger. Play "what would you do if" for a variety of scenarios, including getting lost, being approached by strangers, getting help if mommy is sick, and so on. Children have incredible recall when it comes to role-playing with siblings and parents, and are much more likely to respond appropriately in an actual situation than they will if the same information is presented in a lecture.

PHYSICAL PREPARATION

YOU'LL FIND THAT SOME PHYSICAL CONDITIONING, coupled with a realistic sense of the toll that Walt Disney World takes on your body, will preclude falling apart in the middle of your vacation. As one of our readers put it, "If you pay attention to eat, heat, feet, and sleep, you'll be OK."

If your children (or you, for that matter) do not consider it cool to wear socks, get over it! Bare feet, whether encased in Nikes, Weejuns, Docksides, or Birkenstocks, will turn into lumps of throbbing red meat if you tackle a Disney park without socks.

As you contemplate the stamina of your family, it's important to understand that somebody is going to run out of steam first, and when they do, the whole family will be affected. Sometimes a cold drink or a snack will revive the flagging member. Sometimes, however, no amount of cajoling or treats will work. In this situation it's crucial that you recognize that the child, grandparent, or spouse is at the end of his or her rope. The correct decision is to get them back to the hotel. Pushing the exhausted beyond their capacity will spoil the day for them—and you. Accept that stamina and energy levels vary and be prepared to administer to members of your family who poop out. One more thing: no guilt trips. "We've driven a thousand miles to take you to Disney World and now you're going to ruin everything!" is not an appropriate response.

THE AGONY OF THE FEET

HERE'S A LITTLE FACTOID TO CHEW ON: If you spend a day at Epcot and visit both sections of the park, you will walk 5–9 miles! The walking, however, will be nothing like a 5-mile hike in the woods. At Epcot (and the other Disney parks as well) you will be in direct sunlight most of the time, will have to navigate through huge jostling crowds, will be walking on hot pavement, and will have to endure waits in line between bursts of walking. The bottom line, if you haven't figured it out, is that Disney theme parks (especially in the summer) are not for wimps!

Though most children are active, their normal play usually doesn't condition them for the exertion of touring a Disney theme park. We recommend starting a program of family walks six weeks or more before your trip. A Pennsylvania mom who did just that offers the following:

We had our 6-year-old begin walking with us a bit every day one month before leaving—when we arrived [at Walt Disney World], her little legs could carry her and she had a lot of stamina.

The first thing you need to do, immediately after making your hotel reservation, is to get thee to a "footery." Take the whole family to a shoe store and buy each member the best pair of walking, hiking, or running shoes you can afford. Wear exactly the kind of socks to try on the shoes that you will wear when using them to hike. Do not under any circumstances attempt to tour Walt Disney World shod in sandals, flip-flops, loafers, or any kind of high heel or platform shoe.

Good socks are as important as good shoes. When you walk, your feet sweat like a mule in a peat bog, and moisture increases friction. To minimize friction, wear a pair of SmartWool or Coolmax hiking socks, available at most outdoor retail (camping equipment) stores. To further combat moisture, dust your feet with some antifungal powder.

All right, now you've got some good shoes and socks. The next thing to do is to break the shoes in. You can accomplish this painlessly by wearing the shoes in the course of normal activities for about three weeks.

Once the shoes are broken in, it's time to start walking. The whole family will need to toughen up their feet and build endurance.

Liliane

Be sure to give your kids adequate recovery time between training walks (48 hours will usually be enough), however, or you'll make the problem worse.

As you begin, remember that little people have little strides, and though your 6-year-old may create the appearance of running circles around you, consider that (1) he won't have the stamina to go at that pace very long, and (2) more to the point, he probably has to take two strides or so to every one of yours to keep up when you walk together.

Start by taking short walks around the neighborhood, walking on pavement, and increasing the distance about a quarter of a mile on each outing. Older children will shape up quickly. Younger children should build endurance more slowly and incrementally. Increase distance until you can manage a 6- or 7-mile hike without requiring CPR. And remember, you're not training to be able to walk 6 or 7 miles just once; at Walt Disney World you will be hiking 5–9 miles or more almost *every day*. So unless you plan to crash after the first day, you've got to prepare your feet to walk long distances for three to five consecutive days.

Let's be honest and admit up front that not all feet are created equal. Some folks are blessed with really tough feet, whereas the feet of others sprout blisters if you look at them sideways. Assuming that there's nothing wrong with either shoes or socks, a few brisk walks will clue you in to what kind of feet your family have. If you have a tenderfoot in your family, walks of incrementally increased distances will usually toughen up his or her feet to some extent. For those whose feet refuse to toughen, your only alternative is preventive care. After several walks, you will know where your tenderfoot tends to develop blisters. If you can anticipate where blisters will develop, you can cover sensitive spots in advance with moleskin, a friction-resistant adhesive dressing.

When you initiate your walking program, teach your children to tell you if they feel a hot spot on their feet. This is the warning that a blister is developing. If your kids are too young, too oblivious, too preoccupied, or don't understand the concept, your best bet is to make regular foot checks. Have your children remove their shoes and socks and present their feet for inspection. Look for red spots and blisters, and ask if they have any places on their feet that hurt.

> If your child is age 8 or younger, we recommend regular feet Bob inspections whether he or she understands the hot spot idea or not. Even the brightest and most well-intentioned child will fail to sound off when distracted.

During your conditioning, and also at Walt Disney World, carry a foot emergency kit in your day pack or hip pack. The kit should contain gauze, Betadine antibiotic ointment, moleskin, an assortment of Band-Aid Advance Healing Blister Cushions, scissors, a sewing needle or some such to drain blisters, as well as matches to sterilize the needle. An extra pair of dry socks and foot powder are optional.

If you discover a hot spot, dry the foot and cover the spot immediately with moleskin. Cut the covering large enough to cover the skin surrounding the hot spot. If you find that a blister has fully or partially developed, first air out and dry the foot. Next, using your sterile needle, drain the fluid, but do not remove the top skin. Clean the area with antiseptic cleaner, and place a blister bandage over the blister. If you do not have moleskin or blister bandages, do not try to cover the hot spot or blister with regular Band-Aid bandages. Regular ones slip and wad up.

A stroller will provide the child the option of walking or riding, and, if he collapses, you won't have to carry him. Even if your child hardly uses the stroller at all, it serves as a convenient rolling depository for water bottles and other stuff you may not feel like carrying. Strollers at Walt Disney World are covered in detail on pages 257–259.

> If you have a child who will physically fit in a stroller, rent one, no matter how well conditioned your family is. Liliane

SLEEP, REST, AND RELAXATION

OK, WE KNOW THAT THIS SECTION is about physical preparation *before you go,* but this concept is so absolutely critical that we need to tattoo it on your brain right now.

Physical conditioning is important but is *not* a substitute for adequate rest. Even marathon runners need recovery time. If you push too hard and try to do too much, you'll either crash or, at a minimum, turn what should be fun into an ordeal. Rest means plenty of sleep at night, naps during the afternoon on most days, and planned breaks in your vacation itinerary. And don't forget that the brain needs rest and relaxation as well as the body. The stimulation inherent in touring a Disney theme park is enough to put many children and some adults into system overload. It is imperative that you remove your family from this unremitting assault on the senses, preferably for part of each day, and do something relaxing and quiet like swimming or reading.

The theme parks are huge; don't try to see everything in 1 day. Tour in early morning and return to your hotel around 11:30 a.m. for lunch, a swim, and a nap. Even during off-season, when the crowds are smaller and the temperature more pleasant, the size of the major theme parks will exhaust most children under age 8 by lunchtime. Return to the park in late afternoon or early evening and continue touring. A family from Texas underlines the importance of naps and rest:

> Despite not following any of your "tours," we did follow the theme of visiting a specific park in the morning, leaving midafternoon for either a nap back at the room or a trip to the pool, and then returning to one of the parks in the evening. On the few occasions when we skipped your advice, I was muttering to myself by dinner. I can't tell you what I was muttering . . .

When it comes to naps, this mom does not mince words:

> One last thing for parents of small kids—take the book's advice and get out of the park and take the nap, take the nap, TAKE THE NAP! Never in my life have I seen so many parents screaming at, ridiculing, or slapping their kids. (What a vacation!) Walt Disney World is overwhelming for kids and adults. Even though the rental strollers recline for sleeping, we noticed that most of the toddlers and preschoolers didn't give up and sleep until 5 p.m., several hours after the fun had worn off, and right about the time their parents wanted them to be awake and polite in a restaurant.

A mom from Rochester, New York, was equally adamant:

> [You] absolutely must rest during the day. Kids went 8 a.m.–9 p.m. in the Magic Kingdom. Kids did great that day, but we were all completely worthless the next day. Definitely must pace yourself. Don't ever try to do two full days of park sightseeing in a row. Rest during the day. Go to a water park or sleep in every other day.

If you plan to return to your hotel in midday and would like your room made up, let housekeeping know.

DEVELOPING *a* GOOD PLAN

ALLOW YOUR CHILDREN TO PARTICIPATE in the planning of your time at Walt Disney World. Guide them diplomatically through the options, establishing advance decisions about what to do each day and how the day will be structured. Begin with your trip *to* Walt Disney World, deciding what time to depart, who sits by the window, whether to stop for meals or eat in the car, and so on. For the Walt Disney World part of your vacation, build consensus for wake-up call, bedtime, and building naps into the itinerary, and establish ground rules for eating, buying refreshments, and shopping. Determine the order for visiting the different theme parks and make a list of must-see attractions. To help you with filling in the blanks of your days, and especially to prevent you from spending most of your time standing in line, we offer a number of field-tested touring plans. The plans are designed to minimize your waiting time at each park by providing step-by-step itineraries that route you counter to the flow of traffic. The plans are explained in detail on pages 227–234.

Generally it's better to just sketch in the broad strokes on the master plan. The detail of what to do when you actually arrive at the park can be decided the night before you go or with the help of one of our touring plans once you get there. Above all, be flexible. One important caveat, however: Make sure you keep any promises or agreements that you make when planning. They may not seem important to you, but they will to your children, who will remember for a long, long time that you let them down.

The more that you can agree to and nail down in advance, the less potential you'll have for disagreement and confrontation once you arrive. Because children are more comfortable with the tangible than the conceptual, and also because they sometimes have short memories, we recommend typing up all of your decisions and agreements and providing a copy to each child. Create a fun document, not a legalistic one. You'll find that your children will review it in anticipation of all the things they will see and do, will consult it often, and will even read it to their younger siblings.

By now you're probably wondering what one of these documents looks like, so here's a sample. Incidentally, this itinerary reflects the preferences of its creators, the Langston family, and is not meant to be offered as an example of an ideal itinerary. It does, however, incorporate many of our most basic and strongly held recommendations, such as setting limits and guidelines in advance, getting enough rest, getting to the theme parks early, touring the theme parks in

To keep your thinking fresh and to adequately cover all bases, Bob

develop your plan in a series of family meetings no longer than 30 minutes each. You'll discover that all members of the family will devote a lot of thought to the plan both in and between meetings. Don't try to anticipate every conceivable contingency, or you'll end up with something as detailed and unworkable as the tax code.

shorter visits with naps and swimming in between, and saving time and money by having a cooler full of food for breakfast. As you will see, the Langstons go pretty much full-tilt without much unstructured time and will probably be exhausted by the time they get home, but that's their choice. One more thing—the Langstons visited Walt Disney World in late June, when all of the theme parks stay open late.

THE GREAT WALT DISNEY WORLD EXPEDITION

COCAPTAINS Mary and Jack Langston

TEAM MEMBERS Lynn and Jimmy Langston

EXPEDITION FUNDING The main Expedition Fund will cover everything except personal purchases. Each team member will receive $40 for souvenirs and personal purchases. Anything above $40 will be paid for by team members with their own money.

EXPEDITION GEAR Each team member will wear an official expedition T-shirt and carry a hip pack.

PREDEPARTURE Jack makes priority seating arrangements at Walt Disney World restaurants. Mary, Lynn, and Jimmy make up trail mix and other snacks for the hip packs.

Notice that the Langstons' itinerary on pages 204–205 provides minimal structure and maximum flexibility. It specifies which park the family will tour each day without attempting to nail down exactly what the family will do there. No matter how detailed your itinerary is, be prepared for surprises at Walt Disney World, both good and bad. If an unforeseen event renders part of the plan useless or impractical, just roll with it. And always remember that it's your itinerary; you created it, and you can change it. Just try to make any changes the result of family discussion, and be especially careful not to scrap an element of the plan that your children perceive as something you promised them.

Routines That Travel

If when at home you observe certain routines—for example, reading a book before bed or having a bath first thing in the morning—try to incorporate these familiar activities into your vacation schedule. They will provide your children with a sense of security and normalcy.

Maintaining a normal routine is especially important with toddlers, as a mother of two from Lawrenceville, Georgia, relates:

> The first day, we tried an early start, so we woke the children (ages 2 and 4) and hurried them to get going. BAD IDEA with toddlers. This put them off schedule for naps and meals the rest of the day. It is best to let young ones stay on their regular schedule and see Disney at their own pace, and you'll have much more fun.

We offer a Sleepyhead Touring Plan for each park, perfect for families like this reader's.

LOGISTIC PREPARATION

WHEN WE RECENTLY LAUNCHED into our spiel about good logistic preparation for a Walt Disney World vacation, a friend from Indianapolis said, "Wait, what's the big deal? You pack clothes, a few games for the car, then go!" So OK, we confess, that will work, but life can be sweeter and the vacation smoother (as well as less expensive) with the right gear.

CLOTHING

LET'S START WITH CLOTHES. We recommend springing for vacation uniforms. Buy for each child several sets of jeans (or shorts) and T-shirts, all matching, and all the same. For a one-week trip, as an example, get each child three or so pairs of khaki shorts, three or so light yellow T-shirts, three pairs of SmartWool or

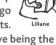

Give your teens the job of coming up with the logo for your shirts. *Liliane* They will love being the family designers.

Coolmax hiking socks. What's the point? First, you don't have to play fashion designer, coordinating a week's worth of stylish combos. Each morning the kids put on their uniform. It's simple, it's time-saving, and there are no decisions to make or arguments about what to wear. Second, uniforms make your children easier to spot and keep together in the theme parks. Third, the uniforms give your family, as well as the vacation itself, some added identity. If you're like the Langston family who created the sample itinerary in the section on organizational planning, you might go so far as to create a logo for the trip to be printed on the shirts.

When it comes to buying your uniforms, we have a few suggestions. Purchase well-made, durable shorts or jeans that will serve your children well beyond the vacation. Active children can never have too many pairs of shorts or jeans. As far as the T-shirts go, buy short-sleeve shirts in light colors for warm weather or long-sleeve, darker-colored T-shirts for cooler weather. We suggest that you purchase your colored shirts from a local T-shirt printing company. Cleverly listed under "T-shirts" (sometimes under "Screen Printing") in the Yellow Pages, these firms will be happy to sell you either printed T-shirts or unprinted T-shirts (called "blanks") with long or short sleeves.

Consider affixing labels to the clothing of young children to *Bob* help in the event that they become separated from the family.

You can select from a wide choice of colors not generally available in retail clothing stores and will not have to worry about finding the sizes you need. Plus, the shirts will cost a fraction of what a clothing retailer would charge. Most shirts come in the more durable 100% cotton or in the more wrinkle-resistant 50% cotton and 50% polyester (50/50s). The cotton shirts are a little cooler and more comfortable in hot, humid weather. The 50/50s dry a bit faster if they get wet.

LABELS A great idea, especially for younger children, is to attach labels

continued on page 206

Langston Family Itinerary

DAY 1: FRIDAY

6:30 p.m. . . . . .Dinner
After dinner . . . . Pack car
10 p.m. . . . . Lights out

DAY 2: SATURDAY

7 a.m. . . . . Wake up!
7:15 a.m. . . . . Breakfast
8 a.m. . . . . Depart Chicago for Hampton Inn, Chattanooga;
                        Confirmation # DE56432; Lynn rides shotgun
About noon . . . . .Stop for lunch; Jimmy picks restaurant
7 p.m. . . . . .Dinner
9:30 p.m. . . . . Lights out

DAY 3: SUNDAY

7 a.m. . . . . Wake up!
7:30 a.m. . . . . .Breakfast
8:15 a.m. . . . . .Depart Chattanooga for Walt Disney World, Port Orleans
            Resort–Riverside; confirmation # L124532; Jimmy rides shotgun
About noon . . . . Stop for lunch; Lynn picks restaurant
5 p.m. . . . . .Check in, buy park admissions, and unpack
6–7 p.m.. . . . . Mary and Jimmy shop for breakfast food for cooler
7:15 p.m. . . . . Dinner at Boatwright's at Port Orleans Riverside
After dinner . . . . Walk along Bonnet Creek
10 p.m. . . . . Lights out

DAY 4: MONDAY

7 a.m. . . . . .Wake up! Cold breakfast from cooler in room
8 a.m. . . . . Depart room to catch bus for Epcot
Noon. . . . . : Lunch at Epcot
1 p.m. . . . . Return to hotel for swimming and a nap
5 p.m. . . . . Return to Epcot for touring, dinner, and *IllumiNations*
9:30 p.m. . . . . .Return to hotel
10:30 p.m.. . . . . Lights out

DAY 5: TUESDAY

7 a.m. . . . . .Wake up! Cold breakfast from cooler in room
7:45 a.m. . . . . Depart room to catch bus for Disney's Hollywood Studios
Noon. . . . . Lunch at Studios
2:30 p.m. . . . . Return to hotel for swimming and a nap
6 p.m. . . . . .Drive to dinner at cafe at Wilderness Lodge
7:30 p.m. . . . . Return to Studios via car for touring and *Fantasmic!*
10 p.m. . . . . .Return to hotel
11 p.m. . . . . Lights out

DAY 6: WEDNESDAY

ZZZZZZ! . . . . Lazy morning—sleep in!
10:30 a.m. . . . . Late-morning swim
Noon. . . . . Lunch at Riverside Mill Food Court at Port Orleans
1 p.m. . .Depart room to catch bus for Animal Kingdom; tour until park closes
8 p.m. . . . . Dinner at Rainforest Cafe at Animal Kingdom
9:15 p.m. . . . . .Return to hotel via bus
10:30 p.m. . . . . Lights out

DAY 7: THURSDAY

6 a.m. . . . . .Wake up! Cold breakfast from cooler in room
6:45 a.m. . . . . Depart via bus for early entry at Magic Kingdom
11:30 a.m. . . . . Return to hotel for lunch, swimming, and a nap
4:45 p.m. . . . . Drive to Contemporary for dinner at Chef Mickey's
6:15 p.m. . . . . .Walk from the Contemporary to the Magic Kingdom
for more touring, fireworks, and parade
11 p.m. . . . . Return to Contemporary via walkway or monorail;
get car, and return to hotel
11:45 p.m. . . . . Lights out

DAY 8: FRIDAY

8 a.m. . . . . .Wake up! Cold breakfast from cooler in room
8:40 a.m. . . . . .Drive to Blizzard Beach water park
Noon. . . . . Lunch at Blizzard Beach
1:30 p.m. . . . . Return to hotel for nap and packing
4 p.m. . . . . .Revisit favorite park or do whatever we want
Dinner . . . . .When and where we decide
10 p.m. . . . . .Return to hotel
10:30 p.m. . . . . Lights out

DAY 9: SATURDAY

7:30 a.m. . . . . Wake up!
8:30 a.m. . . . . . . .After fast-food breakfast, depart for Executive Inn, Nashville;
confirmation # SD234; Lynn rides shotgun
About noon . . . . .Stop for lunch; Jimmy picks restaurant
7 p.m. . . . . .Dinner
10 p.m. . . . . Lights out

DAY 10: SUNDAY

7 a.m. . . . . Wake up!
7:45 a.m. . . . .Depart for home after fast-food breakfast; Jimmy rides shotgun
About noon . . . . Stop for lunch; Lynn picks restaurant
4:30 p.m. . . . . .Home sweet home!

continued from page 203

Liliane

If your kids are little and don't mind a hairdo change, consider getting them a short haircut before you leave home. Not only will they be cooler and more comfortable, but—especially with your girls—you'll save them (and yourselves) the hassle of tangles and about 20 minutes of foo-fooing a day. Don't try this with your confident teen or preteen, though. Braids will do the trick for girls, and your Mick Jagger in the party will be grateful for the bandanna or sports headband, unless of course the hair is meant to keep the monsters and dinosaurs out of sight!

with your family name, hometown, the name of your hotel, the dates of your stay, and your cell phone number inside the shirt. For example:

Carlton Family of Frankfort, KY; Port Orleans Riverside May 5–12; 502-662-2108

Instruct your smaller children to show the label to an adult if they get separated from you. Elimination of the child's first name (which most children of talking age can articulate in any event) allows you to order labels that are all the same, that can be used by anyone in the family, and that can also be affixed to such easily lost items as caps, hats, jackets, hip packs, ponchos, and umbrellas. If fooling with labels sounds like too much of a hassle, check out "When Kids Get Lost" (pages 259–263) for some alternatives.

DRESSING FOR COOLER WEATHER Central Florida experiences temperatures all over the scale from November through March, so it could be a bit chilly if you visit during those months. Our suggestion is to layer: For example, a breathable, waterproof or water-resistant Windbreaker over a light, long-sleeved polypropylene shirt over a long-sleeved T-shirt. As with the baffles of a sleeping bag or down coat, it is the air trapped between the layers that keeps you warm. If all the layers are thin, you won't be left with something bulky to cart around if you want to pull one or more off. Later in this section, we'll advocate wearing a hip pack. Each layer should be sufficiently compactible to fit easily in that hip pack, along with whatever else is in it.

ACCESSORIES

I (BOB) WANTED TO CALL THIS PART "Belts and Stuff," but Liliane (who obviously spends a lot of time at Macy's) thought "Accessories" put a finer point on it. In any event, we recommend pants for your children with reinforced elastic waistbands that eliminate the need to wear a belt (one less thing to find when you're trying to leave). If your children like belts or want to carry an item suspended from their belts, buy them military-style 1-inch-wide web belts at any Army/Navy surplus or camping equipment store. The belts weigh less than half as much as leather, are cooler, and are washable.

SUNGLASSES The Florida sun is so bright and the glare so blinding that we recommend sunglasses for each family member. For children and adults of all ages, a good accessory item is a polypropylene eyeglass strap for spectacles or sunglasses. The best models have a little device for adjusting the amount of slack in the strap. This allows your child to comfortably hang sunglasses from his or her neck when indoors or, alternately, to secure them fast to his or her head while experiencing a fast ride outdoors.

HIP PACKS AND WALLETS Unless you are touring with an infant or toddler, the largest thing anyone in your family should carry is a hip pack, or fanny pack. Each adult and child should have one. They should be large enough to carry at least a half-day's worth of snacks, as well as other items deemed necessary (lip balm, bandanna, antibacterial hand gel, and so on), and still have enough room left to stash a hat, poncho, or light Windbreaker. We recommend buying full-size hip packs as opposed to small, child-size hip packs at outdoor retailers. The packs are light; can be made to fit any child large enough to tote a hip pack; have slip-resistant, comfortable, wide belting; and will last for years.

> Unless you advise the front desk to the contrary, all Disney resort room keys can be used for park admission and as credit cards. They are definitely something you don't want to lose. Our advice is to void the charge privileges on your preteen children's cards, and then collect them and put them together someplace safe when not in use.

Do not carry billfolds or wallets, car keys, Disney Resort IDs, or room keys in your hip packs. We usually give this advice because hip packs are vulnerable to thieves (who snip them off and run), but pickpocketing and theft are not all that common at Walt Disney World. In this instance, the advice stems from a tendency of children to inadvertently drop their wallet in the process of rummaging around in their hip packs for snacks and other items.

You should weed through your billfold and remove to a safe place anything that you will not need on your vacation (family photos, local library card, department store credit cards, business cards, movie rental ID cards, and so on). In addition to having a lighter wallet to lug around, you will decrease your exposure in the event that your wallet is lost or stolen. When we are working at Walt Disney World, we carry a small profile billfold with a driver's license, a credit card, our Disney Resort room key, and a small amount of cash. Think about it: You don't need anything else.

DAY PACKS We see a lot of folks at Walt Disney World carrying day packs (that is, small, frameless backpacks) and/or water bottle belts that strap around the waist. Day packs might be a good choice if you plan to carry a lot of camera equipment or if you need to carry baby supplies on your person. Otherwise, try to travel as light as possible. Packs are hot, cumbersome, not very secure, and must be removed every time you get on a ride or sit down for a show. Hip packs, by way of contrast, can simply be rotated around the waist from your back to your abdomen if you need to sit down. Additionally, our observation has been that the contents of one day pack can usually be redistributed to two or so hip packs (except in the case of camera equipment).

CAPS Caps protect young eyes from damaging ultraviolet rays, but the lifespan of a child's hat is usually pretty short. Simply put, kids pull caps on and off as they enter and exit attractions, restrooms, and restaurants, and . . . big surprise, they lose them. In fact, they lose them by the thousands. You could provide a ball cap for every Little Leaguer in America from the caps that are lost at Walt Disney World each summer.

Equip each child with a big bandanna. Although bandannas come in handy for wiping
Liliane
noses, scouring ice cream from chins and mouths, and dabbing sweat from the forehead, they can also be tied around the neck to protect from sunburn.

If your children are partial to caps, there is a device sold at ski and camping supply stores that might increase the likelihood of the cap returning home with the child. Essentially, it's a short, light cord with little alligator clips on both ends. Hook one clip to the shirt collar and the other to the hat. It's a great little invention. Bob uses one when he skis in case his ball cap blows off.

RAINGEAR Rain in central Florida is a fact of life, although persistent rain day after day is unusual (it is the Sunshine State, after all!). Our suggestion is to check out The Weather Channel or weather forecasts on the Internet for three or so days before you leave home to see if there are any major storm systems heading for central Florida. Weather forecasting has improved to the extent that predictions concerning systems and fronts four to seven days out are now pretty reliable. If it appears that you might see some rough weather during your visit, you're better off bringing raingear from home. If, however, nothing big is on the horizon weather-wise, you can take your chances.

We at the *Unofficial Guide* usually do not bring raingear. First, scattered thundershowers are more the norm than are prolonged periods of rain. Second, raingear is pretty cheap at Walt Disney World, especially the ponchos that sell for about $8 per adult, $7 per child, available in seemingly every retail shop. Third, in the theme parks, a surprising number of attractions and queuing areas are under cover. Fourth, we prefer to travel light.

If you do find yourself in a big storm, however, you'll want to have both a poncho and an umbrella. As one *Unofficial* reader put it:

> Umbrellas make the rain much more bearable. When rain isn't beating down on your ponchoed head, it's easier to ignore.

An advantage of buying ponchos before you leave home is that you can choose the color. At Walt Disney World all the ponchos are clear, and it's quite a sight when 30,000 differently clad individuals suddenly transform themselves into what looks like an army of really big larvae. If your family is wearing blue ponchos, they'll be easier to spot.

And consider this tip from a Memphis, Tennessee, mom:

Scotchgard your shoes. The difference is unbelievable.

MISCELLANEOUS ITEMS

MEDICATION Some parents of hyperactive children on medication discontinue or decrease the child's normal dosage at the end of the school year. If you have such a child, be aware that Walt Disney World might overly stimulate him or her. Consult your physician before altering your child's medication regimen. Also, if your child has attention deficit disorder, remember that especially loud sounds can drive him or her right up the wall. Unfortunately, some Disney theater attractions are almost unbearably loud.

SUNSCREEN Overheating and sunburn are among the most common problems of younger children at Walt Disney World. Carry and use sunscreen of SPF 15 or higher. Be sure to put some on children in strollers, even if the stroller has a canopy. Some of the worst cases of sunburn we've seen were on the exposed foreheads and feet of toddlers and infants in strollers. Protect skin from over-exposure. To avoid overheating, rest regularly in the shade or in an air-conditioned restaurant or show.

Often little ones fall asleep in their strollers (hallelujah!). Bring a large lightweight cloth to drape over the stroller to cover your child from the sun. A few clothespins will keep it in place. — Liliane

WATER BOTTLES Don't count on keeping young children hydrated with soft drinks and stops at water fountains. Long lines may hamper buying refreshments, and fountains may not be handy. Furthermore, excited children may not realize or tell you that they're thirsty or hot. We recommend renting a stroller for children age 6 and younger and carrying plastic bottles of water. Plastic squeeze bottles with caps run about $3 in all major parks.

COOLERS AND MINI-FRIDGES If you drive to Walt Disney World, bring two coolers: a small one for drinks in the car and a large one for the hotel room. If you fly and rent a car, stop and purchase a large Styrofoam cooler, which can be discarded at the end of the trip. If you will be without a car, rent a mini-fridge from your hotel. At Disney Value resorts, mini-refrigerators cost about $15 a day. Make sure you reserve one when you book your room. Refrigerators in all Disney Deluxe and Moderate resort rooms are free of charge. If you arrive at your room and there is no refrigerator, call housekeeping and request one. Along with free fridges, coffeemakers have also been added in the rooms.

About two weeks before I arrive at WDW, I always ship a box to my hotel containing food, plastic cutlery, and toiletries, plus pretty much any other consumables that — Liliane

might come in handy during my stay. If you fly, this helps avoid overweight fees and problems with liquid restrictions for carry-on luggage.

Coolers and mini-fridges allow you to have breakfast in your hotel room, store snacks and lunch supplies to take to the theme parks, and supplant expensive vending machines for snacks

Don't Let the Sun See You Frying

HEALTH-AND-SCIENCE WRITER Avery Hurt sheds some light on the variety of products and often confusing methods for avoiding sunburn.

No matter what time of year you travel to Walt Disney World, don't make the mistake of underestimating the Florida sun. Even in the winter, it can be a problem. And in the summer, old Sol can be wicked indeed.

The most obvious precaution is to slather on the sunscreen. But when you get to the drugstore or discount shop to load up, you may discover that choosing a product is anything but simple. Cream? Lotion? Spray? Waterproof or not? And what's this SPF number all about, anyway?

Making sense of sunscreen is so complex that the dilemma has precipitated lawsuits, required the amendment (and revision of amendments) of Food and Drug Administration (FDA) regulations, and confused officials almost as much as consumers. The sunscreen manufacturers, the FDA, and all of the lawyers involved may have plenty of time to duke it out, but you've got a trip planned! Don't worry. It's not as complicated as it seems. Following is some basic advice from the medical experts:

Choose a sunscreen that is convenient for you to use. Some people prefer sprays, others lotions. The form of the sunscreen doesn't matter as much as the amount of it you use and the technique of its application. Apply sunscreen a half hour before going out, and be sure to get enough on you. One ounce per application is recommended, which means that you should apply the equivalent of a full shot glass each time. The one-ounce amount is the recommendation for average adults in swimsuits; very large adults will need proportionately more. For a 1-year-old child wearing a bathing suit, figure about one-third of an ounce (10 cc) per application. An average 7-year-old child will probably take two-thirds of an ounce (20 cc). It's a good idea to measure that ounce in your hands (at home, when an ounce measure—shot glass or whatever—is handy), so that you will be familiar with what an ounce looks like in your palms. It is far more sunscreen than you tend to think.

and beverages at the hotel. To keep the contents of your cooler cold, we suggest freezing a 2-gallon milk jug full of water before you head out. In a good cooler, it will take the jug five or more days to thaw. If you buy a Styrofoam cooler in Florida, you can use bagged ice and ice from the ice machine at your hotel. Even if you have to rent a mini-fridge, you will save a bundle of cash, as well as significant time, by reducing dependence on restaurant meals and expensive snacks and drinks purchased from vendors.

FOOD PREP KIT If you plan to make sandwiches, bring along your favorite condiments and seasonings from home. A good travel kit will include mayonnaise, ketchup, mustard, salt and pepper, and packets

Be sure not to miss any spots. A few years ago, a group of researchers from Berlin journeyed to the beach to measure how well covered the beachgoers really were. It turned out that even the most dedicated sunscreen users did an abysmal job of applying their chosen brand. Most areas of skin were only sparsely covered, and areas such as the ears and the tops of feet were hardly covered at all. Be sure to get a generous covering on all exposed skin. Then re-apply (another full shot glass) every 2 hours, or after swimming or sweating. No matter what it says on the label, no sunscreen is waterproof, and water resistance is limited. And none of them last all day.

SPF stands for "sun protection factor" and is a measure of how long the protection will last. Geniuses in lab coats come up with this number by calculating how long it will take a person to burn without sunscreen (please don't volunteer me for that study) and comparing that information with how long the same person takes to burn with sunscreen. Theoretically a sunscreen with an SPF of 15 will protect you 15 times longer than if you wear no sunscreen at all.

This might make it sound like the higher the SPF the better, but studies have not borne that out. The effectiveness of the sunscreen diminishes as the number gets higher, and the initial estimate doesn't take into account the fact that during the day your sunscreen rubs off, washes off, and sweats off. In actual practice, there is very little difference in protection between an SPF of 15 or so and an SPF of 45 or 50 or greater. There is no need to spend more for higher SPF numbers. In fact, it is much safer to choose a lower (and typically less expensive) SPF (as long as it is at least 15) and apply it more often. The American Academy of Dermatology (AAD) and the American Academy of Pediatrics (AAP) both recommend an SPF of at least 15. Paying more for a higher SPF will give you very little more protection, and the false sense of security that comes with an SPF of 45 or 50 may do more harm than the (very) slight increase in protection. However, do be sure to choose a product that has "broad-spectrum coverage," meaning that it filters out both UVA and UVB rays.

of sugar or artificial sweetener. Also bring some plastic knives and spoons, paper napkins, plastic cups, and a box of zip-top plastic bags. For breakfast you will need some plastic bowls for cereal. Of course, you can buy this stuff in Florida, but you probably won't consume it all, so why waste the money? If you drink bottled beer or wine, bring a bottle opener and corkscrew.

ENERGY BOOSTERS Kids get cranky when they're hungry, and when that happens, your entire group has a problem. Like many parents you might, for nutritional reasons, keep a tight rein on snacks available to your children at home. At Walt Disney World, however, maintaining energy and equanimity trumps between-meal snack discipline. For maximum

Don't Let the Sun See You Frying (cont'd)

It is best to keep babies under 6 months old covered and out of the sun. However, the AAP condones a small amount of sunscreen on vulnerable areas, such as the nose and chin, when you have the baby out. Be very careful to monitor your baby, even if he or she is wearing a hat and sitting under an umbrella. The sun moves. A spot that was shady when you ordered your funnel cake might be baking by the time you've finished eating it. If your child develops a rash while using sunscreen, get the baby out of the sun, stop using the sunscreen, and call your doctor.

With older children, slather sunscreen liberally and often. Don't make the mistake of thinking that because you've coated your children in a "bazillion-SPF-water-resistant-all-day-protection-top-of-the-line-surfers-use-it-so-should-you" brand of sunscreen that you don't have to worry until dinnertime. Reapply and check for redness often. Sunburn can be sneaky. Children aren't likely to notice the mild discomfort of impending sunburn, especially when they are having fun. Check them often and get them out of the sun as soon as you see even slight redness. You don't have to pay extra for special formulas made for children. As long as the SPF is at least 15 and offers broad-spectrum protection, one brand can serve the whole family.

NOT JUST SKIN DEEP

It is just as important to protect the eyes and lips as the skin. Using a lip balm with an SPF of 15 is pretty easy to do but also easy to forget. Be sure to keep several tubes in your bag or pocket and reapply often to your own lips and

---

zip and contentedness, give your kids snacks containing complex carbohydrates (fruits, crackers, nonfat energy bars, and the like) *before* they get hungry or show signs of exhaustion. You should avoid snacks that are high in fats and proteins because these foods take a long time to digest and will tend to unsettle your stomach if it's a hot day.

Bob enthusiastically recommends Clif Shot Bloks, a chewable cube that replaces electrolytes in the body. They're light, come in several different flavors (all tasty), and don't melt even on the hottest days. Bob uses them when needed on mountain bike rides. They really work wonders.

ELECTRONICS Regardless of your children's ages, always bring a night-light. Flashlights are also handy for finding stuff in a dark hotel room after the kids are asleep. If you are big coffee drinkers and if you drive, bring along a coffeemaker if it's not included in your room.

Portable CD players and iPods with headphones, as well as some electronic games, are often controversial gear for a family outing. We recommend compromise. Headphones allow kids to create their own space even when they're with others, and that can be a safety valve. That said, try to agree before the trip on some headphone parameters, so you those of your kids. Again, the brand is less important than choosing something that you will use and remembering to use it.

Sunglasses are also a must. Too much sun exposure can contribute to age-related macular degeneration, among other things. This may not seem to be much of an issue when you are young and healthy, but when you get old and go blind you'll wish you had remembered to put on some shades. Not all sunglasses filter out damaging rays. Be sure to choose shades (for both the adults and the kids) that have 99-percent-UV protection. Large lenses and wraparound styles might not look as cool, but they offer much better protection. This is one case where you may have to spend a little more to be sure you are getting adequate protection, but you don't want to skimp on this. Much of the damage to the eyes from too much sun is irreversible and, like sun damage to the skin, it starts accumulating in childhood.

If you do slip up and get a burn, cool baths, aloe gels, and ibuprofen (or for the adults, aspirin) usually help ease the suffering. But occasionally sunburns can be as dangerous in the short term as they are in the long term. If you or your child experiences nausea, vomiting, high fever, severe pain, confusion, or fainting, seek medical care immediately.

All of the above is important—and sunscreen is a must if you are headed to Florida after a nice, cushy winter indoors in less sun-drenched climes—but don't let that little bottle with its inscrutable numbers take you off guard. You still need to wear a hat, stay out of the sun during the hottest part of the day (between 10 a.m. and 3 p.m.), and stay well-hydrated.

don't begin to feel as if they're being used to keep other family members and the trip itself at a distance. If you're traveling by car, take turns choosing the radio station or CD for part of the trip.

DON'T FORGET THE TENT This is not a joke and has nothing to do with camping. When Bob's daughter was preschool age, he about went crazy trying to get her to sleep in a shared hotel room. She was accustomed to having her own room at home and was hyperstimulated whenever she traveled. Bob tried makeshift curtains and room dividers and even rearranged the furniture in a few hotel rooms to create the illusion of a more private, separate space for her. It was all for naught. It wasn't until she was around 4 years old and Bob took her camping that he seized on an idea that had some promise. She liked the cozy, secure, womblike feel of a backpacking tent and quieted down much more readily than she ever had in hotel rooms. So the next time the family stayed in a hotel, he pitched his backpacking tent in the corner of the room. In she went, nested for a bit, and fell asleep.

Since the time of Bob's daughter's childhood, there has been an astounding evolution in tent design. Responding to the needs of climbers and paddlers who often have to pitch tents on rocks (where it's impossible to drive stakes), tent manufacturers developed a broad range of tents with self-supporting frames that can be erected virtually anywhere without ropes or stakes. Affordable and sturdy, many are as simple to put up as opening an umbrella. So, if your child is too young for a room of his or her own, or you can't afford a second hotel room, try pitching a small tent. Modern tents are self-contained, with floors and an entrance that can be zipped up (or not) for privacy but cannot be locked. Kids appreciate having their own space and enjoy the adventure of being in a tent, even one set up in the corner of a hotel room. Sizes range from children's play tents with a 2- to 3-foot base to models large enough to sleep two or three husky teens. Light and compact when stored, a two-adult-size tent in its own storage bag (called a stuff sack) will take up about one-tenth or less of a standard overhead bin on a commercial airliner. Another option for infants and toddlers is to drape a sheet over a portable crib or playpen to make a tent.

THE BOX Bob writing: On one memorable Walt Disney World excursion when my children were younger, we started each morning with an immensely annoying, involuntary scavenger hunt. Invariably, seconds before our scheduled departure to the theme park, we discovered that some combination of shoes, billfolds, sunglasses, hip packs, or other necessities were unaccountably missing. For the next 15 minutes we would root through the room like pigs hunting truffles in an attempt to locate the absent items. Now I don't know about your kids, but when my kids lost a shoe or something, they always searched where it was easiest to look, as opposed to where the lost article was most likely to be. I would be jammed under a bed feeling around, while my children stood in the middle of the room intently inspecting the ceiling. As my friends will tell you, I'm as open to a novel theory as the next guy, but we never did find any shoes on the ceiling. Not once. Anyway, here's what I finally did: I swung by a liquor store and mooched a big empty box. From then on, every time we returned to the room, I had the kids deposit shoes, hip packs, and other potentially wayward items in the box. After that the box was off-limits until the next morning, when I doled out the contents.

PLASTIC GARBAGE BAGS There are two attractions, the Kali River Rapids raft ride in the Animal Kingdom and Splash Mountain in the Magic Kingdom, where you are certain to get wet and possibly soaked. If it's really hot and you don't care, then fine. But if it's cool or you're just not up for a soaking, bring a large plastic trash bag to the park. By cutting holes in the top and on the sides, you can fashion a sack poncho that will keep your clothes from getting wet. On the raft ride, you will also get your feet wet. If you're not up for walking around in squishing, soaked shoes, bring a second, smaller plastic bag to wear over your feet while riding.

SUPPLIES FOR INFANTS AND TODDLERS

BASED ON RECOMMENDATIONS FROM HUNDREDS of *Unofficial Guide* readers, here's what we suggest you carry with you when touring with infants and toddlers:

- A disposable diaper for every hour you plan to be away from your hotel room
- A plastic (or vinyl) diaper wrap with Velcro closures
- A cloth diaper or kitchen towel to put over your shoulder for burping
- Two receiving blankets: one to wrap the baby, one to lay the baby on or to drape over you when you nurse
- Ointment for diaper rash
- Moistened towelettes such as Wet Ones
- Prepared formula in bottles if you are not breast-feeding
- A washable bib, baby spoon, and baby food if your infant is eating solids
- For toddlers, a small toy for comfort and to keep them occupied during attractions

Baby Care Centers at the theme parks will sell you just about anything that you forget or run out of. Like all things Disney, prices will be higher than elsewhere, but at least you won't need to detour to a drug store in the middle of your touring day.

TIPS FOR PREGNANT MOTHERS

LET'S FACE IT: A visit to Walt Disney World is not the ideal vacation for an expecting mom, but we also know that quite a lot of pregnant moms visit the World every year. The most important advice for pregnant moms is to take it easy. If you travel by car or plane, make sure you prepare your schedule in such a manner that you have plenty of rest. Don't stay on your feet all day; stick to a healthy, balanced diet;

but most of all don't skip meals; and drink plenty of fluids. Keep the dining options flexible; morning sickness or sudden aversions or preferences to food can be dealt with easily if you don't make reservations and go for whatever you feel like eating. Always carry some snacks and bottled water with you. A plastic bag folded in your pocket in case you feel unwell takes no space but gives peace of mind. You also should discuss your upcoming Walt Disney World visit with your physician. He or she will certainly have valuable tips.

Comfortable clothes are a must and so are well-worn-in supporting shoes. You may consider getting a maternity support belt to keep your back from hurting. If you are using a special pillow to support your belly, this is not the time to leave it at home. If you do not have enough space for it in your suitcase, consider shipping one ahead in a care box. Of course the hotel will provide you with extra pillows if needed.

Maternity bathing suit: If you don't own one, purchase a maternity bathing suit; you will be glad you did. A relaxing afternoon at the pool or a float down the lazy river in the water parks is wonderful.

At the parks take frequent breaks; put your legs up! The Baby Care Centers also welcome expectant moms, and you can sit and relax in a pleasant atmosphere. Go back to the hotel for a nap during the day, and plan a day away from the parks. Go splurge and have a massage; your back and feet will be grateful. Sleep is precious, so don't overdo it; a good night of sleep is better than all the fireworks in the sky.

Heed the warnings! Here is a short list of rides that are absolutely not suitable for expecting moms: Big Thunder Mountain Railroad; DINOSAUR; Expedition Everest; Kali River Rapids; Kilimanjaro Safaris; Mission: SPACE; Rock 'n' Roller Coaster; Star Tours; Space Mountain; Splash Mountain; Test Track; Tomorrowland Speedway; and The Twilight Zone Tower of Terror. Remember, this is just a short list; use your own better judgment.

A word about the water parks: Obviously this is not the time to experience the offerings of Crush 'n' Gusher at Typhoon Lagoon or the moment to come down Summit Plummet at Blizzard Beach, but the water parks offer great lazy rivers and pools, as well as shady beaches where you can relax and let the rest of your family enjoy the wild things.

Tips for Nursing Mothers

Baby Care Centers are available at all Walt Disney World parks, and nursing mothers will not have difficulty finding a comfortable, clean, and pleasant place to take care of their infants. In addition to breast-feeding rooms equipped with rocking chairs and love seats, the child-care facilities have sinks for washing and a room with toys and videos for your older children. Should you need diapers, baby clothes, children's medicines, and other small necessities, Disney has those items available right there for a fee.

Here are some tips to remember when visiting:

- Getting there by plane: Remember to nurse your child at takeoff and landing. It helps to open the baby's ears and so eliminates discomfort due to pressure changes.

- Nurse your infant at the first sign of hunger. You and the baby will be calmer, and you will attract much less attention if you feed the baby before he or she gets fussy and screams at the top of his or her lungs.

- Wear comfortable clothes. While you can access the Baby Care Centers at any time, there is nothing wrong with nursing your infant in a calm, shady spot anywhere at Walt Disney World or at the pool of your hotel. A dress with buttons in the front and a small baby blanket to put over your shoulder will do the trick. A large T-shirt that allows the baby to nurse "from under" is another option. Besides, breast-feeding is completely legal in Florida. As a matter of fact, Florida was the first state to protect breast-feeding in public by law in 1993.

- Pick a quiet place to nurse your baby.

- Adequate rest is another must. Schedule several breaks into your day, and go back to the hotel for a nap.

- Make sure you plan regular healthy meals. A nursing mom, much like an expecting mother, has increased nutritional needs. In addition to eating a well-balanced diet and drinking plenty of fluids, it is always a good idea to take along some snacks.

- It is hot in Florida, and while it is important for all visitors to drink lots of water, it is crucial for nursing moms, so stay hydrated!

- Schedule a down day into your trip. If you have older children, let dad take them to the park while you stay behind with the baby. A day of rest works wonders.

- If you plan on a parent's evening out, consider pumping milk for later use or supplementing breast milk with a bottle of formula.

- Nursing is exhausting, and so is touring Walt Disney World. Fatigue can reduce milk flow. Get enough rest and don't stay up past your bedtime. The night of a nursing mom is already short. Leave the park whenever you feel tired and get enough sleep.

- A bath and a massage calm most fussy babies and are good for mom too.

Enjoy your visit. If you take it easy, Walt Disney World is certainly a magical place to be for expecting and nursing mothers alike. And did we mention the shopping? Of course you will fall for the cute baby clothes, the crib decorations, babies' first Christmas ornament and keepsake, and for at least one of the millions of toys Disney thinks you absolutely need.

Other suggested reading:

- PassPorter's *Open Mouse for Walt Disney World and the Disney Cruise Line: Easy Access Vacations for Travelers With Extra Challenges* has a good section for expectant moms, nursing your baby, and infant travel.

- *Baby Massage: A Practical Guide to Massage and Movement for Babies and Infants* by Peter Walker.

REMEMBERING *Your* TRIP

1. Purchase a notebook for each child and spend some time each evening recording the events of the day. If your children have trouble getting motivated or don't know what to write about, start a discussion; otherwise, let them write or draw whatever they want to remember from the day's events.

2. Collect mementos along the way and create a treasure box in a small tin or cigar box. Months or years later, it's fun to look at postcards, pins, seashells, or ticket stubs to jump-start a memory.

3. Add inexpensive postcards to your photographs to create an album; then write a few words on each page to accompany the images.

4. Give each child a disposable camera to record his or her version of the trip. One 5-year-old snapped an entire series of photos that never showed anyone above the waist—his view of the world (and the photos were priceless).

5. Nowadays, many families travel with a camcorder, though we recommend using one sparingly—parents end up viewing the trip through the lens rather than being in the moment. If you must, take it along, but only record a few moments of major sights (too much is boring anyway). And let the kids tape and narrate. On the topic of narration, speak loudly so as to be heard over the not insignificant background noise of the parks. Make use of lockers at all of the parks when the camcorder becomes a burden or when you're going to experience an attraction that might damage it or get it wet. Unless you've got a camcorder designed for underwater shots, leave it behind on Splash Mountain, the Kali River Rapids, and any other ride where water is involved.

6. Another inexpensive way to record memories is a palm-size voice recorder. Let all family members describe their experiences. Hearing a small child's voice years later is so endearing, and those recorded descriptions will trigger an album's worth of memories, far more focused than what many novices capture with a camcorder.

Finally, when it comes to taking photos and collecting mementos, don't let the tail wag the dog. You're not going to Disney World to build the biggest scrapbook in history. Or as this Houston mom put it:

Tell your readers to get a grip on the photography thing. We were so busy shooting pictures that we kind of lost the thread. We had to get our pictures developed when we got home to see what all we did (while on vacation).

HOW TO HAVE FUN BEFORE AND AFTER YOU VISIT— OR THE THINGS BOB WOULD NEVER DO

PREPARING FOR YOUR Walt Disney World vacation is important, but it is equally important to have a good time. Doing so before you leave is yet another way to get the whole family involved.

The weekend before your departure, plan a party for all who are going to Walt Disney World. Pick a Disney movie the entire family will enjoy and plan a meal in front of the TV. A chocolate cake or cookies shaped like the famous mouse head will be a guaranteed success and add to the fun. This is the perfect time to go over the must-see list and reiterate the dos and dont's.

Don't forget to send Bob an invitation.

Liliane

A similar event can be planned upon your return, when it is time to share the pictures and maybe even the movie you made during your visit to Walt Disney World.

Great Websites:

Arts and crafts and party tips:
disney.go.com/magicartist

For some serious cooking, check out:
magicalkingdoms.com/wdw/recipes

Recommended Books:

The Disney Party Handbook by Alison Boteler

The Disney Bakery by Adrienne Berofsky

Liliane will throw a party with the least provocation—Groundhog Day, National Tulip Day, Bless the Reptiles Day, you name it. But scheduling a wingding the weekend before you go to Disney World is to me like holding an Easter egg hunt in a cattle stampede—just a little too much going on to add one more thing.

Bob

TRIAL RUN

IF YOU GIVE THOUGHTFUL CONSIDERATION to all areas of mental, physical, organizational, and logistical preparation discussed in this chapter, what remains is to familiarize yourself with Walt Disney World itself, and of course, to conduct your field test. Yep, that's right, we want you to take the whole platoon on the road for a day to see if you are combat ready. No joke, this is important. You'll learn who poops out first, who is prone to developing blisters, who has to pee every 11 seconds, and given the proper forum, how compatible your family is in terms of what you like to see and do.

For the most informative trial run, choose a local venue that requires lots of walking, dealing with crowds, and making decisions on how to spend your time. Regional theme parks and state fairs are your best bets, followed by large zoos and museums. Devote the whole day. Kick off the morning with an early start, just like you will at Walt Disney World, paying attention to who's organized and ready to go and who's dragging his or her butt and holding up the group. If you have to drive an hour or two to get to your test venue, no big deal. You'll have to do some commuting at Walt Disney World too. Spend the whole day, eat a couple meals, and stay late.

Don't bias the sample (that is, mess with the outcome) by telling everyone you are practicing for Walt Disney World. Everyone behaves differently when they know they are being tested or evaluated. Your objective is not to run a perfect drill but to find out as much as you can about how the individuals in your family, as well as the family as a group, respond to and deal with everything they experience during the day. Pay attention to who moves quickly and who is slow; to who is adventuresome and who is reticent; to who keeps going and who needs frequent rest breaks; to who sets the agenda and who is content to follow; to who is easily agitated and who stays cool; to who tends to dawdle or wander off; to who is curious and who is bored; to who is demanding and who is accepting. You get the idea.

Discuss the findings of the test run with your spouse the next day. Don't be discouraged if your test day wasn't perfect; few (if any) are. Distinguish between problems that are remediable and problems that are intrinsic to your family's emotional or physical makeup (no amount of hiking, for example, will toughen up some people's feet).

Establish a plan for addressing remediable problems (further conditioning, setting limits before you go, trying harder to achieve family consensus, whatever) and develop strategies for minimizing or working around problems that are a fact of life (waking sleepyheads 15 minutes early, placing moleskin on likely blister sites before setting out, packing familiar food for the toddler who balks at restaurant fare). If you are an attentive observer, a fair diagnostician, and a creative problem solver, you'll be able to work out a significant percentage of the problems you're likely to encounter at Walt Disney World before you ever leave home.

WDW transportation planners use the latest technology
when planning new development of bus routes.

GET *in the* BOAT, MEN!

THE ABOVE IS NOT A *JEOPARDY!* ANSWER, but if it were, the question would be this: "What did George Washington say to his soldiers before they crossed the Delaware?" We share this interesting historic aside as our way of sounding the alarm, blowing the bugle, or whatever. It's time to move beyond preparation and practice and to leap into action. Walt Disney World, here we come! Get in the boat, men!

READY, SET, TOUR!
Some Touring Considerations

HOW MUCH TIME IS REQUIRED TO SEE EACH PARK?

THE MAGIC KINGDOM AND EPCOT offer such a large number of attractions and special live entertainment options that it is impossible to see everything in a single day, with or without a midday break. For a reasonably thorough tour of each, allocate a minimum of one and a half days and preferably two days. The Animal Kingdom and Disney's Hollywood Studios can each be seen in a day, although planning on a day and a half allows for a more relaxed visit.

WHICH PARK TO SEE FIRST?

THIS QUESTION IS LESS ACADEMIC than it appears. Children who see the Magic Kingdom first expect more of the same type of entertainment at the other parks. At Epcot, children are often disappointed by the educational orientation and more serious tone (as are many adults). Disney's Hollywood Studios offers some pretty wild action, but the general presentation is educational and more mature. Though most children enjoy zoos, live animals can't be programmed to entertain. Thus, children may not find the Animal Kingdom as exciting as the Magic Kingdom or the Studios.

First-time visitors should see Epcot first; you will be able to enjoy it fully without having been preconditioned to think of Disney entertainment as solely fantasy or adventure. Children will be more likely to enjoy Epcot on its own merits if they see it first, and they will be more relaxed and patient in their touring.

See the Animal Kingdom second. Like Epcot, it has an educational thrust, but it provides a change of pace because it features live animals. Next, see Disney's Hollywood Studios, which helps all ages make a fluid transition from the educational Epcot and Animal Kingdom to the fanciful Magic Kingdom. Also, because Disney's Hollywood Studios is smaller, you won't walk as much or stay as long. Save the Magic Kingdom for last.

If you can't postpone the Magic Kingdom without a major revolt, at least see Epcot first. Adult orientation notwithstanding, there's lots that children 7 and up will love, younger children not so much. Be sure to participate in the Kim Possible and Kidcot programs, both described in Part 8. They will be the highlight of your child's day. If seeing Mickey is your kid's top priority, be advised that you can see him in each of the four major theme parks. Any cast member can tell you where to find him.

OPERATING HOURS

DISNEY CAN'T BE ACCUSED of being inflexible regarding operating hours at the parks. They run a dozen or more schedules each year, making it advisable to call ☎ 407-824-4321 for the exact hours before you arrive. In the off-season, parks may be open for as few as 8 hours (10 a.m.–6 p.m.). By contrast, at busy times (particularly holidays), they may be open 8 a.m.–2 a.m. the next morning.

Usually, hours approximate the following: September through mid-March, excluding holiday periods, the Magic Kingdom is open from 9 a.m. to 7, 8, or 9 p.m. During the same period, Epcot is open 9 a.m.–9 p.m., and Hollywood Studios is open from 9 a.m. to 7 or 8 p.m. The Animal Kingdom is open from 9 a.m. until 6 or 7 p.m. During summer, expect the Animal Kingdom to remain open until 8 p.m. Epcot and Hollywood Studios are normally open until 9 or 10 p.m., with the Magic Kingdom sometimes open as late as 1 a.m.

We also maintain more easily readable park hours, as well as entertainment and Extra Magic Hour schedules, on our website, **touringplans.com,** and conveniently through our mobile application, Lines (**touringplans.com/lines**).

OFFICIAL OPENING VERSUS REAL OPENING

THE OPERATING HOURS YOU'RE QUOTED when you call are official hours. The parks sometimes open earlier. Many visitors, relying on information from Disney Guest Relations, arrive at the official opening time and find the park packed with people. If the official hours are 9 a.m.–9 p.m., for example, Main Street in the Magic Kingdom opens at 8 or 8:30 a.m., with the remainder of the park opening at 8:30 or 9 a.m. If the official opening for the Magic Kingdom is 8 a.m. and you're eligible for early entry (if you are staying in a Disney resort), you sometimes are able to enter the park as early as 6:30 a.m.

Disney publishes hours of operation well in advance but reserves the flexibility to react daily to gate conditions. Disney traffic controllers survey local hotel reservations, estimate how many visitors they should expect on a given day, and open the theme parks early to avoid bottlenecks at parking facilities and ticket windows and to absorb the crowds as they arrive.

If you're a Disney resort guest and want to take advantage of Extra Magic Hours early entry, arrive 1 hour and 20 minutes before the early-entry park is scheduled to open to the general public. Buses, boats, and monorails will initiate service to the early-entry park about 2 hours before it opens to the general public.

At day's end, rides and attractions shut down at approximately the official closing time. Main Street remains open 30 minutes to an hour after the rest of the Magic Kingdom has closed.

THE RULES

SUCCESSFUL TOURING OF THE MAGIC KINGDOM, Animal Kingdom, Epcot, or Disney's Hollywood Studios hinges on five rules:

1. Determine in Advance What You Really Want To See

What rides and attractions appeal most to you? Which additional rides and attractions would you like to experience if you have some time left? What are you willing to forgo?

To help you set your touring priorities, we describe each theme park and its attractions later in this book. In each description, we include the author's evaluation of the attraction and the opinions of Walt Disney World guests expressed as star ratings. Five stars is the best possible rating.

Finally, because attractions range from midway-type rides and horse-drawn trolleys to colossal, high-tech extravaganzas, we have developed a hierarchy of categories to pinpoint an attraction's magnitude:

SUPER HEADLINERS The best attractions the theme park has to offer. Mind-boggling in size, scope, and imagination. Represents the cutting edge of modern attraction technology and design.

HEADLINERS Full-blown, multimillion-dollar, full-scale themed adventures and theater presentations. Modern in technology and design and employing a complete range of special effects.

MAJOR ATTRACTIONS Themed adventures on a more modest scale but incorporating state-of-the-art technologies. Or, larger-scale attractions of older design.

MINOR ATTRACTIONS Midway-type rides, small dark rides (cars on a track, zigzagging through the dark), small theater presentations, transportation rides, and elaborate walk-through attractions.

DIVERSIONS Exhibits, both passive and interactive. Includes playgrounds, video arcades, and street theater.

Though not every Walt Disney World attraction fits neatly into these descriptions, the categories provide a comparison of attractions' size and scope. Remember that bigger and more elaborate doesn't always mean better. Peter Pan's Flight, a minor attraction in the Magic Kingdom, continues to be one of the park's most beloved rides. Likewise, for many young children, no attraction, regardless of size, surpasses Dumbo.

2. Arrive Early! Arrive Early! Arrive Early!

This is the single most important key to efficient touring and avoiding long lines. There are no lines and fewer people first thing in the morning. The same four rides you can experience in one hour in early morning can take as long as 3 hours to see after 10:30 a.m. Have breakfast before you arrive, so you won't waste prime touring time sitting in a restaurant.

The earlier a park opens, the greater the potential advantage. This is because most vacationers won't make the sacrifice to rise early and get to a theme park before it opens. Fewer people are willing to be on hand for an 8 a.m. opening than for a 9 a.m. opening. On those rare occasions when a park opens at 10 a.m., almost everyone arrives at the same time, so it's almost impossible to get a jump on the crowd. If you're a Disney resort guest and have early-entry privileges, arrive as early as early entry allows (6:30 a.m. if the park opens to the public at 8 a.m. or 7:30 a.m. if the park opens to the public at 9 a.m.). If you are visiting during midsummer, arrive at non-early-entry parks 30 minutes before the official opening time. During holiday periods, arrive at non-early-entry parks 40 minutes before the official opening.

3. Avoid Bottlenecks

Crowd concentrations and/or faulty crowd management cause bottlenecks. Avoiding bottlenecks involves being able to predict where, when, and why they occur. Concentrations of hungry people create bottlenecks at restaurants during lunch and dinner. Concentrations of people moving toward the exit at closing time create bottlenecks in gift shops en route to the gate. Concentrations of visitors at new and popular rides and at rides slow to load and unload create bottlenecks and long lines. To help you get a grip on which attractions cause bottlenecks, we have developed a Bottleneck Scale with a range of one to ten. If an attraction ranks high on the Bottleneck Scale, try to experience it during the first 2 hours the park is open. The scale is included in each attraction profile in Parts Seven through Eleven.

The best way to avoid bottlenecks, however, is to use one of our field-tested touring plans available in clip-out form complete with a map on pages 445–468. The plans will save you as much as 4½ hours of standing in line in a single day.

4. Go Back to Your Hotel for a Rest in the Middle of the Day

Liliane

If you can't calm them—dunk them. Whenever my son was too wound up to nap or go to bed at night, I took him to the pool—water works wonders.

You may think we're beating the dead horse with this midday nap thing, but if you plug away all day at the theme parks, you'll understand how the dead horse feels. No joke; resign yourself to going back to the hotel in the middle of the day for swimming, reading, and a snooze.

5. Let Off Steam

Time at a Disney theme park is extremely regimented for younger children. Often held close for fear of losing them, they are ushered from line to line and attraction to attraction throughout the day. After a couple of hours of being on such a short leash, it's not surprising that they're in need of some physical freedom and an opportunity to discharge that pent-up energy. As it happens, all of the major theme parks except Epcot offer some sort of elaborate, creative playground perfect for such a release. Be advised that each playground (or plaza) is fairly large, and it's pretty easy to misplace a child while they're exploring. All children's playgrounds, however, have only one exit, so although your kids might get lost within the playground, they cannot wander off into the rest of the park without passing through the single exit (usually staffed by a Disney cast member).

YOUR DAILY ITINERARY

PLAN EACH DAY IN THREE BLOCKS:

1. Early morning theme-park touring
2. Midday break
3. Late afternoon and evening theme-park touring

Choose the attractions that interest you most and check their bottleneck ratings along with what time of day we recommend you visit. If your children are 8 years old or younger, review the attraction's fright potential rating. Use one of our touring plans or work out a step-by-step plan of your own and write it down. Experience attractions with a high bottleneck rating as early as possible, transitioning to attractions with bottleneck ratings of six to eight around midmorning. Plan on departing the park for your midday break by 11:30 a.m. or so.

For your late afternoon and evening touring block, you do not necessarily have to return to the same theme park. If you have purchased one of the Disney admission options that allow you to "park hop," that is, visit more than one theme park on a given day, you may opt to spend the afternoon/evening block somewhere different. In any event, as you start your afternoon/evening block, see attractions with low bottleneck ratings until about 5 p.m. After 5 p.m., any attraction with a rating of one to seven is fair game. If you stay into the evening, try attractions with ratings of eight to ten during the hour just before closing.

In addition to attractions, each theme park offers a broad range of special live entertainment events. In the morning block, concentrate on the attractions. For the record, we regard live shows that offer five or more daily performances a day (except for street entertainment) as attractions. Thus, *Indiana Jones* at Disney's Hollywood Studios is an attraction, as is *Festival of the Lion King* at the Animal Kingdom. *IllumiNations* at Epcot or the parades at the Magic Kingdom, on the other hand, are live entertainment events. A schedule of live performances is listed in the *Times Guide* available at the entrance of each park.

We strongly recommend deferring parades, stage shows, and other productions until the afternoon/evening.

When planning your day, also be aware that major live events draw large numbers of guests from the attraction lines. Thus, a good time to see an especially popular attraction is during a parade or other similar event.

TOURING PLANS

OUR TOURING PLANS ARE STEP-BY-STEP GUIDES for seeing as much as possible with a minimum of standing in line. They're designed to help you avoid crowds and bottlenecks on days of moderate-to-heavy attendance. On days of lighter attendance (see "When To Go to Walt Disney World," page 44), the plans will still save time, but they won't be as critical to successful touring.

Don't get obsessed with the touring plans. It's your vacation, after all. You can amend or even scrap the plans if you want.

What You Can Realistically Expect from the Touring Plans

The best way to see as much as possible with the least amount of waiting is to arrive early. Several of our touring plans require that you be on hand when the park opens. Because this is often difficult and sometimes impossible for families with young children or nocturnal teens, we've developed additional touring plans for families who get a late start. You won't see as much as with the early-morning plans, but you'll see significantly more than visitors without a plan.

Variables That Will Affect the Success of the Touring Plans

The plans' success will be affected by how quickly you move from ride to ride; when and how many refreshment and restroom breaks you take; when, where, and how you eat meals; and your ability (or lack thereof) to find your way around. Smaller groups almost always move faster than larger groups, and parties of adults generally cover more ground than families with young children. Switching off (see page 242), also known as baby swapping or child swapping, among other things, inhibits families with little ones from moving expeditiously among attractions.

If you have young children in your party, be prepared for character encounters. The appearance of a Disney character usually stops a touring plan in its tracks. While some characters stroll the parks, it's equally common that they assemble in a specific venue (such as character trails at the Animal Kingdom) where families queue up for photos and autographs. Meeting characters, posing for photos, and collecting autographs can burn hours of touring time. If your kids collect character autographs, you need to anticipate these interruptions and negotiate some understanding with your children about when you will follow the plan and when you will collect autographs. Our advice is to go with the flow or set aside a specific morning or afternoon for photos and autographs. Note that queues for autographs, especially in the Magic Kingdom and Camp Minnie-Mickey at the Animal Kingdom, are sometimes as long as the queues for major attractions. The only time-efficient ways to collect autographs is to use Fastpass where available, such as for Mickey Mouse at the Town Square Theater in the Magic Kingdom, or to line up at the character-greeting areas first thing in the morning. Early morning is also the best time to experience the popular attractions, so you may have tough choices to make.

Liliane

Character meals are another way to collect autographs and might be something you could promise your avid collector in exchange for a full day of touring when the signature hunt is off.

While we realize that following the plans isn't always easy, we nevertheless recommend continuous, expeditious touring until around noon. After noon, breaks and diversions won't affect the plans significantly.

A multigenerational family from Aurora, Ohio, wonders how to know if you are on track or not, writing:

It seems like the touring plans were very time dependent, yet there were no specific times attached to the plan outside of the early morning. On more than one day, I often had to guess as to whether we were on track. Having small children and a grandparent in our group, we couldn't move at a fast pace.

There is no objective measurement for being on track. Each family's or touring group's experience will differ to some degree. Regardless of whether your group is large or small, fast or slow, the sequence of attractions in the touring plans will allow you to enjoy the greatest number of attractions in the least possible amount of time. Two quickly moving adults will probably take in more attractions in a specific time period than will a large group made up of children, parents, and grandparents. However, given the characteristics of the respective groups, each will maximize their touring time and experience as many attractions as possible.

What To Do if You Lose the Thread

Anything from a blister to a broken attraction can throw off a touring plan. If unforeseen events interrupt a plan:

1. Skip one step on the plan for every 15 minutes' delay. If, for example, you lose your billfold and spend an hour finding it, skip four steps and pick up from there.

2. Forget the plan and organize the remainder of your day using the bottleneck ratings in conjunction with the best-times-to-go suggestions in each attraction profile.

What To Expect When You Arrive at the Parks

Because most touring plans are based on being present when the theme park opens, you need to know about opening procedures. Disney transportation to the parks begins 1½–2 hours before official opening. The parking lots open at around the same time.

Each park has an entrance plaza outside the turnstiles. Usually, you're held there until 30 minutes before the official opening time, when you're admitted. What happens next depends on the season and the day's crowds.

1. **LOW SEASON** At slower times, you will usually be confined outside the turnstiles or in a small section of the park until the official opening time. At the Magic Kingdom you might be admitted to Main Street, U.S.A.; at Animal Kingdom, to The Oasis and sometimes to Discovery Island; at Epcot, to the fountain area around Spaceship Earth; and at Disney's Hollywood Studios, to Hollywood Boulevard. Rope barriers supervised by Disney cast members keep you there until the "rope drop," when the barrier is removed and the park and its attractions begin operating at the official opening time.

2. **HIGH-ATTENDANCE DAYS** When large crowds are expected, you will be admitted through the turnstiles 30 minutes before official opening, and the entire park will be operating.

3. **VARIATIONS** Sometimes Disney will run a variation of those two procedures. In this, you'll be permitted through the turnstiles and find that one or several specific attractions are open early. At Epcot, Spaceship Earth and sometimes Test Track or Soarin' will be operating. At Animal Kingdom, you may find Kilimanjaro Safaris and *It's Tough to Be a Bug!* running early. At Disney's Hollywood Studios, look for Tower of Terror and/or Rock 'n' Roller Coaster. The Magic Kingdom almost never runs a variation. Instead, you'll usually encounter plan number one described above or occasionally plan two.

HOW TO FIND THE TOURING PLAN THAT'S BEST FOR YOU

THE DIFFERENT TOURING PLANS FOR EACH PARK are described in the chapter pertaining to that park. The descriptions will tell you for whom (for example, teens, parents with preschoolers, grandparents, and so on) or for what situation (such as sleeping late or enjoying the park at night) the plans are designed. The actual touring plans are located on pages 445–468 at the back of the book. Each plan includes a numbered map of the park in question to help you find your way around. Clip the plan of your choice out of the book by cutting along the line indicated and take it with you to the park.

Will the Plans Continue to Work Once the Secret Is Out?

Yes! First, some of the plans require that a patron be there when a park opens. Many Disney World patrons simply won't get up early while on vacation. Second, less than 1% of any day's attendance has been exposed to the plans—too few to affect results. Last, most groups tailor the plans, skipping rides or shows according to taste.

How Frequently Are the Touring Plans Revised?

Because Disney is always adding new attractions and changing operations, we revise the plans every year, and updates are always available at **touringplans.com.** Most complaints we receive come from readers using out-of-date editions of the *Unofficial Guide*. Be prepared, however, for surprises. Opening procedures and show times may change, for example, and you can't predict when an attraction might break down.

Bouncing Around

Many readers object to crisscrossing a theme park, as our touring plans sometimes require. A lady from Decatur, Georgia, said she "got dizzy from all the bouncing around." We empathize, but here's the rub, park by park.

In the Magic Kingdom, the most popular attractions are positioned across the park from one another. This is no accident. It's a method of more equally distributing guests throughout the park. If you want to experience the most popular attractions in 1 day without long waits, arrive before the park fills and see those attractions first (which requires crisscrossing the park), or enjoy the main attractions on one side of the park first, and then try the most popular attractions on the other side during the hour or so before closing, when crowds presumably have thinned. Using Fastpass lessens the time you wait in line but tends to increase the bouncing around because you must visit the same attraction twice: once to obtain your Fastpass and again to use it.

The best way to minimize bouncing around at the Magic Kingdom is to do half the touring plan on one day and the other half on another. This makes for much more relaxing touring and facilitates returning to your hotel for rest and a swim. Disney's Hollywood Studios is configured in a way that precludes an orderly approach to touring or to a clockwise or counterclockwise rotation. Orderly

We've revised the Epcot plans to eliminate most of the bouncing around and have added instructions to further minimize walking.

touring is further confounded by live entertainment that prompts guests to interrupt their touring to head for whichever theater is about to crank up. At the Studios, therefore, you're stuck with bouncing around, whether you use our plan or not. In our opinion, when it comes to Disney parks, it's best to have a plan.

The Animal Kingdom is arranged in a spoke-and-hub configuration like the Magic Kingdom, simplifying crisscrossing the park. Even so, the only way to catch various shows is to stop what you're doing and troop across the park to the next performance.

Touring Plans and the Obsessive-compulsive Reader

We suggest you follow the touring plans religiously, especially in the mornings, if you're visiting during busy times. The consequence of touring spontaneity in peak season is hours of standing in line. During quieter times, there's no need to be compulsive about following the plans.

A mom in Atlanta suggests:

Emphasize perhaps not following [the touring plans] in off-season. There is no reason to crisscross the park when there are no lines.

A mother in Minneapolis advises:

Please let your readers know to stop along the way to various attractions to appreciate what else may be going on around them. We encountered many families using the Unofficial Guide *[who] became too serious about getting from one place to the next, missing the fun in between.*

Here's a case in point from a Columbia, Missouri, mom:

Getting to the park when it opens is the key to beating the lines. To make that happen pack breakfast on the go—you can eat your PopTarts once you're on the shuttle bus and then drink your juice in line for Dumbo. Send the fastest runner in your party to jump on the shuttle bus or boat; the driver will wait if they see you coming and one of your kids is already hanging on. Skip baths and showers; the pool will do. Showering wastes precious park and rest time. Braid your daughter's hair. My 8-year-old daughter never had to brush her hair in the morning. . . . (Worst case, do her hair on the shuttle bus; don't waste time in your room.) Ball caps for boys also help skip hair brushing and help with the sun.

Yikes! As much as we believe in having a good plan, we probably couldn't keep up with this lady for a day.

When using the plans, relax and always be prepared for surprises and setbacks. When your type-A brain does cartwheels, reflect on the advice of a woman from Trappe, Pennsylvania:

You cannot emphasize enough the dangers of using your touring plans that were printed in the back of the book, especially if the person using them has a compulsive personality. I have a compulsive personality. I planned for this trip for 2 years and researched it by use of guidebooks, computer programs, and information received from WDW. I had a two-page itinerary for our 1-week trip in addition to your touring plans of the theme parks. On night 3 of our trip, I ended up taking an unscheduled trip to the hospital emergency room in Lake Buena Vista. When the doctor asked what seemed to be the problem, I responded with, "I don't know, but I can't stop shaking, and I can't stay here very long because I have to get up in a couple hours to go to the Studios according to my itinerary." Diagnosis: an anxiety attack caused by my excessive itinerary. He gave me a shot of something, and I slept through the first four attractions the next morning. This was our third trip to WDW (not including one trip to Disneyland); on all previous trips I used only the Steve Birnbaum book, and I suffered no ill effects. I am not saying your book was not good. It was excellent! However, it should come with a warning label for people with compulsive personalities.

Touring Plan Rejection

Some folks don't respond well to the regimentation of a touring plan. If you encounter this problem with someone in your party, roll with the punches, as this Maryland couple did:

The rest of the group was not receptive to the use of the touring plans. I think they all thought I was being a little too regimented about planning this vacation. Rather than argue, I left the touring plans behind as we ventured off for the parks. You can guess the outcome. We took our camcorder with us and watched the movies when we returned home. About every 5 minutes or so there is a shot of us all gathered around a park map trying to decide what to do next.

As a Connecticut woman alleges, the plans are incompatible with some readers' bladders and personalities:

I want to know if next year when you write those day schedules you could schedule bathroom breaks in there too. You expect us to be at a certain ride at a certain time and with no stops in between. In one of the letters in your book, a guy writes, "You expect everyone to be theme-park commandos." When I read that, I thought there is a man who really knows what a problem the schedules are if you are a laid-back, slow-moving, careful detail noticer. What were you thinking when you made these schedules?

Finally, note that our mobile app Lines can be used to find attractions with low wait times, even if you're not using a structured touring plan.

Touring Plans for Low-attendance Days

We receive a number of letters each year similar to this one from Lebanon, New Jersey:

The guide always assumed there would be large crowds. We had no lines. An alternate tour for low-traffic days would be helpful.

If attendance is low, you don't need a touring plan. Just go where your taste and instinct direct, and glory in the hassle-free touring. Having said that, however, there are attractions in each park that bottleneck even if attendance is low. These are Space Mountain, Splash Mountain, Dumbo, The Many Adventures of Winnie the Pooh, Peter Pan's Flight, and the Seven Dwarfs Mine Train in the Magic Kingdom; Test Track and Soarin' at Epcot; Kilimanjaro Safaris and Expedition Everest at Animal Kingdom; and Tower of Terror and Rock 'n' Roller Coaster at Disney's Hollywood Studios. Most are Fastpass attractions. Experience them immediately after the parks open or use Fastpass. Remember that crowd size is relative and that large crowds can gather at certain attractions even during less-busy times. We recommend following a touring plan through the first five or six steps. If you're pretty much walking onto every attraction, feel free to scrap the remainder of the plan.

Extra Magic Hours and the Touring Plans

If you're a Disney resort guest and use your morning Extra Magic Hours privileges, complete your early-entry touring before the general public is admitted and position yourself to follow the touring plan. When the public is admitted, the park will suddenly be aswarm. A Wilmington, Delaware, mother advises:

> *The early-entry times went like clockwork. We were finishing up The Great Movie Ride when Disney's Hollywood Studios opened [to the public], and [we] had to wait in line quite a while for* Voyage of the Little Mermaid, *which sort of screwed up everything thereafter. Early-opening attractions should be finished up well before regular opening time so you can be at the plan's first stop as early as possible.*

In the Magic Kingdom, the early-entry attractions are in Fantasyland and Tomorrowland. At Epcot, they're in the Future World section. At Disney's Hollywood Studios, they're dispersed. Practically speaking, see any attractions on the touring plan that are open for early entry, crossing them off as you do. If you finish all early-entry attractions on the touring plan and have time left before the general public is admitted, sample early-entry attractions not included in the plan. Stop touring about 10 minutes before the public is admitted and position yourself for the first attraction on the plan that wasn't open for early entry. During early entry in the Magic Kingdom, for example, you can usually experience Peter Pan's Flight and It's a Small World in Fantasyland, plus Space Mountain and *Stitch's Great Escape!* in Tomorrowland. As official opening nears, go to the boundary between Fantasyland and Liberty Square and be ready to blitz to Splash Mountain and Big Thunder Mountain Railroad, according to the touring plan, when the rest of the park opens.

Evening Extra Magic Hours, when a designated park remains open for Disney resort guests 3 hours beyond normal closing time, have less effect on the touring plans than early entry in the morning does. Parks are almost never scheduled for both early entry and evening Extra Magic Hours on the same day. Thus a park offering evening Extra Magic Hours will enjoy a fairly normal morning and early afternoon. It's not until late afternoon, when park hoppers coming from the other theme parks descend, that the late-closing park will become especially crowded. By that time, you'll be well toward the end of your touring plan.

FASTPASS

IN 1999 DISNEY LAUNCHED A SYSTEM for moderating the wait at many popular attractions. Called Fastpass, it was originally tried at Animal Kingdom and then expanded to attractions at the other parks.

Fastpass works remarkably well, mainly because Fastpass holders get amazingly preferential treatment.

Bob

Here's how it works. Your handout park map and signage at attractions will tell you which attractions are included. Attractions operating Fastpass will have both a regular line and a Fastpass line. A sign at the entrance will say how long the wait is in the regular line. If the wait is acceptable to you, hop in line. If it seems too long, insert your park admission pass into a Fastpass machine and receive an appointment time (for later in the day) to return and ride. When you return at the designated time, you enter the Fastpass line and proceed directly to the attraction's preshow or boarding area. Interestingly, this procedure was pioneered by Universal Studios Hollywood years ago and had been virtually ignored by theme parks since (Universal now has a reworked variation called Universal Express). The system works well and can save a lot of waiting time. There's no extra charge to use Fastpass.

Fastpass is evolving, and attractions continue to be added and deleted from the lineup. Changes aside, here's an example of how to use Fastpass. Say you have only one day to tour the Magic Kingdom. You arrive early and ride Space Mountain and Buzz Lightyear with minimal waits. Then you cross the park to Splash Mountain and find a substantial line. Because Splash Mountain is a Fastpass attraction, you can insert your admission pass into the machine and receive an appointment to come back and ride, thus avoiding a long wait.

The effort to accommodate Fastpass holders makes anyone in the regular line feel second class. And a telling indication of their status is that they're called "standby guests." Indeed, we watched people in regular lines despondently stand by and stand by, while dozens and sometimes hundreds of Fastpass holders were ushered into the boarding area ahead of them. Disney is sending a message here: Fastpass is heaven; anything else is limbo at best and probably purgatory. In any event, you'll think you've been in hell if you're stuck in the regular line during the hot, crowded part of the day.

Readers regularly send standby-line horror stories. Here's one from a Pequea, Pennsylvania, family:

We, a group of four 12-year-olds and five adults, decided to ride Test Track when we arrived at Epcot at 11 a.m. Fastpasses were being issued for [late that night] and the singles line was not open yet, so we decided to brave the 120-minute wait (at MK and the Studios many waits ended up being less than the posted time). What a disaster! Once inside the building, the Fastpass and singles line (which opened when we were very near the building) sped ahead while the standby line barely moved. After 3 hours and 20 minutes, we finally made it to the car! One man who was in the Fastpass line said that he counted a 12:1 ratio between Fastpassers and standby people being let into the [boarding] area. Disney needs to seriously reconsider their boarding policy!

Fastpass doesn't eliminate the need to arrive early at a theme park. Because each park offers a limited number of Fastpass attractions, you still need an early start if you want to see as much as possible in one day. Plus, there's a limited supply of Fastpasses available for each attraction on any day. If you don't arrive until midafternoon, you might find that no more Fastpasses are available. Fastpass does make it possible to see more with less waiting, and it's a great benefit to those who like to sleep late or who choose an afternoon or evening at the parks on their arrival day. It also allows you to postpone wet rides, such as Kali River Rapids at Animal Kingdom or Splash Mountain at the Magic Kingdom, until a warmer time of day.

> Each person in your party must have his or her own Fastpass. — Bob

Understanding the Fastpass System

The purpose of Fastpass is to reduce the wait for designated attractions by distributing guests at those attractions throughout the day. This is accomplished by providing an incentive (a shorter wait) for guests willing to postpone experiencing the attraction until later in the day. The system also, in effect, imposes a penalty (standby status) on those who don't use it. However, spreading out guest arrivals sometimes also decreases the wait for standby guests.

> As a rule of thumb, the earlier in the day you secure a Fastpass, the shorter the interval between time of issue and your 1-hour return window. — Liliane

When you insert your admission pass into a Fastpass time clock, the machine spits out a slip of paper about two-thirds the size of a credit card—small enough to fit in your wallet but also small enough to lose easily. Printed on it is the attraction's name and a time window, for example 1:15–2:15 p.m., during which you can return to ride.

Returning to Ride

In practice, cast members are not very strict about enforcing the return window. They won't let you in before your window begins, but they'll usually admit you after your return window expires. We've used Fastpasses more than 3 years old, and the worst we got was a snarky comment from the cast member minding the line. We'd estimate the probability of being denied entry at 10% or less—it's only happened a couple of times in many dozens of attempts.

At Disneyland in Anaheim, California, the return window expiration time is ignored as a matter of policy, though Disneyland keeps this somewhat of a secret. In other words, a Fastpass is good from the beginning of the return window until closing time. This is shaping up to be the actuality at Walt Disney World, even if not a matter of policy.

When you report back, you'll enter a line marked "Fastpass Return" that routes you more or less directly to the boarding or preshow area. Each person in your party must have his own Fastpass and be ready to show it at the entrance of the Fastpass return line. Before you enter the boarding area or theater, another cast member will collect your Fastpass.

Cast members are instructed to minimize waits for Fastpass holders. Thus, if the Fastpass return line is suddenly inundated (something that occurs by chance), cast members intervene to reduce the Fastpass line. As many as 25 Fastpass holders will be admitted for each standby guest until the Fastpass line is reduced to an acceptable length. Although Fastpass usually eliminates 80% or more of the wait you would experience in the regular line, you can still expect a short wait, usually less than 15 minutes and frequently under 10 minutes.

Obtaining a Fastpass

You can ordinarily obtain a Fastpass anytime after a park opens (some attractions are a little tardy getting their Fastpass system up), but the Fastpass return lines don't usually begin operating until 45–90 minutes after opening.

Regardless of the time of day, if the wait in the regular line at a Fastpass attraction is 25–30 minutes or less, join the regular line.

Whenever you obtain a Fastpass, you can be assured of a period of time between when you receive your Fastpass and when you report back. The interval can be as short as 15 minutes or as long as 7 hours, depending on park attendance and the attraction's popularity and hourly capacity. Generally, the earlier in the day you obtain a Fastpass, the shorter the interval before your return window. If the park opens at 9 a.m. and you obtain a Fastpass for Splash Mountain at 9:25 a.m., your appointment for returning to ride would be 10–11 a.m. or 10:10–11:10 a.m. The exact time will be determined by how many other guests have obtained Fastpasses before you.

The fewer guests who obtain Fastpasses for an attraction, the shorter the interval between receipt of your pass and the return window. Conversely, the more guests issued Fastpasses, the longer the interval. If an attraction is exceptionally popular and/or its hourly capacity is relatively small, the return window might be pushed back almost to park closing time. When this happens, the Fastpass machines shut down and a sign is posted saying all Fastpasses are gone for the day. It's not unusual, for example, for Soarin' at Epcot or Toy Story Mania!

at the Studios to have distributed all available Fastpasses by 1 p.m.

As a reader from Kettle Falls, Washington, explains, there are extra benefits for obtaining Fastpasses as early in the day as possible:

> *When I went to a park, I headed for my favorite ride and got in the standby line while I sent my companion to get us Fastpasses. So we were able to ride twice with almost no wait.*

Rides routinely exhaust their daily Fastpass supply, but shows almost never do. Fastpass machines at theaters try to balance attendance at each show so that the audience for any given performance is divided about evenly between standby and Fastpass guests. Consequently, standby guests for shows aren't discriminated against to the degree that standby guests for rides are. In practice, Fastpass for shows also diminishes the wait for standby guests. With few exceptions, the standby line at theater attractions requires less waiting than using Fastpass.

If you have a Fastpass for an attraction and it breaks down or is closed due to inclement weather, take the Fastpass to Guest Relations. They will issue you Fastpasses for the next day for any park in the World that you plan to visit.

When To Use Fastpass

Except as discussed below, there's no reason to use Fastpass during the first 30–40 minutes a park is open. Lines for most attractions are manageable during this period, and this is the only time of day when Fastpass attractions exclusively serve those in the regular line.

Using Fastpass requires two trips to the same attraction: one to obtain the pass and another to use it. You must invest time to obtain the pass (sometimes Fastpass machines have lines!) and then interrupt your touring later to backtrack to use your Fastpass. The additional time, effort, and touring modification are justified only if you can save more than 30 minutes. Don't forget: Even the Fastpass line requires some waiting.

Nine attractions build lines so quickly in the morning that failing to queue up within the first 6 or so minutes of operation will mean a long wait: Test Track, Soarin', and Mission: SPACE (Epcot); Kilimanjaro Safaris and Expedition Everest (Animal Kingdom); Space Mountain (Magic Kingdom); and Tower of Terror, Toy Story Mania, and Rock 'n' Roller Coaster (Disney's Hollywood Studios). With these, you should race directly to the attractions when the park opens or obtain a Fastpass.

Another four Fastpass attractions—Splash Mountain, The Many Adventures of Winnie the Pooh, Peter Pan's Flight, and the Seven Dwarfs Mine Train in the Magic Kingdom—develop long lines within 30–50 minutes of park opening. If you can get to them before the wait becomes intolerable, great. Otherwise, your options are Fastpass or a long time waiting in line.

You can obtain a second Fastpass at a time printed on the bottom of your most recent Fastpass, usually 2 hours or less from the time the first was issued. Always check the posted return time before obtaining a Fast-pass. If the return time is hours away, forgo Fastpass. Especially in the Magic Kingdom, there will be other Fastpass attractions where the return time is only an hour or so away.

When obtaining Fastpasses, it's quicker and more considerate if one person obtains passes for your entire party. This means entrusting one individual with your valuable park-admission passes and your Fastpasses, so choose wisely.

Obtain Fastpasses for all members of your party, including those who are too short, too young, or simply not interested in riding, as this family of four recommends:

Utilize the Fastpasses of people in your group who don't want to ride. Our 6-year-old didn't want to ride anything rough. All four of us got Fastpasses for each ride. [When] the 6-year-old didn't want to ride, my husband and I took turns riding with the 12-year-old. It was our version of the Fastpass child swap, and the 12-year-old got double rides.

Fastpass Guidelines

- Don't mess with Fastpass unless it can save you 30 minutes or more.
- If you arrive after a park opens, obtain a Fastpass for your preferred Fastpass attraction first thing.
- Do not obtain a Fastpass for a theater attraction until you have experienced all the Fastpass rides on your itinerary. (Using Fastpass at theater attractions usually requires more time than using the standby line.)
- Check the Fastpass return time before obtaining a Fastpass.
- Obtain Fastpasses for Rock 'n' Roller Coaster and Toy Story Mania! at Hollywood Studios; Mission: SPACE, Soarin', and Test Track at Epcot; Expedition Everest at the Animal Kingdom; and The Many Adventures of Winnie the Pooh, Peter Pan's Flight, Space Mountain, and Splash Mountain at the Magic Kingdom as early in the day as possible.
- Try to obtain Fastpasses for rides not mentioned by 1 p.m.
- Don't depend on Fastpasses being available after 2 p.m. during busier times.
- Make sure everyone in your party has his or her own Fastpass.
- You can obtain a second Fastpass at the time printed at the bottom of your first Fastpass.
- Note your Fastpass return slot and plan activities accordingly.

A WORD ABOUT DISNEY THRILL RIDES

READERS OF ALL AGES SHOULD ATTEMPT to be open-minded about the so-called Disney thrill rides. In comparison with rides at other theme parks, most Disney thrill attractions are quite tame, with more emphasis on sights, atmosphere, and special effects than on the motion, speed, or feel of the ride itself. While we suggest you take Disney's preride warnings seriously, we can tell you that guests of all ages report enjoying rides such as Tower of Terror, Big Thunder Mountain Railroad, and Splash Mountain.

A reader from Washington sums up the situation well:

> *Our boys and I are used to imagining typical amusement park rides when it comes to roller coasters. So, when we thought of Big Thunder Mountain [Railroad] and Space Mountain, what came to mind was gigantic hills, upside-down loops, huge vertical drops, etc. I actually hate roller coasters, especially the unpleasant sensation of a long drop, and I have never taken a ride that loops you upside down.*
>
> *In fact, the Disney [rides] are tame in comparison. There are never any long and steep hills (except Splash Mountain, and it is there for anyone to see, so you have informed consent going on the ride). I was able to build up courage to go on all of them, and the more I rode them the more I enjoyed them—the less you tense up expecting a big long drop, the more you enjoy the special effects and even swinging around curves. Swinging around curves is really the primary motion challenge of Disney roller coasters.*

Disney, recognizing that it needs more attractions that appeal to the youth and young adult markets, has added some roller coasters to its parks. The Rock 'n' Roller Coaster at Disney's Hollywood Studios and Expedition Everest at the Animal Kingdom, for example, incorporate at least some of the features our Washington reader seeks to avoid.

A WORD ABOUT HEIGHT REQUIREMENTS

A NUMBER OF ATTRACTIONS REQUIRE children to meet minimum height and age requirements. If you have children too short or too young to ride, you have several options, including switching off (described on page 242). Although the alternatives may resolve some practical and logistical issues, be forewarned that your smaller children might nonetheless be resentful of their older (or taller) siblings who qualify to ride. A mom from Virginia bumped into just such a situation, writing:

> *You mention height requirements for rides but not the intense sibling jealousy this can generate. Frontierland was a real problem in that respect. Our very petite 5-year-old, to her outrage, was stuck hanging around while our 8-year-old went on Splash Mountain and [Big] Thunder Mountain [Railroad] with Grandma and Granddad, and the nearby alternatives weren't helpful (too long a line for rafts to Tom Sawyer Island, etc.). If we had thought ahead, we would have left the younger kid . . . with one of the grown-ups for another roller-coaster ride or two and then met up later at a designated point. The best areas had a playground or other quick attractions for short people near the rides with height requirements, like The Boneyard near the Dinosaur ride at the Animal Kingdom.*

The reader makes a valid point, though in practical terms splitting the group and meeting later can be more complicated than she might imagine. If you choose to split up, ask the Disney greeter at the entrance to the attraction(s) with height requirements how long the wait is. Tack 5 minutes for riding onto the anticipated wait, and then add 5 or so minutes to exit and reach the meeting point for an approximate sense of how long the younger kids (and their supervising adult) will have to do other stuff. Our guess is that even with a long line for the rafts, the reader would have had more than sufficient time to take her daughter to Tom Sawyer Island while the sibs rode Splash Mountain and Big

Thunder Mountain Railroad with the grandparents. For sure she had time to tour the Swiss Family Treehouse in adjacent Adventureland.

WAITING-LINE STRATEGIES FOR ADULTS WITH YOUNG CHILDREN

CHILDREN HOLD UP BETTER THROUGH THE DAY if you minimize the time they spend in lines. Arriving early and using our touring plans immensely reduces waiting. Here are additional ways to reduce stress for children:

1. LINE GAMES Wise parents anticipate restlessness in line and plan activities to reduce the stress and boredom. In the morning, have waiting children discuss what they want to see and do during the day. Later, watch for and count Disney characters or play simple guessing games such as 20 Questions. Lines move continuously, so games requiring pen and paper are impractical. The holding area of a theater attraction, however, is a different story. Here, tic-tac-toe, hangman, drawing, and coloring make the time fly by. As an alternative we've provided a trivia game for each park, developed by Walt Disney World trivia guru Lou Mongello, author of *The Walt Disney World Trivia Book, Volumes 1 and 2*; see **intrepidtraveler.com.**

2. LAST-MINUTE ENTRY If an attraction can accommodate an unusually large number of people at once, it's often unnecessary to stand in line. The Magic Kingdom's *Liberty Belle* Riverboat is a good example. The boat holds about 450 people, usually more than are waiting in line. Instead of standing uncomfortably in a crowd, grab a snack and sit in the shade until the boat arrives and loading is under way. After the line is almost gone, join it.

At large-capacity theaters like that for Epcot's *The American Adventure*, ask the entrance greeter how long it will be until guests are admitted for the next show. If it's 15 minutes or more, take a restroom break or get a snack, returning a few minutes before the show

ATTRACTIONS YOU CAN USUALLY ENTER AT THE LAST MINUTE	
THE MAGIC KINGDOM	
Liberty Square	The Hall of Presidents, *Liberty Belle* Riverboat
Tomorrowland	Walt Disney's Carousel of Progress
EPCOT	
Future World	The Circle of Life (except during mealtimes)
World Showcase	The American Adventure, O Canada!, Reflections of China
DISNEY'S ANIMAL KINGDOM	
Asia	Flights of Wonder
DISNEY'S HOLLYWOOD STUDIOS	
Backlot	Studio Backlot Tour, *Sounds Dangerous*

starts. You aren't allowed to carry food or drink into the attraction, so make sure you have time to finish your snack.

3. THE HAIL MARY PASS Certain lines are configured to allow you and your smaller children to pass under the rail to join your partner just before actual boarding or entry. This technique allows children and one adult to rest, snack, or go to the potty while another adult or older sibling stands in line. Other guests are very understanding about this strategy when used for young children. You're likely to meet hostile opposition, however, if you try to pass older children or more than one adult under the rail. To preempt hostility, tell the folks behind you in line what you are doing and why.

ATTRACTIONS WHERE YOU CAN USUALLY COMPLETE A HAIL-MARY PASS

THE MAGIC KINGDOM

Adventureland Swiss Family Treehouse

Frontierland *Country Bear Jamboree*

Fantasyland Dumbo the Flying Elephant, Mad Tea Party, Peter Pan's Flight, Prince Charming Regal Carrousel, Snow White's Scary Adventures [to close in 2012]

EPCOT

Future World Living with the Land, Spaceship Earth

World Showcase *The American Adventure, O Canada!, Reflections of China*

DISNEY'S ANIMAL KINGDOM

DinoLand U.S.A. TriceraTop Spin

DISNEY'S HOLLYWOOD STUDIOS

Backlot *Sounds Dangerous*

4. SWITCHING OFF (also known as the Baby Swap) Several attractions have minimum height and/or age requirements, usually 40–48 inches tall to ride with an adult or age 7 *and* 40 inches to ride alone. Some couples with children too small or too young forgo these attractions, while others take turns to ride. Missing some of Disney's best rides is an unnecessary sacrifice, and waiting in line twice for the same ride is a tremendous waste of time.

Instead, take advantage of the "switching-off" option, also called "the baby swap." To switch off, there must be at least two adults. Everybody waits in line together, adults and children. When you reach an attendant (called a "greeter"), tell him or her that you want to switch off. The greeter will allow everyone, including the young children, to enter the attraction. When you reach the loading area, one adult rides while the other stays with the kids. Then the riding adult disembarks and takes charge of the children while the other adult rides. A third adult in the party can ride twice, once with each of the switching-off adults, so that the switching-off adults don't have to experience the attraction alone.

ATTRACTIONS WHERE SWITCHING OFF IS COMMON	
MAGIC KINGDOM	**DISNEY'S ANIMAL KINGDOM**
Big Thunder Mountain Railroad	DINOSAUR
Seven Dwarfs Mine Train	Expedition Everest
Space Mountain	Kali River Rapids
Splash Mountain	Primeval Whirl
Stitch's Great Escape!	
	DISNEY'S HOLLYWOOD STUDIOS
EPCOT	Rock 'n' Roller Coaster
Mission: SPACE	Star Tours: The Adventures Continue
Test Track	The Twilight Zone Tower of Terror

On many Fastpass attractions, Disney handles switching off somewhat differently. When you tell the cast member that you want to switch off, he or she will issue you a special "rider exchange" Fastpass good for three people. One parent and the non-riding child (or children) will at that point be asked to leave the line. When those riding reunite with the waiting adult, the waiting adult and two other persons from the party can ride using the special Fastpass. This system eliminates confusion and congestion at the boarding area, while sparing the non-riding adult and child the tedium and physical exertion of waiting in line.

Attractions at which switching off is practiced are oriented to more mature guests. Sometimes it takes a lot of courage for a child just to move through the queue holding dad's hand. In the boarding area, many children suddenly fear abandonment as one parent leaves to experience the attraction. Unless your children are prepared for switching off, you might have an emotional crisis on your hands. A mom from Edison, New Jersey, advises:

> Once my son came to understand that the switch-off would not leave him abandoned, he did not seem to mind. I would recommend to your readers that they practice the switch-off on some dry runs at home so that their child is not concerned that he will be left behind. At the very least, the procedure could be explained in advance so that the little ones know what to expect.

Finally, a mother from Ada, Michigan, who discovered that the procedure for switching off varies from attraction to attraction, offered this suggestion:

> Parents need to tell the very first attendant they come to that they would like to switch off. Each attraction has a different procedure for this. Tell every other attendant too because they forget quickly.

5. COMBINING THE FASTPASS SYSTEM WITH SWITCHING OFF You can incorporate Fastpasses with switching off in order to have Fastpasses for multiple attractions at the same time. This is an enormous benefit for larger groups. In the Fastpass system, each ticket is limited to one

Attractions and Ride Restrictions

MAGIC KINGDOM

Big Thunder Mountain Railroad	40" minimum height
The Great Goofini	35" minimum height
Seven Dwarfs Mine Train.	Not open at press time
Space Mountain	44" minimum height
Splash Mountain.	40" minimum height
Stitch's Great Escape!	40" minimum height
Tomorrowland Speedway . . . . . 32" minimum height (54" to drive unassisted)	

EPCOT

Maelstrom.	3 years minimum age
Mission: SPACE	44" minimum height
Soarin'.	40" minimum height
Test Track	40" minimum height

DISNEY'S HOLLYWOOD STUDIOS

Honey, I Shrunk the Kids Movie Set Adventure	4 years minimum age
Rock 'n' Roller Coaster.	48" minimum height
Star Tours: The Adventures Continue.	40" minimum height
The Twilight Zone Tower of Terror.	40" minimum height

DISNEY'S ANIMAL KINGDOM

DINOSAUR	40" minimum height
Expedition Everest	44" minimum height

Fastpass at a time. The holder of the Fastpass for one attraction may not acquire a Fastpass for a second attraction until the time indicated on the original Fastpass has transpired. Only then can a ticket holder seek a Fastpass for a second attraction, but the rider exchange is a game-changer for those who are serious about time efficiency.

Because the rider exchange pass can be used by the adult holding it as well as three companions, this essentially gives a "four for the price of one" scenario in terms of Fastpass currency. The basic idea is that we're using one one-person Fastpass to get one multiperson rider swap pass. Naturally this gives you more bang for your buck in terms of covering ground during your hours at Disney. An alert reader in Mequon, Wisconsin, discovered this strategy of combining the two time-saving line options to ride more Fastpass attraction headliners:

You advise sending someone to get Fastpasses for Big Thunder and then switching off so all the adults can ride. But if you have at least two adults in a group and one non-riding child, it's possible to use

Kali River Rapids	38" minimum height
Primeval Whirl.	48" minimum height

BLIZZARD BEACH WATER PARK

Chair Lift	32" minimum height
Downhill Double Dipper slide	48" minimum height
Slush Gusher slide	48" minimum height
Summit Plummet slide	48" minimum height
T-Bar (in Ski Patrol Training Camp)	60" maximum height
Tike's Peak children's area	48" maximum height

TYPHOON LAGOON WATER PARK

Bay Slides	60" minimum height
Crush 'n' Gusher	48" minimum height
Humunga Kowabunga slide.	48" minimum height
Ketchakiddee Creek children's area.	48" maximum height
Shark Reef saltwater reef swim	10 years minimum age
	unless accompanied by an adult
Wave Pool.	Adult supervision required

DISNEY QUEST

Buzz Lightyear's AstroBlasters	51" minimum height
CyberSpace Mountain	51" minimum height
Mighty Ducks Pinball Slam	48" minimum height
Pirates of the Caribbean: Battle for Buccaneer Gold	35" minimum height

the switching-off pass to get Fastpasses for more than one attraction at a time.

Our group consisted of two adults, two teens, and two young children. We split our tickets into two groups of three and used one group to get Fastpasses for Big Thunder and one group to get Fastpasses for Splash Mountain. When the half with the Big Thunder Fastpasses went to ride, we asked to switch off and obtained a pass good for one adult and up to three other people. My husband used the three Fastpasses to ride with our two teens. Then, with the switch-off pass, I rode with the teens again and one of our younger sons who was willing to ride.

We did the same thing on Splash Mountain immediately afterwards because the time on our Fastpasses for that ride was already here when we finished riding Big Thunder.

Depending on size and number of ticket bearers, this strategy has the potential to hold Fastpasses for as many as five attractions at any given time while still maintaining the ability to get the entire group on each attraction with a single swap. This mass Fastpass acquisition is accomplished by dividing up the group's tickets for Fastpasses at different attraction kiosks, but the maximum number of attractions a party can exploit this way diminishes as the size of the group increases.

Used at its fullest potential, a family that consists of two adults and four ticket-bearing children, one of whom is not able or willing to ride, can divide their tickets into five groups. One ticket would be used to obtain a Fastpass at Attraction A. One would be used to get a Fastpass at Attraction B. The pattern would continue for acquiring tickets for Attractions C, D, and E simultaneously. With the attraction of the earliest Fastpass time stamp being called Attraction A, an adult wielding the Fastpass for Attraction A would request a rider exchange pass by approaching the cast member at the standby entrance. After securing the rider exchange pass and giving it to the waiting adult, the riding adult would use his or her Fastpass to board the ride. Once he or she rejoins the party, the second adult—accompanied by the three children who are riding—would present the switching-off pass to the cast member guarding the Fastpass return entrance. All four family members would be permitted to enter the Fastpass lane for the ride while the first adult would remain with the non-riding child. Upon the return of the second group, the same procedure could be followed for the remaining four Fastpass attractions without having to wait an extended period for the assigned time frames.

This scenario may seem unappealing, as it would require an adult who was always willing to ride solo as well as some serious team cooperation in gathering the Fastpasses from all corners of the park. For that reason, we see dividing the group's tickets into thirds and using them for three different attractions as a more reasonable option (providing the number of riders in the party doesn't exceed six). Here is how it might play out: Two parents, two adventurous grandparents, two excited teens, and one terrified child named Clarence want to make the most of their time. Dividing their tickets into three groups of two, Dad runs to grab two Fastpasses at Space Mountain and plans to meet up with the rest of the family after they have used two tickets to get Fastpasses at Splash Mountain and two tickets to get Fastpasses at Big Thunder Mountain Railroad. Once the time rolls around, Dad and Grandpa retrieve a rider exchange pass for Mom and use the Fastpasses for Splash Mountain.

After they ride, Mom (who then takes Grandma and the two teens) uses the rider exchange to enter the Fastpass lane. Dad and Grandpa wait with Clarence near the exit, and the group is reunited when Mom, Grandma, and the happy teens emerge. This same scenario would play out for Big Thunder Mountain Railroad and Space Mountain in short duration due to the fact that the Fastpasses for those attractions have already been grabbed and the time for entry has probably arrived.

6. LAST-MINUTE COLD FEET If your young child gets cold feet just before boarding a ride where there is no age or height requirement, you usually can arrange with the loading attendant for a switch off. This is common at Pirates of the Caribbean, where children lose their courage while winding through the dungeon-like waiting area. Additionally, no law says you *have* to ride. If you reach the boarding area and someone is unhappy, tell an attendant you've changed your mind and you'll be shown the way out.

7. CATCH-22 AT TOMORROWLAND SPEEDWAY Though Tomorrowland Speedway is a great treat for young children, they're required to be 52 inches tall in order to drive unassisted. Few children age 6 and younger measure up, so the ride is essentially withheld from the very age group that would most enjoy it. To resolve this catch-22, go on the ride with your small child. The attendants will assume that you will drive. After getting into the car, shift your child over behind the steering wheel. From your position, you will still be able to control the foot pedals. Children will feel like they're really driving, and because the car travels on a self-guiding track, there's no way they can make a mistake while steering.

CHARACTER ANALYSIS

THE LARGE, FRIENDLY COSTUMED VERSIONS of Mickey, Minnie, Donald, Goofy, and others—known as Disney characters—provide a link between Disney animated films and the theme parks. To people emotionally invested, the characters in Disney films are as real as next-door neighbors, never mind that they're just drawings on plastic. In recent years, theme park personifications of the characters also have become real to us. It's not just a person in a mouse costume we see; it is Mickey himself. Similarly, meeting Goofy or Snow White in Fantasyland is an encounter with a celebrity, a memory to be treasured.

If your children can't enjoy things until they see Mickey, ask a cast member where to find him. If the cast member doesn't know right away, he or she can find out quickly. Cast members have a number they can call to learn exactly where the characters are at any time.

While there are hundreds of Disney animated film characters, only about 250 have been brought to life in costume. Of these, a relatively small number (less than a fifth) are greeters (characters who mix with guests). The remaining characters perform in shows or parades. Originally confined to the Magic Kingdom, characters are now found in all the major theme parks and Disney hotels.

CHARACTER WATCHING

CHARACTER WATCHING HAS BECOME A pastime. Families once were content to meet characters only occasionally and by chance. They now pursue them relentlessly, armed with autograph books and cameras. Because some characters are only rarely seen, character watching has become character collecting. (To cash in on character collecting, Disney sells autograph books throughout the World.) Mickey, Minnie, and Goofy are a snap to bag; they seem to be everywhere. But Jiminy Cricket seldom comes out. Other characters appear regularly but only in a location consistent with their starring roles. Cinderella, predictably, reigns at Cinderella Castle in Fantasyland, while Br'er Fox and Br'er Bear frolic in Frontierland near Splash Mountain.

A Brooklyn, New York, dad thinks the character autograph–hunting craze has gotten out of hand, complaining:

> Whoever started the practice of collecting autographs from the characters should be subjected to Chinese water torture! We went to Walt Disney World 11 years ago, with an 8-year-old and an 11-year-old. We would bump into characters, take pictures, and that was it. After a while, our children noticed that some of the other children were getting autographs. We managed to avoid joining in during our first day at the Magic Kingdom and our first day at Epcot, but by day three our children were collecting autographs. However, it did not get too out of hand, since it was limited to accidental character meeting.
>
> This year when we took our youngest child (who is now age 8), he had already seen his siblings' collection and was determined to outdo them. However, rather than random meetings, the characters are now available practically all day long at different locations, according to a printed schedule, which our son was old enough to read. We spent more time standing in line for autographs than we did for the most popular rides!

A family from Birmingham, Alabama, found some benefit in their children's relentless pursuit of characters, writing:

> We had no idea we would be caught up in this madness, but after my daughters grabbed your guidebook to get Pocahontas to sign it (we had no blank paper), we quickly bought a Disney autograph book and gave in. It was actually the highlight of their trip, and my son even got into the act by helping get places in line for his sisters. They LOVED looking for characters. . . . The possibility of seeing a new character revived my 7-year-old's energy on many occasions. It was an amazing, totally unexpected part of our visit.

Our advice for parents with pre-schoolers is to stay with the kids when they meet characters, stepping back only to take a quick picture.

Bob

"THEN SOME CONFUSION HAPPENED" Young children sometimes become lost at character encounters. Usually, there's a lot of activity around a character, with both adults and children touching it or posing for pictures. Most commonly, mom and dad stay in the crowd while Junior approaches to meet the character. In the excitement and with people milling and the character moving around,

Junior heads off in the wrong direction to look for mom and dad. In the words of a Salt Lake City mom: "Milo was shaking hands with Dopey one minute, then some confusion happened and [Milo] was gone." Families with several young children and parents who are busy with cameras can lose track of a youngster in a heartbeat.

CHARACTER DINING: WHAT TO EXPECT

CHARACTER DINING HAS BECOME SO POPULAR that Disney offers character breakfasts, brunches, lunches, and dinners where families can dine in the presence of Mickey, Minnie, Goofy, and other costumed versions of animated celebrities. Besides grabbing customers from Denny's and Hardee's, character meals provide a controlled setting in which young children can warm to the characters. All meals are attended by several characters. Adult prices apply to persons age 10 or older, children's prices to kids ages 3–9. Children younger than 3 years eat free. For more information on character dining, call ☎ 407-WDW-DINE (407-939-3463).

Because character dining is very popular, arrange Advance Reservations as early as possible by calling ☎ 407-WDW-DINE. Advance Reservations aren't reservations, per se—only a commitment to seat you ahead of walk-in patrons at the scheduled date and time. At character meals that are very popular, such as breakfast at Cinderella's Royal Table, you are required to make a for-real reservation and to guarantee it with a for-real deposit.

"Casting? There's been a mistake. We were supposed to get the Assorted Character Package with one Mickey, one Goofy, one Donald . . . "

Liliane

When my son was 3 years old, he was nuts to meet Cinderella. Like so many moms before me, I stood in line at Cinderella Castle to meet her (this was before you had to buy a meal to meet Cinderella). The wait was long, and when it was finally our turn, my boy had fallen asleep. Oh, the agony! Should I wake him? Should I leave the mission unaccomplished? Well, in the end Cinderella came to the rescue. She smiled and asked me to sit down for a chat. She signed my son's autograph book and said, "Tell him to look for me waving at him tonight at the evening parade." And wave she did. I am not even sure it was the same Cinderella, but my son was convinced she was and believed that he had met Cinderella, albeit in his dreams.

Character meals are bustling affairs held in hotels' or theme parks' largest full-service restaurants. Character breakfasts offer a fixed menu served individually, family-style, or on a buffet. The typical breakfast includes scrambled eggs; bacon, sausage, and ham; hash browns; waffles or French toast; biscuits, rolls, or pastries; and fruit. With family-style service, the meal is served in large skillets or on platters at your table. Seconds (or thirds) are free at both family-service and fixed-menu character meals. Buffets offer much the same fare, but you fetch it yourself.

Character dinners range from a set menu served family-style to buffets or ordering off the menu. Character dinner buffets offer separate adults' and children's serving lines. Typically, the children's buffet includes hamburgers, hot dogs, pizza, fish sticks, fried chicken nuggets, macaroni and cheese, and peanut-butter-and-jelly sandwiches. Selections at the adult buffet usually include prime rib or other carved meat, baked or broiled Florida seafood, pasta, chicken, an ethnic dish or two, vegetables, potatoes, and salad.

At all meals characters circulate around the room. During your meal, each of the three to five characters present will visit your table, arriving one at a time to cuddle the kids (and sometimes the adults), pose for photographs, and sign autographs. Keep autograph books (with pens) and loaded cameras handy. For the best photos, adults should sit across the table from their children. Seat the children where characters can easily reach them. If a table is against a wall, for example, adults should sit with their backs to the wall and children on the aisle.

At some larger restaurants, including 'Ohana at the Polynesian Resort and Chef Mickey's at the Contemporary, character meals involve impromptu parades of characters and children around the room, group singing, napkin waving, and other organized mayhem.

Servers don't rush you to leave after you've eaten—you can stay as long as you wish to enjoy the characters. Remember, however, that lots of eager kids and adults are waiting not so patiently to be admitted.

When To Go

Attending a character breakfast usually prevents you from arriving at the theme parks in time for opening. Because early morning is best for

Character-meal Hit Parade

1. CINDERELLA'S ROYAL TABLE

- LOCATION Magic Kingdom
- MEALS SERVED
  Breakfast, lunch, and dinner
- CHARACTERS Cinderella, Fairy Godmother, Aurora, Belle, Jasmine, Snow White
- SERVED Daily
- SETTING ★★★★★
- NOISE LEVEL Quiet
- TYPE OF SERVICE Fixed menu
- FOOD VARIETY AND QUALITY
  ★★★
- CHARACTER–GUEST RATIO 1:26

2. AKERSHUS ROYAL BANQUET HALL

- LOCATION Epcot
- MEALS SERVED Breakfast, lunch, and dinner
- CHARACTERS 4–6 characters chosen from Alice, Ariel, Belle, Jasmine, Mary Poppins, Mulan, Sleeping Beauty, Snow White
- SERVED Daily
- SETTING ★★★★
- TYPE OF SERVICE Family-style and menu *(all you care to eat)*
- FOOD VARIETY AND QUALITY
  ★★★½
- NOISE LEVEL Quiet
- CHARACTER–GUEST RATIO 1:54

3. CHEF MICKEY'S

- LOCATION Contemporary
- MEALS SERVED Breakfast, dinner
- CHARACTERS Mickey, Minnie, Donald, Goofy, Pluto (sometimes Chip 'n' Dale)
- SERVED Daily
- SETTING ★★★
- NOISE LEVEL Loud
- TYPE OF SERVICE Buffet
- FOOD VARIETY AND QUALITY
  breakfast ★★★
  dinner ★★★½
- CHARACTER–GUEST RATIO 1:56

Characters are subject to change, so if your child has his or her heart set on seeing a particular character, make sure you double-check with the restaurant before you go.

4. THE CRYSTAL PALACE

- LOCATION Magic Kingdom
- MEALS SERVED Breakfast, lunch, and dinner
- CHARACTERS Pooh, Eeyore, Piglet, Tigger
- SERVED Daily
- SETTING ★★★
- NOISE LEVEL Very loud
- TYPE OF SERVICE Buffet
- FOOD VARIETY AND QUALITY
  breakfast ★★★½
  lunch and dinner ★★★
- CHARACTER–GUEST RATIO
  breakfast 1:67
  lunch and dinner 1:89

5. 1900 PARK FARE

- LOCATION Grand Floridian
- MEALS SERVED Breakfast, dinner
- CHARACTERS *Breakfast:* Alice Mary Poppins, Mad Hatter, Pooh
  Dinner: Cinderella, Prince Charming, Lady Tremaine, the two stepsisters
- SERVED Daily
- SETTING ★★★
- NOISE LEVEL Moderate
- TYPE OF SERVICE Buffet
- FOOD VARIETY AND QUALITY
  breakfast ★★★
  dinner ★★★½
- CHARACTER–GUEST RATIO
  breakfast 1:54; *dinner* 1:44

6. THE GARDEN GRILL RESTAURANT

- LOCATION Epcot
- MEAL SERVED Dinner
- CHARACTERS Mickey, Pluto, Chip 'n' Dale,
- SERVED Daily
- SETTING ★★★★½
- NOISE LEVEL Very quiet
- TYPE OF SERVICE Family-style
- FOOD VARIETY AND QUALITY
  ★★★½
- CHARACTER–GUEST RATIO 1:46

7. TUSKER HOUSE RESTAURANT

- LOCATION Animal Kingdom
- MEAL SERVED Breakfast
- CHARACTERS Donald, Daisy, Mickey, Goofy
- SERVED Daily
- SETTING ★★★
- NOISE LEVEL Very loud
- TYPE OF SERVICE Buffet
- FOOD VARIETY AND QUALITY
  ★★★
- CHARACTER–GUEST RATIO 1:112

8. CAPE MAY CAFE

- LOCATION Beach Club
- MEAL SERVED Breakfast
- CHARACTERS Goofy, Donald, Minnie
- SERVED Daily
- SETTING ★★★
- NOISE LEVEL Moderate
- TYPE OF SERVICE Buffet
- FOOD VARIETY AND QUALITY
  ★★½
- CHARACTER–GUEST RATIO 1:67

9. 'OHANA

- LOCATION Polynesian Resort
- MEAL SERVED Breakfast
- CHARACTERS Lilo and Stitch, Mickey, Pluto
- SERVED Daily
- SETTING ★★
- NOISE LEVEL Moderate
- TYPE OF SERVICE Family-style
- FOOD VARIETY AND QUALITY
  ★★½
- CHARACTER–GUEST RATIO 1:57

10. HOLLYWOOD & VINE

- LOCATION
  Disney's Hollywood Studios
- MEALS SERVED Breakfast, lunch
- CHARACTERS June, Leo, Handy Manny, Agent Oso
- SERVED Daily
- SETTING ★★½
- NOISE LEVEL Moderate
- TYPE OF SERVICE Buffet
- FOOD VARIETY AND QUALITY
  ★★★
- CHARACTER–GUEST RATIO 1:71

11. GARDEN GROVE

- LOCATION Swan
- MEALS SERVED Breakfast *(Sat & Sun only)*, dinner
- CHARACTERS Rafiki, Timon, Goofy, Pluto
- SERVED Daily
- SETTING ★★★
- NOISE LEVEL Moderate
- TYPE OF SERVICE Buffet
- FOOD VARIETY AND QUALITY
  ★★★½
- CHARACTER–GUEST RATIO
  1:198, but often much better

touring and you don't want to burn daylight lingering over breakfast, we suggest the following:

1. Go to a character dinner or lunch instead of breakfast; it won't conflict with your touring schedule.

2. Substitute a late character breakfast for lunch. Have a light breakfast early from room service or your cooler to tide you over. Then tour the theme park for an hour or two before breaking off around 10:15 a.m. to go to the character breakfast. Make a big brunch of your character breakfast and skip lunch. You should be fueled until dinner.

3. Go on your arrival or departure day. The day you arrive and check in is usually good for a character dinner. Settle at your hotel, swim, then dine with the characters. This strategy has the added benefit of exposing your children to the characters before chance encounters at the parks. Some children, moreover, won't settle down to enjoy the parks until they have seen Mickey. Departure day also is good for a character meal. Schedule a character breakfast on your check-out day before you head for the airport or begin your drive home.

4. Go on a rest day. If you plan to stay five or more days, you'll probably take a day or half day from touring to rest or do something else. These are perfect days for a character meal.

How To Choose a Character Meal

Many readers ask for advice about character meals. This question from a Waterloo, Iowa, mom is typical:

Are all character breakfasts pretty much the same, or are some better than others? How should I go about choosing one?

In fact, some are better, sometimes much better. When we evaluate character meals, we look for these things:

1. **THE CHARACTERS** The meals offer a diverse assortment of characters. Select a meal that features your kids' favorites. Check out our Character-meal Hit Parade chart (see page 251) to see which characters are assigned to each meal. Most restaurants stick with the same characters. Even so, check the lineup when you call to make Advance Reservations.

A mom from Michigan offers this report:

Our character meal at 1900 Park Fare was a DISASTER!!! Please warn other readers with younger children that if they make Advance Reservations and the characters are villains, they may want to rethink their options. We went for my daughter's fifth birthday, and she was scared to death. The Queen of Hearts chased her sobbing and screaming down the hallway. Most young children we saw at the dinner were very frightened. Captain Hook and Prince John were laid-back, but Governor Ratcliff [from Pocahontas] and the Queen were amazingly rude and intimidating.

The villains have abdicated 1900 Park Fare in favor of more benign characters, but you never know where the baddies might show up next. Moral? Call before making Advance Reservations and ask with which characters you'll be dining.

2. **ATTENTION FROM THE CHARACTERS** At all character meals, characters circulate among guests, hugging children, posing for pictures, and signing autographs. How much time a character spends with you and your children depends primarily on the ratio of characters to guests. The more characters and fewer guests, the better. Because many character meals never fill to capacity, the character-to-guest ratios found in our Character-meal Hit Parade chart (see page 251) have been adjusted to reflect an average attendance. Even so, there's quite a range. The best ratio is at Cinderella's Royal Table, where there's approximately one character to every 26 guests.

The worst ratio is theoretically at the Swan Resort's Garden Grove, where there could be as few as 1 character for every 198 guests. We say "theoretically," however, because in practice there are far fewer guests at the Garden Grove than at character meals in Disney-owned resorts, and often more characters. During one recent meal, friends of ours were literally the only guests in the restaurant for breakfast and had to ask the characters to leave them alone to eat.

3. **THE SETTING** Some character meals are in exotic settings. For others, moving the event to an elementary-school cafeteria would be an improvement. Our chart rates each meal's setting with the familiar scale of zero (worst) to five (best) stars. Two restaurants, Cinderella's Royal Table in the Magic Kingdom and The Garden Grill Restaurant in the Land Pavilion at Epcot, deserve special mention. Cinderella's Royal Table is on the first and second floors of Cinderella Castle in Fantasyland, offering guests a look inside the castle. The Garden Grill is a

Many kids take special delight in meeting the face characters, such as Jasmine, Aladdin, and Cinderella, who can speak to them and engage them in a way that the mute animal characters can't.

revolving restaurant overlooking several scenes from the Living with The Land boat ride. Also at Epcot, the popular Princesses Character Breakfast is held in the castlelike Akershus Royal Banquet Hall. Though Chef Mickey's at the Contemporary Resort is rather sterile in appearance, it affords a great view of the monorail running through the hotel. Themes and settings of the remaining character-meal venues, while apparent to adults, will be lost on most children.

4. **THE FOOD** Although some food served at character meals is quite good, most is average (palatable but nothing to get excited about). In variety, consistency, and quality, restaurants generally do a better job with breakfast than with lunch or dinner (if served). Some restaurants offer a buffet, while others opt for one-skillet family-style service, in which all hot items are served from the same pot or skillet. To help you sort it out, we rate the food at each character meal in our chart using the five-star scale.

5. THE PROGRAM Some larger restaurants stage modest performances where the characters dance, head a parade around the room, or lead songs and cheers. For some guests, these activities give the meal a celebratory air; for others, they turn what was already mayhem into absolute chaos. Either way, the antics consume time the characters could spend with families at their table.

6. NOISE If you want to eat in peace, character meals are a bad choice. That said, some are much noisier than others. Our chart gives you an idea of what to expect.

7. WHICH MEAL Although breakfasts seem to be most popular, character lunches and dinners are usually more practical because they don't interfere with early-morning touring. During hot weather, a character lunch can be heavenly.

If you've secured Advance Reservations for a character meal, I **Liliane** say roll out the costume chest. Dress up your little tyke—from princess to pirate, anything goes. As a matter of fact, if your little princess wants to wear her princess dress when visiting the Magic Kingdom for the first time, indulge her. And don't worry about the unavoidable food landing on the precious dress; that is what stain removers are for. Besides, if not today, when?

8. COST Dinners cost more than lunches, and lunches are more than breakfasts. Prices for meals (except those at Cinderella Castle) vary only about $4 from the least expensive to the most expensive restaurant. Breakfasts run $30–$50 for adults and $13–$30 for ages 3–9. For character lunches, expect to pay $25–$55 for adults and $14–$32 for kids. Dinners are $35–$60 for adults and $18–$35 for children. Little ones age 2 and younger eat free. The meals at the high end of the price range are at Cinderella's Royal Table in the Magic Kingdom and Akershus Royal Banquet Hall at Epcot. The reasons for the sky-high prices are (1) Cinderella's Royal Table is small but in great demand, and (2) the prices at Cinderella's and Akershus include a set of photos of your group taken by a Disney photographer. Whereas photos at other venues are optional, at Cindy's and Akershus, you don't have a say in the matter.

9. ADVANCE RESERVATIONS The Disney dining reservations system makes Advance Reservations for character meals up to 180 days before you wish to dine. Advance Reservations for most character meals are easy to obtain, even if you call only a couple of weeks before you leave home. Meals at Cinderella's Royal Table can be another story. To eat at Cinderella's during peak times, you'll need our strategy as well as help from Congress and the Pope. (See page 136 for details.)

10. HOMELESS CHARACTERS Disney periodically pulls the plug on one or another of the character meals. Reconfirm all character-meal Advance Reservations three weeks or so before you leave home by calling ☎ 407-WDW-DINE. In the past year things have been changing more often, so if it must be Pooh and Piglet, double-check before you go to the character meal. And as recommended earlier, it is better to not promise something over which you do not have control.

11. FRIENDS AND PALS For some venues, Disney has stopped specifying characters scheduled for a particular meal. Instead, they say it's a certain character "and friends (or pals)." For example, "Pooh and friends," meaning Eeyore, Piglet, and Tigger, or some combination thereof, or "Mickey's pals" with some assortment chosen among Minnie, Goofy, Pluto, Donald, and Daisy. Most are self-evident, but others such as "Mary Poppins and friends" are unclear. Who knows whom Mary Poppins hangs out with? (Don't expect Dick van Dyke.)

12. THE BUM'S RUSH Most character meals are leisurely affairs, and you can usually stay as long as you want. An exception is Cinderella's Royal Table in the Magic Kingdom. Because Cindy's is in such high demand, the restaurant does everything short of pre-chewing your food to move you through, as this European mother of a 5-year-old can attest:

We dined a lot, did three character meals and a few signature restaurants, and every meal was awesome except for lunch with Cinderella in the castle. While I'd often read it wouldn't be a rushed affair, it was exactly that. We had barely sat down when the appetizers were thrown on our table, the princesses each spent just a few seconds with our daughter—almost no interaction—and the side dishes were cold. We were out of there within 40 minutes and felt very stressed. Considering the price for the meal, I cannot recommend it.

Boosting Sales of Mementos and Souvenirs

Usually when Disney sees a horse carrying moneybags, it rides it until it drops. Disney's latest scheme of bundling photos and souvenirs in the price of character meals at Cinderella's Royal Table and Akershus Royal Banquet Hall is probably something we'll see again at other venues. Adding photos of your group taken by a Disney photographer is Disney's justification for raising the price of the character meals by about 60%. Disney insists that you're getting the photos at a bargain price. This is well and good if you're in the market, but if buying photos was not in your plans, well, they've gotcha. It's a matter of some conjecture how far Disney will run with this idea. Maybe next year the price will be $200 and include fanciful medieval costumes for your entire party (charges for the changing room and locker to store your street clothes not included).

Disney's Royal Alternatives

A Rochester, Michigan, mother of two toddlers suggests a less stressful way to dine with Cinderella:

We went to the Cinderella character dinner at 1900 Park Fare. Once we did this, I stopped trying to get a last-minute reservation at Cinderella's Royal Table. My daughter loved the dinner. The decor of the restaurant was elegant and befitting Cinderella. I think you should emphasize that this is a more easily obtained alternative to

Cinderella's Royal Table. It wasn't easy to get, but I was able to get a reservation only about two months in advance instead of the 180-days-and-atomic-clock routine that the Royal Table requires. Maybe someday we'll do the Royal Table, but this time my daughter was delighted with the dinner at 1900 Park Fare.

If you are unwilling to fund Cinderella's shoe habit or simply were not able to get an Advance Reservation before young Ariel graduates from college, rest assured that there are other venues that will feed you in the company of princesses.

Akershus Royal Banquet Hall in the Norway pavilion of Epcot's World Showcase serves family-style breakfast, lunch, and dinner. Disney tends to define *princess* quite loosely, so you may see any character who's ever donned a dress (with the exception of Cinderella) at this meal. Entrées are a combination of traditional buffet fare and the occasional Scandinavian dish—a nod to the fact that Norway has the only other castle available until the Fantasyland expansion is complete.

Dinner at the Grand Floridian's 1900 Park Fare features the whole crew from *Cinderella,* including Lady Tremaine and the stepsisters (breakfast is a character buffet with Winnie the Pooh and friends). At $36 per adult and $15 for children 9 and under, this is a far more economical option for diners wishing to "get their princess on," and the stepsisters are an absolute hoot. This meal is also a little more boy-friendly if you're entertaining a mixed crowd. Finally, remember that your princess may be feeding off your own excitement over eating in the castle—she might be just as happy with a plastic crown purchased in the gift shop and a hamburger from Cosmic Ray's.

Liliane

I strongly recommend bringing your own stroller. In addition to the parks there is the walk from and to the parking lot or the bus/monorail/boat station to the park entrance, not to mention many other occasions at your hotel or during shopping when you will be happy to have a stroller handy.

OTHER CHARACTER EVENTS

CHIP 'N' DALE'S CAMPFIRE, SING-A-LONG, AND MOVIE are held nightly (times vary with the season) near the Meadow Trading Post and Bike Barn at Fort Wilderness Resort & Campground. Chip 'n' Dale lead the songs, and two Disney films are shown. The program is free and open to resort guests (☎ 407-824-2900).Another character encounter at Fort Wilderness is Mickey's Backyard BBQ, held seasonally on Thursday and Saturday. Prices range $21–$51.

WONDERLAND TEA PARTY Although the name of this enchanting soiree is enough to give most boys hives, it's nevertheless available at the Grand Floridian's 1900 Park Fare restaurant, Monday through Friday, at 1:30 p.m. for about $40 per child (ages 4–12). The program consists of decorating cupcakes and having lunch and tea with characters from *Alice in Wonderland*. Reserve up to 180 days in advance by calling ☎ 407-WDW-DINE.

STROLLERS

STROLLERS ARE AVAILABLE FOR RENT at all four theme parks and the Downtown Disney area (single stroller, $15 per day, no deposit, or $13 per day for the entire stay; double stroller, $31 per day, no deposit, or $27 per day for the entire stay; stroller rentals at Downtown Disney require a $100 credit-card deposit; double strollers are not available at Downtown Disney). Strollers are welcome at Blizzard Beach and Typhoon Lagoon, but no rentals are available. We recommend that you pay in advance for your stroller rentals—this allows you to bypass the paying line and head straight for the pickup line. Make sure that you keep the receipt in a safe place. If you rent a stroller at the Magic Kingdom and decide to go to Epcot, the Animal Kingdom, or Disney's Hollywood Studios, turn in your Magic Kingdom stroller and present your receipt at the next park. You will be issued another stroller without additional charge. Rental at all parks is fast and efficient, and returning the stroller is a breeze.

Readers inform us that there is a lively gray market for strollers at the parks. Families who arrive late look for families who are heading for the exit and "buy" their stroller at a bargain price.

If you do not want to bring your own stroller, you may consider buying one of the umbrella-style collapsible strollers. Walmart retails a very basic collapsible stroller for about $15–$20. You may even consider ordering online at places such as **walmart.com, toysrus.com,** or **sears.com** and shipping it right to your hotel in Orlando. Make sure you leave enough time between your order and arrival dates. When you are ready to go home, keep it or donate it to Goodwill or some other worthy charity.

Rental strollers are too large for all infants and many toddlers. If you plan to rent a stroller for your infant or toddler, bring pillows, cushions, or rolled towels to buttress him in.

Liliane

Another important matter is protection against the sun. Liliane always used a stroller with an adjustable canopy and also had lightweight pieces of cloth handy to protect her child from the sun. You can use anything for that purpose; a receiving blanket works well. Liliane used clothespins and security pins to attach the pieces to the canopy.

Strollers are a must for infants and toddlers, but we have observed many sharp parents renting strollers for somewhat older children (up to age 5 or so). The stroller prevents parents from having to carry children when they sag and provides a convenient place to carry water and snacks.

A family from Tulsa, Oklahoma, recommends springing for a double stroller:

We rent a double for baggage room or in case the older child gets tired of walking.

If you go to your hotel for a break and intend to return to the park, leave your rental stroller by an attraction near the park entrance, marking it with something personal, such as a bandanna. When you return, your stroller will be waiting.

Bringing your own stroller is permitted. However, only collapsible strollers are allowed on monorails, parking-lot trams, and buses. Your stroller is unlikely to be stolen, but mark it with your name.

Having her own stroller was indispensable to a Mechanicsville, Virginia, mother of two toddlers:

How I was going to manage to get the kids from the parking lot to the park was a big worry for me before I made the trip. I didn't read anywhere that it was possible to walk to the entrance of the parks instead of taking the tram, so I wasn't sure I could do it.

I found that for me personally, since I have two kids aged 1 and 2, it was easier to walk to the entrance of the park from the parking lot with the kids in (my own) stroller than to take the kids out of the stroller, fold the stroller (while trying to control the two kids and associated gear), load the stroller and the kids onto the tram, etc. . . No matter where I was parked I could always just walk to the entrance . . . it sometimes took awhile, but it was easier for me.

An Oklahoma mom, however, reports a bad experience with bringing her own stroller:

The first time we took our kids, we had a large stroller (big mistake). It is so much easier to rent one in the park. The large (personally owned) strollers are nearly impossible to get on the buses and are a hassle at the airport. I remember feeling dread when a bus pulled up that was even semifull of people. People look at you like you have a cage full of live chickens when you drag heavy strollers onto the bus.

STROLLER WARS Sometimes strollers disappear while you're enjoying a ride or show. Disney staff will often rearrange strollers parked outside an attraction. This may be done to tidy up or to clear a walkway. Don't assume that your stroller is stolen because it isn't where you left it. It may be neatly arranged a few feet away.

Bob

Sometimes, however, strollers are taken by mistake or ripped off by people not wanting to spend time replacing one that's missing. Don't be alarmed if yours disappears. You won't have to buy it, and you'll be issued a new one.

When you enter a show or board a ride, you must park your stroller, usually in an open area. Bring a cloth or towel to dry it if it rains before you return.

Though most families park their stroller in front of the attraction they're experiencing, a Franklin, Tennessee, family recommends this alternative:

You should feel free to park your stroller at a central attraction in a land, and then retrieve it only when you are leaving the land (with the exception of Epcot). It took us 2 days to figure out that we didn't need to move it every time we moved.

Keep in mind that it is very hard to navigate a stroller in a huge crowd, especially when in a hurry and when trying to exit after the fireworks and shows at closing time. Sometimes guests without strollers may try to get ahead of you, making you wish to use the stroller as a lethal weapon. Don't. Given the number of strollers, pedestrians, and tight spaces, mishaps are inevitable on both sides. A simple apology and a smile are usually the best remediation.

WHEN KIDS GET LOST

IF ONE OF YOUR CHILDREN gets separated from you, don't panic. All things considered, Walt Disney World is about the safest place to get lost we can think of. Disney cast members are trained to watch for seemingly lost kids, and because children become detached from parents so frequently in the theme parks, cast members know exactly what to do.

If you lose a child in the Magic Kingdom, report it to a Disney employee, then check at the Baby Care Center and at City Hall, where lost-children logs are kept. At Epcot, report the loss, then check at the Baby Care Center in the Odyssey Center. At Disney's Hollywood Studios, report the situation at the Guest Relations building at the entrance end of Hollywood Boulevard. At Animal Kingdom, go to the Baby Care Center in Discovery Island. Paging isn't used, but in an emergency an all points bulletin can be issued throughout the park(s) via internal communications. If a Disney employee encounters a lost child, he or she will immediately take the child to the park's Baby Care Center.

As comforting as this knowledge is, however, it's nevertheless scary when a child turns up missing. Fortunately, circumstances surrounding a child becoming lost are fairly predictable and, for the most part, preventable.

For starters, consider how much alike children dress, especially in warm climates where shorts and T-shirts are the norm. Throw your children in with 10,000 other kids the same size and suddenly that cute little outfit turns into theme-park camouflage. It's also smart to sew a label into each child's shirt that states your family name, your hometown, your cell phone number, and the name of your hotel. The same thing can be accomplished by writing the information on a strip of masking tape. Hotel security professionals suggest the information be printed in small letters and the tape be affixed to the outside of the

Bob

We suggest that children younger than age 8 be color-coded by dressing them in vacation uniforms with distinctively colored T-shirts or equally eye-catching apparel.

child's shirt, 5 inches below the armpit or, alternatively, on the tongue of the child's shoe. Another way to skin the cat is to attach a luggage tag to a belt loop. Finally, special name tags can be obtained at the major theme parks.

Other than just blending in, children tend to become separated from their parents under remarkably similar circumstances:

1. PREOCCUPIED SOLO PARENT In this situation, the party's only adult is preoccupied with something like buying refreshments, loading the camera, or using the restroom. Junior is there one second and gone the next.

2. THE HIDDEN EXIT Sometimes parents wait on the sidelines while two or more young children experience a ride together. Parents expect the kids to exit in one place and, lo and behold, the youngsters pop out somewhere else. Exits from some attractions are distant from the entrances. Make sure you know exactly where your children will emerge before letting them ride by themselves. If in doubt, ask a cast member.

3. AFTER THE SHOW At the end of many shows and rides, a Disney staffer will announce, "Check for personal belongings and take small children by the hand." When dozens, if not hundreds, of people leave an attraction simultaneously, it's surprisingly easy for parents to lose contact with their children unless they have them directly in tow.

4. RESTROOM PROBLEMS Mom tells 6-year-old Tommy, "I'll be sitting on this bench when you come out of the restroom." Three possibilities: One, Tommy exits through a different door and becomes disoriented (Mom may not know there is another door). Two, Mom decides she also will use the restroom, and Tommy emerges to find her gone. Three, Mom pokes around in a shop while keeping an eye on the bench but misses Tommy when he comes out.

If you can't be with your child in the restroom, make sure there's only one exit. The restroom on a passageway between Frontierland and Adventureland in the Magic Kingdom is the all-time worst for disorienting visitors. Children and adults alike have walked in from the Adventureland side and walked out on the Frontierland side (and vice versa). Adults realize quickly that something is wrong. Young children, however, sometimes fail to recognize the problem. Designate a meeting spot more distinctive than a bench, and be thorough in your instructions: "I'll meet you by this flagpole. If you get out first, stay right here." Have your child repeat the directions back to you.

5. PARADES There are many parades and shows at which the audience stands. Children tend to jockey for a better view. By moving a little this way and that, the child quickly puts distance between you before either of you notices.

6. MASS MOVEMENTS Be on guard when huge crowds disperse after

"No, no, really, it's OK. It's just not what I was expecting."

fireworks or a parade, or at park closing. With 20,000–40,000 people at once in an area, it's very easy to get separated from a child or others in your party. Use extra caution after the evening parade and fireworks in the Magic Kingdom, *Fantasmic!* at Disney's Hollywood Studios, or *IllumiNations* at Epcot. Families should have specific plans for where to meet if they get separated.

7. CHARACTER GREETINGS Activity and confusion are common when the Disney characters appear, and children can slip out of sight. See "Then Some Confusion Happened" (see page 248).

8. GETTING LOST AT THE ANIMAL KINGDOM It's especially easy to lose a child at the Animal Kingdom, particularly in the Oasis entryway, on the Maharajah Jungle Trek, and on the Pangani Forest Exploration

Trail. Mom and dad will stop to observe an animal. Junior stays close for a minute or so, and then, losing patience, wanders to the other side of the exhibit or to a different exhibit.

9. LOST ... IN THE OZONE More often than you'd think, kids don't realize they're lost. They are so distracted that they sometimes wander around for quite a while before they notice that their whole family has mysteriously disappeared. Fortunately, Disney cast members are trained to look out for kids who have zoned out and will either help them find their family or deposit them at the Baby Care Center. There are times, however, when parents panic during the interval in which these scenarios play out. If you lose a child and he doesn't turn up at the Baby Care Center right away, take a deep breath. He's probably lost in the ozone.

10. TEACH YOUR KIDS WHO THE GOOD GUYS ARE On your very first day in the parks, teach your kids how to recognize a Disney cast member by pointing out the Disney name tags that they all wear. Instruct your children to find someone with such a name tag if they get separated from you.

LILIANE'S TIPS FOR KEEPING TRACK OF YOUR BROOD

ON A GOOD DAY, it's possible for Liliane to lose a cantaloupe in her purse. Being thus challenged, she works overtime developing ways to hang on to her possessions, including her child. Here's what she has to say:

I've seen parents write their cell phone numbers on a child's leg with a felt-tip marker . . . effective but crude. Before you resort to a brand or tattoo, consider some of the tips I've busted my brain dreaming up. My friends (some much ditzier than I) have used them with great success.

- Same-colored T-shirts for the whole family will help you gather your troops in an easy and fun way. You can opt for just a uniform color or go the extra mile and have the T-shirts printed with a logo such as "The Brown Family's Assault on the Mouse." You might also include the date or the year of your visit. Your imagination is the limit. Light-colored T-shirts can even be autographed by the Disney characters.
- Clothing labels are great, of course. If you don't sew, buy labels that you can iron on the garment. If you own a cell phone, be sure to include the number on the label. If you do not own a cell phone, put in the phone number of the hotel where you'll be staying.
- In pet stores you can have name tags printed for a very reasonable price. These are great to add to necklaces and bracelets or attach to your child's shoelace or belt loop.
- When you check into the hotel, take a business card of the hotel for each member in your party, especially those old enough to carry wallets and purses.

- Always agree on a meeting point before you see a parade, fireworks, and nighttime spectacles such as *IllumiNations* and *Fantasmic!* Make sure the meeting place is in the park (as opposed to the car or some-place outside the front gate).
- If you have a digital camera or cell-phone camera, you may elect to take a picture of your kids every morning. If they get lost, the picture will show what they look like and what they are wearing.
- If all the members of your party have cell phones, it's easy to locate each other. Be aware, however, that the ambient noise in the parks is so loud that you probably won't hear your cell phone ring. Your best bet is to carry your phone in a front pants pocket and to program the phone to vibrate. If any of your younger kids carry cell phones, secure the phones with a strap. Even better, send text messages.
- Save key tags and luggage tags for use on items you bring to the parks, including your stroller, diaper bag, and backpack or hip pack.
- Don't underestimate the power of the permanent marker, such as a Sharpie. They are great for labeling pretty much anything. Mini Sharp-ies are sold as clip-ons and are great for collecting character auto-graphs. The Sharpie will also serve well for writing down (Bob suggests on my son's forehead) the location of your car in the parking lot.

A word about keeping track of your park-admission passes. One minute you have them, the next you don't. The passes (which for Dis-ney hotel guests also serve as a credit card and room key) are precious. They are also your key to obtaining Fastpasses and this, typically, is how they get lost. I have tried many ways of keeping track of my passes, but my all-time favorite is a clear badge case that you wear around your neck. It is perfect for holding admission passes, room keys, and some cash; best of all it is completely waterproof, and you can wear the case in the pool or at the water parks.

The MAGIC KINGDOM

OPENED IN 1971, the Magic Kingdom was the first of Walt Disney World's four theme parks to be built. Many of the attractions found here are originals from that park opening, and a few—including Cinderella Castle, Pirates of the Caribbean, and Splash Mountain—have helped define the basic elements of theme-park attractions the world over. Indeed, the Magic Kingdom is undoubtedly what most people think of when Walt Disney World is mentioned.

Much of the Magic Kingdom was built by the same Disney staff that had built Disneyland a little more than a decade earlier. The remarkable achievement that Disney wrought in Orlando isn't that they could build a second, equally compelling theme park; it's that they could do so on a much larger scale while keeping many of the fine details that make visiting a Disney park such a completely immersive experience.

At the Magic Kingdom, stroller and wheelchair rentals are to the right of the train station, and lockers are on the station's ground floor. On your left as you enter Main Street is City Hall, the center for information, lost and found, guided tours, and entertainment schedules. Automated tellers (ATMs) are underneath the Main Street railroad station, near the Transportation and Ticket Center (TTC), near City Hall, near the Frontierland shooting gallery, near Pinocchio Village Haus in Fantasyland, and inside the Tomorrowland Arcade. Down Main Street and left around the central hub (toward Adventureland) are the Baby Care Center and a first-aid post. Disney no longer has pet-care facilities adjacent to the park, but the Best Friends Pet Resort across from Disney's Port Orleans Resort will provide a comfortable home away from home for Fido, Frisky, and all their pet pals.

If you don't already have a handout park map, get one at City Hall. The handout lists all attractions, shops, and eateries; provides helpful information about first aid, baby care, and assistance for the disabled; and gives tips for good photos. It also lists times for the day's special events, live entertainment, Disney character parades, concerts, and other activities. Additionally, it tells when and where to find Disney characters.

Often the guide map is supplemented by a daily entertainment schedule known as a *Times Guide,* which provides info on special Disney character appearances and what Disney calls Extra Magic Hours. This term refers to attractions that open late or close early and to the operating hours of park restaurants. If you are lodging at a Walt Disney World resort hotel and the park is operating on an Extra Magic Hour evening schedule, make sure you also pick up the Extra Magic Hours "Evenings" flyer, which will list which attractions are open late. All members of your party need to present a resort ID and theme-park ticket to participate.

Main Street ends at a central hub from which branch the entrances to the other five sections of the Magic Kingdom: Adventureland, Frontierland, Liberty Square, Fantasyland, and Tomorrowland.

In this and the following three chapters, we rate the individual attractions at each of the four major Disney theme parks. The authors' ratings, as well as ratings according to age group, are given on a scale of zero to five stars—the more stars, the better the attraction. The authors' rating is from the perspective of an adult. The authors, for example, might rate a ride such as Dumbo much lower than the age group for which the ride is intended, in this case, children. This rating, therefore, will more closely approximate how another adult will experience the attraction than how your children will like it. The bottleneck rating ranges 1–10; the higher the rating, the more congested the attraction. In general, try to experience attractions with a high bottleneck rating early in the morning (that is, 8–10:30 a.m.) before the park gets crowded or late in the day when the crowd has diminished.

MAIN STREET, U.S.A.

BEGIN AND END YOUR VISIT ON MAIN STREET, which may open 30 minutes before and closes 30 minutes to 1 hour after the rest of the park. It is easy to get sidetracked when entering Main Street, as this Disney-fied turn-of-the-19th-century small town street is lovely, with exceptional attention to detail. But remember: Time is of the essence, and the rest of the park is waiting to be discovered. The same goes for the one and only Cinderella Castle. Stick with your touring plan and return to Cinderella Castle and Main Street after you've experienced the must-dos on your list.

Character Greetings (Fastpass) ★★

Meet Mickey, Minnie, and other Disney characters throughout the day at the Town Square Theater on Main Street, to your right as you enter the park. Other characters may also be available. Check the *Times Guide* for

The Magic Kingdom

Liberty Square

Frontierland

Adventureland

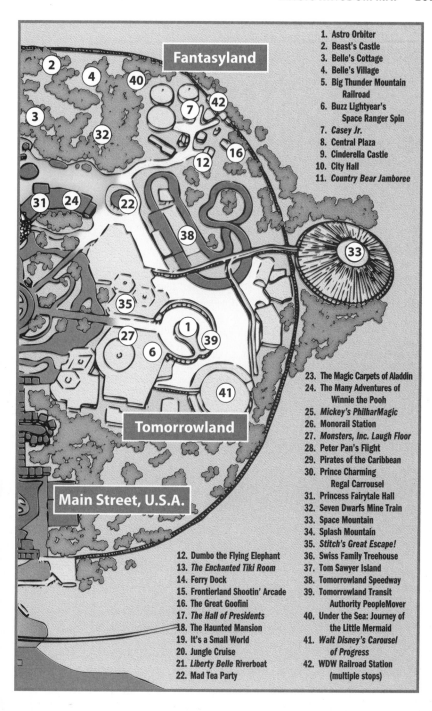

Fantasyland

Tomorrowland

Main Street, U.S.A.

1. Astro Orbiter
2. Beast's Castle
3. Belle's Cottage
4. Belle's Village
5. Big Thunder Mountain Railroad
6. Buzz Lightyear's Space Ranger Spin
7. *Casey Jr.*
8. Central Plaza
9. Cinderella Castle
10. City Hall
11. *Country Bear Jamboree*

12. Dumbo the Flying Elephant
13. *The Enchanted Tiki Room*
14. Ferry Dock
15. Frontierland Shootin' Arcade
16. The Great Goofini
17. *The Hall of Presidents*
18. The Haunted Mansion
19. It's a Small World
20. Jungle Cruise
21. *Liberty Belle* Riverboat
22. Mad Tea Party

23. The Magic Carpets of Aladdin
24. The Many Adventures of Winnie the Pooh
25. *Mickey's PhilharMagic*
26. Monorail Station
27. *Monsters, Inc. Laugh Floor*
28. Peter Pan's Flight
29. Pirates of the Caribbean
30. Prince Charming Regal Carrousel
31. Princess Fairytale Hall
32. Seven Dwarfs Mine Train
33. Space Mountain
34. Splash Mountain
35. *Stitch's Great Escape!*
36. Swiss Family Treehouse
37. Tom Sawyer Island
38. Tomorrowland Speedway
39. Tomorrowland Transit Authority PeopleMover
40. Under the Sea: Journey of the Little Mermaid
41. *Walt Disney's Carousel of Progress*
42. WDW Railroad Station (multiple stops)

details. As we went to press, the Disney princesses are also available at the Town Square Theater until their permanent meet and greet is ready in Fantasyland. If the wait to meet Mickey or the princesses appears long, you can obtain Fastpasses to schedule your visit.

Walt Disney World Railroad ★★½

APPEAL BY AGE	PRESCHOOL ★★★	GRADE SCHOOL ★★★★	TEENS ★★★
YOUNG ADULTS ★★★★		OVER 30 ★★★½	SENIORS ★★★

What it is Scenic railroad ride around perimeter of the Magic Kingdom and transportation to Frontierland and Fantasyland. **Scope and scale** Minor attraction. **Fright potential** Not frightening in any respect. **Bottleneck rating** 6. **When to go** Anytime. **Special comment** Main Street is usually the least congested station. **Authors' rating** Plenty to see; ★★½. **Duration of ride** About 20 minutes for a complete circuit. **Average wait in line per 100 people ahead of you** 8 minutes. **Assumes** Two or more trains operating. **Loading speed** Moderate.

Thumbs Up for the Whole Family

Later in the day when you need a break, this full-circuit ride will give you and your feet 20 minutes of rest. You cannot take your rental stroller on the train; but if you get off short of a complete circuit, you can get a free replacement. Be advised that the railroad shuts down immediately preceding and during parades.

▌ ADVENTURELAND

THE FIRST LAND TO THE LEFT OF MAIN STREET, Adventureland combines an African safari theme with an old New Orleans/Caribbean atmosphere.

Enchanted Tiki Room ★★★½

APPEAL BY AGE	PRESCHOOL ★★★	GRADE SCHOOL ★★★	TEENS ★★½
YOUNG ADULTS ★★★		OVER 30 ★★★	SENIORS ★★★

What it is Audio-animatronic Pacific Island musical theater show. **Scope and scale** Minor attraction. **Fright potential** Young children might be frightened by the thunder and lightning storm, plus the theater is at times plunged into utter darkness. **Bottleneck rating** 4. **When to go** Before 11 a.m. or after 3:30 p.m. **Special comment** Frightens some preschoolers. **Authors' rating** Very, very unusual; ★★★½. **Duration of show** 15½ minutes. **Preshow** Talking birds. **Probable waiting time** 15 minutes.

Dark   Loud

The Tiki birds are a great favorite of the 8-and-under age set. The sarcasm of Iago from *Aladdin* and Zazu from *The Lion King* save the show for older patrons. If you can look beyond the cheese, it is actually hilariously funny. The air-conditioned theater is a great place to cool off and rest your feet.

Jungle Cruise (Fastpass) ★★★

APPEAL BY AGE	PRESCHOOL ★★★★	GRADE SCHOOL ★★★★	TEENS ★★★½
YOUNG ADULTS ★★★½		OVER 30 ★★★½	SENIORS ★★★★

What it is Outdoor safari-themed boat ride adventure. **Scope and scale** Major attraction. **Fright potential** Moderately intense, some macabre sights; a good test attraction for little ones. **Bottleneck rating** 10. **When to go** Before 10 a.m., 2 hours before closing, or use Fastpass. **Authors' rating** An enduring Disney masterpiece; ★★★. **Duration of ride** 8–9 minutes. **Average wait in line per 100 people ahead of you** 3½ minutes. **Assumes** 10 boats operating. **Loading speed** Moderate.

You have to put things into perspective to truly enjoy this ride and realize that it once was a super-headliner attraction at the Magic Kingdom. It still is a relaxing and enjoyable boat ride, but it won't capture the fascination of the high-tech savvy youngsters of the new millennium.

Thumbs Up for the Whole Family

DISNEY DISH WITH JIM HILL

RUMBLE IN THE JUNGLE For more than four decades, skippers have been taking WDW visitors through the Jungle Cruise's supposedly fraught-with-danger hippo pool. Because none of the critters ever touched the boat, the fright factor was, well, kind of *meh*. All of that changes with an upcoming upgrade of this Adventureland classic. The Imagineers plan on adding a system of underwater hydraulic rams to the pool to make it seem as if the hippos are jostling your boat from below and actively trying to sink your skiff. Try yawning through a scene like that!

Magic Carpets of Aladdin ★★★

APPEAL BY AGE	PRESCHOOL ★★★★½	GRADE SCHOOL ★★★★
TEENS ★★★	YOUNG ADULTS ★★½	OVER 30 ★★★	SENIORS ★★½

What it is Elaborate midway ride. **Scope and scale** Minor attraction. **Fright potential** Much like Dumbo; a favorite of most younger children. **Bottleneck rating** 10. **When to go** Before 10 a.m. or in the hour before park closing. **Authors' rating** An eye-appealing children's ride; ★★★. **Duration of ride** 1½ minutes. **Average wait in line per 100 people ahead of you** 16 minutes. **Loading speed** Slow.

Of course the ride is inspired by the 1992 Disney movie *Aladdin*. Did you know that Robin Williams is the voice of the Genie?

Movie Tip

For parents with preschoolers, there's no way out—like Dumbo, it is a must. Try to get your kids to ride in the first 30 minutes the park is open or just before park closing. Beware, the ride has a spitting camel positioned to spray jets of water on riders. The magic-carpet vehicles are rider-controlled, so you can fly your magic carpet up, down, or pitch forward or backward. The front-seat control is for up and down, while the backseat control pitches the carpet forward or backward. Sweet, but oh-so-slow loading. One more tip: Jasmine and Aladdin are often on hand for greeting and meeting.

Pirates of the Caribbean ★ ★ ★ ★ ★

APPEAL BY AGE	PRESCHOOL ★★★½	GRADE SCHOOL ★★★★	TEENS ★★★★
YOUNG ADULTS ★★★★½		OVER 30 ★★★★½	SENIORS ★★★★½

What it is Indoor pirate-themed adventure boat ride. **Scope and scale** Headliner. **Fright potential** Slightly intimidating queuing area; intense boat ride with gruesome (though humorously presented) sights and a short, unexpected slide down a flume. **Bottleneck rating** 7. **When to go** Before noon or after 5 p.m. **Special comment** Frightens some young children. **Authors' rating** Disney audioanimatronics at its best; not to be missed; ★★★★★. **Duration of ride** About 7½ minutes. **Average wait in line per 100 people ahead of you** 1½ minutes. **Assumes** Both waiting lines operating. **Loading speed** Fast.

Dark Loud Scary

Yo ho, yo ho, a pirate's life for me! This indoor ride cruises through a series of sets depicting a pirate raid on an island settlement. It has been a favorite for decades, but with the release of *Pirates of the Caribbean: The Curse of the Black Pearl* (2003), *Pirates of the Caribbean: Dead Man's Chest* (2006), *Pirates of the Caribbean: At World's End* (2007), and *Pirates of the Caribbean: On Stranger Tides* (2011), the popularity of the ride has soared to new heights. Oh yeah, the films' protagonist, Captain Jack Sparrow, has joined the attraction's animatronic cast. A must for all young pirates is Captain Jack Sparrow's Pirate Tutorial, which takes place several times a day next to the Pirates of the Caribbean ride. Check the daily entertainment schedule (*Times Guide*) and arrive 15 minutes in advance if you want your little buccaneer to have a chance of joining the ranks of Captain Jack Sparrow and his faithful companion Mack.

Liliane

Chances of being picked as an apprentice pirate are good at most shows, so don't push your kid in front of Jack and Mack. Dressing up for the part helps, however.

Hannah

When you're entering the ride's line, you can look through the bars in the jail cells and see guns, barrels, and skeletons. The scariest part is when there's a cannon fight between the pirate's boat and the town. And Davy Jones looks kind of creepy.

Movie Tip

For all fans of the *Pirates of the Caribbean* movies, rent the movies before you go to Walt Disney World. They're a blast.

Swiss Family Treehouse ★ ★ ★

APPEAL BY AGE	PRESCHOOL ★★★	GRADE SCHOOL ★★★	TEENS ★★★
YOUNG ADULTS ★★½		OVER 30 ★★★	SENIORS ★★★

What it is Outdoor walk-through tree house. **Scope and scale** Minor attraction. **Fright potential** Not frightening in any respect. **Bottleneck rating** 6. **When to go** Before 11:30 a.m. or after 5 p.m. **Special comment** Requires climbing a lot of stairs. **Authors' rating** A visual delight; ★★★. **Duration of tour** 10–15 minutes. **Average wait in line per 100 people ahead of you** 7 minutes.

This king of all tree houses is perfect for the 10-and-under crowd. Though a minor attraction, it's a great place to expend pent-up energy. Parents might be inclined to sit across the walkway and watch their aspiring Tarzans, but in truth the tree house is fun for adults too.

Thumbs Up for the Whole Family

It's pretty fun to look at, but my sister and I thought it was expendable. However, if you're over 30 years old, you'll probably really appreciate it.

Shelton

Swiss Family Robinson is a 1960 film adaptation of the Johann David Wyss novel and was the inspiration for the Swiss Family Treehouse.

Movie Tip

FRONTIERLAND

FRONTIERLAND ADJOINS ADVENTURELAND as you move clockwise around the Magic Kingdom. The focus is on the Old West, with stockade-type structures and pioneer trappings.

Big Thunder Mountain Railroad (Fastpass) ★★★★

| APPEAL BY AGE | PRESCHOOL ★★★½ | GRADE SCHOOL ★★★★½ | TEENS ★★★★½ |
| YOUNG ADULTS ★★★★ | | OVER 30 ★★★★½ | SENIORS ★★★★ |

What it is Tame, Western-mining-themed roller coaster. **Scope and scale** Headliner. **Fright potential** Visually intimidating from outside, with moderately intense visual effects; the roller coaster is wild enough to frighten many adults, particularly seniors. **Bottleneck rating** 9. **When to go** Before 10 a.m., in the hour before closing, or use Fastpass. **Special comments** Must be 40" tall to ride; children younger than age 7 must ride with an adult. Switching-off option provided (see page 242). **Authors' rating** Great effects; relatively tame roller coaster; not to be missed; ★★★★. **Duration of ride** Almost 3½ minutes. **Average wait in line per 100 people ahead of you** 2½ minutes. **Assumes** 5 trains operating. **Loading speed** Moderate–fast.

Lose Things Rough Scary

Zooming on a runaway train around a mountain and through a deserted mining town is Disney at its best (if only one could concentrate on the scenery). The ride is rough, and if you do not like roller coasters, this one is going to remind you why. If you are a fan, however, the scenery deserves three rides in a row and an extra one for atmosphere after dark. Regardless of when you ride, seats in the back offer a better experience.

Watch out on this one. Sitting in the back jerks me around too much. If you go in the front or the middle, you'll have a smoother ride. It has a lot of dips but no flips because it is more like a wooden roller coaster.

Ian

Hannah

I was not feeling the love the first time I went on this. You always feel like you're going to hit your head on one rock or another, and there are a lot of twists and turns. Eventually, I liked the bumps and how high the ride went, so I went on it again with my dad.

Shelton

My whole family loved the falling rocks and earthquakes. DO NOT duck right near the end. There is a very low rock, which looks like it will hit your head. I ducked, and I got whiplash because there is then a sudden 5-foot drop. It's very small but very quick.

Country Bear Jamboree ★★★

APPEAL BY AGE	PRESCHOOL ★★★½	GRADE SCHOOL ★★★	TEENS ★★
YOUNG ADULTS ★★½		OVER 30 ★★★	SENIORS ★★★½

What it is Audio-animatronic country hoedown theater show. **Scope and scale** Major attraction. **Fright potential** Not frightening in any respect. **Bottleneck rating** 8. **When to go** Before 11:30 a.m., before a parade, or during the 2 hours before closing. **Authors' rating** A Disney classic; ★★★. **Duration of show** 15 minutes. **Probable waiting time** This attraction is not that popular and has a relatively small capacity. Probable waiting time noon–5:30 p.m. on a busy day will average 15–30 minutes.

Kids up to age 10 especially will enjoy this funny country music show. The show is a little dusty, but Teddi Bara, Big Al, Trixie, and the rest of the gang are Disney classics. The *Jamboree* is an air-conditioned refuge during summer afternoons, rainy days, and times of peak attendance. On these days *Country Bear* will draw larger crowds from midmorning on.

Movie Tip

Kids will love watching *The Country Bears,* a live-action film produced by Walt Disney Pictures based loosely on the *Country Bear Jamboree* show. It was Disney's first movie based on a ride or attraction, released in 2002, almost a year before *Pirates of the Caribbean: The Curse of the Black Pearl.*

Frontierland Shootin' Arcade ★½

APPEAL BY AGE	PRESCHOOL ★★½	GRADE SCHOOL ★★★½	TEENS ★★★
YOUNG ADULTS ★★★		OVER 30 ★★½	SENIORS ★★

What it is Electronic shooting gallery. **Scope and scale** Diversion. **Fright potential** Not frightening in any respect. **When to go** Whenever convenient. **Special comment** Costs $1 per play. **Authors' rating** Very nifty shooting gallery; ★½.

Would-be rifle persons get around 30 shots per $1 play. The rifles are set so that each shot must be followed by a short delay before the next shot is taken. This prevents small children from accidentally using all 30 shots in 5 seconds. It's barely noticeable for adults.

Bring quarters. It is big-time fun.

Idan

Splash Mountain (Fastpass) ★★★★★

APPEAL BY AGE	PRESCHOOL† ★★★★	GRADE SCHOOL ★★★★½	TEENS★★★★★
YOUNG ADULTS ★★★★★		OVER 30 ★★★★½	SENIORS ★★★★

† Many preschoolers are too short to meet the height requirement. Among preschoolers who actually ride, most give the attraction high marks.

What it is Indoor/outdoor water-flume adventure ride. **Scope and scale** Super-headliner. **Fright potential** Visually intimidating from outside, with moderately intense visual effects. The ride, culminating in a 52-foot plunge down a steep chute, is somewhat hair-raising for all ages. **Bottleneck rating** 10. **When to go** As soon as the park opens, during afternoon or evening parades, just before closing, or use Fastpass. **Special comments** Must be 40" tall to ride; children younger than 7 must ride with an adult. Switching-off option provided (see page 242). **Authors' rating** A wet winner; not to be missed; ★★★★★. **Duration of ride** About 10 minutes. **Average wait in line per 100 people ahead of you** 3½ minutes. **Assumes** Operating at full capacity. **Loading speed** Moderate.

Lose Things   Wet   Scary

Zip-a-dee-doo-dah, are we having fun yet, my-o-my, did we get wet! The 0.5-mile ride through swamps, caves, and backwoods bayous is wonderful. Based on the 1946 Disney film *Song of the South,* you travel in a log through Uncle Remus's tales of Br'er Rabbit. Three small drops lead up to the big one, a five-story drop at 40 mph.

Ian

Way too cool! If you want to feel what it's like to go over a waterfall, sit in the front, but I prefer the back. I think you get wetter. Get as many big people sitting in front of you as you can. They weigh down the boat and make the biggest splash.

Hannah

You get really wet on this ride, and there are a lot of surprises! When you get in, the seats are going to be really wet.

Shelton

I don't know why people complain about getting wet. You really don't get all that wet. My sister and I were in the front row, and my sister even complained that she didn't get wet enough!

Unavailable in the United States, *Song of the South* will become public domain in 2039, and Disney might re-release the movie before they lose the rights to it. If you are interested in the history of this controversial movie, check out **songofthesouth.net**.

Movie Tip

Tom Sawyer Island and Fort Langhorn ★★★

| APPEAL BY AGE | PRESCHOOL ★★★★ | | GRADE SCHOOL ★★★★ |
| TEENS ★★★ | YOUNG ADULTS ★★★ | OVER 30 ★★★ | SENIORS ★★★ |

What it is Outdoor walk-through exhibit/rustic playground. **Scope and scale** Minor attraction. **Fright potential** Not frightening in any respect. **Bottleneck rating** 4. **When to go** Midmorning through late afternoon. **Special comment** Closes at sunset. **Authors' rating** The place for rambunctious kids; ★★★.

This is a great place for kids age 5 and up to unwind. The wildest and most uncooperative youngster will relax after exploring caves and climbing around in an old fort. While it is also a great place for a picnic, there is no food, so bring your own. Access to the island is by raft with a (usually short) wait both coming and going. Plan to give your kids at least 20 minutes on the island. Left to their own devices, they would likely stay all day.

Thumbs Up for the Whole Family

Each morning, Disney cast members hide about a half-dozen colored paintbrushes around the island for guests to find. (Look for colored handles with white paint on the bristles, on display shelves and in buildings. They'll all be within arm's reach.) Notify a cast member if you find one; you'll be rewarded with a small prize ranging from a front-of-line pass on any Magic Kingdom attraction to free sodas for your entire group. One of each prize is available each day on a first-come basis, so this is a great activity to do early on the second day in the park.

The caves were interesting. It may sound like a little kid's playground, but I think it's worth a look for all ages.

Shelton

I thought this was really cool because I like adventurous stuff like the rope bridges. There's also a playground. You take a boat across the lake to get there.

Hannah

LIBERTY SQUARE

LIBERTY SQUARE RE-CREATES COLONIAL AMERICA at the time of the American Revolution. The architecture is Federal or Colonial. The Liberty Tree, a real live oak that's more than 130 years old, lends dignity and grace to the setting.

The Hall of Presidents ★ ★ ★

| APPEAL BY AGE | PRESCHOOL ★★ | GRADE SCHOOL ★★★ | TEENS ★★★ |
| YOUNG ADULTS ★★★½ | | OVER 30 ★★★★ | SENIORS ★★★★ |

What it is Audio-animatronic historical theater presentation. **Scope and scale** Major attraction. **Fright potential** Not frightening in any respect. **Bottleneck rating** 4. **When to go** Anytime. **Authors' rating** Impressive and moving; ★★★. **Duration of show** Almost 23 minutes. **Probable waiting time** Lines for this attraction look awesome but are usually swallowed up as the theater exchanges audiences. Your wait will probably be the remaining time of the show that's in progress when you arrive. Even during the busiest times, waits rarely exceed 40 minutes.

Thumbs Up for the Whole Family

Disney immortalizes the presidents of the United States with their own audio-animatronic counterparts. In 2009 Disney added Barack Obama and revamped the entire show, which includes a new narration by Morgan Freeman and a new speech by George Washington. The Father of Our Country joins Presidents Lincoln and Obama as the only chief executives with speaking parts. Although the show is revamped roughly every decade, the presentation remains strongly inspirational and patriotic and highlights milestones in American history. *The Hall of Presidents* is a very moving show for Americans and features one of Disney's best and most ambitious audio-animatronic efforts. The show is definitely a must-see for adults. Kids will fidget or fall asleep.

Shelton

Not very interesting, but I thought the presidents were real actors. Very realistic and kind of creepy is what we thought.

If you want to know more about Valerie Edwards, who sculpts presidents, check out **mousetreasures.com/wdcc/valerie**. Her dad was a Disney animator and worked on *Sleeping Beauty*.

Liliane

The Haunted Mansion ★★★★

APPEAL BY AGE	PRESCHOOL ★★★	GRADE SCHOOL ★★★★	TEENS ★★★★½
YOUNG ADULTS ★★★★½		OVER 30 ★★★★½	SENIORS ★★★★½

What it is Haunted-house dark ride. **Scope and scale** Major attraction. **Fright potential** The name raises anxiety, as do the sounds and sights of the waiting area. An intense attraction with humorously presented macabre sights, the ride itself is gentle. **Bottleneck rating** 8. **When to go** Before 11:30 a.m. or after 8 p.m. **Special comment** Frightens some very young children. **Authors' rating** Some of Walt Disney World's best special effects; not to be missed; ★★★★. **Duration of ride** 7-minute ride plus a 1½-minute preshow. **Average wait in line per 100 people ahead of you** 2½ minutes. **Assumes** Both "stretch rooms" operating. **Loading speed** Fast.

Dark Scary

Don't let the apparent spookiness of the old-fashioned Haunted Mansion put you off. This is one of the best attractions in the Magic Kingdom (and, in fact, one that seems to get a few new twists each year). It's not scary, except in the sweetest of ways, but it will remind you of the days before ghost stories gave way to slasher flicks. The Haunted Mansion takes less than 10 minutes to ride, preshow included, but you may have to do it more than once—it's jam-packed with visual puns, special effects, Hidden Mickeys, and really lovely Victorian-spooky sets.

> It's freaky, man. One time I almost chickened out. Real people in costumes stare you down. There's lots of weird stuff going on, like eyes in paintings on the wall following you and a lady's face inside a crystal ball. At the end, a ghost rides in the car with you. Read the funny tombstones before you go in.

Ian

Liberty Belle Riverboat ★★½

APPEAL BY AGE	PRESCHOOL ★★★	GRADE SCHOOL ★★★	TEENS ★★½
YOUNG ADULTS ★★★		OVER 30 ★★★	SENIORS ★★★★

What it is Outdoor scenic boat ride. **Scope and scale** Major attraction. **Fright potential** Not frightening in any respect. **Bottleneck rating** 4. **When to go** Anytime. **Authors' rating** Slow, relaxing, and scenic; ★★½. **Duration of ride** About 16 minutes. **Average wait to board** 10–14 minutes.

This fully narrated 16-minute trip is relaxing and offers great photo ops. It's a good choice also at night when the boat and the attractions along the waterfront are lighted. Did you know that the *Liberty Belle* Riverboat runs on a track hidden just below the water?

Thumbs Up for the Whole Family

FANTASYLAND

FANTASYLAND IS THE HEART of the Magic Kingdom, a truly enchanting place spread gracefully like a miniature Alpine village beneath the lofty towers of the Cinderella Castle. Over the next

DISNEY DISH WITH JIM HILL

TIME TO RESET THE TABLE When the *Beauty and the Beast*–themed Be Our Guest restaurant opens in 2012, look for Cinderella's Royal Table to quietly close for a lengthy rehab. The Imagineers have long wanted to freshen up this Fantasyland staple, but because of continuing high guest demand for the character-dining experience, they just haven't had the chance to do anything of substance until now. So once Beast's Castle opens for business in late 2012, look for Cindy to shutter for at least 6 months so WDI can make this Magic Kingdom must-do even more magical.

2 years Disney will redesign Fantasyland in the largest land expansion in Magic Kingdom history.

The **Princess Fairytale Hall** will be the new elegant home of the Disney princesses. Built on the site of Snow White's Scary Adventures, guests can greet princesses such as Cinderella, Aurora, Rapunzel, and Tiana. Disney scratched the plans for the more-interactive attractions with Cinderella at Dreams Come True, the Briar Rose Cottage with Princess Aurora, and the Pixie Hollow project. It remains to be seen if these changes, which were made to attract more young boys to Fantasyland, are indeed successful.

In **Under the Sea: Journey of the Little Mermaid,** Ariel and friends will entertain in an enclosed ride carrying guests through an underwater world. An Omnimover ride system similar to the one used in The Haunted Mansion will move visitors through adventures featuring favorite songs from the movie.

Inside a castle modeled after the Beast's fortress in *Beauty and the Beast,* the **Be Our Guest** restaurant will feature a lavish dining experience in the elegant ballroom, a gallery, and the mysterious West Wing of the Beast's castle. With seating for 550, the facility will offer fast food by day and full table service in the evening. Nearby, in **Belle's Village,** guests will find **Gaston's Tavern** and **Bonjour! Village Gifts.** Just outside the village is Belle's cottage and **Enchanted Tales with Belle.** The adventure begins in Maurice's workshop, where a magical mirror is the doorway to a captivating new kind of storytelling experience: Guests are transported to the Beast's library to meet Belle and Lumiere and share in a lively, interactive retelling of the "tale as old as time."

The **Seven Dwarfs Mine Train** is a new family coaster coming to the Magic Kingdom. The ride will feature a first-of-its kind ride system, with a train of vehicles that swing back and forth, responding to every twist and turn of the track. The journey will take guests on a mixture of an indoor and outdoor roller coaster accompanied by music and animated figures of Snow White and the Seven Dwarfs.

The sound of the calliope will lead guests into the new **Storybook Circus.** In the new circus grounds you will find not one but two carousels of **Dumbo the Flying Elephant**—all our prayers have been heard—with games and interactive activities inside the big top tent. The

Barnstormer coaster at Goofy's Wiseacre Farm gets a new look, featuring Goofy as the **Great Goofini.** To accommodate the expansion, most of Mickey's Toontown Fair was torn down.

These changes should increase the number of guests heading to Fantasyland, and Fantasyland was already one of the most crowded lands in the park. The good news is that the new attractions and restaurants are well-designed to handle crowds. The ride vehicles in Journey of the Little Mermaid, for example, will board riders almost continuously throughout the day, at a rate of around 2,000 per hour. That's about the number of riders Space Mountain serves in an hour. And the overall size of Fantasyland will double, meaning the crowds will have more room to spread out.

Minnie and Mickey will find new homes near the front entrance of the park. In the meantime, you can meet Mickey, Minnie, and the Disney princesses at the Town Square Theater. Tinker Bell and her fairy friends will be joining the cast of Epcot. Until the completion of the expansion of Fantasyland, the easiest way to meet many princesses and other favorite Disney characters with little waiting in line is in Epcot. We are expecting a few of the new Fantasyland attractions to open late 2011 with most being completed in 2013.

We've updated our Magic Kingdom touring plans to reflect the latest developments with all the attractions. As with any construction project, plans can change. Check **touringplans.com** for the latest developments and touring plan updates.

Dumbo the Flying Elephant ★★★

APPEAL BY AGE	PRESCHOOL ★★★★½	GRADE SCHOOL ★★★★	TEENS ★★½
YOUNG ADULTS ★★½		OVER 30 ★★★	SENIORS ★★½

What it is Disney-fied midway ride. **Scope and scale** Minor attraction. **Fright potential** A tame midway ride; a great favorite of most young children. **Bottleneck rating** 10. **When to go** Before 10 a.m. or after 9 p.m. **Authors' rating** An attractive children's ride; ★★★. **Duration of ride** 1½ minutes. **Average wait in line per 100 people ahead of you** 5 minutes. **Loading speed** Slow.

Making sure your child gets his fill of this tame, happy children's ride is what mother love is all about. The 90-second ride is hardly worth the long lines, unless, of course, you're under 7 years old. If Dumbo's on your must-see list, try to get the kids on board during the first 30 minutes the park is open.

> If you have not seen *Dumbo* (first released in 1941 and winner of an Academy Award for original music score), you have an elephant-size gap in your Disney education. Fun for all ages, rent the movie when you get home.

The Great Goofini
(formerly Barnstormer at Goofy's Wiseacre Farm) ★★

APPEAL BY AGE	PRESCHOOL ★★★★	GRADE SCHOOL ★★★★	TEENS ★★½
YOUNG ADULTS ★★½		OVER 30 ★★★	SENIORS ★★

What it is Small roller coaster. **Scope and scale** Minor attraction. **Fright potential** A children's coaster; frightens some preschoolers. **Bottleneck rating** 9.

When to go Before 10:30 a.m., during parades, or in the evening just before the park closes. **Special comment** Must be 35" tall to ride. **Authors' rating** Great for little ones but not worth the wait for adults; ★★. **Duration of ride** About 53 seconds. **Average wait in line per 100 people ahead of you** 7 minutes. **Loading speed** Slow.

Rough

Scary

Remember that the height requirement for this ride is 35 inches. If you want to see how your child handles riding coasters, The Great Goofini is the perfect testing ground.

Liliane

Yours truly screamed big-time from start to end (thankfully it only lasted a minute), and no way would I let the apple of my eye ride alone unless he or she is 6 years or older.

Liliane is a gentle and sensitive soul. Most kids experience rides wilder than the Great Goofini on their tricycles. When I heard Liliane wailing like a banshee on this little coaster, I thought that her appendix must have ruptured.

Bob

It's a Small World ★★★

APPEAL BY AGE	PRESCHOOL ★★★★½	GRADE SCHOOL ★★★★	TEENS ★★★
YOUNG ADULTS ★★★		OVER 30 ★★★½	SENIORS ★★★★

What it is World brotherhood–themed indoor boat ride. **Scope and scale** Major attraction. **Fright potential** Not frightening in any respect. **Bottleneck rating** 6. **When to go** Anytime. **Authors' rating** Exponentially "cute"; ★★★. **Duration of ride** Approximately 11 minutes. **Average wait in line per 100 people ahead of you** 11 minutes. **Assumes** Busy conditions with 30 or more boats operating. **Loading speed** Fast.

Thumbs Up for the Whole Family

Small boats carry visitors on a tour around the world, with singing and dancing dolls showcasing the dress and culture of each nation. Totally rehabbed in 2005, Small World is one of Disney's oldest entertainments. Did you know that the ride originated at the 1964 New York World's Fair? If you listen closely, you will realize that the theme song is actually sung in numerous languages as your boat is carried from one continent to the next. Of course, there's no escaping the brain-numbing little tune. You'll go home with it lodged in your brain like a bullet, and just when you think you've repressed it, the song will resurface without warning to torture you some more.

Ian

This ride is why MP3 players were invented. Just put on your headphones and listen to Velvet Revolver all the way through the ride. The Small World song won't bother you a bit. Promise.

I must be immune to the tune. I love the ride and would not miss riding It's a Small World anytime I visit.

Idan

Mad Tea Party ★★

APPEAL BY AGE	PRESCHOOL ★★★★	GRADE SCHOOL ★★★★	TEENS ★★★★
YOUNG ADULTS ★★★½		OVER 30 ★★★	SENIORS ★★

What it is Midway-type spinning ride. **Scope and scale** Minor attraction. **Fright potential** Low, but this type of ride can induce motion sickness in all ages. **Bottleneck rating** 9. **When to go** Before 11 a.m. or after 5 p.m. **Special comment** You can make the teacups spin faster by turning the wheel in the center of the cup. **Authors' rating** Fun but not worth the wait; ★★. **Duration of ride** 1½ minutes. **Average wait in line per 100 people ahead of you** 7½ minutes. **Loading speed** Slow.

Queasy

It's a party, and a mad one at that. Prepare yourself for a whirling adventure inside a giant teacup (also known as the human centrifuge). Teenagers love to lure adults into the spinning teacups and then turn the wheel in the middle (making the cup spin faster) until the adults are plastered against the sides and on the verge of throwing up. The only sane way to experience this ride with teenagers is, paradoxically, to put them in straitjackets so they can't spin the wheel. We're dying to try this. Volunteers, anyone?

Liliane

My son loves this ride, but then again he is a teenager. As for me, I love the ride too. I'll take the Mad Tea Party over Big Thunder Mountain any day. Plus, it's good training for experiencing Mission: SPACE at Epcot.

Bob

Researchers at NASA determined that you're less likely to experience motion sickness if you don't ride on an empty stomach.

Movie Tip

The Mad Tea Party is inspired by the unusual tea party scene in the 1951 Disney adaptation of Lewis Carroll's *Alice in Wonderland.* Did you know that the voice of Alice, British voice actress and schoolteacher Kathryn Beaumont, is also the voice of Wendy in *Peter Pan*?

The Many Adventures of Winnie the Pooh ★★★½ (Fastpass)

APPEAL BY AGE	PRESCHOOL ★★★★	GRADE SCHOOL ★★★★	TEENS ★★★
YOUNG ADULTS ★★★		OVER 30 ★★★½	SENIORS ★★★½

What it is Indoor track ride. **Scope and scale** Minor attraction. **Fright potential** Not frightening in any respect. **Bottleneck rating** 8. **When to go** Before 10 a.m., in the 2 hours before closing, or use Fastpass. **Authors' rating** Cute as the Poohbear himself; ★★★½. **Duration of ride** About 4 minutes. **Average wait in line per 100 people ahead of you** 4 minutes. **Loading speed** Moderate.

Thumbs Up for the Whole Family

This ride is a romp through the Hundred-Acre Wood on a blustery day. The visuals are gentle and charming without being saccharine. The Many Adventures of Winnie the Pooh is a perfect test to assess how your very young children will react to the indoor, so-called dark rides.

Movie Tip

The ride is based on a 1977 Disney animated feature, *The Many Adventures of Winnie the Pooh.* The movie and Winnie the Pooh books are perfect for very young children. Did you know that Paul Winchell won a Grammy for his voicing of Tigger? Other Disney roles of Paul Winchell include parts in *The Aristocats* as a Chinese cat and *The Fox and the Hound* as Boomer the woodpecker. He also lends his voice to evil Gargamel in the Smurfs TV show (not the movie).

Mickey's PhilharMagic (Fastpass seasonally) ★★★★

APPEAL BY AGE	PRESCHOOL ★★★★	GRADE SCHOOL ★★★★½	TEENS ★★★★
YOUNG ADULTS ★★★★½		OVER 30 ★★★★½	SENIORS ★★★★★

What it is 3-D movie. **Scope and scale** Major attraction. **Fright potential** Some preschoolers may be scared at first, but taking off the 3-D glasses tones down the effect. **Bottleneck rating** 6. **When to go** Before 11 a.m., during parades, or use Fastpass if available. **Authors' rating** Not to be missed; a masterpiece; ★★★★. **Duration of show** About 12 minutes. **Probable waiting time** 12–25 minutes.

A real stunner, *Mickey's PhilharMagic* combines three fabulous ideas: Mickey and Donald mix and meet with latter-day Disney stars such as Aladdin, Jasmine, Ariel, the Beast's pantry servants (such as Lumiere and Mrs. Potts), and Simba; it employs a form of computer-enhanced 3-D video technology that is truly impressive (it's the first time most of these characters have been digitally animated, which will make them more "flexible," so to speak, in the future); and the whole shebang is projected on a 150-foot-wide, 180-degree screen. *Mickey's PhilharMagic* even employs some of those famous Disney scent effects and turns the old *Sorcerer's Apprentice* trick back on Mickey.

You want to duck when corks and other things come flying out at you. I loved the part with Aladdin, when they were flying on their magic carpet. It felt very real!

Shelton

Peter Pan's Flight (Fastpass) ★★★★

APPEAL BY AGE	PRESCHOOL ★★★★	GRADE SCHOOL ★★★★	TEENS ★★★½
YOUNG ADULTS ★★★★		OVER 30 ★★★★	SENIORS ★★★★

What it is Indoor track ride. **Scope and scale** Minor attraction. **Fright potential** Not frightening in any respect. **Bottleneck rating** 8. **When to go** Before 10 a.m., after 6 p.m., or use Fastpass. **Authors' rating** Happy, mellow, and well done; ★★★★. **Duration of ride** A little more than 3 minutes. **Average wait in line per 100 people ahead of you** 5½ minutes. **Loading speed** Moderate–slow.

Take a snort of pixie dust and off you go soaring over London and on to Never Land.

Thumbs Up for the Whole Family

Disney's animated film version of *Peter Pan* is, of course, the inspiration for this wonderful ride. While the original is easy to find, the sequel, *Return to Never*

Movie Tip

Land, is not. Try to get a copy at a library or find a used one at **amazon.com** and reunite with Peter, Wendy, Tinker Bell, Mr. Smee, the Lost Boys, and Captain Hook. But most of all: Don't grow up.

Prince Charming Regal Carrousel ★★★

APPEAL BY AGE	PRESCHOOL ★★★★½	GRADE SCHOOL ★★★½
TEENS ★★	YOUNG ADULTS ★★★	OVER 30 ★★★	SENIORS ★★★

What it is Merry-go-round. **Scope and scale** Minor attraction. **Fright potential** Not frightening in any respect. **Bottleneck rating** 9. **When to go** Before 11 a.m. or after 8 p.m. **Special comment** Adults enjoy the beauty and nostalgia of this ride. **Authors'**

rating A beautiful children's ride; ★★★. **Duration of ride** About 2 minutes. **Average wait in line per 100 people ahead of you** 5 minutes. **Loading speed** Slow.

It is a long wait, but the beauty of the carousel (formerly known as Cinderella's Golden Carrousel) captures everyone. The carousel, built in 1917, was discovered in New Jersey, where it was once part of an amusement park. It is beautifully maintained and especially magical at night when all the lights are on. Check out your children's delighted expressions as the painted ponies go up and down.

Princess Fairytale Hall (opens 2012) ★★

What it is Character greeting venue. **Scope and scale** Minor attraction. **Fright potential** Not frightening in any respect. **Bottleneck rating** 9. **When to go** Before 10:30 a.m. or after 4:30 p.m. **Authors' rating** You want princesses? We got 'em; ★★. **Duration of experience** About 7–10 minutes (estimated). **Average wait in line per 100 people ahead of you** 35 minutes (estimated). **Touring speed** Slow.

Scheduled to open in 2012 on the site of Snow White's Scary Adventures, Fairytale Hall will be the central location for meeting Disney's princesses in the Magic Kingdom. While Disney has not yet released details, we think the meeting-and-greeting process will work similar to other Magic Kingdom meet and greets: The princesses occupy a greeting room where 15–20 guests are admitted at a time. They're allowed about 7–10 minutes, long enough for a photo, autograph, and a hug from each princess.

Seven Dwarfs Mine Train (opens 2012)

What it is Indoor/outdoor roller coaster. **Scope and scale** Major attraction. **When to go** Before 10 a.m., during parades, or in the evening.

The Mine Train looks to appeal to the entire family. Although the attraction had not opened as we went to press, the concept art shows a set of small mine trains running through the Seven Dwarfs workplace and around the forest above the ground. As far as we can tell, the experi-

Thumbs Up for the Whole Family

ence looks relatively tame—there are no loops, inversions, or rolls in the track, with no massive hills or steep drops. The attraction seems geared to tweens and those slightly younger.

We've also heard that the ride vehicles will swing back and forth around the track. Disney hasn't said, but we suspect that this means your seats pitch left and right while your ride vehicle barrels down the track. It should make the ride's tight turns all the more fun.

Under the Sea may be the big draw, but we'd bet that the Mine Train will have longer lines throughout the day.

Snow White's Scary Adventures ★★½

APPEAL BY AGE	PRESCHOOL ★★★	GRADE SCHOOL ★★★	TEENS ★★★
YOUNG ADULTS ★★★	OVER 30 ★★★		SENIORS ★★★

What it is Indoor track ride. **Scope and scale** Minor attraction. **Fright potential** Moderately intense spook-house-genre attraction with some grim characters. Terrifies many preschoolers. **Bottleneck rating** 8. **When to go** Before 11 a.m. or

DISNEY DISH WITH JIM HILL

DOC, HAPPY, SNEEZY, . . . AND SPEEDY So how exactly is the Magic Kingdom's new Seven Dwarfs Mine Train ride going to differ from Snow White's Scary Adventures? Not as much as you might think. I'm told that many of the show scenes from this Fantasyland classic will be replicated—at least in part—within this new thrill ride. The key difference is that as you zoom through this enormous show building aboard your swaying ore car, you'll be moving past Grumpy, Dopey, and Bashful at dwarf, er, warp speed. So don't expect to be like Sleepy and be able to catch a nap while experiencing this family-friendly thrill ride.

after 6 p.m. **Authors' rating** Worth seeing if the wait isn't long; ★★½. **Duration of ride** Almost 2½ minutes. **Average wait in line per 100 people ahead of you** 6¼ minutes. **Loading speed** Moderate–slow.

Dark   Scary

"I'm Wishing" is one of the most beloved songs from Disney's first animated feature, but experiencing Snow White's Scary Adventures gives this song a new twist. You end up wishing not for the Prince to come but for the wicked witch to GO AWAY. The ride is intimidating to many young children because Snow White's Scary Adventures is more about the witch, who's more persistent than a time-share salesman, than about Snow White.

Note: Snow White will close to make way for the construction of the Princess Fairytale Hall. No closing date was announced before we went to press.

Movie Tip

The movie, a classic of course, is scary for preschoolers but a timeless must-see for older children. Walt Disney won an honorary Academy Award for significant screen innovation with this film and received a full-size Oscar statuette with seven miniature ones. The honorary award was presented in 1938 to Walt Disney by Shirley Temple; the seven miniatures represented Doc, Grumpy, Happy, Sneezy, Bashful, Sleepy, and Dopey.

Under the Sea: Journey of the Little Mermaid
(opens 2012) ★★★½ *(Rating based on its sister attraction at Disneyland)*

What it is Indoor dark ride retelling the film's story. **Scope and scale** Major attraction. **Fright potential** Moderately intense effects; Ursula may frighten children under 7 years of age. **Bottleneck rating** 6. **When to go** Before 11 a.m., during parades, or in the evening. **Authors' rating** ★★★½. **Duration of ride** 5½ minutes. **Average wait in line per 100 people ahead of you** 3 minutes. **Loading speed** Fast.

Under The Sea takes riders through almost a dozen scenes retelling the story of *The Little Mermaid* film, this time with audio-animatronics, video effects, and a vibrant three-dimensional set the size of a small theater.

Guests board a clam-shell-shaped ride vehicle running along a continuously moving track (similar to the Haunted Mansion's). Once on board, the ride descends "underwater" past Ariel's grotto and to King Triton's undersea kingdom. This setting is the ride's centerpiece, including detailed animatronics of Ariel, plus a school of singing lobsters, octopuses, and a conga line of cod. Other scenes hit the film's highlights, including Ariel meeting Prince Eric, her deal with Ursula to become human, and, of course, the happy couple at the end.

 # TOMORROWLAND

TOMORROWLAND IS A MIX OF RIDES and experiences relating to the technological development of humankind and what life will be like in the future. When Disney overhauled Tomorrowland a few years back, it bailed on trying to predict how the future might appear, opting instead for a timeless, retro Buck Rogers look.

Keep an eye out for PUSH, the talking trash can of Tomorrowland. Kids love PUSH and delight in the opportunity to talk trash with the real thing.

Astro Orbiter ★★

APPEAL BY AGE	PRESCHOOL ★★★½		GRADE SCHOOL ★★★½
TEENS ★★★	YOUNG ADULTS ★★	OVER 30 ★★½	SENIORS ★★

What it is Buck Rogers–style rockets revolving around a central axis. **Scope and scale** Minor attraction. **Fright potential** Visually intimidating waiting area for a relatively tame ride. **Bottleneck rating** 10. **When to go** Before 11 a.m. or after 5 p.m. **Special comment** This attraction is not as innocuous as it appears. **Authors' rating** Not worth the wait; ★★. **Duration of ride** 1½ minutes. **Average wait in line per 100 people ahead of you** 13½ minutes. **Loading speed** Slow.

 Parents beware! If you are prone to motion sickness, this ride a) spins round and round; b) is faster than Dumbo; and c) for added "fun," there's a joystick that lets you raise and lower the rocket throughout your 1½-minute journey. We like to ride the Astro Orbiter at night. The combination of lighting and the view are spectacular.

I don't have a fear of heights, but I get scared when something that's moving up and down is leaning outwards like it's going to dump you out. It's very scary for me.

Shelton

Buzz Lightyear's Space Ranger Spin (Fastpass) ★★★★

APPEAL BY AGE	PRESCHOOL ★★★★	GRADE SCHOOL ★★★★½	TEENS ★★★★
YOUNG ADULTS ★★★★		OVER 30 ★★★★	SENIORS ★★★★

What it is Combination space travel–themed indoor ride and shooting gallery. **Scope and scale** Minor attraction. **Fright potential** Dark ride with cartoonlike aliens may frighten some preschoolers. **Bottleneck rating** 8. **When to go** Before 10:30 a.m., after 6 p.m., or use Fastpass. **Authors' rating** A real winner! ★★★★. **Duration of ride** About 4½ minutes. **Average wait in line per 100 people ahead of you** 3 minutes. **Loading speed** Fast.

Once you get the hang of it, you will come back for more, to infinity and beyond.

 Totally awesome! I earned my Space Ranger Wings on my first ride. Use the joystick to spin and set up your shots, but don't spin too much

Ian

because that uses up time and energy. Always aim and never stop shooting, especially at the big alien targets. Those are the ones with lots of arms and legs, and four eyes. They get you the most points.

Hannah

You'll see Zurg in jail at the end of the ride. Little kids can squeeze through the bars and pretend that they're in jail too.

Movie Tip

The ride is based on the space-commando character Buzz Lightyear from the 1995 Disney/Pixar feature *Toy Story.* Did you know that Tom Hanks and Tim Allen are the voices of Woody and Buzz?

Monsters, Inc. Laugh Floor ★★★½

APPEAL BY AGE	PRESCHOOL ★★★★	GRADE SCHOOL ★★★★	TEENS ★★★★
YOUNG ADULTS ★★★★		OVER 30 ★★★★	SENIORS ★★★★

What it is Interactive animated comedy routines. **Scope and scale** Major attraction. **Fright potential** Not much is frightening, but they are monsters, after all. **Bottleneck rating** 8. **When to go** Before 11 a.m. or after 4 p.m. **Special comment** Audience members may be asked to participate in skits. **Author's rating** Good concept; jokes are hit-and-miss; ★★★½. **Duration of show** About 15 minutes including preshow. **Probable waiting time** 25 minutes.

We learned in Disney/Pixar's *Monsters, Inc.* that children's screams could be converted into electricity, which was used to power a town inhabited by monsters. During the film, the monsters discovered that children's laughter was an even better source of energy. In this attraction, the monsters have set up a comedy club to capture as many laughs as possible. Mike Wazowski, the one-eyed character from the film, emcees the club's three comedy acts. Each consists of an animated monster (most not seen in the film) trying out various bad puns, knock-knock jokes, and Abbott and Costello–like routines. Using the same cutting-edge technology as Epcot's popular *Turtle Talk with Crush,* behind-the-scenes Disney employees voice the characters and often interact with audience members during the skits. As with any comedy club, some performers are funny and some are not. A good thing about this attraction is that Disney has shown a willingness to try new routines and jokes, so the show should remain fresh to repeat visitors. A Sioux Falls, South Dakota, mom is a big fan:

> The Laugh Floor was great. It's amazing how the on-screen characters interact with the audience—I got picked on twice without trying. This should definitely be seen; plus, kids are able to text jokes to Roz.

Movie Tip

The show is based on the 2001 Pixar film *Monsters, Inc.,* starring Billy Crystal (voice) in the role of Mike Wazowski and won an Oscar for Best Song.

Space Mountain (Fastpass) ★★★★

APPEAL BY AGE†	PRESCHOOL ★★½	GRADE SCHOOL ★★★★½	TEENS ★★★★½
YOUNG ADULTS ★★★★½		OVER 30 ★★★★½	SENIORS ★★★

† Some preschoolers love Space Mountain; others are frightened. The sample size of senior citizens who experienced this ride was too small to develop an accurate rating.

What it is Roller coaster in the dark. **Scope and scale** Super-headliner. **Fright potential** Very intense roller coaster in the dark; the Magic Kingdom's wildest

A PEEK BEHIND THE SCENES WITH JIM HILL

LOST HORIZON As you exit Space Mountain, keep an eye out for a warm tribute to a long-gone Epcot attraction. In a pile of luggage alongside the speed ramp that whisks you out, the Imagineers placed a sticker reading MESA VERDE on the side of one suitcase. Mesa Verde was one of three destinations that you were able to choose at the end of Horizons, a classic Future World attraction that closed in January 1999 to make way for Mission: SPACE.

ride and a scary roller coaster by any standard. **Bottleneck rating** 10. **When to go** When the park opens, between 6 and 7 p.m., during the hour before closing, or use Fastpass. **Special comments** Great fun and action; much wilder than Big Thunder Mountain Railroad. Must be 44" tall to ride; children younger than age 7 must be accompanied by an adult. Switching-off option provided (see page 242). **Authors' rating** An unusual roller coaster with excellent special effects; not to be missed; ★★★★. **Duration of ride** Almost 3 minutes. **Average wait in line per 100 people ahead of you** 3 minutes. **Assumes** Two tracks, one dedicated to Fastpass riders, dispatching at 21-second intervals. **Loading speed** Moderate–fast.

    Space Mountain is one of the zippiest (and darkest) rides in Walt Disney World, lasting just under 3 minutes and including several abrupt turns and plummets. So those with neck or back problems or vertigo should probably skip it. However, this ride achieves "only" about 28 mph, a leisurely pace by 21st-century standards.

Space Mountain also involves sudden blackouts, as do many thrill rides at Disney World. Those who suffer from claustrophobia (Liliane), tend to panic in the dark (Liliane), or have vision problems with extremes of light and darkness (Liliane) should avoid this attraction. Plunged into darkness and bouncing around like a marble in a spittoon, many warmly recall Space Mountain as the longest 3 minutes of their lives. Your kids will love it, of course.

Refurbished in 2009, Space Mountain got a smoother track and larger ride vehicles, as well as interactive video games to pass time in the standby line. Then in 2010, a soundtrack was added to the ride that accented high-octane music with sounds of speeding rocket ships and other intergalactic occurrences. It is difficult to know if it is just from hearing asteroids whiz past your vehicle, but we think the new ride is slightly faster than it was.

 If you're not sure that you are brave enough to ride Space Mountain, you can always take the Tomorrowland Transit Authority People-Mover and watch the actual ride in action before you get in line.

Ian

I dream of riding Space Mountain at the pace of Spaceship Earth in Epcot. At last, I would be able to enjoy the twinkling lights.

Liliane

 All of the people screaming sort of scared me at first. I did like all the flashing lights and the astronaut stuff. Look for the giant chocolate-chip cookies flying by on the ceiling when you're in line.

Hannah

Stitch's Great Escape! ★★

APPEAL BY AGE	PRESCHOOL ★½	GRADE SCHOOL ★★½	TEENS ★★
YOUNG ADULTS ★★		OVER 30 ★★	SENIORS ★★

What it is Theater-in-the-round sci-fi adventure show. **Scope and scale** Major attraction. **Fright potential** Frightens children of all ages; must be 40" tall. **Bottleneck rating** 6. **When to go** Before 11 a.m. or after 6 p.m.; try during parades. **Authors' rating** A cheap coat of paint on a broken car; ★★. **Duration of show** About 12 minutes. **Preshow** About 6 minutes. **Probable waiting time** 12–35 minutes.

Dark Loud Scary

Disney's press release touting *Stitch* as a child-friendly attraction was about as accurate as Lehman Brothers bookkeeping. You are held in your seat by overhead restraints and subjected to something weird clambering around you and whispering to you in a theater darker than a stack of black cats. Enough to scare the pants off many kids age 10 and younger.

Not fair! I love *Stitch* but agree with parents of young children who have complained about how scary the show is, especially because the overhead restraint prevents you from leaving your seat to comfort your child if need arises. Preteens and up, however, will enjoy the wicked fun of the show. All I could think of was the Pink Floyd song "Comfortably Numb": "Is there anybody in there?"

Liliane

This should be scrapped. My dad thought it was mediocre, but everyone else hated it.

Shelton

Movie Tip

Skip the show, but do not discount the movie. *Lilo & Stitch* (released in 2002) is a great family movie. The Hawaiian culture of 'Ohana, which in Hawaiian means extended family including friends, is the cornerstone philosophy of this wonderful flick. The movie reminds children about the importance of good behavior and points out to adults that there is good inside every child, no matter how rotten he or she may behave at times.

A PEEK BEHIND THE SCENES WITH JIM HILL

SOUNDS KIND OF FAMILIAR The voice of Sarge, the animatronic figure featured in the *Stitch* preshow, should ring a bell for most of you. The actor behind the character is Richard Kind, best known for playing nerdy Paul Lassiter on the long-running 1990s sitcom *Spin City*. The kids in your family will know this Second City vet as the voice of grasshopper Molt in *A Bug's Life* and, more recently, the Bookworm in *Toy Story 3*.

Tomorrowland Speedway ★★

APPEAL BY AGE	PRESCHOOL ★★★★		GRADE SCHOOL ★★★★
TEENS ★★★	YOUNG ADULTS ★★½	OVER 30 ★★★	SENIORS ★★½

What it is Drive-'em-yourself miniature cars. **Scope and scale** Major attraction. **Fright potential** Not frightening in any respect. **Bottleneck rating** 9. **When to go**

Before 11 a.m. or after 5 p.m. **Special comment** Must be 54" tall to drive unassisted. **Authors' rating** Boring for adults; great for preschoolers; ★★★ **Duration of ride** About 4¼ minutes. **Average wait in line per 100 people ahead of you** 4½ minutes. **Assumes** 285-car turnover every 20 minutes. **Loading speed** Slow.

The sleek cars and racetrack noise will get your younger kids hopped up to ride this extremely prosaic attraction. The minimum height requirement of 54 inches means that the younger (or shorter) set will have to ride with an adult. We suggest that you work the accelerator and brakes and let your future Kasey Kahne steer the car. Resist the urge to dispatch your little one with a taller sibling, unless the sibling is willing to hand over the steering wheel. The loading and unloading speed is excruciatingly slow, and the attraction offers hardly any protection from the sun.

What I like about this ride is you don't have to be 16 years old to drive! Dude, you have total control . . . well, almost. Pretend that you're an Indy car driver like Sam Hornish Jr. Turn the steering wheel, put your foot on the gas, and even hit the brakes . . . just like a go-cart. Sweet!

Ian

Tomorrowland Transit Authority PeopleMover ★★★

APPEAL BY AGE	PRESCHOOL ★★★★	GRADE SCHOOL ★★★½	TEENS ★★★½
YOUNG ADULTS ★★★★	OVER 30 ★★★★		SENIORS ★★★★

What it is Scenic tour of Tomorrowland. **Scope and scale** Minor attraction. **Fright potential** Not frightening in any respect. **Bottleneck rating** 3. **When to go** During hot, crowded times of day (11:30 a.m.–4:30 p.m.). **Special comment** A good way to check out the Fastpass line at Space Mountain. **Authors' rating** Scenic, relaxing, informative; ★★★. **Duration of ride** 10 minutes. **Average wait in line per 100 people ahead of you** 1½ minutes. **Assumes** 39 trains operating. **Loading speed** Fast.

Thumbs Up for the Whole Family

There is never a line, and the ride is ideal for taking a break. It's also a great way to see Tomorrowland all aglow at night. The route gives a sneak preview of Buzz Lightyear's Space Ranger Spin, and you can check on those screams emanating from Space Mountain. Most of the time cast members will let you ride several times in a row without having to get off. This last thing, according to many moms, makes the ride a great option for nursing.

It's good because you don't have to scream at anything, and there are no hills.

Hannah

Walt Disney's Carousel of Progress ★★★

APPEAL BY AGE	PRESCHOOL ★★★	GRADE SCHOOL ★★★	TEENS ★★★
YOUNG ADULTS ★★★½	OVER 30 ★★★½		SENIORS ★★★★

What it is Audio-animatronic theater production. **Scope and scale** Major attraction. **Fright potential** Not frightening in any respect. **Bottleneck rating** 4. **When to go** Anytime. **Authors' rating** Nostalgic, warm, and happy; ★★★. **Duration of show** 21 minutes. **Preshow** Documentary on the attraction's long history. **Probable waiting time** Less than 10 minutes.

A piece of Disney history not to be missed. The attraction offers a nostalgic look at how technology and electricity have changed the lives of an audio-animatronic family over several generations.

> My dad forced us all to see it, and
> we're glad he did. It was very good!

Shelton

LIVE ENTERTAINMENT *and* PARADES *in the* MAGIC KINGDOM

IT'S IMPOSSIBLE TO TAKE IN ALL THE MANY LIVE entertainment offerings at the Magic Kingdom in a single day. To experience both the attractions and the live entertainment, we recommend that you allocate at least 2 days to this park. In addition to parades, stage shows, and fireworks, check the daily entertainment schedule (*Times Guide*) or ask a cast member about concerts in Fantasyland, the Flag Retreat at Town Square, and the appearances of the various bands, singers, and street performers that roam the park daily. WDW live-entertainment guru Steve Soares usually posts the Magic Kingdom's performance schedule about a week in advance at **wdwent.com.**

Following is a short list of daily events with special appeal for families with children:

CASTLE FORECOURT STAGE "DREAM-ALONG WITH MICKEY" A daytime stage show in front of Cinderella Castle featuring a veritable pantheon of Disney characters and music.

RAPUNZEL AND FLYNN RIDER PLAY AND GREET AT THE FAIRYTALE GARDEN The garden, formerly the site of Storytime with Belle, has now been transformed into a stone castlelike setting. You are admitted to the courtyard, where cast members assist the children, helping them color pictures of Rapunzel, as they await her arrival. Rapunzel and Flynn arrive, and after a 5-minute show, they join the children for a dance around the table. Very young children will be happy with the activity, but it isn't a very interactive experience. The activity targets the under-5 age group. After the dance, while waiting to meet the characters, cast members walk through the line introducing Pascal, Rapunzel's faithful companion. They play a game with the children called Pass Pascal, much like Hot Potato.

If you plan on meeting Rapunzel and Flynn, arrive at least 20–30 minutes early to the staging area. Once the area is at capacity, after usually about 20 children and parents, cast members rope it off. Be forewarned that the entire experience will take a whole hour out of your day. The play and greet takes places six to eight times a day; check the daily entertainment schedule (*Times Guide*) for showtimes.

FAVORITE EATS IN MAGIC KINGDOM

LAND	SERVICE LOCATION	FOOD ITEM

MAIN STREET

Main Street Bakery | Homemade goodies & crisped-rice treats

ADVENTURELAND

Tortuga Tavern | Quesadillas for kids

FANTASYLAND

Pinocchio Village Haus | Mac and cheese & pizza
Friar's Nook | Fries

FRONTIERLAND

Pecos Bill Tall Tale Inn & Café | Burgers & great fixin's station

LIBERTY SQUARE

Columbia Harbour House | Soup & sandwiches
Sleepy Hollow | Funnel cake

TOMORROWLAND

Cosmic Ray's Starlight Café | Rotisserie chicken, ribs, & kosher choices
The Lunching Pad | Designer dogs, pretzels, & frozen soda

Liliane

Disney should revisit the entertainment presented here. While meeting Rapunzel and Flynn is a real treat (they both take great pains in interacting with the children), the wait time makes for some very cranky kids. Unlike Storytime with Belle, there are no benches for the parents to sit.

MOVE IT! SHAKE IT! CELEBRATE IT! PARADE Starting at the train station end of Main Street, U.S.A., and working toward the central hub, this short walk incorporates about a dozen guests with a handful of floats, Disney characters, and entertainers. Music is provided by one of Disney's latest artists (Miley Cyrus currently), and there's a good amount of interaction between the entertainers and the crowd.

MAIN STREET ELECTRICAL PARADE The more-dazzling-than-ever Main Street Electrical Parade is back by popular demand. Last seen at Walt Disney World 1999–2001, the parade with 23 illuminated floats and 80 performers twinkles with about half a million lights. New additions are floats inspired by Pinocchio and Snow White. Check the daily entertainment schedule (*Times Guide*) for parade days and times.

FLAG RETREAT At 4:45 p.m. daily at Town Square (railroad-station end of Main Street). Sometimes performed with great fanfare and college marching bands, sometimes with a smaller Disney band.

MAGIC KINGDOM BANDS Banjo, Dixieland, steel drum, marching, and fife-and-drum bands play daily throughout the park.

CAPTAIN JACK SPARROW'S PIRATE TUTORIAL Sign up with Captain Jack Sparrow and his crewman Mack for a hilarious pirate one-on-one. Check your *Times Guide* for the scheduled daily encounters and meet

Liliane

The show is wonderful for little wannabe pirates and grown-ups alike and draws quite a crowd, especially ladies. I signed up for the pirate's life in a jiffy.

the Johnny Depp look-alike right next to the Pirates of the Caribbean ride. The lucky chosen buccaneers are taught how to be pirates and receive an honorary pirate certificate at the end of the show.

ENCHANTED TALES WITH BELLE (OPENS 2012) Disney hasn't promoted this interactive storytelling session as much as other parts of the Fantasyland expansion, but something similar was held in another part of Fantasyland for years before the construction. Then, Belle and several helpers selected children from the audience and dressed them up as characters from *Beauty and the Beast.* As Belle told the story, the children acted out the roles. There was a 3- to 5-minute meet and greet with photo and autograph opportunities afterward. The show was staged six to eight times each day. We expect Disney to retain much of these details when Enchanted Tales opens in a dedicated location near Beasts' Castle in 2012.

PARADES Parades at the Magic Kingdom are full-fledged spectaculars with dozens of Disney characters and amazing special effects. An outstanding new afternoon parade is introduced every year or two; while some elements such as the Disney characters remain constant, the theme, music, and float design change. The evening parade is a high-tech affair and not to be missed. Always check your entertainment schedule (*Times Guide*) to make sure what parade is happening when, as well as the guide map for the parade route.

Remember, parades disrupt traffic, and it is nearly impossible to move around the park when one is going on. Parades also draw thousands of guests away from the attractions, making parade time the perfect moment to catch your favorite attraction with a shorter line. Finally, be advised that the Walt Disney World Railroad shuts down during parades.

The best place to view a parade is the upper platform of the Walt Disney Railroad station, but you will have to stake out your position 30–45 minutes before the event. Try also, especially on rainy days, the covered walkway between Liberty Tree Tavern and The Diamond Horseshoe Saloon on the border of Liberty Square and Frontierland.

Liliane

If all you want is a serene spot to watch the fireworks or the Bay Lake and Seven Seas Floating Electrical Pageant, you do not need to spend big bucks. The gardens of the Grand Floridian are perfect for the fireworks, and the beach of the Polynesian Resort does the trick for the electrical pageant.

TINKER BELL'S FLIGHT This nice special effect in the sky above Cinderella Castle heralds the beginning of the fireworks show (when the park is open late).

FIREWORKS The nightly fireworks show starts just after Tinker Bell's flight in the sky above Cinderella Castle. The fireworks are synchronized to music from beloved Disney films.

View the fireworks from the upper platform of the railroad station. This vantage point also provides an easy path to the park exit when the fireworks are over. Our favorite spot, if we intend to remain in the park after the fireworks, is between Plaza Restaurant on Main Street and the Tomorrowland Terrace area to its right (if you're facing the castle).

A very special spot to view the fireworks is atop the nearby Contemporary Resort at the California Grill. Once the fireworks begin, the restaurant dims its lights and broadcasts the music from the show.

THE MAGIC, THE MEMORIES, AND YOU! At 7:45 p.m. every night, the show turns Cinderella Castle into a canvas where guests can view photos taken earlier that day by a Disney PhotoPass photographer and projected onto the castle's exterior. The show, which lasts approximately 10 minutes, takes place before *Wishes! Nighttime Spectacular* and features a new song written exclusively for the show called "Let the Memories Begin."

FIREWORKS CRUISE For a different view, you can watch the fireworks from the Seven Seas Lagoon aboard a chartered pontoon boat. The charter comes with a price (about $350 for up to 10 people and includes chips and drinks), of course. Your Disney captain will take you for a little cruise and then position the boat in a perfect place to watch the fireworks. For an additional cost, you can arrange for more substantial food items through the catering department. Life jackets are provided, but wearing them is at your discretion. To reserve, call 407-WDW-PLAY 180 days prior to your visit. Similar charters are available for viewing *IllumiNations* at Epcot.

BAY LAKE AND SEVEN SEAS LAGOON FLOATING ELECTRICAL PAGEANT Performed at nightfall at about 9 p.m. most of the year on Seven Seas Lagoon and Bay Lake, this pageant is the perfect culmination of a wonderful day. You have to leave the Magic Kingdom to see this floating electric light show. Take the monorail to the Polynesian Resort, get the kids a snack and yourself a drink, and walk to the end of the pier to watch the show. Pure magic, less the crowds. You can also watch the show at the Grand Floridian at 9:15 p.m. and at the Contemporary at 10:05 p.m.

EXIT STRATEGIES

LEAVING THE PARK AFTER EVENING PARADES AND FIREWORKS is no small matter. Huge throngs depart the Magic Kingdom after parades, fireworks, and at closing. Trust us, with small children, you don't want to be among them. The best strategy for avoiding the mass exodus is to view both fireworks and parades from the upper platform of the railroad station at the Town Square end of Main Street. As soon as the performance concludes, beat feet to the park exits. If you remain in the park after the fireworks and parades, don't wait until closing time to leave. On a busy day give yourself a 30- to 40-minute cushion.

Another strategy for beating the masses out of the park (if your car is in the TTC lot) is to watch the early parade and then leave before the fireworks begin. Line up for the ferry instead of the monorail. A ferry departs about every 8–10 minutes. Try to catch the ferry that will be crossing Seven Seas Lagoon while the fireworks are in progress. The best vantage point is on the top deck to the right of the pilothouse. Your chances are about 50/50 of catching it just right. If you are in front of the line for the ferry and you don't want to board the boat that's loading, stop at the gate and let people pass you. You'll be the first to board the next boat.

MAGIC KINGDOM TOURING PLANS

OUR STEP-BY-STEP TOURING PLANS are field-tested, independently verified itineraries that will keep you moving counter to the crowd flow and allow you to see as much as possible in a single day with minimum time wasted in line.

We developed many of these plans when preparing to visit the Magic Kingdom with our own children (ages 2–8). Some plans offer a midday break of at least 3 hours back at your hotel. It's debatable whether the kids will need the nap more than you, but you'll thank us later, we promise. Our kids are picky eaters too: One went through a phase where she ate nothing but beige food (chicken fingers, pasta, macaroni and cheese, and the like). The restaurants we recommend in these plans are all kid-friendly and should work for almost everyone.

Don't worry that other people will be following the plans and render them useless. Fewer than 1 in every 350 people in the park will have been exposed to this information.

Bob

If you have just 1 day to spend in the Magic Kingdom, our single-day plans will allow you to see the best attractions for kids while avoiding crowds and long waits in line. If you're looking for a more relaxed, less structured tour of the park, try the 1-and-a-half, 2-day, or Sleepyhead plans. These alternatives have less backtracking, the same midday breaks, and a much more casual feel. The Sleepyhead plans assume that you'll get to the park around 11 a.m., so they're great for mornings when you don't feel like getting out of bed early.

The different touring plans for each park are described below. The descriptions will tell you for whom (for example, tweens, parents with preschoolers, grandparents, and so on) or for what situation (such as sleeping late) the plans are designed. The actual touring plans are located on pages 445–453. Each plan includes a numbered map of the park in question to help you find your way around. Clip the plan of your choice out of the book by cutting along the line indicated, and take it with you to the park.

MAGIC KINGDOM HAPPY FAMILY 1-DAY TOURING PLAN This is a 1-day touring plan of the Magic Kingdom that includes something for everyone in the family: small children, tweens (children ages 8–12), teenagers, parents, and seniors. The plan keeps the entire family together for most of the day, plus lunch and dinner. A midday break is integrated into the day's touring.

Switching off allows adults to enjoy the more adventuresome attractions while keeping the group together.

Liliane

The plan includes attractions very popular with small children, such as Dumbo in Fantasyland and the Magic Carpets of Aladdin in Adventureland. For older kids and teenagers, we recommend thrill rides such as Space Mountain and Big Thunder Mountain, with both groups getting back together when each is done.

MAGIC KINGDOM 1-DAY TOURING PLAN FOR GRANDPARENTS WITH SMALL CHILDREN The attractions in this touring plan are generally those rated at least three stars (out of five) by both seniors and small children, plus a handful of senior-friendly attractions that children just love. Specifically designed to minimize walking, this plan also includes a midday break of at least 3 hours and dining recommendations for lunch and dinner. We don't try to cover the entire park, either: Most of Tomorrowland is left as an option if everyone's feeling up for it.

To convert this itinerary into a 2-day plan, one option is to do steps 1–14 on Day 1. If you're returning in the morning of Day 2, do steps 25 and 26 first, then steps 16–24. An alternate strategy for a morning and afternoon is to do steps 1–14 on the morning of Day 1 and steps 15–28 on the afternoon of Day 2.

MAGIC KINGDOM 1-DAY TOURING PLAN FOR TWEENS AND THEIR PARENTS A 1-day plan for parents with children ages 8–12, it includes every attraction rated three stars and higher by this age group and sets aside ample time for lunch and dinner.

MAGIC KINGDOM 2-DAY TOURING PLAN FOR PARENTS WITH SMALL CHILDREN This is a 2-day touring plan designed specifically to eliminate extra walking and backtracking. It is a comprehensive touring plan of the Magic Kingdom and includes every child-friendly attraction in the park. The plan features long midday breaks for rest and naps outside the park, as well as recommendations for good dining choices inside the park.

MAGIC KINGDOM 2-DAY SLEEPYHEAD TOURING PLAN FOR PARENTS WITH SMALL CHILDREN Another version of the 2-day touring plan described above, this plan allows families with young children to sleep in, arrive at the park in the late morning, and still see the very best attractions in the Magic Kingdom over 2 days. Each day also contains a 1-hour break inside the park, and we've made specific recommendations on the best spots to rest and cool off. The plan includes lunch and dinner suggestions for both days, with plenty of time to explore the park on either day.

PARENT'S MAGIC KINGDOM TOURING PLAN—1 AFTERNOON AND 1 FULL DAY This day-and-a-half plan works perfectly if you're arriving in Orlando late in the morning of your first vacation day and can't wait to start touring. It also works great for families who want to sleep in one morning after spending a full day in the Magic Kingdom the day before.

The attractions in these plans are the same as those found in the standard 1-day plans for parents with small children, so these day-and-a-half itineraries also work as relaxed versions of those plans. Both plans employ Fastpass and some version of a "wait 'em out" crowd strategy, whereby you'll take advantage of lower evening crowds to visit the more popular attractions. The plans should work well during the more crowded times of the year, and we've provided Fastpass alternatives for the more popular attractions in case they're out of passes by the time you arrive.

PRELIMINARY INSTRUCTIONS FOR
ALL MAGIC KINGDOM TOURING PLANS

ON DAYS OF MODERATE-TO-HEAVY ATTENDANCE, follow your chosen touring plan exactly, deviating only:

1. When you aren't interested in an attraction it lists. For example, the plan may tell you to go to Tomorrowland and ride Space Mountain, a roller coaster. If you don't enjoy roller coasters, skip this step and proceed to the next.

2. When you encounter a very long line at an attraction the touring plan calls for. Crowds ebb and flow at the park, and an unusually long line may have gathered at an attraction to which you're directed. For example, you arrive at The Haunted Mansion and find extremely long lines. It's possible that this is a temporary situation caused by several hundred people arriving en masse from a recently concluded performance of *The Hall of Presidents* nearby. If this is the case, skip The Haunted Mansion and go to the next step, returning later to retry.

WHAT TO DO IF YOU GET OFF TRACK

IF AN UNEXPECTED INTERRUPTION or problem throws the touring plan off, consult the recommended attraction visitation times in the attraction profile for the preferred times of day to visit.

BEFORE YOU GO

1. Call ☎ 407-824-4321 the day before you go to check the official opening time.

2. Purchase admission before you arrive.

3. Familiarize yourself with park-opening procedures (described on page 229) and reread the touring plan you've chosen so that you know what you're likely to encounter.

MAGIC KINGDOM
TRIVIA QUIZ

By Lou Mongello

1. WHAT IS THE NAME OF SONNY ECLIPSE'S (UNSEEN) BACKUP GROUP AT COSMIC RAY'S STARLIGHT CAFÉ?

a. The Space Cadets

b. The Sun Bonnets

c. Space Angels

d. Cranium Commandos

2. WHAT IS THE NAME OF THE RIVERBOAT AT LIBERTY SQUARE?

a. *Joe Fowler*

b. *Mark Twain*

c. *Liberty Belle*

d. *Lily Belle*

3. WHAT IS THE NAME OF MIKE WAZOWSKI'S NEPHEW IN *MONSTERS, INC. LAUGH FLOOR*?

a. Roz

b. Henry

c. Bob

d. Marty

4. WHERE IN THE MAGIC KINGDOM CAN YOU FIND A DOG NAMED NANA?

a. *The Hall of Presidents*

b. The Haunted Mansion

c. *Walt Disney's Carousel of Progress*

d. Peter Pan's Flight

5. IN WHAT SCENE CAN YOU FIND A BRIDE IN THE HAUNTED MANSION?

a. The ballroom

b. The séance room

c. The attic

d. The graveyard

6. THE NUMBER ON THE FRONT OF *THE HALL OF PRESIDENTS* BUILDING REPRESENTS:

a. The year Walt Disney World opened

b. The current year

c. The year America gained its independence

d. The year the Constitution was ratified

7. THE NARRATOR ON THE LIBERTY SQUARE RIVERBOAT IS:

a. Mark Twain

b. Ben Franklin

c. Prince Naveen

d. Paul Revere

8. ABOUT HOW MANY LEAVES CAN YOU FIND ON THE SWISS FAMILY TREEHOUSE?

a. 3,000

b. 30,000

c. 300,000

d. 3,000,000

9. AT THE END OF *MICKEY'S PHILHARMAGIC*, HOW DOES MICKEY WAKE UP DONALD?

a. Blowing a trumpet in his face

b. Grabbing his feet

c. Tickling him

d. Banging a drum

10. THE MAIN STREET ELECTRICAL PARADE FEATURES A FLOAT BASED ON A CHARACTER FROM WHICH OF THESE MOVIES:

a. *Pete's Dragon*

b. *The Sword in the Stone*

c. *The Incredibles*

d. *101 Dalmations*

Answers can be found on page 426.

Trivia content courtesy of Lou Mongello, author of Walt Disney World Trivia Books *(Volumes I and II), as well as the* Audio Guides to WDW. *Lou is also the host and producer of WDW Radio (**wdwradio.com**) and is the publisher of* Celebrations *magazine (**celebrations press.com**). Dream Team Project (**dreamteamproject.org**), which Mongello founded, helps raise money for the Make-A-Wish Foundation of America to send seriously ill children and their families to Walt Disney World.*

EPCOT

EDUCATION, INSPIRATION, AND CORPORATE IMAGERY are the focus at Epcot, the most adult of the Walt Disney World theme parks. What it gains in taking a futuristic, visionary, and technological look at the world, it loses, just a bit, in warmth, happiness, and charm. Some people find the attempts at education to be superficial; others want more entertainment and less education. Most visitors, however, are in between, finding plenty of amusement *and* information alike.

Epcot's theme areas are distinctly different. Future World combines Disney creativity and major corporations' technological resources to examine where humankind has come from and where we're going. World Showcase features landmarks, cuisine, and culture from almost a dozen nations and is meant to be a sort of permanent World's Fair.

So you thought that the Magic Kingdom was big? Epcot is more than twice as large as the Magic Kingdom, so unless 1 day is all you have, plan on spending 2 days at Epcot to savor all it has to offer. While Epcot, unlike the Magic Kingdom, does not stand out as a natural for kids, rest assured that families can have as much fun at Epcot as at any of the other theme parks.

Now for the practical stuff: Future World always opens first; that is where you start your day. The World Showcase opens later at 11 a.m. But first things first: Call ☎ 407-824-4321 for exact park hours. If you are lodging at a Disney hotel, consider visiting when the park offers morning or evening Extra Magic Hours. Once you arrive, pick up a park map and the daily entertainment schedule (*Times Guide*). If you are a Disney hotel guest and the park offers Extra Magic (morning or evening) Hours, grab the extra flyer that lists all the attractions open during the additional hours. If you intend to stay for Extra Magic Hours in the evening, each member of your party will need to have his or her resort ID.

Stroller and wheelchair rentals are available inside the main entrance to the left, toward the rear of the Entrance Plaza. For storage lockers, turn right at Spaceship Earth. The Baby Care Center is on the

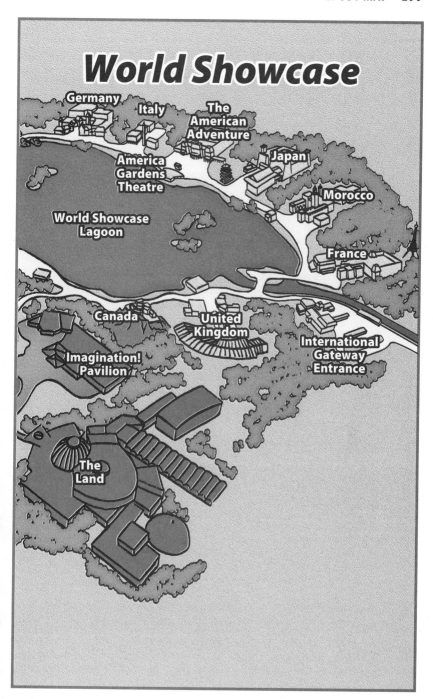

World Showcase side of the Odyssey Center complex, to the rear of Test Track. At the same location are first-aid and lost-persons services. For a live-entertainment schedule and dining reservations, stop at Guest Relations to the left of Spaceship Earth. Lost and found is located at the main entrance. Banking services (ATMs) are available outside the main entrance, on the Future World Bridge, and in World Showcase at the Germany Pavilion. Disney no longer has pet-care facilities adjacent to the park, but the Best Friends Pet Resort across from Disney's Port Orleans Resort will provide a comfortable home away from home for Fido, Frisky, and all their pet pals.

KIDCOT FUN STOPS

THIS PROGRAM, DESIGNED TO MAKE EPCOT more interesting for younger visitors, is basically a movable feast of simple arts and crafts projects. Tables are set up at some locations in Future World and at each pavilion in World Showcase. The tables are staffed by cast members who discuss their native country with the children and engage them in a craft project. Look for the brightly colored Kidcot signs. Participation is free. For a memento and to augment the experience, you can purchase a World Showcase Passport for your children. The passports are sold for $10 at most stores throughout Epcot. As you visit the different lands, cast members at the Kidcot stations will stamp the passport. If your child is really interested in different lands, Guest Relations offers free fact sheets for each country.

Children as young as age 3 will enjoy the Kidcot Fun Stops. If you do not want to spring for the passport, the Disney folks will be happy to stamp an autograph book or just about anything else, including your child's forehead.

Bob

FUTURE WORLD
Innoventions ★★★½

APPEAL BY AGE	PRESCHOOL ★★★½	GRADE SCHOOL ★★★★	TEENS ★★★½
YOUNG ADULTS ★★★		OVER 30 ★★★	SENIORS ★★★

What it is Static and hands-on exhibits relating to products and technologies of the near future. **Scope and scale** Major diversion. **Fright potential** Not frightening in any respect. **Bottleneck rating** 8. **When to go** On your second day at Epcot or after seeing all major attractions. **Special comments** Most exhibits demand time and participation to be rewarding; not much gained here by a quick walk-through. **Authors' rating** Vastly improved; ★★★½.

Innoventions—a huge, busy collection of walk-through, hands-on exhibits—consists of two huge, crescent-shaped, glass-walled structures separated by a central plaza. Exhibits, many of which are changed each year, demonstrate such products as virtual-reality games, high-definition TV, voice-activated appliances, future cars, medical diagnostic equipment, and Internet applications. Each of the major exhibit areas is sponsored by a different manufacturer or research lab, emphasizing the effect of the products or technology on daily living. The most popular Innoventions attraction is an arcade of video and simulator games. One of the coolest exhibits, however, is the demonstration area for the Segway Human Transporter, the much-publicized two-wheeled vehicle that makes riders look as if they're standing on top of a push lawn mower. A limited number of brief test rides are also offered to the general public. The Sum of All Thrills is a design-your-own roller-coaster simulator.

The newer exhibits are certainly more compelling, but they require waiting in line to be admitted. Because the theater at each exhibit is quite small, you often wait as long for an Innoventions infomercial as for a real attraction elsewhere in the park. We observed a wide range of reactions by visitors to the exhibits and can suggest only that you form your own opinion. We suggest skipping exhibits with waits of more than 10 minutes or experiencing them first thing in the morning when there are no lines.

Liliane

This is a great place for parents to abandon their teenagers—at least for a while—to enjoy a meal of escargot at Bistro de Paris in France.

Whoa! You gotta check out the e-mail postcards. Star in your own cartoon and e-mail it to all your friends. The best is in Innoventions. I put myself in an alien movie and landed on Mars! On the way home, we couldn't wait to get there to see it on our computer. A very cool souvenir—and it's free.

Ian

Spaceship Earth ★★★★

APPEAL BY AGE	PRESCHOOL ★★★★	GRADE SCHOOL ★★★★	TEENS ★★★★
YOUNG ADULTS ★★★★		OVER 30 ★★★★	SENIORS ★★★★½

What it is Educational dark ride through past, present, and future. **Scope and scale** Headliner. **Fright potential** Dark and imposing presentation intimidates a few preschoolers. **Bottleneck rating** 7. **When to go** Before 10 a.m. or after 4 p.m. **Special comment** If lines are long when you arrive, try again after 4 p.m. **Authors' rating** One of Epcot's best; not to be missed; ★★★★. **Duration of ride** About 16 minutes. **Average wait in line per 100 people ahead of you** 3 minutes. **Loading speed** Fast.

Thumbs Up for the Whole Family

This ride spirals through the 18-story interior of Epcot's premier landmark, taking guests through audio-animatronic scenes depicting mankind's development in communications from cave painting to the Internet. It's actually more fun than it sounds and is carried off with a lot of humor. Spaceship Earth draws crowds like a magnet first thing in the morning because it is so close to the park entrance.

I hate this ride because it's boring. Most of these people didn't have cars or TV or anything we have today.

Hannah

CLUB COOL

ATTACHED TO THE FOUNTAIN SIDE OF INNOVENTIONS WEST is a sort of international soda fountain called Club Cool. The exhibit provides free unlimited samples of soft drinks from around the world. Kids will love to fill their own tasting cups and move from one sampling station to the next. Mix lemon, water, and honey and you get Kinley, popular in Israel. In Mozambique Krest Ginger Ale is in; in China a drink based on watermelon is highly popular. The Japanese recommend the nutrition and health benefits of a vitamin drink, and the Italians are in love with a beverage that could chalk up great sales as an emetic in the U.S. VegitaBeta, anyone? Club Cool also lives up to its name; it is cool inside and makes for a good meeting place.

Club Cool is my favorite place to go when I'm thirsty, and the drinks are FREE. You can have as much as you want, soft drinks that is, from all over the world. Some are pretty yucky, but some are pretty good. Give it a try and see what you think. Coke from China is not bad.

Ian

THE SEAS WITH NEMO AND FRIENDS PAVILION

THE SEAS IS HOME TO ONE OF AMERICA'S top marine aquariums, a ride, an interactive animated film, and a number of first-class educational exhibits. Featuring characters from the animated feature *Finding Nemo*, it brings some whimsy and much-needed levity to what was heretofore educationally brilliant but somewhat staid. Before the makeover, The Seas (or The Living Seas, as it was previously known) was a snoozer for children. Now it ranks near the top of the kids' list.

The Seas Main Tank and Exhibits ★★★½

APPEAL BY AGE	PRESCHOOL ★★★★	GRADE SCHOOL ★★★★	TEENS ★★★★
YOUNG ADULTS ★★★★		OVER 30 ★★★★	SENIORS ★★★★

What it is A huge saltwater aquarium, plus exhibits on oceanography, ocean ecology, and sea life. **Scope and scale** Major attraction. **Fright potential** Not frightening in any respect. **Bottleneck rating** 7. **When to go** Before 11:30 a.m. or after 5 p.m. **Authors' rating** An excellent marine exhibit; ★★★½. **Average wait in line per 100 people ahead of you** 3½ minutes. **Loading speed** Fast.

Take a *Finding Nemo*–themed ride to Sea Base to start your discovery of The Seas' main tank and exhibits. Watch scientists and divers conduct actual marine experiments in the main tank, containing fish, mammals, and crustaceans in a simulation of an ocean ecosystem. Visitors can observe

Thumbs Up for the Whole Family

the activity through windows below the surface (including inside the Coral Reef restaurant). Children will be enchanted to discover the substantial fish population and the many exhibits offered. With the addition of *Turtle Talk with Crush* and The Seas with Nemo & Friends, The Seas has been transformed from a Future World backwater into one of Epcot's most popular venues. We recommend experiencing the ride and *Turtle Talk* in the morning before the park gets crowded, saving the excellent exhibits for later.

The Seas with Nemo & Friends ★★★

| APPEAL BY AGE | PRESCHOOL ★★★★ | GRADE SCHOOL ★★★★ | TEENS ★★★ |
| YOUNG ADULTS ★★★ | | OVER 30 ★★★½ | SENIORS ★★★½ |

What it is Ride through a tunnel in The Seas' main tank. **Scope and scale** Major attraction. **Fright potential** Not frightening in any respect. **Bottleneck rating** 7. **When to go** Before 11 a.m. or after 5 p.m. **Authors' rating** Educational *and* fun; ★★★½. **Duration of ride** 4 minutes. **Average wait in line per 100 people ahead of you** 3½ minutes. **Loading speed** Fast.

Upon entering The Seas, you proceed to the loading area, where you'll be made comfortable in a "clamobile" for your journey through the aquarium. The technology used makes it seem as if the animated characters are swimming with the live fish. Meet characters from *Finding Nemo,* such as Mr. Ray, and help Dory, Bruce, Marlin, Squirt, and Crush find Nemo. This cool ride attracts lots of the lovable clown fish's fans, so ride early.

Clamobiles! This ride is fun because it shows real fish and real dolphins, and sometimes real scuba divers! I still get really cautious when I see real sharks, but they can't break the glass and attack you.

Hannah

See *Finding Nemo* prior to your visit if you have not already. You will not soon forget this superb family movie that won the 2004 Oscar for best animated feature. Did you know that Alexander Gould, who gives his voice to little Nemo, is also the voice behind Bambi in the Disney animated sequel *Bambi II*?

Movie Tip

Turtle Talk with Crush ★★★★

| APPEAL BY AGE | PRESCHOOL ★★★★½ | GRADE SCHOOL ★★★★½ | TEENS ★★★★ |
| YOUNG ADULTS ★★★★ | | OVER 30 ★★★★ | SENIORS ★★★★ |

What it is An interactive animated film. **Scope and scale** Minor attraction. **Fright potential** Not frightening in any respect. **Bottleneck rating** 9. **When to go** Before 11 a.m. or after 5 p.m. **Special comments** Get there early to avoid long lines; a real spirit lifter. **Authors' rating** Amazing technology; ★★★★. **Duration of show** 17 minutes. **Probable waiting time** 10–20 minutes before 11 a.m. and after 5 p.m.; as much as 40–60 minutes during the more crowded part of the day.

This interactive theater show starring the 153-year-old surfer turtle from *Finding Nemo* starts like a typical Disney theme-park movie but quickly turns into an interactive encounter, as Crush begins conversations with guests in the audience. Not to be missed! The capacity of the attraction is relatively small, and the show is a big hit, so get here as early as you can to avoid long lines.

Thumbs Up for the Whole Family

I like this show a lot. Don't miss it. You actually feel as if you're in the movie *Finding Nemo*. *Turtle Talk* comes alive when Crush swims up on the movie screen and talks to people. I mean really talks to people. He saw me raise my hand and—Dude!—he said my name and we had a conversation. I don't know how they do it. It was great.

Ian

THE LAND PAVILION

THE LAND IS A HUGE PAVILION containing three attractions and several restaurants. When the pavilion was originally built, its emphasis was on farming, but now it focuses on environmental concerns. Dry as that sounds, kids really enjoy The Land's attractions, especially Soarin', a thrill ride where the operative word is *thrill*, not *terror*. The Land Pavilion is a great place to grab a fast-food lunch. If you're here to see the attractions, however, stay away during mealtimes, as the place is super crowded.

The Circle of Life ★★★½

APPEAL BY AGE	PRESCHOOL ★★★	GRADE SCHOOL ★★★	TEENS ★★★
YOUNG ADULTS ★★★		OVER 30 ★★★	SENIORS ★★★

What it is Film exploring man's relationship with his environment. **Scope and scale** Minor attraction. **Fright potential** Not frightening in any respect. **Bottleneck rating** 5. **When to go** Before 11 a.m. or after 2 p.m. **Authors' rating** Highly interesting and enlightening; ★★★½. **Duration of show** About 20 minutes. **Probable waiting time** 10–15 minutes.

The Swahili saying *hakuna matata* ("don't worry") does not apply to this movie. On the contrary, Simba, Pumbaa, and Timon from Disney's animated feature *The Lion King* offer a sugar-coated lesson on how to protect and care for the environment.

Did you know that Elton John wrote the music to the song "Hakuna Matata"?

Living with the Land (Fastpass seasonally) ★★★★

APPEAL BY AGE	PRESCHOOL ★★★½	GRADE SCHOOL ★★★½	TEENS ★★★½
YOUNG ADULTS ★★★★		OVER 30 ★★★★	SENIORS ★★★★

What it is Indoor boat-ride adventure through the past, present, and future of U.S. farming and agriculture. **Scope and scale** Major attraction. **Fright potential** Not frightening in any respect, but loud. **Bottleneck rating** 9. **When to go** Before 10:30 a.m., after 5 p.m., or use Fastpass if available. **Authors' rating** Interesting and fun; not to be missed; ★★★★. **Duration of ride** About 14 minutes. **Average wait in line per 100 people ahead of you** 3 minutes. **Assumes** 15 boats operating. **Loading speed** Moderate.

Thumbs Up for the Whole Family

This boat ride through four experimental growing areas is inspiring and educational. Kids like seeing the giant pumpkins and hearing about the tomato tree that produced 32,000 tomatoes. Teens will be fascinated by the imaginative ways to grow crops—without soil, hanging in the air, and even on a space station. A lot of the fruits and vegetables grown here are served to guests in the restaurants at Epcot, such as the Garden Grill and the Coral Reef.

I like the gardening part and looking at the fruits and vegetables. They need to make Living with the Land into a rock song.

Hannah

Soarin' (Fastpass) ★★★★½

APPEAL BY AGE	PRESCHOOL ★★★★	GRADE SCHOOL ★★★★★	TEENS ★★★★★
YOUNG ADULTS ★★★★★		OVER 30 ★★★★★	SENIORS ★★★★★

What it is Flight simulation ride. **Scope and scale** Super-headliner. **Fright potential** Frightens almost no one who meets the minimum height requirements. **Bottleneck rating** 10. **When to go** First 30 minutes the park is open or use Fastpass. **Special comments** Entrance on the lower level of The Land Pavilion. May induce motion sickness; must be 40" tall to ride; switching-off option provided (see page 242). **Authors' rating** Exciting and mellow at the same time; not to be missed; ★★★★½. **Duration of ride** 5½ minutes. **Average wait in line per 100 people ahead of you** 4 minutes. **Assumes** 2 concourses operating. **Loading speed** Moderate.

This is the closest to hang gliding you will come without trying the real thing. Once airborne, you are flying over California with IMAX-quality images projected all around you, while a flight simulator moves your hang glider in sync with the movie. The experience is extremely mellow and nonthreatening. Any child (or adult) who meets the 40-inch minimum height requirement will love Soarin'. If you opt for Fastpass, make sure to get one before lunch, as there may not be any passes left after 12:30 p.m. or so. As a matter of fact, Liliane had to be rescued by her son during one of her visits, as a mob of gone-wild guests nearly ran her over on her way to the Fastpass machine. Gaming stations have been added to keep visitors entertained while waiting in line.

Now I know what it feels like to be a kite. Fly high into the clouds and soar like a bird! It's like you have a front-row seat to see the world. You feel the wind in your face and smell the oranges as you fly over the trees. I'll never forget flying through the golf course when all of a sudden—oh, dude!—a golf ball whooshed by my head.

Ian

It's a ride, but you don't really move that much. There's a huge movie screen in front of you. You go past an orange farm in the ride, and it starts to smell like oranges. It's a good thing you don't go near any wet dogs!

Hannah

IMAGINATION! PAVILION

THIS MULTIATTRACTION PAVILION is situated on the west side of Innoventions West and down the walk from The Land. Outside is an "upside-down waterfall" and one of our favorite Future World landmarks, the "jumping water," a fountain that hops over the heads of unsuspecting passersby.

When it's hot, all I want to do is wear my swim trunks and get wet. One of the best places is outside of the Imagination! Pavilion. They have dancing waters skipping through the air. I like to follow where the water is flying and let it splash my face. Another place to get wet is near Test Track. Water shoots up from the ground. It's fun!

Ian

Honey, I Shrunk the Audience ★★★★½
Captain EO ★★★★

APPEAL BY AGE	PRESCHOOL ★★★★½	GRADE SCHOOL ★★★★	TEENS ★★★
YOUNG ADULTS ★★		OVER 30 ★★½	SENIORS ★★

What they are 3-D films with special effects. **Scope and scale** Headliners. **Fright potential** Extremely intense visual effects and loudness frighten young children. **Bottleneck rating** 8. **When to go** Before noon or after 4 p.m. **Special comments** Adults should not be put off by the sci-fi theme (or rock music, for *Captain EO*). The high decibels and *Honey*'s tactile effects frighten some young children. **Authors' rating** *Honey:* An absolute hoot! Not to be missed; ★★★★½. *EO:* ★★★★. **Duration of show** About 17 minutes. **Preshow** 8 minutes. **Probable waiting time** 15 minutes (at suggested times).

Dark Loud Scary

In response to Michael Jackson's death in 2009, Disney brought back his 3-D space-themed musical film *Captain EO* for a "limited engagement" in its theme parks; at Epcot, it has temporarily supplanted *Honey, I Shrunk the Audience*. *Captain EO* originally ran here 1986–1994; there's no telling how long it will last on its second run, but we've heard that Disney will yank the film as soon as its audience numbers begin to drop. Both films share very loud sound tracks and a propensity to frighten small kids.

HONEY, I SHRUNK THE AUDIENCE A 3-D offshoot of Disney's feature film *Honey, I Shrunk the Kids, Honey, I Shrunk the Audience* features an array of special effects, including simulated explosions, smoke, fiber optics, lights, water spray, and moving seats. This attraction is played strictly for laughs—a commodity that's in short supply when it comes to Epcot entertainment.

CAPTAIN EO The ultimate music video. Starring the late Michael Jackson and directed by Francis Ford Coppola, this 3-D space fantasy is augmented by lasers, fiber optics, cannons, and a host of other special effects in the theater, as well as by some audience participation. There's not much of a story, but there's plenty of music and dancing performed by some of the most unlikely creatures ever to shake a tail feather. If nothing else, *Captain EO* reminds us that music videos once contained more than young urbanites dancing in clubs or five ill-dressed, unshaven guys whining onstage.

Liliane

Young children will be frightened at times. If, however, they want to see the show, I recommend letting them watch first without the 3-D glasses and with earplugs.

Yikes, Liliane, you could cover them up with a blanket too! About those mice in *Honey:* If the thought of several thousand (simulated) mice loose in the theater gives you the willies, sit with your feet crossed in a yoga position. You'll never know that the mice are there (except for the screaming of everyone around you, of course).

Bob

Journey into Imagination with Figment ★★½

APPEAL BY AGE	PRESCHOOL ★★★½	GRADE SCHOOL ★★★½	TEENS ★★★
YOUNG ADULTS ★★★		OVER 30 ★★★	SENIORS ★★★

What it is Dark fantasy-adventure ride. **Scope and scale** Major attraction wannabe. **Fright potential** Frightens a small percentage of preschoolers. **Bottleneck rating** 6. **When to go** Anytime. **Authors' rating** Vacuous; ★★½. **Duration of ride** About 6 minutes. **Average wait in line per 100 people ahead of you** 2 minutes. **Loading speed** Fast.

"One little spark of inspiration is at the heart of all creation," croons the ever-popular Figment, as he takes you on a tour of the zany Imagination Institute with the help of your five senses. Young children will love the little purple dragon, but grown-ups and teens will be mildly amused at best.

Mission: SPACE (Fastpass) ★★★★

APPEAL BY AGE	PRESCHOOL ★★★	GRADE SCHOOL ★★★★	TEENS ★★★★½
YOUNG ADULTS ★★★★		OVER 30 ★★★★	SENIORS ★★★

What it is Space flight simulation ride. **Scope and scale** Super-headliner. **Fright potential** Intense thrill ride may frighten guests of any age. Switching-off option provided (see page 242). **Bottleneck rating** 9. **When to go** First 30 minutes the park is open, or use Fastpass. **Special comments** Not recommended for pregnant women or people prone to motion sickness; must be 44" tall to ride; a gentler, non-spinning version is also available. **Authors' rating** Impressive; ★★★★. **Duration of ride** About 5 minutes plus preshow. **Average wait in line per 100 people ahead of you** 4 minutes.

A PEEK BEHIND THE SCENES WITH JIM HILL

AND IT'S $25 PER BAG, ONE-WAY
Mission: SPACE is supposed to simulate what an astronaut might experience during a trip to Mars. But once you're stuck on the red planet, how do you get back home? Simple. Just head for the attraction's postshow area, where you can play the Mission: SPACE Race game. You and your friends compete against another team to see who will be the first to get their rocket from Mars back to Earth.

Rough   Queasy

In this attraction, you join three other guests in a four-man crew to fly a space mission. Each guest plays a role (commander, pilot, navigator, or engineer) and is required to perform certain functions during the flight. A cleverly conceived, technological marvel, Mission: SPACE made national news when, in separate incidents, two guests died after riding it. While neither of the deaths were linked to the attraction (the victims had unknown preexisting conditions), the negative publicity caused many guests to skip it entirely. In response, Disney has added a less stressful non-spinning version of Mission: SPACE. If you want to experience the spinning version of the ride, join the orange team, and if you prefer to check it out without those pesky g-forces, join the green team.

Follow the orange brick road because it's much more fun. The ride is too intense for little ones and people prone to motion sickness, but grade-schoolers, teens, and brave moms and dads will love it! And don't worry

Liliane

about the job assignments. Do you really think that Disney is going to let you meddle around with their multimillion-dollar high-tech toys?

The host during your expedition is Gary Sinise, known for his roles in the space flicks *Apollo 13* and *Mission to Mars*.

The "Mom, I Can't Believe It's Disney!" Fountain ★★★★

APPEAL BY AGE	PRESCHOOL ★★★★★	GRADE SCHOOL ★★★★★
TEENS ★★★★	YOUNG ADULTS ★★★★	OVER 30 ★★★★ SENIORS ★★★★★

What it is Combo fountain/shower. **Scope and scale** Diversion. **Fright potential** Not frightening in any respect. **Bottleneck rating** 2. **When to go** When it's hot. **Special comment** Secretly installed by Martians during *IllumiNations*. **Authors' rating** Yes! ★★★★★.

On a broiling Florida day, when you think you might suddenly combust, fling yourself into the fountain and dance, skip, sing, jump, splash, stick your toes down the spouts, or catch the water in your mouth! Toddlers and pre-

schoolers, along with hippies, especially love the fountain. We know that your kids will be right in the middle of this thing before your brain sounds the alert. Our advice: Pack a pair of dry shorts and turn the kids loose. Make sure that they don't go into the fountain with sneakers, as wet sneakers are a recipe for blisters.

Thumbs Up for the Whole Family

Test Track (Fastpass) ★★★½

APPEAL BY AGE	PRESCHOOL ★★★★	GRADE SCHOOL ★★★★½	TEENS ★★★★★
YOUNG ADULTS ★★★★½		OVER 30 ★★★★½	SENIORS ★★★★

What it is Automobile test-track simulator ride. **Scope and scale** Super-headliner. **Fright potential** Intense thrill ride may frighten guests of any age. Switching-off option provided (see page 242). **Bottleneck rating** 10. **When to go** First 30 minutes the park is open, just before closing, or use Fastpass. **Special comment** Must be 40" tall to ride. **Authors' rating** Good but not worth a 40-minute or longer wait; ★★★½. **Duration of ride** About 4 minutes. **Average wait in line per 100 people ahead of you** 4½ minutes. **Loading speed** Moderate–fast.

Visitors test a future model car at high speeds through hairpin turns, up and down steep hills, and over rough terrain. The six-guest vehicle is a motion simulator that rocks and pitches. The grand finale is a spin around a steep-

Rough   Scary

banked loop at 65 mph! It is much fun if you meet the height requirements. Test Track is a favorite attraction of teens.

Man, this is about as scary as driving with my 17-year-old sister! The ride is pretty cool, especially driving in a car that nearly wipes out and hits a truck. If you like those test dummies, you'll know what it's like to be one. The best time is when you hit the speed track outside and rip around an oval like you're a NASCAR driver.

Ian

If nobody in your family wants to join you on the ride and you don't have a Fastpass, join the singles line. It moves much faster.

Idan

I love fast things, and this was more than fast! You ride in a really cool car on what looks like a real road. There's no radio, but it's a convertible, and I like convertibles!

Hannah

It was pretty fun but not as exciting as I thought it would be. The thought of going 65 miles an hour was amazing, but you might as well get in a convertible and go down the highway.

Shelton

There is a Kidcot Fun Stop at Test Track where those too short to ride can occupy themselves with arts and crafts. When the temperature's boiling, try the neighboring Cool Wash misting station.

Liliane

Universe of Energy: *Ellen's Energy Adventure* ★★★★

APPEAL BY AGE	PRESCHOOL ★★★	GRADE SCHOOL ★★★½	TEENS ★★★
YOUNG ADULTS ★★★		OVER 30 ★★★½	SENIORS ★★★½

What it is Combination ride/theater presentation about energy. **Scope and scale** Major attraction. **Fright potential** Dinosaur segment frightens some preschoolers; visually intense, with some intimidating effects. **Bottleneck rating** 7. **When to go** Before 11:15 a.m. or after 4:30 p.m. **Special comment** Don't be dismayed by long lines; 580 people enter the pavilion each time the theater changes audiences. **Authors' rating** The most unique theater in Walt Disney World; ★★★★. **Duration of presentation** About 26½ minutes. **Preshow** 8 minutes. **Probable waiting time** 20–40 minutes.

Scary

Join Ellen DeGeneres and Bill Nye, the science guy, who star in this 26-minute presentation about energy. Visitors are seated in what appears to be an ordinary theater. After a short film, the theater seats divide into six 97-passenger traveling cars that glide among swamps and through a prehistoric forest full of animatronic dinosaurs. The ride itself is smooth and not scary at all, though some children are frightened by the dinosaurs.

Ellen DeGeneres lent her voice to the role of Dory, a fish with short-term memory loss, in the animated Disney/Pixar film *Finding Nemo*.

Movie Tip

WORLD SHOWCASE

WORLD SHOWCASE, EPCOT'S SECOND THEME AREA, is an ongoing World's Fair encircling a picturesque, 40-acre lagoon. The cuisine, culture, history, and architecture of almost a dozen countries are permanently displayed in individual national pavilions spaced along a 1.2-mile promenade. Pavilions replicate familiar landmarks and street scenes from the host countries. Until the Fantasyland expansion is complete, the best places to see characters are in Epcot. Mulan and Musha appear regularly in China; Snow White in Germany; Mickey at the American Adventure; Donald in Mexico; Pinocchio in Italy; Alice and Mary Poppins in the United Kingdom; Marie, Remy, Belle, and the Beast in France; and Aladdin, Jasmine, and the Genie in

Morocco. Now moving clockwise around the World Showcase promenade, here are the nations represented and their attractions.

Kim Possible World Showcase Adventure ★★★★

APPEAL BY AGE	PRESCHOOL ★★★½	GRADE SCHOOL ★★★★½	TEENS ★★★
YOUNG ADULTS ★★★		OVER 30 ★★★½	SENIORS ★★

What it is Interactive scavenger hunt in select World Showcase pavilions. **Scope and scale** Minor attraction. **Fright potential** Not frightening in any respect. **Bottleneck rating** 1. **When to go** Anytime. **Authors' rating** One of our favorite additions to the parks; ★★★★. **Duration of experience** Allow 30 minutes per adventure.

Disney Channel's *Kim Possible* show follows the teen heroine as she battles the forces of evil in exotic locations while trying to navigate typical teen challenges such as proms, parents, and homework. In the Kim Possible World Showcase Adventure, you play the part of Kim and are given a cell phone–like "Kimmunicator" before being dispatched on a mission to your choice of seven World Showcase pavilions. Once you arrive at the pavilion, the Kimmunicator's video screen and audio provide various clues about the adventure. As you discover each clue, you'll find special effects such as talking statues and flaming lanterns, plus live "secret agents" stationed in the pavilions just for this game.

Idan

Kim Possible opens up a world of adventure for little ones and ones who are young at heart. It's most fun if you are in at least two pairs. Split up in teams and see who can solve the most missions first!

Kim Possible is Disney's attempt at making static World Showcase pavilions more interactive and kid-friendly. It succeeds wildly, even as Disney is still ironing out all the technological kinks. The adventures have relatively simple clues, fast pacing, and neat rewards for solving the puzzles. Since the experience debuted, reader reviews have been uniformly positive, with the Japan adventure being the most popular.

Playing the game is free, and no deposit is required for the Kimmunicator. You'll need a valid theme-park ticket to sign up before you play, and you can choose both the time and location of your adventure. Register at either Future World's Innoventions East or Innoventions West buildings, along the main walkway from Future World to World Showcase, or on the Odyssey Bridge. You'll report to the Italy, Norway, or

---

A PEEK BEHIND THE SCENES WITH JIM HILL

GET READY FOR A JUNGLE ODYSSEY For far too many years, the Odyssey restaurant between Test Track and Mexico was open only seasonally. Instead of serving food, it's now used intermittently as a location for Food & Wine and Flower & Garden festival seminars. Imagineers are now eyeballing this prime piece of real estate as a possible location for World Showcase's next international pavilion. Which country, you ask? Think south of the border. To be specific: a nation famous for its rain forests, one that would be a natural neighbor for the Mexico Pavilion.

United Kingdom Pavilion to pick up your Kimmunicator before heading off to your chosen country.

Each group can have up to three Kimmunicators for the same adventure. Because you're working with a device about the size of a cell phone, it's best if you have one Kimmunicator for every two people in your group.

MEXICO PAVILION

PRE-COLUMBIAN PYRAMIDS dominate the architecture of this exhibit. Inside you will find authentic and valuable artifacts, a village scene complete with restaurant, and the boat ride.

SPANISH 101	
Hello: *Hola*	**Pronunciation:** *Oh-la*
Goodbye: *Adios*	**Pronunciation:** *Ah-dee-ohs*
Thank you: *Gracias*	**Pronunciation:** *Grah-see-ahs*
Mickey Mouse: *El Ratón Miguelito*	**Pronunciation:** *El Rah-tone Mee-gell-lee-toe*

Gran Fiesta Tour Starring the Three Caballeros ★★½

APPEAL BY AGE	PRESCHOOL ★★★★	GRADE SCHOOL ★★★½	TEENS ★★★
YOUNG ADULTS ★★★		OVER 30 ★★★	SENIORS ★★★

What it is Indoor scenic boat ride. **Scope and scale** Minor attraction. **Fright potential** Not frightening in any respect. **Bottleneck rating** 5. **When to go** Before noon or after 5 p.m. **Authors' rating** New role for classic Disney characters; ★★½. **Duration of ride** About 7 minutes (plus 1½-minute wait to disembark). **Average wait in line per 100 people ahead of you** 4½ minutes. **Assumes** 16 boats in operation. **Loading speed** Moderate.

Thumbs Up for the Whole Family

Gran Fiesta Tour's story line features Donald Duck, José Carioca (a parrot), and Panchito (a Mexican charro rooster) from the 1944 Disney film *The Three Caballeros;* the story has our heroes racing to Mexico City for a gala reunion performance. Guests are treated to detailed scenes done in eye-catching colors.

NORWAY PAVILION

SURROUNDING A COURTYARD is an assortment of traditional Scandinavian buildings, including a replica of the 14th-century Akershus Castle, now home to princess-hosted character meals. Other attractions include Maelstrom (a ride) and a Viking ship playground (the only dedicated playground at Epcot).

It is hard to say no to the mouthwatering pastries at Kringla Bakeri og Kafe.

Liliane

Maelstrom (Fastpass) ★★★

APPEAL BY AGE	PRESCHOOL ★★★	GRADE SCHOOL ★★★½	TEENS ★★★½
YOUNG ADULTS ★★★½		OVER 30 ★★★½	SENIORS ★★★½

What it is Indoor adventure boat ride. **Scope and scale** Major attraction. **Fright potential** Dark; visually intense in parts. Ride ends with a plunge down a 20-foot

NORWEGIAN 101

Hello: *God dag*	Pronunciation: *Good dagh*
Goodbye: *Ha det*	Pronunciation: *Hah deh*
Thank you: *Takk*	Pronunciation: *Tahk*
Mickey Mouse: *Mikke Mus*	Pronunciation: *Mikeh Moose*

flume. **Bottleneck rating** 9. **When to go** Before noon, after 4:30 p.m., or use Fastpass. **Authors' rating** Too short but has its moments; ★★★. **Duration of ride** 4½ minutes, followed by a 5-minute film with a short wait in between; about 14 minutes for the ride and show combo. **Average wait in line per 100 people ahead of you** 4 minutes. **Assumes** 12 or 13 boats operating. **Loading speed** Fast.

Dark

Scary

Board a dragon-headed ship for a voyage through the fabled seas of Viking history and legends with brave trolls, rocky gorges, and a storm at sea. Sounds dangerous? The ride can be intense at times, but the only hold-your-breath moment is when your boat descends a 20-foot slide. The rather short ride is followed by a 5-minute film on Norway, but if you don't want to see the film, you will be given the opportunity to exit before it begins.

CHINA PAVILION

THERE IS NO RIDE AT THE CHINA PAVILION, but the majestic half-size replica of the Temple of Heaven in Beijing will surely make it into your photo album. Inside the pavilion, see *Reflections of China*, an impressive film about the people and natural beauty of China. Children will enjoy the regularly scheduled performances of Chinese acrobats. Check your entertainment schedule (*Times Guide*) for showtimes.

CHINESE (MANDARIN) 101

Hello: *Ni hao*	Pronunciation: *Knee how*
Goodbye: *Zai jian*	Pronunciation: *Zy jehn*
Thank you: *Xiè xie*	Pronunciation: *Chi-eh chi-eh*
Mickey Mouse: *Mi Lao Shu*	Pronunciation: *Me Lah-oh Su*

Reflections of China ★★★½

APPEAL BY AGE	PRESCHOOL ★★	GRADE SCHOOL ★★★	TEENS ★★★
YOUNG ADULTS ★★★½		OVER 30 ★★★★	SENIORS ★★★½

What it is Film about the Chinese people and country. **Scope and scale** Major attraction. **Fright potential** Not frightening in any respect. **Bottleneck rating** 4. **When to go** Anytime. **Special comment** Audience stands throughout performance. **Authors' rating** This beautifully produced film was introduced in 2003; ★★★½. **Duration of presentation** About 14 minutes. **Probable waiting time** 10 minutes.

GERMANY PAVILION

THE GERMANY PAVILION DOES NOT HAVE RIDES. The main focus is Biergarten, a full-service (reservations suggested) restaurant serving German food and beer. Yodeling, folk dancing, and oompah-band music are regularly performed during mealtimes. Be sure to check out the large, elaborate model railroad located just beyond the restrooms as you walk from Germany toward Italy.

GERMAN 101	
Hello: *Hallo*	Pronunciation: *Hall-o*
Goodbye: *Auf wiedersehen*	Pronunciation: *Ow-f veeh-der-zain*
Thank you: *Danke*	Pronunciation: *Dan-keh*
Mickey Mouse: *Micky Maus*	Pronunciation: *Me-key Mouse*

Biergarten German restaurant: The best party I ever went to. My dad liked the beer band, and so did I. They shouted, "Ticky tocky, ticky tocky!" and we yelled back, "Oy, oy, oy!" (whatever that means). Everybody raised their beer glasses, sang songs, and did goofy dances. I think I had one too many root beers.

Ian

The Germany Pavilion is the perfect place to introduce your kids to a great snack: *Gummibaerchen* (gummy bears), my favorite childhood candy.

Liliane

ITALY PAVILION

THE ENTRANCE TO ITALY IS MARKED by an 83-foot-tall campanile (bell tower) intended to mirror the tower in St. Mark's Square in Venice. Left of the campanile is a replica of the 14th-century Doge's Palace.

Streets and courtyards in the Italy Pavilion are among the most realistic in the World Showcase. You really feel as if you're in Italy. Because there's no film or ride, tour any time.

ITALIAN 101	
Hello: *Buon giorno*	Pronunciation: *Bon jor-no*
Goodbye: *Ciao* (informal)	Pronunciation: *Chow*
Thank you: *Grazie*	Pronunciation: *Grah-zee-eh*
Mickey Mouse: *Topolino*	Pronunciation: *To-po-lee-no*

I don't know how they do this, but I couldn't stop watching. A lady statue comes alive and messes with people. She stands perfectly still in front of Italy. When people have their pictures taken next to her, she moves and does crazy things to them. My family laughed a lot, but I was too chicken to go up to her.

Ian

UNITED STATES PAVILION

THE UNITED STATES PAVILION is an imposing brick structure reminiscent of colonial Philadelphia and is home to a very moving and patriotic, albeit sanitized, retrospective of U.S. history. Street entertainment outside includes the Voices of Liberty choral ensemble and the Spirit of America Fife & Drum Corps, among others. Across the plaza is the America Gardens Theatre, Epcot's premier venue for concerts and stage shows.

The American Adventure ★★★★

APPEAL BY AGE   PRESCHOOL ★★½   GRADE SCHOOL ★★★   TEENS ★★★
YOUNG ADULTS ★★★½   OVER 30 ★★★★   SENIORS ★★★★

What it is Patriotic mixed-media and audio-animatronic theater presentation on U.S. history. **Scope and scale** Headliner. **Fright potential** Not frightening in any respect. **Bottleneck rating** 6. **When to go** Anytime. **Authors' rating** Disney's best historic/patriotic attraction; not to be missed; ★★★★. **Duration of presentation** About 29 minutes. **Preshow** Voices of Liberty chorale singing. **Probable waiting time** 25 minutes.

Thumbs Up for the Whole Family

The 29-minute multimedia show is narrated by animatronic Mark Twain and Ben Franklin. *The American Adventure* reminds you of a contest: Tell us everything you love about America in 30 minutes or less. Only four female figures are among the 12 personified ideals around the theater, one of them representing the rather ambiguous "tomorrow" by virtue of holding a baby. The North American continent seemingly does not exist prior to the landing of the *Mayflower*.

JAPAN PAVILION

THE FIVE-STORY, BLUE-ROOFED PAGODA, inspired by a 17th-century shrine in Nara, sets this pavilion apart. A hill garden behind it encompasses waterfalls, rocks, flowers, lanterns, paths, and rustic bridges. There are no attractions unless you count the huge Japanese retail venue. Not to be missed, though, are the Matsuriza Taiko drummers. The drums can often be heard throughout the World Showcase, but you need to be up close to see the graceful way the drums are played. Check the *Times Guide* for scheduled performances.

JAPANESE 101	
Hello: *Konnichiwa*	Pronunciation: *Ko-nee-chee wah*
Goodbye: *Sayonara*	Pronunciation: *Sigh-yo-nah-ra*
Thank you: *Arigato*	Pronunciation: *Ah-ree-gah-to*
Mickey Mouse: *Mikki Mausu*	Pronunciation: *Mikkee Mou-su*

MOROCCO PAVILION

THE BUSTLING MARKET, WINDING STREETS, lofty minarets, and stuccoed archways re-create the romance and intrigue of Marrakech and Casablanca. Attention to detail makes Morocco one of the most exciting World Showcase pavilions, but there are no attractions.

ARABIC 101		
Hello: *Salaam alekoum*	**Pronunciation:** *Sah-lahm ah-leh-koom*
Goodbye: *Ma'salama*	**Pronunciation:** *Mah sah-lah-mah*
Thank you: *Shoukran*	**Pronunciation:** *Shoe-krah-n*
Mickey Mouse: *Mujallad Miki*	**Pronunciation:** *Muh-jahl-lahd Me-key*

I love Middle Eastern food and enjoy the music and belly dancing at Restaurant Marrakesh. Try the falafel; it's delicious. In the courtyard, Aladdin and Jasmine come to greet kids several times a day. I wish Disney would bring out Jaffar, my favorite character from *Aladdin,* more often.

Idan

FRANCE PAVILION

WELCOME AND BIENVENUE to Paris, Eiffel Tower, and all. There is not much to do for the kids here, but you won't have any trouble luring them into Boulangerie Patisserie for a scrumptious French pastry. Givenchy, the famed French perfume empire, opened a shop at the France Pavilion and is the only retail location in the United States offering the full line of Givenchy make-up and skin-care products, as well as a large selection of Givenchy fragrances.

Here is something for mom.... Seriously, do they really think that this is why we go to Epcot?

Liliane

Impressions de France ★★★½

APPEAL BY AGE	PRESCHOOL ★★	GRADE SCHOOL ★★★	TEENS ★★★
YOUNG ADULTS ★★★½		OVER 30 ★★★½	SENIORS ★★★★

What it is Film essay on the French people and country. **Scope and scale** Major attraction. **Fright potential** Not frightening in any respect. **Bottleneck rating** 7. **When to go** Anytime. **Authors' rating** Exceedingly beautiful film; not to be missed; ★★★½. **Duration of presentation** About 18 minutes. **Probable waiting time** 15 minutes (at suggested times).

France, here I come! This truly lovely 18-minute movie will make you want to pack your suitcase. An added bonus is that the showing is *très civilizé,* as you get to sit down and rest your weary feet.

FRENCH 101	
Hello: *Bonjour*	**Pronunciation:** *Bon-jure*
Goodbye: *Au revoir*	**Pronunciation:** *Oh reh-vwa*
Thank you: *Merci*	**Pronunciation:** *Maer-si*
Mickey Mouse: *Mickey*	**Pronunciation:** *Mee-keh*

FAVORITE EATS AT EPCOT

LAND | SERVICE LOCATION | FOOD ITEM

THE SEAS PAVILION
Coral Reef Restaurant* | Food with a view—fish menu. The aquarium will keep the kids happy for quite some time

THE LAND PAVILION
Sunshine Seasons | Healthy choices—our all-time favorite

MEXICO
La Cantina de San Angel | Children's plate with burrito, chips, & beverage

NORWAY
Kringla Bakeri og Kafe | Salmon sandwiches & pastries

CHINA
Lotus Blossom Café | Beef & chicken rice bowls, vegetable lo mein, & egg rolls

GERMANY
Sommerfest | Bratwurst & frankfurter with kraut & apple strudel

ITALY
Tutto Italia* | Reasonable pasta & kids' menu

UNITED STATES
Liberty Inn | If you are craving all-American food

JAPAN
Yakitori House | Beef & chicken teriyaki

MOROCCO
Tangierine Café | *Shawarma,* hummus, couscous, & kids' meals; outdoor seating

FRANCE
Boulangerie Patisserie | Croissants, chocolate mousse, & yummy sandwiches on baguettes

Crêpes des Chefs de France | Crêpes & espresso

UNITED KINGDOM
The Tea Caddy | You must have an English Cadbury bar once in your life.

* table service only–Advance Reservations highly recommended

UNITED KINGDOM PAVILION

A BLEND OF ARCHITECTURE ATTEMPTS to capture Britain's city, town, and rural atmospheres. One street alone has a thatched-roof cottage, four-story timber-and-plaster building, pre-Georgian plaster building, formal Palladian exterior of dressed stone, and a city square with a Hyde Park bandstand (whew!). There are no attractions.

If your child loves Mary Poppins, your best chance to meet her is here.

Liliane

CANADA PAVILION

CANADA'S CULTURAL, NATURAL, AND architectural diversity is reflected in this large and impressive pavilion. Older kids will be interested in the 30-foot-tall totem poles that embellish a Native American village. Canada is also home to a sort of punk-Celtic-country band called Off Kilter—yes, the lead singer wears a kilt—that performs in front of the showcase entrance. Check your entertainment schedule (*Times Guide*) for performance times.

O Canada! ★★★½

APPEAL BY AGE	PRESCHOOL ★★½	GRADE SCHOOL ★★★	TEENS ★★★½
YOUNG ADULTS ★★★½		OVER 30 ★★★★	SENIORS ★★★★

What it is Film essay on the Canadian people and their country. **Scope and scale** Major attraction. **Fright potential** Not frightening in any respect. **Bottleneck rating** 5. **When to go** Anytime. **Special comment** Audience stands during performance. **Authors' rating** Makes you want to catch the first plane to Canada! ★★★½. **Duration of presentation** About 18 minutes. **Probable waiting time** 10 minutes.

O Canada! showcases Canada's natural beauty and population diversity and demonstrates the immense pride that Canadians have in their country. An updated film replaced the decades-old original in 2007. Starring Martin Short, it features additional clips and dialogue interspersed with some of the original film's scenes. Visitors leave the theater through Victoria Gardens, which was inspired by the famed Butchart Gardens of British Columbia.

Cast members often run a preshow quiz on Canadian trivia outside the theater before the show. Here are some helpful tips: Canada's capital is Ottawa; its $1 coin is nicknamed the Loonie, after the bird engraved on it; and the $2 coin is the Toonie—not, unfortunately, the Doubloonie.

This large-capacity attraction (guests must stand) gets fairly heavy late-morning attendance, as Canada is the first pavilion encountered as one travels counterclockwise around World Showcase Lagoon.

LIVE ENTERTAINMENT *at* EPCOT

IN FUTURE WORLD

KIDS WILL LOVE THE CREW OF DRUMMING JANITORS (The JAMMitors), as well as the Krystos gymnasts in alien attire and the dancing fountains show in the plaza between the Innoventions East and West buildings.

Combine a rest break with a little fun. Let your kids experience one of the special talking water fountains at Epcot (located outside the Mouse Works shop, behind Innoventions West; between Innoventions and *Honey, I Shrunk the Audience* or *Captain EO* in the Imagination Pavilion; and next to the play fountain between Future World and World Showcase). For a hilarious chat, seek out PUSH the talking trash can at the Electric Umbrella Restaurant in Innoventions East.

Liliane

AROUND THE WORLD SHOWCASE

STREET PERFORMANCES IN AND AROUND the World Showcase are what set live entertainment at Epcot apart from the other Disney parks. A strolling mariachi group can be found in Mexico; street actors in Italy; a fife-and-drum corps or The Voices of Liberty in the United States; traditional songs, drums, and dances in Japan; street comedy in the United Kingdom; white-faced mimes in France; and bagpipes and Celtic bands in Canada, among other performances. Check your entertainment schedule *(Times Guide)* for performance times. Some restaurants get in on the act too. You can dine among singing waiters in Italy, enjoy Oktoberfest entertainment in Germany, and see belly dancing in Morocco. WDW live-entertainment guru Steve Soares usually posts the Epcot performance schedule about a week in advance at **wdwent.com.**

AMERICA GARDENS THEATRE

THE AMERICA GARDENS THEATRE, an amphitheater on the lagoon across from the U.S. Pavilion, features stage shows (all free, of course) with Disney characters, international dance troupes, acrobatic companies, choruses, musical groups, dinosaur rock bands (particularly appropriate), comedians who book engagements of several weeks, and even cheerleading competitions. Some of these are very good indeed, though whether you're interested in a particular show may depend on how tired you are and what else you have scheduled. Showtimes are listed on a board outside the exits and in the daily *Times Guide.*

ILLUMINATIONS

A NIGHTLY CAPSTONE EVENT AT EPCOT called *IllumiNations* features a program of music, fireworks, erupting fountains, special lighting, and laser technology performed on World Showcase Lagoon. This enchanting and ambitious show (it tells the history of the universe starting with the Big Bang) is well worth keeping the kids up late. The best place to view the show is from the lakeside veranda of La Hacienda at the Mexico Pavilion or Rose & Crown Pub at the United Kingdom Pavilion. Come early and relax with a drink or snack. The drawback is, you guessed it, that you will have to claim this spot at least 90 minutes before *IllumiNations.*

For other great viewing spots, check out our "Where to View *IllumiNations*" map. Note that the boat dock opposite Germany may be exposed to a lot of smoke from the fireworks because of Epcot's prevailing winds.

IllumiNations is the climax of every day at Epcot, so keep in mind that once the show is over, you will be leaving the park and so will almost everybody else. For suggested exit strategies, see the opposite page.

For a really good view of the show, you can charter a pontoon boat for about $350. Captained by a Disney cast member, the boat holds up to 10 guests. Your captain will take you for a little cruise and then

Where to View IllumiNations

position the boat in a perfect place to watch *IllumiNations*. For more information, call ☎ 407-WDW-PLAY.

IllumiNations ★★★★½

APPEAL BY AGE	PRESCHOOL ★★★½	GRADE SCHOOL ★★★★	TEENS ★★★★½
YOUNG ADULTS ★★★★½		OVER 30 ★★★★½	SENIORS ★★★★½

What it is Nighttime fireworks and laser show at World Showcase Lagoon. **Scope and scale** Super-headliner. **Fright potential** Not frightening in any respect. **When to go** Stake out viewing position 20–40 minutes before showtime. **Special comments** Showtime is listed in the daily entertainment schedule on the handout park map. Audience stands during performance. **Authors' rating** Epcot's most impressive entertainment event; ★★★★½. **Duration of show** About 18 minutes.

EXIT STRATEGIES

MORE GROUPS GET SEPARATED and more children lost after *IllumiNations* than at any other time. Make sure that you have preselected a meeting point in the Epcot entrance area. Warn your group not to leave through the exit turnstiles until everyone is reunited.

Suggested meeting point: the fountain just inside the main entrance.

- If you are staying at the Swan, Dolphin, Yacht & Beach Club Resorts, or BoardWalk Inn & Villas, watch *IllumiNations* from somewhere between Italy and the United Kingdom, and exit the park through the International Gateway between France and the United Kingdom. You can walk or take a boat back to your hotel.

- If you have a car in the Epcot lot, find a viewing spot at the Future World end of World Showcase Lagoon (Showcase Plaza) and leave immediately after *IllumiNations* ends. The problem is not the traffic in the parking lot—it actually moves pretty well—it's making your way to, and finding, your car. Make sure that you write down where you are parked—this is not the time to rely on your memory. If you are parked near the entrance, skip the tram and walk. If you walk, watch your children closely and hang on to them for all you're worth. The parking lot is pretty wild at this time of night.

EPCOT TOURING PLANS

OUR STEP-BY-STEP TOURING PLANS ARE FIELD-TESTED, independently verified itineraries that will keep you moving counter to the crowd flow and allow you to see as much as possible in a single day with minimum time wasted in line. We present three Epcot 1-day touring plans specifically geared toward visiting with children. We also offer, and recommend, a 2-day touring plan that is much more relaxing and far less tiring.

Touring Epcot is much more strenuous and demanding than touring the other theme parks. Epcot requires about twice as much walking. And, unlike the Magic Kingdom, Epcot has no effective in-park transportation—wherever you want to go, it's always quicker to walk. Our plans will help you avoid crowds and bottlenecks on days of moderate to heavy attendance, but they can't shorten the distance you have to walk. (Wear comfortable shoes.) On days of lighter attendance, when crowd conditions aren't a critical factor, the plans will help you organize your tour.

As a group, the *Unofficial Guide* research staff loves Epcot. Because we spend so much time there, we really wanted our small children to enjoy it too. The challenge was figuring out how to get the kids connected to the theme or presentation at each pavilion, especially in Future World. Let's face it—a 7-year-old is only going to take so much talk about hydroponic vegetables, nuclear fission, or communication systems before tuning out.

The key for us was to brief our children on what they were likely to see in each attraction and then tie it back to something they could relate to in their everyday lives. During the tour of the greenhouse in Living with the Land, for example, we made a game of finding foods they like. (They have cocoa beans—chocolate—so we think that covers almost everyone.) While riding Test Track, we asked our daughter to figure out which parent's driving was most like the ride's. (To avoid further sleeping in the garage, we'll not disclose who "won" that contest.) Our point here is that Epcot's Future World attractions can be a lot more palatable to young children if they're engaged and prepared going in. It's all about presentation.

The different touring plans are described below. The descriptions will tell you for whom (for example, tweens, parents with preschoolers, and so on) or for what situation (such as sleeping late) the plans are designed. The actual touring plans are located on pages 454–458. Each plan includes a numbered map of the park in question to help you find your way around. Clip the plan of your choice out of the book by cutting along the line indicated, and take it with you to the park.

EPCOT 1-DAY TOURING PLAN FOR PARENTS WITH SMALL CHILDREN This plan is designed for parents of children ages 3–8 who wish to see the very best age-appropriate attractions in Epcot. Every attraction has a rating of at least three stars (out of five) from preschool and grade-school children surveyed by the *Unofficial Guide*. Special advice is provided for touring the park with small children, including restaurant recommendations. The plan keeps walking and backtracking to a minimum.

EPCOT 1-DAY SLEEPYHEAD TOURING PLAN FOR PARENTS WITH SMALL CHILDREN A relaxed plan that allows families with small children to sleep late and still see the highlights of Epcot. The plan begins around 11 a.m., sets aside ample time for lunch, and includes the very best child-friendly attractions in the park. The plan also points out where Fastpass can best be used.

EPCOT 1-DAY TOURING PLAN FOR TWEENS AND THEIR PARENTS A 1-day touring plan for parents with children ages 8–12. It includes every attraction rated three stars and higher by this age group, and it sets aside ample time for lunch and dinner.

PARENT'S EPCOT TOURING PLAN—1 AFTERNOON AND 1 FULL DAY This touring plan is for families who want to tour Epcot comprehensively over 2 days. Day 1 uses early-morning touring opportunities. Day 2 begins in the afternoon and continues until closing.

BEFORE YOU GO

1. Call ☎ 407-824-4321 in advance for the hours of operation on the day of your visit.

2. Make reservations at the Epcot full-service restaurant(s) of your choice in advance of your visit.

EPCOT TRIVIA QUIZ

By Lou Mongello

1. IN WHAT WORLD SHOWCASE PAVILION CAN YOU MEET DONALD DUCK?

a. United States

b. Germany

c. United Kingdom

d. Mexico

2. IN SOARIN', WHAT U.S. STATE DO YOU SOAR OVER?

a. Florida

b. California

c. Texas

d. The entire nation

3. *CAPTAIN EO* IS PLAYED BY WHICH OF THESE FAMOUS STARS?

a. Michael Jordan

b. Michael Jackson

c. Robin Williams

d. Joe Jonas

4. WHAT COUNTRY IS FOUND BETWEEN GERMANY AND THE UNITED STATES?

a. France

b. Morocco

c. Japan

d. Italy

5. WHAT IS THE LARGEST PAVILION AT EPCOT?

a. The Seas with Nemo & Friends

b. Mission: SPACE

c. Universe of Energy

d. The Land

6. HOW MANY DIFFERENT INTERNATIONAL PAVILIONS CAN BE FOUND IN EPCOT?

a. 7

b. 9

c. 11

d. 13

7. WHAT IS UNIQUE ABOUT THE WATERFALLS OUTSIDE THE IMAGINATION! PAVILION?

a. They flow upwards.

b. The water is purple.

c. They are holograms.

d. They only flow at night.

8. WHAT DOES EPCOT STAND FOR?

a. Employee Paychecks Come On Tuesday

b. Every Person Comes Out Tired

c. Experimental Prototype Community of Tomorrow

d. Economic Private City of Orlando Taxation

9. KIDS OF ALL AGES CAN PARTICIPATE IN AN ADVENTURE THROUGH WORLD SHOWCASE BASED ON WHICH DISNEY CHANNEL SHOW?

a. *Phineas and Ferb*

b. *Wizards of Waverly Place*

c. *Kim Possible*

d. *The Replacements*

10. THE GRAN FIESTA TOUR FEATURES DONALD AND:

a. Daisy and Goofy.

b. José Carioca and Panchito.

c. Pepe and Pancho.

d. José Carioca and Marco.

11. WHAT COLOR ARE FIGMENT'S EYES?

a. Red

b. Orange

c. Yellow

d. Green

12. IN THE UNIVERSE OF ENERGY, WHAT DOES ELLEN NICKNAME HER COLLEGE ROOMMATE?

a. Jumpin' Judy

b. Stupid Judy

c. Smarty Pants

d. Einstein

Answers can be found on page 426.

ANIMAL KINGDOM

WITH ITS LUSH FLORA, WINDING STREAMS, meandering paths, and exotic setting, the Animal Kingdom is a stunningly beautiful theme park. The landscaping alone conjures images of a rain forest, veld, and even formal gardens. Add to this loveliness a population of more than 1,700 animals, replicas of Africa's and Asia's most intriguing architecture, and a diverse array of singularly original attractions, and you have the most unique of all Walt Disney World theme parks. The Animal Kingdom's seven sections, or "lands," are Oasis, Discovery Island, DinoLand U.S.A., Camp Minnie-Mickey, Africa, Asia, and Rafiki's Planet Watch.

On Discovery Island, behind the Creature Comforts Shop, is the Baby Care Center with supplies, changing tables, and a quiet place to nurse, as well as a first-aid center. Garden Gate Gifts at the main entrance and Duka La Filimu in Africa will save the day if you run out of film or other camera supplies.

At the entrance plaza, ticket kiosks front the main entrance. To your right before the turnstiles, you'll find an ATM. Passing through the turnstiles, wheelchair and stroller rentals (at Garden Gate Gifts) are to your right. Guest Relations—the park headquarters for information, handout park maps, entertainment schedules, missing persons, and lost and found—is to the left. Lockers are just inside the main entrance to the left. Disney no longer has pet-care facilities adjacent to the park, but the Best Friends Pet Resort across from Disney's Port Orleans Resort will provide a comfortable home away from home for Fido, Frisky, and all their pet pals.

The park is arranged somewhat like the Magic Kingdom. The lush, tropical Oasis serves as Main Street, funneling visitors to Discovery Island at the center of the park. Discovery Island is the park's retail and dining center. From Discovery Island, guests can access the respective theme areas: Africa, Camp Minnie-Mickey, Asia, and DinoLand U.S.A. Rafiki's Planet Watch is accessed from Africa.

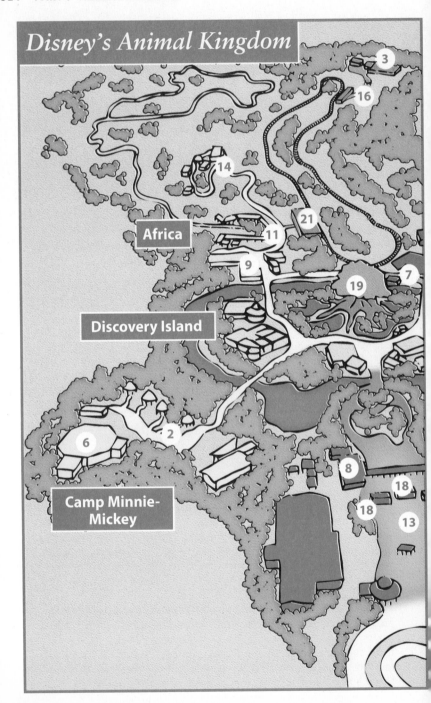

Disney's Animal Kingdom

Africa

Discovery Island

Camp Minnie-Mickey

1. The Boneyard
2. Character Greeting Trails
3. Conservation Station
4. DINOSAUR
5. Expedition Everest
6. *Festival of the Lion King*
7. *Flights of Wonder*
8. Guest Relations
9. Harambe Village
10. Kali River Rapids
11. Kilimanjaro Safaris
12. Maharajah Jungle Trek
13. Main Entrance
14. Pangani Forest
    Exploration Trail
15. Primeval Whirl
16. Rafiki's Planet Watch
17. Theater in the Wild/
    *Finding Nemo—
    The Musical*
18. Ticket Booths
19. The Tree of Life/
    *It's Tough to
    Be a Bug!*
20. TriceraTop Spin
21. Wildlife Express
    Train

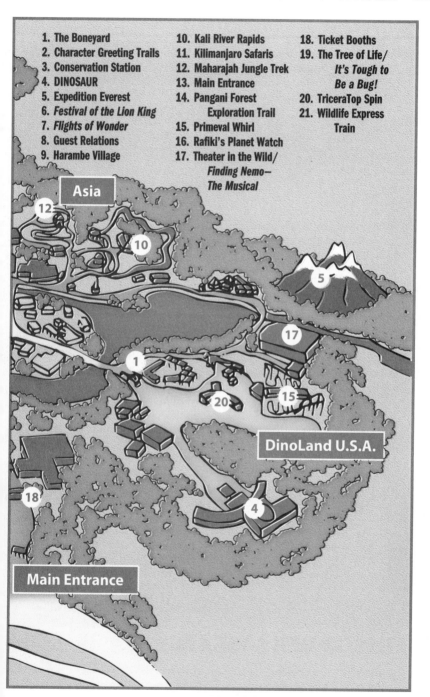

Extra Magic Hours are offered to guests lodging at the Disney hotels. However, our testing has shown that the early-entry program doesn't really save you any time waiting in line. In addition, Evening Magic Hours are no longer offered. We're not sure whether this is a temporary cost-cutting move or a permanent change, so check the Disney website as you plan your visit.

Kilimanjaro Safaris and Pangani Forest Exploration Trail close about 30–60 minutes before sunset. Thus, as days get shorter with the change of seasons, the attractions close earlier in the day. In the fall, when the clocks are rolled back, Disney closes all animal exhibits as early as 4:45 p.m.

Kali River Rapids in Asia—as well as the Boneyard playground, the Wildlife Express Train, and Conservation Station—are sometimes not opened until 30 minutes or longer after the rest of Animal Kingdom opens. It is not clear if these delayed openings are temporary, permanent, seasonal, or year-round. Check before you run to ride Kali River Rapids!

The OASIS

THOUGH THE FUNCTIONAL PURPOSE OF THE OASIS is to funnel guests to the center of the park, it also sets the stage and gets you into the right mood to enjoy Animal Kingdom. The Oasis immediately envelops you in an environment that is replete with choices. There is not one broad thoroughfare but rather multiple paths. Each will deliver you to Discovery Island at the center of the park, but which path you choose and what you see along the way is up to you. The natural-habitat zoological exhibits are primarily designed for the comfort and well-being of the animals. A sign will identify the animal(s) in each exhibit, but there's no guarantee that the animals will be immediately visible. Because most habitats are large and provide ample terrain for the occupants to hide, you must linger and concentrate, looking for small movements in the vegetation. The Oasis is a place to linger and appreciate, and although this is exactly what the designers intended, it will be largely lost on Disney-conditioned guests who blitz through at warp speed to queue up for the big attractions. If you are a blitzer in the morning, plan to spend some time in The Oasis on your way out of the park. The Oasis usually closes 30–60 minutes after the rest of the park.

We thought the animals were very cool. But don't get too close to the spoonbills. One squawked at me!

Shelton

DISCOVERY ISLAND

DISCOVERY ISLAND IS AN ISLAND OF TROPICAL GREENERY and whimsical equatorial African architecture, executed in vibrant hues of teal, yellow, red, and blue. Connected to the other lands by bridges, the island is the hub from which guests can access the park's various theme areas. Discovery Island is the park's central shopping, dining, and services headquarters. It is here that you will find the first-aid and Baby Care centers. For the best selection of Disney trademark merchandise, try the Island Mercantile shop. Counter-service food and snacks, but no full-service restaurants, are available. In addition to several wildlife exhibits, Discovery Island's Tree of Life hosts the film *It's Tough to Be a Bug!*

The Tree of Life/*It's Tough to Be a Bug!* ★★★★

APPEAL BY AGE	PRESCHOOL ★★★	GRADE SCHOOL ★★★★	TEENS ★★★★
YOUNG ADULTS ★★★★		OVER 30 ★★★★	SENIORS ★★★★

What it is 3-D theater show. **Scope and scale** Major attraction. **Fright potential** Very intense and loud, with special effects that startle viewers of all ages and potentially terrify young children. **Bottleneck rating** 9. **When to go** Before noon or after 4 p.m. **Special comment** The theater is inside the tree. **Authors' rating** Zany and frenetic; ★★★★. **Duration of show** Approximately 8 minutes. **Probable waiting time** 12–30 minutes.

Before entering the show, take a close look at The Tree of Life, the remarkable home of this 3-D movie. The primary icon and focal point of the Animal Kingdom, the tree features a trunk with high-relief carvings depicting 325 animals.

It's Tough to Be a Bug! is a zany, cleverly conceived, but very intense 3-D show housed below The Tree of Life. For starters, the show is about bugs, and bugs always rank high on the ick-factor scale. That, coupled with some startling special effects and a very loud sound track, make *It's Tough to Be a Bug!* a potential horror show for the age-7-and-under crowd. Tread cautiously, but don't write off the attraction. You can prepare by watching the animated feature *A Bug's Life* before you leave home—many of the characters are the same.

The closing lines of the show tipped me off when it was announced that "honorary bugs (read: audience members) remain seated while all the lice, bed bugs, maggots, and cockroaches exit first." In plain English, this means that if you don't like bugs crawling on you, even simulated ones, keep your feet off the floor. And thanks to Disney ingenuity, the bugs sting too—they do, they do.

I saw different things on The Tree of Life each time I looked. It was great!

CAMP MINNIE-MICKEY

THIS LAND IS DESIGNED TO BE THE DISNEY characters' Animal Kingdom headquarters. A small land, Camp Minnie-Mickey has a rustic and woodsy theme like a summer camp. In addition to a character meeting and greeting area, Camp Minnie-Mickey is home to a live stage production featuring Disney characters.

Character Trails

Characters can be found at the end of each of several character trails. Each trail has its own private reception area and, of course, its own queue. Unless your child is really into character autograph and photo-op sessions, skip this part of Camp Minnie-Mickey and experience the real gem, the *Festival of the Lion King* stage show.

Festival of the Lion King ★★★★

APPEAL BY AGE		PRESCHOOL ★★★★½		GRADE SCHOOL ★★★★½
TEENS ★★★★½	YOUNG ADULTS ★★★★½		OVER 30 ★★★★½	SENIORS ★★★★★

What it is Theater-in-the-round stage show. **Scope and scale** Major attraction. **Fright potential** A bit loud, but otherwise not frightening in any respect. **Bottleneck rating** 9. **When to go** Before 11 a.m. or after 4 p.m. **Special comment** Performance times are listed in the handout park map or *Times Guide*. **Authors' rating** Upbeat and spectacular; not to be missed; ★★★★. **Duration of show** 30 minutes. **Probable waiting time** 20–35 minutes.

Great pageantry, dazzling costumes, a mini–Broadway show, and air-conditioning too. *Festival of the Lion King* at the Animal Kingdom was the precursor of the Broadway production of *The Lion King*.

Thumbs Up for the Whole Family

This was one of my favorite things I did on the whole trip. It was cool how they put us on teams.

Shelton

Try to score front-row seats. Kids are invited to play musical instruments and join the performance.

Liliane

The show is based on the animated feature *The Lion King*, a must-see movie. Did you know that James Earl Jones, the voice behind Mufasa (father of Simba), is also the voice behind Darth Vader in *Star Wars*?

Movie Tip

▐ AFRICA

AFRICA IS THE LARGEST OF THE ANIMAL KINGDOM'S lands, and guests enter through Harambe, Disney's idealized and immensely sanitized version of a modern, rural African town. A market (with modern cash registers), a sit-down buffet, limited counter service, and snack stands are available.

Kilimanjaro Safaris (Fastpass) ★★★★★

APPEAL BY AGE	PRESCHOOL ★★★★½	GRADE SCHOOL ★★★★½	TEENS ★★★★½
YOUNG ADULTS ★★★★★		OVER 30 ★★★★½	SENIORS ★★★★★

What it is Truck ride through an African wildlife reservation. **Scope and scale** Super-headliner. **Fright potential** A "collapsing" bridge and the proximity of real animals make a few young children anxious. **Bottleneck rating** 10. **When to go**

As soon as the park opens, in the 2 hours before closing, or use Fastpass. **Authors' rating** Truly exceptional; ★★★★★. **Duration of ride** About 20 minutes. **Average wait in line per 100 people ahead of you** 4 minutes. **Assumes** Full-capacity operation with 18-second dispatch interval. **Loading speed** Fast.

Off you go in an open safari vehicle through a simulated African savanna. Preschoolers will enjoy looking for hippos, zebras, giraffes, lions, and rhinos, while the older kids will get a kick out of the story line about poachers. Many readers have asked us whether fewer animals are visible from Kilimanjaro Safaris around lunchtime than at park opening, out of concern that the animals might be less active in the midday heat. To help answer that question, we sent a team of researchers to ride continuously during 1 week in the summer and had

Thumbs Up for the Whole Family

them count the number of animals visible at different times of day. We subdivided our counting into large animals (elephants, hippos, and lions, for example), small (deer and other ungulates), and birds. Our results indicate that you'll probably see the same number of animals regardless of when you visit. This finding is almost certainly due to Disney's deliberate placement of water, food, and shade near the safari vehicles.

Feast your eyes on the habitat and the animals and forget the story (which can really get to you if you ride more than once). The experience would be infinitely more educational if Disney ditched the hokey poacher plot and replaced it with interesting facts about the animals.

Liliane

There are animals here that I've never heard of. It was cool to discover new animals, learn about them, and see what they look like. I didn't know how big a baby giraffe really is!

Hannah

Pangani Forest Exploration Trail ★★★★

APPEAL BY AGE	PRESCHOOL ★★★★	GRADE SCHOOL ★★★★	TEENS ★★★½
YOUNG ADULTS ★★★★	OVER 30 ★★★★		SENIORS ★★★★

What it is Walk-through zoological exhibit. **Scope and scale** Major attraction. **Fright potential** Not frightening in any respect. **Bottleneck rating** 9. **When to go** Before 10 a.m. and after 2:30 p.m. **Authors' rating** ★★★. **Duration of tour** About 20–25 minutes.

The Pangani Forest Exploration Trail is lush, beautiful, and jammed to the gills with people much of the time. This is particularly unpleasant if you have to wiggle your way through with a stroller. Walk the trail before 11 a.m. or after 2:30 p.m.

If you are more into the wildlife than the thrill rides, head to Kilimanjaro Safaris as soon as the park opens and get a Fastpass. Early in the morning, the return window will be short—just long enough, in fact, for an uncrowded, leisurely tour of the Pangani Forest Exploration Trail before you go on safari.

Rafiki's Planet Watch

Rafiki's Planet Watch is not a "land" and not really an attraction either. Our best guess is that Disney is using the name as an umbrella for Conservation

Station, the petting zoo, and the environmental exhibits accessible from Harambe via the Wildlife Express train. Presumably, Disney hopes that invoking Rafiki (a beloved character from *The Lion King*) will stimulate guests to make the effort to check out things in this far-flung corner of the park. As for your kids seeing Rafiki, don't bet on it. The closest likeness we've seen here is a two-dimensional wooden cutout.

I think we went to this, but I'm not sure. It wasn't very memorable.

Shelton

Conservation Station and Affection Section ★★★

APPEAL BY AGE	PRESCHOOL ★★★½	GRADE SCHOOL ★★★½	TEENS ★★★
YOUNG ADULTS ★★★		OVER 30 ★★★	SENIORS ★★★

What it is Behind-the-scenes walk-through educational exhibit and petting zoo. **Scope and scale** Minor attraction. **Fright potential** Not frightening in any respect. **Bottleneck rating** 6. **When to go** Anytime. **Special comment** Opens 30 minutes after rest of park. **Authors' rating** Evolving; ★★★.

This is the Animal Kingdom's veterinary and conservation headquarters. Guests can meet wildlife experts, observe some of the ongoing projects, and learn about the operations of the park. A rehabilitation area for injured animals, a nursery for recently born or hatched critters, and a petting zoo are included. Conservation Station is interesting, but you have to invest a little effort, and it helps to be inquisitive. What you see at Conservation Station will largely depend on what happens to be going on when you arrive. Because it's so removed from the rest of the park, you'll never bump into Conservation Station unless you take the train round-trip from Harambe.

Habitat Habit!

Located on the pedestrian path between the train station and Conservation Station, and listed on the park maps as an attraction, Habitat Habit! consists of a tiny collection of signs (about coexistence with wildlife) and a few cotton-top tamarins. To call it an attraction is absurd.

Wildlife Express Train ★★

APPEAL BY AGE	PRESCHOOL ★★★½	GRADE SCHOOL ★★★	TEENS ★★★
YOUNG ADULTS ★★½		OVER 30 ★★★	SENIORS ★★★

What it is Scenic railroad ride to Rafiki's Planet Watch and Conservation Station. **Scope and scale** Minor attraction. **Fright potential** Not frightening in any respect. **Bottleneck rating** 7. **When to go** Anytime. **Special comment** Opens 30 minutes after the rest of the park. **Authors' rating** Ho hum; ★★. **Duration of ride** About 5–7 minutes one way. **Average wait in line per 100 people ahead of you** 9 minutes. **Loading speed** Moderate.

Take the train only if you have small kids who would really enjoy the Affection Section petting zoo at Rafiki's Planet Watch. If you have a future veterinarian in your family, it is also well worth checking out the behind-the-scenes exhibits at Conservation Station.

ASIA

CROSSING THE ASIA BRIDGE FROM DISCOVERY ISLAND, you enter Asia through the village of Anandapur, a veritable collage of Asian themes inspired by the architecture and ruins of India, Thailand, Indonesia, and Nepal.

Expedition Everest (Fastpass) ★★★★½

APPEAL BY AGE	PRESCHOOL ★★★	GRADE SCHOOL ★★★★½	TEENS ★★★★★
YOUNG ADULTS ★★★★★		OVER 30 ★★★★★	SENIORS ★★★★

What it is High-speed roller coaster through Mount Everest. **Scope and scale** Super-headliner. **Fright potential** Frightens guests of all ages. **Bottleneck rating** 8. **When to go** Before 9:30 a.m., after 3 p.m., or use Fastpass. **Special comments** Contains some of the park's most stunning visual elements. Must be 44" tall to ride. **Authors' rating** ★★★★½. **Duration of ride** 4 minutes. **Average wait in line per 100 people ahead of you** Just under 4 minutes. **Assumes** 2 tracks operating. **Loading speed** Moderate–fast.

A PEEK BEHIND THE SCENES WITH JIM HILL

SEND IN THE STUNT SNOWMAN Expedition Everest's yeti: He's big. He's furry. He's ferocious. Or at least he would be, had he not been out of commission for much of the past 2 years. To divert the public's attention, the Imagineers are now considering placing a second audio-animatronic Abominable Snowman somewhere else in this ride. The second yeti won't be as technologically sophisticated as the original, but he'll still surprise guests when he suddenly pops up along the track for this runaway train.

Lose Things

Scary

As you enjoy one of the most spectacular panoramas in Walt Disney World, you wish this expedition would never end. But you get over that in a hurry as the train starts whirring through the guts of Disney's largest man-made mountain (not only the largest in Florida, but it also beats out Mount Petty Poot Poot in Kansas by 2 feet). After a high-speed encounter with a large, smelly yeti and a dead stop at the top of the mountain, the 50-mile-per-hour chase continues backward. The ride is very smooth and rich both in visuals and special effects. The backward segment is one of the most creative and exciting 20 seconds in roller coaster annals.

I think it's cool because there are a lot of big hills. There's a Yeti, and he tries to eat you. If you're a big screamer like me, you'll probably just close your eyes and open your mouth.

Hannah

Flights of Wonder ★★★★

APPEAL BY AGE	PRESCHOOL ★★★★	GRADE SCHOOL ★★★★	TEENS ★★★★
YOUNG ADULTS ★★★★		OVER 30 ★★★★	SENIORS ★★★★

What it is Stadium show about birds. **Scope and scale** Major attraction. **Fright potential** Swooping birds startle some younger children. **Bottleneck rating** 6.

When to go Anytime. **Special comment** Performance times are listed in the handout park map or *Times Guide*. **Authors' rating** Unique; ★★★★. **Duration of show** 30 minutes. **Probable waiting time** 20–30 minutes.

Thumbs Up for the Whole Family

Humorously presented, the show is ideal for kids. Don't expect parrots riding unicycles though. *Flights of Wonder* is about the natural talents and characteristics of various bird species. If your child is comfortable with you sitting a few rows behind, encourage him or her to take a seat in the up-front "for kids only" section. When the show is over, stick around and talk to the bird trainers and meet the feathery cast of the show up close and personal. It is a great opportunity to ask questions and take pictures. *Flights of Wonder* plays at the stadium located near the Asia Bridge on the walkway between Asia and Africa. Though the stadium is covered, it's not air-conditioned; thus, early-morning and late-afternoon performances are more comfortable. To ensure finding a seat, arrive about 10–15 minutes before showtime.

Kali River Rapids (Fastpass) ★★★½

APPEAL BY AGE	PRESCHOOL ★★★★	GRADE SCHOOL ★★★★½	TEENS ★★★★½
YOUNG ADULTS ★★★★		OVER 30 ★★★★	SENIORS ★★★★

What it is White-water raft ride. **Scope and scale** Headliner. **Fright potential** Potentially frightening and certainly wet for guests of all ages. **Bottleneck rating** 9. **When to go** Before 10:30 a.m., after 4:30 p.m., or use Fastpass. **Special comments** Must be 38" tall to ride; guaranteed to get wet; opens 30 minutes after the rest of the park. Switching-off option provided (see page 242). **Authors' rating** Short but scenic; ★★★½. **Duration of ride** About 5 minutes. **Average wait in line per 100 people ahead of you** 5 minutes. **Loading speed** Moderate.

Wet

Scary

The ride itself is tame and allows you to take in the outstanding scenery as you drift through a dense rain forest, past waterfalls and temple ruins. There are neither big drops nor terrifying rapids waiting to swallow the raft and all inside. The foregoing information notwithstanding, Disney still manages to drench you. Nonriding park guests will take great pleasure squirting water at the rafters from above. The water-squirting elephant stations are a great consolation prize for young ones who do not meet the 38-inch height requirement.

Hannah

Don't wear anything fancy because you're going to get soaked.

Liliane

If you ride early in the morning or on a cool day, use raingear and make sure that your shoes stay dry. Touring in wet clothes is unpleasant, and walking all day in soaked sneakers is a recipe for blisters.

Maharajah Jungle Trek ★★★★

APPEAL BY AGE	PRESCHOOL ★★★★	GRADE SCHOOL ★★★★	TEENS ★★★★
YOUNG ADULTS ★★★★		OVER 30 ★★★★	SENIORS ★★★★

What it is Walk-through zoological exhibit. **Scope and scale** Headliner. **Fright potential** Some children may balk at the bat exhibit. **Bottleneck rating** 5. **When**

to go Anytime. **Special comment** Opens 30 minutes after the rest of the park. **Authors' rating** A standard-setter for natural habitat design; ★★★★. **Duration of tour** About 20–30 minutes.

The Jungle Trek is less congested than the Pangani Forest Exploration Trail and is a good choice for midday touring. Tigers, gibbons, bats, and birds are waiting to be discovered along a path winding through the fabulous ruins of the maharajah's palace.

> The bat enclosure is outstanding and my favorite section of the trek. This is the opportunity to increase your knowledge, from Batman to Dracula, of these mysterious mammals.

Liliane

DINOLAND U.S.A.

THIS MOST TYPICALLY DISNEY of the Animal Kingdom's lands is a cross between an anthropological dig and a quirky roadside attraction. Accessible via the bridge from Discovery Island, DinoLand U.S.A. is home to a children's play area, a nature trail, a 1,500-seat amphitheater, and DINOSAUR, one of the Animal Kingdom's three thrill rides. Children ages 4–12 will feel right at home at DinoLand U.S.A. *Finding Nemo—The Musical* is shown at the Theater in the Wild.

The Boneyard ★★★½

APPEAL BY AGE	PRESCHOOL ★★★★½		GRADE SCHOOL ★★★★
TEENS ★★	YOUNG ADULTS ★★	OVER 30 ★★½	SENIORS ★★

What it is Elaborate playground. **Scope and scale** Diversion. **Fright potential** Not frightening in any respect. **Bottleneck rating** 5. **When to go** Anytime. **Special comment** Opens 30 minutes after the rest of the park. **Authors' rating** Stimulating fun for children; ★★★½.

It's playtime! The Boneyard is an elaborate playground for the kids age 12 and younger and is a great place for them to let off steam and get dirty (or at least sandy). The playground equipment consists of skeletal replicas of triceratops, Tyrannosaurus rex, Brachiosaurus, and the like. In addition, there are climbing mazes, as well as sand pits, where little ones can scrounge around for bones and fossils.

The Boneyard can get very hot in the scorching Florida sun, so make sure that your kids are properly hydrated and protected against sunburn. The playground is huge and parents might lose sight of a small child. Fortunately, however, there's only one entrance and exit. Your little ones are going to love the Boneyard, so resign yourself to staying awhile.

DINOSAUR (Fastpass) ★★★★½

APPEAL BY AGE	PRESCHOOL ★★½	GRADE SCHOOL ★★★½	TEENS ★★★★
YOUNG ADULTS ★★★★		OVER 30 ★★★★	SENIORS ★★★★

What it is Motion-simulator dark ride. **Scope and scale** Super-headliner. **Fright potential** High-tech thrill ride rattles riders of all ages. **Bottleneck rating** 8. **When to go** Before 10:30 a.m., in the hour before closing, or use Fastpass. **Special**

A PEEK BEHIND THE SCENES WITH JIM HILL

CORNY COASTER REPLACEMENT UNDER CONSIDERATION In the wake of the second Primeval Whirl–related accident in 4 years, WDW officials have been looking at a carnival-themed substitute for the troubled kids' coaster. The problem is that it's hard to conjure another attraction that would fit in with DinoLand U.S.A.'s cheesy design sense. One idea being bandied about is a Carnotaurus Corn Maze, with a silly-looking walk-around version of this DINO-SAUR character lurking at its corn-filled center, ready to jump out and scare the tourists.

comments Must be 40" tall to ride. Switching-off option provided (see page 242). **Authors' rating** Really improved; ★★★★½. **Duration of ride** 3½ minutes. **Average wait in line per 100 people ahead of you** 3 minutes. **Assumes** Full-capacity operation with 18-second dispatch interval. **Loading speed** Fast.

Dark   Rough   Scary

Here you board a time capsule to return to the Jurassic age in an effort to bring back a live dinosaur before a meteor hits the Earth and wipes them out. The bad guy in this epic is the little-known carnotaurus, an evil-eyed, long in the tooth, Tyrannosaurus rex–type fellow. A combination track ride and motion simulator, the DINOSAUR ride is not for the faint-hearted. You get tossed and pitched around in the dark with pesky dinosaurs jumping out at you. DINOSAUR has left many an adult weak-kneed. Most kids under age 9 find it terrifying.

DINOSAUR is an absolute no-no for preschoolers and any child easily frightened. The carnotaurus, unlike Barney and Figment, did not make my favorite dino list.

Liliane

It doesn't really go up any hills, and it didn't make me scream, but it scared my cousin half to death when she was 4. Even if you're 5 or 6, the dinosaurs might scare you.

Hannah

Shelton

I love the story line, which is thick and detailed and not thin, like the stories for some other rides. I love the part where you just barely escape and you go under a carnotaurus's belly!

Primeval Whirl ★★★

APPEAL BY AGE	PRESCHOOL ★★	GRADE SCHOOL ★★★★	TEENS ★★★★
YOUNG ADULTS ★★★½		OVER 30 ★★★	SENIORS ★★½

What it is Small coaster. **Scope and scale** Minor attraction. **Fright potential** Scarier than it looks. **Bottleneck rating** 9. **When to go** During the first 2 hours the park is open or in the hour before park closing. **Special comments** Must be 48" tall to ride. Switching-off option provided (see page 242). **Authors' rating** Wild Mouse on steroids; ★★★. **Duration of ride** Almost 2½ minutes. **Average wait in line per 100 people ahead of you** 4½ minutes. **Loading speed** Slow.

Scary Rough Queasy

This is a tricky little coaster with short drops, curves, and tight loops. As if that's not enough, the coaster cars also spin. The problem is that unlike with the evil teacups, guests cannot control the spinning. Complete spins are fun, but watch out for the screeching-stop half-spins.

Theater in the Wild/*Finding Nemo–The Musical* ★★★★

APPEAL BY AGE	PRESCHOOL ★★★★	GRADE SCHOOL ★★★★	TEENS ★★★★
YOUNG ADULTS ★★★★		OVER 30 ★★★★	SENIORS ★★★★

What it is Open-air venue for live stage shows. **Scope and scale** Major attraction. **Fright potential** Not frightening in any respect. **Bottleneck rating** 6. **When to go** Anytime. **Special comment** Performance times are listed in the handout park map or *Times Guide*. **Authors' rating** ★★★★. **Duration of show** 30 minutes. **Probable waiting time** About 30 minutes.

Thumbs Up for the Whole Family

Based on the Disney/Pixar animated feature, *Finding Nemo–The Musical* is an elaborate stage show headlining puppets, dancing, acrobats, and special effects. *Finding Nemo* is arguably the most elaborate live show in any Disney World theme park. A few scenes, such as one in which Nemo's mom is eaten (!!!), may be too intense for some very small children. Some of the mid-show musical numbers slow the pace, so the main concern for parents is whether the kids can sit still for an entire show. With that in mind, we advise parents to catch an afternoon performance—around 3 p.m. would be great—after seeing the rest of Animal Kingdom.

To get a seat, show up 20–25 minutes in advance for morning and late-afternoon shows and 30–35 minutes in advance for shows scheduled noon–4:30 p.m. Access to the theater is via a relatively narrow pedestrian path; if you arrive as the previous show is letting out, you will feel like a salmon swimming upstream.

When the line is very long, don't assume that you will get into the next show just by queuing up. Disney cast members monitor the line; ask them if you are likely to get into the next show.

Liliane

TriceraTop Spin ★★

APPEAL BY AGE	PRESCHOOL ★★★★	GRADE SCHOOL ★★★★	TEENS ★★★
YOUNG ADULTS ★★		OVER 30 ★★½	SENIORS ★★

What it is Hub-and-spoke midway ride. **Scope and scale** Minor attraction. **Fright potential** May frighten preschoolers. **Bottleneck rating** 9. **When to go** First 90 minutes the park is open and in the hour before park closing. **Authors' rating** Dumbo's prehistoric forebear; ★★. **Duration of ride** 1½ minutes. **Average wait in line per 100 people ahead of you** 10 minutes. **Loading speed** Slow.

Instead of Dumbo, you get Dino spinning around a central axis. The ride is fun for young children, but this slow loader is infamous for inefficiency and long waits.

FAVORITE EATS AT ANIMAL KINGDOM

LAND | SERVICE LOCATION | FOOD ITEM

DISCOVERY ISLAND

Flame Tree Barbecue | Ribs & chicken with beans
Pizzafari | Pizza & chicken Caesar salad, breadsticks

AFRICA

Tamu Tamu | Milk shakes
Tusker House Restaurant | Marrakech couscous with roasted veggies
Donald's Safari Breakfast at-Tusker House is a character breakfast including
Donald, Daisy, Goofy, and Mickey. All-you-can-eat buffet, 8 a.m.–10:30 a.m.

ASIA

Royal Anandapur Tea Company | Teas & specialty coffees
Yak & Yeti | Shaoxing steak & shrimp

DINOLAND U.S.A.

Restaurantosaurus | Kid's cheeseburger comes with choice of two sides
(grapes, carrot sticks, or applesauce) & choice of 1% milk, bottled water,
or apple juice

OUTSIDE ENTRANCE

Rainforest Cafe* | Breakfast, lunch, & dinner in a tropical rain forest setting
with a huge saltwater aquarium, gorillas going wild once in a while, & simulated thunderstorms. The place to take the kids if you want to sit down!
They'll love you for it—cross my heart, and hope to die.

table service only

Tusker House is my favorite. It has a lot of choices, and
there are always a lot of people there because the food is good.
You can get cinnamon rolls here as big as a stuffed animal!

Hannah

LIVE ENTERTAINMENT
at ANIMAL KINGDOM

STAGE SHOWS ARE PERFORMED DAILY at the Animal Kingdom;
check your entertainment schedule (*Times Guide*) for showtimes.
Street performers can be found most of the time at Discovery Island;
in Harambe, Africa; Anandapur, Asia; and in DinoLand U.S.A. For an
updated listing of live entertainment at Animal Kingdom, check out
Steve Soares's website **wdwent.com.**

LOOK WHO'S TALKING At The Oasis, don't miss introducing your kids
to **Wes Palm,** the talking palm tree who loves to poke fun at unsuspecting guests. At Conservation Station have a silly-dilly (Liliane's term)
chat with **Pipa,** the recycling trash can.

Though Wes Palm and Pipa will have you roaring with laughter, **DiVine** will leave you speechless. A perfect fusion between fantasy and reality, DiVine is an artist in a garb half-vine and half-creeping plant. She blends perfectly with the foliage at the Animal Kingdom and is only noticeable when she moves (which can be quite startling if you're not aware of her presence). DiVine travels around the park but seems to love the vicinity of the Rainforest Cafe entrance. The silent gracefulness of her movements and the serenity of her demeanor are totally captivating. If you don't encounter her, ask a cast member where she can be found. There is a video of DiVine on **youtube.com.**

ANIMAL ENCOUNTERS Throughout the day, Disney staff conduct impromptu short lectures on specific animals at the park. Look for a cast member in safari garb holding a bird, reptile, or small mammal. If you see a cast member being strangled or eaten by a reptile or large animal, keep walking.

GOODWILL AMBASSADORS A number of Asian and African natives are on hand throughout the park. Both gracious and knowledgeable, they are delighted to discuss their countries. Look for them in Harambe and along the Maharajah Jungle Trek in Asia. They can also be found near the main entrance and at The Oasis.

KIDS' DISCOVERY CLUB Activity stations offer kids ages 4–8 a structured learning experience as they tour Animal Kingdom. Set up along walkways in six themed areas, Discovery Club stations are manned by cast members who supervise a different activity at each station. A souvenir logbook is available at no charge and will be stamped at each station when the child completes a craft or exercise. Kids enjoy collecting the stamps and completing logbook puzzles while in attraction lines.

AFTERNOON PARADE Mickey's Jammin' Jungle Parade features characters from *The Lion King* and other Disney stories. The parade starts in Africa, crosses the bridge to Discovery Island, proceeds counterclockwise around the island, and then crosses the bridge to Asia. In Asia, the parade turns left and follows the walkway paralleling the river back to Africa.

The walking path between Africa and Asia has small cutouts that offer good views of the parade and excellent sun protection. Most guests scramble to Harambe, the starting point of the parade, and leave this area as soon as the parade crosses over the bridge to Discovery Island. Because guests don't realize that the parade cycles back through Harambe, there is never much of a crowd when the parade rumbles through the second time en route to going offstage. Therefore, if you make your way to Harambe about 20 minutes after the parade time listed in the *Times Guide,* you'll be able to score a super vantage point at the last minute.

ANIMAL KINGDOM
TOURING PLANS

OUR STEP-BY-STEP TOURING PLANS ARE FIELD-TESTED, independently verified itineraries that will keep you moving counter to the crowd flow and allow you to see as much as possible in a single day with minimum time wasted in line. You can take in all the attractions at the Animal Kingdom in a single day even when traveling with young children.

If you are not interested in an attraction listed on the touring plan, just skip that step and proceed to the next one. Should you encounter a very long line at an attraction the touring plan calls for, skip the attraction and go to the next step, returning later to retry. The use of Fastpass is factored into the touring plans.

The different touring plans are described below. The descriptions will tell you for whom (for example, tweens, parents with preschoolers, and so on) or for what situation (such as sleeping late) the plans are designed. The actual touring plans are located on pages 459–462. Each plan includes a numbered map of the park in question to help you find your way around. Clip the plan of your choice out of the book by cutting along the line indicated, and take it with you to the park.

ANIMAL KINGDOM 1-DAY TOURING PLAN FOR PARENTS WITH SMALL CHILDREN This plan is designed for parents of children ages 3–8 who wish to see the very best age-appropriate attractions in the Animal Kingdom. Every attraction has a rating of at least three stars (out of five) from preschool and grade-school children surveyed by the *Unofficial Guide*. Special advice is provided for touring the park with small children, including restaurant recommendations. The plan keeps walking and backtracking to a minimum, with no crisscrossing of the park.

ANIMAL KINGDOM 1-DAY SLEEPYHEAD TOURING PLAN FOR PARENTS WITH SMALL CHILDREN A relaxed plan that allows families with small children to sleep late and still see the highlights of the Animal Kingdom. The plan begins around 11 a.m., sets aside ample time for lunch, and includes the very best child-friendly attractions in the park.

ANIMAL KINGDOM 1-DAY TOURING PLAN FOR TWEENS AND THEIR PARENTS A 1-day plan for parents with children ages 8–12. It includes every attraction rated three stars and higher by this age group and sets aside ample time for lunch and dinner.

ANIMAL KINGDOM 1-DAY HAPPY FAMILY TOURING PLAN A plan for families of all ages. Includes time-saving tips for teens and adults visiting the Animal Kingdom's thrill rides, as well as age-appropriate attractions for parents with small children. The entire family stays together as much as possible (including lunch), but this plan allows groups with different interests to explore their favorite attractions without having everyone wait around.

BEFORE YOU GO

1. Call ☎ 407-824-4321 before you go for the park's operating hours.
2. Purchase your admission prior to arrival.

DISNEY'S ANIMAL KINGDOM TRIVIA QUIZ

By Lou Mongello

1. WHO ARE THE PROPRIETORS OF DINORAMA?
a. Mickey and Minnie
b. Wes Palm and Dr. Seeker
c. Chester and Hester
d. Freddy the Yeti

2. DISNEY SPENDS MORE THAN $1,700,000 YEARLY ON WHAT FOR DISNEY'S ANIMAL KINGDOM?
a. Worms
b. Manure
c. Transportation costs to import new animals from overseas
d. Plant food

3. ABOUT HOW MANY BRANCHES ARE ON THE TREE OF LIFE?
a. 500
b. 1,000
c. 3,000
d. 8,000

4. WHAT ARE THE RIDE VEHICLES IN DINOSAUR CALLED?
a. Jurassic Jeeps
b. Time Rovers
c. XP-37s
d. Omnimovers

5. WHAT LAND IN DISNEY'S ANIMAL KINGDOM HAS THE GREATEST NUMBER OF ATTRACTIONS?
a. Discovery Island
b. Asia
c. Africa
d. DinoLand U.S.A.

6. WHICH OF THESE ATTRACTIONS IS THE LARGEST IN ALL OF WALT DISNEY WORLD?
a. Maharajah Jungle Trek
b. Kilimanjaro Safaris
c. Pangani Forest Exploration Trail
d. Primeval Whirl

7. WHAT ATTRACTION'S RIDE VEHICLES ARE KNOWN AS STEAM DONKEYS?
a. Wildlife Express Train
b. Expedition Everest
c. Kali River Rapids
d. Kilimanjaro Safaris

8. WHERE CAN YOU FIND GUANO JOE?
a. Pangani Forest Exploration Trail
b. Rafiki's Planet Watch
c. Maharajah Jungle Trek
d. Flights of Wonder

9. AS YOU ENTER DISNEY'S ANIMAL KINGDOM, WHAT IS THE FIRST LAND THAT YOU REACH?
a. Africa
b. Discovery Island
c. The Oasis
d. Harambe Village

10. ABOUT HOW MANY DIFFERENT FOOD ITEMS ARE AVAILABLE IN WALT DISNEY WORLD?
a. 400
b. 1,600
c. 3,000
d. 6,000

Answers can be found on page 426.

DISNEY'S HOLLYWOOD STUDIOS

ABOUT HALF OF DISNEY'S HOLLYWOOD STUDIOS is set up as a theme park. The other half is off-limits except by guided tour. Though modest in size, the Studios' open-access areas are confusingly arranged (a product of the park's hurried expansion in the early 1990s). As at the Magic Kingdom, you enter the park and pass down a main street, only this time it's Hollywood Boulevard of the 1920s and 1930s. Though the park is largely organized by street names rather than by "lands," the easiest way to navigate it is by landmarks and attractions using the park map.

After Disney severed its relationship with MGM in 2008, the park formerly known as Disney-MGM Studios was renamed Disney's Hollywood Studios. Though the attraction lineup is essentially unchanged, the vision for the park going forward is to develop themes and attractions based on Pixar films and characters. The use of Hollywood in the park's name represents a more generic reference to moviemaking. In popular usage, however, many folks drop the Hollywood entirely, referring to the park simply as Disney Studios or The Studios.

While it is true that Disney's Hollywood Studios educates and entertains, what it does best is promote. Self-promotion of Disney films and products was once subtle and in context but is now blatant, inescapable, and distracting. Although most visitors are willing to forgive Disney its excesses, Studios veterans will lament the changes and remember how good it was when education was the park's goal instead of the medium.

Guest Relations, on your left as you enter, serves as the park headquarters and information center, similar to City Hall in the Magic Kingdom. Go there for a schedule of live performances, lost persons, package pickup, lost and found (on the right side of the entrance), general information, or in an emergency. If you haven't received a map of the Studios, get one here. To the right of the entrance are locker, stroller, and wheelchair rentals.

A Baby Care Center is located at Guest Relations, and Oscar's sells baby food and other necessities. Camera supplies for those precious moments can be purchased at The Darkroom on the right side of Hollywood Boulevard, just past Oscar's. Oddly enough the closest ATM is located outside the park to the right of the turnstiles. Disney no longer has pet-care facilities adjacent to the park, but the Best Friends Pet Resort across from Disney's Port Orleans Resort will provide a comfortable home away from home for Fido, Frisky, and all their pet pals.

Guests enter the park on Hollywood Boulevard, a palm-lined street reminiscent of the famous Hollywood main avenue of the 1930s. The best way to navigate is to decide what you really want to see and go for it! If you want the whole enchilada, it can be done in 1 day. But, as with the other parks, this is best accomplished by using one of our touring plans.

Architecture on Hollywood Boulevard is streamlined modern with Art Deco embellishments. Most service facilities are here, interspersed with eateries and shops. Merchandise includes Disney trademark items, Hollywood and movie-related souvenirs, and one-of-a-kind collectibles obtained from studio auctions and estate sales. Hollywood characters and roving performers entertain on the boulevard, and daily parades and other happenings pass this way.

Sunset Boulevard, evoking the 1940s, is a major component of DHS. The first right off Hollywood Boulevard, Sunset Boulevard provides another venue for dining, shopping, and street entertainment.

The American Idol Experience ★★★★

APPEAL BY AGE	PRESCHOOL ★★★	GRADE SCHOOL ★★★★	TEENS ★★★★
YOUNG ADULTS ★★★★		OVER 30 ★★★★	SENIORS ★★★

What it is Theme-park version of the popular TV show, with guests doing the singing. **Scope and scale** Major attraction. **Fright potential** Some of the singing would frighten Frankenstein. **Bottleneck rating** 5. **When to go** Anytime. **Special comments** All shows except the finale last 20 minutes; the finale can last around 40. **Authors' rating** Even if you don't watch the show, you'll find someone to cheer for; ★★★★. **Duration of show** About 20–30 minutes. **When to arrive** 25–30 minutes before showtime.

Based on the successful *American Idol* television show, *The American Idol Experience* is your chance to showcase your karaoke abilities to the world. Your path to stardom goes something like this: Potential singers of all ages will select a song and audition in front of a live judge. Most singers will receive a "thanks for auditioning" message from the judge, but a handful will be selected to perform in the attraction's next stage show, held several times per day. During the show, contestants repeat their songs in front of a live audience of theme-park guests. As with American Idol, three judges (Disney cast members here) provide feedback. Don't worry that your operatic rendition of "Achy Breaky Heart" will meet with critical disdain. For the most part, the Disney panel uses humor to tell you not to quit your day job. Audience members vote to decide the winner. During the last show of the

Disney's Hollywood Studios

Streets of America

Echo Lake

1. *The American Idol Experience*
2. *Disney Junior— Live on Stage!*
3. *Fantasmic!*
4. Food and shopping
5. *The Great Movie Ride*
6. Guest Relations
7. *Honey, I Shrunk the Kids Movie Set Adventure*
8. *Indiana Jones Epic Stunt Spectacular!*
9. *Jim Henson's Muppet-Vision 3-D*
10. *Lights, Motors, Action! Extreme Stunt Show*
11. *The Magic of Disney Animation*
12. *Rock 'n' Roller Coaster*
13. *Sounds Dangerous with Drew Carey*
14. *Star Tours—The Adventures Continue/ Jedi Training Academy*
15. *Studio Backlot Tour*
16. *Theater of the Stars/Beauty and the Beast—Live on Stage*
17. *Toy Story Mania!*
18. *The Twilight Zone Tower of Terror*
19. *Voyage of the Little Mermaid*
20. *Walt Disney: One Man's Dream*
21. *Oscar's Super Service*

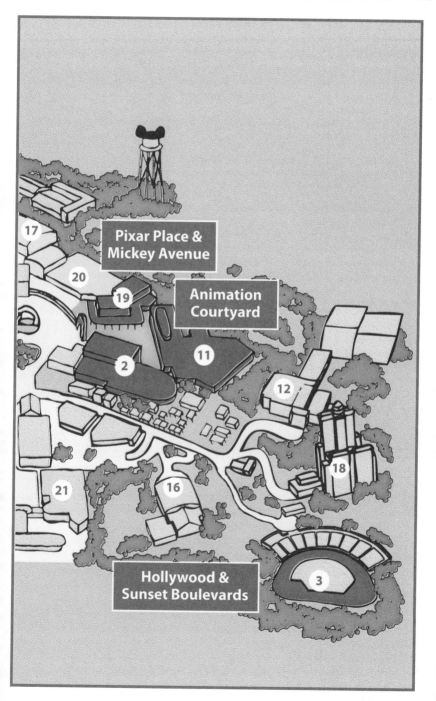

Pixar Place &
Mickey Avenue

Animation
Courtyard

Hollywood &
Sunset Boulevards

night, all of the winners from throughout the day meet for one final competition. The winner of that show receives a front-of-the-line pass for the next season's audition of *American Idol* in their local city. The last show of the day offers (ostensibly) the best talent but is twice the length of the daytime shows. If you don't want to commit to the entire show inside the auditorium, the final show (usually around 7 p.m.) can be viewed from outside on a Jumbotron screen. This is a wise option (as is catching one of the daytime shows) for those who have to leave for a dinner reservation or line up early for *Fantasmic!*

Beauty and the Beast—Live on Stage/ Theater of the Stars ★★★★

APPEAL BY AGE	PRESCHOOL ★★★★	GRADE SCHOOL ★★★★	TEENS ★★★★
YOUNG ADULTS ★★★★		OVER 30 ★★★★	SENIORS ★★★★½

What it is Live musical, featuring Disney characters; performed in an open-air theater. **Scope and scale** Major attraction. **Fright potential** Not frightening in any respect. **Bottleneck rating** 5. **When to go** Anytime; evenings are cooler. **Special comment** Performances are listed in the daily *Times Guide*. **Authors' rating** Excellent; ★★★★. **Duration of show** 25 minutes. **Preshow** Sometimes. **Probable waiting time** 20–30 minutes.

Join Cogsworth, Lumiere, Chip, and Mrs. Potts as they help Belle to break the spell. This 25-minute musical stage show of Disney's *Beauty and the Beast* feature will charm everybody. The show is popular, so show up 30 minutes early to get a seat.

> The decor and the costumes, the actors and the music: Everything is in perfect harmony. Little girls fond of Belle will want to have that ball gown, and young boys will be eager to teach that mean Gaston a lesson!
>
> Liliane

Disney Junior—Live on Stage! ★★★★

APPEAL BY AGE	PRESCHOOL ★★★★½	GRADE SCHOOL ★★★½	TEENS ★½
YOUNG ADULTS ★★		OVER 30 ★★½	SENIORS ★★½

What it is Live show for children. **Scope and scale** Minor attraction. **Fright potential** Not frightening in any respect. **Bottleneck rating** 8. **When to go** Per the daily entertainment schedule. **Special comment** Audience sits on the floor. **Authors' rating** A must for families with preschoolers; ★★★★. **Duration of show** 20 minutes. **Probable waiting time** 30 minutes.

The show features characters from the Disney Channel's *Little Einsteins*, *Mickey Mouse Clubhouse*, *Jake and the Never Land Pirates*, and *Handy Manny*, plus other Disney Channel characters. Reengineered in 2011, *Disney Junior* uses elaborate puppets instead of live characters on stage. A simple plot serves as the platform for singing, dancing, some great puppetry, and a great deal of audience participation. The characters, who ooze love and goodness, rally throngs of tots and preschoolers to sing and dance along with them. All the jumping, squirming, and high-stepping is facilitated by having the audience sit on the floor so that kids can spontaneously erupt into motion when the mood strikes. Even for adults without children, it's a treat to watch the tykes rev up. If you have a younger child in your party, all the better: Just stand back and let the video roll. For preschoolers, *Disney Junior* will be the highlight of their day, as a Thomasville, North Carolina, mom attests:

> [The show] was fantastic! My 3-year-old loved it. The children danced, sang, and had a great time.

Disney Junior is the second iteration of the stage show since 2007. Both versions replaced live characters with puppets, a fact that has left some parents less than enthralled. These comments from a Virginia Beach, Virginia, couple are typical:

> We were disappointed with the newly updated [show]. This did not consist of live characters, and I think the level of excitement from the kids was lower because of this. I mean, the kids enjoyed it, but you would think they would be more excited when it's a show with some of their favorite characters.

The show is headquartered in what was formerly the Soundstage Restaurant, located to the right of the Animation Tour. Show up at least 30 minutes before showtime. Once inside, pick a spot on the floor and take a breather until the performance begins.

The Great Movie Ride ★★★½

| APPEAL BY AGE | PRESCHOOL ★★★ | GRADE SCHOOL ★★★½ | TEENS ★★★½ |
| YOUNG ADULTS ★★★½ | | OVER 30 ★★★½ | SENIORS ★★★★ |

What it is Movie-history indoor adventure ride. **Scope and scale** Headliner. **Fright potential** Intense in parts, with very realistic special effects and some visually intimidating sights. **Bottleneck rating** 8. **When to go** Before 11 a.m. or after 4:30 p.m. **Special comment** Elaborate, with several surprises. **Authors' rating** Unique; ★★★½. **Duration of ride** About 19 minutes. **Average wait in line per 100 people ahead of you** 2 minutes. **Assumes** All trains operating. **Loading speed** Fast.

 Inside the re-creation of Hollywood's Chinese Theater awaits a trip down memory lane. From *Casablanca* to *Raiders of the Lost Ark,* classic movies are showcased in this ride through some of the movies' most memorable sets. Young movie buffs might be flipped out along the way (*Alien* is one of the movies represented), but the wonderful Munchkins from *The Wizard of Oz* scene will make up for it—the Wicked Witch of the North notwithstanding.

 I've only seen some of these movies, so I like how it's not just a ride, but a hostess who tells you about the movies, like if it's a Western or something. There's the yellow-brick road from *The Wizard of Oz,* and the Munchkins sing "Follow the Yellow Brick Road."

Hannah

Honey, I Shrunk the Kids Movie Set Adventure ★★½

| APPEAL BY AGE | PRESCHOOL ★★★★½ | GRADE SCHOOL ★★★★ | TEENS ★★★ |
| YOUNG ADULTS ★★ | | OVER 30 ★★½ | SENIORS ★★ |

What it is Small but elaborate playground. **Scope and scale** Diversion. **Fright potential** Everything is oversize, but nothing is scary. **Bottleneck rating** 8. **When to go** Before 11 a.m. or after dark. **Special comment** Opens 1 hour later than the rest of the park. **Authors' rating** Great for young children, more of a curiosity for adults; ★★½. **Average wait in line per 100 people ahead of you** 20 minutes.

This elaborate playground appeals particularly to kids age 11 and younger. Tunnels, slides, rope ladders, and a variety of oversize props offer lots of playtime fun. There are a few problems with the attraction, though. The place is too small to accommodate all the children who would like to play, and supervision inside the jam-packed and poorly ventilated playground can be trying. Last but not least, kids play as long as parents allow, so be prepared for this stop to take a big chunk of time out of your touring day. If you visit during the warmer months and want your children to experience the playground, get them in and out before 11 a.m. By late morning, this attraction is way too hot and crowded for anyone to enjoy. A mom from Tolland, Connecticut, found the playground exasperating:

> We let the kids hang out at [Honey, I Shrunk the Kids] because we thought it would be relaxing. NOT! You have three choices here: (1) Let your kids go anywhere and hope that if they try to get out without your permission, someone will stop them. Also hope that someone else will help your kids if they get caught up in the exhibit. (2) Go everywhere with your kids—this takes a lot of stamina and some athleticism. If you care about appearances, this could be a problem because you look pretty stupid coming down those slides. (3) Try to visually keep track of your kids. This is impossible, so you will be either on the edge of or in the middle of an anxiety attack the whole time you are there.

Indiana Jones Epic Stunt Spectacular! ★★★★

APPEAL BY AGE	PRESCHOOL ★★★½	GRADE SCHOOL ★★★★	TEENS ★★★★
YOUNG ADULTS ★★★★		OVER 30 ★★★★	SENIORS ★★★★

What it is Movie-stunt demonstration and action show. **Scope and scale** Headliner. **Fright potential** An intense show with powerful special effects, including explosions. Presented in an educational context that young children generally handle well. **Bottleneck rating** 8. **When to go** First three morning shows or last evening show. **Special comment** Performance times posted on a sign at the entrance to the theater. **Authors' rating** Done on a grand scale; ★★★★. **Duration of show** 30 minutes. **Preshow** Selection of "extras" from audience. **Probable waiting time** None.

Professional stunt men and women demonstrate dangerous stunts with a behind-the-scenes look at how it is done. Most kids handle the show well. The show always needs a few "extras." To be chosen from the audience, arrive early, sit down front, and display unmitigated enthusiasm. Unfortunately "victims" must be 18 years old and up.

Idan

An amazing show with fiery explosions and nonstop action. Did you know that the folks at Disney have a vault filled with sound-effects CDs ranging from gunshots to magical twinkles? When a show is created, they pick and choose from this treasure chest and upload the sounds into their state-of-the-art computerized mixing table.

Huh? What's a magical twinkle sound like? But now that I think about it, I sure remember the noise my innards made after eating about a dozen magical twinkles.

Bob

Liliane

Those were Twinkies, Mr. Tiki-Birdbrain!

Jedi Training Academy ★★★

APPEAL BY AGE	PRESCHOOL ★★★★★	GRADE SCHOOL ★★★★★	TEENS ★★
YOUNG ADULTS ★★★		OVER 30 ★★★★	SENIORS ★★★★

What it is Outdoor stage show. **Scope and scale** Minor attraction. **Fright potential** It does involve battle with Darth Vader, but the good guys always win; children typically love it. **Bottleneck rating** 8. **When to go** First two shows of the day. **Special comment** Volunteers from the audience are chosen to go on stage to fight Darth Vader. **Authors' rating** A treat for young *Star Wars* lovers; ★★★. **Duration of show** About 15 minutes. **When to arrive** 15 minutes before showtime.

Jedi Training Academy is to the left of the Star Tours building entrance, opposite Backlot Express. Young Skywalkers-in-training are selected from the audience to train in the ways of The Force and do battle against Darth Vader. If all this sounds too intense, it's not—Storm Troopers provide comic relief and, just as in the movies, the Jedi always wins. Kids are chosen at random from the audience to appear on stage. Sitting in the front two rows or putting your child on your shoulders may increase his or her chances of being picked.

Jim Henson's Muppet-Vision 3-D ★★★★½

APPEAL BY AGE	PRESCHOOL ★★★★	GRADE SCHOOL ★★★★	TEENS ★★★★
YOUNG ADULTS ★★★★		OVER 30 ★★★★	SENIORS ★★★★

What it is 3-D movie starring the Muppets. **Scope and scale** Major attraction. **Fright potential** Intense and loud but not frightening. **Bottleneck rating** 8. **When to go** Before 11 a.m. or after 3 p.m. **Authors' rating** Uproarious; not to be missed; ★★★★½. **Duration of show** 17 minutes. **Preshow** Muppets on television. **Probable waiting time** 12 minutes.

Thumbs Up for the Whole Family

Kermit, Miss Piggy, and the rest of the gang will lift your spirits as they unleash their hilarious mayhem. Because adults tend to associate Muppet characters with the children's show *Sesame Street,* many bypass this attraction. Big mistake. *Muppet-Vision 3-D* operates on several planes, and there's as much here for oldsters as for youngsters. The presentation is intense and sometimes loud, but most preschoolers handle it well. If your child is a little scared, encourage him to watch without the 3-D glasses at first.

Lights, Motors, Action! Extreme Stunt Show ★★★½

APPEAL BY AGE	PRESCHOOL ★★★½	GRADE SCHOOL ★★★★½	TEENS ★★★★½
YOUNG ADULTS ★★★★		OVER 30 ★★★★	SENIORS ★★★★

What it is Auto stunt show. **Scope and scale** Headliner. **Fright potential** Loud with explosions but not scary. **Bottleneck rating** 5. **When to go** First show of the day or after 4 p.m. **Authors' rating** Good stunt work, slow pace; ★★★½. **Duration of show** 33 minutes. **Preshow** Selection of audience "volunteers." **When to arrive** 25–30 minutes before showtime.

Loud

This show features cars and motorcycles in a blur of chases, crashes, jumps, and explosions. The secrets behind the special effects are explained after each stunt sequence. The show runs about 30 minutes, and small children may become restless. Teens, however, will be gobsmacked.

The show left me speechless. This is one of the most amazing, unbelievable shows of all. You won't believe your eyes.

Maybe it's an age thing, but I'm less impressed than Idan. The stunts are super, but there's too much dead time and redundancy in this show.

Idan

Bob

The Magic of Disney Animation ★★½

APPEAL BY AGE	PRESCHOOL ★★★	GRADE SCHOOL ★★★½	TEENS ★★★½
YOUNG ADULTS ★★★½		OVER 30 ★★★½	SENIORS ★★★½

What it is Overview of Disney Animation process with limited hands-on demonstrations. **Scope and scale** Minor attraction. **Fright potential** Not frightening in any respect. **Bottleneck rating** 7. **When to go** Before 11 a.m. or after 5 p.m. **Special comment** Opens 1 hour later than the rest of the park. **Authors' rating** Not as good as previous renditions; ★★½. **Duration of presentation** 20 minutes. **Preshow** Gallery of animation art in waiting area. **Average wait in line per 100 people ahead of you** 7 minutes.

The consolidation of Disney Animation at the Burbank, California, studio has left this attraction without a story to tell. A shadow of its former self, the attraction doesn't warrant waiting in line. Guests learn very little about animation. The only interesting part, especially for children, is Animation Academy, an optional stop after the presentation. Here, kids and grown-ups alike can draw their own cartoon with the help of an animator. (Space is limited and on a first-come, first-serve basis.) The compelling presentation provides a good idea of how difficult hand-drawn animation is. Children who need more time or assistance with their drawing may become frustrated.

Movie Promo Soundstage

Disney uses this soundstage to promote its latest films. Disney's biggest effort went into building the set's doors in the shape of the wardrobe described in *The Chronicles of Narnia*. To call this anemic offering an attraction would be a stretch. If you are a C. S. Lewis fan, see the attraction; it has some behind-the-scenes footage and concept art from the films, as well as props and costumes. Otherwise, skip it.

Rock 'n' Roller Coaster (Fastpass) ★★★★

APPEAL BY AGE	PRESCHOOL ★	GRADE SCHOOL ★★★★½	TEENS ★★★★★
YOUNG ADULTS ★★★★★		OVER 30 ★★★★★	SENIORS ★★★

What it is Rock music–themed roller coaster. **Scope and scale** Headliner. **Fright potential** Extremely intense for all ages; the ride is one of Disney's wildest. **Bottleneck rating** 10. **When to go** Before 10 a.m., in the hour before closing, or use Fastpass. **Special comments** Must be 48" tall to ride; children younger than age 7 must ride with an adult. Switching-off option provided (see page 242). **Authors' rating** Disney's wildest American coaster; not to be missed; ★★★★. **Duration**

of ride Almost 1½ minutes. **Average wait in line per 100 people ahead of you** 2½ minutes. **Assumes** All trains operating. **Loading speed** Moderate–fast.

Dark Lose Things Rough Queasy Scary

Aerosmith once did a tour called Route of All Evil, and the notorious ride at the Studios will make good on fans' expectations. Loops, corkscrews, and drops that make Space Mountain seem like the Jungle Cruise is what to expect and what is delivered—pronto. You will be launched from 0 to 57 miles per hour in less than 3 seconds, and by the time you enter the first loop, you'll be pulling five g's. By comparison, that is two more g's than astronauts experienced at liftoff on a space shuttle.

Aerosmith describes this ride best in one of their songs: "Living on the Edge."

Liliane

Sounds Dangerous with Drew Carey ★★★ (open seasonally)

APPEAL BY AGE	PRESCHOOL ★½	GRADE SCHOOL ★★	TEENS ★★★
YOUNG ADULTS ★★		OVER 30 ★★	SENIORS ★★

What it is Show demonstrating sound effects. **Scope and scale** Minor attraction. **Fright potential** Sounds in darkened theater frighten some preschoolers. **Bottleneck rating** 6. **When to go** Before 11 a.m. or after 4 p.m. **Authors' rating** Funny and informative; ★★★. **Duration of show** 12 minutes. **Preshow** Video introduction to sound effects. **Probable waiting time** 15–30 minutes.

Dark

Put on your headphones, turn off the lights, and join Drew Carey in a hilarious presentation about sound effects. The show is not geared toward preschoolers. The theater is completely dark during much of the presentation, and the sound effects are very realistic and not a little disconcerting.

Star Tours: The Adventures Continue (Fastpass) ★★★★

APPEAL BY AGE	PRESCHOOL ★★★★	GRADE SCHOOL ★★★★	TEENS ★★★★
YOUNG ADULTS ★★★★		OVER 30 ★★★★	SENIORS ★★★★

What it is Indoor space flight–simulation ride. **Scope and scale** Headliner. **Fright potential** Extremely intense visually for all ages; too intense for children under age 8. Likely to cause motion sickness. Switching-off option provided (see page 242). **Bottleneck rating** 8. **When to go** First 90 minutes after opening, or use Fastpass. **Special comments** Expectant mothers and anyone prone to motion sickness are advised against riding. Must be 40" tall to ride. **Authors' rating** Not to be missed; ★★★★. **Duration of ride** About 7 minutes. **Average wait in line per 100 people ahead of you** 5 minutes. **Assumes** All simulators operating. **Loading speed** Moderate–fast.

Rough Queasy Scary

Based on the *Star Wars* movie series, the new ride, overhauled in 2011 and based on the pod racing scene from *Star Wars Episode 1: The Phantom Menace*, uses 3-D special effects and interactive elements. The ride has lots of dips, turns, twists, and climbs as your vehicle goes through an intergalactic version of the chariot race in *Ben-Hur*. Characters

A PEEK BEHIND THE SCENES WITH JIM HILL

SOUNDS LIKE A TOUGH DECISION As with all *Star Wars*–related stories, this one has a good side—in this case, what the Imagineers want to do—and a dark side—what Disney's accountants would prefer the Imagineers do. What WDI would like to do with the *Sounds Dangerous* show building is gut its interior to make it the new indoor home of the popular *Jedi Training Academy* show. What the pencil pushers want is for all of *Sounds'* audio equipment to be left in place so that the building can house a new audio-based show built around the *Star Wars: The Clone Wars* animated series. Of course, only one of these show concepts can ultimately be realized.

from the prequel films released 1999–2005 were included in the makeover. The ride has more than 50 combinations of scenes!

Disney, I am watching you. I am still demanding that you put *Star Wars* characters back on the streets of DHS now!

Oh, no! We're caught in a tractor beam!

Idan

Liliane

Star Wars weekends are a must for any and all *Star Wars* fans. Shame on Disney for keeping Darth Vader away from his fans. While he appears in *Jedi Training Academy*, he is no longer part of the parade.

Idan

Movie Tip

Every year (usually mid-May to mid-June) Walt Disney World hosts four Star Wars weekends. Celebrities from the saga and fans converge at the park in celebration of George Lucas's epic series. Even Mickey turns into a Jedi and joins Ewoks, Jawas, and Wookies for a ride to a galaxy far, far away.

Streets of America ★★★

APPEAL BY AGE	PRESCHOOL ★★½	GRADE SCHOOL ★★★	TEENS ★★★
YOUNG ADULTS ★★★		OVER 30 ★★★½	SENIORS ★★★½

What it is Walk-through backlot movie set. **Scope and scale** Diversion. **Fright potential** Not frightening in any respect. **Bottleneck rating** 1. **When to go** Anytime. **Authors' rating** Interesting, with great detail; ★★★. **Probable waiting time** None.

There is never a wait to enjoy the Streets of America; save your visit here until you have seen those attractions that develop long lines. During the Christmas season, Streets of America are decorated with millions of Christmas lights and serve as a backdrop for the Osborne Family Spectacle of Lights.

Studio Backlot Tour ★★★★

APPEAL BY AGE	PRESCHOOL ★★★	GRADE SCHOOL ★★★½	TEENS ★★★½
YOUNG ADULTS ★★★		OVER 30 ★★★½	SENIORS ★★★½

What it is Combination tram and walking tour of modern film and video production. **Scope and scale** Headliner. **Fright potential** Sedate and nonintimidating except for Catastrophe Canyon, where an earthquake and flash flood are simulated. Prepare

A PEEK BEHIND THE SCENES WITH JIM HILL

SO LONG, BACKLOT; HELLO, BLACKTOP If you're a devotee of the Studio Backlot Tour, you might want to get in a few extra trips through this 35-minute guided walk and tram ride the next time you're in the park. The Imagineers have penciled in this corner of the Studios as a possible location for the WDW version of Radiator Springs Racers, the centerpiece attraction of Cars Land, the new Pixar-themed area that's opening at Disney California Adventure in 2012. Given that Cars Land is in the American Southwest, there's a very good chance that Catastrophe Canyon will survive this radical retheming in some form. But as for the rest of DHS's Studio Backlot? It's most likely going bye-bye.

younger children for this part of the tour. **Bottleneck rating** 6. **When to go** Anytime. **Special comment** Use the restroom before getting in line. **Authors' rating** Educational and fun; not to be missed; ★★★★. **Duration of tour** About 35 minutes. **Preshow** A video before the special effects segment and another video in the tram boarding area. **Probable waiting time** Usually less than 10 minutes.

About two-thirds of Disney's Hollywood Studios was once a film and television facility. The tour is an absolute must. Special effects are explained with demonstrations of rain and a naval battle. Next, visitors board a tram that takes them through wardrobe and craft shops, where costumes, sets, and props are designed. The tour continues through the backlot, where western canyons exist side by side with New York City brownstones. The tour's highlight is Catastrophe Canyon, an elaborate special-effects movie set where a thunderstorm, earthquake, oil-field fire, and a flash flood are simulated. Prepare young children for Catastrophe Canyon, as the rattling earthquake and the sudden flood shake the tram, and yes, if you are sitting on the left side facing the canyon, you will get wet.

> I took the tour first at age 3 and was very scared. Now, of course, Catastrophe Canyon is my favorite part of the ride. I also love to see the costumes and props and wish I could pack all of it up to take home with me.

Idan

Toy Story Mania! (Fastpass) ★★★★½

APPEAL BY AGE	PRESCHOOL ★★★★★	GRADE SCHOOL ★★★★★	TEENS ★★★★★
YOUNG ADULTS ★★★★★		OVER 30 ★★★★★	SENIORS ★★★★½

What it is 3-D ride through indoor shooting gallery. **Scope and scale** Headliner. **Fright potential** Not frightening in any respect. **Bottleneck rating** 10. **When to go** Before 10:30 a.m., after 6 p.m., or use Fastpass (if available). **Authors' rating** ★★★★½. **Duration of ride** About 6½ minutes. **Average wait in line per 100 people ahead of you** 4½ minutes. **Loading Speed** Fast.

This is an interactive shooting gallery much like Buzz Lightyear's Space Ranger Spin, but in Toy Story Mania! your vehicle passes through a totally virtual midway, with booths offering such games as the ring toss and ball throw. You use a cannon on your ride vehicle to play as you move along from booth to booth. The pull-string cannon takes advantage of computer-graphic image technology to toss rings, shoot balls, and even throw eggs and pies. Each game booth is manned by a *Toy Story* character who is right beside you in 3-D glory cheering you on. In addition to 3-D imagery, you experience vehicle motion, wind, and water spray. The ride begins with a training round to familiarize you with the nature of the games and then continues through a number of games that count for score, in which you compete against your riding mate. The technology has the ability to self-adjust the level of difficulty, and there are plenty of easy targets for small children to reach. Tip: Let the pull-string retract all the way back into the cannon before pulling it again.

Toy Story Mania! is the hottest ticket in the park and stays packed all day. Ride first thing after the park opens or use Fastpass. Regarding the latter, pick up your Fastpasses before 11 a.m. or they may be exhausted for the day. Following are reports from readers. First from a Cold Spring, New York, mom:

> There was a 20-minute wait just for Fastpasses as soon as the park opened, and by 11 [a.m.] Fastpasses were gone for the day. Thanks to the DIS forums I was aware of how popular the ride was though, so I got Fastpasses for it first, then followed the touring plan, and everything fell into place nicely.

A Nashville, Tennessee, mom shared this:

> Toy Story Mania! was swamped by the time we got to it, still fairly early in the day. We had to resort to getting some of the last Fastpasses, and it elongated our day to wait until our [return] time came up. But, oh my gosh, what fun! It was worth the wait!

An Ontario, Canada, mom observed :

> By 10 a.m. the line was 50 minutes long and we got Fastpasses for 2 in the afternoon. At 2 p.m. the line was 80 minutes and there were no more Fastpasses left.

From an Evansville, Indiana, mom:

> We immediately went to Toy Story Mania! and found a HUGE line for the ride. We figured we'd be smart and get a Fastpass. Turns out the HUGE line WAS the Fastpass line! The FP return time was already at 12:45. Unfortunately we had to skip this ride due to the long wait.

Toy Story Mania! has become the biggest bottleneck in Walt Disney World, surpassing even Test Track at Epcot. The only way to get aboard without a horrendous wait is to be one of the first through the turnstiles when the park opens and zoom to the attraction. Another alternative is to obtain Fastpasses for Toy Story Mania! as soon as the park opens, and then backtrack to ride the Rock 'n' Roller Coaster and Tower of Terror. Expect long queues at the Fastpass kiosks. If you decide to get Fastpasses, spare your family the extra legwork and dispatch the fittest member to get Fastpasses for all while you get in line to ride Tower of Terror or Rock 'n' Roller Coaster. If you have a cell phone, text your location in line to the brave warrior getting the Fastpasses and reunite to ride together.

The Twilight Zone Tower of Terror (Fastpass) ★★★★★

| APPEAL BY AGE | PRESCHOOL ★★½ | GRADE SCHOOL ★★★★ | TEENS ★★★★★ |
| YOUNG ADULTS ★★★★★ | | OVER 30 ★★★★★ | SENIORS ★★★★ |

What it is Sci-fi-theme indoor thrill ride. **Scope and scale** Super-headliner. **Fright potential** Visually intimidating to young children; contains intense and realistic special effects. The plummeting elevator at the ride's end frightens many adults. Switching-off option provided (see page 242). **Bottleneck rating** 10. **When to go** Before 9:30 a.m., after 6 p.m., or use Fastpass. **Special comment** Must be 40" tall to ride. **Authors' rating** Walt Disney World's best attraction; not to be missed; ★★★★★. **Duration of ride** About 4 minutes plus preshow. **Average wait in line per 100 people ahead of you** 4 minutes. **Assumes** All elevators operating. **Loading speed** Moderate.

Dark

Rough

Scary

And suddenly the cable went *snap*. If riding a capricious elevator in a haunted hotel sounds like fun to you, this is your ride. Erratic yet thrilling, the Tower of Terror is an experience to savor. The Tower has great potential for terrifying young children and rattling more mature visitors. Random ride-and-drop sequences make the attraction wilder and keep you guessing about when, how far, and how many times the elevator drops. We suggest that you use teenagers in your party as experimental probes. If they report back that they really, really liked the Tower of Terror, run as fast as you can in the opposite direction. Tower of Terror is one of the hottest tickets in the park. If you're up to it, experience the ride first thing in the morning or use Fastpass.

Hannah

Another ride that gives you surprises. I like it when you go up and think you're going to stay up but end up zooming down. There's a part of the ride where it looks like you're in outer space, and then it turns back into the hotel.

The part where you get up and then suddenly start moving through the floor is cool. I did not see that coming. I consider it a thrill ride for people who don't like thrill rides. You can easily trick someone into going on it.

Shelton

Voyage of the Little Mermaid ★★★★

| APPEAL BY AGE | PRESCHOOL ★★★★ | GRADE SCHOOL ★★★★ | TEENS ★★★ |
| YOUNG ADULTS ★★★½ | | OVER 30 ★★★★ | SENIORS ★★★★ |

What it is Musical stage show featuring characters from the Disney movie *The Little Mermaid*. **Scope and scale** Major attraction. **Fright potential** Ursula the sea witch may frighten preschoolers. **Bottleneck rating** 10. **When to go** Before 9:45 a.m. or just before closing. **Authors' rating** Romantic, lovable, and humorous in the best Disney tradition; not to be missed; ★★★★. **Duration of show** 15 minutes. **Preshow** Taped ramblings about the decor in the preshow holding area. **Probable waiting time** Before 9:30 a.m., 10–30 minutes; after 9:30 a.m., 35–70 minutes.

Thumbs Up for the Whole Family

This most tender and romantic stage show is a winner, appealing to every age. Once inside the theater, the audience is transported into the wonderful underwater world of Ariel and her friends. Very young children might be frightened by Ursula the sea witch (she is actually a puppet standing 12 feet tall).

Because it's well done and located at a busy pedestrian intersection, *Voyage of the Little Mermaid* plays to capacity crowds all day. When the theater doors open, pick a row of seats, and let 6–10 people enter the row ahead of you. The strategy is twofold: to obtain a good seat and be near the exit.

> The scary characters like the eels just show up on the side— they don't come out at you. Ariel's hair is really, really bright red.
>
> **Hannah**

Walt Disney: One Man's Dream ★★★

APPEAL BY AGE	PRESCHOOL ★★	GRADE SCHOOL ★★★	TEENS ★★★½
YOUNG ADULTS ★★★★		OVER 30 ★★★★	SENIORS ★★★★

What it is Tribute to Walt Disney. **Scope and scale** Minor attraction. **Fright potential** Not frightening in any respect. **Bottleneck rating** 2. **When to go** Anytime. **Authors' rating** Excellent! ★★★ and about time. **Duration of presentation** 25 minutes. **Preshow** Disney memorabilia. **Probable waiting time** For film, 10 minutes.

One Man's Dream is a long-overdue tribute to Walt Disney. The attraction consists of an exhibit area showcasing Disney memorabilia, followed by a film documenting Disney's life. Teens and adults, especially those old enough to remember Walt Disney, will enjoy this homage to the man behind the Mouse.

> Hands off! Don't even think of packing this gem off. I pay tribute every time I visit and discover something I had not noticed before.
>
> **Idan**

A PEEK BEHIND THE SCENES WITH JIM HILL

IF EVER, OH EVER A WIZ THERE WAS Get ready to go over the rainbow in 2013, as Disney's Hollywood Studios becomes the home of *Oz: The Great and Powerful*. This prequel to *The Wizard of Oz*—which will be directed by Sam Raimi, who helmed the *Spider-Man* trilogy—will be celebrated at the Studios in a very big way. Current plans call for a daily Oz-themed parade, which will feature appearances by many of the beloved characters from the L. Frank Baum books. There's even talk of *Walt Disney: One Man's Dream* being replaced by a exhibit that would celebrate some of the best-known Oz movies.

LIVE ENTERTAINMENT *at* DISNEY'S HOLLYWOOD STUDIOS

WHEN THE STUDIOS OPENED, live entertainment, parades, and special events weren't as fully developed or impressive as those at the Magic Kingdom or Epcot. With the introduction of an afternoon parade and elaborate shows at **Theater of the Stars,** the Studios joined the big leagues. In 1998 DHS launched a new edition of *Fantasmic!* (see page 356), a water, fireworks, and laser show that draws rave reviews. Staged in its own specially designed 10,000-person amphitheater, *Fantasmic!* makes the Studios the park of choice for spectacular nighttime entertainment. WDW live-entertainment guru Steve Soares usually posts the DHS performance schedule about a week in advance at **wdwent.com.**

AFTERNOON PARADE Staged once a day, the parade begins near the park's entrance, continues down Hollywood Boulevard, and circles in front of the giant hat. From there, it passes in front of *Sounds Dangerous* and ends by Star Tours. An alternate route begins at the far end of Sunset Boulevard and turns right onto Hollywood Boulevard.

Pixar Pals Countdown to Fun features characters from the Pixar films *Up!* and *Ratatouille,* which have never appeared in a Disney parade before. The parade replaces the popular Block Party Bash and lacks originality. It is really not that different from its predecessor except that the parade is very short. Many of the floats are the same; the rest are simply repainted. Cast members' costumes and props are also unchanged.

DISNEY CHANNEL ROCKS! A replacement for the former High School Musical Pep Rally, this live show is Disney's attempt to bring their Disney Channel original movies and sitcoms to the parks. Parading to their stage underneath the Sorcerer's Hat, the four singers and dozen dancers put on a mildly entertaining "rock concert" for approximately 15 minutes and perform hit songs promoted by the channel's programs. Expect the material of this show to change in accordance with the latest Disney Channel fare.

DISNEY CHARACTERS Find characters in front of the Sorcerer's Hat, in front of the Magic of Disney Animation building, the Cars Meet and Greet (near Mama Melrose's on Streets of America), in the Animation Courtyard, along Pixar Place, and in parades. Characters from *Monsters, Inc.* can sometimes be found near the Backlot Tour. Times and locations for character appearances are listed in the *Times Guide.*

STREET ENTERTAINMENT With the possible exception of Epcot's World Showcase Players, the Studios has the best collection of roving street performers in all of Walt Disney World. Appearing primarily on Hollywood and Sunset boulevards, the cast of characters includes Hollywood stars and wannabes, their agents, film directors, and gossip columnists, as well as various police officers and Hollywood public-works crews.

The performers are not shy about asking you to join in their skits, and you may be asked anything from explaining why you came to "Hollywood" all the way to reciting a couple of lines in one of the directors' new films. If you're looking for a spot to rest and a bit of entertainment, grab a drink and seek out these performers.

Fantasmic! ★★★★★

APPEAL BY AGE	PRESCHOOL ★★★★	GRADE SCHOOL ★★★★½	TEENS ★★★★½
YOUNG ADULTS ★★★★★		OVER 30 ★★★★½	SENIORS ★★★★½

What it is Mixed-media nighttime spectacular. **Scope and scale** Super-headliner. **Fright potential** Loud and intense with fireworks and some scary villains, but most young children like it. **Bottleneck rating** 9. **When to go** Only staged in the evening. **Special comment** Disney's best nighttime event. **Authors' rating** Not to be missed; ★★★★. **Duration of show** 25 minutes. **Probable waiting time** 50–90 minutes for a seat; 35–40 minutes for standing room.

  Until recently, *Fantasmic!* was staged nightly and always played to a full house. Presumably as a cost-containment measure, Disney has cut performances to 2 evenings a week, or 3 nights a week during busier times. As you might imagine, trying to cram 7 nights of capacity crowds into 2 nights is not working very well, as a reader from Sandwich, Illinois, reports:

Loud   Scary

> *The reduction in* Fantasmic! *shows per week is ridiculous to me. The Studios is an absolute ghost town on nights it doesn't show and packed to capacity on nights when it does! There has to be a happy medium.*

Nonetheless, *Fantasmic!* is far and away the most unique outdoor spectacle ever attempted in any theme park and a must-see for the whole family. Starring Mickey Mouse in his role as the sorcerer's apprentice from *Fantasia,* the production uses lasers, images projected on a shroud of mist, dazzling fireworks, lightning effects, and powerful music. *Fantasmic!* has the potential to frighten young children. Prepare your children for the show, and make sure that they know that in addition to all the favorite Disney characters, the maleficent dragon and the evil Jafar will make appearances. To give you an idea, just picture this: The evil Jafar turns into a cobra 100 feet long and 16 feet high. Rest assured, however, that during the final parade your kids will cheer on Cinderella and Prince Charming, Belle, Snow White, Ariel and Prince Eric, Jasmine and Aladdin, Donald Duck, Minnie, and Mickey. You can alleviate the fright factor somewhat by sitting back a bit. Also, if you are seated in the first 12 rows, you will get sprayed with water at times.

The theater is huge, but so is the popularity of the show. If there are two performances, the second show will almost always be less crowded. If you attend the first (or only) scheduled performance, show up at least 60–80 minutes in advance. Plan to use that time for a picnic. Bring food and drinks and something to entertain the younger kids. If you forget to bring munchies, not to worry; there are food concessions in the theater. As a cost-cutting measure, since 2009 Disney has staged *Fantasmic!* on only 2 nights a week. This makes it almost impossible to see the show without lining up 90 minutes to 2 hours in advance. Yes, *Fantasmic!* is a great show, but is it worth a 2-hour wait?

Unless you buy a *Fantasmic!* dinner package, you will not have assigned seats, so arrive early for best choice. Try to sit in the middle three or four sections, a bit off-center. Finally, understand that you are out of luck if *Fantasmic!* is cancelled due to weather or other circumstances.

Fantasmic! Dinner Packages

Three restaurants offer a ticket voucher for the members of your dining party to enter *Fantasmic!* via a special entrance and sit in a reserved section of seats. The package consists of a buffet at Hollywood & Vine, or a fixed-price dinner at Mama Melrose's Ristorante Italiano or The Hollywood Brown Derby (full-service restaurants). You can call ☎ 407-WDW-DINE up to 180 days in advance and request the *Fantasmic!* Dinner Package. This is a real reservation and must be guaranteed by a credit card at the time of booking. There's a 48-hour cancellation policy.

Included in the package are fixed-price menus for all three restaurants as follows; respective prices are for adults and kids ages 3–9: *Hollywood & Vine:* lunch, $26–$35/$15–$20, dinner, $30–$40/$15–$19; *The Hollywood Brown Derby:* lunch and dinner, $50–$57/$13–$19; *Mama Melrose's:* lunch and dinner, $35–$39/$13–$19. Nonalcoholic drinks and tax are included; park admission and gratuity are not. Please note that prices fluctuate according to season, so call ☎ 407-WDW-DINE if you want to know exactly what

FAVORITE EATS AT DISNEY'S HOLLYWOOD STUDIOS

LAND	SERVICE LOCATION	FOOD ITEM

ECHO LAKE

ABC Commissary | Chicken nuggets with fruit or veggies
Backlot Express | Great burgers & fixin's

STREETS OF AMERICA

Pizza Planet | THE place for pizza
Sci-Fi Dine-In Theater* | It's not about the food (dismal) but about eating in a vintage convertible car watching old sci-fi movie previews. Teens love it! Great place to cool off.

SUNSET BOULEVARD

Studio Catering Co. | Good place for a break while your kids check out Honey, I Shrunk the Kids playground

* table service only

the dinner charge will be for a particular date.

Allow yourselves a minimum of 2 hours to eat. You will receive the vouchers (tickets for the show) at the restaurants. After dinner, report to the *Fantasmic!* sign on Hollywood Boulevard next to Oscar's filling station (just inside the front entrance to the park) no later than 35 minutes prior to showtime. A cast member will collect the vouchers and escort you to the reserved section. If *Fantasmic!* is cancelled for any reason, such as weather, technical problems, and the like, you'll not receive a refund or even a voucher for another performance.

EXIT STRATEGIES

EXITING THE STUDIOS at the end of the day following *Fantasmic!* is not nearly as difficult as leaving Epcot after *IllumiNations*. We recommend that you take it easy and make your way out of the park after the first wave of guests has departed. Pick a spot inside the park and give instructions that nobody is to go through the turnstiles before the group is reunited. Most important, latch on to your kids.

DISNEY'S HOLLYWOOD STUDIOS TOURING PLANS

OUR STEP-BY-STEP TOURING PLANS ARE FIELD-TESTED, independently verified itineraries that will keep you moving counter to the crowd flow and allow you to see as much as possible in a single day with a minimum of time wasted in line.

The different touring plans are described below. The descriptions will tell you for whom (for example, tweens, parents with preschoolers, and so on) or for what situation (such as sleeping late) the plans are designed. The actual touring plans are located on pages 463–466. Each plan includes a numbered map of the park in question to help you find your way around. Clip the plan of your choice out of the book by cutting along the line indicated, and take it with you to the park.

You can take in all the attractions at the Disney's Hollywood Studios in 1 day, even when traveling with young children. If you are not interested in an attraction listed on the touring plan, just skip that attraction and proceed to the next step. Likewise, should you encounter a very long line at an attraction, skip it. Use of Fastpass is factored into the touring plans.

DISNEY'S HOLLYWOOD STUDIOS 1-DAY TOURING PLAN FOR PARENTS WITH SMALL CHILDREN This plan is designed for parents of children ages 3–8 who wish to see the very best age-appropriate attractions and shows in Disney's Hollywood Studios. Every attraction has a rating of at least three stars (out of five) from preschool and grade-school children surveyed by the *Unofficial Guide*. The plan includes a midday break inside the park so families can rest, relax, and regroup. The plan keeps walking and backtracking to a minimum, with no crisscrossing of the park.

DISNEY'S HOLLYWOOD STUDIOS 1-DAY SLEEPYHEAD TOURING PLAN FOR PARENTS WITH SMALL CHILDREN A relaxed plan that allows families with small children to sleep late and still see the highlights of Disney's Hollywood Studios. The plan begins around 11 a.m., sets aside ample time for lunch, and includes the very best child-friendly attractions and shows in the park. Special advice is provided for touring the park with small children. The plan points out where Fastpass can best be used.

DISNEY'S HOLLYWOOD STUDIOS 1-DAY TOURING PLAN FOR TWEENS AND THEIR PARENTS A 1-day plan for parents with children ages 8–12. It includes every attraction rated three stars and higher by this age group and sets aside ample time for lunch and dinner.

DISNEY'S HOLLYWOOD STUDIOS 1-DAY HAPPY FAMILY TOURING PLAN A 1-day itinerary for multigenerational families, this plan allows teens and older children to experience the Studios' thrill rides while parents and small children visit more age-appropriate attractions. The family stays together most of the day, including lunch and dinner, and each attraction in the plan is rated three stars or higher.

BEFORE YOU GO

1. Call ☎ 407-824-4321 to verify the park's hours.
2. Buy your admission before arriving.
3. Make lunch and dinner advance reservations or reserve the *Fantasmic!* dinner package (if desired) before you arrive by calling ☎ 407-WDW-DINE.
4. The schedule of live entertainment changes from month to month and even from day to day. Review the daily *Times Guide* handout to get a fairly clear picture of your options.

DISNEY'S HOLLYWOOD STUDIOS TRIVIA QUIZ

By Lou Mongello

1. IN *MUPPET-VISION* 3-D, SAM THE EAGLE STATES THAT THE FINALE WILL BE "A SALUTE TO ALL NATIONS BUT MOSTLY . . . ":

a. America

b. Muppets

c. Florida

d. Walt Disney World

2. WHAT IS THE NAME OF THE HOTEL FEATURING THE TWILIGHT ZONE TOWER OF TERROR?

a. Hollywood Tower Hotel

b. Hollywood Hills Hotel

c. Hightower Hotel

d. The Sunset Hotel

3. AT THE END OF *MUPPET-VISION* 3-D, WHAT "CRASHES" THROUGH THE SCREEN?

a. A monorail

b. An animal

c. A fire engine

d. Dumbo

4. WHAT COLOR ARE YOUR 3-D GLASSES IN TOY STORY MANIA!?

a. Yellow

b. Black

c. Blue

d. Purple

5. WHAT BAND IS FEATURED IN ROCK 'N' ROLLER COASTER?

a. Jonas Brothers

b. Aerosmith

c. U2

d. Guns 'n Roses

6. THE MR. POTATO HEAD FIGURE IN THE QUEUE FOR TOY STORY MANIA! IS ABLE TO:

a. Remove his ear

b. Tip his hat

c. Walk up stairs

d. Moonwalk

7. HOW MANY PEOPLE DISAPPEAR IN THE ELEVATOR OF THE TWILIGHT ZONE TOWER OF TERROR?

a. 0

b. 1

c. 5

d. 7

8. MANY WALT DISNEY WORLD ATTRACTIONS ARE BASED ON MOVIES, BUT WHICH OF THESE ATTRACTIONS HAD A MOVIE MADE ABOUT IT AFTER IT OPENED AT DISNEY'S HOLLYWOOD STUDIOS?

a. *Muppet-Vision 3-D*

b. The Twilight Zone Tower Of Terror

c. The Great Movie Ride

d. *Sounds Dangerous*

9. THE GIANT REPLICA OF A *STAR WARS* VEHICLE OUTSIDE THE STAR TOURS ATTRACTION IS:

a. A landspeeder

b. A Star Destroyer

c. An AT-AT walker

d. A probe droid

10. WHAT IS THE NAME OF THE DINOSAUR THAT IS ALSO AN ICE CREAM STAND?

a. Deeno

b. Gertie

c. Diner-Saur

d. Hector

11. WHAT ANIMALS MAKE UP THE ORCHESTRA IN *MUPPET-VISION* 3-D?

a. Penguins

b. Rats

c. Frogs

d. Bunnies

Answers can be found on page 426.

UNIVERSAL ORLANDO
and SEAWORLD

UNIVERSAL ORLANDO

UNIVERSAL ORLANDO HAS TRANSFORMED into a complete desti-nation resort, with two theme parks, three hotels, and a shopping, dining, and entertainment complex. The second theme park, Islands of Adventure, opened in 1999 with five themed areas.

A system of roads and two multistory parking facilities are con-nected by moving sidewalks to **CityWalk,** a shopping, dining, and nighttime-entertainment complex that also serves as a gateway to the **Universal Studios Florida** and **Islands of Adventure** theme parks.

LODGING AT UNIVERSAL ORLANDO

UNIVERSAL CURRENTLY HAS THREE OPERATING resort hotels. The 750-room **Portofino Bay Hotel** is a gorgeous property set on an artificial bay with an Italian coastal town theme. The 650-room **Hard Rock Hotel** is an ultracool Hotel California replica, with slick contemporary design and a hip, friendly attitude. The 1,000-room, Polynesian-themed **Loews Royal Pacific Resort** is sumptuously deco-rated and richly appointed. All three are excellent hotels; the Por-tofino and the Hard Rock are on the pricey side, and the Royal Pacific ain't exactly cheap.

ARRIVING AT UNIVERSAL ORLANDO

THE UNIVERSAL ORLANDO COMPLEX can be accessed directly from I-4. Once on site, you will be directed to park in one of two multitiered parking garages. Parking runs $15 for cars and $20 for RVs. Be sure to write down the location of your car before heading for the parks. From the garages, moving sidewalks deliver you to the Universal CityWalk dining, shopping, and entertainment venue described above. From City-Walk, you can access the main entrances of both Universal Studios Florida and Islands of Adventure theme parks.

Universal offers 1-day, 2-day, 3-day, and 4-day passes for one park or two parks, as well as annual passes for both parks.

Passes can be obtained in advance on the phone with your credit card at ☎ 800-711-0080 or **universalorlando.com.** Prices include tax but not applicable fees.

UNIVERSAL ORLANDO ADMISSION	ADULTS	CHILDREN (3–9)
1-day, One-park Pass	$90.53	$84.14
1-day, Two-park Pass	$127.80	$121.41
2-day, Two-park Pass	$166.13	$155.48
2-week, Three-park Pass (includes Wet ' Wild)	$186.36	$170.39

Be sure to check Universal's website for seasonal deals and specials. You can save as much as 25% by buying your tickets in advance on Universal's website. A five-park, 14-day pass called the Orlando Flex Ticket allows unlimited entry to Universal Studios, Islands of Adventure, SeaWorld, Aquatica, and Wet 'n Wild and costs about $293 for adults and $272 for children (ages 3–9). A six-park, 14-day pass called the Orlando Flex Ticket Plus provides unlimited entry to Universal Studios, Islands of Adventure, SeaWorld, Aquatica, Wet 'n Wild, and Busch Gardens for about $336 for adults and $314 for children. The six-park ticket includes a free shuttle to Busch Gardens. At Undercover Tourist, a reputable wholesaler, you can obtain the Flex tickets at substantial savings. Visit **undercovertourist.com.**

The main Universal Orlando information number is ☎ 407-363-8000. Reach Guest Services at ☎ 407-224-4233, or schedule a character lunch at **universalorlando.com**. The numbers for lost and found are ☎ 407-224-4244 (Universal Studios) and 407-224-4245 (Islands of Adventure).

UNIVERSAL EXPRESS

DISNEY'S FASTPASS AND UNIVERSAL EXPRESS were once roughly comparable. They both offered a system whereby a guest could schedule an appointment to experience an attraction later in the day with little or no waiting. The Universal Express program is actually two programs: one for Universal hotel guests, called Universal Express, and one available to everyone for an additional fee, called Universal Express Plus. There is no longer a basic program similar to Disney's Fastpass.

If you're willing to drop the extra cash, you can upgrade your regular ticket to Universal Express Plus, which allows you to use the Express entrance one time only at each designated Universal Express attraction (although we have found that the one-time use policy is loosely enforced, except for major attractions on crowded days). Universal Express Plus is good only for the date of purchase *at one park* (though there's a more expensive two-park option) and can be used only by one person, and for one ride only on each participating attraction. The number of Plus passes is limited each day, and they can sell out. Increase your chances of securing passes by buying them in advance online.

Universal Express Plus prices vary $21–$64, plus tax; they're cheaper in the off-seasons and more expensive during peak seasons and holidays. You can purchase Universal Express Plus online or at the theme park's ticket windows, just outside the front gates. Once in the Universal Studios theme park, Universal Express Plus is available at NickStuff or Sahara Traders. Inside Islands of Adventure, you can buy Universal Express Plus at Jurassic Outfitters, Toon Extra, and the Marvel Alterniverse Store. Universal Express Plus is available on the Internet up to 8 months in advance. You must know what date you plan on using Universal Express Plus because different dates have different prices.

Be aware that neither Hollywood Rip Ride Rockit at Universal Studios nor Harry Potter and the Forbidden Journey at Islands of Adventure are Universal Express attractions. However, Universal hotel guests are eligible to enter the Harry Potter theme area 1 hour before the park opens to the public.

The Universal Express program for Universal resort guests allows guests to bypass the regular line anytime and as often as desired by simply showing their room keys. This perk far surpasses any perk accorded to guests of Disney resorts.

In 2010 Universal initiated an early-entry program in conjunction with its Wizarding World of Harry Potter Exclusive Vacation Package. Purchasers of the package can enter The Wizarding World section of Islands of Adventure theme park 1 hour before the general public. As it stands the vacation package was still available at press time.

IS UNIVERSAL EXPRESS PLUS WORTH IT?

THE ANSWER DEPENDS ON THE SEASON you visit, hours of park operation, and crowd levels. Because The Wizarding World of Harry Potter is new, crowd levels are expected to increase dramatically at Islands of Adventure while remaining steady or declining slightly at Universal Studios. In the Studios, only one attraction, Hollywood Rip Ride Rockit, might be difficult to ride without waiting an unacceptable length of time. However, if you arrive 30 minutes before park opening and use our touring plan (see page 467), you should experience it with a minimal wait. For the Studios, therefore, you shouldn't need Universal Express Plus.

Islands of Adventure is a different story because of the hoopla surrounding Harry Potter and the lack of high-capacity theater shows at IOA to siphon off crowds (one show at IOA compared to six shows at the Studios). Using our touring plan will cut your waiting to a minimum, so our advice is to try it first. The beauty of Universal Express Plus is that you can purchase it in the park if waits for the rides become intolerable.

UNIVERSAL MEAL DEALS

AT UNIVERSAL'S ISLANDS OF ADVENTURE try the character breakfast at Confisco Grille. For $18 for those age 10 and older (age 9 and under pay $12), you can enjoy a buffet breakfast in the presence of Universal characters. A character breakfast is offered each Thursday and Sunday 9 a.m.–10:30 a.m. Character breakfast prices do not include theme-park admission. Call ☎ 407-224-4012 for reservations after purchasing your ticket. Reservations must be made at least 1 day prior to your visit. Tickets are nonrefundable.

ONE-PARK MEAL DEAL With your Universal Meal Deal ticket, enjoy as much food as you would like all day long at participating Meal Deal locations in one park only. Meal includes one entrée and one dessert. Food service ends 30 minutes before theme-park closing time; children under age 9 must eat from a kid's menu. Guests will receive a wristband in exchange for the Meal Deal coupon at the first participating restaurant they visit in the park. Costs (before tax) for adults are $21, $10 for children.

TWO-PARK MEAL DEAL With your Universal Meal Deal ticket, enjoy as much food as you would like all day long at participating Meal Deal locations in both parks. Meal includes one entrée and one dessert. Food service ends 30 minutes before theme-park closing time; children under age 9 must eat from a kid's menu. Guests must order from a limited menu. Guests will receive a wristband in exchange for the Meal Deal coupon at the first participating restaurant they visit that day in either park. Costs for adults are $25 and $12 for children.

1-DAY MEAL DEAL SOUVENIR CUP This ticket entitles you to 1 day of unlimited soft-drink fountain beverages at all participating Meal Deal locations at either Universal Studios Florida OR Islands of Adventure. Cost is $9 for all ages.

CITYWALK MEAL AND MOVIE DEAL This deal includes a ticket to any movie playing at the Universal Cineplex and a meal from a limited menu at participating CityWalk restaurants. The meal includes one entrée and a coffee, tea, or soft drink. This combination costs $21 for all ages. Buy your Meal and Movie Deal tickets at the CityWalk Guest Services ticket window, at all Destination Universal locations, or call a CityWalk sales coordinator at ☎ 407-224-2691. Additional charges apply for IMAX, IMAX 3-D, and 3-D movies.

UNIVERSAL, KIDS, AND SCARY STUFF

ALTHOUGH THERE'S PLENTY for younger children to enjoy at the Universal parks, the majority of their attractions have the potential for wigging out kids less than 8 years of age. At Universal Studios

Florida, forget Hollywood Rip Ride Rockit, Revenge of the Mummy, *TWISTER . . . Ride It Out*, *Disaster!*, JAWS, Men in Black Alien Attack, and *Terminator 2: 3-D*. The Simpsons Ride is not too scary but very intense and rough. At Universal's Islands of Adventure, watch out for The Incredible Hulk Coaster, Doctor Doom's Fearfall, The Amazing Adventures of Spider-Man, the Jurassic Park River Adventure, Harry Potter and the Forbidden Journey, Dragon Challenge, and *Poseidon's Fury*. Popeye & Bluto's Bilge-Rat Barges is wet and wild, but younger children handle it well. Dudley Do-Right's Ripsaw Falls is a toss-up, to be considered only if your kids like water-flume rides. *The Eighth Voyage of Sindbad* stunt show includes some explosions and startling special effects, but once again, children tolerate it well. Nothing else should pose a problem.

TNA IMPACT! AND BLUE MAN GROUP

UNIVERSAL ORLANDO OFFERS theater productions that do not require theme-park admission. At Soundstage 21, guests can sit in on the taping of Spike TV's TNA iMPACT! professional-wrestling program. There is no admission for the rasslin'; a taping calendar and directions to Soundstage 21 can be found at **universalorlando.com/ shows/tna_wrestling.aspx.** The minimum age required for audience members is 14 years.

Universal Studio's Sharp Aquos Theater, near CityWalk, is home to the Blue Man Group. Tickets for shows start at $64 for adults and $25 for children ages 3–9 and can be purchased online or at the Universal box office; tickets purchased at the box office are $10 higher. Upon presenting a valid International Student Identity Card, students can purchase tickets for $30. The show can be accessed from inside or outside the Universal Studios theme park. We recommend seats at least 15 rows back from the stage.

UNIVERSAL STUDIOS FLORIDA

UNIVERSAL STUDIOS FLORIDA OPENED IN JUNE 1990. At that time, it was almost four times the size of Disney's Hollywood Studios (The Studios has since expanded somewhat), with much more of the facility accessible to visitors. Like its sister facility in Hollywood, Universal Studios Florida is spacious, beautifully landscaped, meticulously clean, and delightfully varied in its entertainment. Rides are exciting and innovative and, as with many Disney rides, focus on familiar and/or beloved movie characters or situations.

Universal Studios Florida is laid out in an upside-down-L configuration. Beyond the main entrance, a wide boulevard stretches past several shows and rides to Streets of America. Branching off this pedestrian thoroughfare to the right are five streets that access other areas of the studios and intersect a promenade circling a large lake.

The park is divided into six sections: Production Central, New York, Hollywood, San Francisco–Amity, Woody Woodpecker's Kid-Zone, and World Expo. Where one section begins and another ends is blurry, but no matter. Guests orient themselves by the major rides, sets, and landmarks and refer, for instance, to New York, the water-front, over by E. T., or by Mel's Diner. The area of Universal Studios Florida open to visitors is about the size of Epcot.

The park offers all standard services and amenities, including stroller and wheelchair rentals, lockers, diaper-changing and infant-nursing facilities, car assistance, and foreign-language assistance. Most of the park is accessible to disabled guests, and TDDs are available for the hearing impaired. Almost all services are in the Front Lot, just inside the main entrance.

DISNEY'S HOLLYWOOD STUDIOS *versus* UNIVERSAL STUDIOS FLORIDA

DISNEY'S HOLLYWOOD STUDIOS (DHS) and Universal Studios Florida are direct competitors. Because both are large and expensive and they take at least 1 day to see, some guests must choose one park over the other. In the summer of 1999, Universal launched its second major theme park, Universal's Islands of Adventure, which competes directly with Disney's Magic Kingdom. (Universal Studios Florida theme park, Islands of Adventure theme park, the three Universal hotels, and the CityWalk complex are collectively known as Universal Orlando.)

Half of Disney's Hollywood Studios is off-limits to guests—except by guided tour—while most of Universal Studios Florida is open to exploration.

Both Disney's Hollywood Studios and Universal Studios Florida draw their themes and inspiration from film and television. Both offer movie- and TV-themed rides and shows, some of which are just for fun, while others provide an educational, behind-the-scenes introduction to the cinematic arts.

Unlike Disney's Hollywood Studios, Universal Studios Florida's open area includes the entire back lot, where guests can walk at leisure among movie sets. Universal Studios Florida is about twice as large as the Studios, and because almost all of it is open to the public, the crowding and congestion so familiar at Disney's Hollywood Studios are largely mitigated. Universal Studios has plenty of elbow room.

Both parks include film and television-production studios. Guests are more likely, however, to see a movie, commercial, or television production in progress at Universal Studios than at Disney's

Mickie & Minny travel incognito to Universal Studios.

Hollywood Studios. On most days, production crews will be shooting on the Universal back lot in full view of guests who care to watch.

Attractions are excellent at both parks, though Disney's Hollywood Studios attractions are on average engineered to move people more efficiently. Each park offers stellar attractions that break new ground, transcending in power, originality, and technology any prior standard for theme-park entertainment. Universal offers Revenge of the Mummy, an indoor roller coaster that combines space-age robotics with live effects and pyrotechnics; *Terminator 2: 3-D,* which we consider the most extraordinary theater attraction in any American theme park; and Men in Black Alien Attack, an interactive high-tech ride where guests' actions determine the ending of the story. The Studios features The Twilight Zone Tower of Terror, Disney's best attraction to date in our book; Rock 'n' Roller Coaster, an indoor coaster that's launched like a jet off an aircraft carrier; and *Jim Henson's Muppet-Vision 3-D,* a zany theater attraction.

Amazingly, and to the visitor's advantage, each park offers a completely different product mix, so there is little or no redundancy for a person who visits both. Disney's Hollywood Studios and Universal Studios Florida each provide good exposure to the cinematic arts. Disney's Hollywood Studios over the years has turned several of its better tours into infomercials for Disney films. At Universal, you can still learn about postproduction, soundstages, set creation, and special effects without being bludgeoned by promotional hype.

Finally the muggles completed the long-awaited Wizarding World of Harry Potter at Islands of Adventure, which opened its doors in June 2010. It is crowded, it is packed, and no magic will save you from the long lines unless you stay in one of the three Universal resort hotels, as the Universal Express program allows you to bypass the regular lines any time and as often as you like. Another solution, though pricier and less satisfactory, is to buy a Universal

continued on page 372

Universal Orlando

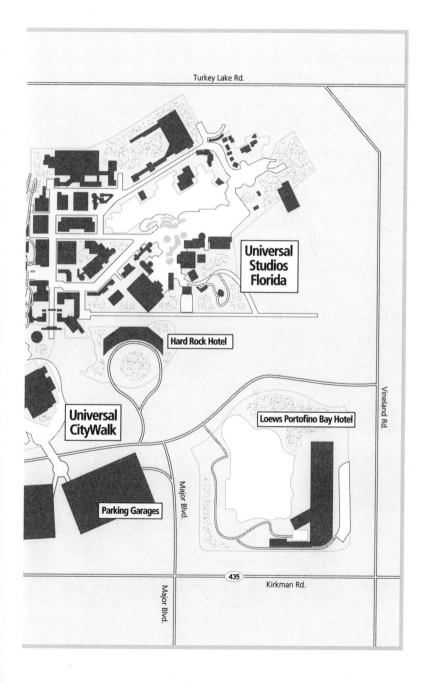

Universal Studios Florida

1. *Animal Actors on Location*
2. *Beetlejuice's Graveyard Revue*
3. *A Day in the Park with Barney*
4. Despicable Me
5. *Disaster!*
6. *E.T. Adventure*
7. *Fear Factor Live* (open seasonally)
8. *Fievel's Playland*
9. *Hollywood Rip Ride Rockit*
10. JAWS
11. *Lucy—A Tribute*
12. Men in Black Alien Attack
13. *Revenge of the Mummy*
14. *Shrek 4-D*
15. The Simpsons Ride

16. *Terminator 2: 3-D*
17. *TWISTER . . . Ride It Out*
18. *Universal 360: A Cinesphere Spectacular* (summer only)
19. *Universal Orlando's Horror Make-Up Show*
20. Woody Woodpecker's Nuthouse Coaster, Curious George Goes to Town

continued from page 367

Express Plus pass, which allows you to bypass the lines, but only once per Universal Express attraction.

We recommend trying one of the studios. If you enjoy one, you'll probably enjoy the other. If you have to choose, consider the following:

1. TOURING TIME If you tour efficiently, it takes about 8–10 hours to see Disney's Hollywood Studios (including a lunch break). Because Universal Studios Florida is larger and contains more rides and shows, touring, including one meal, takes about 9–11 hours.

2. CONVENIENCE If you're lodging along International Drive, I-4's northeast corridor, the Orange Blossom Trail (US 441), or in Orlando, Universal Studios Florida is closer. If you're lodging along US 27 or FL 192 or in Kissimmee or Walt Disney World, Disney's Hollywood Studios is more convenient.

3. ENDURANCE Universal Studios Florida is larger and requires more walking than Disney's Hollywood Studios, but it is also much less congested, so the walking is easier. Both parks offer wheelchairs and disabled access.

4. COST Both parks cost about the same for 1-day admission, food, and incidentals, though Universal admission can be purchased in combo packages that include discounted passes to SeaWorld, Busch Gardens, and/or Wet 'n Wild. When Disney instituted the multiday Magic Your Way admission system in which you pay extra for park-hopping privileges, admissions to the minor parks, and the no-expiration pass option, Universal was quick to follow. However, multiday one-park passes are significantly less at Universal. Park-hopping (or "park to park" in Universal parlance) passes are comparable to Disney. In this category, the one admission where Universal seriously underprices Disney is for 1-day park-hopping passes, which are $25 less at Universal than at Disney. As at Disney, passes expire 14 days after first use.

5. BEST DAYS TO GO In order, Mondays, Sundays, and Saturdays are best to visit Universal Studios Florida. The best day to visit DHS depends on whether *Fantasmic!* is playing and on the Extra Magic Hours rotation. Expressed differently, it changes from week to week. Daily crowd forecasts are available at **touringplans.com.**

6. WHEN TO ARRIVE For Disney's Hollywood Studios, arrive with your ticket in hand 30–40 minutes before official opening time. For Universal Studios, arrive with your admission already purchased about 30 minutes before official opening time.

7. YOUNG CHILDREN Both DHS and Universal Studios Florida are relatively adult entertainment offerings. By our reckoning, half the rides and shows at DHS and about two-thirds at Universal Studios have a significant potential for frightening young children.

8. FOOD For counter-service food, Universal Studios has a decided edge. Disney's Hollywood Studios full-service restaurants are marginally better.

9. LOCKERS Universal has instituted a mandatory locker system at its big thrill rides. Bags and other items must be placed in lockers outside the attractions. Lockers are free for the first hour, and then $3 for each half hour after that, with a $20 maximum.

The locker banks are easy to find; each bank has a small computer in the center. When the sun is bright, the screen is almost impossible to read, so have someone block the sun or use a different computer. After selecting your language, press your thumb onto the keypad and have your fingerprints scanned. We've seen people walk off cursing at this step, having repeated it over and over with no success. Most patrons press their thumb down too hard. The computer cannot read your thumbprint if it's squished onto the scanner, so take a deep breath and just lightly place your thumb on the designated spot.

After your thumb scans, you will receive a locker number. Write it down! When you return from your ride, go to the same kiosk machine, enter your locker number, and scan your thumb again. At Guest Services, family-size lockers are available for $8 for the entire day, but remember that only the person who scanned his or her thumb can open it.

UNIVERSAL STUDIOS FLORIDA ATTRACTIONS

Animal Actors on Location (Universal Express) ★★★

APPEAL BY AGE	PRESCHOOL ★★★★	GRADE SCHOOL ★★★★	TEENS ★★★
YOUNG ADULTS ★★★		OVER 30 ★★★	SENIORS ★★★★

What it is Animal tricks and comedy show. **Scope and scale** Major attraction. **Fright potential** Not frightening in any respect. **Bottleneck rating** 4. **When to go** After you have experienced all rides. **Authors' rating** Cute li'l critters; ★★★. **Duration of show** 20 minutes. **Probable waiting time** 25 minutes.

This show integrates video segments with live sketches, jokes, and animal tricks performed onstage. Live animals, some of which are veterans of television and movies, take part, and kids are invited to participate. Where else can you get the chance to hold an 8-foot albino reticulated python in your lap? Check the daily entertainment schedule for showtimes.

Successful touring of Universal Studios with young children is absolutely possible, and this show is a must-see!

Liliane

Beetlejuice's Graveyard Revue (Universal Express) ★★★½

APPEAL BY AGE	PRESCHOOL ★★★★	GRADE SCHOOL ★★★★	TEENS ★★★★
YOUNG ADULTS ★★★★		OVER 30 ★★★★	SENIORS ★★★★

What it is Rock-and-roll stage show. **Scope and scale** Almost major attraction. **Fright potential** Costumes and loud noises scare the under-7 crowd. **Bottleneck rating** 2. **When to go** At your convenience. **Authors' rating** Outrageous; ★★★½. **Duration of show** 18 minutes. **Probable waiting time** None.

This high-powered rock-and-roll stage show stars Beetlejuice, Frankenstein, the Bride of Frankenstein, Wolfman, and Dracula. Mercifully, this attraction is under cover. If you have small children, tell them beforehand that it is a live show with "monsters," but that they are all really very funny and totally nice, albeit a little loud. Rock on!

The show is based on the popular movie *Beetlejuice*, which won an Oscar in 1989 for Best Makeup.

The Blues Brothers ★★★½

APPEAL BY AGE	PRESCHOOL ★★★	GRADE SCHOOL ★★★½	TEENS ★★★½
YOUNG ADULTS ★★★½	OVER 30 ★★★★		SENIORS ★★★★

What it is Blues concert. **Scope and scale** Diversion. **Fright potential** Not frightening in any respect. **Bottleneck rating** 1. **When to go** Scheduled showtimes. **Special comment** A party in the street. **Authors' rating** ★★★½. **Duration of presentation** 15 minutes.

An impromptu concert featuring live singing and saxophone playing with a background track. The concert is a great pick-me-up, and the short runtime keeps the energy high.

A Day in the Park with Barney (Universal Express) ★★★★

APPEAL BY AGE	PRESCHOOL ★★★★★	GRADE SCHOOL ★★★	TEENS ★★
YOUNG ADULTS ★★★	OVER 30 ★★★		SENIORS ★★★

What it is Live character stage show. **Scope and scale** Major children's attraction. **Fright potential** Toddlers may balk at Barney's size. **Bottleneck rating** 4. **When to go** Anytime. **Authors' rating** A great hit with preschoolers; ★★★★. **Duration of show** 20 minutes plus preshow and character greeting. **Probable waiting time** 15 minutes.

Barney, the purple dinosaur of public-television fame, leads a sing-along with the help of the audience and sidekicks Baby Bop and BJ. A short preshow gets the kids lathered up before they enter Barney's Park (the theater). Interesting theatrical effects include wind, falling leaves, clouds and stars in the simulated sky, and snow. After the show, Barney exits momentarily to allow parents and children to gather along the stage. He then returns and moves from child to child, hugging each and posing for photos. If your child likes Barney, this show is a must. It's happy and upbeat, and the character greeting that follows is the best organized we've seen in any theme park. There's no line and no fighting for Barney's attention. Just relax by the rail and await your hug.

I love you, and you love me. This show should be a top priority if you have little ones.

Liliane

Despicable Me

APPEAL BY AGE	PRESCHOOL ★★★	GRADE SCHOOL ★★★½	TEENS ★★★½
YOUNG ADULTS ★★★½	OVER 30 ★★★★		SENIORS ★★★★

What it is Motion simulator 3-D ride. **Scope and scale** Major attraction. **Fright potential** Ride is wild and jerky but not frightening. **Bottleneck rating** 10. **When to go** First hour after park opening or after 5 p.m. **Special comment** Expect *long* waits in line. **Authors' rating** Not yet open at press time. **Duration of ride** 4 minutes. **Average wait in line per 100 people ahead of you** 5 minutes. **Assumes** All simulators in use. **Loading speed** Moderate–slow.

Rough   Queasy

This motion-simulator system premiered in the Funtastic World of Hanna-Barbera when the park opened in 1990; was used again in Jimmy Neutron's Nicktoon Blast, which replaced the former in 2003; and is being retained for the attraction's third incarnation as Despicable Me, scheduled to open in 2012.

As with the former attractions, Despicable Me involves the motion simulators moving and reacting in sync with a cartoon projected on an IMAX-like screen. Though the simulators have been updated, the most significant upgrade is incorporated in the projection system, which employs high-definition 3-D digital technology. The story line combines elements from the animated movie *Despicable Me,* starring Gru, the villain, along with his adopted daughters and his diminutive yellow minions.

All new attractions draw large crowds, and Despicable Me won't be any different. Compounding the crowding is the ride's location just inside the main entrance. Be aware that the simulators cause motion sickness in a very small percentage of riders. Stationary seating is available for those prone to motion sickness and for children less than 40 inches tall.

Disaster! (Universal Express) ★★★★

What it is Combination theater presentation and adventure ride. **Scope and scale** Major attraction. **Fright potential** Special effects frighten those age 8 and under. **Bottleneck rating** 7. **When to go** In the morning or late afternoon. **Special comment** May frighten young children. **Authors' rating** Shaken, not stirred; ★★★★. **Duration of presentation** 20 minutes. **Probable waiting time** 18 minutes. **Loading speed** Moderate.

Loud   Scary

Disaster! is an updated version of *Earthquake: The Big One.* Guests are recruited for roles in a film called *Mutha Nature,* directed by an overbearing and conceited director. After the recruiting, the audience enters a soundstage where a number of scenes are filmed starring the guests/volunteers. If you ever wondered about special effects, this is the show to see. Next, guests board a faux subway where they experience a simulated earthquake. For younger children the earthquake is pretty intense. Older kids will love it! Following the quake, while the subway returns to the station, guests view a finished cut of *Mutha Nature* that incorporates all the soundstage shots.

Yours truly was recruited for a part in *Mutha Nature.* I am so happy that the movie is shown only once!

Yep, I saw that movie. Liliane starred as the earthquake.

Bob

Liliane

E. T. Adventure (Universal Express) ★★★½

APPEAL BY AGE	PRESCHOOL ★★★★	GRADE SCHOOL ★★★★	TEENS ★★★
YOUNG ADULTS ★★★		OVER 30 ★★★★	SENIORS ★★★★

What it is Indoor adventure ride based on the *E. T.* movie. **Scope and scale** Major attraction. **Fright potential** Too intense for some preschoolers. **Bottleneck rating 8. When to go** Before noon; before 10 a.m. if you have small children. **Authors' rating** A happy reunion; ★★★½. **Duration of ride** 4½ minutes. **Average wait in line per 100 people ahead of you** 5 minutes. **Loading speed** Moderate.

Guests aboard a bicycle-like conveyance escape with E. T. from earthly law enforcement officials and then journey

Thumbs Up for the Whole Family

to E. T.'s planet. The attraction is similar to Peter Pan's Flight at the Magic Kingdom but is longer and has more elaborate special effects. Make sure that you give the attendant your name—we recommend that you just state your name; don't try to spell it—and relish the end of the ride as E. T. will personalize his good-bye message. Lines build quickly after 10 a.m., and waits can be more than 2 hours on busy days. Ride in the morning or late afternoon.

Very cute. Liliane wants to phone home . . .

E. T. is based on Steven Spielberg's film *E. T.: The Extra-Terrestrial*—a great family movie that won four Oscars in 1982.

Liliane

Fear Factor Live (Universal Express) ★★★★ (open seasonally)

APPEAL BY AGE	PRESCHOOL ½	GRADE SCHOOL ★★	TEENS ★★★★
YOUNG ADULTS ★★★		OVER 30 ★★★	SENIORS ★½

What it is Live version of the gross-out-stunt television show on NBC. **Scope and scale** Headliner. **Fright potential** Stuff of nightmares. **Bottleneck rating 6. When to go** Six to eight shows daily; crowds are smallest at the first and second-to-last shows. **Authors' rating** Great fun if you love the TV show; ★★★★. **Duration of show** 30 minutes. **Probable waiting time** 25 minutes.

Fear Factor Live is a live stage show in which up to six volunteers compete for one prize by doing dumb and yucky things such as swimming with eels and eating bugs. The show is really payback for adults; adolescents will enjoy watching mom squirm during the icky parts. For children age 8 and under, *Fear Factor Live* is nightmare material. Whether you participate or simply watch, this show will keep your innards in an uproar.

Fievel's Playland ★★★★

APPEAL BY AGE	PRESCHOOL ★★★★	GRADE SCHOOL ★★★★
TEENS —	YOUNG ADULTS —	OVER 30 —	SENIORS —

What it is Children's play area with waterslide. **Scope and scale** Minor attraction. **Fright potential** Not frightening in any respect. **Bottleneck rating 1. When to go** Anytime. **Authors' rating** A much-needed attraction for preschoolers; ★★★★. **Probable waiting time** 20–30 minutes for the waterslide; otherwise, no waiting.

This is a great playground that features ordinary household items reproduced on a giant scale, seen as a mouse would experience them. Preschoolers and grade-schoolers can climb nets, walk through a huge boot, splash in a sardine-can fountain, seesaw on huge spoons, and climb onto a cow skull. Most of the playground is reserved for preschoolers, but a waterslide/raft ride is open to all ages. There's almost no waiting in queue here, and you can stay as long as you want. Younger children love the oversize items, and there's enough to keep teens and adults busy while little ones let off steam. The waterslide/raft ride is open to everyone but is extremely slow loading and carries only 300 riders per hour. With an average wait of 20–30 minutes, we don't think the 16-second ride is worth the trouble and, yes, you will get soaked.

Fievel's Playland is another must for a successful visit to Universal Studios with small children. The playground is themed after the 1991 Spielberg movie *Fievel Goes West*. Young children will love to identify with the tales of Fievel Mousekewitz.

Liliane

Hollywood Rip Ride Rockit ★★★★

APPEAL BY AGE	PRESCHOOL —	GRADE SCHOOL ★★★★	TEENS ★★★★½
YOUNG ADULTS ★★★★½		OVER 30 ★★★★	SENIORS ★★★½

What it is Super-high-tech roller coaster. **Scope and scale** Headliner. **Fright potential** Frightening for all ages. **Bottleneck rating** 9. **When to go** Immediately after park opening. **Special comments** Expect long waits in line; must be 51" tall to ride. **Authors' rating** ★★★★. **Duration of ride** 2½ minutes. **Average wait in line per 100 people ahead of you** 6–8 minutes. **Loading speed** Fast.

Rough

Queasy

Opened in the summer of 2009, Hollywood Rip Ride Rockit has some features that we've never seen before. Let's start with the basics: Rip Ride Rockit is a sit-down X-Car coaster that runs on a 3,800-foot steel track, with a maximum height of 167 feet and a top speed of 65 miles an hour. X-Car vehicles are more maneuverable than most other kinds and use less restrictive restraints, making for an exhilarating ride.

You ascend—vertically—at 11 feet per second to crest the 17-story-tall first hill, the highest point reached by any roller coaster in Orlando. The drop is almost vertical, too, and launches you into Double Take, a loop inversion in which you begin on the inside of the loop, twist to the outside at the top (so you're upright), and then twist back inside the loop for the descent. Double Take stands 136 feet tall, and its loop is 103 feet in diameter at its widest point. You next hurl (not that hurl—it comes later) into a stretch of track shaped like a musical treble clef. As on Double Take, the track configuration on Treble Clef is a first. Another innovation is Jump Cut, a spiraling negative-gravity maneuver. Usually on coasters, you experience negative gravity on long, steep vertical drops; with Jump Cut you feel as though you're in a corkscrew inversion, but you never actually go upside down. Other high points include a 95-degree turn, a downhill into an "underground chasm" (gotta love those Universal PR wordsmiths!), and a final incline loop banked at 150 degrees.

The ride starts in the Production Central area; weaves into the New York area near *TWISTER*, popping out over the heads of guests in the square below; and then storms out and over the lagoon separating Universal Studios from Islands of Adventure. Each row is outfitted with color-changing LEDs and high-end audio and video technology for each seat. Like the Rock 'n' Roller Coaster at Disney's Hollywood Studios, this coaster features a musical sound track. With Rip Ride Rockit, however, you can choose the genre of music you want to hear as you ride: classic rock, country, disco, pop, or rap. After the ride, Universal flogs a digital-video "rip" of your ride, complete with the sound track you chose, that you can upload to websites such as YouTube.

No, Liliane, don't even ask. I'm still half-deaf from the last roller coaster I rode with you.

Bob

Liliane

The incentive to try out this thingy has not been invented. Therefore, Bob, stop asking me to ride the monster. The answer is NO.

JAWS (Universal Express) ★★★★

| APPEAL BY AGE | PRESCHOOL ★★★ | GRADE SCHOOL ★★★★ | TEENS ★★★★ |
| YOUNG ADULTS ★★★★ | | OVER 30 ★★★★ | SENIORS ★★★★ |

What it is Adventure boat ride. **Scope and scale** Headliner. **Fright potential** Frightening for all ages. **Bottleneck rating** 8. **When to go** Before 11 a.m. or after 5 p.m. **Special comments** Will frighten young children; must be 42" tall to ride. **Authors' rating** Not to be missed; ★★★★. **Duration of ride** 5 minutes. **Average wait in line per 100 people ahead of you** 3 minutes. **Assumes** All 8 boats are running. **Loading speed** Fast.

Wet   Scary

JAWS delivers 5 minutes of nonstop action, with the huge shark repeatedly attacking. The attraction builds an amazing degree of suspense. It isn't just a cruise into the middle of a pond with a scary rubber fish. People on the boat's left side tend to get splashed more. If you have young children, consider switching off (see page 242). If you want to add a little extra suspense, go for a ride after dark.

The ride is based on the 1975 Spielberg film *Jaws*. All that panic earned him *three* Oscars!

Movie Tip

Lucy—A Tribute ★★★

| APPEAL BY AGE | PRESCHOOL ★ | GRADE SCHOOL ★★ | TEENS ★★ |
| YOUNG ADULTS ★★★ | | OVER 30 ★★★ | SENIORS ★★★ |

What it is Walk-through tribute to Lucille Ball. **Scope and scale** Diversion. **Fright potential** Not frightening in any respect. **Bottleneck rating** 0. **When to go** Anytime. **Authors' rating** A touching remembrance; ★★★.

This museumlike exhibit spotlights the life and career of comedienne Lucille Ball. See Lucy during the hot, crowded mid-afternoon or on your way out of the park.

The well-deserved tribute is not for young children, and most teenagers will lack a frame of reference. As for me: "I love Lucy."

Men in Black Alien Attack
(Universal Express) ★★★★½

| APPEAL BY AGE | PRESCHOOL † | GRADE SCHOOL ★★★★★ | TEENS ★★★★★ |
| YOUNG ADULTS ★★★★★ | | OVER 30 ★★★★★ | SENIORS ★★★★ |

† Due to height requirement, sample size too small for an accurate rating.

What it is Interactive dark thrill ride. **Scope and scale** Super-headliner. **Fright potential** Dark and intense; frightens many children age 10 and under. **Bottleneck rating** 9. **When to go** In the morning after Revenge of the Mummy. **Special comments** May induce motion sickness; must be 42" tall to ride. Switching-off option provided (see page 242). **Authors' rating** Buzz Lightyear on steroids; not to be missed; ★★★★½. **Duration of ride** 2½ minutes. **Average wait in line per 100 people ahead of you** 5 minutes. **Loading speed** Moderate–fast.

  Based on the movie of the same name, the story line has you volunteering as a Men in Black (MIB) trainee. After an introduction warning that aliens "live among us" and articulating MIB's mission to round them up, Zed expands on the finer points of alien spotting and familiarizes you with your training vehicle and your weapon, an alien "zapper." Following this, you load up and are dispatched on an innocuous training mission that immediately deteriorates into a situation where only you are in a position to prevent aliens from taking over the universe. Now, if you saw the movie, you understand that the aliens are mostly giant exotic bugs and cockroaches and that zapping the aliens involves exploding them into myriad, gooey body parts. Thus, the meat of the ride (no pun intended) consists of careening around Manhattan in your MIB vehicle and shooting aliens. Each of the 120 or so alien figures has sensors that activate special effects and respond to your zapper. Aim for the eyes and keep shooting until the aliens' eyes turn red. To avoid a long wait, hotfoot it to MIB immediately after riding Mummy in the first 30 minutes the park is open.

Bugs are everywhere. The ride is really fun, especially if you have seen the movie. Can't wait to go back and shoot some aliens.

Ian

Revenge of the Mummy (Universal Express) ★★★★½

| APPEAL BY AGE | PRESCHOOL ★★ | GRADE SCHOOL ★★★★ | TEENS ★★★★★ |
| YOUNG ADULTS ★★★★½ | | OVER 30 ★★★★ | SENIORS ★★★½ |

What it is Combination dark ride and roller coaster. **Scope and scale** Super-headliner. **Fright potential** Scary for all ages. **Bottleneck rating** 8. **When to go** The first hour the park is open or after 6 p.m. **Special comment** Must be 48" tall to ride. **Authors' rating** Killer! ★★★★½. **Duration of ride** 4 minutes. **Average wait in line per 100 people ahead of you** 7 minutes. **Loading speed** Moderate.

   Revenge of the Mummy is an indoor dark ride based on the *Mummy* flicks, where guests fight off "deadly curses and vengeful creatures" while flying through Egyptian tombs and other spooky places on a high-tech roller coaster. The special effects are cutting edge, integrating the best technology from such attractions as *Terminator 2: 3-D* and Spider-Man (the ride). The ride begins slowly, passing through various chambers, including one where flesh-eating scarab beetles descend on you. Suddenly your vehicle stops, and then drops backward and rotates. Next thing you know, you're shot at high speed up the first hill of the roller coaster. Though it's a wild ride by anyone's definition, the emphasis remains as much on the visuals, robotics, and special effects as on the ride itself.

> The mummy scared the willies out of me. This one is definitely not for young children.
>
> Liliane

Shrek 4-D (Universal Express) ★★★½

APPEAL BY AGE	PRESCHOOL ★★★★	GRADE SCHOOL ★★★★★	TEENS ★★★★★
YOUNG ADULTS ★★★★★		OVER 30 ★★★★★	SENIORS ★★★★

What it is 3-D movie. **Scope and scale** Headliner. **Fright potential** Loud but not frightening. Preshow area is a little macabre. **Bottleneck rating** 7. **When to go** The first hour the park is open or after 4 p.m. **Authors' rating** Warm, fuzzy mayhem; ★★★★½. **Duration of show** 20 minutes. **Probable waiting time** 16 minutes.

This attraction is a real winner. It's irreverent, frantic, laugh-out-loud funny, and iconoclastic. In contrast to Disney's *It's Tough to Be a Bug!*, *Shrek 4-D* doesn't generally frighten children under age 7.

> Children under age 7 might be frightened at times. Take off the 3-D glasses if it is all too scary, and consider earplugs. Did you know that Shrek in German means "the scare"?
>
> Liliane

The Simpsons Ride (Universal Express) ★★★★

APPEAL BY AGE	PRESCHOOL —	GRADE SCHOOL ★★★★	TEENS ★★★★
YOUNG ADULTS ★★★★		OVER 30 ★★★★	SENIORS ★★★½

What it is Mega-simulator ride. **Scope and scale** Super-headliner. **Fright potential** Visuals not scary but very wild ride. **Bottleneck rating** 9. **When to go** First thing after park opening. **Special comments** Must be 40" tall to ride; not recommended for pregnant women or people prone to motion sickness. Switching-off option provided (see page 242). **Authors' rating** Despicable Me with attitude; ★★★★. **Duration of ride** 4⅓ minutes. **Average wait in line per 100 people ahead of you** 5 minutes. **Loading speed** Moderate.

Rough   Queasy

Two preshows involve Simpsons characters speaking sequentially on different video screens around the line area. Their comments help define the characters for guests who are unfamiliar with the TV show. The attraction is a simulator ride, similar to Star Tours at Disney's Hollywood Studios and Despicable Me at Universal, but with a larger screen more like that of Soarin' at Epcot. The attraction takes a wild and humorous poke at thrill rides, dark rides, and live shows. Like the show on which it's based, The Simpsons Ride definitely has an edge—and more than a few wild hairs. Like *Shrek 4-D*, it operates on several levels. There will be jokes and visuals that you'll get but will fly over your children's heads—and most assuredly vice versa. You can expect large crowds all day.

The ride is a long way from being tame. Skip it if you're an expectant mom or prone to motion sickness. Several families we interviewed found the humor a little too adult for their younger children.

Bob

Street Scenes ★★★★★

APPEAL BY AGE	PRESCHOOL ★★★	GRADE SCHOOL ★★★★★	TEENS ★★★★★
YOUNG ADULTS ★★★★★		OVER 30 ★★★★★	SENIORS ★★★★

What it is Elaborate outdoor sets for making films. **Scope and scale** Diversion. **Fright potential** Not frightening in any respect. **Bottleneck rating** 0. **When to go** Anytime. **Special comment** You'll see most sets without special effort as you tour the park. **Authors' rating** One of the park's great assets; ★★★★★.

Unlike at Disney's Hollywood Studios, all Universal Studios Florida's backlot sets are accessible for guest inspection. You'll see most as you walk through the park. Enjoy a New York City street, San Francisco's waterfront, a New England coastal town, Rodeo Drive, and Hollywood Boulevard. The sets make for great photo ops!

Terminator 2: 3-D (Universal Express) ★★★★

APPEAL BY AGE	PRESCHOOL ★★★	GRADE SCHOOL ★★★★	TEENS ★★★★
YOUNG ADULTS ★★★★★		OVER 30 ★★★★★	SENIORS ★★★★

What it is 3-D thriller mixed-media presentation. **Scope and scale** Superheadliner. **Fright potential** Intense; will frighten children age 7 and under. **Bottleneck rating** 7. **When to go** After 3:30 p.m. **Special comments** The nation's best theme-park theater attraction; very intense for some preschoolers and grade-schoolers. **Authors' rating** Furiously paced high-tech experience; not to be missed; ★★★★. **Duration of show** 20 minutes, including an 8-minute preshow. **Probable waiting time** 20–40 minutes.

Dark

Loud

Scary

The attraction, like the films, is all action, and you really don't need to understand much. What's interesting is that it uses 3-D film and a theater full of sophisticated technology to integrate the real with the imaginary. Images seem to move in and out of the film, not only in the manner of traditional 3-D but also in actuality. Remove your 3-D glasses momentarily and you'll see that the guy on the motorcycle is actually onstage. *Terminator 2: 3-D* has been eclipsed a bit by newer attractions such as Revenge of the Mummy, Hollywood Rip Ride Rockit, and The Simpsons Ride. We suggest that you save *Terminator* and other theater presentations until you have experienced all of the rides. Families with young children should know that the violence characteristic of the *Terminator* movies is largely absent from the attraction. There's suspense and action but not much blood and guts.

Greatest show ever! Saw it twice on the same day and will go back for more next time I visit. Of all the shows I've seen, this one is the most impressive ever.

Idan

TWISTER . . . Ride It Out (Universal Express) ★★★½

APPEAL BY AGE	PRESCHOOL ★★	GRADE SCHOOL ★★★★	TEENS ★★★★
YOUNG ADULTS ★★★★		OVER 30 ★★★★	SENIORS ★★★

What it is Theater presentation featuring special effects from the movie *Twister*. **Scope and scale** Major attraction. **Fright potential** Will frighten children age 7 and under. **Bottleneck rating** 7. **When to go** Should be your first show after experiencing all rides. **Special comment** High potential for frightening young children. **Authors' rating** Gusty; ★★★½. **Duration of show** 15 minutes. **Probable waiting time** 26 minutes.

Loud   Scary

Twister combines an elaborate set and special effects, climaxing with a five-story-tall simulated tornado created by circulating more than 2 million cubic feet of air per minute. The wind, pounding rain, and freight-train sound of the tornado are deafening, and the entire presentation is exceptionally intense. Schoolchildren are mightily impressed, while younger children are terrified and overwhelmed. Unless you want the kids hopping in your bed whenever they hear thunder, try this attraction yourself before taking your kids.

Universal Orlando's Horror Make-Up Show ★★★½ (Universal Express)

APPEAL BY AGE	PRESCHOOL ★★★	GRADE SCHOOL ★★★★	TEENS ★★★★
YOUNG ADULTS ★★★★		OVER 30 ★★★★	SENIORS ★★★★

What it is Theater presentation on the art of makeup. **Scope and scale** Major attraction. **Fright potential** Gory but not frightening. **Bottleneck rating** 6. **When to go** After you have experienced all rides. **Special comment** May upset young children. **Authors' rating** A gory knee-slapper; ★★★½. **Duration of show** 25 minutes. **Probable waiting time** 20 minutes.

Thumbs Up for the Whole Family

Lively, well-paced look at how makeup artists create film monsters, realistic wounds, severed limbs, and other unmentionables. Exceeding most guests' expectations, the *Horror Make-Up Show* is the sleeper attraction at Universal. Its humor and tongue-in-cheek style transcend the gruesome effects, and most folks (including preschoolers) take the blood and guts in stride. It usually isn't too hard to get into.

Universal 360: A Cinesphere Spectacular (open seasonally) ★★★½

APPEAL BY AGE	PRESCHOOL ★★★	GRADE SCHOOL ★★★★	TEENS ★★★½
YOUNG ADULTS ★★★★		OVER 30 ★★★★	SENIORS ★★★★

What it is Fireworks, lasers, and movies. **Scope and scale** Major attraction. **Fright potential** Fireworks and scary movie footage frighten preschoolers. **Bottleneck rating** 7. **When to go** One show a day, usually 10 minutes before park closes. **Special comment** Movie trailers galore. **Authors' rating** Good effort; ★★★½. **Duration of show** 10 minutes.

Bob

If you want to beat the crowds out of the park after *Universal 360*, watch the show from the Mel's Diner end of the lagoon.

A nighttime spectacular presented at the Universal Studios lagoon, the presentation is a celebration of hit movies and is built around four 360-degree projection cinespheres, each 36 feet tall and 30 feet wide. The cinespheres project images relating to the chosen films, augmented by lasers and fireworks. Realize that not all of the movie clips may be suitable for young viewers. During the horror movie montage, parents may want to cover some eyes. The action movie montage is also stuffed with gunplay and gore. The ends of the lagoon are not recommended for viewing. The best spot is directly across the lagoon from Richter's Burger Co. in the San Francisco area, where the sidewalk juts out over the water. This side of the lagoon also offers the best view of the projections on the buildings and cinespheres. Scoring a viewing spot here can be very difficult. We recommend arriving at least 45 minutes ahead of time and taking turns holding the spot while the rest of your crew rides JAWS at night! *Universal 360* is presented during the summer and holiday periods.

Woody Woodpecker's Nuthouse Coaster and Curious George Goes to Town ★★★

APPEAL BY AGE	PRESCHOOL ★★★★		GRADE SCHOOL —		TEENS —
YOUNG ADULTS —		OVER 30 —		SENIORS —	

What it is Interactive playground and kid's roller coaster. **Scope and scale** Minor attraction. **Fright potential** Not frightening in any respect. **Bottleneck rating** 5. **When to go** Anytime. **Special comment** Must be 36" tall to ride coaster. **Authors' rating** A good place to turn the kids loose; ★★★.

The KidZone consists of Woody Woodpecker's Nuthouse Coaster and an interactive playground called Curious George Goes to Town. The child-size roller coaster is small enough for kids, though its moderate speed might unnerve some smaller children. The Curious George playground exemplifies the Universal obsession with wet stuff; in addition to innumerable spigots, pipes, and spray guns, two giant roof-mounted buckets periodically dump *a thousand gallons* of water on unsuspecting visitors below. Kids who want to stay dry can mess around in the foam-ball playground, also equipped with chutes, tubes, and ball-blasters. The playground is creatively designed and a great place for kids to cut loose after being in tow all day.

Have the kids wear a bathing suit under their clothes so they can enjoy the water features. Simpler still, let the 4-and-unders frolic in their underwear (bring an extra pair).

Liliane

LIVE ENTERTAINMENT *at* UNIVERSAL STUDIOS

IN ADDITION TO THE SHOWS profiled above, Universal offers a wide range of street entertainment. Costumed comic-book and cartoon characters (Shrek, Donkey, SpongeBob SquarePants, and Woody Woodpecker) roam the park for photo ops, along with movie star look-alikes, plus the Frankenstein monster, who can be said to be neither. The handout park map has a section called "Character Zones" that provides times and places for character appearances and shows.

Musical acts include Blues Brothers impersonators dancing and singing in the New York section of the park.

UNIVERSAL STUDIOS FLORIDA TOURING PLAN

UNIVERSAL STUDIOS FLORIDA 1-DAY TOURING PLAN FOR FAMILIES

THIS PLAN IS FOR FAMILIES. If a ride or show is listed that you don't want to experience, skip that step and proceed to the next. Move quickly from attraction to attraction and, if possible, don't stop for lunch until after Step 9. Minor street shows occur at various times and places throughout the day; check the daily schedule for details. The actual touring plan in clip-out version with a map is on page 467. The touring plan is geared toward the whole family. Because there are so many attractions with the potential to frighten young children, be prepared to skip a few things and to practice switching off (works the same way as at Walt Disney World; see page 242). For the most part, attractions designed especially for young children, such as playgrounds, can be enjoyed anytime. Work them into the plan at your convenience.

UNIVERSAL'S ISLANDS *of* ADVENTURE

WHEN UNIVERSAL'S ISLANDS OF ADVENTURE theme park opened in 1999, it provided Universal with enough critical mass to actually compete with Disney. Universal finally has on-site hotels, a shopping and entertainment complex, and two major theme parks. Doubly interesting is that Islands of Adventure is pretty much just for fun—in other words, a direct competitor to Disney's Magic Kingdom, the most visited theme park in the world.

Disney and Universal officially downplay their fierce competition, pointing out that any new theme park or attraction makes central Florida a more marketable destination. Behind closed doors, however, it's a Pepsi versus Coke–type rivalry that will keep both companies working hard to gain a competitive edge. The good news, of course, is that all this translates into better and better attractions for you to enjoy.

In 2010, in one of the greatest seismic shifts in theme-park history, Universal secured the rights to build a Harry Potter theme area within the park. This is proving to be a competitive game changer. Harry Potter is possibly the only character extant capable of trumping Mickey Mouse, and Universal has gone all out (under author J. K. Rowling's watchful and very particular eye) to create a setting and attractions designed to be the envy of the industry.

Consider yourself warned: Several attractions at Islands of Adventure will drench you to the bone.

Liliane

If you're having trouble sizing up how big a deal The Wizarding World is, you need only to check the discussion boards of any website associated with Orlando, theme parks, Harry Potter, Daniel Radcliffe, J. K. Rowling, or dozens of other tenuously related topics. What you're likely to see is a billion or so postings like this:

> *OMG!!!!!!!!!!!!! I CAN'T WAIT!!!!!!!!! I LOVE Harry Potter SOOOOOOOO much you wouldn't BELIEVE!!!!!!!!!!!!!!!!!! I was just looking for Harry Potter stuff and I saw a link to this!! I am so EXCITED!!!!*

BEWARE OF THE WET AND WILD

ALTHOUGH WE HAVE DESCRIBED Universal's Islands of Adventure as a direct competitor to the Magic Kingdom, there is one major qualification you should be aware of. Whereas most Magic Kingdom attractions are designed to be enjoyed by guests of any age, attractions at Islands of Adventure are largely created for an under-40 population. The roller coasters at Universal are serious with a capital S, making Space Mountain and Big Thunder Mountain look about as tough as Dumbo. In fact, seven out of the nine top attractions at Islands are thrill rides, and of these, there are three that not only scare the bejeebers out of you but also drench you with water.

For families, there are three interactive playgrounds, as well as six rides, that young kids will enjoy. Of the thrill rides, only the two in Toon Lagoon (described later) are marginally appropriate for young children, and even on these rides your child needs to be fairly stalwart.

GETTING ORIENTED AT ISLANDS OF ADVENTURE

Roller coasters at Islands of Adventure are the real deal— not for the timid or for little ones.

Bob

BOTH UNIVERSAL THEME PARKS are accessed via the Universal CityWalk entertainment complex. Crossing CityWalk from the parking garages, you can bear right to Universal Studios Florida or left to Universal's Islands of Adventure.

Islands of Adventure is arranged much like Epcot's World Showcase is—in a large circle surrounding a lake. Unlike Epcot, however, the Islands of Adventure areas evidence the sort of thematic continuity pioneered by Disneyland and the Magic Kingdom. Each "land," or island in this case, is self-contained and visually consistent in its theme, though you can see parts of the other islands across the lake.

You first encounter the Moroccan-style Port of Entry, where you'll find Guest Services, lockers, stroller and wheelchair rentals, ATM banking, lost and found, and shopping. From the Port of Entry, moving clockwise around the lake, you can access Marvel Super Hero Island, Toon Lagoon, Jurassic Park, The Wizarding World of Harry Potter, the Lost Continent, and Seuss Landing.

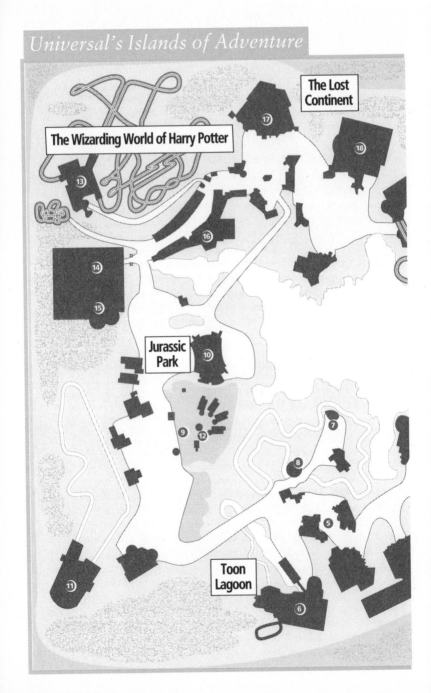

Universal's Islands of Adventure

The Lost Continent

The Wizarding World of Harry Potter

Jurassic Park

Toon Lagoon

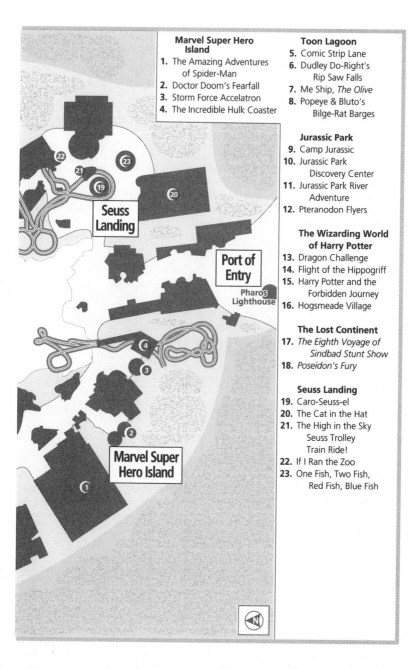

Marvel Super Hero Island
1. The Amazing Adventures of Spider-Man
2. Doctor Doom's Fearfall
3. Storm Force Accelatron
4. The Incredible Hulk Coaster

Toon Lagoon
5. Comic Strip Lane
6. Dudley Do-Right's Rip Saw Falls
7. Me Ship, *The Olive*
8. Popeye & Bluto's Bilge-Rat Barges

Jurassic Park
9. Camp Jurassic
10. Jurassic Park Discovery Center
11. Jurassic Park River Adventure
12. Pteranodon Flyers

The Wizarding World of Harry Potter
13. Dragon Challenge
14. Flight of the Hippogriff
15. Harry Potter and the Forbidden Journey
16. Hogsmeade Village

The Lost Continent
17. *The Eighth Voyage of Sindbad Stunt Show*
18. *Poseidon's Fury*

Seuss Landing
19. Caro-Seuss-el
20. The Cat in the Hat
21. The High in the Sky Seuss Trolley Train Ride!
22. If I Ran the Zoo
23. One Fish, Two Fish, Red Fish, Blue Fish

ISLANDS *of* ADVENTURE
ATTRACTIONS

MARVEL SUPER HERO ISLAND

THIS ISLAND, WITH ITS FUTURISTIC AND RETRO-FUTURE design and comic-book signage, offers shopping and attractions based on Marvel Comics characters.

The Amazing Adventures of Spider-Man ★★★★★ (Universal Express)

APPEAL BY AGE	PRESCHOOL ★★★	GRADE SCHOOL ★★★★★	TEENS ★★★★★
YOUNG ADULTS ★★★★★		OVER 30 ★★★★★	SENIORS ★★★★

What it is Indoor adventure simulator ride based on Spider-Man. **Scope and scale** Super-headliner. **Fright potential** Intense; kids tall enough to ride usually take it in stride. **Bottleneck rating** 9. **When to go** Before 10 a.m. **Special comment** Must be 40" tall to ride. **Authors' rating** One of the best attractions anywhere; ★★★★★. **Duration of ride** 4½ minutes. **Average wait in line per 100 people ahead of you** 4 minutes. **Loading speed** Fast.

Dark   Rough   Scary

Covering 1½ acres and combining moving ride vehicles, 3-D film, and live action, Spider-Man is frenetic, fluid, and astounding. The visuals are rich, and the ride is wild but not jerky. Spider-Man is technologically on a par with Disney's Hollywood Studios' Tower of Terror, which is to say that it will leave you in awe. Ride as early in the morning as possible or in the hour before closing. Already considered by many to

---

FAVORITE EATS AT UNIVERSAL STUDIOS

LAND	SERVICE LOCATION	FOOD ITEM
PRODUCTION CENTRAL		
	Classic Monsters Cafe	Chicken, salads, & fresh fruit
NEW YORK		
	Louie's Italian Restaurant	Pasta
	Finnegan's Bar & Grill	Irish pub, frequently with live music *(table service only)*
SAN FRANCISCO		
	Richter's Burger Co.	Burgers
WORLD EXPO		
	International Food & Film Festival	Asian food & ice cream
WOODY WOODPECKER'S KIDZONE		
	KidZone Pizza Company	Pizza
HOLLYWOOD		
	Mel's Drive-In	Chocolate chip cookies

be the best theme-park attraction on the planet, Spider-Man is being enhanced for 2012 with a complete high-definition digital upgrade, including 13 reanimated 3-D scenes.

An absolute must. Soar above buildings without ever leaving the ground! Kudos to Universal; this is the ultimate deception, and I loved every turn. Must ride several times to take in all the details. And do hold on to your personal belongings, as I managed to lose my room key (still wondering how I did it).

Doctor Doom's Fearfall (Universal Express) ★★★

APPEAL BY AGE	PRESCHOOL —	GRADE SCHOOL ★★★	TEENS ★★★★
YOUNG ADULTS ★★★★		OVER 30 ★★★	SENIORS —

What it is Lunch liberator. **Scope and scale** Headliner. **Fright potential** Frightening for all ages. **Bottleneck rating** 10. **When to go** Before 9:15 a.m. **Special comment** Must be 52" tall to ride. **Authors' rating** More bark than bite; ★★★. **Duration of ride** 40 seconds. **Average wait in line per 100 people ahead of you** 18 minutes. **Loading speed** Slow.

Here you are strapped into a seat with your feet dangling, blasted 200 feet up in the air, and then allowed to partially free-fall back down. We've seen glaciers that move faster than the line to Doctor Doom. If you want to ride without investing half a day, be one of the first in the park to ride.

This attraction is best experienced with your mother right next to you. Hold her hand for personal comfort (it makes you look good too) and brace for her expression of absolute terror.

The Incredible Hulk Coaster (Universal Express) ★★★★½

APPEAL BY AGE	PRESCHOOL ★	GRADE SCHOOL ★★★★★	TEENS ★★★★★
YOUNG ADULTS ★★★★		OVER 30 ★★★★	SENIORS ★★★

What it is Roller coaster. **Scope and scale** Super-headliner. **Fright potential** Frightening for all ages. **Bottleneck rating** 10. **When to go** Before 9:30 a.m. **Special comments** Must be 54" tall to ride. **Authors' rating** A coaster-lover's coaster; ★★★★½. **Duration of ride** 2¼ minutes. **Average wait in line per 100 people ahead of you** 9 minutes. **Loading speed** Moderate.

The Hulk is a great roller coaster, one of the best in Florida, providing a ride comparable to Montu (Busch Gardens) with the added thrill of an accelerated launch (instead of the more typical uphill crank). Plus, like Montu, this coaster has a smooth ride. The Hulk gives Dragon Challenge a run as the park's most popular coaster. Ride first thing in the morning.

You-know-who made me ride it, and for the duration of the ride I lost my very polite European ways.

Unfortunately, Liliane lost her very polite European ways at about 100 decibels. My ears hurt for days.

Storm Force Accelatron (Universal Express) ★★★

APPEAL BY AGE	PRESCHOOL ★★★★	GRADE SCHOOL ★★★	TEENS ★★★
YOUNG ADULTS ★★★		OVER 30 ★★★	SENIORS ★★★

What it is Indoor spinning ride. **Scope and scale** Minor attraction. **Fright potential** Nauseating but not frightening. **Bottleneck rating** 9. **When to go** Before 10:30 a.m. **Authors' rating** Teacups in the dark; ★★★. **Duration of ride** 1½ minutes. **Average wait in line per 100 people ahead of you** 21 minutes. **Loading speed** Slow.

Storm Force is a spiffed-up indoor version of Disney's nausea-inducing Mad Tea Party. Ride early or late to avoid long lines. Skip it if you're prone to motion sickness.

Dark   Queasy

TOON LAGOON

TOON LAGOON IS CARTOON ART TRANSLATED into real buildings and settings. Whimsical and gaily colored, with rounded and exaggerated lines, Toon Lagoon was Universal's answer to Mickey's Toontown Fair in the Magic Kingdom. The main difference was that (as you will see) you have about a 60% chance of drowning at Universal's version.

Comic Strip Lane

What it is Walk-through exhibit and shopping and dining venue. **Scope and scale** Diversion. **Fright potential** Not frightening in any respect. **Bottleneck rating** 0. **When to go** Anytime.

This is the main street of Toon Lagoon. Here you can visit the domains of Beetle Bailey, Hagar the Horrible, Krazy Kat, the Family Circus, and Blondie and Dagwood, among others of whom your kids have never heard. Shops and eateries tie into the cartoon strip theme. This is a great place for photo ops with cartoon characters.

Dudley Do-Right's Ripsaw Falls ★★★½
(Universal Express)

APPEAL BY AGE	PRESCHOOL ★★★	GRADE SCHOOL ★★★★	TEENS ★★★★
YOUNG ADULTS ★★★		OVER 30 ★★★★	SENIORS ★★★

What it is Flume ride. **Scope and scale** Major attraction. **Fright potential** The big drop frightens guests of all ages. **Bottleneck rating** 8. **When to go** Before 11 a.m. **Special comments** Must be 44" tall to ride. **Authors' rating** A minimalist Splash Mountain; ★★★½. **Duration of ride** 5 minutes. **Average wait in line per 100 people ahead of you** 9 minutes. **Loading speed** Moderate.

Inspired by the *Rocky and Bullwinkle* cartoons, this ride features Canadian Mountie Dudley Do-Right as he attempts to save Nell from evil Snidely Whiplash. Story line aside, it's a flume ride, with the inevitable big drop at the end. Universal claims that this is the first flume ride to "send riders plummeting 15 feet below the surface of the water." In reality, though, you're just plummeting into a tunnel. This ride will get you wet, but on average not as wet as you might expect (it looks worse than it is). If you want to stay dry, however,

Wet   Scary

arrive prepared with a poncho or at least a big garbage bag with holes cut out for your head and arms. While younger children are often intimidated by the big drop, those who ride generally enjoy themselves. Ride first thing in the morning after experiencing the Marvel Super Hero rides.

Small children will be intimidated by the big drop. Try Popeye & Bluto's Bilge-Rat Barges first.

Liliane

Right, Liliane. Popeye & Bluto's Bilge-Rat Barges is perfect for small children . . . as long as they have wet suits and life jackets.

Bob

Me Ship, *The Olive* ★★★

APPEAL BY AGE		PRESCHOOL ★★★★		GRADE SCHOOL ★★★★
TEENS ½	YOUNG ADULTS ½		OVER 30 ½	SENIORS —

What it is Interactive playground. **Scope and scale** Minor attraction. **Fright potential** Not frightening in any respect. **Bottleneck rating** 4. **When to go** Anytime. **Authors' rating** Colorful and appealing for kids; ★★★.

The Olive is Popeye's three-story boat come to life as an interactive playground. Younger children can scramble around in Swee'Pea's Playpen, while older sibs shoot water cannons at riders trying to survive the adjacent Bilge-Rat raft ride. If you're into the big rides, save this for later in the day.

Popeye & Bluto's Bilge-Rat Barges ★★★★ (Universal Express)

APPEAL BY AGE	PRESCHOOL ★★★	GRADE SCHOOL ★★★★★	TEENS ★★★★
YOUNG ADULTS ★★★★		OVER 30 ★★★★	SENIORS ★★★

What it is White-water raft ride. **Scope and scale** Major attraction. **Fright potential** Ride is wild and wet but not frightening. **Bottleneck rating** 8. **When to go** Before 10:30 a.m. **Special comment** Must be 42" tall to ride. **Authors' rating** Bring your own soap; ★★★★. **Duration of ride** 4½ minutes. **Average wait in line per 100 people ahead of you** 7 minutes. **Loading speed** Moderate.

This white-water raft ride for the whole family is engineered to ensure that everyone gets drenched; the ride even provides water cannons for highly intelligent nonparticipants ashore to fire at those aboard. The rapids are rougher and

Rough   Wet

more interesting, and the ride longer, than the Animal Kingdom's Kali River Rapids. If you didn't drown on Dudley Do-Right, here's a second chance.

Remember you will get wet. It is OK on a hot summer day, unless it's first thing in the morning. Now is the time to use the raingear or plastic bags to protect yourselves. Most important, keep your footwear dry.

Liliane

JURASSIC PARK

JURASSIC PARK (FOR ANYONE WHO'S BEEN ASLEEP for 20 years) is a Steven Spielberg film franchise about a fictitious theme park with real dinosaurs. Jurassic Park at Universal's Islands of Adventure is a real theme park (or at least a section of one) with fictitious dinosaurs.

Camp Jurassic ★★★

| APPEAL BY AGE | PRESCHOOL ★★★ | | GRADE SCHOOL ★★★ |
| TEENS — | YOUNG ADULTS — | OVER 30 — | SENIORS — |

What it is Interactive play area. **Scope and scale** Minor attraction. **Fright potential** Not frightening in any respect. **Bottleneck rating** 3. **When to go** Anytime. **Authors' rating** Creative playground; confusing layout; ★★★.

Camp Jurassic is a great place for children to run and explore. Sort of a Jurassic version of Tom Sawyer Island, kids can explore lava pits, caves, mines, and a rain forest.

Very small children should not be left to explore this place alone, as they will get lost inside the playground and might get very scared. Kids over age 8 are guaranteed an adventure and lots of fun. I loved the playground and regret that, due to my height, I was not allowed on the pteranodon whatchamacallit.

Ian

Jurassic Park Discovery Center ★★★

| APPEAL BY AGE | PRESCHOOL ★★★ | GRADE SCHOOL ★★★★ | TEENS ★★★ |
| YOUNG ADULTS ★★★ | | OVER 30 ★★★ | SENIORS ★★★ |

What it is Interactive natural history exhibit. **Scope and scale** Minor attraction. **Fright potential** Not frightening in any respect. **Bottleneck rating** 3. **When to go** Anytime. **Authors' rating** ★★★.

The Discovery Center is an interactive, educational exhibit that mixes fiction from the movie *Jurassic Park,* such as using fossil DNA to bring dinosaurs to life, with various skeletal remains and other paleontological displays. Cycle back after experiencing all the rides or on a second day. Most folks can digest this exhibit in 10–15 minutes.

Don't skip the Discovery Center. On a hot summer day, it is a great place to cool off. The best exhibit of all is the one where an animatronic raptor hatches from an egg. Young children will delight in the hatching and are afforded an opportunity to name the baby dino.

Liliane

Jurassic Park River Adventure ★★★★
(Universal Express)

| APPEAL BY AGE | PRESCHOOL ★★★ | GRADE SCHOOL ★★★★★ | TEENS ★★★★★ |
| YOUNG ADULTS ★★★★ | | OVER 30 ★★★★ | SENIORS ★★★★ |

What it is Indoor-outdoor adventure river-raft ride based on the *Jurassic Park* movies. **Scope and scale** Super-headliner. **Fright potential** Visuals and big drop frighten guests of all ages. **Bottleneck rating** 9. **When to go** Before 11 a.m. **Special comment** Must be 42" tall to ride. **Authors' rating** Better than its Hollywood cousin; ★★★★. **Duration of ride** 6½ minutes. **Average wait in line per 100 people ahead of you** 5 minutes. **Loading speed** Fast.

Guests board boats for a water tour of Jurassic Park. Everything is tranquil as the tour begins, and then, as word is received that some of the carnivores have escaped their enclosure, the tour boat is accidentally diverted into Jurassic Park's maintenance facilities. Here, the boat and its riders are menaced by

Wet   *Scary*

an assortment of hungry meat-eaters. At the climactic moment, the boat and its passengers escape by plummeting over an 85-foot drop. Young children must endure a double whammy on this ride. First, they are stalked by giant, salivating (sometimes spitting) reptiles, and then they're sent catapulting over the falls. Unless your children are fairly stalwart, wait a year or two before you spring the River Adventure on them.

Pteranodon Flyers ½

APPEAL BY AGE	PRESCHOOL ★★★	GRADE SCHOOL ★★★	TEENS ★
YOUNG ADULTS ★★		OVER 30 ★	SENIORS ★★

What it is Slow as Christmas. **Scope and scale** Minor attraction. **Fright potential** Not frightening in any respect. **Bottleneck rating** 10. **When to go** When there's no line. **Authors' rating** All sizzle, no steak; ½. **Duration of ride** 1¼ minutes. **Average wait in line per 100 people ahead of you** 28 minutes. **Loading speed** Slower than a hog in quicksand.

This ride swings you along a track that passes over a small part of Jurassic Park. We recommend that you skip this one. Why? Because the Jurassic period will probably end before you reach the front of the line! And your reward for all that waiting? A 1-minute-and-15-second ride.

THE LOST CONTINENT

THIS AREA IS AN EXOTIC MIX of Silk Road bazaar and ancient ruins, with Greco-Moroccan accents. (And you thought your decorator was nuts.) This is the land of mythical gods, fabled beasts, and expensive souvenirs.

The Eighth Voyage of Sindbad (Universal Express) ★★

APPEAL BY AGE	PRESCHOOL ★★★	GRADE SCHOOL ★★★★	TEENS ★★★
YOUNG ADULTS ★★★		OVER 30 ★★★	SENIORS ★★★

What it is Theater stunt show. **Scope and scale** Major attraction. **Fright potential** Special effects startle preschoolers. **Bottleneck rating** 4. **When to go** Anytime as per the daily entertainment schedule. **Authors' rating** Not inspiring; ★★. **Duration of show** 17 minutes. **Probable waiting time** 15 minutes.

A story about Sindbad the Sailor is the glue that (loosely) binds this stunt show featuring water explosions, 10-foot-tall circles of flame, and various other daunting eruptions and perturbations. It's billed as a stunt show, but the production is so vacuous and redundant that it's hard to get into the action. See *Sindbad* after you've experienced the rides and the better-rated shows. The theater seats 1,700.

Not to be missed is the Mystic Fountain at the entrance to the theater. The fountain may not grant you wishes, but it will talk to you. But watch out, it's a fountain with attitude. Keep your umbrella handy.

Liliane

Poseidon's Fury (Universal Express) ★★★★

APPEAL BY AGE	PRESCHOOL ★★	GRADE SCHOOL ★★★★	TEENS ★★★★
YOUNG ADULTS ★★★★		OVER 30 ★★★★	SENIORS ★★★★

What it is High-tech theater attraction. **Scope and scale** Headliner. **Fright potential** Intense visuals and special effects frighten some preschoolers. **Bottleneck rating** 7. **When to go** After experiencing all the rides. **Special comment** Audience stands throughout. **Authors' rating** Much improved; ★★★★. **Duration of show** 17 minutes, including preshow. **Probable waiting time** 25 minutes.

The Greek god Poseidon tussles with an evil wizard-ish guy using fire, water, lasers, smoke machines, and angry lemurs. (*Note:* Lemurs are not actually used—just seeing if you're paying attention.) The plot unravels in installments as you pass from room to room and finally into the main theater preshow. There's some great technology at work here. *Poseidon* is by far and away the best of the Islands of Adventure theater attractions. Frequent explosions and noise may frighten younger children, so exercise caution with preschoolers. We recommend catching *Poseidon* after experiencing your fill of the rides.

THE WIZARDING WORLD OF HARRY POTTER

IN WHAT MAY PROVE TO BE the competitive coup of all time between archrivals Disney and Universal, the latter inked a deal with Warner Brothers Entertainment to create a fully immersive Harry Potter–themed environment based on the best-selling children's books by J. K. Rowling and the companion blockbuster movies from Warner Brothers. The project was blessed by Rowling, who is known for tenaciously protecting the integrity of her work. In the case of the films, she demanded that Warner Brothers be true, almost to an unprecedented degree, to the books on which the films were based. She had many suitors over the years vie for the rights to translate her novels into a theme park, but she never consented until now.

The 20-acre Wizarding World draws its inspiration from all the Harry Potter movies and books, creating an amalgamation of landmarks, sights, creatures, and themes that are faithful to the films. The Wizarding World is situated in the northwest corner of the park between The Lost Continent and Jurassic Park. Let's begin our exploration at Wizarding World's main entrance on the Lost Continent side of the theme area.

Passing beneath a stone archway, you enter the village of **Hogsmeade.** The **Hogwarts Express** locomotive belches steam on your right, and the village, depicted in winter, stretches before you, following the contours of a gently curving street. While decidedly different and visually rich, the winter thing seems like a stretch in the dog days of August. On your left opposite the train station is **Zonko's,** a joke and novelty shop specializing in such necessities as shrunken heads, extendable ears, and screaming yo-yos. If your sweet tooth is on a rampage, the shop also sells sweets such as Fever Fudge, Nosebleed Nougat, and our personal favorite, Puking Pastilles. Connected to

The Wizarding World will suck up guests like a vacuum on steroids. This means, among other things, that crowds will be considerably lighter in other sections of Islands of Adventure, especially in the morning.

Bob

Zonko's through an interior passage is **HoneyDukes**. For those whose appetite has recovered from disgorging their Puking Pastilles, Honey-Dukes—specializing in Acid Pops, Exploding Bonbons, and Fizzing Whizbees—offers another opportunity to expand your midriff.

Across the street from HoneyDukes next to the train station is the entrance to the Dragon Challenge dueling roller coasters. Next door to HoneyDukes and set back from the main street is the **Three Broomsticks,** a rustic tavern serving English staples such as fish-and-chips, shepherd's pie, Cornish pastry, and turkey legs. A children's menu includes standards such as mac and cheese and the obligatory chicken fingers. The Three Broomsticks is also a good, albeit expensive, venue for ice cream and dessert treats. Adjacent to the restaurant is the **Hog's Head** pub with a nice selection of beer, as well as The Wizarding World's signature nonalcoholic beverage, Butterbeer. Except for some meager snacks from vendor carts, no other hot food or sandwiches are available in The Wizarding World. The Three Broomsticks doesn't participate in any of Universal's meal plans.

Down the street from the Hog's Head are restrooms. Roughly across the street from the pub, you'll find benches in the shade at the **Owlery,** where animatronic owls (complete with owl poop) ruffle and hoot from the rafters.

Next to the Owlery is the **Owl Post,** a functioning post office where any postcards you mail will be delivered with a Hogsmeade postmark. The Owl Post also sells stationery, toy owls, and the like. To access the Owl Post, enter through an interior door following the wand-choosing demonstration at **Ollivanders** (see below) or through **Dervish and Banges,** a magical supplies and equipment shop, which is interconnected with the Owl Post. The Owl Post front door is used exclusively as an exit. Because it's so difficult to get into the Owl Post, Universal sometimes stations a team member outside to stamp your postcards with The Wizarding World postmark.

Next to the Owl Post is the above-mentioned Ollivanders magic wand shop. Here, following a script from the Potter books, you can buy a wand. You can pick it out yourself, or in an interactive experience, a wand will choose you. This is one of the most truly imaginative elements of The Wizarding World. The store is musty and stacked to the ceiling with boxes of wands. A wand keeper sizes you up and presents a wand, inviting you to try it out. Naturally your attempted spells produce unintended, unwanted, and very amusing consequences. The experience is delightful, but the tiny shop can accommodate only about 24 guests at a time. Usually only one person in each group goes through the process of being chosen by a wand, and then the whole group is dispatched to the Owl Post and Dervish and Banges to actually make purchases. Wands run upwards of $19 with most in the $28–$38 range. If Ollivanders is a priority, experience it first thing in the morning or after 7:30 p.m. Average wait time during summer and other busy periods is 60–120 minutes 9:30 a.m.–7:30 p.m.

At the far end of the village is the massive **Hogwarts Castle,** set atop a rock face and towering over Hogsmeade and the entire Wizarding World. Follow the path through the gates of Hogwarts to the Harry Potter and the Forbidden Journey attraction. To the right of the castle and at the base of the cliff are the Forbidden Forest, Hagrid's Hut, and the Flying Hippogriff children's roller coaster. Located in the village near the gate to Hogwarts Castle is **Filch's Emporium of Confiscated Goods.** The shop offers all manner of Potter-themed gifts and apparel, including Quidditch clothing, magical creature toys, film-based chess sets, and of course, Death Eater masks (breath mints extra). Because the shops are so jammed, Universal sells some merchandise, including wands, through street vendors. Wizarding World items are also for sale in Port of Entry shops.

Accessing Wizarding World

Wizarding World crowd management has been a work in progress for Universal. Trying to herd tens of thousands of guests, all wanting to alight in the same few acres of the park, has been a monumental challenge. A variety of measures have been tried, abandoned, modified, and run up the flagpole yet again, all with mixed success. Now, with more than a year and a half of Wizarding World operation under its belt, Universal has settled on a flexible system with three basic crowd-control options predicated on the expected level of attendance for any given day. No matter what the crowd level, however, if you're staying in one of Universal's three on-site hotels and have early-entry privileges for The Wizarding World, use them, arriving as early in the early-entry period as possible.

Crowd Control Option One is for off-season and slow days when the park is not crowded. On these days you can enter and depart The Wizarding World as you please. The waits for the rides will still be over an hour at times, but gaining entry to The Wizarding World is not an issue. Sometimes Option One will be in force in the morning, transitioning to Option Two as crowds build through the course of the day.

Crowd Control Option Two is for days when attendance is high and the park is nearly full to capacity, for example spring break or the days before or after a large holiday. It is at this level that barricades are placed at both entrances to The Wizarding World. You can go to either entrance and obtain a pass to come back into the Harry Potter area at a designated time. The pass is free and similar to Disney's Fastpass. This option allows you to enjoy other areas of the park while waiting for your scheduled time in The Wizarding World. At the specified time, return to either Wizarding World entrance and present the pass to the barricade crew.

Once admitted to the Harry Potter theme area, you will still have to wait for each ride, store, and concessions, as well as for the one restaurant in the area. It's common when Option Two is in effect for the entrance barricades to be removed during the last hour or two the park is open, thus allowing you to come and go as you please.

Crowd Control Option Three is for when the park is at full capacity, usually during holidays such as Easter, Christmas, Thanksgiving, and New Year's Eve. On these days the barricades around Wizarding World are in place all day, and the demand to get into the area is much higher.

On an Option Three day you will be directed toward the Jurassic Park entrance to The Wizarding World. There will also be a standby line to enter the area. You can choose between the standby line, with waits as long as 2–3 hours, or you can obtain a pass with a designated return time as described under Option Two.

Be forewarned that on Option Three days, return passes are fully distributed by noon or earlier. This means that if you are not in line to enter Islands of Adventure before the park opens, there is a chance that you might not be able to enter The Wizarding World at all. We strongly counsel you to arrive an hour before opening on these busiest of days and, once admitted, immediately obtain a return pass. For the first year and a half, return passes were distributed by cast members. In the summer of 2010, automatic machines resembling Disney Fastpass machines were installed in Jurassic Park near the Triceratops exhibit (just past the Jurassic Park River Adventure) and in Lost Continent close to the entrance to the *Sindbad* show. At both locations there is no need to use a park entrance ticket (as with Disney's Fastpass) to obtain a return pass. The machines use touch screens, and you can get one ticket for your whole party. The touch screen asks two questions, starting with how many are in your party. It then allows you to select one of two return times. After answering the questions, a ticket is printed.

On Option Two and Option Three days, do not exit The Wizarding World until you have done and seen everything of interest. This applies to both day guests and hotel guests. Do not defer anything in the area for later in the day or depend on being able to get back in. Schedule food breaks before or after your visit. If you leave Wizarding World, you'll have to obtain a new pass to reenter.

Dragon Challenge (Universal Express) ★★★½

APPEAL BY AGE	PRESCHOOL —	GRADE SCHOOL ★★★★	TEENS ★★★★
YOUNG ADULTS ★★★★		OVER 30 ★★★★	SENIORS ★★

What it is Roller coaster. **Scope and scale** Headliner. **Fright potential** Frightening to guests of all ages. **Bottleneck rating** 4. **When to go** After Harry Potter and the Forbidden Journey. **Special comment** Must be 54" tall to ride. **Authors' rating** As good as the Hulk coaster; ★★★½. **Duration of ride** 2½ minutes. **Average wait in line per 100 people ahead of you** 9 minutes. **Loading speed** Moderate.

Lose Things   Rough   Queasy

This high-tech coaster launches two trains, the Chinese Fireball and the Hungarian Horntail, at the same time on tracks that are closely intertwined. Each track is configured differently so that you get a different experience on each. A collision with the other train sometimes seems imminent—a catastrophe that seems all the more real because the coasters are suspended from above so that you sit with your feet dangling. At times the two trains and their passengers are separated by a mere 12 inches. Because this is an inverted coaster, your view of the action is limited unless you're sitting in the front row. This means that most passengers miss seeing all these near collisions. Dragon Challenge is the highest coaster in the park and also claims the longest drop at 115 feet, not to mention five inversions.

Dragon Challenge, formerly Dueling Dragons, was renamed and incorporated into the new Wizarding World of Harry Potter in 2010. The story line is that you are preparing to compete in the Tri-Wizard Tournament (from *Harry Potter and the Goblet of Fire*). As you wind through the long, long queue, you pass through tournament tents and dark passages. You'll see the Goblet of Fire on display and hear the distant roar of the crowd in the supposed stadium above you.

We prefer the front row on either train, but coaster loonies hype the front row of Chinese Fireball and the last row of Hungarian Horntail.

Flight of the Hippogriff (Universal Express) ★★½

APPEAL BY AGE	PRESCHOOL ★★★★		GRADE SCHOOL ★★★★
TEENS ★★	YOUNG ADULTS ★★	OVER 30 ★	SENIORS ★

What it is Children's roller coaster. **Scope and scale** Minor attraction. **Fright potential** Frightens a small percentage of preschool riders. **Bottleneck rating** 5. **When to go** First 90 minutes the park is open. **Special comment** Must be 36" tall to ride. **Authors' rating** A good beginner coaster; ★★½. **Duration of ride** 1 minute. **Average wait in line per 100 people ahead of you** 14 minutes. **Loading speed** Slow.

Previously called the Flying Unicorn, the coaster underwent a name and theme change when it was incorporated into The Wizarding World. Located below and to the right of Hogwarts Castle next to Hagrid's Hut, the Hippogriff is short and sweet but not worth much of a wait. Fortunately, waits usually don't exceed 20 minutes, even in the non-Express line. Have your children ride soon after the park opens, while older sibs enjoy Dragon Challenge. Even if you don't ride, it's worth a stroll down to see Hogwarts Castle from the cliff bottom and to check out Hagrid's Hut situated above the path for the regular line.

Harry Potter and the Forbidden Journey ★★★★½

APPEAL BY AGE	PRESCHOOL –	GRADE SCHOOL ★★★★★	TEENS ★★★★★
YOUNG ADULTS ★★★★★		OVER 30 ★★★★★	SENIORS ★★★★★

What it is Motion simulator dark ride. **Scope and scale** Super-headliner. **Fright potential** Intense special effects and wild ride. **Bottleneck rating** Off the chart. **When to go** Immediately after park opening or after 8 p.m. The ride has a Universal Express line, but for the time being, it is not being used. **Special comments** Expect *long* waits in line; must be 48" tall to ride. The seats are designed for certain body types. Sample seats are at the beginning of the queue, and just before the boarding area is a bench with four fully functional seats. To ride, the overhead restraint has to click three times. If you don't pass muster, you'll be escorted to a place where you can wait for the rest of your party. **Authors' rating** ★★★½. **Duration of ride** 4⅓ minutes. **Average wait in line per 100 people ahead of you** 4 minutes. **Loading speed** Moderate.

    This attraction is the big banana of The Wizarding World and provides the only opportunity to actually come in contact with the Harry Potter characters. Half of the attraction is a series of preshows that sets the stage for the main event, a dark ride. To understand the story line and get the most out of the attraction, it's critical to see and hear the entire presentation in each of the queue's preshow rooms. You can get on the ride in only 10–20 minutes using the single-riders line, but everyone should go through the main queue at least once. If you see a complete iteration of each of the preshows in the queue and then experience the 4⅓-minute ride, you'll invest 25–35 minutes even if you don't have to wait.

From Hogsmeade you reach the attraction through the imposing Winged Boar gate and progress along a winding path. Entering the castle on a lower level, you walk through a sort of dungeon with various icons and prop replicas from the Potter flicks, including the Mirror of Erised from *Harry Potter and the Sorcerer's Stone* (*Harry Potter and the Philosopher's Stone* outside the United States). Later you emerge outside and into the Hogwarts' greenhouses, which comprise the larger part of the Forbidden Journey's queuing area. The greenhouses are not air-conditioned, but fans move the (hot) air around. Also, blessedly, drinking fountains are in the greenhouse, but no restrooms—take care of that before getting in line for the attraction.

Once through horticulture purgatory, you reenter the castle, moving along its halls and passageways. One chamber you'll probably remember from the films is a multistory gallery of portraits, many of whose subjects come alive when they take a notion. The four founders of Hogwarts—Rowena Ravenclaw, Helga Hufflepuff holding her famous cup, Godric Gryffindor nearby, and the tall, moving portrait of Salazar Slytherin straight ahead—argue about Quidditch and Dumbledore's controversial decision to host an open house for muggles (garden-variety humans who are neither wizards nor witches) at Hogwarts. Don't rush through the gallery—the effects are very cool and the conversation among the portraits is essential to understanding the rest of the attraction.

After navigating some more passages, you reach Dumbledore's office, where Dumbledore appears on a balcony and welcomes you to Hogwarts. The headmaster's appearance is your introduction to Musion Eyeliner® technology, a high-definition video projection system that produces breathtakingly realistic, three-dimensional, moving, life-size holograms. After his welcoming remarks, Dumbledore dispatches you to the Defence Against the Dark Arts classroom to hear a presentation on the history of Hogwarts.

As you await the lecturer, Harry, Ron Weasley, and Hermione Granger pop out from under an invisibility cloak. They suggest that you ditch the lecture in favor of joining them for a proper tour of Hogwarts, including a Quidditch match. After some repartee between the characters and a couple of special effects surprises, it's off to the Hogwarts Official Attraction

Safety Briefing and Boarding Instructions Chamber—OK, we made up the name of the room, but that's what goes on there. The briefing and instructions are presented by talking portraits including an etiquette teacher. Later on, even the famed Sorting Hat gets into the act. All this leads to the Requirement Room with hundreds of candles floating overhead. This is where you board the ride.

After all the high-tech stuff in your queuing odyssey, you will naturally expect to be wowed by your ride vehicle. Surely it's a Nimbus 3000 turbo-broom, a Phoenix, a Hippogriff, or at least the Weasleys' flying car. But no, what you will ride in the most technologically advanced theme-park attraction in America is, ta-da . . . a bench!?! Yes, you heard right, a bench. Not that there's anything wrong with a bench. We're just saying that maybe the well ran a little dry in the imagination department.

But as benches go, it's a doozy, mounted to a Kuka robotic arm that can be programmed to replicate all the sensations of flying, including broad swoops, steep dives, sharp turns, sudden stops, and fast acceleration. The ride vehicle moves you through a series of alternating sets and domes where scenes are projected all around you. The movement of the Kuka arm is synchronized to create the motion that corresponds to what is happening in the set or film. When everything works correctly, it's mind blowing. You'll soar over Hogwarts Castle, get tossed into a Quidditch match, spar with the Whomping Willow, narrowly evade an attacking dragon, and fight off Dementors.

Many riders experience various degrees of motion sickness on Forbidden Journey. The best defense against motion sickness is not to ride on an empty stomach. If you have a child who doesn't meet the minimum-height requirement of 48 inches, a child-swapping option is provided at the loading area. Be advised that the seats on each bench are compartmentalized, so your child will not be able to see you or hold your hand.

Upon entering Forbidden Journey's outside queue, you have two choices, left line or right line. They are unmarked, but the right line is for those who have bags or loose items (and therefore *require* a locker). Our wait-time research has shown that, in some cases, not having a bag (and not needing a locker) can save you as much as 30 minutes of standing in line! The locker area is small, crowded, and confusing. Given this, it may make more sense to risk paying the $3 and stashing your things at the lockers beside Dragon Challenge.

The single-rider line is equally unmarked and relatively few guests use it. Typically, on most attractions, the wait in the singles line is one-third the wait of the standby line. At Forbidden Journey it can be as much as one-tenth! Because the ride experience is individual (you can't see the other riders, including members of your party), the singles line is a great option. To access the singles line, enter the left line (no bags) and stay to the left all the way into Hogwarts Castle. After passing the locker area, take the first left into the unmarked single-rider line. If you use the singles line, however, you will miss much of the interior of the castle.

SEUSS LANDING

A 10-ACRE THEMED AREA BASED ON Dr. Seuss's famous children's books. As at the old Mickey's Toontown in the Magic Kingdom, all of the buildings and attractions replicate a whimsical, brightly colored cartoon style with exaggerated features and rounded lines. There are four rides at Seuss Landing (described below) and an interactive play area, **If I Ran the Zoo,** populated by Seuss creatures.

If you have only young children in your party, Seuss Landing is the place to spend lots of happy time. A great stop in Seuss Landing is Dr. Seuss's All the Books You Can Read bookstore. Last but not least, if your kids cannot get enough of Dr. Seuss, check out **seussville.com.**

Liliane

Caro-Seuss-El (Universal Express) ★★★½

APPEAL BY AGE	PRESCHOOL ★★★★	GRADE SCHOOL ★★★★
TEENS —	YOUNG ADULTS —	OVER 30 —	SENIORS —

What it is Merry-go-round. **Scope and scale** Minor attraction. **Fright potential** Not frightening in any respect. **Bottleneck rating** 8. **When to go** Before 11 a.m. **Authors' rating** Wonderfully unique; ★★★½. **Duration of ride** 2 minutes. **Average wait in line per 100 people ahead of you** 9 minutes. **Loading speed** Slow.

Totally outrageous, the Caro-Seuss-El is a full-scale, 56-mount merry-go-round made up exclusively of Dr. Seuss characters. If you are touring with young children, try to get them on early in the morning.

The Cat in the Hat (Universal Express) ★★★½

APPEAL BY AGE	PRESCHOOL ★★★★	GRADE SCHOOL ★★★★	TEENS ★★★
YOUNG ADULTS ★★★★	OVER 30 ★★★★	SENIORS ★★★★

What it is Indoor adventure ride. **Scope and scale** Major attraction. **Fright potential** Not frightening in any respect. **Bottleneck rating** 8. **When to go** Before 11:30 a.m. **Authors' rating** Seuss would be proud; ★★★½. **Duration of ride** 3½ minutes. **Average wait in line per 100 people ahead of you** 5 minutes. **Loading speed** Moderate.

A must for preschoolers, guests ride on "couches" through 18 different sets inhabited by animatronic Seuss characters, including The Cat in the Hat, Thing 1, Thing 2, and the beleaguered goldfish who tries to maintain order in the midst of bedlam. Well done overall, with nothing that should frighten younger children. This is fun for all ages. Try to ride early.

The High in the Sky Seuss Trolley Train Ride! ★★★½
(Universal Express)

APPEAL BY AGE	PRESCHOOL ★★★★	GRADE SCHOOL ★★★½	TEENS ★
YOUNG ADULTS ★★½	OVER 30 ★★½	SENIORS ★★★

What it is Elevated train. **Scope and scale** Major attraction. **Fright potential** Not frightening in any respect. **Bottleneck rating** 8. **When to go** Before 11:30 a.m. **Authors' rating** ★★★½. **Special comments** Relaxed tour of Seuss Landing; must be 34" tall to ride. **Duration of ride** 3½ minutes. **Average wait in line per 100 people ahead of you** 11 minutes. **Average wait in line per 100 people**

ahead of you 9 minutes. **Loading speed** Molasses.

Trains putter along elevated tracks, while a voice reads one of four Dr. Seuss stories over the train's speakers. As each train makes its way through Seuss Landing, it passes a series of animatronic characters in scenes that are part of the story being told. The trains are small, fitting about 20 people, and the loading speed is glacial. Save the train ride for the end of the day or ride first thing in the morning.

If I Ran the Zoo ★★★ (Universal Express)

APPEAL BY AGE	PRESCHOOL ★★★★★	GRADE SCHOOL ★★★	TEENS —
YOUNG ADULTS —		OVER 30 —	SENIORS —

What it is Interactive playground. **Scope and scale** Minor attraction. **Fright potential** Not frightening in any respect. **Bottleneck rating** 2. **When to go** Any time. **Authors' rating** Whimsical and funny; great for preschoolers; ★★★★.

A playground with 19 different interactive elements, this area is great silly-dilly fun for little tykes. How silly? The sign at the entrance of this crazy zoo should give you a clue: "Keep track of adults. They get lost all the time." And yes, you should know by now that there is no way the kids will stay dry.

One Fish, Two Fish, Red Fish, Blue Fish ★★★½ (Universal Express)

APPEAL BY AGE	PRESCHOOL ★★★★	GRADE SCHOOL ★★★★	TEENS ★★★
YOUNG ADULTS ★★★		OVER 30 ★★★	SENIORS ★★★

What it is Wet version of Dumbo the Flying Elephant. **Scope and scale** Minor attraction. **Fright potential** Not frightening in any respect. **Bottleneck rating** 8. **When to go** Before 10 a.m. **Authors' rating** Who says you can't teach an old ride new tricks? ★★★½. **Duration of ride** 2 minutes. **Average wait in line per 100 people ahead of you** 9 minutes. **Loading speed** Slow.

Wet

Imagine Dumbo with Seuss-style fish instead of elephants, and you have half the story. Guests steer their fish up or down 15 feet in the air while traveling in circles trying to avoid streams of water projected from "squirt posts."

I followed Dr. Seuss's advice: If you never did, you should. These things are fun. These things are good. And all wet there I stood! My favorite ride in Seuss Landing!
Liliane

ISLANDS *of* ADVENTURE TOURING PLAN

ISLANDS OF ADVENTURE 1-DAY TOURING PLAN FOR FAMILIES

WE PRESENT ONE ISLANDS OF ADVENTURE TOURING PLAN geared toward the whole family. Because there are so many attractions with the potential to frighten young children, be prepared to skip a

FAVORITE EATS AT UNIVERSAL'S ISLANDS OF ADVENTURE

| LAND | SERVICE LOCATION | FOOD ITEM |

PORT OF ENTRY

Croissant Moon Bakery | Croissants & panini

TOON LAGOON

Ale to the Chief | Nathan's hot dogs
Blondie's: Home of the Dagwood | Sandwiches

JURASSIC PARK

Pizza Predattoria | Pizza

WIZARDING WORLD

Three Broomsticks | Fish-and-chips

LOST CONTINENT

Fire Eater's Grill | Gyro
Mythos Restaurant | Risotto & pizza

SEUSS LANDING

Circus McGurkus Cafe Stoo-pendous | Fried chicken; mashed potatoes with gravy
Green Eggs and Ham Cafe | Green eggs & ham sandwich platter (*Green herbs are the reason for the green eggs, not food coloring.*)

few things and to practice switching off (works the same way as at Walt Disney World; see page 242). For the most part, attractions designed especially for young children, such as playgrounds, can be enjoyed anytime. Work them into the plan at your convenience.

Be aware that in this park there are an inordinate number of attractions that will get you wet. If you want to experience them, come armed with ponchos, large plastic garbage bags, or some other protective covering. Failure to follow this prescription will make for a squishy, sodden day.

This plan is for families of all sizes and ages and includes thrill rides that may induce motion sickness or get you wet. If the plan calls for you to experience an attraction that does not interest you, simply bypass that attraction and proceed to the next step. Be aware that the plan calls for some backtracking. The plan can be found in clip-out form with a map on page 468.

UNIVERSAL CITYWALK

AT CITYWALK you will find a number of great restaurants, clubs, shops, outdoor entertainment, a concert hall (Hard Rock Live), and the Universal Cineplex 20 movie theater. CityWalk has a number of combination restaurants and clubs. Open to families with kids until 9 p.m.,

If you want to have a good time at one of the clubs or a calm dinner, consider sending your teen to the movies or to Teen Night at The Groove. The movie theater, restaurants, and clubs are all centrally located, and it is easy to have a controlled night out.

Liliane

many of the venues offer live entertainment. Teens can sample a taste of the club scene and still be in bed by 10 p.m.

For mom's and dad's night out, great entertainment is available at Rising Star, a karaoke bar where a live band backs the singers; reggae at Bob Marley—A Tribute to Freedom; Pat O'Brien's dueling-piano club; Jimmy Buffett's Margaritaville; the Latin Quarter for Nuevo Latino music; the Red Coconut Club, an upscale lounge with cocktails and dancing; and The Groove, a club with high-tech lighting and visual effects. If you want to go clubbing, $12 plus tax admits you to all of the clubs.

On designated nights, teens ages 15–19 (school ID or driver's license is required for admission) can get into the teen spirit at Teen Night at The Groove. A DJ spins the latest hits; admission is $10–$15, and the first soft drink is included. For details and a schedule, call Universal CityWalk information at ☎ 407-224-2691.

How To Make it Work

CityWalk is open daily 11 a.m.–2 a.m., and parking is available in the same garages that serve the theme park at the rate of $15 a day; parking is $10 from 3 p.m. until park closing. If you park before 3 p.m., you can receive an $8 cinema parking rebate with movie ticket purchase; after 3 p.m., receive a $5 rebate with movie ticket purchase. If you stay at one of the Universal resorts, it's a short walk, but water taxi and bus transportation are also available to transport you to CityWalk. For added fun, try one of the pedicabs that will take you from CityWalk to your resort for a modest tip. Call ☎ 407-224-FOOD for dinner reservations. Visit **universalorlando.com** and select "At CityWalk" under "Events" for special events.

SEAWORLD

Discount coupons for SeaWorld admission are available in the free visitor magazines found in most (but not Disney) hotel lobbies.

MANY DOZENS OF READERS HAVE WRITTEN to extol the virtues of SeaWorld. The following are representative. An English family writes:

The best-organized park [is] SeaWorld. The computer printout we got on arrival had a very useful show schedule, told us which areas were temporarily closed due to construction, and had a readily understandable map. Best of all, there was almost no queuing. Overall, we rated this day so highly that it is the park we would most like to visit again.

A woman in Alberta, Canada, gives her opinion:

We chose SeaWorld as our fifth day at the "World." What a pleasant surprise! It was every bit as good (and in some ways better) than WDW itself. Well worth the admission, an excellent entertainment value,

STAR RATINGS FOR SEAWORLD ATTRACTIONS

★★★★★	Manta (roller coaster)
★★★★½	*One Ocean* (high-tech Shamu and killer-whale show)
★★★★	Kraken (roller coaster)
★★★★	*Shamu Rocks* (killer-whale movements synchronized to rock music; seasonal after dark)
★★★½	*Clyde and Seamore Take Pirate Island* (sea lion, walrus, and otter show)
★★★½	Key West at SeaWorld (dolphin, stingray, and turtle viewing)
★★★½	Shamu's Happy Harbor (children's play area)
★★★½	Shark Encounter
★★★½	Wild Arctic (simulation ride and Arctic wildlife viewing)
★★★	*A'lure: The Call of the Ocean* (Cirque du Soleil–type presentation)
★★★	*Blue Horizons* (whale, dolphin, and bird show)
★★★	*Elmo and Abby's Treasure Hunt* (stage show featuring *Sesame Street* characters; seasonal)
★★★	Manatee Rescue (manatee viewing)
★★★	Pacific Point Preserve (sea lions and seals)
★★★	Penguin Encounter
★★★	*Pets Ahoy!* (show with performing birds, cats, dogs, and a pig)
★★½	Journey to Atlantis (combination roller coaster–flume ride)
★★	Skytower (400-foot-tall observation tower)

educational, well run, and better value for the dollar in food services. Perhaps expand your coverage to give them their due!

OK, here's what you need to know (for additional information, call ☎ 407-351-3600, 888-800-5447, or visit **seaworld.com**). SeaWorld is a world-class marine-life theme park near the intersection of I-4 and the Beachline Expressway. It's about 10 miles east of Walt Disney World. Opening daily at 9 a.m. and closing between 6 p.m. and 11 p.m., depending on the season, SeaWorld charges about $80 admission for adults and $72 for children ages 3–9. Five-park combination passes (called the Orlando Flex Ticket), which include admission to SeaWorld, Universal

If you don't purchase your admission in advance, take advantage of Bob the automatic admission machines located to the right of the main entrance. The machines are a pain in the rear, asking for your name, age, home zip code, and billing zip code, but if you have a credit card, the machines are a lot faster than standing in line at the ticket windows.

FAVORITE EATS AT SEAWORLD

LAND	SERVICE LOCATION	FOOD ITEM

KEY WEST AT SEAWORLD
Captain Pete's Island Eats | Hot dogs & fresh funnel cakes

THE WATERFRONT
Voyager's Smokehouse | Barbecue ribs & chicken

SHARK ENCOUNTER
Sharks Underwater Grill | Floor-to-ceiling glass allows guests to dine and observe some 50 sharks and other fish. *(table service only)*

WILD ARCTIC
Mango Joe's | Fajita sandwiches

FRONT GATE PLAZA
Sweet Sailin' Candy Shop | Candies & hand-dipped chocolate turtles

Studios, Islands of Adventure, Wet 'n Wild, and Busch Gardens, are also available. Sea World offers some super advance purchase discounts on its website. Parking is $14 per car, $15 per RV or camper.

Figure 8–9 hours or more to see everything, 6 or so if you stick to the big deals. Discovery Cove is directly across the Central Florida Parkway from SeaWorld. Parking at Discovery Cove is free.

With a focus on personal guest service and one-on-one animal encounters, Discovery Cove admits only 1,000 guests per day.

SeaWorld is about the size of the Magic Kingdom and requires about the same amount of walking. In terms of size, quality, and creativity, it's unequivocally on par with Disney's major theme parks. Unlike Walt Disney World, SeaWorld primarily features stadium shows or walk-through exhibits. This means that you will spend about 80% less time waiting in line during 8 hours at SeaWorld than you would for the same-length visit at a Disney park.

But, you'll notice immediately as you check the performance times that the shows are scheduled so that it's almost impossible to see them back to back. A Cherry Hill, New Jersey, visitor confirms this rather major problem, complaining:

The shows were timed so we could not catch all the major ones in a 7-hour visit.

Much of the year, you can get a seat for the stadium shows by showing up 10 or so minutes in advance. When the park is crowded, however, you need to be at the stadiums at least 20 minutes in advance (30 minutes in advance for a good seat). All of the stadiums have splash zones, specified areas where you're likely to be drenched with ice-cold saltwater by whales, dolphins, and sea lions. Finally, SeaWorld has three of the best coasters—Journey to Atlantis, Manta, and Kraken—in the county. If you're a coaster lover, be on hand before park opening and ride all three rides as soon as the park opens.

DISCOVERY COVE

THIS INTIMATE PARK is a welcome departure from the hustle and bustle of other Orlando parks; its slower pace could be the overstimulated family's ticket back to mental health.

The main draw at Discovery Cove is the chance to swim with an Atlantic bottlenose dolphin, from among the 30 here. The 30-minute experience is open to visitors age 6 and up who are comfortable in the water. Discovery Cove is located across the street from SeaWorld.

Other exhibits at Discovery Cove include the Grand Reef, the Tropical Reef, the Explorer's Aviary, the Ray Pool, and the Freshwater Lagoon. Snorkel or swim in the Tropical Reef, which houses thousands of exotic fish, as well as an underwater shipwreck and hidden grottoes. In the Aviary, you can touch and feed gorgeous tropical birds. The park is threaded by a "tropical river" in which you can float or swim and is dotted with beaches that serve as pathways to the attractions.

Discovery Cove is open 9 a.m.–5:30 p.m. daily. Admission is limited, so purchase tickets well in advance; call ☎ 877-4-DISCOVERY or visit **discoverycove.com.** Prices vary seasonally $211.94–$414.29 per person, including tax (no children's discount). Admission includes the dolphin swim, self-parking, Continental breakfast, lunch, drinks, snacks, and use of beach umbrellas, lounge chairs, towels, lockers, and swim and snorkel gear. Discovery Cove admission also includes a 7-day pass to SeaWorld Orlando, Aquatica, *or* Busch Gardens Tampa. If you're not interested in the dolphin swim, you can visit Discovery Cove for the day for $137.39–$211.94 per person, depending on the season.

The price is high, but the prize is right. Swimming with a dolphin across the bay was one of the most amazing things I have ever done in my life.

Liliane

THE REST *of* *the* WORLD

The WATER THEME PARKS

WALT DISNEY WORLD HAS TWO SWIMMING THEME PARKS. Typhoon Lagoon is the most diverse Disney splash pad, while Blizzard Beach takes the prize for the most slides and most bizarre theme (a ski resort in meltdown). Blizzard Beach has the best slides, but Typhoon Lagoon has a surf pool where you can bodysurf. Both parks have excellent and elaborate themed areas for toddlers and preschoolers.

Disney water parks allow one cooler per family or group, but no glass and no alcoholic beverages. Both parks charge the following rental prices: towels, $2; lockers are $13 small, $15 large (plus $5 refundable deposit); life jackets are available at no cost. Strollers are welcome but are not available for rent. Admission costs for each park are $49 per day for adults and $43 per day for children (ages 3–9).

During summer and holiday periods, Typhoon Lagoon and Blizzard Beach fill to capacity on weekdays and close their gates before 11 a.m.

The best way to avoid standing in lines is to visit the water parks when they're less crowded. We recommend going on a Saturday or Sunday, when most visitors are traveling, or on a Monday—very few guests go to a water park on their first day at Walt Disney World. Like the four major Disney parks, the water parks participate in the Extra Magic Hours program, but on a limited and seasonal basis. Typhoon Lagoon has Extra Magic Hour mornings on Wednesdays and Blizzard Beach on Thursdays during the summer and busy spring periods 8–9 a.m. Evening Extra Magic Hours are not currently offered at the water parks. If you are a Disney resort guest, by all means visit on the day the water park of your choice offers Extra Magic Hours.

If you have a car, drive instead of taking a Disney bus.

Just like at the major theme parks, the key to a successful visit to the water parks is to arrive early. If you are going to Blizzard Beach or Typhoon Lagoon, get up early, have breakfast, and arrive at the park 30 minutes before opening. Wear your bathing suit under shorts and a T-shirt so you don't need to use lockers or dressing rooms. Wear shoes. The paths are relatively easy on bare feet, but there's a lot of ground to cover. If you or your children have tender feet, wear protective footwear that can be worn in and out of the water as you move around the park. Shops in the parks sell sandals and waterproof shoes.

You will need a towel, sunblock, and money. Carry enough money for the day and your Disney resort ID (if you have one) in a plastic bag or Tupperware container. Though nowhere is completely safe, we felt comfortable hiding our plastic money bags in our cooler. Nobody disturbed our stuff, and our cash was easy to reach. However, if you're carrying a wad or

Wallets and purses get in the way, so lock them in your car's trunk or leave them at your hotel.

Liliane

worry about money anyway, rent a locker. Another great device is a waterproof card case with a lanyard to hold park tickets, a credit card, some cash, and your hotel key. You can buy them at the water parks for about $10; more sophisticated versions are available at any good outdoors or sport shop.

Personal swim gear (fins, masks, rafts, and so on) is not allowed. Everything you need is either provided or available to rent. If you forget your towel, you can rent one (cheap!). If you forgot your swimsuit or lotion, they're available for sale. So are disposable, waterproof cameras, which are especially fun to have at Typhoon Lagoon Shark Reef.

Establish your base for the day. Many beautiful sunning and lounging spots are

Lost children stations at the water parks are so out of the way that neither you nor your child will find them without help from a Disney cast member. Explain to your children how to recognize a Disney cast member (by their distinctive name tags) and how to ask for help.

Liliane

scattered throughout both swimming parks. Arrive early, and you can have your pick. The breeze is best along the beaches of the lagoon at Blizzard Beach and the surf pool at Typhoon Lagoon. At Typhoon Lagoon, if children younger than age 6 are in your party, choose an area to the left of Mount Mayday near the children's swimming area.

Though Typhoon Lagoon and Blizzard Beach are huge parks with many slides, armies of guests overwhelm them almost daily. If your main reason for going is the slides and you hate long lines, try to be among the first guests to enter the park. Go directly to the slides and ride as many times as you can before the park fills. When lines for the slides become intolerable, head for the surf or wave pool or the tube-floating streams. The lazy rivers at both parks are perfect for relaxation. Float

While I do not feel any better on a water roller coaster than I do on the dry thing, I love the water parks. My all-time favorite water ride is Teamboat Springs, the 1,200-foot white-water raft flume at Blizzard Beach.

Liliane

through caves, beneath waterfalls, past gardens, and under bridges. Life is beautiful and the water is soothing. Did you know that in the winter months Disney actually heats all the water park pools?

Both water parks are large and require almost as much walking as the major theme parks. Add to this wave surfing, swimming, and climbing to reach the slides, and you'll definitely be pooped by day's end. Consider a low-key activity for the evening.

Grab an inner tube and go on Cross Country Creek or Castaway Creek. It's best when you go with a group like your family. Sometimes I hop off the tube and find an underwater jet on the side of the bank. If you go underwater, the jet will shoot you out really fast. It's a blast! Don't worry; the water isn't deep. A good trick to play on someone in your family is to push their inner tube under a cave waterfall. The water is ice cold. It's fun to watch them freak out.

Ian

It's as easy to lose a child or become separated from your party at one of the water parks as it is at a major theme park. On arrival, pick a very specific place to meet in the event you are separated. If you split up on purpose, establish times for checking in.

Children under age 10 must be accompanied by an adult. The water parks are great fun for the whole family, but if you have very young children or if you are not a thrill-seeking water puppy, the pool of your hotel might serve just as well. The water parks, however, were made to order for teens. Note that during the winter months, Disney closes Blizzard Beach and Typhoon Lagoon for refurbishing, alternating maintenance in such a way that one water park will be open at all times. If it is very wintry, Disney will close both parks.

Captain Nemo surfaces by mistake at Blizzard Beach.

Blizzard Beach

ATTRACTION | HEIGHT REQUIREMENT | WHAT TO EXPECT

CHAIR LIFT UP MT. GUSHMORE | 32 inches | Great ride even if you only go up for the view. When the park is packed, use the single-riders line.

CROSS COUNTRY CREEK | None | Lazy river circling the park; grab a tube.

DOWNHILL DOUBLE DIPPER | 48 inches | Side-by-side tube-racing slides. At 25 mph, the tube races through water curtains and free falls. It's a lot of fun but rough.

MELT-AWAY BAY | None | Wave pool with gentle, bobbing waves. The pool is great for younger swimmers.

RUNOFF RAPIDS | None | Three corkscrew tube slides to choose from. The center slide is for solo raft rides; the other two slides offer one-, two-, or three-person tubes. The dark, enclosed tube makes the ride feel as if you've been flushed down a toilet.

SKI PATROL TRAINING CAMP | 48 inches and shorter | A place for kids a little too old for Tike's Peak but not tall enough yet for the adult slides.

SLUSH GUSHER | 48 inches | A 90-foot double-humped slide. Ladies, cling to those tops—all others hang on to live.

SNOW STORMERS | None | Three mat-slide flumes; down you go on your belly.

SUMMIT PLUMMET | 48 inches | A 120-foot free fall at 60 mph. This ride is very intense. Make sure that your child knows what to expect. Being over 48 inches tall does not guarantee an enjoyable experience. If you think you'd enjoy washing out of a 12th-floor window during a heavy rain, then this slide is for you.

TEAMBOAT SPRINGS | None | 1,200-foot white-water group raft flume. Wonderful ride for the whole family.

TIKE'S PEAK | 48 inches and under only | Kid-size version of Blizzard Beach. This is the place for little ones.

TOBOGGAN RACERS | None | Eight-lane race course. You go down the flume on a mat. The ride is less intense than Snow Stormers.

BEFORE YOU GO

1. Call ☎ 407-824-4321 the day before you go to find out the official park opening time.
2. Purchase admission tickets online before you arrive.
3. Decide if you want to picnic or not, and then plan or pack accordingly. Pets are not allowed at the water parks.

A WORD FROM THE WEATHERMAN

THUNDERSTORMS ARE COMMON in Florida. On summer afternoons such storms often occur daily, forcing the water parks to

The Slush Gusher at Blizzard Beach is really cool. It's really steep and wavy on the way down. You have to cross your arms and legs because water will rush up your swimsuit. Stay as still as possible, and you will go really fast. A speed sign at the bottom shows how fast you came down. Be careful, because if you try to open your eyes, water goes in, and sometimes water goes up your nose.

— Ian

Typhoon Lagoon

ATTRACTION | HEIGHT REQUIREMENT | WHAT TO EXPECT

CASTAWAY CREEK | None | Half-mile lazy river in a tropical setting. Wonderful!

CRUSH 'N' GUSHER | 48 inches | Water roller coaster where you can choose from among three slides: Banana Blaster, Coconut Crusher, and Pineapple Plunger, ranging 410–420 feet long. This thriller leaves you wondering what exactly happened—if you make it down in one piece, that is. It's not for the faint of heart. If your kids are new to water-park rides, this is not the place to break them in, even if they're tall enough to ride.

GANG PLANK FALLS | None | White-water raft flume in a multiperson tube.

HUMUNGA KOWABUNGA | 48 inches | Speed slides that hit 30 mph. A five-story drop in the dark rattles the most courageous rider. Ladies should ride this in a one-piece swimsuit.

KEELHAUL FALLS | None | Fast white-water ride in a single-person tube.

KETCHAKIDDEE CREEK | 48 inches and under only | Toddlers and preschoolers love this area reserved only for them. Say "splish splash" and have lots of fun.

MAYDAY FALLS | None | The name says it all. Wild single-person tube ride. Hang on!

SHARK REEF | None | After you're equipped with fins, mask, snorkel, and a life vest, you get a brief lesson in snorkeling. Then off you go for about 60 feet to the other side of the saltwater pool, where you swim with small colorful fish, rays, and very small leopard and hammerhead sharks. If you don't want to swim with the fish, visit the underwater viewing chamber anytime during the day. Surface Air Snorkeling—a SCUBA-like pursuit involving a "pony" tank, a small regulator, and a buoyancy vest—is also offered. Participants must be at least 5 years old. To sign up and get more information, visit the kiosk near the entrance to Shark Reef.

STORM SLIDES | None | Three body-slides down and thru Mount Mayday.

SURF POOL | None | World's largest inland surf facility with waves up to 6 feet high. Adult supervision required. Four summer mornings each week at 5:45 a.m. (before the park opens), surfing lessons are offered (surfboard provided). Cost is $150 for 2½ hours; minimum age is 8; class size is 12. Call ☎ 407-WDW-SURF. The price does not include park admission.

close temporarily while the threatening weather passes. If the storm is severe and prolonged, it can cause a great deal of inconvenience. The park may actually close for the day, launching a legion through the turnstiles to compete for space on the Disney resort buses. If you depend on Disney buses, leave the park earlier, rather than later, when you see a storm moving in. Most important though, instruct your children to immediately return to home base at the sight of lightning or when they hear the first rumble of thunder.

We recommend that you monitor the local weather forecast the day before you go, checking again in the morning before leaving for the water park. Scattered thunderstorms are to be expected and usually cause no more than temporary inconvenience, but moving storm fronts are to be avoided.

FAVORITE EATS AT THE WATER PARKS

LAND | SERVICE LOCATION | FOOD ITEM

BLIZZARD BEACH

Avalunch | Hot dogs & cheesecake
Cooling Hut | Popcorn, nachos, & Itzakadoozie
Lottawatta Lodge | Pizza, burgers, salads, & kids' meals
Warming Hut | Hot dogs & chicken wraps

TYPHOON LAGOON

Happy Landings | Ice cream, cookies, & waffle cones. *Garbage pail:* Ice cream pieces, fudge, nuts, and sprinkles in pail with shovel.
Leaning Palms | Pizza & kids' meals inside sand pail with shovel
Lowtide Lou's (seasonal) | Chicken wraps & tuna sandwiches
Typhoon Tilly's | Fish, barbecued pork, & kids' meals inside sand pail with shovel

Refillable mugs: If you or the kids enjoy soda, your best bet is to get a refillable mug, available at both water parks. For the price of the mug ($10), you are entitled to free refills throughout the day (only on the day of purchase). Select locations.

SAFETY FIRST

TOO MUCH FUN IN THE SUN isn't a good thing if you get sunburned or become dehydrated. Drink lots of fluids, use sunscreen, and bring a T-shirt and a hat for extra protection. Read all signs and follow the rules. Lifeguards are on duty throughout the parks. At Typhoon Lagoon, a first-aid station is located behind Leaning Palms. The Blizzard Beach first-aid station is between Lottawatta Lodge and Beach Haus.

WET 'N WILD

WET 'N WILD (ON INTERNATIONAL DRIVE IN ORLANDO, one block east of I-4 at Exit 75A; ☎ 800-992-WILD or 407-351-1800; **wetnwildorlando.com**) is a non-Disney water-park option. If you are looking for a colorful atmosphere, Wet 'n Wild will not deliver; however, the park is packed with incredible slides, flumes, and activities for all ages. Water puppies will get their fill, and kids can go wild.

Tickets with tax at the main gate are $48 for adults and $42 for kids ages 3–9. Always call or check online for special deals and discounts (especially for AAA members, Florida residents, and members of the military). An annual pass is $80 if purchased online, and an annual pass for weekdays runs $70 (both are plus tax and include parking). In recent years Wet 'n Wild has offered unlimited admission for the rest of the year or the rest of your stay for the price of a 1-day ticket. The park also regularly offers half-price admission in the

Wet 'n Wild

ATTRACTION | HEIGHT REQUIREMENT | WHAT TO EXPECT

THE BLACK HOLE | 48 inches if riding alone; 36 inches if riding with an adult | Two-person tube; 1,000 gallons of water per minute; all this in the dark. Do we need to say more? While not the wildest ride in town, it sure is dark in there.

THE BLAST | 48 inches if riding alone; 36 inches if riding with an adult | Two-person tube ride inside a waterworks where all the pipes are broken. You cannot get any wetter.

THE BOMB BAY | 48 inches | You stand on a pair of doors that open, dropping you down a 76-foot slide. You're gonna need a lot of nerve to stand on those doors and wait for the drop.

BRAIN WASH | 48 inches | Extreme six-story tube ride with a 53-foot vertical drop into a 65-foot funnel; tube holds two or four riders.

BUBBA TUB | 48 inches if riding alone; 36 inches if riding with an adult | Long straight track with three hummocks to impede momentum.

DER STUKA | 48 inches | Speed flume descending from a six-story tower.

DISCO H2O | 48 inches if riding alone; 36 inches if riding with an adult | Four persons in a raft are ushered down a tube into a 1970s-era nightclub complete with lights, music, and a disco ball.

THE FLYER | 48 inches if riding alone; 36 inches if riding with an adult | A calmer toboggan-style ride more suitable for families with smaller children.

MACH 5 | 48 inches | Mat slide. For a really fast ride, grab a newer mat.

THE STORM | 48 inches | Half slide, half toilet bowl. This ride is exhilarating and disorienting; when the lifeguard begins hollering, just stumble toward his voice and give him a thumbs-up.

THE SURGE | 48 inches if riding alone; 36 inches if riding with an adult | Four-person raft ride sends you flying down 600 feet of banked turns. Wild!

afternoon. Parking fees are $10 for cars and vans and $12 for RVs. Lockers can be rented for $5–$10 depending on size, and towel rental is $4; both require a refundable deposit of $3. Life vests are provided for free. Pets are not allowed inside the park, and there is no kennel.

Mears Transportation operates a shuttle to Wet 'n Wild that stops three times a day at Disney hotels. It's the same shuttle that commutes between Walt Disney World and Universal Orlando. Cost is $18 for guests age 3 and older. There is no transportation to Wet 'n Wild from Disney property. If you are staying in Walt Disney World, in Lake Buena Vista, or along US 192, you will need a car. If you are staying on International Drive, you can take the International Drive trolley (visit **iridetrolley.com** for schedules and fees).

As with all thrill slides, lines can become unbearably long, so arrive early. Also keep in mind that most slides are geared more toward older children. All the slides outside the Kids' Park have a

48-inch height requirement, except for multipassenger slides, for which the minimum height is 36 inches if an adult accompanies the short rider. The only exceptions to this policy are the rides at Wake Zone, with a height requirement of 51 inches (The Wild One) and 56 inches (Knee Ski and Wake Skating).

Other Wet n' Wild attractions include a 3,200-square-foot **Kids' Park** with a smaller-scale version of the adult menu. It's located to the left of the main gate; look for the oversize sand castle capped off with a big blue bucket. The bucket actually fills with water and tips over, soaking the people in front of the castle. The area has slides, a mini-wave pool, a kid-size climbing net, a junior river ride, and two very short zip lines.

Much fun for the younger crowd is **Bubble Up**—a large, wet, inflated bubble made just for kids to climb, bounce, and slide down into 3 feet of water. Kids must be 42–64 inches tall and under 13 years of age to ride this attraction.

The 17,000-square-foot wave pool at **Surf Lagoon** is perfect for body bobbing. If you prefer to ride the waves with tubes, you can rent those at the main rental stand. Another great way to relax is the **Lazy River.** Be forewarned though: The circuit is short and the current fast. If you lose your tube, swim down the river or wait patiently until an empty one passes within reach.

Wake Zone, situated on a lake roughly the same size as the rest of the park, offers wakeboarding, knee-boarding, and tubing. The lines can be considerable, especially since the attraction only runs from noon until dusk and is open on weekends only from mid-March to June, daily during the summer, and weekends only from September to mid-October. Be sure to call before going to Wet 'n Wild to see if the area is open on the day of your visit.

What I like best about Wet 'n Wild is that the park is open 9:30 a.m.–9 p.m. daily throughout the summer. This is a huge advantage over the Disney water parks that generally close 6–7 p.m.

When you get hungry, the main food pavilions are the centrally located **Bubba's BBQ, Manny's Pizza,** and **Surf Grill,** together offering such staples as burgers, pizza, and barbecued-pork sandwiches, as well as more-nutritious (and nontraditional) items such as veggie burgers and tabbouleh. Wait times are long, and prices are high but not outrageous. Guests may bring a picnic, but alcohol and glass containers are not allowed (although beer can be purchased inside the park).

You can take in all the attractions at Wet 'n Wild in 1 day, especially in the summer when the park is open until 9 p.m. It is a huge park, and a whole day playing in the water under the hot Florida sun will poop you out. Try to get back to the hotel for a midday nap, and don't plan on dragging already tired kids to a restaurant for a sit-down dinner.

BEFORE YOU GO

1. Call ☎ 800-992-WILD or 407-351-1800, or visit **wetnwildorlando.com,** the day before you go to find out the official park opening time.

2. Purchase admission tickets online before you arrive.

3. Visit the website to determine what attractions are appropriate for the kids in your party.

▌ AQUATICA *by* SEAWORLD

AQUATICA, ORLANDO'S FIRST NEW SWIMMING PARK to open in more than a decade, is located across International Drive from the backside of SeaWorld. From Kissimmee, Walt Disney World, and Lake Buena Vista, take I-4 East, exit onto the Central Florida Parkway, and then bear left on International Drive. From Universal Studios, take I-4 West to FL 528 and from there exit onto International Drive. Admission costs about the same as at the Disney water parks and at Wet 'n Wild: $48 for adults and $42 for kids. If you don't want to wait in a queue to purchase tickets, buy them in advance at **aquatica byseaworld.com** or use the credit-card ticket machines to the left of Aquatica's main entrance.

Aquatica is comparable in size to other water theme parks in the area. Attractively landscaped with palms, ferns, and tropical flowers, it's far less themed than Disney's Typhoon Lagoon and Blizzard Beach but much greener and more aesthetically appealing than Wet 'n Wild. You can take in all the attractions in 1 day but, as with all water parks, remember that an entire day of action in the Florida sun will wear out the most active kids and most grown-ups too.

Admission, including the Banana Beach Cookout All-You-Care-to-Eat Deal, is $60 for adults and $50 for kids. The deal includes all-you-can-drink Pepsi products and is by far the most economical package for any water park. Parking fees are $11.26 per day.

As at other water parks, there are lockers, towels, wheelchairs, and strollers to rent, gift shops to browse, and places to eat. The three restaurants at Aquatica are **WaterStone Grill,** offering specialty sandwiches, fried fish, wraps, and salads; **Banana Beach Cookout,** an all-you-can-eat venue dishing up burgers, hot dogs, and chicken; and **Mango Market,** a diminutive eatery serving pizza and chicken tenders. WaterStone Grill and Mango Market serve beer.

BEFORE YOU GO

1. Call ☎ 888-800-5447 or 407-351-3600, or visit **aquatica byseaworld.com** the day before you go to find out the official park opening time.

2. Purchase admission tickets online before you arrive.

3. Visit the website to determine what attractions are appropriate for the kids in your party.

Aquatica by SeaWorld

ATTRACTION | HEIGHT REQUIREMENT* | WHAT TO EXPECT

CUTBACK COVE AND BIG SURF SHORES | None | One cove serves up bodysurfing waves, while the other puts out gently bobbing floating waves. A spacious beach arrayed around the coves is the park's primary sunning venue. Shady spots, courtesy of beach umbrellas, ring the perimeter of the area for sun-sensitive guests.

DOLPHIN PLUNGE | Guests must be at least 48 inches tall and be able to maintain proper riding position unassisted | Corkscrewing romp through a totally arced tube until you blast through the clear tube at the end. The viewing of the dolphins is nearly impossible because you're flushed through the clear tube so fast and with so much water splashing in your face, the ride is over before you've seen anything.

HOOROO RUN | 42 inches | A six-story open-air run down a steep, straight, undulating slide.

KATA'S KOOKABURRA COVE | 48 inches and under only | Wading pool and slides for the preschool crowd.

LOGGERHEAD LANE | Guests must be in a single or double tube | Take a tube and enjoy this lazy river, which at one point passes through the Fish Grotto, a tank populated by hundreds of exotic tropical fish.

ROA'S RAPIDS | Guests under 51 inches are required to wear a life vest | Floating stream with a very swift current but without any rapids. There is only one place to get in and out.

TASSIE'S TWISTERS | Guests must be able to maintain proper riding position while holding on to both handles unassisted | An enclosed slide tube spits you into an open bowl, where you careen around the bowl's edge much in the manner of the ball in a roulette wheel.

TAUMATA RACER | Guests must be at least 42 inches tall and be able to maintain proper riding position unassisted | A high-speed mat ride down a steep hill.

WALHALLA WAVE | Guests must be at least 42 inches tall and be able to maintain proper riding position unassisted | Circular raft that can accommodate up to four people and splashes down a six-story enclosed twisting tube.

WALKABOUT WATERS | Guests must be 36–42 inches for slides into main pool and over 42 inches tall for larger slides | 15,000-square-foot children's adventure area. If your children are under the age of 10, this alone may be worth the admission price. It's impossible not to get wet and impossible not to have fun!

WHANAU WAY | Guests must be able to maintain the proper riding position while holding on to both handles unassisted | Tubes carry one or two passengers down one of four slides with a few twists and one corkscrew.

Guests under 48 inches are required to wear a life vest.

DOWNTOWN DISNEY

DOWNTOWN DISNEY COMPRISES THE Disney Village Marketplace, Pleasure Island, and Disney's West Side. All three are shopping, dining, and entertainment complexes. You can roam, shop, and dine without paying any sort of entrance fee.

Downtown Disney

Downtown Disney West Side

Parking

1. Cirque du Soleil *La Nouba*
2. DisneyQuest
3. House of Blues
4. Ridemakerz *(moves to Marketplace late 2011)*
5. Wolfgang Puck Grand Cafe
6. Specialty shopping:
   Disney's Candy Cauldron
   D-Street
   Hoypoloi
   Magic Masters
   Magnetron Magnetz
   Orlando Harley-Davidson
   Pop Gallery
   Sosa Family Cigars
   Sunglass Icon
7. Bongos Cuban Cafe
8. AMC Downtown Disney 24 Theatres
9. Wetzel's Pretzels/Häagen-Dazs
10. Characters In Flight
11. Planet Hollywood
12. Curl by Sammy Duvall
13. Paradiso 37
14. Fuego by Sosa Cigars
15. Raglan Road/Cookes of Dublin
16. Portobello

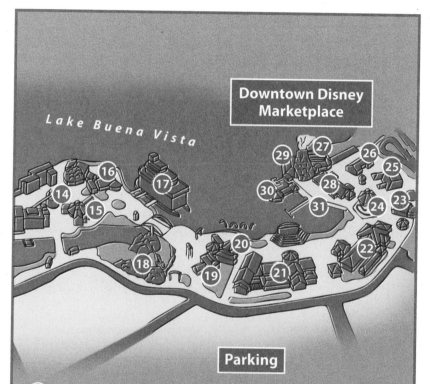

Downtown Disney Marketplace

Lake Buena Vista

Parking

17 Fulton's Crab House

18 T-REX

19 Pollo Campero

20 LEGO Imagination Center

21 World of Disney

22 Specialty shopping:
Arribas Brothers
Basin
Ghirardelli Soda Fountain
& Chocolate Shop
Team Mickey
Tren-D

23 Once Upon a Toy

24 Disney's Pin Traders

25 Earl of Sandwich Restaurant/
Mickey's Pantry

26 Wolfgang Puck Express Cafe

27 Specialty shopping:
The Art of Disney
Disney's Design-a-Tee
Disney's Wonderful World
of Memories

28 Specialty shopping:
Goofy's Candy Co.
littlemissmatched
Mickey's Mart
Pooh Corner

29 Rainforest Cafe

30 Cap'n Jack's Restaurant

31 Cap'n Jack's Marina

I love the LEGO Imagination Center at Downtown Disney. You can make your own LEGO cars and drop them down a slope. Better watch out because it gets crowded with kids. One kid ran off with my car. There are cool LEGO statues outside and a LEGO dragon on the lake. It's a good place to take pictures.

My all-time favorite toy at Once Upon a Toy is a miniature version of Wilderness Lodge made of Lincoln Logs.

If you have a car, use it. There is bus transportation from all the Disney resorts to Downtown Disney, and some resorts (Old Key West and Port Orleans) offer boat transportation. The problem is that buses make stops at a number of locations at Downtown Disney, so you might sit on the bus for 20 minutes or more before you finally depart for your destination. The boats are better than the buses but take about four times as long as driving your car. The boat route, however, is very pretty and a good choice if you're not in a hurry. Shops open as early as 9:30 a.m., but there is really no reason to arrive at the crack of dawn—for once.

MARKETPLACE HIGHLIGHTS

KIDS WILL PARTICULARLY ENJOY the **LEGO Imagination Center**. You'll know you're there when you see the 30-foot sea serpent made out of more than a million LEGO blocks that lives in the lake right in front of the store. Outside the store is a play area filled with LEGO blocks for children to enjoy.

Once Upon a Toy is a joy. The biggest draws at this 16,000-square-foot store are classic toys with a Disney twist. Here you can find Mr. Potato Head with Mickey Ears or a sorcerer's hat and the classic game Clue set in The Haunted Mansion.

Bibbidi Bobbidi Boutique transforms your little girl into a princess, albeit for a price. A Fairy Godmother-in-training (the shop owner) and her helpers offer salon services for princesses age 3 and up. Hairstyle and makeup cost $53, adding a manicure will cost you $58, and the royal makeover (including your choice of a princess costume with accessories and a photo shoot with imaging package) starts at $202. Prices include tax.

I say go for the hairstyle and makeup only at Bibbidi Bobbidi and take your own pictures. Disney princess costumes are available at a reasonable rate at your hometown Halloween shop (best buys just after the holiday) or on eBay. While the salon also offers a "cool dude" makeover for boys, this place is a serious girl's thing.

THE WEST SIDE HIGHLIGHTS

THE BEST THING at Downtown Disney and probably in all of Walt Disney World is **Cirque du Soleil's La Nouba**. Mesmerizing, thrilling, superb, and beautiful hardly do the show justice, but it's all of those and more. Tickets range $91–$128 for adults and $74–$104 for kids ages 3–9 (tax included). Florida residents are eligible for a 20% discount. If you are not familiar with Cirque du Soleil, visit the website at **cirquedusoleil.com.** You can book online or call ☎ 407-939-7600.

The place for wannabe magicians is **Magic Masters,** where the store interior is a re-creation of

Houdini's personal library. If you buy a magic trick, you are taken behind a hidden panel in the bookcase to learn its secret. **Pop Gallery** is the place to go for high-end paintings and sculpture.

Catch all the latest box office hits at the **AMC Downtown Disney** state-of-the-art, 24-movie theater complex, all under one roof and offering flicks in an Art Deco setting. For information on showtimes and tickets, log on to **amctheatres.com** and select AMC Downtown Disney 24.

Weekdays before 4 p.m. are least crowded at DisneyQuest.

Bob

Restaurants include the **House of Blues,** which serves Cajun specialties; **Planet Hollywood,** offering movie memorabilia and basic American fare; **Bongos Cuban Cafe,** serving Cuban favorites; and **Wolfgang Puck Cafe,** featuring California cuisine.

DISNEYQUEST If your children are age 11 or older, DisneyQuest on Disney's West Side is a special treat you might want to consider. DisneyQuest is Disney's pioneering prototype of a theme park in a box, or more literally, in a modest five-story building.

DisneyQuest contains all the elements of the larger Disney theme parks. An entrance area facilitates your transition into the park environment and leads to the gateways of four distinct themed lands, referred to here as zones. As at other Disney parks, everything is included in the price of your admission.

It takes about 2–3 hours to experience DisneyQuest once you get in. Disney limits the number of guests admitted to ensure that queues are manageable and that guests have a positive experience.

DisneyQuest is aimed at a youthful audience, say 8–35 years of age, though younger and older patrons will enjoy much of what it offers. The feel is dynamic, bustling, and noisy. Those who haunt the electronic games arcades at shopping malls will feel most at home at DisneyQuest.

From the turnstile, you enter the Departure Lobby and a "Cyberlator"—a sort of "transitional attraction" (read: elevator) hosted by the genie from *Aladdin*—that delivers you to an entrance plaza called Ventureport. From here you can enter the four zones: Explore Zone, Score Zone, Create Zone, and Replay Zone. As in the larger parks, each zone is distinctively themed. Some zones cover more than one floor, so looking around, you can see things going on

Ian

You've got to try Cyberspace Mountain at DisneyQuest! Ride the roller coaster you design on a computer. You can choose to ride in space, the jungle, or inside a volcano. Space is the coolest. I picked barrel rolls, backflips, a dive into a black hole, twists and turns, and a dip down under the track. You sit in a simulator and feel like an astronaut flying through space. And don't miss the Virtual Jungle Cruise. It's totally wild! I worked up a sweat on this one. Feels like you're in a real video game. It's a simulator raft ride and you paddle through river rapids with a group of people. Everybody is yelling and screaming as you try to paddle in the right direction. Watch out for dinosaurs and waterfalls. You will get wet, really, but not too much.

both above and below you. In addition, DisneyQuest offers two restaurants and the inevitable gift shop.

Each zone offers several attractions, most based on technologies such as simulators that work well in confined spaces. The Explore Zone is representative. You enter through a re-creation of the tiger's-head cave from *Aladdin*. The headline attraction in Explore Zone is the Virtual Jungle Cruise, where you paddle a six-person raft. The raft is a motion simulator perched on top of blue air bags that replicate the motion of water. Responding to the film of the river projected before you, you can choose several routes through the rapids. The motion simulator responds to sensors on your paddle. As if navigating the river isn't enough, man-eating dinosaurs and a cataclysmic comet are tossed in for good measure.

Pinball wizard, here I come! Seriously, DisneyQuest is great for a rainy day or arrival and departure days.

— Liliane

Some DisneyQuest attractions tap your imagination. In the Create Zone, for example, you can use a computer to design your own roller coaster, including 360-degree loops, and then take a virtual reality ride on your creation in a motion simulator. Sid's Make-a-Toy, also in the Create Zone, lets you design a toy and receive the parts to actually construct it at home. Other creative attractions include virtual beauty salon makeovers and painting on an electronic canvas.

Like all things Disney, admission to DisneyQuest is not cheap. But especially for teens and technology junkies, it's an eye-opening experience and a fun time.

A 1-day admission ranges $35–$45. Children under age 10 must be accompanied by a responsible person 16 years and older. Kids under the age of 3 are admitted free of charge, but strollers are not permitted inside

The Rainforest Cafe is like having dinner in a tree house. Tree branches are everywhere. Birds are chirping, and there are humongous mushrooms. Monkeys, orangutans, and gorillas are all around too. Don't worry; they're not real. While you're eating, every once in a while thunder and lightning appear and a rainstorm happens. The ribs are very good. You have to get the chocolate volcano for dessert. It's incredible!

— Ian

DisneyQuest. You can leave and re-enter anytime you want on the day of your visit: Just make sure your wrist gets stamped upon arrival. Annual passes are available.

Believe it or not, there are height restrictions at DisneyQuest, and here is the countdown: **Cyberspace Mountain:** 51 inches; **Pirates of the Caribbean—Battle for Buccaneer Gold:** 35 inches; and **Buzz Lightyear's Astro Blasters:** 51 inches.

No need to leave DisneyQuest when hunger strikes. Wonderland Cafe and FoodQuest serve the usual fare, and once you are ready to leave, the exit is through the obligatory gift shop.

PLEASURE ISLAND HIGHLIGHTS

AFTER A 20-YEAR RUN, Disney all but shut down the Pleasure Island nighttime entertainment complex. Recently scheduled to be rethemed as Hyperion Wharf, Disney has chunked the wharf theme and gone back to the drawing board. In any event, the focus is on family-friendly shops and restaurants, including **Raglan Road,** an Irish pub and restaurant featuring live Celtic music; **Fuego by Sosa Cigars,** a posh cigar bar; **Curl by Sammy Duval,** a surf shop; a Harley-Davidson apparel store; and several outdoor food-and-beverage locations. **Paradiso 37,** opened in 2010, features the cuisines of the Americas (that would be North, Central, and South) served both indoors and out. Disney remains mum regarding the future of the four former nightclubs that have not been demolished. As a side note, some shops in Downtown Disney contain props from the old clubs of Pleasure Island. One such example is the split zebra cabinet in D-Street. It is a remnant from the Adventurer's Club.

Ian's tip gives you a good example of how most kids feel about the Downtown Disney Rainforest Cafe. Getting a table during normal dinner hours, however, is only slightly less difficult than eloping with Daisy Duck. If the kids are all over you to go, try the saner, more manageable Rainforest Cafe at the Animal Kingdom. You'll be done and out the door in less time than it takes to get seated at the Downtown Disney location.

HOW TO MAKE IT WORK

IT REALLY DOES NOT MATTER if you make Downtown Disney your destination for the day or if you decide to go on the spur of the moment. Fun can be had by all anytime. Family restrooms (with a changing and nursing area) are located in the Marketplace near Once Upon a Toy and the Art of Disney.

SHOPPING There are five ATMs at Downtown Disney. All major credit cards are accepted, and if you are a Disney resort guest, you can

---

FAVORITE EATS AT DOWNTOWN DISNEY

LAND | SERVICE LOCATION | FOOD ITEM

MARKETPLACE

Earl of Sandwich | Sandwich paradise
Ghirardelli Soda Fountain & Chocolate Shop | Ice cream & chocolate treats
Rainforest Cafe* | Burgers & kids' menu in Jurassic setting with T-Rex dinosaurs
Wolfgang Puck Express | Soups, salads, & pizza

WESTSIDE

FoodQuest | Pizza, pasta, & salads
Forty-Thirst Street | Mini-doughnuts & coffee
House of Blues* | Cajun food & kids' menu. For shows in the music hall next door, check out **hob.com.**
Planet Hollywood* | Burgers. Great for teens who will love checking out the Hollywood memorabilia.
Wetzel's Pretzels | Pretzels with a twist

PLEASURE ISLAND

Raglan Road | Irish food & live music

---

* table service only

have your shopping purchases delivered to your hotel (this only works if you are not checking out the next day). Pickup is usually at the primary gift shop of your resort (no room delivery), but even so, it sure beats lugging stuff around.

BEFORE YOU GO

1. Determine in advance what all members in your party want to do. Pick up a map at Guest Relations and enjoy the area.

2. Downtown Disney is a great place to give your teenagers some space. Agree on a time and place to reunite and turn them loose. While teens enjoy DisneyQuest or the latest flick at the AMC movie theater, mom and dad can have a peaceful dinner at the Portobello Yacht Club or Wolfgang Puck Cafe.

3. Pets are not allowed at Downtown Disney. Best Friends Pet Care (**bestfriendspetcare.com**) is located near Port Orleans Resort.

The **BEST** of the **REST**

UNLESS YOU'RE A GAMBLER OR A NUDIST, you'll probably find your favorite activity offered at Walt Disney World. You can fish, canoe, hike, bike, boat, play tennis and golf, ride horses, work out, take cooking lessons, and even drive a real race car or watch the Atlanta Braves' spring training.

Your kids will go nuts for the **Wilderness Lodge Resort,** and so will you. While you're there, have a family-style meal at the kid-friendly Whispering Canyon restaurant and rent bikes for a ride on the paved paths of adjacent Fort Wilderness campground. The outing will be a great change of pace. The only downside is that your kids might not want to go back to their own hotel.

More fun is available at **The ESPN Wide World of Sports,** a 220-acre competition and training complex. During late winter and early spring, the venue is the spring training home of the Atlanta Braves. Disney guests are welcome at the sports complex as paying spectators, but none of the facilities are available for guests to use.

To learn what events, including Major League Baseball exhibition games, are scheduled during your visit, call ☎ 407-939-GAME or visit **disneyworldsports.com.** Admission is $14.38 for adults, $10.65 for children ages 3–9. Some events carry an extra charge, and dining options are available.

Located 40–60 minutes south of Walt Disney World is the **Disney Wilderness Preserve,** a wetlands-restoration area operated by the Nature Conservancy in partnership with Disney. There are hiking trails, an interpretive center, guided outings on weekends, and buggy rides. Trails wind through grassy savannas, beneath ancient cypress trees, and along the banks of pristine Lake Russell. The preserve is open daily, 9 a.m.–5 p.m.; closed on Thanksgiving and Christmas

ARNOLD PALMER'S BAY HILL CLUB & LODGE ★★★★
bayhill.com; ☎ 407-876-2429

CHAMPIONSGATE INTERNATIONAL COURSE ★★★★
championsgategolf.com; ☎ 407-787-4653

CHAMPIONSGATE NATIONAL COURSE ★★★½
championsgategolf.com; ☎ 407-787-4653

CROOKED CAT ★★★★ ☎ 407-656-2626

GRAND CYPRESS GOLF CLUB ★★★★½
grandcypress.com; ☎ 407-239-4700

INDEPENDENCE ★★★★ ☎ 407-662-1100

LEGACY ★★★★½ ☎ 407-662-1100

METROWEST GOLF CLUB ★★★½ metrowestgolf.com; ☎ 407-299-1099

PANTHER LAKE ★★★★½ ☎ 407-656-2626

days. General admission is $3 for adults and $2 for children ages 6–17. Guided trail walks are offered on Saturday at no extra cost. Reservations are highly recommended. Disney cast members and information operators don't know squat about the Wilderness Preserve, so if you're interested, call the preserve directly at ☎ 407-935-0002.

GOLF

IF GOLF IS YOUR THING, call ☎ 407-938-GOLF for information, tee times, and greens fees at Palm Golf Course (★★★★), Magnolia Golf Course (★★★½), Lake Buena Vista Golf Course (★★★), or Oak Trail Golf Course (★★½).

There is, of course, golf beyond Mickey's Kingdom. The greater Orlando area has enough high-quality courses to rival better-known golfing meccas, such as Scottsdale and Palm Springs. But unlike these destinations with their endless private country clubs, Orlando is unique because almost all its courses are open for some sort of public play. We compiled a list of off-Disney golf courses for dad's or mom's special day off (see the chart above).

The 900-page *Unofficial Guide to Walt Disney World*, by Bob Sehlinger and Len Testa, contains an entire chapter on Walt Disney World and Orlando-area golf, with in-depth profiles of all the best golf courses.

MINIATURE GOLF

CONSIDER MINIATURE GOLF FOR THE WHOLE FAMILY at **Fantasia Gardens Miniature Golf,** located across the street from the Walt Disney World Swan or at **Winter Summerland** right next to Blizzard Beach. Fantasia Gardens Miniature Golf is a beautifully landscaped garden with fountains, animated statues, topiaries, and flower beds. At Winter Summerland the Christmas holiday theme is prevalent, with ornaments hanging from palm trees. At Castle Hole watch out for a snowman that sprays water on unsuspecting guests when their golf balls pass beneath him.

Fantasia Gardens is quite demanding and not nearly as whimsical as Winter Summerland. Adults and older teens will enjoy the challenge of Fantasia Gardens, but if your group includes children younger than 12, head to Winter Summerland. Another Winter Summerland plus is that it can be reached easily via Disney transportation. To access Fantasia Gardens you must take a bus to the Walt Disney World Swan Resort and walk to the course from there. Admission with tax to both courses is $12 for adults and $10 for children ages 3–9. Opening hours are 10 a.m.– 11 p.m. For more information call ☎ 407-WDW-PLAY.

THEME PARK TRIVIA QUIZ ANSWERS

MAGIC KINGDOM	DISNEY'S ANIMAL KINGDOM
1. (C)	1. (C)
2. (C)	2. (A)
3. (D)	3. (D)
4. (D)	4. (B)
5. (C)	5. (D)
6. (D)	6. (B)
7. (A)	7. (B)
8. (C)	8. (D)
9. (B)	9. (C)
10. (A)	10. (D)

EPCOT	DISNEY'S HOLLYWOOD STUDIOS
1. (D)	1. (A)
2. (B)	2. (A)
3. (B)	3. (C)
4. (D)	4. (A)
5. (D)	5. (B)
6. (C)	6. (A)
7. (A)	7. (C)
8. (C)	8. (B)
9. (C)	9. (C)
10. (B)	10. (B)
11. (C)	11. (A)
12. (B)	

INDEX

A

AAA Dream Homes, 127
ABC Commissary, 163
accommodations, 72–128
    Animal Kingdom, 100–101
    babysitting in, 87
    Bonnet Creek, 95–100
    child-care options, 87
    childproofing, 127–128
    commuting time to/from, 76–78
    condominiums, 124–127
    costs, 73–75, 124–125
    dining in, 78–79, 145
    discounts, 107–110
    Downtown Disney, 95–100, 106–107
    ease of access, 79
    Epcot, 93–95
    Extra Magic Hours with.
        See Extra Magic Hours.
    good deals, 122–124
    group size and, 79–80
    guaranteed admission with, 87
    holiday decorations in, 55
    information chart, 102–104
    International Drive, 111, 113–116
    Internet sites, 123–124
    Lake Buena Vista, 111, 116–120
    locations, 75–76
    Magic Kingdom, 88–93
    Magical Express service, 85–87
    parking with, 87
    reservations for, 123–124
    selection, 73–81
    sharing with parents, 87
    swimming areas, 85
    tents for, 213–214
    themes, 82–85
    transportation options, 75–76, 81
    travel agent help with, 109–110
    near Universal Orlando, 111–112
    Universal Studios, 361
    US 192, 111, 120–122
    vacation homes, 124–127
    in Walt Disney World, 81–110
    outside Walt Disney World, 76–81, 110–127
admission, 57–65
    Aquatica by SeaWorld, 417
    Discovery Cove, 407
    DisneyQuest, 422
    Disney's Hollywood Studios, 362
    guaranteed, 87
    lost pass replacement, 263
    SeaWorld, 405–406
    Universal Orlando, 362
    water parks, 408
    Wet 'n Wild, 413–414
Advance Reservations, for dining, 136–143,
        249–250, 254
Adventureland (Magic Kingdom)
    attractions, 186, 266–271
        Enchanted Tiki Room, 186, 266–268
        Jungle Cruise, 186, 266–267, 269
        Magic Carpets of Aladdin, 186, 266–270
        Pirates of the Caribbean, 186, 266–267, 270
        Swiss Family Treehouse, 186, 266–267,
            270–271
    dining, 289
Affection Station (Animal Kingdom), 190, 324–
        325, 330
Africa (Animal Kingdom), 324, 328–330, 336
Africa Coolpost, 159
age considerations, 21
    expectations, 184–185
    four to six, 24–25
    ideal, 2
    infants, 21–24, 127–128, 215
    teenagers, 25–26, 421–422
    toddlers, 21–24, 127–128, 215
agriculture exhibit (Epcot), 299, 304–305
airports, transportation to/from, 85–87

A *(continued)*

Akershus Royal Banquet Hall, 167, 251

All About Kids, 67–68

All Star Vacation Homes, 125–126

allears.net, 40

All-Star Resorts, 84, 101–102

Amaura (restaurant), 132

Amazing Adventures of Spider-Man, The (Islands of Adventure), 386–389

AMC Downtown Disney movie theater, 421

America Gardens Theatre (Epcot), 318

American Adventure, The (Epcot), 188, 241–242, 299, 314

American Adventure Rotunda, Christmas at, 54

American Idol Experience, The (DHS), 189, 341–344

Andanapur Local Foods Cafes, 162

animal(s). *See also* Animal Kingdom.

   Animal Actors on Location (Universal Studios), 370–371, 373

   SeaWorld, 404–407

Animal Actors on Location (Universal Studios), 370–371, 373

Animal Kingdom, 323–339

  accommodations, 100–102

  attractions, 324–335

    Affection Section, 30, 188, 190, 324–325

    Boneyard, The, 190, 325, 333

    Camp Minnie-Mickey, 324–325, 327–328

    Conservation Station, 190, 324–325, 330

    DINOSAUR, 190, 324–325, 333–334

    Discovery Island, 324–327, 336

    Expedition Everest, 190, 324–325, 331

    Festival of the Lion King, 190, 324–325, 328

    Finding Nemo: The Musical, 190, 324–325, 335

    Flights of Wonder, 190, 324–325, 331–332

    fright potential, 190

    Habitat Habit!, 330

    height requirements, 244–245

    It's Tough to Be a Bug!, 190, 324–326

    Kali River Rapids, 190, 324–325, 332

    Kilimanjaro Safaris, 190, 324–325, 328–329

    Maharajah Jungle Trek, 190, 324–325, 332–333

    Pangani Forest Exploration Trail, 324–325, 329–330

    Primeval Whirl, 190, 325, 334–335

    Rafiki's Planet Watch, 324–325, 329–330

    Theater in the Wild, 324–325, 335

    Tree of Life, The, 324–326

    TriceraTop Spin, 190, 324–325, 335

    waiting line strategies, 241–243

    Wildlife Express Train, 190, 324–325, 330

  Christmas celebration, 54–55

  dining, 145, 155, 162–163, 166–167, 251, 336

  Extra Magic Hours, 326

  live entertainment, 336–337

  lost persons, 259, 261–262

  map, 324–325

  opening procedures and operating hours, 222, 229

  overview, 13–14, 323, 326

  parades, 54–55, 337

  services, 322

  time required for, 221

  touring order, 221–222

  touring plans, 338–339

  trivia quiz, 339

Animal Kingdom Lodge & Villas, 82, 100, 102

animation, The Magic of Disney Animation (DHS), 189, 342–343, 348

Animation Courtyard (DHS), 343

Annual Passes, 61–62

aquariums, The Seas with Nemo and Friends Pavilion (Epcot), 188, 298, 302–303, 316

Aquatica by SeaWorld, 416–417

Aquos Theater (Universal Studios), 365

Art of Animation Resort, 103, 8499–100

Artist Point, 168

Artist's Palette, 168

Asia (Animal Kingdom), 324–325, 331–333, 336

Astro Orbiter (Magic Kingdom), 187, 266–267, 283

ATMs. *See* Banking services.

attractions. *See also* specific locations.

  dark, 193

  Fastpass for. *See* Fastpass.

  fright potential, 185–194

  hail Mary pass for, 242

  height requirements, 239–241, 244–245

  hidden exits at, 260

  intensity, 193

  last-minute cold feet, 247

  last-minute entry, 241–242

  loud, 193–194

  switching off, 243–246

  thrill rides, 238–239

  types, 223–224

  visual impact, 193

  water protection for, 215

autographs, 196, 228, 248

aviary (Discovery Cove), 407

B

baby care centers, 23

  Animal Kingdom, 322

  Disney's Hollywood Studios, 341

  Epcot, 300

  Magic Kingdom, 264

  supplies at, 215

  Universal Studios Florida, 366

babysitting, 66–70, 87

Backlot Express, 163

Backlot Tour (DHS), 189, 342–343, 350–351

Ball, Lucille, tribute to (Universal Studios), 370–371, 378

banking services

  Animal Kingdom, 322

Disney's Hollywood Studios, 341
Downtown Disney, 423
Epcot, 300
Islands of Adventure, 385
Magic Kingdom, 264
Barney show (Universal Studios), 370–371, 374
baseball spring training, 49
Bay Lake (Magic Kingdom), 290–291
Bay Lake Tower, 89–90, 103
Be Our Guest restaurant, 276
Beach Club Resort & Villas, 82, 91–93, 103
Beaches & Cream, 149
bears, *Country Bear Jamboree* (Magic Kingdom),
    186, 266–267, 272
Beast's Castle (Magic Kingdom), 266–267
Beauty and the Beast—Live on Stage (DHS),
    341–344
Beetlejuice's Graveyard Revue (Universal Studios),
    370–371, 373–374
behavior, 31–36
Belle, Enchanted Tales with (Magic Kingdom), 276,
    290
Belle's Cottage (Magic Kingdom), 266–267
Belle's Village (Magic Kingdom), 266–267, 276
Best Friends Pet Resort, 264, 341
Bibbidi Bobbidi Boutique (Downtown Disney),
    418–420
Bice Orlando Ristorante, 132
Biergarten, 139, 165
Big Thunder Mountain Railroad (Magic Kingdom),
    186, 266–267, 271–272
birds
    Enchanted Tiki Room (Magic Kingdom), 186,
        266–268
    Flights of Wonder (Animal Kingdom), 190, 324–
        325, 331–332
birthdays, 70–71
Bistro de Paris, 166–167
blisters, 197–199
Blizzard Beach, 58–59, 245, 408–413
blogs, 42–43
Blue Man Group (Universal Studios), 365
Blues Brothers, The (Universal Studios), 374
bluezoo, 166
Boardwalk, Disney's, 14–15
BoardWalk Inn & Villas, 82, 93, 102
boat rides
    Gran Fiesta Tour Starring the Three Caballeros
        (Epcot), 188, 311
    IllumiNations (Epcot), 53, 188, 318–319
    It's a Small World (Magic Kingdom), 187,
        266–267, 278
    JAWS (Universal Studios), 370–371, 378
    Jungle Cruise (Magic Kingdom), 186, 266–267,
        269
    Jurassic Park River Adventure (Islands of
        Adventure), 386–387, 392–393
    Kali River Rapids (Animal Kingdom), 190,
        324–325, 332

Liberty Belle Riverboat (Magic Kingdom), 186,
    241, 266–267, 275
Living with the Land (Epcot), 304
Maelstrom (Epcot), 189, 298, 311–312
Pirates of the Caribbean (Magic Kingdom), 186,
    266–267, 270
Popeye & Bluto's Bilge-Rat Barges (Islands of
    Adventure), 386–387, 391
Splash Mountain (Magic Kingdom), 186, 266–
    267, 272–273
to Tom Sawyer Island (Magic Kingdom), 266–
    267, 273–274
Bonefish Grill, 133
Boneyard, The (Animal Kingdom), 190, 325, 333
Bongos Cuban Cafe, 166, 421
Bonnet Creek, accommodations, 95–100
Boo to You Parade, 51
Boston Lobster Feast, 131
bottlenecks, avoiding, 224, 226
Boulangerie Patisserie, 159
breakfast, 131, 134, 151–152, 250–254
breast-feeding, 23–24, 216–217
Bubbalou's Bodacious Bar-B-Que, 132
Buena Vista Palace Hotel & Spa, 116
buffets, 130–131, 134, 145–146
Buzz Lightyear's Astro Blasters (DisneyQuest), 422
Buzz Lightyear's Space Ranger Spin (Magic
    Kingdom), 187, 266–267, 283–284

C

California Grill, 166, 168
Camp Jurassic (Islands of Adventure), 386–387,
    392
Camp Minnie-Mickey (Animal Kingdom), 324–325,
    327–328
campfire, Fort Wilderness Resort, 256
camping, 91–92
Canada Pavilion (Epcot), 53, 189, 299, 316–317
Candlelight Processional (Epcot), 53
Cantina Laredo, 133
Cape May Cafe, 251
Capital Grille, The, 133
caps, as sun protection, 208
Captain EO (Epcot), 188, 306
Carey, Drew, *Sounds Dangerous,* 189, 342–343, 349
Caribbean Beach Resort, 84, 95, 103
Caro-Seuss-El (Islands of Adventure), 386–387, 401
carousel(s)
    Caro-Seuss-El (Islands of Adventure), 386–387,
        401
    Prince Charming's Regal Carrousel (Magic
        Kingdom), 187, 266–267, 280–281
Carousel of Progress (Magic Kingdom), 187, 266–267,
    287–288
cars
    Test Track (Epcot), 188, 298, 308–309
    Tomorrowland Speedway (Magic Kingdom),
        188, 247, 266–267, 286–287
Casey's Corner, 157

C *(continued)*

Castaway Cay, 17

Castaway Creek (Typhoon Lagoon), 412

castles
Beast's, 266–267
Cinderella, 266–267, 288, 290–291
Hogwarts, 396

Cat in the Hat, The (Islands of Adventure), 386–387, 401

Central Plaza (Magic Kingdom), 266–267

Chair Lift up Mt. Gushmore (Blizzard Beach), 411

characters. *See* Disney characters.

Chef Mickey's, 139, 251

Chefs de France, 166

Chevy's Fresh Mex, 133

child-care centers, 67, 87

childproofing rooms, 127–128

Chinese Fireball (Islands of Adventure), 386–387, 397–398

"Choose Kissimmee" Guide, 39

Christmas celebration, 52–55

Cinderella Castle, 139, 266–267, 288, 290–291

Cinderella's Royal Table, 139, 165, 251, 253, 255

Circle of Life, The (Epcot), 188, 304

Cirque du Soleil (Downtown Disney), 420

Citricos, 168

CityWalk (Universal Orlando), 55, 361, 368–369, 403–404

clothing, 143, 203, 206

Club Cool (Epcot), 302

Columbia (restaurant), 132

Columbia Harbour House, 157

comedy, *Monsters, Inc. Laugh Floor* (Magic Kingdom), 187, 266–267, 284

Comfort Suites Maingate, 120

Comic Strip Lane, 386–387, 390–391

Commissary Lane (DHS), dining, 357

communication, devices for, 212–213

condominiums, 124–127

Conservation Station (Animal Kingdom), 190, 324–325, 330

Contemporary Resort, 85, 89–90, 103

convention schedule, 47

coolers, 209–210

Coral Reef (Discovery Cove), 407

Coral Reef restaurant, 165

Coronado Springs Resort, 84, 101, 103

Cosmic Ray's Starlight Cafe, 157

costs
accommodations, 73–75, 124–125
admission, 57–65
Aquatica by SeaWorld, 417
condominiums, 124–125
dining
character meals, 251–254
counter-service, 146–147
by cuisine, 179–181
discounts in, 129–130, 134–136
saving, 151–153

Discovery Cove, 407

DisneyQuest, 422

Disney's Hollywood Studios, 362
typical day at WDW, 65–66
Universal Studios Florida, 362
vacation home rental, 124–125
water parks, 408

Country Bear Jamboree (Magic Kingdom), 186, 266–267, 272

Create Zone (DisneyQuest), 422

credit cards, 207

Crêpes des Chefs de France, 159

Cross Country Creek (Blizzard Beach), 411

crowds
avoiding, 224, 226
day of week, 56, 372
Extra Magic Hours. *See* Extra Magic Hours.
holiday, 48–56
lost children in, 260–261
seasonal, 44–48
water parks, 408
Wizarding World, 396

cruise line, 15–17, 38

Crush 'n' Gusher (Typhoon Lagoon), 412

Crystal Palace, 165, 251

Curious George Goes To Town (Universal Studios), 383

Cyberlator (DisneyQuest), 421

D

daily itinerary, planning, 226–227

Day in the Park with Barney, A (Universal Studios), 370–371, 374

day of week, 56
Disney's Hollywood Studios, 372
Universal Studios Florida, 372

day packs, 207–208

dehydration, 209

Del Frisco's, 133

Dervish and Banges (Islands of Adventure), 395

Despicable Me (Universal Studios), 370–371, 374–375

DHS. *See* Disney's Hollywood Studios.

diapers, 215

dining, 129–181
in accommodations, 78–79, 145
Advance Reservations for, 136–143, 249–250, 254
Animal Kingdom, 145, 155, 162–163, 167, 336
Blizzard Beach, 413
breakfast, 131, 134, 151–152, 250–254
buffets, 130–131, 134, 145–146
caveats, 144
choices, 146
CityWalk, 403–404
costs, 129–130, 134–136, 146–147, 151–153, 179–181
counter service, 146–147, 156–164
by cuisine, 179–181

discounts for, 129–130, 134–135
  with Disney characters, 148–149, 178, 249–257
  Disney's Hollywood Studios, 145, 154–155,
    163–166, 357, 364
  Downtown Disney, 166–167, 423
  dress recommendations, 143
  Epcot, 145, 153–154, 159–162, 165–168, 316
  ethnic foods, 130–134, 179–181
  family-style, 145
  Fantasyland, 276
  fast casual, 146
  fast food, 149–153
  food allergies, 143–144
  food courts, 146
  full-service restaurants, 144, 159–162
  healthful, 150–151
  Islands of Adventure, 403–404
  Magic Kingdom, 145, 153, 157–159, 165–166,
    289
  Magic Your Way plan, 168–177
  meal deals, 134
  money-saving, 151–153, 210–212
  Pleasure Island, 423
  quality, 129–130, 134–135, 155–156
  ratings and ranking, 179–181
  readers' comments, 155–156
  restaurant categories in, 144–146
  romantic, 194
  smoking in, 143
  snacks, 148–149, 151–152
  special diets, 143
  surcharges for, 144
  Thanksgiving, 52
  time saving in, 151
  touring plans and, 148
  Typhoon Lagoon, 413
  Universal Orlando, 364
  Universal Studios Florida, 364, 388
  vendor food, 146
  outside Walt Disney World, 129–134
  water parks, 413
Dinoland U.S.A. (Animal Kingdom), 325, 333–335
DINOSAUR (Animal Kingdom), 190, 325, 333–334
disabled visitors
  guidebook for, 39
  Universal Studios Florida, 366
Disaster! (Universal Studios), 370–371, 375
discipline, 31–36
discounts
  accommodations, 107–110
  admission, 64–65
  dining, 129–130, 134
  on websites, 40
Discovery Center, Jurassic Park (Islands of
  Adventure), 386–387, 392
Discovery Cove (SeaWorld), 407
Discovery Island (Animal Kingdom), 324–327,
  336
discussion boards, 41

Disney, Walt, tribute to, *One Man's Dream* (DHS),
  190, 342–343, 354
Disney Channel Rocks! (DHS), 355
Disney characters, 247–257
  Animal Kingdom, 327–328
  autographs, 196, 228, 248
  Camp Minnie-Mickey, 324–325, 327–328
  costumes, 194–195
  dining with, 148–149, 178, 249–257
  Disney's Hollywood Studios, 355
  face, 195
  friends of, 255
  greeting, 265, 268
  headpiece, 195
  "homeless," 254–255
  lost children and, 248–249, 261
  meeting, 194–196
  Princess Fairytale Hall, 187, 266–267, 276, 281
  types, 195
  watching, 247–248
Disney Cruise Lines, 15–17, 48
Disney Junior–Live on Stage! (DHS), 189, 342–345
Disney Vacation Club Points, 108–109
Disney Village Marketplace, 419–420, 423
Disney Wilderness Preserve, 424–425
DisneyQuest, 245, 421–422
Disney's Boardwalk, 14–15
Disney's Hollywood Studios, 340–360
  attractions, 351–354
    American Idol Experience, The, 189, 341–344
    Backlot Tour, 342–343, 350–351
    Beauty and the Beast–Live on Stage, 342–344
    Disney Junior–Live on Stage!, 189, 342–345
    Fantasmic!, 189, 356–358
    fright potential, 189–190
    Great Movie Ride, The, 189, 342–343, 345
    height requirements, 244
    Honey, I Shrunk the Kids Movie Set Adven-
      ture, 189, 342–343, 345–346
    Indiana Jones Epic Stunt Spectacular, 189,
      342–343, 346
    Jedi Training Academy, 188, 347
    Jim Henson's Muppet-Vision 3-D, 189, 342–343,
      347–348
    Lights! Motors! Action! Extreme Stunt Show,
      189, 342–343, 347–348
    Magic of Disney Animation, The, 189,
      342–343, 348
    Mickey Avenue Movie Promo Soundstage,
      348
    One Man's Dream, 190, 342–343, 354
    Rock 'n' Roller Coaster, 189, 342–343,
      348–349
    Sounds Dangerous with Drew Carey, 189,
      342–343, 349
    Star Tours: The Adventures Continue, 189,
      342–343, 349–350
    Streets of America, 342–343, 350
    Studio Backlot Tour, 342–343, 350–351

D *(continued)*

Disney's Hollywood Studios *(continued)*
  attractions *(continued)*
    Theater of the Stars, 344
    Toy Story Mania!, 189, 342–343, 351–352
    Twilight Zone Tower of Terror, The, 190, 342–343, 353
    vs. Universal Studios Florida, 366–367, 372–373
    Voyage of the Little Mermaid, 190, 342–343, 353–354
    waiting line strategies, 241–243
  Christmas celebration, 54
  dining, 145, 154–155, 163–166, 251, 357
  Disney characters in, 355
  exit strategies, 358
  Extra Magic Hours, 233–234
  Halloween parade, 51
  live entertainment, 356–358
  lost persons, 259, 261
  map, 342–343
  opening procedures and operating hours, 222, 229
  overview, 13, 340–341
  parades, 355
  services, 340–341
  time required for, 221
  touring order, 221–222
  touring plans, 358–359
  trivia quiz, 360
  vs. Universal Studios Florida, 366–367, 372–373
Disney's West Side, 14, 418–423
Disneyspeak, 17–18
diversions, 224
DiVine (Animal Kingdom), 337
Dr. Doom's Fearfall (Islands of Adventure), 386–387, 389
dolphin(s)
  Aquatica by SeaWorld, 416–417
  SeaWorld, 407
Dolphin Resort, 85, 94–95, 102
Don Pablo's, 133
DoubleTree Resort Orlando–International Drive, 113
Downhill Double Dipper (Blizzard Beach), 411
Downtown Disney, 14, 417–426
  accommodations, 95–100, 106–107
  Christmas celebration, 55
  dining, 166–167
Dragon Challenge (Islands of Adventure), 386–387, 397–398
"Dream-Along with Mickey" (Magic Kingdom), 288
dress recommendations, 143, 203, 206
drugs, 209
Dudley Do-Right's Ripsaw Falls (Islands of Adventure), 386–387, 390–391
Dumbledore's Office (Islands of Adventure), 399
Dumbo the Flying Elephant (Magic Kingdom), 187, 266–267, 277

E

Easter celebration, 49
eating. *See* dining.
Echo Lake (DHS), 342, 357
educational programs, 68–70
Eighth Voyage of Sindbad, The (Islands of Adventure), 386–387, 393
El Patron, 133
Electric Umbrella Restaurant, 159
electronic devices, 212–213
elephant ride, 266–267, 277
Ellen's Energy Adventure (Epcot), 188, 298, 309
Empress Package (Magic Kingdom), 69
Enchanted Tales with Belle (Magic Kingdom), 276, 290
Enchanted Tiki Room (Magic Kingdom), 186, 266–268
energy presentation, Epcot, 188, 298, 309
Epcot, 297–322. *See also* Future World; World Showcase.
  accommodations, 93–95
  attractions
    fright potential, 188–189
    height requirements, 244
    waiting line strategies, 241–243
  Christmas celebration, 53–54
  dining, 145, 153–154, 159–162, 165–168, 251–256, 316
  exit strategies, 319–320
  Extra Magic Hours, 233–234
  Kidcot Fun Stops, 300
  live entertainment, 317–320
  lost persons, 259
  map, 298–299
  New Year celebration, 55
  opening procedures and operating hours, 222, 229, 297
  overview, 12–13, 297
  services, 300
  time required for, 221
  touring order, 221–222
  touring plans, 320–321
  trivia quiz, 322
  World Showcase attractions, 299, 310–317
ESPN Wide World of Sports, 15, 424
E. T. Adventure (Universal Studios), 370–371, 376
ethnic foods, 130–134, 179–181
expectant mothers, tips for, 215–216
Expedition Everest (Animal Kingdom), 190, 324–325, 331
Explore Zone (DisneyQuest), 421–422
Extra Magic Hours, 56–57, 82
  Animal Kingdom, 326
  Epcot, 297
  Magic Kingdom, 265
  opening hours and, 222–223
  touring plans with, 233–234
  water parks, 408

F

Facebook, 40–41
Fairfax Fare, 164
Fairy Godmothers, 67–68
Fairytale Garden (Magic Kingdom), 288–289
Fantasia Gardens Miniature Golf, 425–426
Fantasmic! (DHS), 189, 356–358
Fantasyland (Magic Kingdom)
  attractions, 187, 275–283
    Beast's Castle, 266–267
    Belle's Cottage, 266–267
    Belle's Village, 266–267, 276
    Dumbo the Flying Elephant, 187, 266–267, 277
    Enchanted Tales with Belle, 276
    Great Goofini, The, 187, 266–267, 277–278
    It's a Small World, 187, 266–267, 278
    Mad Tea Party, 187, 266–267, 278–279
    Many Adventures of Winnie the Pooh, The, 187, 266–267, 279
    Mickey's PhilarMagic, 266–267, 280
    Peter Pan's Flight, 187, 266–267, 280
    Prince Charming's Regal Carrousel, 187, 266–267, 280–281
    Princess Fairytale Hall, 187, 266–267, 276, 281
    Seven Dwarfs Mine Train, 187, 266–267, 276, 281
    Snow White's Scary Adventures, 187, 281
    Storybook Circus, 276–277
    Under the Sea: Journey of the Little Mermaid, 266–267, 276, 282–283
  dining, 276, 289
fast food, 149–153
Fastpass, 232–238
  attractions using, 238
  guidelines, 238
  obtaining, 236–237
  purpose, 235
  returning to ride, 235–236
  switching off with, 243–246
  vs. Universal Express, 362–364
  when to use, 237–238
Fear Factor Live (Universal Studios), 370–371, 376
ferry dock, 266–267
Festival of the Lion King (Animal Kingdom), 190, 324–325, 328
Fievel's Playland (Universal Studios), 370–371, 376–377
Fife & Drum Tavern, 159
50's Prime Time Cafe, 154, 165
Figment (Epcot), 188, 306–307
Filch's Emporium of Confiscated Goods (Islands of Adventure), 386–387, 398
films
  at AMC Downtown Disney movie theater, 421
  Captain EO (Epcot), 188, 306
  Circle of Life, The (Epcot), 188, 304
  Honey, I Shrunk the Audience (Epcot), 188, 306

Impressions de France (Epcot), 188, 299, 315
It's Tough to Be a Bug! (Animal Kingdom), 190, 324–326
Jim Henson's Muppet-Vision 3-D (DHS), 189, 342–343, 347–348
Mickey's PhilarMagic (Magic Kingdom), 266–267, 280
O Canada (Epcot), 189, 299, 316–317
One Man's Dream (DHS), 190, 342–343, 354
Reflections of China (Epcot), 189, 298, 312
Shrek 4-D (Universal Studios), 370–371, 380
Terminator 2:3-D (Universal Studios), 370–371, 381
Turtle Talk with Crush (Epcot), 298–299, 303
Universal 360° (Universal Studios), 370–371, 382–383
Finding Nemo: The Musical (Animal Kingdom), 190, 324–325, 335
fireworks
  Fantasmic! (DHS), 189, 356–358
  IllumiNations (Epcot), 53, 188, 318–319
  Magic Kingdom, 290–291
  New Year celebration, 55
  Universal 360° (Universal Studios), 370–371, 382–383
flag retreat, 289
Flame Tree Barbecue, 162
Flight of the Hippogriff (Islands of Adventure), 386–387, 398
flight simulation rides
  Mission: SPACE (Epcot), 188, 307–308
  Soarin' (Epcot), 306
  Star Tours: The Adventures Continue (DHS), 189, 342–343, 349–350
Flights of Wonder (Animal Kingdom), 190, 324–325, 331–332
Florida Roomsaver, 123
Florida-resident passes, 62
flower festival, 49
flume rides
  Dudley Do-Right's Ripsaw Falls (Islands of Adventure), 386–387, 390–391
  Jurassic Park River Adventure (Islands of Adventure), 386–387, 392–393
  Splash Mountain (Magic Kingdom), 186, 266–267, 272–273
Flying Fish Cafe, 168
Flynn Rider, 288–289
foot care and footwear, 197–199
Forbidden Journey, Harry Potter and (Islands), 386–387, 398–400
Forest Exploration Trail, Pangani (Animal Kingdom), 324–325, 329–330
Fort Langhorn (Magic Kingdom), 266–267, 273–274
Fort Wilderness Campground, 91–92, 102
Fort Wilderness Resort, 256
fountain(s), Epcot, 188, 308
Fountain View Ice Cream, 160
Fourth of July celebration, 50

F *(continued)*
France Pavilion (Epcot), 54, 189, 299, 315
French Quarter, Port Orleans Resort, 95–96, 104
Friar's Nook, 157
friends, inviting, 26–28
Frontierland (Magic Kingdom)
   attractions, 186, 266–267, 271–274
      Big Thunder Mountain Railroad, 186,
        266–267, 271–272
      Country Bear Jamboree, 186, 266–267, 272
      Frontierland Shootin Arcade, 266–267, 272,
        286
      Splash Mountain, 266–267, 272–273
      Tom Sawyer Island, 266–267, 273–274
   dining, 289
Frontierland Shootin Arcade (Magic Kingdom),
   266–267, 272
Future World
   attractions, 298–309
      Captain EO, 188, 306
      Circle of Life, The, 188, 304
      Club Cool, 302
      fright potential, 188
      Honey, I Shrunk the Audience, 188, 306
      Imagination Pavilion, 299, 305–309
      Innoventions, 188, 298–301, 316
      Journey into Imagination with Figment, 188,
        306–307
      Living with the Land, 188, 304
      Mission: SPACE, 188, 307–308
      "Mom, I Can't Believe It's Disney" Fountain,
        188, 308
      Seas with Nemo and Friends Pavilion, The,
        188, 298, 302–303, 316
      Soarin', 188, 306
      Spaceship Earth, 188, 298–299, 301
      Test Track, 188, 298, 308–309
      Turtle Talk with Crush, 188, 298–299, 303
      Universe of Energy: Ellen's Energy Adven-
        ture, 188, 298, 309
      waiting line strategies, 241–243
   dining, 154
   live entertainment in, 317

G
games, DisneyQuest, 421–422
Gang Plank Falls (Typhoon Lagoon), 412
garden festival, 44
Garden Grill Restaurant, The, 251, 253
Garden Grove Cafe, 251, 253
Gaylord Palms Hotel & Convention Center,
   120–121
gays and lesbians
   Gay Days, 50
   guidebook for, 39
Germany Pavilion (Epcot), 54, 188, 299, 313, 316
Ghirardelli Soda Fountain and Chocolate Shop, 149
Golden Oak Outpost, 157
golf, 425

goodwill ambassadors, 337
Gran Fiesta Tour Starring the Three Caballeros
   (Epcot), 188, 311
Grand Floridian Resort & Spa, 82, 88, 102
grandparents, 29–31, 185
Great Goofini, The (Magic Kingdom), 187, 266–
   267, 277–278
Great Movie Ride, The (DHS), 189, 342–343, 345
grocery stores, 152–153
Guest Relations
   Animal Kingdom, 322
   Disney's Hollywood Studios, 340
   Epcot, 300
Guest Services, Islands of Adventure, 385
Guidebook for Guests with Disabilities, 39

H
Habitat Habit! (Animal Kingdom), 330
hail Mary pass, for waiting lines, 242
haircuts and hairdos, 70–71
Hall of Presidents, The (Magic Kingdom), 186,
   266–267, 274
Halloween Party, 51–52
Hanamazuki, 132
Harambe Village (Animal Kingdom), 324–325
Hard Rock Hotel, 113–114
Harry Potter and the Forbidden Journey (Islands of
   Adventure), 386–387, 398–400
hats, 208
Haunted Mansion, The (Magic Kingdom), 51, 186,
   266–267, 275
hayrides, haunted, 51
headliners, 223
height requirements, 239–241, 244–245
High in the Sky Seuss Trolley Train Ride, The (Is-
   lands of Adventure), 386–387, 401–402
Hilton Walt Disney World, 117
hip packs, 207
Hippogriff ride (Islands of Adventure), 386–387,
   398
Hog's Head pub (Islands of Adventure), 394–395
Hogsmeade Village (Islands of Adventure), 386–
   387, 394–395
Hogwarts Castle (Islands of Adventure), 396
Hogwarts Express (Islands of Adventure), 394–395
holiday(s), 48–56
Holiday Inn Castle Hotel, 114
Holiday Inn SunSpree Resort Lake Buena Vista, 117
Holidays from Around the World, 53–54
Hollywood (Universal Studios), 370–371, 388
Hollywood & Vine, 165, 251
Hollywood Boulevard (DHS), 341, 343
Hollywood Brown Derby, 154
Hollywood Rip Ride Rockit (Universal Studios),
   370–371, 377–378
Honey, I Shrunk the Audience (Epcot), 188, 306
Honey, I Shrunk the Kids Movie Set Adventure
   (DHS), 189, 342–343, 345–346
HoneyDukes (Islands of Adventure), 395

horror, make-up for, 370–371, 382
hotels. See accommodations.
House of Blues, 166, 421
Humunga Kowabunga (Typhoon Lagoon), 412
Hungarian Horntail (Islands of Adventure), 386–387, 397–398
Hyatt Regency Grand Cypress, 117–118

I

If I Ran the Zoo (Islands of Adventure), 386–387, 402
IllumiNations (Epcot), 53, 188, 318–319
Imagination Pavilion (Epcot), 299, 305–309
Impressions de France (Epcot), 188, 299, 315
Incredible Hulk Coaster, The (Islands of Adventure), 386–387, 389
Indiana Jones Epic Stunt Spectacular (DHS), 189, 342–343, 346
infants, 21–24. See also baby care centers.
 childproofing rooms for, 127–128
 strollers for. See strollers.
 supplies for, 215
information, 37–43
 accommodations, 122–124
 Animal Kingdom, 322
 blogs, 42–43
 Disney's Hollywood Studios, 340
 Epcot, 300
 Magic Kingdom, 264
 planning DVDs and videos, 194, 196
 podcasts, 41–42
 publications, 38–39
 websites, 37–43
Innoventions (Epcot), 188, 298–301, 316
International Drive, accommodations, 111, 113–116
Irlo Bronson Memorial Highway, accommodations, 111, 120–122
Islands of Adventure, 384–404
 admission, 362
 arrival, 362
 attractions, 386–402
  Amazing Adventures of Spider-Man, The, 386–389
  Camp Jurassic, 386–387, 392
  Caro-Seuss-El, 386–387, 401
  Cat in the Hat, The, 386–387, 401
  Comic Strip Lane, 386–387, 390–391
  Dr. Doom's Fearfall, 386–387, 389
  Dragon Challenge, 386–387, 397–398
  Dudley Do-Right's Ripsaw Falls, 386–387, 390–391
  Eighth Voyage of Sindbad, The, 386–387, 393
  Flight of the Hippogriff, 386–387, 398
  Harry Potter and the Forbidden Journey, 386–387, 398–400
  High in the Sky Seuss Trolley Train Ride, The, 386–387, 401–402
  If I Ran the Zoo, 386–387, 402

  Incredible Hulk Coaster, The, 386–387, 389
  Jurassic Park Discovery Center, 386–387, 392
  Jurassic Park River Adventure, 386–387, 392–393
  Me Ship, *The Olive*, 386–387, 391
  One Fish, Two Fish, Red Fish, Blue Fish, 386–387, 402
  Popeye & Bluto's Bilge-Rat Barges, 386–387, 391
  Poseidon's Fury, 386–387, 393–394
  Pteranodon Flyers, 386–387, 393
  Storm Force Accelatron, 386–387, 390
 dining, 403–404
 Lost Continent, The, 386–387, 393–394
 maps, 368–369, 386–387
 Marvel Super Hero Island, 386–390
 overview, 384–385
 services, 385
 Seuss Landing, 386–387, 401–402
 Toon Lagoon, 386–387, 390–391
 touring plans, 402–404
Italy Pavilion (Epcot), 54, 188, 299, 313, 316
It's a Small World (Magic Kingdom), 187, 266–267, 278
It's Tough to Be a Bug! (Animal Kingdom), 190, 324–326

J

J. Alexander's (restaurant), 132
Jambo House, Animal Kingdom, 100
Jammin' Jungle Parade (Animal Kingdom), 337
Japan Pavilion (Epcot), 54, 188, 299, 314, 316
JAWS (Universal Studios), 370–371, 378
Jedi Training Academy (DHS), 188, 347
Jiko, 168
Jim Henson's Muppet-Vision 3-D (DHS), 189, 342–343, 347–348
Jingle Jungle Parade (Animal Kingdom), 54–55
Journey into Imagination with Figment (Epcot), 188, 306–307
Jungle Cruise (Magic Kingdom), 186, 266–267, 269
Jurassic Park (Islands of Adventure), 386–387, 391–393
Jurassic Park River Adventure (Islands of Adventure), 386–387, 392–393

K

Kaki Gori, 148
Kali River Rapids (Animal Kingdom), 190, 324–325, 332
Keelhaul Falls (Typhoon Lagoon), 412
Ketchakiddee Creek (Typhoon Lagoon), 412
Kidani Village, Animal Kingdom, 100
Kidcot Fun Stops, 300
Kid's Discovery Club (Animal Kingdom), 337
Kid's Night Out, 67–68
Kilimanjaro Safaris (Animal Kingdom), 190, 324–325, 328–329

K *(continued)*

Kim Possible World Showcase Adventure (Epcot), 188, 310–311

Kimonos, 166

Kouzzina, 166

Kringla Bakeri og Kafe, 160

Kuka arm, in Harry Potter attraction (Islands of Adventure), 400

Kusafiri Coffee Shop, 162

L

La Cantina de San Angel, 159, 166

La Hacienda de San Angel, 166

La Nouba (Downtown Disney), 420

labels, for clothing, 203, 206

Lake Buena Vista, accommodations, 111, 116–120

Land Pavilion, The (Epcot), 188, 299, 304–305, 316

laser shows

 IllumiNations (Epcot), 53, 188, 318–319

 Universal 360° (Universal Studios), 370–371, 382–383

Last Minute Villas, 126

Le Cellier Steakhouse, 139, 166

Le Coq au Vin, 132

LEGO Imagination Center (Disney Village Market-place), 420

Les Chefs de France, 165–167

Liberty Belle Riverboat (Magic Kingdom), 186, 241, 266–267, 275

Liberty Inn, 160

Liberty Square (Magic Kingdom)

 attractions, 266–267, 274–275

  fright potential, 186

  Hall of Presidents, The, 186, 266–267, 274

  Haunted Mansion, The, 51, 186, 266–267, 275

  Liberty Belle Riverboat, 186, 241, 266–267, 275

  waiting-line strategies, 242–246

 dining, 289

Liberty Tree Tavern, 139, 165

Lights! Motors! Action! Extreme Stunt Show (DHS), 189, 342–343, 347–348

Lion King, Festival of the (Animal Kingdom), 190, 324–325, 328

Little Mermaid, Journey of the (Magic Kingdom), 266–267, 276, 282–283

live entertainment

 Animal Kingdom, 336–337

 Disney's Hollywood Studios, 355–358

 Epcot, 317–320

 on holidays, 48–56

 Magic Kingdom, 288–291

 SeaWorld, 404–407

 Universal Studios, 383

Living with the Land (Epcot), 188, 304

lobster buffets, 131

lockers

 Disney's Hollywood Studios, 340

 Epcot, 297

 Islands of Adventure, 385

 Magic Kingdom, 264

 Universal Studios Florida, 373

 water parks, 409

lodging. *See* accommodations.

Loews Portofino Bay Hotel, 114–115

Look Who's Talking (Animal Kingdom), 336

lost and found

 Animal Kingdom, 322

 Disney's Hollywood Studios, 340

 Epcot, 300

 Islands of Adventure, 385

 Magic Kingdom, 264

 phone numbers, 45

 Universal Studios Florida, 366

Lost Continent, The (Islands of Adventure), 386–387, 393–394

lost persons, 259–263

 Animal Kingdom, 259, 261–262, 322

 Disney character meeting and, 248–249

 Disney's Hollywood Studios, 259, 261, 340

 Epcot, 259, 300

 Magic Kingdom, 259–261

 water parks, 410

Lotus Blossom Cafe, 160

Lucy, A Tribute (Universal Studios), 370–371, 378

Lunching Pad, The, 158

M

Mad Tea Party (Magic Kingdom), 187, 266–267, 278–279

Maelstrom (Epcot), 189, 298, 311–312

The Magic, the Memories, and You! (Magic Kingdom), 291

Magic Carpets of Aladdin (Magic Kingdom), 186, 266–267, 269–270

Magic Kingdom, 264–296

 accommodations, 88–93

 attractions, 187

  Adventureland, 186, 266–271

  Fantasyland, 187, 275–283

  Frontierland, 186, 266–267, 271–274

  height requirements, 244

  Liberty Square, 186, 241, 266–267, 274–275

  Main Street, U.S.A., 186, 265–268

  Tomorrowland, 266–267, 283–288

  waiting line strategies, 241–242

 Christmas celebration, 53

 dining, 145, 153, 157–159, 165–166, 251–256, 289

 exit strategies, 291–292

 Extra Magic Hours, 233–234, 265

 family magic tour, 69–70

 live entertainment, 288–291

 lost children, 259–261

 map, 266–267

 opening procedures and operating hours, 222, 229

 overview, 12, 264–265

parades, 289–290
services, 264
time required for, 221
touring order, 221–222
touring plans, 292–295
trivia quiz, 295–296
Magic Masters (Disney's West Side), 420–421
Magic of Disney Animation, The (DHS), 189,
    342–343, 348
magic theme park (Islands of Adventure), 386–
    387, 394–400
Magic Your Way Deluxe Dining, 169–170
Magic Your Way Premium Package, 175–176
Magic Your Way program, 58–65, 168–177
Magical Express service, 85–87
Maharajah Jungle Trek (Animal Kingdom), 190,
    324–325, 332–333
Main Street, U.S.A. (Magic Kingdom), 186, 265–
    268, 289
Main Street Bakery, 148
major attractions, 223
make-up shows, Universal Horror Make-up Show
    (Universal Studios), 370–371, 382
Mama Melrose's, 165
Many Adventures of Winnie the Pooh, The (Magic
    Kingdom), 187, 266–267, 279
maps. See specific locations.
marine animals, SeaWorld, 404–407
Marketplace, Disney Village, 418–419, 423
Marketplace, Downtown Disney, 14
Marriott Village at Lake Buena Vista, 118
Marvel Super Hero Island (Islands of Adventure),
    386–390
Mayday Falls (Typhoon Lagoon), 412
Me Ship, The Olive (Islands of Adventure), 386–387,
    391
medication, 209
Mei Asian Bistro, 130
Melt-Away Bay (Blizzard Beach), 411
memories, 218–219
Men in Black Alien Attack (Universal Studios),
    370–371, 379
Mermaid, Little, Journey of the (Magic Kingdom),
    266–267, 276, 282–283
Mermaid, Little, Voyage of the (DHS), 190, 342–343,
    353–354
merry-go-rounds
    Caro-Seuss-El (Islands of Adventure), 386–387,
        401
    Prince Charming's Regal Carrousel, 187,
        266–267, 280–281
Mexico Pavilion (Epcot), 54, 189, 298, 311, 316
Mickey Avenue (DHS), 343
Mickey Avenue Movie Promo Soundstage, 348
Mickey's PhilharMagic (Magic Kingdom), 266–267, 280
Min and Bill's Dockside Diner, 164
Ming Court, 132, 134
miniature golf, 425–426
minor attractions, 223–224

Mission: SPACE (Epcot), 188, 307–308
Mobile Magic app, 41
Moe's Southwest Grill, 133
"Mom, I Can't Believe It's Disney" Fountain
    (Epcot), 188, 308
Monorail Station, 266–267
Monsters, Inc. Laugh Floor (Magic Kingdom), 187,
    266–267, 284
Morocco Pavilion (Epcot), 54, 189, 299, 314–316
mousesavers.com, 40
Move It! Shake It! Celebrate It! parade (Magic
    Kingdom), 289
movies. See films.
Muppet-Vision 3-D, Jim Henson's (DHS), 189,
    342–343, 347–348
music, Magic Kingdom, 289
My Disney Girl's Perfectly Princess Tea Party
    (Magic Kingdom), 69

N

Nagoya Sushi, 133
naps, 226
natural history exhibit, Discovery Center (Islands of
    Adventure), 386–387, 392
nature reserves, 424–425
Nemo and Friends, The Seas with (Epcot), 188,
    298, 302–303, 316
Never Land Club, 67
New Year celebration, 55–56
New York (Universal Studios), 370–371, 388
Nickelodeon Suites Resort Orlando, 115–116
Night of Joy music festival, 50
1900 Park Fare, 251
Nine Dragons, 139, 167
no expiration date, for admission, 58–59, 61
Norway Pavilion (Epcot), 54, 189, 251, 298,
    311–312, 316

O

O Canada (Epcot), 189, 299, 316–317
Oasis, The, 190, 323, 326
Odyssey Center (Epcot), 298
'Ohana, 251
Old Key West Resort, 84, 96–97, 103
Olive, The (Islands of Adventure), 386–387, 391
Ollivanders (Islands of Adventure), 395
Once Upon a Toy (Downtown Disney Market-
    place), 420
One Fish, Two Fish, Red Fish, Blue Fish (Islands of
    Adventure), 386–387, 402
One Man's Dream (DHS), 190
opening procedures, 222–223, 229
operating hours
    Animal Kingdom, 222
    Aquatica by SeaWorld, 417
    Disney's Hollywood Studios, 222
    Epcot, 222, 297
    Magic Kingdom, 222
    with small crowds, 47
Orange Lake Resort, 121

◐ *(continued)*
Orlando, map, 8–9
Orlando Magicard, 38–39, 122–123
Orlando–Orange County Convention and Visitors
    Bureau, 126
Orlando's Finest Vacation Homes, 126
Osborne Family Spectacle of Lights, 94
Owlery and Owl Post (Islands of Adventure), 395

P
Pangani Forest Exploration Trail (Animal Kingdom),
    190, 324–325, 329–330
parades
    Animal Kingdom, 54–55, 337
    Christmas, 68
    Disney's Hollywood Studios, 355
    Halloween, 51
    lost children at, 260
    Magic Kingdom, 53, 289–290
Paradiso 37 restaurant, 423
parents
    activities for, 194
    children sharing room with, 87
    single, 28–29
park hopping, 60
parking
    at accommodations, 87
    Universal Orlando, 361
*PassPorters Open Mouse for Walt Disney World and
    the Disney Cruise Line,* 39
passports, World Showcase, 300
Pecos Bill Tall Tale Inn & Café, 158
pet care services, 341
Peter Pan's Flight (Magic Kingdom), 187, 266–267,
    280
petting zoos
    Affection Section (Animal Kingdom), 190, 330
    Rafiki's Planet Watch (Animal Kingdom), 324–
        325, 329–330
phone numbers, Walt Disney World, 44–45
photos, 218–219, 255
Pinocchio Village Haus, The, 158
Pipa, the trash can (Animal Kingdom), 336
pirate activities
    adventures, 68–69
    Captain Jack Sparrow's pirate tutorial (Magic
        Kingdom), 289–290
Pirates of the Caribbean (Magic Kingdom), 186,
    266–267, 270
Pixar Pals Countdown to Fun (DHS), 355
Pixar Place (DHS), 343
Pizza Planet, 164
Pizzafari, 162–163
Planet Hollywood, 166, 421
Planet Watch (Animal Kingdom), 324–325, 329–
    330
planning, 37–71
    accessories, 206–209
    admission options, 57–65
    attraction suitability, 185–194

    for attractions, 223–224, 226
    babysitting, 66–70
    birthdays, 70–71
    clothing, 203, 206
    daily itinerary, 226–227
    day of week, 56, 372
    Disney character meeting, 194–196
    emotional preparation, 183–196
    Extra Magic Hours.
        See Extra Magic Hours.
    holidays, 48–56
    importance, 183
    information for, 37–43
    logistic preparation, 203–218
    master plan, 201–202
    memory recording, 218–219
    mental preparation, 183–196
    for parents' enjoyment, 194
    physical preparation, 196–200
    for rest, 199–200
    role-playing in, 196
    seasons to visit, 44–48
    special events, 48–50
    special programs, 68–70
    telephone numbers, 44–45
    time allocation, 43–57
    trial run, 219–220
Platinum Package, 176
playgrounds
    Boneyard, The (Animal Kingdom), 190, 325, 333
    Camp Jurassic (Islands of Adventure), 386–387,
        392
    Curious George Goes To Town (Universal
        Studios), 383
    Fievel's Playland (Universal Studios), 370–371,
        376–377
    Honey, I Shrunk the Kids Movie Set Adventure
        (DHS), 189, 342–343, 345–346
    If I Ran the Zoo (Islands of Adventure), 386–387,
        402
    Me Ship, *The Olive* (Islands of Adventure),
        386–387, 391
    for relaxation, 226
    Tom Sawyer Island (Magic Kingdom), 186,
        266–267, 273–274
    Woody Woodpecker's KidZone (Universal
        Studios), 383
Pleasure Island, 14, 422–423
podcasts, 41–42
Polynesian Resort, 82, 89, 103
ponchos, 208–209
Pop Century Resort, 84, 98–99, 103
Popeye & Bluto's Bilge-Rat Barges (Islands of
    Adventure), 386–387, 391
Port of Entry (Universal Orlando), 385
Port Orleans Resort, 83, 95–96
Portofino Bay Hotel, 114–115
Poseidon's Fury (Islands of Adventure), 386–387,
    393–394

post office, Wizarding World of Harry Potter, 395

Potter, Harry, The Wizarding World of (Islands of Adventure), 386–387, 394–400

pregnant visitors, tips for, 215–216

Presidents, The Hall of (Magic Kingdom), 186, 266–267, 274

Primeval Whirl (Animal Kingdom), 190, 324–325, 334–335

Prince Charming's Regal Carrousel (Magic Kingdom), 186, 266–267, 280–281

Princess Fairytale Hall (Magic Kingdom), 187, 266–267, 276, 281

Production Central (Universal Studios), 370–371, 388

Promenade Refreshments, 160

Pteranodon Flyers (Islands of Adventure), 386–387, 393

Q

Quick Service dining plan, 169

Quidditch match (Islands of Adventure), 399–400

R

radio stations, 42–43

Radisson Resort Orlando-Celebration, 122

Rafiki's Planet Watch (Animal Kingdom), 324–325, 329–330

railroads

High in the Sky Seuss Trolley Train Ride, The (Islands of Adventure), 386–387, 401–402

Seven Dwarfs Mine Train (Magic Kingdom), 187, 266–267, 276, 281

Tomorrowland Transit Authority PeopleMover (Magic Kingdom), 187, 266–267, 287

Walt Disney World Railroad (Magic Kingdom), 70, 186, 266–268

Wildlife Express Train (Animal Kingdom), 190, 324–325, 330

raingear, 208–209

Rainforest Cafe, 155, 167, 422

Rapunzel and Flynn Rider Play and Greet (Magic Kingdom), 288–289

Ravenous Pig, The, 132

Red Bamboo, 133

Reflections of China (Epcot), 189, 298, 312

Refreshment Port, The, 160

relaxation, 199–200

reservations

for accommodations, 123–124

for dining, 136–143, 249–250, 254

rest, 199–200, 226

restrooms

diaper changing facilities in, 23

lost children at, 260

Restaurantosaurus, 163

restaurants. *See* dining.

Revenge of the Mummy (Universal Studios), 370–371, 379–380

rides. *See* attractions.

River Adventure, Jurassic Park (Islands of Adventure), 386–387, 392–393

Riverside, Port Orleans Resort, 95–96, 104

Rock 'n' Roller Coaster (DHS), 190, 342–343, 348–349

roller coasters, 238–239

Big Thunder Mountain Railroad (Magic Kingdom), 186, 266–267, 271–272

Dragon Challenge (Islands of Adventure), 386–387, 397–398

Expedition Everest (Animal Kingdom), 190, 324–325, 331

Great Goofini, The (Magic Kingdom), 187, 266–267, 277–278

Hollywood Rip Ride Rockit (Universal Studios), 370–371, 377–378

Incredible Hulk Coaster, The (Islands of Adventure), 386–387, 389

Primeval Whirl (Animal Kingdom), 190, 324–325, 334–335

Revenge of the Mummy (Universal Studios), 370–371, 379–380

Rock 'n' Roller Coaster (DHS), 189, 342–343, 348–349

Space Mountain (Magic Kingdom), 187, 266–267, 284–285

Woody Woodpecker's Nuthouse Coaster (Universal Studios), 370–371, 383

romantic activities, 194

Rose & Crown Pub, 161

Rosen Shingle Creek, 116

routines, in vacation schedule, 201

Rowling, J. K., 394

Royal Anandapur Tea Company, 163

rumors, 40

Runoff Rapids (Blizzard Beach), 411

S

safety

childproofing rooms for, 127–128

for teenagers, 26

water parks, 413

San Angel Inn, 165, 167

San Francisco/Amity (Universal Studios), 370–371, 388

Sanaa, 168

Saratoga Springs Resort & Spa, 82, 97–98, 104

scavenger hunts, 188, 310–311

school work, 65–67

Sci-Fi Dine-In Restaurant, 154, 165–166

seafood buffets, 131

Seas, The (Epcot), 188

Seas with Nemo and Friends Pavilion, The (Epcot), 188, 298, 302–303, 316

seasons

opening procedures and, 229

to visit, 44–48, 222

Seasons 52 restaurant, 132

SeaWorld, 404–407

Aquatica by, 416–417

S *(continued)*

senior citizens, 29–31, 185

Serenity Bay, 17

services
  Animal Kingdom, 322
  Disney's Hollywood Studios, 340–341
  Epcot, 297, 300
  Islands of Adventure, 385
  Magic Kingdom, 264
  Universal Studios Florida, 366

Seuss Landing (Islands of Adventure), 386–387, 401–402

Seven Dwarfs Mine Train (Magic Kingdom), 187, 266–267, 276, 281

Seven Seas Lagoon Floating Electrical Pageant (Magic Kingdom), 291

Shades of Green, 91, 104

Shark Reef (Typhoon Lagoon), 412

Sharp Aquos Theater (Universal Studios), 365

Sheraton Safari Hotel & Suites Lake Buena Vista, 118–119

Sheraton Vistana Resort Villas, 119

shoes, 197–199

Shootin' Arcade (Magic Kingdom), 186, 266–267, 272

shooting galleries, Toy Story Mania! (DHS), 189, 342–343, 351–352

shopping
  Disney Village Marketplace, 420–421
  Disney's West Side, 418–423
  Downtown Disney, 423–424
  Islands of Adventure, 385, 390
  Wizarding World of Harry Potter, 396

shows
  America Gardens Theatre (Epcot), 318
  American Adventure, The (Epcot), 188, 241–242, 299, 314
  American Idol Experience (DHS), 189
  Animal Actors on Location (Universal Studios), 370–371, 373
  Aquos Theater (Universal Studios), 365
  Beauty and the Beast–Live on Stage (DHS), 342–344
  Beetlejuice's Graveyard Revue (Universal Studios), 370–371, 373–374
  Blue Man Group (Universal Studios), 365
  Blues Brothers, The (Universal Studios), 374
  Cirque du Soleil (Downtown Disney), 420
  Country Bear Jamboree (Magic Kingdom), 186, 266–267, 272
  Day in the Park with Barney, A (Universal Studios), 370–371, 374
  Disaster! (Universal Studios), 370–371, 375
  Disney Junior–Live on Stage! (DHS), 189, 342–345
  Eighth Voyage of Sindbad, The (Islands of Adventure), 386–387, 393
  Enchanted Tales with Belle (Magic Kingdom), 276, 290
  Enchanted Tiki Room (Magic Kingdom), 186, 266–268

Fantasmic! (DHS), 189, 356–358

Fear Factor Live (Universal Studios), 370–371, 376

Festival of the Lion King (Animal Kingdom), 190, 324–325, 328

Finding Nemo: The Musical (Animal Kingdom), 190, 324–325, 335

Flights of Wonder (Animal Kingdom), 190, 324–325, 331–332

Hall of Presidents, The (Magic Kingdom), 186, 266–267, 274

Indiana Jones Epic Stunt Spectacular (DHS), 189, 342–343, 346

Jedi Training Academy (DHS), 188, 347

Little Mermaid, Voyage of the (DHS), 190, 342–343, 353–354

The Magic, the Memories, and You! (Magic Kingdom), 291

Poseidon's Fury (Islands of Adventure), 386–387, 393–394

SeaWorld, 404–407

Stitch's Great Escape (Magic Kingdom), 187, 266–267, 286

TWISTER (Universal Studios), 370–371, 381–382

Universal Horror Make-up Show (Universal Studios), 370–371, 382

Voyage of the Little Mermaid (DHS), 190, 342–343, 353–354

Walt Disney's Carousel of Progress (Magic Kingdom), 187, 266–267, 287–288

Shrek 4-D (Universal Studios), 370–371, 380

Shula's Steakhouse, 166

shuttle services, to/from accommodations, 75–76, 81

Simpsons Ride, The (Universal Studios), 370–371, 380–381

simulator rides
  Despicable Me (Universal Studios), 370–371, 374–375
  Harry Potter and the Forbidden Journey (Islands of Adventure), 386–387, 398–400

Sindbad, The Eighth Voyage of (Islands of Adventure), 386–387, 393

single parents, 28–29

Ski Patrol Training Camp (Blizzard Beach), 411

sleep, 199–200

Slush Gusher (Blizzard Beach), 411

Small World, It's A (Magic Kingdom), 187, 266–267, 278

smoking, in restaurants, 143

snacks, 148–149, 210–212

snorkeling (Typhoon Lagoon), 412

Snow Stormers (Blizzard Beach), 411

Snow White's Scary Adventures (Magic Kingdom), 187, 281

Soarin' (Epcot), 188, 306

soda fountains, Epcot, 302

Sommerfest, 161

Sonny's Real Pit Bar-B-Q, 134

Sounds Dangerous with Drew Carey (DHS), 189, 342–343, 349

soundstages, Disney's Hollywood Studios, 189

souvenirs, 255

Space Mountain (Magic Kingdom), 187, 266–267, 284–285

Spaceship Earth (Epcot), 188, 298–299, 301

special children's programs, 68–70

Spider-Man, The Amazing Adventures of (Islands of Adventure), 386–389

Splash Mountain (Magic Kingdom), 186, 266–267, 272–273

sports, Wide World of Sports, 19, 424

Star Tours: The Adventure Continues (DHS), 189, 342–343, 349–350

Star Wars weekends, 49

Starring Rolls Cafe, 164

Stitch's Great Escape (Magic Kingdom), 187, 266–267, 286

Storm Force Accelatron (Islands of Adventure), 386–387, 390

Storm Slides (Typhoon Lagoon), 412

Storybook Circus (Magic Kingdom), 276–277

Storybook Treats, 158

Street Scenes (Universal Studios), 381

Streets of America (DHS), 342–343, 350, 357

strollers, 23, 199, 257–259

   Animal Kingdom, 322

   Disney's Hollywood Studios, 340

   Epcot, 297

   Islands of Adventure, 385

   Magic Kingdom, 264

   sunburn in, 209

   Universal Studios Florida, 366

Studio Backlot Tour (DHS), 342–343, 350–351

Studio Catering Co., 146, 164

stunt shows

   Eighth Voyage of Sindbad, The (Islands of Adventure), 386–387, 393

   Indiana Jones Epic Stunt Spectacular (DHS), 189, 342–343, 346

   Lights! Motors! Action! Extreme Stunt Show (DHS), 189, 342–343, 347–348

Summit Plummet (Blizzard Beach), 411

sunglasses, 206–207

sunscreen, 209–213

Sunset Boulevard (DHS), 341, 343, 357

Sunset Ranch Market, 164

Sunshine Seasons, 146, 161, 168

super-headliners, 223

Surf Pool (Typhoon Lagoon), 412

Swan, 85, 94–95, 104

Sweet Tomatoes (restaurant), 131

swimming, 85. *See also* water parks.

Swiss Family Treehouse (Magic Kingdom), 186, 266–267, 270–271

T

Tabla Bar and Grill, 132

Tamu Tamu, 163

Tangierine Cafe, 161

tantrums, 35–36

tea cup ride, Magic Kingdom, 187, 266–267, 278–279

tea party, 69, 256–257

Teamboat Springs (Blizzard Beach), 411

teenagers, 25–26, 421–422

telephone numbers, Walt Disney World, 44–45

tents, 213–214

Teppan Edo, 139, 166–167

Terminator 2:3-D (Universal Studios), 370–371, 381

Test Track (Epcot), 188, 298, 308–309

Texas de Brazil, 133

Thanksgiving celebration, 52

Theater in the Wild (Animal Kingdom), 324–325, 335

Theater of the Stars (DHS), 342–344

Three Broomsticks (Islands of Adventure), 395

Three Caballeros, Gran Fiesta Tour Starring (Epcot), 188, 311

thrill rides, 238–239

tickets. *See* admission.

Tike's Peak (Blizzard Beach), 411

Tinker Bell's flight, 290

TNA iMPACT (Universal Studios), 365

Toboggan Racers (Blizzard Beach), 411

toddlers, 21–24. *See also* baby care centers.

   childproofing rooms for, 127–128

   strollers for. *See* strollers.

   supplies for, 215

Tom Sawyer Island (Magic Kingdom), 186, 266–267, 273–274

Tomorrowland (Magic Kingdom)

   attractions, 187, 266–267, 283–288

      Astro Orbiter, 187, 266–267, 283

      Buzz Lightyear's Space Ranger Spin, 187, 266–267, 283–284

      Carousel of Progress, 187, 266–267, 287–288

      Monsters, Inc. Laugh Floor, 187, 266–267, 284

      Space Mountain, 187, 266–267, 284–285

      Stitch's Great Escape, 187, 266–267, 286

      Tomorrowland Speedway, 187, 247, 266–267, 286–287

      Tomorrowland Transit Authority People-Mover, 187, 266–267, 287

   dining, 289

Tomorrowland Speedway (Magic Kingdom), 187, 247, 266–267, 286–287

Tomorrowland Terrace Noodle Station, 146, 158

Tomorrowland Transit Authority PeopleMover (Magic Kingdom), 187, 266–267, 287

Toon Lagoon (Islands of Adventure), 386–387, 390–391

Tortuga Tavern, 158–159

tour(s)

   magic, 69–70

   steam trains, 70

touring plans

   Animal Kingdom, 338–339

T (continued)
touring plans (continued)
bouncing around with, 230–231
dining time and, 148
Disney's Hollywood Studios, 358–359
Epcot, 320–321
with Extra Magic Hours, 233–234
for high-attendance days, 229
interruption, 229
Islands of Adventure, 402–404
for low-attendance days, 229, 232–233
Magic Kingdom, 292–295
for obsessive-compulsive reader, 231–232
opening procedures and, 229
rejection, 232
revision, 230
selection, 229–234
Universal Studios, 384
variables affecting, 227–228
touringplans.com, 37–38
Tower of Terror (DHS), 190, 342–343, 353
Toy Story Mania! (DHS), 189, 342–343, 351–352
trains
High in the Sky Seuss Trolley Train Ride, The (Islands of Adventure), 386–387, 401–402
Hogwarts Express (Islands of Adventure), 394–395
Seven Dwarfs Mine Train (Magic Kingdom), 187, 266–267, 276, 281
Tomorrowland Transit Authority PeopleMover (Magic Kingdom), 187, 266–267, 287
Universal Studios, 394–395
Walt Disney World Railroad (Magic Kingdom), 70, 186, 266–268
Wildlife Express Train (Animal Kingdom), 190, 324–325, 330
transportation
to/from accommodations, 75–76, 81
for teenagers, 26
travel agents, 109–110
Tree of Life, The (Animal Kingdom), 324–326
Treehouse, Swiss Family (Magic Kingdom), 186, 266–267, 270–271
Treehouse Villas at Disney's Saratoga Springs Resort & Spa, 82, 104
T-REX restaurant, 167
TriceraTop Spin (Animal Kingdom), 190, 324–325, 335–336
trivia, website for, 42
truck rides, Kilimanjaro Safaris (Animal Kingdom), 190, 324–325, 328–329
Turf Club Bar & Grill, 168
turkey legs, 148
Turtle Talk with Crush (Epcot), 188, 298–299, 303
Tusker House Restaurant, 155, 166, 251
Twilight Zone Tower of Terror, The (DHS), 190, 342–343, 353
TWISTER (Universal Studios), 370–371, 381–382
Twitter, 40–41

Typhoon Lagoon, 58–59, 245, 408–413

U

Under the Sea: Journey of the Little Mermaid (Magic Kingdom), 266–267, 276, 282–283
United Kingdom Pavilion (Epcot), 53–54, 189, 299, 315–316
United States Pavilion (Epcot), 54, 188, 299, 314, 316
Universal 360°: A Cinesphere Spectacular (Universal Studios), 370–371, 382–383
Universal CityWalk, 55–56, 361, 403–404
Universal Express, vs. Fastpass, 362–364
Universal Horror Make-up Show (Universal Studios), 370–371, 382
Universal Orlando. See also Islands of Adventure; Universal Studios Florida.
accommodations near, 111–112, 362
admission, 362
arrival, 361–362
dining, 364
map, 368–369
overview, 361
parking, 361
Universal Studios Florida, 365–384
accommodations, 361
admission, 362
arrival, 362
attractions, 373–383
Animal Actors on Location, 370–371, 373
Beetlejuice's Graveyard Revue, 370–371, 373–374
Blues Brothers, 374
Day in the Park with Barney, A, 370–371, 374
Despicable Me, 370–371, 374–375
Disaster!, 370–371, 375
vs. Disney's Hollywood Studios, 366–367, 372–373
E. T. Adventure, 370–371, 376
Fear Factor Live, 370–371, 376
Fievel's Playland, 370–371, 376–377
frightening, 364–365
Hollywood Rip Ride Rockit, 370–371, 377–378
JAWS, 370–371, 378
Lucy, A Tribute, 370–371, 378
Men in Black Alien Attack, 370–371, 379
Revenge of the Mummy, 370–371, 379–380
Shrek 4-D, 370–371, 380
Simpsons Ride, The, 370–371, 380–381
Street Scenes, 381
Terminator 2:3-D, 370–371, 381
TWISTER, 370–371, 381–382
Universal 360°: A Cinesphere Spectacular, 370–371, 382–383
Universal Horror Make-up Show, 370–371, 382
Woody Woodpecker's KidZone, 370–371, 383

costs, 362
dining, 388
vs. Disney's Hollywood Studios, 366–367,
    372–373
live entertainment, 383
maps, 368–369
overview, 365–366
services, 366
touring plans, 384
touring time, 372
Universal Express, 362–364
Universe of Energy: Ellen's Energy Adventure
    (Epcot), 188, 298, 309
US 192 (Irlo Bronson Memorial Highway),
    accommodations, 111, 120–122

V

vacation home rental, 124–127
Vacation Planning Kit, 194
vacation rentals, 126
vendor food, 146
Very Merry Christmas Parade, 53
Via Napoli, 139, 166
Victoria & Albert's, 167–168
video cameras, 218
virtual games, DisneyQuest, 421–422
Vito's Chop House, 133
Vittorio's, 131
Voyage of the Little Mermaid (DHS), 190, 342–343,
    353–354

W

waiting-line strategies, 241–247
walking, foot care for, 197–199
wallets, 207
Walt Disney Travel Company Florida Vacations
    Brochure and DVD, 38
Walt Disney World Railroad (Magic Kingdom), 70,
    186, 266–268
Walt Disney's Carousel of Progress (Magic Kingdom),
    187, 266–267, 287–288
wand store (Islands of Adventure), 395
water bottles, 209
water parks, 404–407
admission, 58–59
Aquatica by SeaWorld, 416–417
Blizzard Beach, 58–59, 245, 408–413
costs, 408
eating in, 413
height requirements, 245
overview, 14
safety in, 413
Typhoon Lagoon, 58–59, 245, 408–413
weather and, 411–412
Wet 'n Wild, 413–416
weather
cool, 206
raingear, 208–209
seasonal, 44–48
for water park use, 411–412

websites, 37–43
Wes Palm (Animal Kingdom), 336
West Side, Disney's, 14, 418–423
Wet 'n Wild water park, 413–416
whales, SeaWorld, 405–406
wheelchairs
Animal Kingdom, 322
Disney's Hollywood Studios, 340
Epcot, 297
Islands of Adventure, 385
Magic Kingdom, 264
Universal Studios Florida, 366
white-water raft rides
Kali River Rapids (Animal Kingdom), 190,
    324–325, 332
Popeye & Bluto's Bilge-Rat Barges (Islands of
    Adventure), 386–387, 391
Wide World of Sports, 15, 424
Wild Jack's Steaks & BBQ, 134
Wilderness Lodge Resort and Villas, 90–91, 104,
    424
Wilderness Preserve, 424–425
Wildlife Express Train (Animal Kingdom), 190,
    324–325, 330
wine festivals, 50–51
Winnie the Pooh, The Many Adventures of (Magic
    Kingdom), 187, 266–267, 279
Winter Summerland miniature golf, 425–426
Wizarding World of Harry Potter, The (Islands of
    Adventure), 386–387, 394–400
attractions, 386–387, 398–400
shopping in, 396
touring plans, 402–403
Wonderland Tea Party (Magic Kingdom), 69,
    256–257
Woody Woodpecker's KidZone (Universal Studios),
    370–371, 383
World Expo (Universal Studios), 370–371, 388
World Showcase
attractions, 299, 310–317
    American Adventure, The (Epcot), 188,
        241–242, 299, 314
    China Pavilion, 54, 189, 298, 312, 316
    France Pavilion, 54, 188, 299, 315
    fright potential, 188–189
    Germany Pavilion, 54, 188, 299, 313, 316
    Gran Fiesta Tour Starring the Three
        Caballeros, 188, 311
    Impressions de France, 188, 299, 315
    Italy Pavilion, 54, 188, 299, 313, 316
    Japan Pavilion, 54, 188, 299, 314, 316
    Kim Possible World Showcase Adventure,
        188, 310–311
    Maelstrom, 189, 298, 311–312
    Mexico Pavilion, 54, 188, 298, 311, 316
    Morocco Pavilion, 54, 189, 299, 314–316
    Norway Pavilion, 94, 189, 251, 298, 311–312,
        316
    O Canada, 189, 299, 316–317

W *(continued)*
World Showcase *(continued)*
   attractions *(continued)*
      Reflections of China, 189, 298, 312
      United Kingdom Pavilion, 53–54, 189, 299, 316
      United States Pavilion, 54, 188, 299, 314, 316
      waiting line strategies, 241–243
   dining, 154
   live entertainment in, 318–319
Wyndham Bonnet Creek Resort, 119–120

Y
Yacht Club Resort & Villas, 82, 91–93, 104
Yachtsman Steakhouse, 166

Yak & Yeti, 155, 166
Yakitori House, 161–162
Yorkshire County Fish Shop, 162
YouTube attraction previews, 4

Z
Zonko's (Islands of Adventure), 394–395
zoologic exhibits, Maharajah Jungle Trek (Animal Kingdom), 190, 324–325, 332–333

Magic Kingdom

Magic Kingdom Happy Family 1-Day Touring Plan

1. If you are a Disney resort guest, arrive at the entrance to the Magic Kingdom 30 minutes prior to opening. Guests staying off-site should arrive at the Ticket and Transportation Center 40 minutes prior to opening. Obtain park maps and a copy of the daily entertainment schedule when you pass through the turnstiles. Stroller rentals are under the train station on Main Street.

2. **PARENTS:** As soon as the park opens, ride Dumbo the Flying Elephant in Fantasyland.

3. **TEENS:** As soon as the park opens, ride Space Mountain in Tomorrowland.

4. **FAMILY:** Ride The Many Adventures of Winnie the Pooh in Fantasyland.

5. **FAMILY:** Ride the Seven Dwarfs Mine Train in Fantasyland.

6. **FAMILY:** Ride Peter Pan's Flight in Fantasyland.

7. **PARENTS:** Ride The Magic Carpets of Aladdin in Adventureland.

8. **TEENS:** Ride Splash Mountain in Frontierland. If the wait exceeds 30 minutes, use Fastpass.

9. **TEENS:** Ride Big Thunder Mountain Railroad in Frontierland. Tip: Get Fastpasses for Splash or Big Thunder now if you want to ride again later.

10. **FAMILY:** Ride Pirates of the Caribbean in Adventureland.

11. **FAMILY:** See *The Enchanted Tiki Room.*

12. **FAMILY:** Eat lunch. Good nearby dining choices include Pecos Bill Tall Tale Inn & Café and the top floor of the Columbia Harbour House.

13. **PARENTS:** After lunch, return to your hotel for a break. We recommend allowing at least 3 hours.

14. **TEENS:** Ride Splash Mountain again in Frontierland. If you have Fastpasses, use those. Otherwise, obtain Fastpasses if the wait exceeds 30 minutes.

15. **TEENS:** Ride Big Thunder Mountain Railroad again in Frontierland. If you have Fastpasses, use those. Otherwise, obtain Fastpasses (if you can) if the wait exceeds 30 minutes.

16. **TEENS:** See The Haunted Mansion in Liberty Square.

17. **TEENS:** Explore the rest of the park, or revisit favorite attractions until the rest of the family returns.

18. **PARENTS:** Return to the Magic Kingdom and take the WDW Railroad from Main Street to Frontierland.

19. **FAMILY:** Tour Tom Sawyer Island. Allow at least 30–45 minutes to run around the island. Be sure to try the barrel bridges and tour Fort Langhorn.

20. **FAMILY:** Eat dinner.

21. **FAMILY:** See *Monsters, Inc. Laugh Floor* in Tomorrowland.

22. **FAMILY:** Ride Buzz Lightyear's Space Ranger Spin.

23. **PARENTS:** In Fantasyland, ride The Great Goofini.

24. **FAMILY:** Ride Journey of the Little Mermaid.

25. **FAMILY:** See *Mickey's PhilharMagic.*

26. **FAMILY:** Ride the Mad Tea Party.

27. **PARENTS:** If time permits, check the daily entertainment schedule for locations and times to meet Disney characters. The most common character greeting locations are Main Street and Fantasyland.

28. **FAMILY:** See the evening parade and/or fireworks on Main Street. A good viewing location for the fireworks is on the right-hand side of the end of Main Street, near the walkway to Tomorrowland Terrace.

29. **FAMILY:** Depart the Magic Kingdom.

If you have a Web-enabled cell phone, you can view current and future wait times for every attraction—and add the times you see in the parks—at **m.touringplans.com.**

Magic Kingdom

Magic Kingdom 1-Day Touring Plan for Grandparents with Small Children

1. If you are a Disney resort guest, arrive at the entrance to the Magic Kingdom 30 minutes prior to opening. Guests staying off-site should arrive at the Ticket and Transportation Center 40 minutes prior to opening. Obtain park maps and a copy of the daily entertainment schedule when you pass through the turnstiles. Stroller rentals are under the train station on Main Street.

2. As soon as the park opens, ride Dumbo the Flying Elephant in Fantasyland. To get to Fantasyland, go down Main Street and either through or around the castle.

3. Ride The Many Adventures of Winnie the Pooh.

4. Experience The Seven Dwarfs Mine Train, also in Fantasyland.

5. Ride Peter Pan's Flight.

6. See *Mickey's PhilharMagic*.

7. Take a spin on Prince Charming's Regal Carrousel.

8. Take the It's a Small World boat ride.

9. Give the Mad Tea Party a spin. It's located near the Winnie the Pooh ride.

10. If your grandkids are interested in meeting Disney characters, princesses, or fairies, do so now. Check the daily entertainment schedule for times and locations of each character. The most common locations are in Fantasyland and on Main Street.

11. Eat lunch outside of the park and return to your hotel for a break of 3–4 hours.

12. Return to the Magic Kingdom and take the WDW Railroad from Main Street to Frontierland.

13. Tour Tom Sawyer Island. Allow at least 30–45 minutes to run around the island. Be sure to try the barrel bridges and tour Fort Langhorn.

14. Return to Frontierland for the Frontierland Shootin' Arcade. Cost is $1 per play.

15. See the *Country Bear Jamboree*. If possible, send one member of your party into Adventureland to check on Fastpasses for Jungle Cruise. If they're available for return in around an hour, get Fastpasses for everyone.

16. Eat dinner if you've not already done so. The nearest counter-service restaurant is Pecos Bill Tall Tale Inn & Café in Frontierland.

17. Ride The Magic Carpets of Aladdin.

18. Take the Jungle Cruise if lines are short or you have Fastpasses; otherwise, see *The Enchanted Tiki Room*.

19. Ride Pirates of the Caribbean.

20. Tour the Swiss Family Treehouse.

21. If the evening parade or fireworks will start within the next hour, find a spot on Main Street for the evening parade and fireworks. Grab the kids an ice cream and take a break. Otherwise, try the next few steps.

22. In Fantasyland, ride Journey of the Little Mermaid.

23. Try Buzz Lightyear's Space Ranger Spin in Tomorrowland, and then ride the Tomorrowland Transit Authority PeopleMover across from Buzz in the center of Tomorrowland.

24. Take a spin on the Tomorrowland Speedway.

25. See *Monsters, Inc. Laugh Floor*.

26. See the evening parade and fireworks from Main Street. The right side of the end of Main Street is a good viewing location.

27. If time permits and you've not already done so, obtain character autographs for any characters your grandchildren wish to meet.

28. Depart the Magic Kingdom.

If you have a Web-enabled cell phone, you can view current and future wait times for every attraction—and add the times you see in the parks—at **m.touringplans.com**.

Magic Kingdom

Magic Kingdom 1-Day Touring Plan
for Tweens and Their Parents

1. If you are a Disney resort guest, arrive at the entrance to the Magic Kingdom 30 minutes prior to opening. Guests staying off-site should arrive at the Ticket and Transportation Center 40 minutes prior to opening. Obtain park maps and a copy of the daily entertainment schedule when you pass through the turnstiles.
2. As soon as the park opens, ride Space Mountain in Tomorrowland.
3. Ride Buzz Lightyear's Space Ranger Spin.
4. Ride The Many Adventures of Winnie the Pooh in Fantasyland.
5. Ride the Seven Dwarfs Mine Train.
6. Ride Peter Pan's Flight.
7. See The Haunted Mansion in Liberty Square.
8. Ride Splash Mountain. If the wait exceeds 30 minutes, consider using Fastpass.
9. Ride Big Thunder Mountain Railroad.
10. Ride Pirates of the Caribbean.
11. Eat lunch. Good nearby counter-service restaurants include Pecos Bill Tall Tale Inn & Café in Frontierland and the Columbia Harbour House in Liberty Square.
12. Ride the Jungle Cruise in Adventureland. If the wait exceeds 30 minutes, use Fastpass.
13. Tour the Swiss Family Treehouse.

14. See The Enchanted Tiki Room.
15. See the Country Bear Jamboree in Frontierland.
16. Try the Frontierland Shootin' Arcade. Cost is $1 per play.
17. Experience The Hall of Presidents.
18. See Mickey's PhilharMagic in Fantasyland.
19. Ride Journey of the Little Mermaid.
20. Eat dinner. The closest sit-down restaurant is Cinderella's Royal Table (reservations required). For counter-service, try Pinocchio Village Haus in Fantasyland.
21. Take a ride on the Walt Disney World Railroad. Stations are located in Frontierland and on Main Street.
22. If time permits, see Monsters, Inc. Laugh Floor in Tomorrowland.
23. See the evening parade on Main Street.
24. See the evening fireworks on Main Street. A good viewing spot is to the right of the end of Main Street, near the Tomorrowland Terrace.
25. Depart the Magic Kingdom.

If you have a Web-enabled cell phone, you can view current and future wait times for every attraction—and add the times you see in the parks—at **m.touringplans.com.**

Magic Kingdom

Magic Kingdom 2-Day Touring Plan for Parents with Small Children—Day 1

(Review the Small-child Fright-potential Chart on pages 186-190)

1. If you are a Disney resort guest, arrive at the entrance to the Magic Kingdom 30 minutes prior to opening. Guests staying off-site should arrive at the Ticket and Transportation Center 40 minutes prior to opening. Obtain park maps and a copy of the daily entertainment schedule when you pass through the turnstiles. Stroller rentals are under the train station on Main Street.

2. As soon as the park opens, ride Dumbo the Flying Elephant in Fantasyland.

3. Ride Peter Pan's Flight.

4. Ride the Seven Dwarfs Mine Train.

5. Ride The Many Adventures of Winnie the Pooh.

6. Obtain Fastpasses for Splash Mountain in Frontierland.

7. Tour Tom Sawyer Island. Allow 30–45 minutes to run around the island. Be sure to try the barrel bridges and tour Fort Langhorn.

8. See the *Country Bear Jamboree.*

9. Take a round-trip on the Walt Disney World Railroad from the Frontierland station. The station is accessed by stairs located to the right of the entrance to Splash Mountain.

10. Ride Splash Mountain.

11. Eat lunch. Good nearby dining choices include Pecos Bill Tall Tale Inn & Café, with ample seating and air-conditioning. In Liberty Square, the top floor of the Columbia Harbour House is usually less crowded.

12. After lunch, return to your hotel for a midafternoon break. We recommend allowing at least 3 hours,

including transportation—4 hours would be better.

13. Return to the Magic Kingdom.

14. Experience *The Hall of Presidents* and the *Liberty Belle* riverboat in Liberty Square. These attractions are located across from each other in Liberty Square; see first the attraction that begins soonest, then see the other.

15. Eat dinner. The closest counter-service restaurant is Pinocchio Village Haus in Fantasyland. The nearest sit-down restaurant is Liberty Tree Tavern in Liberty Square.

16. Enjoy Prince Charming's Regal Carrousel in Fantasyland.

17. Ride It's a Small World.

18. See *Mickey's PhilharMagic.*

19. Ride Journey of the Little Mermaid. This is the last attraction in today's touring. Use extra time to revisit favorite attractions or explore the rest of the park.

20. See the evening parade and/or fireworks. A good viewing location for the fireworks is on the right-hand side of the end of Main Street, near Tomorrowland Terrace.

21. Depart the Magic Kingdom.

If you have a Web-enabled cell phone, you can view current and future wait times for every attraction—and add the times you see in the parks—at **m.touringplans.com.**

Magic Kingdom

Magic Kingdom 2-Day Touring Plan for Parents with Small Children—Day 2

(Review the Small-child Fright-potential Chart on pages 186-190)

1. If you are a Disney resort guest, arrive at the entrance to the Magic Kingdom 30 minutes prior to opening. Guests staying off-site should arrive at the Ticket and Transportation Center 40 minutes prior to opening. Obtain park maps and a copy of the daily entertainment schedule when you pass through the turnstiles. Stroller rentals are under the train station on Main Street.

2. As soon as the park opens, ride the Tomorrowland Speedway in Tomorrowland.

3. Ride the Astro Orbiter.

4. Ride Buzz Lightyear's Space Ranger Spin. If the wait exceeds 30 minutes, obtain Fastpasses for each member of your party.

5. Ride the Tomorrowland Transit Authority PeopleMover.

6. See *Monsters, Inc. Laugh Floor.*

7. In Fantasyland, ride The Great Goofini.

8. Ride Mad Tea Party.

9. If your children are interested in meeting Disney characters, princesses, or fairies, do so now. Check the daily entertainment schedule for times and locations of each character. The most common locations are in Fantasyland and on Main Street.

10. Ride Pirates of the Caribbean in Adventureland. While most children will take this attraction in stride,

the skeletons in some of the scenes may frighten a few children.

11. Eat lunch. Good sit-down restaurants include Liberty Tree Tavern in Liberty Square and the Crystal Palace on Main Street. For burgers, try Pecos Bill Tall Tale Inn & Café in Frontierland.

12. Return to your hotel for a mid-day break. Allow at least 3 hours for your break—4 hours would be better.

13. Return to the Magic Kingdom and explore the Swiss Family Treehouse in Adventureland.

14. Ride the Jungle Cruise. If the wait time exceeds 30 minutes, use Fastpass.

15. Ride The Magic Carpets of Aladdin.

16. See *The Enchanted Tiki Room.* This is the last attraction in today's touring. Use extra time to revisit favorite attractions or explore the rest of the park.

17. If you have not already done so, see the evening parade and/or fireworks.

18. Depart the Magic Kingdom.

If you have a Web-enabled cell phone, you can view current and future wait times for every attraction—and add the times you see in the parks—at **m.touringplans.com**.

Magic Kingdom

Magic Kingdom 2-Day Sleepyhead Touring Plan for Parents with Small Children—Day 1

(Review the Small-child Fright-potential Chart on pages 186-190)

1. Arrive at the entrance to the Magic Kingdom around 11 a.m. Obtain park maps and a copy of the daily entertainment schedule when you pass through the turnstiles. Stroller rentals are under the train station on Main Street.

2. Obtain Fastpasses for Splash Mountain in Frontierland.

3. Tour Tom Sawyer Island. Allow at least 30–45 minutes to see the island, including the barrel bridges and Fort Langhorn.

4. See the *Country Bear Jamboree.*

5. Ride Splash Mountain. Use the Fastpasses obtained in Step 2.

6. Send one member of your party to obtain Fastpasses for Peter Pan's Flight in Fantasyland.

7. Eat a late lunch. Good nearby dining choices include Pecos Bill Tall Tale Inn & Café, with ample seating and air-conditioning. In Liberty Square, the top floor of the Columbia Harbour House is usually less crowded.

8. Take a round-trip on the Walt Disney World Railroad from the Frontierland station. The station is accessed by stairs located to the right of the entrance to Splash Mountain.

9. Experience *The Hall of Presidents* and the *Liberty Belle* riverboat in Liberty Square. These attractions are located across from each other in Liberty Square; see first the attraction that begins soonest, then see the other.

10. See the afternoon parade from Frontierland or Liberty Square.

11. Send one member of your party to obtain Fastpasses for The Many Adventures of Winnie the Pooh in Fantasyland. Check your Fastpasses for Peter Pan's Flight for the exact time you can obtain Fastpasses for Pooh.

12. Take a 1-hour break inside the park. Good rest areas include the second floor of the Columbia Harbour House in Liberty Square and the walkway near the candy store in Frontierland.

13. Ride Peter Pan's Flight using the Fastpasses obtained in Step 6.

14. Ride It's a Small World.

15. See *Mickey's PhilharMagic.*

16. Enjoy Prince Charming's Regal Carrousel.

17. Ride Dumbo the Flying Elephant.

18. Ride the Mad Tea Party.

19. Ride The Many Adventures of Winnie the Pooh using the Fastpasses obtained in Step 11.

20. Ride Journey of the Little Mermaid.

21. Try the Seven Dwarfs Mine Train.

22. Eat dinner. Nearby choices include Pinocchio Village Haus (counter-service) and Cinderella's Royal Table (sit-down; reservations required).

23. See the evening parade and fireworks from Main Street. A good viewing location for the fireworks is on the right-hand side of the end of Main Street, on the walkway to Tomorrowland Terrace.

24. Depart the Magic Kingdom.

If you have a Web-enabled cell phone, you can view current and future wait times for every attraction—and add the times you see in the parks—at m.touringplans.com.

Magic Kingdom 2-Day Sleepyhead Touring Plan for Parents with Small Children—Day 2

(Review the Small-child Fright-potential Chart on pages 186–190)

1. Arrive at the entrance to the Magic Kingdom around 11 a.m. Obtain park maps and a copy of the daily entertainment schedule when you pass through the turnstiles. Stroller rentals are under the train station on Main Street.
2. Obtain Fastpasses for the Jungle Cruise in Adventureland.
3. Explore the Swiss Family Treehouse.
4. Ride The Magic Carpets of Aladdin.
5. See *The Enchanted Tiki Room*.
6. Ride Pirates of the Caribbean.
7. Ride the Jungle Cruise using the Fastpasses obtained in Step 2.
8. Eat lunch. Good nearby dining choices include Pecos Bill Tall Tale Inn & Café, with ample seating and air-conditioning. In Liberty Square, the top floor of the Columbia Harbour House is usually less crowded.
9. If your children are interested in meeting Disney characters, princesses, or fairies, do so now. Check the daily entertainment schedule for times and locations of each character. The most common locations are in Fantasyland and on Main Street.
10. In Fantasyland, ride The Great Goofini.

11. Take a 1-hour break inside the park. A good resting spot is inside Cosmic Ray's Starlight Café in Tomorrowland. If possible, send one member of your family to obtain Fastpasses for Buzz Lightyear's Space Ranger Spin in Tomorrowland.
12. Ride the Tomorrowland Speedway.
13. Ride the Tomorrowland Transit Authority PeopleMover.
14. Ride the Astro Orbiter.
15. See *Monsters, Inc. Laugh Floor.*
16. Ride Buzz Lightyear's Space Ranger Spin using the Fastpasses obtained in Step 11.
17. Eat dinner. The closest counter-service restaurant is Cosmic Ray's Starlight Café in Tomorrowland. Or try The Plaza Restaurant on Main Street.
18. See the evening parade on Main Street.
19. Depart the Magic Kingdom.

If you have a Web-enabled cell phone, you can view current and future wait times for every attraction—and add the times you see in the parks—at **m.touringplans.com**.

Magic Kingdom

Parent's Magic Kingdom Plan—1 Afternoon and 1 Full Day (Full Day)

(Review the Small-child Fright-potential Chart on pages 186–190)

1. If you are a Disney resort guest, arrive at the entrance to the Magic Kingdom 30 minutes prior to opening. Guests staying off-site should arrive at the Ticket and Transportation Center 40 minutes prior to opening. Obtain park maps and a copy of the daily entertainment schedule when you pass through the turnstiles. Stroller rentals are under the train station on Main Street.
2. As soon as the park opens, ride Dumbo the Flying Elephant in Fantasyland.
3. Ride Peter Pan's Flight.
4. Ride the Seven Dwarfs Mine Train.
5. Ride The Many Adventures of Winnie the Pooh. Unless the wait exceeds 30 minutes, do not use Fastpass.
6. Ride It's a Small World.
7. See *Mickey's PhilharMagic*.
8. If possible, send one member of your party to obtain Fastpasses for Buzz Lightyear's Space Ranger Spin in Tomorrowland.
9. Ride The Great Goofini.
10. Ride the Tomorrowland Transit Authority PeopleMover in Tomorrowland.
11. See *Monsters, Inc. Laugh Floor*.
12. Ride Buzz Lightyear's Space Ranger Spin, using the Fastpasses obtained in Step 8.
13. Eat lunch. The nearest counter-service restaurant is Cosmic Ray's Starlight Café, across from the

Tomorrowland Speedway. Good sandwiches can be found at The Plaza Restaurant on Main Street.
14. Leave the park for a nap back at your hotel. Allow at least 3 hours for this break—4 would be better.
15. Return to the park. If you want to experience any ride again, see if Fastpasses are still available for it. Good evening rides include Splash Mountain in Frontierland and Prince Charming's Regal Carrousel in Fantasyland.
16. Ride Journey of the Little Mermaid in Fantasyland.
17. Eat dinner if you have not already done so. Most kids will find something they like at the sit-down Liberty Tree Tavern. Reservations are recommended.
18. See The Haunted Mansion in Liberty Square.
19. See the evening parade on Main Street. Liberty Square is a good alternate viewing location if you're already there.
20. See the evening fireworks on Main Street. A good viewing spot is to the right of the end of Main Street, on the walkway toward Tomorrowland Terrace.
21. Depart the Magic Kingdom.

If you have a Web-enabled cell phone, you can view current and future wait times for every attraction—and add the times you see in the parks—at **m.touringplans.com**.

Parent's Magic Kingdom Plan—1 Afternoon and 1 Full Day (Afternoon)

(Review the Small-child Fright-potential Chart on pages 186–190)

1. Arrive at the entrance to the Magic Kingdom around 2 p.m. Obtain park maps and a copy of the daily entertainment schedule when you pass through the turnstiles. Stroller rentals are under the train station on Main Street.

2. Obtain Fastpasses for Splash Mountain in Frontierland. If the wait is 20 minutes or less, ride now instead of using Fastpass.

3. In Frontierland, take the raft over to Tom Sawyer Island. Be sure to explore the barrel bridges and Fort Langhorn. If your kids are especially adventurous, explore the caves too!

4. Ride the Jungle Cruise in Adventureland. If the wait exceeds 30 minutes, use Fastpass.

5. See the *Country Bear Jamboree*. It's a short walk from the Jungle Cruise if you cut through Adventureland to Frontierland. Keep *The Enchanted Tiki Room* on your left, Magic Carpets of Aladdin on your right, and walk straight toward Frontierland. *CBJ* will be on your left.

6. Ride Pirates of the Caribbean in Adventureland.

7. Explore the Swiss Family Treehouse.

8. Ride Splash Mountain, using the Fastpasses obtained in Step 2.

9. Eat dinner. The closest counter-service restaurant is Pecos Bill Tall Tale Inn & Café in Frontierland. The closest sit-down restaurant is the Liberty Tree Tavern in Liberty Square. Reservations are recommended.

10. If you want to leave the park now, take the Walt Disney World Railroad from Frontierland to Main Street. The Frontierland station is located just above the entrance to Splash Mountain.

11. See the evening parade from Frontierland. Good viewing spots are along the storefronts of Frontierland—try in front of the candy store.

12. See the evening fireworks on Main Street. A good viewing spot is to the right of the end of Main Street, on the walkway toward Tomorrowland.

13. Depart the Magic Kingdom.

If you have a Web-enabled cell phone, you can view current and future wait times for every attraction—and add the times you see in the parks—at **m.touringplans.com**.

Epcot 1-Day Touring Plan for Parents with Small Children

1. Arrive at the entrance to Epcot 30 minutes prior to opening. Pick up a park map and daily entertainment schedule when entering the park. Stroller rentals are just inside the main entrance and to the left.

2. If your children are tall enough, ride Soarin' at the Land pavilion in Future World West. If your children aren't yet tall enough, skip this step and continue to Living with the Land.

3. Ride Living with the Land, also at the Land pavilion. Use Fastpass if the wait exceeds 30 minutes. Exit the pavilion and turn left to get to the Seas pavilion.

4. See The Seas with Nemo and Friends. Be sure to catch *Turtle Talk with Crush*.

5. Ride Journey Into Your Imagination.

6. See the film at the Imagination pavilion, to the right after you exit the post-show area for Journey Into Your Imagination.

7. See *The Circle of Life* in the Land pavilion.

8. Eat lunch. The closest (and best) restaurant will be Sunshine Seasons in the Land pavilion. For burgers, try the Electric Umbrella in Future World East.

9. If your kids are tall enough, try the Sum of All Thrills roller coaster simulator at Innoventions East in Future World East.

10. Ride Universe of Energy in Future World East. This ride can also be seen after Spaceship Earth later today.

11. Sign up for a Kim Possible World Showcase Adventure on the way to World Showcase. Look for the Kim Possible booth on the left side of the main walkway from Future World to World Showcase. The Mexico and

Norway adventures will be the closest to the next few steps; France and the United Kingdom will be better choices for the afternoon.

12. Ride the Gran Fiesta Tour at Mexico in World Showcase.

13. Ride Maelstrom at Norway. If the wait exceeds 30 minutes, consider using Fastpass.

14. Return to your hotel for a mid-day break.

15. Return to Epcot and ride Spaceship Earth.

16. See the *O Canada!* film at Canada in World Showcase. Eat dinner. Le Cellier, Canada's sit-down restaurant, is a popular choice. Reservations are required.

17. See *The American Adventure* at the United States pavilion.

18. If you've not already done so, try a Kim Possible World Showcase Adventure. The closest sign-up booth is between France and the United Kingdom in World Showcase.

19. If time permits, explore the Morocco, France, and United Kingdom pavilions.

20. See *IllumiNations*. Excellent viewing locations can be found along the walkway between Canada and France in World Showcase.

21. Depart Epcot.

If you have a Web-enabled cell phone, you can view current and future wait times for every attraction—and add the times you see in the parks—at **m.touringplans.com**.

Epcot

Epcot 1-Day Sleepyhead Touring Plan for Parents with Small Children

1. Arrive at the entrance to Epcot around 11 a.m. Pick up a park map and daily entertainment schedule when entering the park. Stroller rentals are just inside the main entrance and to the left.

2. If your children are tall enough, obtain Fastpasses for Soarin' at the Land pavilion in Future World West. If the wait is 25 minutes or less, ride now instead of using Fastpass.

3. Ride Living with the Land at the Land pavilion.

4. See The Seas with Nemo and Friends, and then tour the Seas pavilion. Be sure to try Turtle Talk with Crush.

5. Ride Journey into Your Imagination.

6. See the film at the Imagination pavilion, to the right after you exit the post-show area for Journey Into Your Imagination.

7. If you have not already done so, eat lunch. Sunshine Seasons at the Land pavilion offers the best selection in Future World.

8. Ride Soarin' using the Fastpasses obtained in Step 2.

9. If your children are tall enough, try the Sum of All Thrills roller coaster simulator at Innoventions East in Future World East.

10. Ride Universe of Energy in Future World East.

11. Ride Spaceship Earth.

12. Sign up for a Kim Possible World Showcase Adventure mission on the way to World

Showcase. A Kim Possible sign-up station is on the left side of the main walkway leading from Future World to World Showcase.

13. Ride the Gran Fiesta Tour boat ride at Mexico.

14. Ride Maelstrom at Norway. Because of the walk back, we do not recommend using Fastpass unless the wait exceeds 45 minutes.

15. See The American Adventure at the United States pavilion. The Liberty Inn is a convenient counter-service restaurant.

16. Eat dinner. Good sit-down restaurants include Restaurant Marrakesh in Morocco and Le Cellier in Canada. Reservations are strongly recommended for Le Cellier.

17. See the O Canada! film at Canada in World Showcase.

18. See IllumiNations. The best viewing spots are along the border between World Showcase and Future World, and between Canada and France in World Showcase.

19. Depart Epcot.

If you have a Web-enabled cell phone, you can view current and future wait times for every attraction—and add the times you see in the parks—at **m.touringplans.com.**

Epcot

Epcot 1-Day Touring Plan for Tweens and Their Parents

1. Arrive at the entrance to Epcot 30 minutes prior to opening. Pick up a park map and daily entertainment schedule when entering the park.

2. As soon as the park opens, obtain Fastpasses for Soarin' at the Land pavilion in Future World West.

3. In Future World East, ride Test Track.

4. Ride Mission: SPACE. Do not use Fastpass.

5. In Innoventions East, ride Sum of All Thrills.

6. Ride Living with the Land in the Land Pavilion.

7. Now might be a good time to pick up a second Fastpass for Soarin', if available.

8. See The Seas with Nemo and Friends and *Turtle Talk with Crush*.

9. Ride Journey into Imagination.

10. See the film at the Imagination pavilion, to the right after you exit the post-show area for Journey Into Your Imagination.

11. Ride Soarin' using the Fastpasses obtained in Step 2.

12. Eat lunch. Sunshine Seasons has the best food in Future World. The Garden Grill in the Land pavilion is the closest sit-down restaurant.

13. Ride Spaceship Earth.

14. Ride Universe of Energy in Future World East.

15. Tour the remaining exhibits in Innoventions East.

16. Sign up for the Kim Possible World Showcase Adventure on the walk to World Showcase.

17. Experience the Gran Fiesta Tour boat ride at Mexico. This begins a clockwise tour of World Showcase.

18. Ride Maelstrom and tour the stave church in Norway.

19. See *Reflections of China.*

20. Tour Germany.

21. Visit Italy.

22. See *The American Adventure.*

23. Explore Japan.

24. Visit Morocco, including the small museum on the left side of the pavilion.

25. See *Impressions de France* at the France pavilion. Children give the film average marks, but the film is shown in an air-conditioned theater with comfortable seating, and everyone might need this kind of break about now.

26. Eat dinner. Good sit-down restaurants include Le Cellier at Canada and the Rose and Crown at the United Kingdom. Reservations are strongly recommended.

27. Visit the United Kingdom.

28. Tour Canada and see *O Canada!*

29. See *IllumiNations.* Prime viewing spots are along the lagoon between Canada and France.

30. Depart Epcot.

If you have a Web-enabled cell phone, you can view current and future wait times for every attraction—and add the times you see in the parks—at **m.touringplans.com.**

Parent's Epcot Touring Plan — 1 Afternoon and 1 Full Day (Full Day)

1. Arrive at the entrance to Epcot 30 minutes prior to opening. Pick up a park map and daily entertainment schedule when entering the park.

2. As soon as the park opens, obtain Fastpasses for Soarin' at the Land pavilion in Future World West.

3. In Future World East, ride Test Track.

4. Ride Mission: SPACE. Do not use Fastpasses.

5. In Innoventions East, ride Sum of All Thrills.

6. Ride Living with the Land in the Land Pavilion.

7. Now might be a good time to pick up a second Fastpass for Soarin', if available.

8. Ride Journey into Imagination.

9. See the film at the Imagination pavilion, to the right after you exit the post-show area for Journey Into Your Imagination.

10. Ride Soarin' using the Fastpasses obtained in Step 2.

11. Eat lunch. Sunshine Seasons has the best food in Future World. The Garden Grill in the Land pavilion is the closest sit-down restaurant. Or try the counter-service restaurant at Mexico in World Showcase.

12. Sign up for the Kim Possible World Showcase Adventure on the walk to World Showcase.

13. Experience the Gran Fiesta Tour boat ride at Mexico. This begins a clockwise tour of World Showcase.

14. Ride Maelstrom and tour the stave church in Norway.

15. See *Reflections of China*.

16. Tour Germany.

17. Visit Italy.

18. See *The American Adventure*.

19. Explore Japan.

20. Visit the Morocco pavilion.

21. Depart Epcot.

If you have a Web-enabled cell phone, you can view current and future wait times for every attraction—and add the times you see in the parks—at **m.touringplans.com**.

Epcot

Epcot

Parent's Epcot Touring Plan— 1 Afternoon and 1 Full Day (Afternoon)

1. Arrive at Epcot at 1 p.m. Pick up a park map and daily entertainment schedule when entering the park. Make dining reservations by calling (407) WDW-DINE if you have not already done so.

2. Ride Spaceship Earth.

3. Tour the remaining attractions in Future World East.

4. See the Universe of Energy.

5. See The Seas with Nemo and Friends in Future World West. If you have young children, also see *Turtle Talk with Crush* at the Seas pavilion.

6. See *The Circle of Life* at the Land pavilion in Future World West.

7. If you have not already done so, sign up for the Kim Possible World Showcase Adventure on the walk to World Showcase.

8. See *O Canada!* at the Canada pavilion in World Showcase.

9. Visit the United Kingdom pavilion.

10. In France, see *Impressions de France*.

11. Eat dinner. Good nearby restaurants include Le Cellier at Canada, Restaurant Marrakesh at Morocco, and Teppan Edo at Japan. Reservations are recommended.

12. See *IllumiNations*. Good viewing spots can be found along the waterway between France and Canada.

13. Depart Epcot.

If you have a Web-enabled cell phone, you can view current and future wait times for every attraction—and add the times you see in the parks—at **m.touringplans.com**.

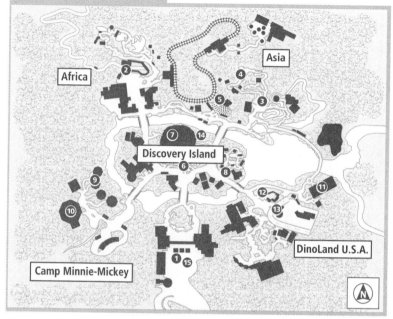

Animal Kingdom 1-Day Touring Plan
for Parents with Small Children

1. Arrive at the entrance to Disney's Animal Kingdom 25 minutes prior to opening. Pick up a park map and entertainment schedule. Stroller rentals are just past the entrance, to the right.
2. As soon as the park opens, experience the Kilimanjaro Safaris in Africa.
3. Ride Kali River Rapids in Asia. You will get wet. Use ponchos or plastic bags to keep dry.
4. Walk the Maharajah Jungle Trek.
5. See *Flights of Wonder*. Check the daily entertainment schedule for performance times.
6. See *It's Tough To Be a Bug* in Discovery Island. If the wait exceeds 30 minutes, use Fastpass.
7. See the exhibits at the Tree of Life.
8. Eat lunch. Good nearby locations include Flame Tree Barbecue and Pizzafari.
9. Explore the Camp Minnie-Mickey Character Trails in Camp Minnie-Mickey.

10. See the *Festival of the Lion King*.
11. Check the next performance time of *Finding Nemo: The Musical* at the Theater in the Wild in DinoLand. If the next show is within 25 minutes, see *Nemo* now. Otherwise, see The Boneyard in DinoLand.
12. Check out The Boneyard in DinoLand.
13. Ride TriceraTop Spin in DinoLand.
14. If it's near parade time, find a good viewing spot on Discovery Island for the Afternoon Parade from Discovery Island. The parade is usually performed around 4 p.m.
15. Depart Disney's Animal Kingdom. The Animal Kingdom is a theme park to be savored. Take time to explore the exhibits and speak with the cast members.

Animal Kingdom

Asia

Africa

Discovery Island

DinoLand U.S.A.

Camp Minnie-Mickey

N

Animal Kingdom 1-Day Sleepyhead Touring Plan for Parents with Small Children

1. Arrive at the entrance to Disney's Animal Kingdom around 11 a.m. Pick up a park map and entertainment schedule. Stroller rentals are just past the entrance, to the right.

2. Send one member of your party to obtain Fastpasses for the Kilimanjaro Safari in Africa.

3. See *Flights of Wonder*. Check the daily entertainment schedule for show times.

4. Eat lunch. The nearest counter-service restaurants are the Flame Tree Barbecue on Discovery Island, and Anandapur Local Foods Cafés in Asia.

5. Ride Kali River Rapids in Asia. You can leave this step for last if you'd rather not walk around the park wet.

6. Walk the Maharajah Jungle Trek in Asia.

7. Check the next performance time of *Finding Nemo: The Musical* at the Theater in the Wild in DinoLand. If the next show is within 25 minutes, see *Nemo* now. Otherwise, see *It's Tough to Be a Bug* first, then see *Nemo*.

8. See *It's Tough To Be a Bug*. Also see the exhibits at the Tree of Life in Discovery Island.

9. Explore the Camp Minnie-Mickey Character Trails in Camp Minnie-Mickey.

10. See the *Festival of the Lion King*.

11. Experience the Kilimanjaro Safaris in Africa using the Fastpasses from Step 2.

12. If desired, see the Afternoon Parade.

13. Depart Disney's Animal Kingdom.

Animal Kingdom 1-Day Touring Plan for Tweens and Their Parents

1. Arrive 40 minutes before official opening mid-June through mid-August and during all holiday periods. At other times arrive 30 minutes early.
2. As soon as the park opens, send one member of your party to get Fastpasses for Expedition Everest in Asia. The shortest route to Everest is from Discovery Island through Asia, not DinoLand U.S.A.
3. Ride Primeval Whirl in DinoLand U.S.A.
4. Ride DINOSAUR.
5. Ride Kali River Rapids in Asia. You will get wet. Ponchos or plastic bags are advised. If you don't feel like getting soaked right now, skip this attraction or obtain Fastpasses for later in the day.
6. See *Flights of Wonder* in Asia if the next show is within 20 minutes from now. Otherwise, walk the Maharajah Jungle Trek, and then see the show.
7. Walk the Maharajah Jungle Trek in Asia if you have not already done so.
8. Ride Expedition Everest in Asia. Don't worry if your Fastpass times have past; Disney rarely enforces the times, as long as you're not trying to get in early.
9. If possible, send one member of your party to obtain Fastpasses for the Kilimanjaro Safaris in Africa.
10. Eat lunch. The closest counter-service restaurant is Tusker House in Africa.
11. Walk the Pangani Forest Exploration Trail.

12. Experience Kilimanjaro Safaris using the Fastpasses obtained earlier. Don't worry if the Fastpass return times have past; Disney rarely enforces them.
13. See the *Festival of the Lion King* in Camp Minnie-Mickey.
14. Meet the characters at Camp Minnie-Mickey.
15. Check the next performance time of *Finding Nemo: The Musical* at the Theater in the Wild in DinoLand. If the next show is within 25 minutes, see *Nemo* now. Otherwise, see *It's Tough to Be a Bug* first, then see *Nemo*.
16. See *It's Tough to Be a Bug* on Discovery Island. Use Fastpass if the wait exceeds 30 minutes. Also check out the exhibits at the Tree of Life.
17. Shop, snack, or repeat any attractions you especially enjoyed. Visit the zoological exhibits in The Oasis, and depart the Animal Kingdom. This plan should work well with Extra Magic Hour mornings. The only exception might be Kali River Rapids, which may open later than the rest of the attractions in Asia. If that happens, skip the attraction and return to it after all the other Asia attractions are done.

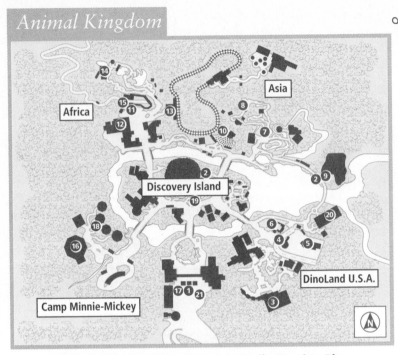

Animal Kingdom

Animal Kingdom 1-Day Happy Family Touring Plan

1. **FAMILY:** Arrive 40 minutes before official opening mid-June through mid-August and during all holiday periods. At other times arrive 30 minutes early.
2. **TEENS:** As soon as the park opens, obtain Fastpasses for Expedition Everest in Asia. The fastest way to Everest is through Asia, not DinoLand.
   PARENTS: Don't feel the need to rush to an attraction. Explore The Oasis on Discovery Island, pointing out any unusual animals. Hungry? Look for the Royal Anandapur Tea Company in Asia between Kali River Rapids and Expedition Everest.
3. **TEENS:** Ride DINOSAUR in DinoLand U.S.A.
4. **PARENTS:** Ride TriceraTop Spin in DinoLand U.S.A.
5. **TEENS:** Ride Primeval Whirl in DinoLand U.S.A.
6. **PARENTS:** Check out The Boneyard in DinoLand.
7. **FAMILY:** If everyone's up for it, ride Kali River Rapids in Asia. You will get wet. Ponchos or plastic bags are advised. If you don't feel like getting soaked right now, save this attraction for later in the day.
8. **FAMILY:** Walk the Maharajah Jungle Trek.
9. **TEENS:** Ride Expedition Everest, using the Fastpasses obtained earlier. Don't worry if your Fastpass times have past; Disney rarely enforces the times, as long as you're not trying to get in early.
10. **PARENTS:** See *Flights of Wonder*. If the next show time is too far away, check out other nearby exhibits.
11. **FAMILY:** Send one member of your party to obtain Fastpasses for the Kilimanjaro Safaris in Africa.
12. **FAMILY:** Eat lunch. The closest counter-service restaurant is Tusker House in Africa.
13. **FAMILY:** Take the Wildlife Express train to Rafiki's Planet Watch/Conservation Station. See the exhibits. Note the writing on the bathroom walls. Take the train back to Africa when you're done.
14. **FAMILY:** Walk the Pangani Forest Exploration Trail. If teens want to, they could obtain more Fastpasses for Expedition Everest near the entrance to Kilimanjaro Safaris. Meet back at the entrance to Kilimanjaro Safaris.
15. **FAMILY:** Experience Kilimanjaro Safaris using the Fastpasses obtained earlier. Don't worry if the Fastpass return times have past; Disney rarely enforces them.
16. **FAMILY:** See the *Festival of the Lion King* in Camp Minnie-Mickey.
17. **TEENS:** Free time. Revisit favorite attractions or explore the rest of the park.
18. **PARENTS:** Meet the characters at Camp Minnie-Mickey.
19. **FAMILY:** See *It's Tough to Be a Bug* on Discovery Island. Use Fastpass if the wait exceeds 30 minutes. Also check out the exhibits at the Tree of Life.
20. **FAMILY:** See *Finding Nemo: The Musical.*
21. **FAMILY:** Shop, snack, or repeat any attractions you especially enjoyed. Visit the zoological exhibits in The Oasis, and depart the Animal Kingdom.

Disney's Hollywood Studios

Disney's Hollywood Studios 1-Day Touring Plan for Parents with Small Children

1. Arrive at the entrance to Disney's Hollywood Studios 30 minutes prior to opening. Grab a park map and daily entertainment schedule when you enter the park. Rent strollers as needed at the gas station on the right side of the park entrance, just past the turnstiles.
2. As soon as the park opens, ride Toy Story Mania! at Pixar Place near the back center of the park.
3. If your kids are up for it, ride the Tower of Terror on Sunset Boulevard.
4. See *Voyage of the Little Mermaid.*
5. See *Disney Junior—Live on Stage!* Check the daily entertainment schedule for showtimes.
6. Ride Star Tours. Use Fastpass if the wait exceeds 25 minutes.
7. See the *Jedi Training Academy* show near Star Tours, either before or after you ride. Check the entertainment schedule for showtimes.
8. See *Muppet-Vision 3-D.*
9. Explore the Honey, I Shrunk the Kids Movie Set.
10. Eat lunch. The Backlot Express and Mama Melrose's are good nearby choices.
11. Take a midday break of around 3 hours.
12. Return to the park and see *Beauty and the Beast.* Check the daily entertainment schedule for showtimes.
13. See the *Lights, Motors, Action! Extreme Stunt Show* or the *Indiana Jones Epic Stunt Spectacular.* Check the daily entertainment schedule for showtimes.
14. If time permits, take the Studio Backlot Tour.
15. Eat dinner. Good nearby selections include the counter-service eateries on Sunset Boulevard. The Hollywood Brown Derby and the 50's Prime Time Café are the closest sit-down choices. Reservations are recommended.
16. See *Fantasmic!* if it's playing. Plan on arriving 30–40 minutes early to get decent seats, and up to an hour in advance for good seats.
17. Depart Disney's Hollywood Studios.

If you have a Web-enabled cell phone, you can view current and future wait times for every attraction—and add the times you see in the parks—at **m.touringplans.com.**

Disney's Hollywood Studios

Disney's Hollywood Studios 1-Day Sleepyhead Touring Plan for Parents with Small Children

1. Arrive at the entrance to Disney's Hollywood Studios around 11 a.m. Grab a park map and entertainment schedule when you enter the park. Rent strollers as needed at the gas station on the right side of the park entrance, just past the turnstiles.

2. If your kids are up for it, obtain Fastpasses for the Tower of Terror on Sunset Boulevard.

3. Ride Star Tours. Use Fastpass if the wait exceeds 25 minutes.

4. See the *Jedi Training Academy* show near Star Tours, either before or after you ride. Check the entertainment schedule for showtimes.

5. See *Muppet-Vision 3-D.*

6. Explore the Honey, I Shrunk the Kids Movie Set.

7. Eat lunch. The Backlot Express and Mama Melrose's are good nearby choices.

8. See *Disney Junior—Live on Stage!* Check the daily entertainment schedule for showtimes.

9. Ride the Tower of Terror using the Fastpasses obtained in Step 2.

10. See *Beauty and the Beast*. Check the daily entertainment schedule for showtimes.

11. See *The American Idol Experience* or the *Indiana Jones Epic Stunt Spectacular*. Check the daily entertainment schedule for showtimes.

12. Eat dinner. Good nearby selections include the counter-service eateries on Sunset Boulevard. The Hollywood Brown Derby and the 50's Prime Time Café are the closest sit-down choices. Reservations are recommended.

13. Ride Toy Story Mania! at Pixar Place at the back of the park.

14. See *Fantasmic!* if it's playing. Plan on arriving 30–40 minutes early to get decent seats, and up to an hour in advance for good seats.

15. Depart Disney's Hollywood Studios.

If you have a Web-enabled cell phone, you can view current and future wait times for every attraction—and add the times you see in the parks—at **m.touringplans.com.**

Disney's Hollywood Studios

Disney's Hollywood Studios 1-Day Touring Plan for Tweens and Their Parents

1. Arrive at the park 30–40 minutes prior to opening. Grab a park map and entertainment schedule when you enter the park.
2. As soon as the park opens, ride Toy Story Mania! at Pixar Place.
3. Ride Rock 'n' Roller Coaster.
4. Ride the Tower of Terror. Use Fastpass if wait exceeds 30 minutes.
5. Ride The Great Movie Ride.
6. Ride Star Tours. If you have small children, check the daily entertainment schedule for the next performance of the *Jedi Training Academy* and work Star Tours in around that show. Use Fastpass for Star Tours if wait exceeds 20 minutes.
7. Check your entertainment schedule for the next performance of the *Lights, Motors, Action! Extreme Stunt Show.* Either see the show or eat lunch. Good nearby restaurants include Backlot Express and Mama Melrose's.
8. Take the Studio Backlot Tour.

9. Explore the rest of the Streets of America on the way to *Muppet-Vision 3-D.*
10. See *Muppet-Vision 3-D.*
11. Head toward Echo Lake. Check your entertainment schedule for the next performance of the *Indiana Jones* show. If the next show is within 25 minutes, get in line now. See *Walt Disney: One Man's Dream* between *Little Mermaid* and Toy Story Mania!
12. Check your entertainment schedule for the next performance of *The American Idol Experience.*
13. Work in *Voyage of the Little Mermaid!* if you have small children and time permits.
14. See *Beauty and the Beast.*
15. Tour Hollywood and Sunset boulevards.
16. Enjoy *Fantasmic!* if it's playing.
17. Depart Disney's Hollywood Studios.

If you have a Web-enabled cell phone, you can view current and future wait times for every attraction—and add the ones you see in the parks—at **m.touringplans.com.**

Disney's Hollywood Studios

Disney's Hollywood Studios
1-Day Happy Family Touring Plan

1. Arrive at the park 30–40 minutes prior to opening. Grab a park map and entertainment schedule when you enter the park. Rent strollers or wheelchairs as needed at the gas station on the right side of the park entrance, just past the turnstiles.
2. **FAMILY:** As soon as the park opens, ride Toy Story Mania! at Pixar Place.
3. **TEENS:** Ride Rock 'n' Roller Coaster. Consider using the single-rider line or Fastpass if the standby wait exceeds 25 minutes.
4. **PARENTS:** *See Voyage of the Little Mermaid* in the Animation Courtyard.
5. **TEENS:** Ride the Tower of Terror. Use Fastpass if wait exceeds 30 minutes.
6. **FAMILY:** Ride The Great Movie Ride.
7. **PARENTS:** See *Disney Junior—Live on Stage!* Check the daily entertainment schedule for showtimes.
8. **TEENS:** Ride Star Tours.
9. **PARENTS:** Check the daily entertainment schedule for the next performance of the *Jedi Training Academy* near Star Tours.
10. **FAMILY:** See *Muppet-Vision 3-D.*
11. **FAMILY:** Eat lunch. The best nearby counter-service restaurant is the Studio Catering Co. Now would be a good time to check the daily entertainment schedule for showtimes for *Lights, Motors, Action!, Beauty and the Beast, Indiana*

Jones, and *The American Idol Experience.*
12. **TEENS:** See the *Lights, Motors, Action!* stunt show.
13. **PARENTS:** Explore the Honey, I Shrunk the Kids Movie Set.
14. **FAMILY:** Explore the Streets of America if you didn't get enough on the way to the *Muppets.*
15. **FAMILY:** Take the Studio Backlot Tour.
16. **FAMILY:** See *Walt Disney: One Man's Dream* near Toy Story Mania! at Pixar Place.
17. **FAMILY:** See the next showing of *The American Idol Experience.* For any show except the last of the day, plan on arriving around 15 minutes in advance to get a seat. Arrive 25 minutes early for the last show.
18. See *Beauty and the Beast* or the *Indiana Jones Epic Stunt Spectacular.*
19. Eat dinner. Good sit-down choices include Mama Melrose's and The Hollywood Brown Derby.
20. Tour Hollywood and Sunset boulevards.
21. Enjoy *Fantasmic!* if it's playing.
22. Depart Disney's Hollywood Studios.

If you have a Web-enabled cell phone, you can view current and future wait times for every attraction—and add the ones you see in the parks—at **m.touringplans.com**.

Universal Studios Florida
1-day Touring Plan

1. Call ☎ 407-363-8000 the day before your visit for the official opening time.
2. Arrive 50 minutes before opening and pick up a map and entertainment schedule.
3. Line up at the turnstile. Ask if any rides or shows are closed, and adjust touring plan.
4. Ride Hollywood Rip Ride Rockit.
5. Ride Revenge of the Mummy.
6. Ride The Simpsons Ride.
7. Ride E.T. Adventure (expendable if there are no young kids in your group).
8. Ride Men in Black Alien Attack.
9. Ride JAWS.
10. Experience *Disaster!*
11. See *TWISTER . . . Ride It Out.*
12. See *Shrek 4-D.*
13. Take a break for lunch.
14. See *Animal Actors on Location* **(14a)**, *Beetlejuice's Graveyard Revue* **(14b)**, *Universal Orlando's Horror Make-Up Show* **(14c)**, and *Fear Factor Live* **(14d)** as convenient according to the daily entertainment schedule. See *Terminator 2: 3-D* **(14e)** after 3:30 p.m.
15. Take preschoolers to see Barney **(15a)** after riding E.T., and then head for Woody Woodpecker's KidZone **(15b).**
16. Revisit favorite rides and shows. See any live performances you may have missed.

If you have a Web-enabled cell phone, you can view current and future wait times for every attraction—and add the ones you see in the parks—at **m.touringplans.com.**

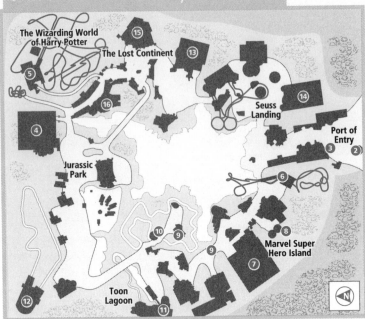

Universal's Islands of Adventure

The Wizarding World of Harry Potter

The Lost Continent

Seuss Landing

Port of Entry

Jurassic Park

Marvel Super Hero Island

Toon Lagoon

Universal's Islands of Adventure
1-day Touring Plan

1. Call ☎ 407-363-8000 the day before your visit for the official opening time.
2. Arrive 60 minutes before opening time, and pick up a map and daily entertainment schedule.
3. Line up at the turnstiles. Ask if any attractions are closed; adjust touring plan accordingly.
4. Hurry to Harry Potter and the Forbidden Journey as soon as you clear the turnstiles, and ride. Be warned that even without much waiting, you'll invest at least 35–40 minutes here.
5. Ride Dragon Challenge if the wait is 30 minutes or less. Otherwise skip to Step 6.
6. At Marvel Super Hero Island, ride The Incredible Hulk Coaster.
7. Exit left and experience The Adventures of Spider-Man.
8. On exiting Spider-Man, backtrack right and ride Doctor Doom's Fearfall. Skip it if the wait exceeds 20 minutes.
9. Depart Super Hero Island and cross into Toon Lagoon.
10. On your right, ride Popeye & Bluto's Bilge-Rat Barges.
11. Continue your clockwise circuit of the park. Ride Dudley Do-Right's Ripsaw Falls.
12. Continue around the lake to Jurassic Park. Ride the Jurassic Park River Adventure.
13. Pass through The Wizarding World to The Lost Continent. Experience *Poseidon's Fury.*
14. Continue clockwise to Seuss Landing and ride The Cat in the Hat.
15. Check the daily entertainment schedule for performances of *The Eighth Voyage of Sindbad Stunt Show* in The Lost Continent. See the show when convenient.
16. Return to The Wizarding World and explore Hogsmeade Village.
17. Revisit favorite rides and check out attractions you may have missed.

If you have a Web-enabled cell phone, you can view current and future wait times for every attraction—and add the ones you see in the parks—at **m.touringplans.com**.

Unofficial Guide Reader Survey

If you would like to express your opinion in writing about Walt Disney World or this guidebook, complete the following survey and mail it to:

Unofficial Guide Reader Survey
P.O. Box 43673
Birmingham, AL 35243

Or fill out the survey online at **touringplans.com.**

Inclusive dates of your visit: _____

Your hometown: _____

Your e-mail address: _____

Members of your party: Person 1   Person 2   Person 3   Person 4   Person 5
            Gender: M   F   M   F   M   F   M   F   M   F
              Age: _____   _____   _____   _____   _____

How many times have you been to Walt Disney World? _____
On your most recent trip, where did you stay? _____

Concerning accommodations, on a scale with 100 being best and 0 being worst, how would you rate:

- the quality of your room_____
- the quietness of your room _____
- shuttle service to parks _____
- the value for the money _____
- check-in/checkout efficiency _____
- swimming pool facilities _____

What transportation did you use to get to Orlando? (circle one)
            Car / Airplane / Train / Cruise / Other

For your trip going to Orlando, what day(s) of the week did you travel?
            (circle all that apply)   Sun Mon Tue Wed Thu Fri Sat

What day(s) of the week did you start your trip home?
            (circle all that apply)   Sun Mon Tue Wed Thu Fri Sat

Did you rent a car? _____ From whom? _____
Concerning your rental car, on a scale with 100 being best and 0 being worst, how would you rate:

- pickup processing efficiency_____
- condition of the car _____
- airport shuttle efficiency _____
- return processing efficiency _____
- cleanliness of the car _____

Concerning touring:
  Who in your party was most responsible for planning the itinerary?_____
  What time did you normally get started in the morning?_____
  Did you usually arrive at the theme parks before opening?_____
  Did you return to your hotel for rest during the day?_____
  What time did you normally go to bed at night?_____

If you remember the days of the week and times you visited the theme parks, indicate those on the chart below. Use the a.m. column for morning visits and p.m. for afternoon/evening visits.

	Sun AM	Sun PM	Mon AM	Mon PM	Tue AM	Tue PM	Wed AM	Wed PM	Thu AM	Thu PM	Fri AM	Fri PM	Sat AM	Sat PM
MK														
Epcot														
AK														
DHS														
Universal														
IOA														

On a scale with 100 being best and 0 being worst, please rate how the touring plans worked:

Park	Name of Plan	Rating
Magic Kingdom		
Epcot		
Animal Kingdom		
Hollywood Studios		
Universal Studios		
Islands of Adventure		

Concerning your dining experiences:
How many restaurant meals (including fast food) did you average per day? ___
How much (approximately) did your party spend on meals per day? _____
Favorite restaurant outside of Walt Disney World? _____

Did you buy this guide: Before leaving? _____ While on your trip? _____
How did you hear about this guide?
Loaned or recommended by a friend _____ Radio or TV _____
Newspaper or magazine _____ Bookstore salesperson _____
Just picked it out on my own _____ Library _____
Internet _____

What other guidebooks or websites did you use on this trip? On the 100-as-best, 0-as-worst scale, how would you rate them?

	Name	Rating
Guidebooks		
Websites		

Using the same scale, how would you rate the *Unofficial Guide*? _____
Are *Unofficial Guides* readily available at bookstores near you? _____
Have you used other *Unofficial Guides*? Which ones? _____
Comments about your Walt Disney World vacation or about the *Unofficial Guide*:
_____
_____